Arbitration in Mexico

Arbitration in Mexico

Edited by

Gloria M. Alvarez
Carlos Alvarado

Associate Editor

Celia Cañete

Wolters Kluwer

Published by:
Kluwer Law International B.V.
PO Box 316
2400 AH Alphen aan den Rijn
The Netherlands
E-mail: lrs-sales@wolterskluwer.com
Website: www.wolterskluwer.com/en/solutions/kluwerlawinternational

Sold and distributed by:
Wolters Kluwer Legal & Regulatory U.S.
920 Links Avenue
Landisville, PA 17538
United States of America
E-mail: customer.service@wolterskluwer.com

ISBN 978-94-035-2527-3

e-Book: ISBN 978-94-035-2537-2
web-PDF: ISBN 978-94-035-2547-1

Editors

Dr. Gloria M. Alvarez, FCIArb, is a qualified Mexican lawyer and a leading academic in international arbitration. She is a dual Mexican and U.S. national and holds both a master's and a doctorate degree from the School of International Arbitration, Queen Mary University of London. She is the founding partner of GM Arbitration, with a presence in Mexico City and London, where she serves as an independent arbitrator, arbitration secretary, and expert in dispute resolution under various institutions, including ICC, ICSID, LCIA, and CANACO. Dr. Alvarez is an Associate Professor in Dispute Resolution and Energy Law at the University of Aberdeen in the United Kingdom and a Visiting Professor at the University of Lausanne (Switzerland) and Osgoode Hall Law School (Canada). Dr. Alvarez is a member of the steering committee for the Academic Forum for the UNCITRAL Working Group III and sits on the editorial board of *ICSID Review and the Journal of International Arbitration*. Her notable publications include *ICSID Practical Commentary, Energy Arbitration in Latin America*, and the *Routledge Handbook on Energy Law*. Her work has been quoted by national courts and international tribunals. Since 2023, the Mexican Agency for International Development Cooperation has included Dr. Alvarez in its list of 'Mexican Women in Science,' where she is the only representative in the legal sciences. She is also the co-founder of Arbitration Links, an initiative to promote free knowledge of international arbitration in Mexico. In 2024, Gloria was selected to take part in the prestigious ICC Academy for Latin America and the Special Editor on Energy Transition and Investment Arbitration for ICSID Review.

Carlos Alvarado is a founding partner at Alvarado Moreno Abogados in Mexico City, where he focuses his practice on commercial arbitration and litigation before national courts. He has extensive experience in international arbitrations conducted under the rules of the ICC, CAM, ICDR, LMAA, UNCITRAL, CANACO, and others. He also frequently serves as an arbitrator. Carlos combines his arbitration expertise with over fifteen years of experience in civil, constitutional (amparo), and commercial litigation before national courts, including proceedings in aid of arbitration. Before founding Alvarado Moreno Abogados, Carlos worked for ten years at Hogan Lovells in Mexico

City, and in 2017, he was an International Associate in their London office. He studied law at the Universidad Autónoma de San Luis Potosí, holds an LLM from Queen Mary University of London in International and Comparative Dispute Resolution, and a Master's in Finance from EGADE Business School. Currently, he is part of the ICC Advanced Arbitration Academy for Latin America. Carlos served as Co-chair of the Spanish Club of Arbitration-40 (2021-2022) and Chair of the Young Arbitrators Forum CAM-CANACO (2018-2020). He has published articles and chapters on arbitration, international law, and litigation in national and international publications and frequently participates as a speaker at conferences in Mexico and abroad.

Associate Editor

Celia Cañete is an associate in the dispute resolution practice at Pérez-Llorca, with prior experience in the energy and corporate practice within the same firm. Her expertise spans international and domestic arbitration proceedings administered by the ICC, CAM, SCAI, and CAS, as well as Spanish civil and commercial litigation. Before joining Pérez-Llorca, Celia served as a law clerk at a Swiss international arbitration boutique. She is co-director of the GoArb International Arbitration course organized by International Arbitration Seminars & Courses (IASC) and University Carlos III (UC3M). Additionally, she is co-founder of the Sports Arbitration Moot (SAM) and Secretary General of IASC. For over two years, she acted as coordinator of Madrid Very Young Arbitration Practitioners (MAD VYAP) and represented the Spanish local chapter within Global VYAP's Steering Committee. Celia frequently contributes to publications and participates in conferences and projects led by professional associations. She holds a Master's degree in Spanish Legal Practice and works in English, Spanish, and French.

Contributors

Michelle Carrillo's practice is focused on international dispute resolution in complex commercial and investment arbitrations. With over ten years of experience, Michelle has deep-rooted knowledge of arbitral proceedings, having conducted arbitrations under all major arbitral institutions, including the ICC, LCIA, ICDR/AAA, CAM, CANACO, SIAC, ICSID, as well as ad hoc arbitrations under the UNCITRAL Rules. She has acquired thorough experience as a party representative, administrative secretary, and general tribunal assistant. Her experience covers numerous governing laws, substantive and procedural, and she has managed complex, high-value disputes under multiple jurisdictions, conducted in both English and Spanish.

Orlando Federico Cabrera Colorado, Having studied law in Canada, Mexico, and the United States of America, and fluent in English, Spanish, Portuguese, and French, Orlando counsels governments and corporate investors in international dispute resolution across borders and languages at Hogan Lovells. Orlando represents clients in CAM, CANACO, ICC, ICDR, ICSID, LCIA, and UNCITRAL arbitrations in mining, energy, telecommunications, finance, construction, transport, national security, real estate assets, and government contracting. Prior to joining the Hogan Lovells Mexico City office, Orlando started in the international arbitration practice of the firm's Miami office. Orlando also previously served as a legal intern in the New York State Supreme Court.

Fernanda Serrano Cortez, Prior to joining Hogan Lovells, Fernanda clerked at the Mexican Supreme Court of Justice Nation. Having experience in the judiciary and as a party counsel has allowed her to have a comprehensive vision for resolving the disputes in which she participates. Fernanda has represented a wide range of clients, multinational and domestic, in various legal disputes, including civil, commercial, and administrative litigation and domestic and international arbitration. Fernanda's academic profile includes her participation as a member of her university's representative team in international commercial arbitration competitions, as well as her membership in her Law School's Academic Excellence Program.

Francisco González de Cossío is an expert in arbitration dedicated to acting as arbitrator, advocate, and Dispute Board Member in mostly construction, energy, and complex cases, having acted in more than two hundred such cases. Law Degree, Universidad Iberoamericana; Master's (LLM) and doctoral (JSD) degrees from the University of Chicago; Master's Degree in History of Thought, Universidad Panamericana; Business degree (OPM) from Harvard Business School. Author of twelve books and more than two hundred specialized articles. Professor of arbitration at the Universidad Iberoamericana, Universidad Panamericana, and Escuela Libre de Derecho. Arbitrator, Court of Arbitration for Sport. President, Mexican Arbitration Institute (IMA), Arbitration Commission, Mexican Bar Association, Mexican Chapter of the CEIA.

René Irra de la Cruz is a partner at Cuatrecasas and leads the international litigation and arbitration practice of the Mexico City office. He is an expert in judicial proceedings and international arbitrations conducted under institutional rules and ad hoc norms, acting as counsel or arbitrator and as an expert in Mexican law in proceedings abroad. René has participated in more than fifty international arbitrations with seats in Canadian, American, Latin American, and European cities, resolved according to the law of more than eighteen countries. His expertise covers sectors such as M&A, foreign investment, international trade, investor-State dispute settlement, energy (electricity, oil and gas), construction, and infrastructures, among others.

Ana María Castro Dosal, Ana María is an associate in both the Arbitration and the Commercial Litigation practices at Galicia. She began her professional experience at Bufete Asali, where she represented clients from the financial, real estate, and trade industries. Ana then clerked for Justice Javier Laynez Potisek at the Mexican Supreme Court of Justice, where she participated in drafting decisions as well as concurring and dissenting opinions. Ana María studied law at the Instituto Tecnológico Autónomo de México, earned a diploma in Insurance and Sureties Law at Escuela Libre de Derecho, and has an LLM from Columbia University. Ana is authorized to practice in Mexico and New York.

Ana Sofía Sapiña Errecart obtained her law degree at Universidad Panamericana and is a Masters in Law (LLM) candidate at Harvard Law School. Before her LLM she was an associate at Galicia Abogados arbitration and commercial litigation practice. Before joining Galicia, she was a law clerk at Bufete Asali. With over six years of experience in dispute resolution, Ana Sofía has focused her practice in complex commercial arbitrations in the construction, infrastructure, and energy sectors. Ana Sofía has experience acting as counsel and administrative secretary for the arbitral tribunal in multiple cases.

Diana María Pineda Esteban is a partner at Sainz Abogados. She advises national and international clients in the energy sector on project development, regulatory compliance, administrative litigation, and arbitration. She focuses on the energy transition, helping companies adapt to new regulations and sustainable technologies, and promoting energy sufficiency with a lower carbon footprint. She is an expert in negotiating complex structures and resolving disputes in the energy sector. She has been a professor of Obligations Law and Energy Law at Universidad Iberoamericana. She wrote this chapter during her maternity leave for the birth of her daughter Ana Jose.

Rodrigo Zamora Etcharren, Rodrigo co-heads the Arbitration and leads the Civil and Commercial Litigation practices at Galicia. He has appeared before various local and federal trial and appellate courts throughout Mexico, including the Supreme Court, representing both plaintiffs and defendants. Rodrigo has also been involved in numerous arbitrations, serving as both counsel and arbitrator. Rodrigo has participated as an expert in Mexican law in numerous arbitrations and judicial proceedings before the courts of the United States and other nations and before arbitral tribunals, including investor-state cases. Rodrigo is authorized to practice in Mexico and New York.

Alejandro Flores Patiño, Partner of the law firm Loperena Lerch y Martín del Campo. From 2006 to date he has worked in the areas of commercial arbitration, corporate law, and intellectual property. In the area of arbitration, he has participated as sole arbitrator, co-arbitrator, administrative secretary of the arbitration court, and party lawyer in various national commercial arbitrations (CANACO and CAM) and international (ICC, ICDR, and LCIA). Intellectual Property, and issues related to advertising. He has been a consulting lawyer for advertising and entertainment companies and has experience in consulting, drafting, and reviewing contracts involving copyright, right of publicity, and neighboring rights.

Jorge Escalona Gálvez is an associate at Alvarado Moreno Abogados in Mexico City. A boutique law firm specialized in international arbitration and litigation. He has solid experience in investment arbitration assisting Mexico's defense in its ICSID-administered proceedings when working at the Ministry of Economy. Prior to joining Alvarado Moreno Abogados, he also worked at Von Wobeser y Sierra, Malpica Iturbe Buj y Paredes in the energy and litigation practices. He is a law graduate from Universidad Panamericana (UP). He has furthered his knowledge by successfully completing diplomas in ADR, Public International Law, International Commercial Arbitration, and Investor-State Dispute Settlement from esteemed institutions such as the CIArb, Queen Mary University, Washington College of Law, University of Aberdeen, British Institute of International and Comparative Law, and King's College London. He is a Fellow of CIArb and a member of its Young Members Group Global Steering Committee.

Salvador Fonseca González, Salvador is a partner at the dispute resolution firm Fonseca, Rodríguez & Perchemlian and has more than twenty-eight years of experience as counsel, sole arbitrator, and president of arbitration tribunals in multiple international and local cases under the arbitration rules of the main arbitration institutions. Salvador graduated with honors from the University of Guadalajara, he has an LLM from New York University and is a professor of arbitration and alternative dispute resolution at the Universidad Panamericana and other prestigious universities. Salvador chairs the Advisory Committee of ICDR in Mexico, and he is a member of the

Arbitration Commission of the ICC, and the Mediation and Arbitration Commission of CANACO.

Eduardo Lobatón Guzmán, Eduardo Lobatón Guzman is a Senior Associate at Hogan Lovells and Professor of International Law and Arbitration at Instituto Tecnológico y de Estudios Superiores de Monterrey. Eduardo focuses his practice in international commercial and investment arbitration, as well as civil and commercial litigation. Eduardo is skilled in both civil and common law. Eduardo has represented and advised clients in ICSID, ICC, LCIA, ICDR, UNCITRAL, CANACO, and CAM arbitrations, and commercial litigations in diverse industries, including energy, construction, infrastructure, insurance, food, automotive, and IT. Eduardo regularly writes and speaks on international arbitration and litigation topics.

Luis Jardón is counsel at Creel, García-Cuéllar, Aiza y Enríquez, S.C., in the firm's arbitration and dispute resolution practice. His practice is focused on structuring transnational mechanisms for the protection of foreign investment in Mexico and designing alternatives directed to the early solution of complex regulatory and contractual disputes. Luis frequently acts as counsel in crisis management situations and in the development of multi-tiered strategies by which national remedies are combined with recourse to international arbitration. Luis obtained his law degree from the Centro de Investigación y Docencia Económicas (CIDE), where he has also been a lecturer for over ten years. He also holds an LLM in international law from the University of Cambridge.

Adrián Magallanes is Co-Head of the Litigation and Arbitration Practice Groups of Von Wobeser y Sierra, S.C. He is admitted to practice in Mexico and New York and has twenty years of experience. He has acted as counsel in ad hoc and institutional arbitrations (ICC, LCIA, ICSID, AAA, ICDR, UNCITRAL, CAM, CANACO) in the commercial, construction, infrastructure, and energy sectors, and has also acted as arbitrator in these types of cases. Adrián appears before Mexican courts in various types of litigation proceedings, particularly in commercial, administrative, and constitutional law-related disputes. His experience also includes several class actions and has acted as an expert on Mexican law before the Courts of the United States.

Montserrat Manzano is a partner in the dispute resolution practice of Von Wobeser y Sierra, S.C., appointed in 2017 as the first woman partner in its thirty-year history. She is part of the ESG and Energy & Natural Resources practice groups. Additionally, she co-leads the firm's Diversity & Inclusion and Ethics Committees. Ms. Manzano acts as counsel in international commercial and investor-State disputes. She has experience in a broad range of sectors. She represents clients before Mexican courts in proceedings in support of arbitration. Ms. Manzano also sits as an arbitrator to international commercial disputes and is specializing in arbitrating investor-State disputes.

Cecilia Azar Manzur joined Galicia as a partner in 2018, where she has focused her practice on complex domestic and international commercial disputes. Acting as arbitrator, counsel, mediator, and expert in Mexican law, she has developed extensive experience, particularly in cases related to energy, infrastructure, construction, and commercial mediation. Currently, Cecilia is president of the Mexican Institute of Mediation (IMM). She is on Mexico's list of conciliators in ICSID proceedings and is a member of ICC´s International Arbitration Court. Recently, she was appointed as co-chair of the ICC Advanced Arbitration Academy for Latin America.

Elsa Ortega López has more than twenty years of experience in large and complex cases of international commercial arbitration, both ad hoc and administered under the arbitration rules of several arbitral institutions, such as the International Court of Arbitration of the International Chamber of Commerce (ICC), the International Centre for Dispute Resolution (ICDR), and the London Court of International Arbitration (LCIA), acting as party counsel, arbitrator and chair of arbitral tribunals in numerous cases in diverse sectors and industries. She is the head of the arbitration practice of Creel, García-Cuellar, Aiza y Enriquez in Mexico City.

Andrés Peña Loyo graduated top of his class and summa cum laude from Instituto Tecnológico y de Estudios Superiores de Monterrey. He also studied international law at Universidad Pontificia Comillas. Andrés is passionate about the Arts and seeks to reconcile his passion with his law practice in trial advocacy and legal design. He was awarded by his alma mater for his contributions to Arts and Culture and has received diverse recognitions for his oral trial advocacy skills at domestic and international arbitration competitions. Andrés has represented and advised clients in complex domestic and international disputes. He focuses his practice in diverse industries, including construction, energy, infrastructure, automotive, insurance, IT, and health sciences, among others.

Andrea Orta, Partner at Orta González Sicilia Abogados, S.C. Director of the Mediation and Arbitration Commission of CANACO. Second Vice President of the Executive Committee of CIAC. Member of the Steering Committee of the Mexican Chapter of CEIA. Representative of CEIA Women Mexico. Co-Coordinator of the Arbitration Commission of the BMA. Member of the ICC Task Force on Disability Inclusion in Arbitration. Member of the Award Scrutiny Commission (CIAM-CIAR). Participates in national and international arbitrations as party counsel, sole arbitrator, chair of the arbitral tribunal, co-arbitrator, or emergency arbitrator, in ad hoc arbitrations and arbitrations under different institutional rules.

Elisa Legorreta Pastor is an accomplished professional specializing in civil and commercial litigation, as well as domestic and international arbitration (administered by CCI, LCIA, CAM, and CANACO or ad hoc procedures). She has extensive experience in sectors such as M&A, finance, infrastructure, construction, energy, and security and bonds disputes. Elisa holds a bachelor's degree in law from Universidad Iberoamericana in Mexico City, where she graduated with honors, and a Master's in Laws from Duke University, where she graduated with distinction. She has co-authored numerous articles on product liability and arbitration and is a co-author of the book *Strategic Leadership for Women in the Legal Sector* published by Tirant Editorial.

Alan Bonfiglio Ríos is the General Counsel ("Director General") of the Legal Office for International Trade Law ("Consultoría Jurídica de Comercio Internacional") at the Ministry of Economy of Mexico ("Secretaría de Economía"). He represents the United Mexican States in investor-State arbitration proceedings covering various industries and economic sectors. He provides counsel within the Ministry of Economy and to other government agencies about public international law, international trade law, market access, and dispute settlement. Mr. Bonfiglio also advises on negotiating and implementing free trade agreements and bilateral investment treaties. Previously, he was part of Hogan Lovells' (Mexico City) litigation and arbitration practice.

Adriana San Román Rivera is co-founder of Wöss & Partners with vast experience as party counsel and damages expert in international arbitration, administrative, mercantile, and civil litigations. She is recognized as a Leading Individual by the Legal 500 and an outstanding party counsel in international arbitration by the Who's Who Legal. The Legal 500 has named her and her partner as "the foremost experts in Mexico for complex arbitrations involving damages." As an attorney at law as first profession, she also obtained an MA in Finance and Investment from the University of Exeter and passed the first level of the Chartered Financial Analyst exam.

Vicente Bañuelos Rizo, Graduated from Escuela Libre de Derecho. LLM in International Commercial Arbitration from UC Davis. PhD course at the Universidad Panamericana (thesis in progress). Has been a Law Professor in the ITESM, Universidad Panamericana, and Universidad Iberoamericana, in civil and commercial procedure and arbitration. Over twenty-seven years of experience in the areas of commercial litigation & arbitration. He has been counsel, co-arbitrator, sole arbitrator, and president of Arbitral Tribunals, in more than fifty arbitrations (ICC, AAA, ICDR, LCIA, CAM, and CANACO), and more than twenty judicial procedures assisting or supervising arbitrations. Currently the arbitration and complex litigation equity partner at Clyde & Co. (Mexico).

Luis Omar Guerrero Rodríguez, Based in Mexico City, Omar co-heads the arbitration and litigation practice and co-heads the antitrust practice of our Mexico offices. Omar knows the importance of being a team player, providing bold solutions for clients, and the merits of being a fierce competitor. Omar joined Hogan Lovells (formerly Barrera, Siqueiros y Torres Landa) in 1993, immediately after graduating top of his class and summa cum laude. He became partner in 2000. He holds three post-graduate degrees including an LM from LSE (with merits). He has advised companies in the pharmaceutical, hospitality, telecom, food, construction, IT, and agro-business industries to advance their business objectives whether in a dispute or antitrust matters.

Julia González Romero, Specialized attorney in energy and litigation, focusing on social impact. Julia actively participates in international and national-level boards and relevant networks, contributing significantly to various sectors. With eighteen years in the public sector and eight years in private practice, Julia is known for innovating and successfully implementing solutions, establishing herself as a trusted voice in the energy sector. She serves as Counsel at Gonzalez Calvillo, designing strategies covering regulation, conflict resolution, and risk prevention, particularly in infrastructure projects and environmental law challenges. She holds a law degree from the Instituto Tecnológico Autónomo de México (ITAM), with specializations and a master's degree from the Universidad Nacional Autónoma de México (UNAM).

Carlos Manuel Loperena Ruiz was President of the Mexican Bar Association (Barra Mexicana). Member of the ICC International Court of Arbitration. Former President of the IMA (Mexican Arbitration Institute). President of the ICC Mexico Commission on Arbitration and ADR. Professor of Arbitration and ADR at Escuela Libre de Derecho (Mexico City). Member of the 31.22 USMCA Committee. He has intervened in several international commercial arbitration cases under the rules of the ICC, the LCIA, the UNCITRAL, the ICSID, the AAA (ICDR), the CAM, the U.S. Mexico Dispute Resolution Center, the CAMCA, and the IACAC as attorney, expert witness, and arbitrator.

Víctor M. Ruiz acts as counsel and as arbitrator in domestic and international arbitrations, and in judicial proceedings before local and federal courts involving disputes under contracts for the international sale of goods, contracts for sale of shares, mergers and acquisitions, shareholder agreements, joint venture agreements, distribution and franchise agreements, as well as energy and infrastructure projects. A relevant part of his practice focuses on corporate governance issues, which has enabled him to assist in the resolution of disputes between shareholders, or between shareholders and the Board of Directors, and to advise companies on the implementation of mechanisms for the prevention and effective resolution of their disputes.

Claudia T. Salomon is an independent arbitrator, specializing in international, investor-State and complex commercial disputes. She is widely recognized as one of the leading arbitration practitioners of her generation. Ms. Salomon has experience as arbitrator and counsel in some of the most complex, high value and significant disputes. Her cases span a broad range of industry sectors including construction, energy and natural resources, financial services, hospitality, life sciences, technology, and telecommunications. Ms. Salomon has been recommended for election as President of the ICC International Court of Arbitration, effective July 1, 2021, putting her on the path to becoming the first woman President of the ICC Court in its almost 100-year history.

Fernando Navarro Sánchez is an experienced international mediator and conflict resolution professional from Mexico. He has acted as mediator and organizational ombudsperson on cases and with parties from a diverse range of cultural and legal backgrounds. In recent years, he has had extensive experience working in the United Nations system.

Bernardo Sepúlveda, Bernardo Sepúlveda Amor is of counsel at Creel, García-Cuéllar, Aiza y Enríquez, S.C., in the firm's arbitration and dispute resolution practice, which he founded. He has vast experience as an arbitrator, including acting as chair on several high-stake investment treaty arbitration tribunals. He served as judge of the International Court of Justice (ICJ) for the period 2006–2015 and was elected as vice president of the ICJ from 2012 to 2015. From 1982 to 1986 he served as Mexico's lead diplomat during his tenure as Mexico's Secretary of Foreign Affairs.

Eduardo Siqueiros T., Recently retired as a partner from the law firm of Hogan Lovells in Mexico City (previously Barrera, Siqueiros y Torres Landa), where he practiced law for approximately forty years in commercial, joint ventures, investment, insurance, and infrastructure law. He received his law degree from Escuela Libre de Derecho in Mexico City and subsequently an LLM degree from Harvard Law School. Has been a professor of law at several law schools in Mexico, and a frequent speaker on commercial law and arbitration in diverse fora in Mexico and abroad. He actively participates as arbitrator in domestic and international commercial disputes, as well as investor-State disputes.

Camilo Soto is an Associate at Creel, García-Cuéllar, Aiza y Enríquez, S.C. and is regularly involved in handling cases and transactions for the Arbitration and Dispute Settlement, Energy and Infrastructure, and Financial Regulatory Services groups. Camilo obtained his law degree (LLB) from the Centre of Economic Research and Teaching (CIDE) in Mexico City in 2012. In addition, he completed his Master of Laws (LLM) in international legal studies at New York University School of Law in 2016.

Marco Tulio Venegas is one of the founding partners of LITREDI, S.C., a firm specialized in the areas of arbitration, litigation, and dispute resolution. Mr. Venegas has advised and litigated for more than twenty-eight years before Jurisdictional Courts and Arbitral Tribunals in various areas of law (including commercial, administrative, and constitutional law). His experience includes participation in at least seventy arbitrations, including the most important energy arbitrations (and subsequent award enforcement proceedings) in the history of Mexico, both for their amount and for their legal and political relevance. More recently, he has participated in ten arbitrations as co-arbitrator, Chair or Sole Arbitrator.

Dr. Herfried Wöss is a leading international arbitrator ranked in the Hall of Fame by The Legal 500 with his law firm in the Top Tier in Arbitration and frequently sits as president, co-arbitrator, adjudicator, or acts as party counsel with respect to large and complex infrastructure, energy and damages disputes (gas pipelines, power plants, energy tariffs, oil platforms, refineries, renewable energies) both with respect to commercial and investment arbitrations. He started his career at the Legal Service of the European Commission and holds a Magister iuris and a doctorate with honors in international and European economic law in Austria, and an LLM in international business at the University of Exeter. He is a professorial lecturer on Damages in International Arbitration at The Hague Academy of International Law.

Summary of Contents

Table of Contents

Foreword

Mexico stands out as one of the world's leading jurisdictions in arbitration, a distinction that should not escape the attention of the global arbitration community. Recent statistics demonstrate the significant role arbitration plays in that country. Over the last five years, Mexico has consistently ranked within the top ten countries with the most parties participating in arbitration proceedings administrated under the Arbitration Rules of the International Chamber of Commerce (ICC Arbitration) reaching fifth place in 2021, with the involvement of 91 Mexican parties in ICC arbitrations and in 2023 reached, for the first time, the second place, together with Germany, with 111 parties.

In Latin America, Mexico undoubtedly is first among the Spanish-speaking countries, as the country with the highest representation in ICC Arbitration for the last decade, with a total of 344 Mexican parties involved in ICC Arbitration. More recently, from 2018 to 2022, a total of eighty-one were, what we could consider "domestic" disputes in which both parties were of Mexican nationality.

Mexico is also among the countries most selected as a place of arbitration, holding the sixth place in ICC Arbitration in 2022. This fact reflects the importance of Mexico in the region and its attractive legal framework for arbitration.

Understanding the legal, economic, and social factors that make Mexico such an attractive jurisdiction for domestic and international arbitration is vital, not only for those already immersed in Mexican-related disputes but also for those not familiar with it and who might be seeking to broaden their understanding of the region.

The prominence of Mexico in the field of domestic and international arbitration arises from multiple factors. The country's growing economic relevance on a global scale and its wealth in natural resources position it as an attractive jurisdiction in terms of investment and development of extractive and production industries, as well as its solid industrial development, significantly contribute to its importance in the arbitration scene.

This book presents a remarkable collection of twenty-one chapters written by some of the most distinguished minds in the field of international arbitration in Mexico, fulfilling the objective of providing a deep understanding of arbitration in this country.

This work addresses relevant aspects from the regulatory, economic, and political framework of the country, offering a comprehensive view of the development of international arbitration in Mexico. It also illustrates the evolution in the relationship between Mexican courts and arbitration practice, the approach toward investment arbitration in the country, as well as its practical aspects. The authors also touch upon other contemporary issues such as the participation of state entities in commercial arbitrations, disputes in the country's main economic sectors, the particularities of corporate disputes under Mexican law, the impact of technology on Mexican international arbitration practice, and the different dispute resolution options available in Mexico.

This book covers a wide range of current topics of interest that reveal the peculiarities of Mexico through the eyes of those specialists in the region who, in addition to providing their valuable knowledge, help identify possible future challenges. Undoubtedly, this collection will be of great utility for those interested in entering the Mexican arbitration practice in the coming years.

Mexico has unique legal, cultural, and commercial practices. Understanding the functioning of international arbitration in such a jurisdiction has significant practical advantages, especially considering the importance of Mexico in international arbitration. In an increasingly globalized world, it is gradually more common for disputes to involve parties from different countries. Therefore, understanding the particularities of arbitration in the most representative jurisdictions in the world, among which Mexico undoubtedly stands out, is a valuable tool for all practitioners of international arbitration, and this book undoubtedly achieves that objective.

Claudia T. Salomon

PART I Introduction and Regulatory Framework

CHAPTER 1

Arbitration in Mexico: An Overview

Bernardo Sepúlveda, Luis Jardón & Camilo Soto[*]

[A] INTRODUCTION

For more than three decades, Mexico has embraced commercial and investment arbitration. Coinciding with the transformation from an import-substitution industrialization economy to an outward, export-oriented economy in the 1970s, Mexico began a series of legal changes that included adopting the prime multilateral treaties on international commercial arbitration and enacting domestic law reforms to the Commercial Code in 1989 and 1993 to regulate commercial arbitration.[1] In the 1990s, alongside the signing of the North American Free Trade Agreement (NAFTA), Mexico enacted reforms that further liberalized its economy and embraced international scrutiny for the state through investment arbitration. This led to the signing of several bilateral investment treaties (BITs) and free trade agreements (FTAs) with investment chapters that provide for arbitration.[2] Such reforms also opened commercial arbitration for specific kinds of public contracts entered into with state-owned entities (SOE) and

* The authors wish to thank Sara Contreras, Junior Associate at the firm, for her invaluable research assistance during the writing of the article.

1. *See* Margarita Trevino Balli & David S. Coale, *Recent Reforms to Mexican Arbitration Law: Is Constitutionality Achievable* 30 Tex. Int'l L. J. 535, 536 (1995); *see also* Jorge A. Vargas, *Enforcement of Judgments and Arbitral Awards in Mexico* 5 U.S.-Mex. L.J. 137, 141, footnote 18 (1997) (arguing that "Mexico's adhesion in 1971 to the United Nations Convention on the Recognition and Enforcement of Foreign Arbitral Awards ... signals the initiation of a more active role on private international law matters on the part of this country."); *see also* Leonel Pereznieto Castro, *Commercial Arbitration in Mexico* 13 Fla. J. Int'l L. 29 (2000) (pinpointing Mexico's turning point toward opening to commercial arbitration to Mexico's joining of the General Agreement on Tariffs and Trade in 1986).
2. *See generally* Camilo Soto, *A Mexican Outlook on NAFTA, TPP and their Renegotiation: Investment Arbitration's Transparency and International Supervision, at Peril?* 40 Hou. J. Int'l L. 937 (2018).

state instrumentalities,[3] permitting arbitration today generally for all public works, procurement and public-partnership contracts entered into by the federal government and its SOEs.[4]

Today, Mexico is party to most of the relevant international treaties for the enforcement of arbitral awards and most innovative BITs and FTAs, and its domestic legislation regulates favorably the use of arbitration. Consequently, arbitration is nowadays deeply embedded in the Mexican legal system. Recent decisions by Mexican courts confirm the general arbitration-friendly environment.

The termination of NAFTA and the advent of the United States-Mexico-Canada Agreement (USMCA) was a recent major turning point for Mexico. With more limited protections for the investor and novel rules, the USMCA's investment arbitration chapter will change the landscape of the practice for years to come.

This article gives a brief overview of arbitration in Mexico and the challenges that the practice will encounter in the near future.

[B] OVERVIEW

[1] Mexican Legal Framework

[a] Commercial Arbitration

[i] Constitution

The regulation of commercial arbitration in Mexico is underpinned at the highest echelons of the legal system: the Mexican Constitution, international treaties, and laws enacted by Congress.[5]

Since 2008, the Constitution provides for the obligation to establish alternative dispute resolution mechanisms in law.[6] Through a 2017 amendment to the Constitution, the right to a fair trial and access to justice, provided in Article 17, requires

3. *See Decreto que reforma, adiciona y deroga disposiciones de diversas leyes relacionadas con el Tratado de Libre Comercio de América del Norte* [Decree that reforms, amends, and repeals provisions of various laws related to the North American Free Trade Agreement], published in the Federal Official Gazette on Dec. 22, 1993, Arts. seventh and eighth.
4. *See Ley de Adquisiciones, Arrendamientos y Servicios del Sector Público* [*Public Sector Procurement, Leasing and Services Law*], published in the Federal Official Gazette on Jan. 4, 2000, last amended on May 20, 2021, Arts. 80-86; *Ley de Obras Públicas y Servicios Relacionados con las Mismas* [*Public Works and Related Services Law*], published in the Federal Official Gazette on Jan. 4, 2000, last amended on May 20, 2021, Arts. 98–104; *Ley de Asociaciones Público-Privadas* [*Public-Private Partnership Law*], published in the Federal Official Gazette on Jan. 16, 2012, last amended on Jun. 15, 2018, Arts. 138-139.
5. *See Constitución Política de los Estados Unidos Mexicanos* [Mexican Constitution], published in the Federal Official Gazette on Feb. 5, 1917, last amended on Nov. 18, 2022, Art. 133.
6. "*Decreto por el que se reforman y adicionan diversas disposiciones de la Constitución Política de los Estados Unidos Mexicanos*" [Decree whereby the Mexican Constitution is amended], published in the Federal Official Gazette on Jun. 18, 2008, Art. 17, para. third.

authorities to privilege conflict resolution over procedural formalities.[7] Therefore, authorities at all levels of government are granted more flexibility and discretion to reach more equitable decisions, subject to not affecting due process of law and equality of arms.[8] In this regard, there is a recent judicial decision extending this obligation to arbitrators.[9] Moreover, the Mexican Constitution has been amended to empower Congress to legislate a general law that regulates alternative dispute-resolution mechanisms.[10] However, to this date, Congress has been remiss in enacting such legislation.

[ii] International Treaties

Along with the Commercial Code, commercial arbitration in Mexico is governed by the international treaties to which Mexico is a party. Other than the current bilateral treaty with Spain, Mexico has not entered into bilateral treaties for the recognition and enforcement of commercial arbitral awards, but has rather entered into the following three multilateral conventions:[11]

(1) Convention on the Recognition and Enforcement of Foreign Arbitral Awards (New York Convention), since 1971.
(2) Inter-American Convention on International Commercial Arbitration (Panama Convention), since 1978.
(3) Inter-American Convention on Extraterritorial Validity of Foreign Judgments and Arbitral Awards (Montevideo Convention), since 1987.

7. "*Decreto por el que se reforman y adicionan los artículos 16, 17 y 73 de la Constitución Política de los Estados Unidos Mexicanos, en materia de Justicia Cotidiana (Solución de Fondo del Conflicto y Competencia Legislativa sobre Procedimientos Civiles y Familiares)*" [Decree that amends Arts. 16, 17 and 73 of the Mexican Constitution in matters of daily justice (solution of the merits of the conflict, and legislative jurisdiction over civil and family procedures)], published in the Federal Official Gazette on Sep. 15, 2017, Art. 17, para. third.
8. *See ibid.*
9. "*Arbitral Award. Articles 1457, section i, item b), final part, and 1434, both of the commercial code, which regulate the cause of nullity for violation of equal treatment and the full opportunity to validate rights in arbitration proceedings, are not unconstitutional for not allowing a judicial control of the merits of the award.*" Mexican Supreme Court of Justice's First Chamber, Isolated Thesis: 1a. XXX/2022 (10a.), Judicial Weekly of the Federation, Eleventh Epoch, Digital Registry: 2025648 (original in Spanish).
10. *Decreto por el que se declaran reformadas y adicionadas diversas disposiciones de la Constitución Política de los Estados Unidos Mexicanos, en materia de Mecanismos Alternativos de Solución de Controversias, Mejora Regulatoria, Justicia Cívica e Itinerante y Registros Civiles* [*Decree whereby various provisions of the Mexican Constitution are amended regarding alternative dispute resolution mechanisms, regulatory improvement, civic and itinerant justice and civil registries*], published in the Federal Official Gazette on Feb. 5, 2017, Art. 73, section XXIX-A, and Transitory Arts. second, fourth and fifth.
11. *See* Jose Luis Siqueiros, *Mexican Arbitration: The New Statute* 30 Tex. Int'l L. J. 227, 244-245 (referring to the Convention on the Recognition and Execution of Judicial Judgments and Arbitral Awards in Civil and Commercial Matters, signed on Apr. 17, 1989); cf. Mexican Ministry of Foreign Affairs, *Búsqueda de Tratados* [Treaty Search], https://aplicaciones.sre.gob.mx/tratados/consulta_nva.php (last visited on Dec. 19, 2022).

[iii] Domestic Legislation

Most of the substantive regulation of arbitration in Mexico is embedded in the Commercial Code, which essentially adopted the United Nations Commission on International Trade Law (UNCITRAL) Model Law on International Commercial Arbitration (Model Law).[12] Chapter IV of the Commercial Code is applicable to both national and international arbitrations.[13] Such provisions were first enacted into law in 1989[14] and were later amended in 1993.[15] In 2011, the Commercial Code was again modified to include the amendments to the UNCITRAL Model Law on International Commercial Arbitration adopted on 7 July 2006.[16]

Pursuant to the Commercial Code, Mexican courts are obliged to recognize arbitral awards as binding and enforce them upon written request[17] but may deny their enforcement for a limited set of reasons.[18] Such provisions echo the grounds provided by Article V of the New York Convention on the Recognition and Enforcement of Foreign Arbitral Awards and Article 36 of the UNCITRAL Model Law. Accordingly, a judge may deny the enforcement for the following reasons:

(1) By request of the resisting party because: (i) the parties to the arbitral agreement lacked the capacity to enter into the arbitral agreement or such agreement was invalid; (ii) the party against whom the award is invoked was not given proper notice of the appointment of arbitrators or of the arbitration proceedings or was otherwise unable to present his/her case; (iii) the award deals with matters that fall outside of the arbitration agreement; (iv) the composition of the arbitral tribunal or the arbitral procedure was not in accordance with the parties' agreement or the law of the country where the arbitration took place; or (v) the award is not yet binding on the parties or has been set aside or suspended by a competent authority.

(2) By decision of the Mexican court because: (i) the subject matter of the dispute is considered non-arbitrable under the laws of Mexico; or (ii) the recognition or enforcement of the award would be contrary to Mexico's public policy.

12. *See Código de Comercio* [Commercial Code], published in the Federal Official Gazette on Oct. 7, 1889, last amended on Dec. 30, 2021.
13. *Ibid.*, at Art. 1415.
14. *See Decreto por el que se reforma, adiciona y deroga diversas disposiciones del Código de Comercio* [Decree that amends the Commercial Code], published in the Federal Official Gazette on Jan. 4, 1989.
15. *See Decreto por el que se reforman y adicionan diversas disposiciones del Código de Comercio y del Código Federal de Procedimientos Civiles* [Decree that amends the Commercial Code and the Federal Code on Civil Procedure], published in the Federal Official Gazette on Jul. 22, 1993; Siqueiros, *supra* n. 11, at 230-231. This reform substantially incorporated other elements of the UNCITRAL Model Law that had not been fully integrated; incorporated certain principles of the UNCITRAL Arbitration Rules as well; made the Commercial Code applicable to both domestic and international arbitrations; and made editorial and typographical changes.
16. *Decreto por el que se reforman, adicionan y derogan diversas disposiciones del Código de Comercio* [Decree that amends the Commercial Code], published in the Federal Official Gazette on Jan. 27, 2011.
17. Commercial Code, at Art. 1461.
18. *Ibid.*, at Art. 1462.

There are no specialized tribunals on arbitration in Mexico. Pursuant to the Commercial Code, judicial intervention in aid of arbitration can be either sought through a federal or a local judge at the place of the seat of the arbitration.[19] National courts in general have ruled favorably for the enforcement of national and international arbitral awards. Overall, under the Commercial Code, the enforcement of foreign commercial awards is easier than that of foreign judgments.[20] The merits of the award have not been a valid reason to reject its recognition and enforcement, which has been reinforced in judicial precedents.[21] *Amparo* proceedings may be filed against a judgment rendered in the special trial for the nullity, recognition, or execution of the arbitral award, but only for violations of the plaintiffs' Constitutional and human rights.[22]

[b] Investment Arbitration

Mexico has thirty BITs in force.[23] The last BIT signed by Mexico was with Hong Kong in 2020, which entered into force in 2021.[24]

Mexico is also a party to the International Convention on the Settlement of Investment Disputes between States and Nationals of Other States (ICSID Convention) since 2018,[25] which benefits both Mexico and foreign investors by "ground[ing] the award interpretation, revision and annulment motions, as well as award recognition and enforcement, in a single statute, all wrapped up in a single package": the International Centre for Settlement of Investment Disputes (ICSID).[26] (The first arbitration against Mexico under the ICSID Convention was filed in 2019 by Legacy Vulcan LLC.[27]) The

19. *Ibid.*, at Art. 1422.
20. Siqueiros, *supra* n. 11, 245.
21. *See, e.g.*, Mexican Supreme Court of Justice's First Chamber, *supra* n. 9.
22. *See* "Arbitral Award. The indirect Amparo can be filed against the judgment issued in the special trial in which its nullity, or recognition and execution, is decided." Mexican Supreme Court of Justice's First Chamber, Jurisprudence: 1a./J. 87/2019 (10a.), Judicial Weekly of the Federation and its Gazette, Book 73, December 2019, Ch. I, 253, Tenth Epoch, Digital Registry: 2021235 (original in Spanish).
23. Mexican Ministry of Economy, *Entra en vigor el Acuerdo para la Protección y Promoción Recíproca de las Inversiones (APPRI) entre México y Hong Kong* [The Mexico-Hong Kong BIT enters into force] (Jun. 16, 2021), https://www.gob.mx/se/es/articulos/entra-en-vigor-el-acuerdo-para-la-proteccion-y-promocion-reciproca-de-las-inversiones-appri-entre-mexico-y-hong-kong-274825?idiom=es (last visited on Dec. 22, 2022).
24. *See Decreto Promulgatorio del Acuerdo entre el Gobierno de los Estados Unidos Mexicanos y el Gobierno de la Región Administrativa Especial de Hong Kong de la República Popular China para la Promoción y Protección Recíproca de Inversiones, hecho en Davos, Suiza, el veintitrés de enero de dos mil veinte* [Promulgatory Decree of the BIT Between Mexico and Hong Kong, signed in Davos, Switzerland, on Jan. 23, 2020], published in the Federal Official Gazette on Jun. 11, 2021.
25. *See* ICSID, *Database of ICSID Member States*, https://icsid.worldbank.org/about/member-states/database-of-member-states (last visited on Dec. 19, 2022).
26. Bernardo Sepúlveda, *Mexico and the Settlement of Investment Disputes: ICSID as the Recommended Option*, 5 Pepp. Disp. Resol. L.J. 407, 410 (2005).
27. *See Legacy Vulcan, LLC v. United Mexican States* (ICSID Case No. ARB/19/1), https://icsid.worldbank.org/cases/case-database/case-detail?CaseNo=ARB/19/1.

adhesion to the ICSID Convention occurred within the NAFTA renegotiation process that led to the USMCA with the intention of strengthening Mexico's position as an investor-friendly country.[28]

Given its close commercial links with the United States and Canada, NAFTA Chapter XI quickly became the basis for most investor-State disputes against Mexico. However, on July 1, 2020, the USMCA entered into force and NAFTA was terminated. Under NAFTA, the United States (U.S.), Canada, and Mexico had the same set of protections and arbitration procedural rules. This changed with the USMCA, reducing the investor-friendlier climate that existed with NAFTA:

(1) Although the USMCA was signed by the U.S., Mexico and Canada, investment arbitration thereunder will only exist for Mexico and the U.S. and both countries' investors. As between the U.S. and Canada, no investment arbitration will exist pursuant to the USMCA's rules; and as between Mexico and Canada, the Comprehensive and Progressive Agreement for Trans-Pacific Partnership (CPTPP) will be applicable for investor-State disputes.

(2) While the USMCA has the same general investor protections as NAFTA—i.e., protection against direct and indirect expropriation,[29] fair and equitable treatment,[30] full protection and security,[31] most-favored-nation,[32] and national treatment[33]—the protections provided under the USMCA are written more restrictively.[34] In addition, the USMCA restricts the protections that can be claimed in an arbitration to the type of arbitration pursued.

Under the USMCA, the following three alternative (either or) investment arbitration procedures exist:

(1) *Legacy investment arbitration*: Although the NAFTA was terminated with the entry into force of the USMCA, the USMCA provides that NAFTA will still apply beyond its termination only to arbitrations filed between 1 July 2020—the entry into force of the USMCA—until July 1, 2023— "three years

28. *See* Mexican Ministry of Economy, *México Firma el Convenio sobre Arreglo de Diferencias Relativas a Inversiones entre Estados Nacionales y de Otros Estados* [Mexico signs the ICSID Convention] (Jan. 11, 2018), https://www.gob.mx/se/prensa/mexico-firma-el-convenio-sobre-arreglo-de-diferencias-relativas-a-inversiones-entre-estados-nacionales-y-de-otros-estados (last visited on Dec. 22, 2022).
29. USMCA, Annex 14-B, at Art. 14.8.1.
30. *Ibid.*, at Art. 14.6.
31. *Ibid.*, at Art. 14.6.1.
32. *Ibid.*, at Art. 14.5.
33. *Ibid.*, at Art. 14.4.
34. For instance, the USMCA clarifies that the minimum standard of treatment does not require treatment beyond that required by customary international law; the *national treatment* and *most-favored-nation treatment* clauses include a definition of treatment accorded in *like circumstances*; and the scope of direct and indirect expropriation is expressly defined, among others.

after the termination of NAFTA."[35] Such arbitrations refer to the legacy investments, which are defined as those "established or acquired between January 1, 1994, and [1 July 2020], and in existence on [the latter date]," i.e., made under the NAFTA.[36] The request for arbitration has to be filed on or before June 30, 2023 (three years after NAFTA's termination),[37] which means that the notice of arbitration has to be filed on or before April 1, 2023,[38] and therefore that the contravening state act must have occurred on or before January 1, 2023, at the latest, but not before July 1, 2020, at the earliest.[39]

Since the legacy investment arbitration is governed by NAFTA, its provisions control the proceedings, and therefore the applicable protections are those provided by NAFTA and the three states' investors can have recourse thereunder.[40] This is the only existent recourse for Canadian investors against the U.S., whereas against Mexico Canadian investors can also recur to the CPTPP. Mexican and U.S. investors will only have recourse to the legacy investment arbitration if they cannot submit claims based on the USMCA's covered government contracts dispute mechanism, explained below.[41]

(2) *Special arbitration for investment disputes related to covered government contracts:* It is restricted to investors that have a covered government contract, i.e., "a *written agreement* between a *national authority* of an Annex Party and a covered investment or investor of the other Annex Party, on which the covered investment or investor relies in establishing or acquiring a covered investment other than the written agreement itself, that grants rights to the covered investment or investor in a *covered sector*."[42] In addition, since this arbitration is fully governed by the USMCA's provisions, the factual pattern must have taken place after July 1, 2022, i.e., after the date the USMCA entered into force.[43] This mechanism permits investors to submit claims for breaches to any and all of the protections provided under the USMCA.[44]

The underscored terms, in turn, are defined in the USMCA, but are not self-evident, and have no resemblance to NAFTA or other treaties in force.[45]

35. Protocol replacing the NAFTA with the USMCA, para. 3.
36. USMCA, Annex 14-C para. 6(a).
37. Protocol replacing the NAFTA with the USMCA, para. 3.
38. NAFTA, Art. 1119.1.
39. *Ibid.*, at Arts. 1116.2, 1117.2, 1120.1.
40. USMCA, Annex 14-C, para. 3.
41. *Ibid.*, Annex 14-C, footnote 21.
42. *Ibid.*, Annex 14-C, para. 6.a (emphasis added).
43. *Ibid.*, Annex 14-C, at Art. 14.2, para. 3.
44. *Ibid.*, Annex 14-E, para. 2.
45. The Trans-Pacific Partnership Agreement (TPP) provides a definition for written agreement and uses the term national authority (although it is not defined) while defining the term investment agreement. Although the TPP does not use the term covered sector in the definition of investment agreement, the manner in which paragraphs (a), (b) and (c) of such definition is written has a similar resemblance with the definition provided in the USMCA for covered sectors. *See* TPP, Chapter 9, section. A; cf. USMCA, Annex 14-E, para. 6.b. The TPP never

As such, they are novel concepts that are yet to be construed by either the Free Trade Commission or arbitral tribunals. The way they will be interpreted in the future has the potential to either widen the already limited investors' access to arbitration or restrict it more.

A *written agreement* is defined as "an agreement in writing, negotiated, and executed by two or more parties, whether in a single instrument or in multiple instruments."[46] Consequently, the following are not considered written agreements: "(a) a unilateral act of an administrative or judicial authority, such as a permit, license, certificate, approval, or similar instrument issued by an Annex Party in its regulatory capacity, or a subsidy or grant, or a decree, order or judgment, standing alone; and (b) an administrative or judicial consent decree or order."[47] It seems that only public contracts or concessions entered into with national authorities would cover such a definition.

A *national authority* is defined as that "at the central level of government," which "includes any person, including a state enterprise or another body, when it exercises governmental authority delegated to it by an authority at the central level of government."[48] National authorities also mean "a state enterprise or another body, when it exercises governmental authority delegated to it by an authority at the central level of government," which can be delegated in the applicable legal framework.[49] The USMCA's Article 1.5.b defines central level of government as the federal government.

And a *covered sector* is defined as any of the following five:

(i) activities with respect to oil and natural gas that a national authority of an Annex Party controls, such as exploration, extraction, refining, transportation, distribution, or sale;
(ii) the supply of power generation services to the public on behalf of an Annex Party;
(iii) the supply of telecommunications services to the public on behalf of an Annex Party;
(iv) the supply of transportation services to the public on behalf of an Annex Party; or
(v) the ownership or management of roads, railways, bridges, or canals that are not for the exclusive or predominant use and benefit of the government of an Annex Party.[50]

(3) *Investment disputes mechanism for all other arbitrations*: It applies generally to all investments that do not fall under the purview of a covered government contracts' investment dispute. Similarly to the covered government contracts' arbitration, since this venue is fully governed by the USMCA's provisions, the

entered into force; however, its provisions were incorporated by reference *mutatis mutandis* in the CPTPP. Some of the TPP's provisions were suspended in the CPTPP until the parties thereto agree otherwise, and therefore they never entered into force. That is the case with the definitions of investment agreement and written agreement. *See* CPTPP, Arts. 1.1, 2, Annex, para. 2(a)(i).

46. USMCA, Annex 14-E, para. 6.c.
47. *Ibid.*, Annex 14-E, footnote 34.
48. *Ibid.*, Annex 14-E, para. 6.c, and footnote 33.
49. *See ibid.*, footnotes 5 and 33.
50. *Ibid.*, Annex 14-E, para. 6.b.

factual pattern must have taken place after July 1, 2022, i.e., after the date of entry into force of the USMCA.[51]

The main differences between the covered government contracts and the legacy investment arbitrations are the following two: On the one hand, the claimant is limited in submitting a claim for breaches to the following three protections: national treatment, most-favored-nation, or direct expropriation.[52] And, on the other hand, the investor cannot gain access directly to arbitration, but is rather required to exhaust litigation before national courts prior to filing an arbitration—"the claimant [must] obtain[] a final decision from a court of last resort of [Mexico] or 30 months have elapsed from the date the proceeding ... was initiated."[53]

NAFTA became almost synonymous with an effective recourse for foreign investors, which led it to contribute as a tool to contrast the state's deviances to the rule of law.[54] Compared to both the CPTTP and the USMCA, it is clear that NAFTA was a more investor-friendly treaty.[55] Although not a negative trait in and of itself, the fact that the USMCA limits investors' protections and recourse to arbitration will certainly affect the view foreign investors have in Mexico and their means to attempt to enforce the rule of law.

[2] Trends in Arbitration

[a] Commercial Arbitration

The most-used arbitration institution in Mexico with an international component is the International Chamber of Commerce's International Court of Arbitration (ICC).[56] The most recent available statistics of the ICC, which pertain to the year 2020, consider Mexico as a high-ranking status country worldwide. In the Americas, Mexico is usually

51. *Ibid.*, at Art. 14.2, para. 3.
52. *Ibid.*, Annex 14-D, para. 1.a.b.
53. *Ibid.*, Annex 14-D, para. 1.b.
54. *See* Sergio Puig, *Is Investment Arbitration Good or Bad for Developing Countries? The Mexican Experience in the North American Free Trade Agreement Context*, 4 L. & Prac. Int'l Cts. & Tribunals 61, 67 (2005) (arguing that the positive effect of Chapter XI "for Mexico relies on the availability of a process to combat political power deviations, which process produces information about State behavior and exposes violators.").
55. *See, e.g.*, David Gantz, *The Spaghetti Bowl Revisited: Coexistence of Regional Trade Agreements such as NAFTA with the Trans-Pacific Partnership*, 48 Geo. J. Int'l L. 557, 569 (2017) (suggesting that most investors would prefer the earlier treaty in lieu of TPP, such as the NAFTA, because preceding treaties are more investor friendly than TPP). Because it incorporated reservations that were not existent in the TPP, the CPTPP limits more restrictively the kind of disputes a foreign investor could claim against Mexico. CPTPP, Annex 9-L (laying out Mexico's laundry list of reservations to its consent on investment arbitration, related to specific acts of authority, such as the administrative rescission for certain public contracts, which were not contemplated under TPP).
56. Pereznieto, *supra* n. 1, at 31.

only surpassed by the U.S. and Brazil. Other numbers regarding Mexico include the following:

(1) most selected country as a place of arbitration: Mexico ranked 13th with eighteen arbitrations;[57]
(2) most frequent nationality of the parties to an arbitration: Mexico ranked 10th with seventy-eight parties, out of which thirty-seven were claimants and forty-one respondents (compared to a total of fifty-one in 2019);[58]
(3) most frequent nationality of the arbitrator: Mexico ranked 8th worldwide with forty-seven arbitrators (compared to thirty-six in 2019);[59] and
(4) most disputes between parties of the same nationality: Mexico ranked 3rd with over twenty cases.[60]

Other centers for arbitrations with an international component that are usually sought include the American Arbitration Association's International Centre for Dispute Resolution (ICDR) and the London Court of International Arbitration (LCIA). Such centers have the following numbers regarding Mexico:

(1) Data from the ICDR considers that, for 2020, Mexico ranked 8th in terms of top nationality with twenty-five parties (compared to ranking number 7 for 2019 with thirty-six parties).[61]
(2) Information from the LCIA considers that the percentage of Mexican parties in arbitration proceedings increased from 1.3% in 2020 to 2.1% in 2021.[62] In addition, in five arbitrations the parties selected Mexico as the place of the seat of the arbitration and applicable law (same number as in 2020);[63] and seven arbitrators had Mexican nationality (compared to fourteen in 2020, when it ranked the 6th most sought nationality).[64]

At the purely national level, arbitrations with Mexican parties in Mexico are commonly handled by one of the following two Mexican arbitration institutions: the National Chamber of Commerce of Mexico City (CANACO), and the Mexican Arbitration Centre (CAM). CAM very recently updated its Rules of Arbitration.[65] Beginning on December 1, 2022, CAM's new Rules of Arbitration include simplified, expedited

57. ICC, *ICC Dispute Resolution 2020 Statistics*, http://iccwbo.org/dr-stat (last visited on Dec. 15, 2022), 30.
58. *Ibid.*, at 10, 25.
59. *Ibid.*, at 27-28.
60. *Ibid.*, at 11.
61. ICDR, *2020 ICDR Case Data Infographic* (2021), https://www.adr.org/research (last visited on Dec. 15, 2022); ICDR, *2019 ICDR Case Data Infographic* (2021), https://www.adr.org/research (last visited on Dec. 15, 2022).
62. LCIA, *2021 Annual Casework Report*, 12.
63. *Ibid.*, at 15; LCIA, *2020 Annual Casework Report*, 17.
64. LCIA, *2021 Annual Casework Report*, 18; LCIA, *2020 Annual Casework Report*, 19.
65. *See* CAM, *Rules of Arbitration*, (Dec. 1, 2022), https://camex.com.mx/reglas-de-arbitraje-del-cam/ (last visited on Dec. 15, 2022).

proceedings for arbitrations under MXN 3,000,000 (approximately USD 150,000);[66] the use of electronic communications and remote and hybrid hearings;[67] an obligation to disclose third-party funding and funders;[68] and the power of the tribunal to order the parties to maintain the status quo situation between them while deciding on a request for a precautionary measure.[69]

Although neither CANACO nor CAM publishes their statistics, from informal talks with practitioners it can roughly be estimated that CANACO receives approximately ten new cases each year, while CAM confirmed to the authors of this article that in 2022 they received thirty-six new cases.

Mexico's federal legislation allows the use of arbitration in public contracts generally.[70] Given that the first federal laws to provide for the use of arbitration in public contracts were those concerning contracts entered into by the National Oil Company, *Petróleos Mexicanos*, and the power utility, *Comisión Federal de Electricidad* (CFE), and due to the sheer amount of contracts such SOEs enter into, it is not uncommon to refer to them as "Mexico's most recurrent users of arbitration."[71] In recent years, CFE's arbitrations in particular have gained notoriety in national media. In 2021, CFE began publishing the numbers of its arbitrations in its quarterly public financial statements. According to the most recent financial statement, they amount to thirty-four arbitrations, out of which twenty-four are international.[72] This is a sheer increase from 2021, where CFE reported only twenty arbitrations (without giving more specifics).[73]

For commercial arbitration, there is no single, specialized legal unit within the federal government that litigates all arbitrations related to all SOE or state instrumentalities, but rather each one of them litigates their cases individually.[74] Accordingly, there is no single figure for all the arbitrations to which the federal government's SOEs and instrumentalities are a party.

66. *Ibid.*, at Appendix III.
67. *Ibid.*, at Arts. 3, 20.2, 28.1.
68. *Ibid.*, at Art. 13.4. Third-party funding has not been established yet in Mexico as a general sought practice for neither arbitration nor domestic court litigation; however, its use is "widely expected ... to continue to progress in the coming years," especially for arbitration. Paloma Castro, *The Third Party Litigation Funding Law Review: Mexico* (Dec. 8, 2022), The Law Reviews, https://thelawreviews.co.uk/title/the-third-party-litigation-funding-law-review/mexico (last visited on Dec. 15, 2022).
69. CAM, *supra* n. 65, at Art. 30.1.
70. *See* Public Sector Procurement, Leasing and Services Law, *supra* n. 4, at Arts. 80-86; Public Works and Related Services Law, *supra* n. 4, at Arts. 98-104; Public-Private Partnerships Law, *supra* n. 4, at Arts. 138-139.
71. *See* Victor Ruiz, *Time for a Mexican "Procuración" to Litigate Its Arbitrations?* (May 23, 2012), http://arbitrationblog.kluwerarbitration.com/2012/05/23/time-for-a-mexican-procuracion-to-litigate-its-arbitrations/ (last visited on Dec. 21, 2022).
72. *See* CFE, *Estados Financieros Consolidados Condensados: al 30 de septiembre de 2022 y 31 de diciembre de 2021*, 50-51, https://www.cfe.mx/finanzas/reportes-financieros/pages/estados-financieros.aspx (last visited on Dec. 21, 2022).
73. *See* CFE, *Estados Financieros Consolidados Condensados por los dos años terminados el 31 de diciembre de 2021 y 2020*, 87, https://www.cfe.mx/finanzas/reportes-financieros/pages/estados-financieros.aspx (last visited on Dec. 21, 2022).
74. *See* Ruiz, *supra* n. 71.

[b] Investment Arbitration

There are currently two ongoing negotiations to sign the following FTAs with potential investment chapters:

(1) *European Union (EU)*: In May 2016, Mexico and the European Union (EU) started the negotiation process for the update of the EU-Mexico Global Agreement, which came into force in 2000.[75] In April 2018, Mexico and the EU reached an agreement on the most important elements of the treaty, which has been made publicly available.[76] The new agreement would make duty-free practically all trade in goods between them and would open trade in services.[77] Such text has not been signed yet by the EU and Mexico, and no formal date of signature has been announced.

On the investment arbitration side, its most salient trait is the incorporation of the EU's new Investment Court System, which would differ greatly from the current investment arbitration system contained in other BITs and FTAs with an investment chapter that Mexico has signed.[78] There will be two tribunals: The Tribunal, which will be competent to hear investment claims, will be composed of three Mexican nationals, three nationals of a Member State of the EU, and three nationals of third countries;[79] and the Appeal Tribunal, which will be competent to hear appeals against awards rendered by the Tribunal, will be composed of six members, out of which two will be Mexican nationals, two nationals of a Member State of the EU, and two nationals of third countries.[80] ICSID's secretariat will act as the secretariat for both tribunals.[81]

In addition, "[o]n the date of entry into force of th[e EU-Mexico Global] Agreement, the agreements between Member States of the European Union and Mexico ... including the rights and obligations derived therefrom shall cease to have effect and shall be replaced and superseded by th[e EU-Mexico Global] Agreement."[82] Similarly to the USMCA's legacy investment claims, the EU-Mexico Global Agreement permits the submission of claims pursuant to the BITs signed by EU Member States with Mexico if (i) "the claim arises from an alleged breach of that agreement that took place prior to the date of

75. European Commission, *EU and Mexico reach new agreement on trade*, (Apr. 21, 2018), https://ec.europa.eu/commission/presscorner/detail/en/IP_18_782 (last visited on Dec. 15, 2022).
76. *See* European Commission, *EU-Mexico agreement: The agreement in principle*, https://policy.trade.ec.europa.eu/eu-trade-relationships-country-and-region/countries-and-regions/mexico/eu-mexico-agreement/agreement-principle_en (last visited in Dec. 15, 2022).
77. European Commission, *EU and Mexico reach new agreement on trade*, *supra* n. 75.
78. *Ibid.*
79. Modernization of the Trade part of the EU-Mexico Global Agreement, S. X: Resolution of Investment Disputes, Art. 11.1.2, https://policy.trade.ec.europa.eu/eu-trade-relationships-country-and-region/countries-and-regions/mexico/eu-mexico-agreement/agreement-principle_en (last visited in Dec. 21, 2022).
80. *Ibid.*, S. X: Resolution of Investment Disputes, at Art. 12.1.2.
81. *Ibid.*, S. X: Resolution of Investment Disputes, at Arts. 11.17 and 12.15.
82. *Ibid.*, Ch. XX: Investment, S. A: General Provisions, at Art. 22.1.

suspension of the [BIT]" and (ii) "no more than three years have elapsed from the date of suspension of the [BIT]."[83]

(2) *United Kingdom*: The United Kingdom and Mexico were both part of the EU-Mexico Global Agreement. As a consequence of Brexit, on February 1, 2020, the Withdrawal Agreement between the EU and the United Kingdom entered into force, which establishes the terms of the United Kingdom's orderly withdrawal from the EU.[84] Under such a treaty, a transition period was provided until December 31, 2020, during which time the United Kingdom still benefited as if being party to treaties with third states, including the EU-Mexico Global Agreement.[85]

On December 15, 2020, Mexico and the United Kingdom entered into an Agreement for Commercial Continuity between both countries, which preserves the preferential trade conditions between both countries as provided in the EU-Mexico Global Agreement, and foresees the commencement of negotiations between both parties to reach an FTA.[86]

On May 20, 2022, the negotiation process toward an FTA between Mexico and the United Kingdom officially began.[87] On July 11, 2022, the first round of negotiations was held.[88]

It is unclear whether such FTA will comprehend an investment chapter, considering that a BIT between Mexico and the United Kingdom has been in force since 2007.

---

83. *Ibid.*, Ch. XX: Investment, S. A: General Provisions, Art. 22.3.a.b.
84. European Commission, *The EU-UK Withdrawal Agreement*, https://commission.europa.eu/strategy-and-policy/relations-non-eu-countries/relations-united-kingdom/eu-uk-withdrawal-agreement_en (last visited on Dec. 19, 2022).
85. *See ibid.*; *see also* Mexican Ministry of Economy, *Ante la salida del Reino Unido de la Unión Europea, la relación comercial preferencial con México se mantiene* [Upon the United Kingdom's exit of the EU, the preferential commercial relationship with Mexico is maintained], (Jan. 30, 2020), Press communiqué 012, https://www.gob.mx/se/articulos/ante-la-salida-del-reino-unido-de-la-union-europea-la-relacion-comercial-preferencial-con-mexico-se-mantiene?idiom=es (last visited in Dec. 20, 2022).
86. *See* "*Decreto Promulgatorio del Acuerdo de Continuidad Comercial entre los Estados Unidos Mexicanos y el Reino Unido de la Gran Bretaña e Irlanda del Norte, hecho en la Ciudad de México el quince de diciembre de dos mil veinte*" [Promulgatory Decree of the Agreement between Mexico and the United Kingdom of Great Britain and Northern Ireland for the Commercial Continuity, signed in Mexico City on Dec. 15, 2020], published in the Federal Official Gazette on Jun. 1, 2021.
87. Mexican Ministry of Economy, *México y Reino Unido inician formalmente negociaciones hacia un nuevo Tratado de Libre Comercio* [Mexico and the United Kingdom commence formal negotiations toward a new FTA], Press communiqué 027, (May 20, 2022), https://www.gob.mx/se/es/articulos/mexico-y-reino-unido-inician-formalmente-negociaciones-hacia-un-nuevo-tratado-de-libre-comercio-302568?idiom=es (last visited in Dec. 20, 2022).
88. Mexican Ministry of Economy, *México y el Reino Unido llevarán a cabo la Primera Ronda de Negociaciones para un Tratado de Libre Comercio entre ambos países* [Mexico and the United Kingdom will undertake the First Round of Negotiations toward an FTA between both countries], Press communiqué 043 (Jul. 11, 2022), https://www.gob.mx/se/prensa/mexico-y-el-reino-unido-llevaran-a-cabo-la-primera-ronda-de-negociaciones-para-un-tratado-de-libre-comercio-entre-ambos-paises?idiom=es (last visited in Dec. 20, 2022).

Mexico attracts much more FDI than what its national companies invest abroad. This is reflected in the times Mexico has been a respondent compared to the number of arbitrations where the claimant has been a Mexican national: thirty-eight times as respondent, and only five as the home state of the investor (of the cases that have been made public).[89] The nationality of the claimants roughly reflects Mexico's trade relationship, which has the U.S. as the main trade partner (by a sheer amount), followed by Canada, and China:[90] the great majority of claimants are U.S. nationals (57.8%), followed by Canadians (13.1%); however, no Chinese claimant has instituted an arbitration against Mexico.[91]

In 2022, ICSID reports that two investment arbitrations were filed against Mexico, compared to three filed in 2021;[92] IA Reporter informed that two notices of intention were submitted against Mexico,[93] although none are mentioned in the Mexican Ministry of Economy's webpage.[94] Per the latter's official figures, Mexico has fifteen active notices of arbitration and thirteen active cases.[95]

Mexico litigates investment arbitration cases with both in-house and external legal counsel: the Mexican Ministry of Economy's International Trade Legal Counsel acts as leading counsel with the assistance of external counsel from international law firms, which have changed from time to time.[96] Mexico is reported to have a perfect compliance record, having paid the awards rendered against it in all instances.[97]

89. UNCTAD, *Investment Policy Hub: Investment Dispute Settlement Navigator*, https://investmentpolicy.unctad.org/investment-dispute-settlement/country/136/mexico (last visited Dec. 15, 2022).
90. *See* Mexican Central Bank, *Cubo de Información de Comercio Exterior: Septiembre 2022*, [Trade Informational Cube: September 2022], https://www.banxico.org.mx/CuboComercioExterior/participacion (last visited Dec. 15, 2022).
91. *See* UNCTAD, *supra* n. 89.
92. *See* ICSID, *Search Cases*, https://icsid.worldbank.org/cases/case-database (last visited on Dec. 22, 2022) (noting that on 2022 Doups Holdings LLC and Consolidated Water Coöperatief, U.A. filed claims against Mexico, whereas in 2021 the following companies filed claims: L1bre Holding, LLC, Finley Resources Inc., MWS Maņagement Inc., and Prize Permanent Holdings, LLC, and First Majestic Silver Corp).
93. *See* Lisa Bohmer, *US Company Puts Mexico ON Notice of a 667 Million USD NAFTA Legacy Dispute*, IA Reporter, (Feb. 22, 2022), https://www.iareporter.com/articles/us-company-puts-mexico-on-notice-of-a-667-million-usd-nafta-legacy-dispute/ (last visited in Dec. 22, 2022) (informing that "Monterra Energy, an oil and infrastructure company, has submitted a NAFTA/USMCA notice of dispute to Mexico over the state's decision to close a fuel storage terminal located in the Mexican province of Veracruz, the Tuxpan terminal"); *see also* Damien Charlotin, *Mexico Is Put on Notice of a 3 Billion USD NAFTA Legacy Dispute*, IA Reporter, (Nov. 2, 2022), https://www.iareporter.com/articles/mexico-is-put-on-notice-of-a-3-billion-usd-nafta-legacy-dispute/ (last visited in Dec. 22, 2022) (reporting that "Access Business Group (ABG), a US entity based in Michigan, has filed a Notice of Intent (NoI) to submit a NAFTA legacy claim against Mexico, in relation to a dispute over a large agricultural venture.").
94. *See* Mexican Ministry of Economy, *Comercio Exterior, Solución de Controversias* [Foreign Trade: Dispute Resolution], (May 10, 2015), https://www.gob.mx/se/acciones-y-programas/comercio-exterior-solucion-de-controversias?state=published (last visited on Dec. 22, 2022).
95. *Ibid.*
96. *See* Rodrigo Polanco, *Systems of Legal Defence Used by Latin American Countries in Investment Disputes*, 17 J. World Inv. & Trade 562, 580-581 (2016) https://doi.org/10.1163/22119000-12340004 (noting that, since Mexico began contracting external counsel in 2004, it has never retained a domestic law firm, which is consistent with the strategy used by the majority of the Latin American states with the highest amounts of investment arbitration cases); *see also* Cosmo

[C] OUTLOOK AND CONCLUSIONS

Mexico's decades-long history with arbitration has positioned it as an arbitration-friendly jurisdiction. Its network of multilateral commercial treaties, coupled with its BITs and FTAs with investment chapters, along with the Constitutional and legal frameworks that underpin them, have granted foreign and national investors alike the confidence that arbitration will continue to be the go-to dispute resolution method for parties that prefer an alternative method of resolution over domestic courts.

The increasing number of arbitrations for both state and private parties alike is most likely to continue its steady growth in the following years.

Anderson, *Curtis Wins Bid to Advise Mexico in 13 Disputes*, GAR (Oct. 7, 2022), https://globalarbitrationreview.com/article/curtis-wins-bid-advise-mexico-in-13-disputes (last visited in Dec. 22, 2022) (informing that Curtis, Mallet-Prevost Colt & Mosle will be the new external legal counsel to advise the Mexican Ministry of Economy in investment arbitration disputes after winning a tender).

97. *See* Jan Paulsson, *The Power of States to Make Meaningful Promises to Foreigners*, 1 J. Int'l Disp. Settlement 341, 346 (2010) https://doi.org/10.1093/jnlids/idq013 (praising Mexico's legal defense in NAFTA arbitrations for being competent, obtaining moderate losses, and paying unfavorable awards, all of which has enhanced its reputation as an investor-friendly country); *see also* Emmanuel Gaillard& Ilija Mitrev Penushliski, *State Compliance with Investment Awards*, 35 ICSID Rev. 540, 564 (2020) https://doi.org/10.1093/icsidreview/siaa034 (noting that "[a]lthough in some cases it initially pursued annulment, Mexico has voluntarily complied with the adverse awards, and often within a year of the final decision"); *see also* Nikos Lavranos, *Report on Compliance with Investment Treaty Arbitration Awards 2022*, International Law Compliance (October 2022), 11, https://www.internationallawcompliance.com/ (last visited on Dec. 22, 2022).

CHAPTER 2

Regulatory Framework in Mexico: The National and International Dimensions

Ana Sofía Sapiña Errecart & Cecilia Azar Manzur[*]

We can safely say that Mexico is a pro-arbitration jurisdiction. Mexico has adopted an arbitration legal framework that conforms with the highest international standards and has ratified a considerable number of treaties with investment protection provisions. Apart from having two growing local institutions, Mexicans are among the top users of the most renowned international arbitration institutions. The inclusion of arbitration agreements in government contracts is only one of the many factors that contribute to the extensive use of arbitration in Mexico; which is predicted to keep growing in the next couple of years.

In this chapter, we will provide an overview of the national and international dimensions of the Mexican commercial and investment arbitration legal framework (section [A]). Then, we will describe some key trends that contribute to the increase in the use of arbitration in Mexico (section [B]). Lastly, we will outline some of the most imminent challenges that commercial and investment arbitration will face in the foreseeable future in Mexico (section [C]).

[A] MEXICO'S ARBITRATION LEGAL FRAMEWORK

Mexico has adopted and ratified a comprehensive and sophisticated set of arbitration legislations and international treaties. In this chapter, we provide an overview of Mexico's pro-arbitration legal framework. We first describe the different elements that, together, comprise the Mexican commercial arbitration regulation (section [1]). Then, we describe Mexico's robust framework of investment treaties; many of which contain

* We would like to thank Ana Sofía Mosqueda from Galicia Abogados, S.C. for her collaboration in researching and compiling judicial precedents issued by Mexican Courts regarding arbitration.

investment arbitration provisions for the settlement of investment disputes (section [2]).

[1] Commercial Arbitration

Mexico's commercial arbitration practice is primarily regulated by the Mexican *lex arbitri*; which is a verbatim adoption of the UNCITRAL Model Law on International Commercial Arbitration (the "*Model Law*") with very specific and harmless amendments (section [a]). The Mexican *lex arbitri* is complemented with a second element: international conventions ratified by Mexico for the recognition and enforcement of foreign arbitral awards (section [c]). These two elements make the Mexican arbitration legal framework conform to the highest standards of international arbitration practice.

Another essential element of this framework should not be overlooked: judicial precedents. Mexican Courts have consistently interpreted and applied the Mexican *lex arbitri* and these interpretations have shaped the arbitration practice in Mexico (section [b]). Even if Mexico can pride itself on its considerable number of pro-arbitration precedents; several national Courts still issue decisions that directly violate some of the most basic principles of international arbitration.

[a] Mexican Lex Arbitri

Mexico is a Model Law jurisdiction. However, the Model Law was not adopted as an independent arbitration statute but in a chapter of the Mexican Code of Commerce.[1] Some provisions of the Model Law had already been partially adopted in 1989[2] to modernize the national arbitration legislation.[3] However, the most relevant reform of the Mexican *lex arbitri* did not arrive until 1993[4] when most of the Model Law[5] and some provisions from the UNCITRAL Arbitration Rules[6] were adopted in the Code of Commerce.[7]

One of the most relevant variations of the original text of the Model Law introduced by the Mexican legislator is that the Mexican *lex arbitri* is applicable to both domestic and international commercial arbitrations seated in Mexico[8] (with the exception of specific provisions that apply regardless of the fact that the seat of

1. *See* the chapter titled "Commercial Arbitration" within the "Commercial Proceedings" section of the Code of Commerce (Código de Comercio) including Arts. 1415 to 1480.
2. 1989 Code of Commerce Reform Decree.
3. Treviño Azcué, J., "The New Mexican Legislation on Commercial Arbitration," Journal of International Arbitration in Kluwer Law International, 5-29 (1994) https://doi.org/10.54648/joia 1994026.
4. 1993 Code of Commerce Reform Decree.
5. Model Law (1985).
6. UNCITRAL Arbitration Rules (1976).
7. Treviño Azcué, J., "The New Mexican Legislation on Commercial Arbitration," Journal of International Arbitration in Kluwer Law International, 5 (1994): "[t]he new law substantially incorporates the Model Law plus several provisions from the UNCITRAL Arbitration Rules of 1976 regarding costs, and a few procedural rules."
8. Code of Commerce, Art. 1415.

arbitration is not Mexico).[9] This means that Mexico has a single statute, unlike other countries with a dualist system with independent legislations for domestic and international arbitrations.[10]

Years after it was adopted in Mexico, the Model Law was amended in 2006. The amendments sought to "modernize the form required of an arbitration agreement to better conform with international contract practices" [11] and "establishe[d] a more comprehensive legal regime dealing with interim measures in support of arbitration."[12] These amendments have not been introduced to the Code of Commerce.

After the inclusion of the Model Law in 1993, the text of the arbitration chapter of the Code of Commerce has only been reformed once in 2011. Two major changes were introduced in that 2011 reform. First, the reform allows judges to suspend the recognition and enforcement of the award while set aside proceedings are pending.[13] Second, a chapter was included to adapt the Mexican judicial procedure to the limited situations in which judicial intervention is permitted in arbitration.[14] The second element of the reform is transcendental since it provided the arbitration regime with autonomy from the procedural rules that apply to judicial proceedings not related to arbitration; by including in the *lex arbitri* specific procedural rules to be followed by judges in the limited cases in which judicial intervention is permitted in arbitration.

In addition to the commercial arbitration *lex arbitri*, some local civil procedure legislations currently allow parties to settle their disputes through civil arbitrations in very specific circumstances in the context of contractual relationships between private, non-merchant, parties. An example of that is the legislation in Mexico City.[15] However, civil arbitration will soon have a uniform regulation since it will be exclusively governed by the National Civil and Family Procedural Code, which will gradually enter into force in the upcoming years in every state in Mexico.[16]

However, as stated by renowned Mexican arbitration practitioner Julio César Treviño Azcué "[i]n the international sphere, it is difficult to conceive of civil arbitrations taking place in Mexico and, as regards domestic arbitration, the great majority of domestic arbitrations that take place in the country are also commercial."[17]

9. *Ibid.* The second paragraph of this article provides that Arts. 1424, 1425, 1461, 1462, and 1463 will apply regardless of the fact that the seat of arbitration is not Mexico. Said provisions refer to matters such as the issuance of interim measures in support of arbitration, and the recognition and enforcement of foreign awards, among other things.
10. For instance, Argentina, Chile, Uruguay, and France have separate international and domestic arbitration statutes.
11. Model Law (2006), Art. 7.
12. Model Law (2006), Art. IV-A.
13. Code of Commerce, Art. 1463.
14. Code of Commerce, Arts. 1464 to 1480.
15. *See* Mexico City Civil Code (*Código de Procedimientos Civiles para la Ciudad de México*), Arts. 609 to 636.
16. *See* National Civil and Family Procedural Code (Código Nacional de Procedimientos Civiles y Familiares), Arts. 63 VIII, 386, 533-549 and 1182.
17. Treviño Azcué, J., "The New Mexican Legislation on Commercial Arbitration," Journal of International Arbitration in Kluwer Law International, 8 (1994).

This makes sense since, "[i]n Mexico there is no juridical tradition among Mexican litigation parties to submit civil matters to arbitration."[18]

[b] Judicial Precedents Related to Arbitration

The understanding of the Mexican *lex arbitri* cannot be complete without considering judicial precedents issued by Mexican Courts to interpret and apply it. The provisions of the Code of Commerce and the decisions of judges, jointly, are what truly represent Mexican arbitration practice.

For purposes of clarity, it is necessary to take a broad look at how the system of judicial precedent works in Mexico. The Mexican Constitution *(Constitución Política de los Estados Unidos Mexicanos)* regulates those cases in which a judicial decision by a federal Court will either bind or guide lower Courts.[19] There are two kinds of precedents in Mexico. There are precedents that are non-binding for lower Courts but are certainly used as authoritative guides (known as *tesis aisladas)*. There are also precedents that become binding for lower Courts (known as *jurisprudencias)* after going through one of the mechanisms provided by the law.

For instance, a binding precedent is created: (i) when the Supreme Court issues a judgment with favorable votes from a certain number of justices; (ii) when five consecutive *tesis* decide or interpret a legal question in the same way, creating a "precedent by repetition"; or (iii) when two *tesis* have decided the same legal matter in a contradictory way and the competent authority decides which decision shall prevail, creating a "precedent by contradiction."

That being said, some binding and non-binding judicial precedents issued by Mexican Courts can be considered pro-arbitration since they have contributed to the application of the *lex arbitri* pursuant to the spirit of the Model Law. However, some Mexican Courts have issued precedents and established practices that threaten our arbitration regime and violate international arbitration principles.

We provide a table summarizing some examples of both kinds of precedents, highlighting in gray precedents and practices that, considering the international principles applicable to arbitration, threaten the arbitration regime:

18. Silva J., "Arbitraje Comercial Internacional en México," Pereznieto Editores, 29 (1994).
19. Mexican Constitution (*Constitución Política de los Estados Unidos Mexicanos*), Art. 94 & Amparo Law (*Ley de Amparo, Reglamentaria de los Artículos 103 y 107 de la Constitución Política de los Estados Unidos Mexicanos*), Arts. 215-230.

Table 2.1 Precedents Regarding Arbitration Issued by Mexican Courts

Issue	*Article CC*	*Precedent or Practice*
Judicial intervention in arbitrations seated in Mexico	Article 1424[20]	**Limited extent of judicial intervention in arbitrations:** In several non-binding precedents,[21] Mexican Courts have reaffirmed the principle of minimum judicial intervention in arbitration and invited judges to only intervene in arbitration in the limited circumstances allowed by the *lex arbitri*. In another non-binding precedent,[22] a Mexican Court went even further by clarifying that Mexican Courts had no jurisdiction to decide procedural aspects of arbitrations or review interim procedural decisions made by arbitral tribunals. The Court reasoned that arbitration proceedings should have no judicial intervention (with specific exceptions) to guarantee the efficiency and autonomy of arbitration from Court proceedings.

20. Adoption of Model Law (2006), Art. 5: "Extent of Court intervention. In matters governed by this Law, no Court shall intervene except where so provided in this Law."
21. Seventh Civil Collegiate Court of the First Circuit, non-binding precedent number 163413 (2010) titled "Arbitraje comercial. Su legislación es especializada y por ende, excluyente de normas generales"; Civil Plenary of the First Circuit, non-binding precedent 2022901 (2021) titled "Juicio arbitral. Se rige por los principios de autonomía de la voluntad o voluntariedad y de mínima intervención."
22. Third Civil Collegiate Court of the First Circuit, non-binding precedent number 172973 (2006) titled "Nulidad de actos dentro del procedimiento arbitral mercantil. No corresponde su conocimiento a un tribunal judicial."

Issue	*Article CC*	*Precedent or Practice*
Interim measures in support of arbitrations	Articles 1425,[23] 1433[24] & 1478[25]	**Discretion of Mexican Courts to grant interim measures in support of arbitration:** In a non-binding precedent,[26] a Mexican Court reaffirmed that Mexican Courts have broad discretion to grant interim measures in support of arbitration due to the diversity and unpredictability of situations that may require said kind of relief. However, the Court clarified that Courts must conform to standards of reasonability and coherence when issuing these orders.
		***Ex parte* interim measures issued by Mexican Courts in support of arbitration:** In a non-binding precedent,[27] a Mexican Court interpreted that interim measures issued by Mexican Courts in support of arbitration could be initially issued ex parte to secure the effectiveness of the measure. The affected party by the interim measure will then be called to the interim measures proceeding, be heard, and have an opportunity to combat the initial interim measures. The judge will eventually issue a final interim measures decision.

23. Adoption of Model Law (2006), Art. 9: "Arbitration agreement and interim measures by Court. It is not incompatible with an arbitration agreement for a party to request, before or during arbitral proceedings, from a Court an interim measure of protection and for a Court to grant such measure."
24. Adoption of Model Law (2006), Art. 17(1): "Power of arbitral tribunal to order interim measures. (1) Unless otherwise agreed by the parties, the arbitral tribunal may, at the request of a party, grant interim measures." Art. 17 of the Model Law was reformed in 2006 and that reform has not been included in the Code of Commerce.
25. Article 1478 of the Code of Commerce is not an adoption of any provision of the Model Law and was introduced by the Mexican Congress in the 2011 reform of the Code of Commerce.
26. Fourth Civil Collegiate Court of the First Circuit, non-binding precedent number 2012480 (2016) titled "Procedimiento para la adopción judicial de medidas cautelares vinculadas al arbitraje. Está sujeto a discreción amplia del juzgador."
27. Second Civil Collegiate Court of the First Circuit, non-binding precedent number 2002829 (2012) titled "Medidas cautelares. Para su adopción, reconocimiento y ejecución en el procedimiento arbitral, no rige la garantía de audiencia previa a favor del afectado en aras de preservar el derecho de quien las solicita y en cumplimiento de la jurisprudencia p./j. 21/98."

Issue	*Article CC*	*Precedent or Practice*
		This possibility is a blessing and a curse for arbitration practitioners in Mexico, depending on the position of their clients in a given case. If your client is the one requesting interim measures, this precedent will allow it to get immediate ex parte interim relief. However, if interim measures are granted against your client, it will be notified and given an opportunity to present its case only after the preliminary interim measures have already been issued.
		Anti-arbitration injunctions issued by Mexican Courts: Sadly, some Mexican Courts still issue anti-arbitration injunctions forcing arbitral tribunals to suspend arbitrations. These orders are issued, for instance, so that arbitral tribunals suspend arbitrations while a judge is deciding on the existence and validity of an arbitration agreement. This directly violates Article 1424 of the Code of Commerce, which provides that arbitrations may be commenced or continued, and an award may be issued, even when a matter involving an arbitration agreement is pending before the Court. Yet, when arbitral tribunals have decided to continue with the arbitration regardless of an anti-arbitration injunction, some Mexican Courts have threatened to sanction the arbitral tribunal and consider it in contempt, which could lead to the arbitrators facing criminal charges for disobeying a judicial order. Even if these judicial orders have eventually been deemed unconstitutional when challenged through *amparos*, they have forced arbitrators to suspend arbitration or, in some cases, to spend time and money litigating and have distracted them from their true objective: settling the dispute.
		Denial of interim measures requested in support of arbitrations against state-owned companies or government agencies: We have seen a trend in the last couple of years in which Mexican Courts are frequently denying interim measures requested in support of arbitrations against state-owned companies. The reasoning provided by the Courts in these cases is usually ill-founded and forces litigators to challenge the decision which takes time. These delays are not ideal in the context of interim measures requests.

Issue	*Article CC*	*Precedent or Practice*
Competence-competence and referral to arbitration by Mexican Courts	Articles 1424,[28] 1432[29] and 1464[30]	**Standard of judicial review of the existence and validity of an arbitration agreement when deciding a request for referral to arbitration:** In a non-binding precedent,[31] a Mexican Court determined that the threshold to determine that an arbitration agreement is null and void, inoperative, or incapable of being performed when deciding not to refer a dispute to arbitration should be high.

28. Adoption of Model Law (2006), Art. 8: "Arbitration agreement and substantive claim before Court (1) A Court before which an action is brought in a matter which is the subject of an arbitration agreement shall, if a party so requests not later than when submitting his first statement on the substance of the dispute, refer the parties to arbitration unless it finds that the agreement is null and void, inoperative or incapable of being performed. (2) Where an action referred to in paragraph (1) of this article has been brought, arbitral proceedings may nevertheless be commenced or continued, and an award may be made, while the issue is pending before the Court."
29. Adoption of Model Law (2006), Art. 16: "Competence of arbitral tribunal to rule on its jurisdiction. (1) The arbitral tribunal may rule on its own jurisdiction, including any objections with respect to the existence or validity of the arbitration agreement. For that purpose, an arbitration clause which forms part of a contract shall be treated as an agreement independent of the other terms of the contract. A decision by the arbitral tribunal that the contract is null and void shall not entail ipso jure the invalidity of the arbitration clause. (2) A plea that the arbitral tribunal does not have jurisdiction shall be raised not later than the submission of the statement of defence. A party is not precluded from raising such a plea by the fact that he has appointed, or participated in the appointment of, an arbitrator. A plea that the arbitral tribunal is exceeding the scope of its authority shall be raised as soon as the matter alleged to be beyond the scope of its authority is raised during the arbitral proceedings. The arbitral tribunal may, in either case, admit a later plea if it considers the delay justified. (3) The arbitral tribunal may rule on a plea referred to in paragraph (2) of this article either as a preliminary question or in an award on the merits. If the arbitral tribunal rules as a preliminary question that it has jurisdiction, any party may request, within thirty days after having received notice of that ruling, the Court specified in article 6 to decide the matter, which decision shall be subject to no appeal; while such a request is pending, the arbitral tribunal may continue the arbitral proceedings and make an award."
30. Article 1464 of the Code of Commerce is not an adoption of any provision of the Model Law and was introduced by the Mexican Congress in the 2011 reform of the Code of Commerce.
31. Second Civil and Labor Collegiate Court of the Seventh Circuit, non-binding precedent number 2021255 (2019) titled "Remisión al arbitraje internacional. El procedimiento previsto en el Código de Comercio para resolver de inmediato esa solicitud, garantiza el derecho de audiencia, al dar oportunidad de alegar mediante la vista que se otorga a las partes."

Issue	*Article CC*	*Precedent or Practice*
		The judge ruled that said decision could only be reached if: (i) there is evidence that the arbitration agreement was nullified by a judicial ruling or arbitration award; or (ii) if the arbitration agreement notoriously meets any of the abovementioned grounds. This precedent is relevant since it favors the application of the competence-competence principle with the exception of very specific circumstances. Another non-binding precedent related to this issue[32] determined that the inability of one party to pay the fees of the arbitration institution does not make the arbitration agreement impossible to perform.
		Standard of judicial review of a jurisdiction determination made by an arbitral tribunal: In a non-binding precedent,[33] a Mexican Court determined that a judge must refrain from analyzing a jurisdiction decision from an arbitral tribunal as if it were analyzing an appeal. The Court reasoned that the judicial review of said decisions should have two steps. First, the judge must review the text of the arbitration agreement to determine if it is clearly valid. Second, if the agreement is not clearly valid, the judge must verify if the decision of the arbitral tribunal to deem it valid is reasonable. In the second step, the judge may only consider the arbitration clause invalid if it finds that the reasoning of the arbitral tribunal was arbitrary or insufficient.

32. Third Civil and Labor Collegiate Court of the Seventh Circuit, non-binding precedent number 176594 (2005) titled “Arbitraje mercantil. La insolvencia económica de alguna de las partes que impida cubrir los honorarios de los árbitros no es una causa de ineficacia del acuerdo de.”
33. Mexican Supreme Court, non-binding precedent number 2014012 (2016) titled “Laudos arbitrales. Estándar de revisión judicial para determinar la validez de la decisión de un tribunal arbitral sobre su propia competencia.”

Issue	*Article CC*	*Precedent or Practice*
		Res judicata effects of the judicial review of the jurisdiction of an arbitral tribunal: In a couple of non-binding precedents,[34] Mexican Courts have determined that any decision reached by a judge in the exercise of its judicial review of a jurisdiction decision by an arbitral tribunal has res judicata effects and cannot be revisited. This means that if, for instance, a judge has already ruled that an arbitral tribunal had jurisdiction when reviewing a jurisdiction award pursuant to Article 1432, then that decision cannot be revisited by a Court in set-aside proceedings of the final award.
		Procedural timeframe to request a Mexican judge to refer a dispute to arbitration: There is an apparent contradiction in the Mexican *lex arbitri* regarding the procedural timeframe to request a judge to refer a dispute to arbitration. It was unclear if a party had to request the referral to arbitration in its first motion before the Court or at any time during the Court proceedings. In a non-binding precedent,[35] a Mexican Court decided that said request can be made at any time before the final ruling is issued by the Court. This precedent is relevant because the Court reasoned that judges should not favor their jurisdiction over that of an arbitral tribunal when the parties have concluded an arbitration agreement.

34. Fourth Civil Collegiate Court of the First Circuit, non-binding precedent number 162932 (2010) titled “Arbitraje comercial. El control judicial de la competencia para conocer de la validez del acuerdo arbitral puede ejercerse sólo en una de las oportunidades previstas.”
Fourth Civil Collegiate Court of the First Circuit, non-binding precedent number 162931 (2010) titled “Arbitraje comercial. El juzgador debe limitarse a conocer de la pretensión de nulidad del acuerdo arbitral cuando se ejerce junto con la de cumplimiento contractual y decidirla en la resolución sobre el fondo del juicio.”
35. Third Civil Collegiate Court of the First Circuit, non-binding precedent number 2021586 (2019) titled “Remisión al arbitraje. Puede solicitarse en cualquier etapa del procedimiento, hasta antes del dictado de la sentencia definitiva (alcance de las tesis aisladas i.3o.c.503 c y i.3o.c.504 c).”

Issue	*Article CC*	*Precedent or Practice*
Set aside arbitral awards	Articles 1457 to 1459[36]	**Standard of judicial review of awards by Mexican Courts in set-aside proceedings**: There are several binding and non-binding precedents[37] that have reaffirmed that judges cannot revisit the merits of the case in set-aside proceedings and can only analyze if the award meets one of the grounds for set aside provided by Article 1457 of the Code of Commerce. In another non-binding precedent,[38] a Mexican Court reaffirmed that the burden of proof of demonstrating that one of the grounds for set aside is met is on the party that requests the annulment of the award and that, if that burden of proof is not met, then the award will be deemed valid. Recently, in two non-binding precedents,[39] the Mexican Supreme Court specifically analyzed the standard of judicial review of an award when a party argues that the arbitral tribunal violated due process due to an incorrect analysis of the relevance and weight of the evidence. The Supreme Court determined that the arbitral tribunal has the power to **determine the admissibility and weight of** evidence and, therefore, if a **Court reviewed this issue, it would be revisiting the** decision on the merits of the case, **which is not allowed.**

36. Adoption of Model Law (2006), Art. 16: "Application for setting aside as exclusive recourse against arbitral award."
37. Mexican Supreme Court, binding precedent 2021235 (2019) titled "Laudo arbitral. En contra de la sentencia emitida en el juicio especial en que se dilucide su nulidad, o bien, su reconocimiento y ejecución, procede el juicio de amparo indirecto"; Mexican Supreme Court, non-binding precedent 2014012 (2017) titled "Laudos arbitrales. Estándar de revisión judicial para determinar la validez de la decisión de un tribunal arbitral sobre su propia competencia"; Seventh Civil Collegiate Court of the First Circuit, non-binding precedent 2002333 (2012) titled: "Laudo Arbitral. Denegación de su ejecución. Análisis sobre la actualización de la hipótesis señalada en el inciso c) de la fracción I del artículo 1462 del Código de Comercio"; Seventh Civil Collegiate Court of the First Circuit, non-binding precedent 2001131 (2012) titled "Laudo Arbitral. Cuándo, por qué y en qué condiciones se deben analizar las consideraciones que lo sustentan."
38. Sixth Civil Collegiate Court of the First Circuit, non-binding precedent 2010751 (2013) titled: "Acción de nulidad de laudo arbitral. Cuando no se acredita, éste resulta válido y surte sus efectos legales."
39. Mexican Supreme Court, non-binding precedents number 2025648 & 2025652 (2022) titled "Laudo arbitral. Los artículos 1457, fracción i, inciso b), parte final, y 1434, ambos del código de comercio que regulan la causa de nulidad por violación a la igualdad de trato y la plena oportunidad de hacer valer

Issue	*Article CC*	*Precedent or Practice*
		Preclusion of filing several set-aside requests against the same award: In a non-binding precedent,[40] a Mexican Court reasoned that a party that wishes to set aside an award must include all the grounds it considers are met in its initial set aside request. The Court considers that a party should not be allowed to file several set-aside requests against the same award invoking different grounds (even if it does so within the three-month period provided for that purpose).
		Inclusion of arbitrators and arbitration institutions as parties in set-aside proceedings: Regrettably, some parties tend to include arbitrators and arbitration institutions as respondents in setting aside proceedings. Even if some Courts exclude them from the proceedings in the initial act, others notify them as respondents and force them to act within the proceedings. Once again, this forces arbitrators and institutions to spend time and money litigating. This is especially burdensome for foreign arbitrators who have to retain local counsel for this purpose. Some arbitrators even include a section in their first procedural order of the arbitration that provides a waiver by the parties to sue arbitrators in set-aside proceedings. If the parties do not accept this waiver, arbitrators may decide to resign.

los derechos en el procedimiento arbitral, no son inconstitucionales por no permitir un control judicial del fondo del laudo bajo sus hipótesis normativas" & "Nulidad de laudo arbitral. La causa prevista en el artículo 1457, fracción i, inciso b), parte final, en relación con el diverso 1434, ambos del código de comercio, se refiere a la igualdad de trato y la plena oportunidad de hacer valer los derechos de las partes durante la sustanciación del procedimiento de arbitraje."

40. Third Civil Collegiate Court of the First Circuit, non-binding precedent 167443 (2008) titled: "Nulidad de laudo arbitral. Principios de concentración y celeridad."

Issue	*Article CC*	*Precedent or Practice*
Enforcement of arbitral awards	Articles 1461 to 1463[41]	**Formalities for the enforcement of an arbitration award in Mexico:** In a non-binding precedent,[42] a Mexican judge interpreted that the reference to an authenticated original award made in Article 1461 implied an additional formality, in accordance with Mexican law, that calls for the certification by a notary public that the signatures contained therein correspond to those of the arbitrators. As stated by Ruiz and Orta, internationally renowned Mexican arbitration practitioners, "[t]his unfortunate decision departed from the spirit of the New York Convention and the [Code of Commerce]" and "Mexican courts [were] burdened by additional formalities and requirements for the recognition and enforcement of awards."[43] However, the Mexican Supreme Court eventually reversed this reasoning in a non-binding precedent.[44] The Court ruled that a party seeking the recognition and enforcement of an award only needed to submit the original of the award or a certified copy thereof by the arbitral institution. No authentication of the arbitrators' signatures by a notary public was needed.

41. Adoption of Model Law (2006), Arts. 35 & 36: "Recognition and enforcement" & "Grounds for refusing recognition or enforcement."
42. Fourteenth Civil Collegiate Court of the First Circuit, non-binding precedent 2017915 (2018) titled: "Laudo arbitral. Autenticación a que se refiere el artículo 1461 del código de comercio para su ejecución."
43. Ruiz, V. & Orta, A., "The Arbitration Review of the Americas 2022: Mexico," Global Arbitration Review (2021).
44. Mexican Supreme Court, non-binding precedent 2025614 (2020) titled "Reconocimiento y ejecución de laudo arbitral. El artículo 1461, párrafo segundo, del código de comercio, al prever como requisito presentar el original del laudo 'debidamente autenticado' o copia certificada del mismo, vulnera el derecho de acceso a la justicia tutelado por el artículo 17 constitucional."

Issue	*Article CC*	*Precedent or Practice*
Role of arbitrators in the Mexican legal framework	–	**Arbitrators may not be considered "authorities" for purposes of amparo proceedings:** In Mexico, individuals and companies have access to *amparo* actions to combat unconstitutional acts from public entities (*acts of authorities* or *acts du prince*). The Amparo Law provides the possibility of considering private parties as authorities if they perform acts that are equivalent to those of public entities. This possibility triggered a debate regarding the fact that arbitrators could be considered authorities and *amparo* actions could be initiated against their decisions. Thankfully, in non-binding precedents,[45] Mexican Courts have ruled that arbitrators may not be considered authorities for the purpose of *amparo* actions. This precedent has very important implications for arbitration practice in Mexico since it prevents parties from filing *amparo* actions against decisions of the arbitral tribunal. Today, parties may only file *amparo* actions against judicial decisions issued in support of arbitration (for instance, set-aside or enforcement decisions, interim measures orders, etc.).
The *lex arbitri* as a self-contained statute	–	**The Mexican *lex arbitri* as a self-contained statute:** In a non-binding precedent,[46] a Mexican Court determined that the chapter of the Code of Commerce that contains the Mexican *lex arbitri* should be deemed as a self-contained specialized legislation that does not need to be supplemented by other domestic laws or principles for its effective application.

Source: Table created by authors.

45. Twelfth Civil Collegiate Court of the First Circuit, non-binding precedent 2018229 (2018) titled "Árbitros y secretaria de acuerdos designados en el procedimiento arbitral. No son autoridades para efectos del juicio de amparo."
46. Seventh Civil Collegiate Court of the First Circuit, non-binding precedent 163413 (2010) titled "Arbitraje comercial. Su legislación es especializada y por ende, excluyente de normas generales."

[c] *Conventions for the Recognition and Enforcement of Awards*

Mexico is part of several international conventions for the recognition and enforcement of foreign arbitral awards. Most importantly, Mexico ratified the 1958 Convention on the Recognition and Enforcement of Foreign Arbitral Awards (known as the "*New York Convention*") on April 14, 1971, with no reservations, and it entered into force on July 13, 1971.[47] Since this convention was adopted without reservations, Mexico may enforce awards issued in arbitrations seated in non-Contracting States of the New York Convention as well as awards issued to settle non-commercial matters.[48]

Mexico is also a Member State to the 1975 Inter-American Convention on International Commercial Arbitration (known as the "*Panama Convention*"), which it signed on October 27, 1977 and ratified on February 15, 1978,[49] and the 1979 Inter-American Convention on Exterritorial Validity of Foreign Judgments and Arbitral Awards (known as the "*Montevideo Convention*"), which it signed on February 12, 1986 and ratified on November 2, 1987.[50]

[2] Investment Arbitration

Mexico also has a robust investment arbitration regime. Mexico has ratified a considerable number of bilateral investment treaties (BITs)[51] and free trade agreements (FTAs)[52] with investment protection chapters. These treaties generally provide for investment arbitration as the mechanism to settle disputes between investors and the host state of the investment.

Although a little late considering that its main free trade agreements were signed by Mexico in the 1990s, Mexico has also ratified the Convention on the Settlement of Investment Disputes between States and National of Other States (the "*ICSID Convention*"); which entered into force in Mexico on August 26, 2018.

Mexico has faced more than fifty investment arbitrations from 1997 to 2024 (some of them are still pending).[53] Some arbitration practitioners predict that Mexico may lead the next wave of investment arbitrations due to the current political climate (section [C][1][b]),[54] but only the future will tell.

47. *See* the status page of the New York Convention.
48. New York Convention, Art. I-3.
49. *See* the status page of the Panama Convention.
50. *See* the status page of the Montevideo Convention.
51. *See* the list of BITs ratified by Mexico.
52. See the list of FTAs ratified by Mexico.
53. *See* the list of investment arbitrations faced by Mexico.
54. Vallejo, D. "Will Mexico Lead The Next Wave of Investment Arbitration Claims?", Kluwer Arbitration Blog (2018); Flores Rueda, C., "Fact Summary: Legal Actions Taken by Mexico on the Energy Sector since 2018," Mealey's International Arbitration Report.

[B] CURRENT TRENDS IN MEXICO'S ARBITRATION PRACTICE

In this section, we outline how, apart from the existence of a pro-arbitration legal framework in Mexico, there are some national trends that have contributed to and may contribute to an increase in arbitration users.

One factor that seems to have contributed to the increase in the use of arbitration in Mexico is the inclusion of arbitration clauses in contracts by foreign investors, government agencies, and state-owned companies (section [1]). Another factor that may contribute to strengthening arbitration in Mexico could be the efforts made by Mexican arbitration institutions to adapt their rules and practices to international arbitration developments (section [2]).

[1] Increase in the Inclusion of Arbitration Agreements in Contracts

In the past years, the number of commercial arbitrations has increased due to the arrival of foreign investors who requested the inclusion of arbitration agreements as part of their negotiation strategy in their contracts.[55] The increase in foreign investment may be attributed to the adoption of a comprehensive investment protection legal framework in Mexico (section [A][2]); and the Energy Reform that opened the energy market to foreign investors (section [C][1]); among other factors.

In addition, several government agencies, such as the Mexican Hydrocarbons Commission, and state-owned entities, such as *Comisión Federal de Electricidad* (CFE) and *Petróleos Mexicanos* (PEMEX), consistently include arbitration clauses in a significant number of contracts.

The abovementioned factors have contributed to Mexican private and state-owned companies becoming top users of international arbitration institutions such as the ICC, the ICDR,[56] and the LCIA.

For instance, in the "ICC Dispute Resolution 2020 Statistics" Mexico ranked 10th in the list of most frequent nationalities among parties to ICC arbitrations that year. Also, the ICC noted that "[p]arties from Latin America and the Caribbean represented approximately 15% of all parties. ... Within Latin America, Brazil was followed by Mexico with 78 parties (compared to 51 in 2019), which ranked 10th in the worldwide."[57]

[2] Modernization of Mexican Arbitration Institutions

Mexico has two national arbitration institutions: the Mexican Arbitration Centre *(Centro de Arbitraje de México)* (CAM) and Mexico City's Commercial Chamber *(Cámara de Comercio de la Ciudad de México)* (CANACO). Both institutions administer a considerable number of arbitrations each year.

55. Zamora, R., et al., "Law and Practice—Mexico," Chambers International Arbitration Global Practice Guides (2022).
56. 2018 ICDR Case Data Infographic, p. 1.
57. ICC Dispute Resolution 2020 Statistics, p. 10.

We have seen worth noting efforts by Mexican arbitration institutions to conform with the highest international arbitration standards. CANACO, for instance, has taken impressive steps toward the efficiency of arbitration by issuing a specific set of Expedited Arbitration Rules; which are specially designed for cases with a low quantum.[58] These rules have been incredibly valuable since they contribute to the efficiency of arbitration and make it more accessible for smaller transactions.

Also, this year, CAM reformed its arbitration rules (which had been in force since 2009)[59] in order to modernize them and adapt them to current arbitration best practices.[60] We believe this reform could be CAM's next step in the journey to handle larger and more complex cases in the following years.

[C] CHALLENGES FOR ARBITRATION IN MEXICO

Even if it may seem that Mexican arbitration is in its prime; that does not mean that this dispute-resolution mechanism is not facing considerable challenges.

In this section, we identify three main categories of hardships that are affecting and will continue to affect the arbitration regime in Mexico in the foreseeable future: challenges caused by the current political climate in the country (section [1]); challenges caused by the Mexican judiciary (section [2]); and challenges caused by the global pandemic (section [3]).

[1] Challenges Caused by the Current Political Climate

The current political climate has had a direct impact on arbitration in Mexico. Every arbitration practitioner in the country can attest that, since President Andrés Manuel López Obrador (commonly known as "*AMLO*") came into power, arbitration has become a strategic dispute resolution mechanism to counter his administration's actions; especially in the energy sector.

As context, in 2013, during Enrique Peña Nieto's administration,[61] Mexico passed a constitutional reform to allow free competition in the energy industry (the "*First Energy Reform*").[62] The energy industry in Mexico had been a State monopoly controlled by *Comisión Federal de Electricidad* (CFE) and *Petróleos Mexicanos* (PEMEX), state-owned entities in the electricity, oil, and gas sectors, for many years. The First Energy Reform was comprised of a complex system of legislation and regulations that reshaped the energy industry in Mexico.

The reform sought to incentivize private investments to introduce renewable energies into the market. A national renewable energy target of 35% in 2024 was set and the consumption of renewable energy (vis-à-vis electricity generated by CFE) was

58. CANACO Expedited Arbitration Rules, last reformed Jun. 1, 2018.
59. Rules of Arbitration of the Arbitration Center of Mexico, in force as of Jul. 1, 2009.
60. *Ibid.*
61. Enrique Peña Nieto's presidency lasted from Dec. 1, 2012 to Nov. 30, 2018.
62. 2013 Constitutional Reform Decree.

meant to be favored. The reform boosted foreign investments of billions of dollars[63] and was internationally appraised. For instance, the International Energy Agency ("*IEA*") in the World Energy Investment 2018 report stated that the Energy Reform was a model for the world to follow.[64]

However, in 2018, when AMLO came into power, his administration started pursuing energy policies to reinstate the State monopoly and reverse the Energy Reform. AMLO has substantially changed the rules of the game for long-term financed investments in the sector. AMLO first started reforming regulations or issuing orders, which were mostly blocked by Mexican Courts. As a consequence, AMLO tried to pass a constitutional reform that would reverse the Energy Reform (the "*Energy Counter Reform*"). Despite the current administration's efforts, the Energy Counter Reform was not passed by Congress. However, the government is still performing actions to favor CFE and PEMEX. Many renewable energy projects are now near bankruptcy.

This administration's policies have brought a wave of litigations against the State. Administrative and constitutional litigation has been the first line of defense to counter the immediate effects of these policies. However, we have also seen a considerable rise in commercial arbitrations against government agencies and state-owned entities in the energy sector (section [a]). Some say that the current political climate may even provoke a wave of investment arbitrations initiated by foreign investors against Mexico (section [b]).

Also, we can predict reactions by the international community. For instance, the United States has already initiated consultations under the United States-Mexico-Canada Agreement (the "*USMCA*") against AMLO's policies (section [c]).

[a] Commercial Arbitrations

As previously stated (section [B][1]), before the current Mexican administration, Mexico had seen a boom in commercial arbitrations due to the inclusion of arbitration agreements in contracts concluded by foreign investors, government agencies, and state-owned entities. However, the policies of this administration have further triggered disputes against government agencies and state-owned companies pursuant to these arbitration agreements.

PEMEX had always been represented by its internal counsel in commercial arbitrations, while CFE used to retain outside specialized arbitration firms. During this administration, CFE has followed PEMEX's footsteps and has developed an in-house team that represents the state-owned company in commercial arbitrations.

Even if in the past the Mexican government was known for voluntarily complying with arbitration awards, we have seen a recent trend in which state-owned companies are seeking to set aside or refuse the recognition and enforcement of awards. We will see if this trend is also present in potential investment arbitrations that may be initiated

63. Jaramillo, E., "Mexico's Efforts to Undo the 2013 Energy Reform: Substantives and Procedural Protections for 'Covered Investments' under the USMCA," Kluwer Arbitration Blog (2021).
64. Andrew B., "IEA Hails Mexico Energy Reform as World's 'Most Successful,' Natural Gas Intelligence."

by Mexico; which would damage the country's reputation as a voluntary compiler of investment awards (section [C][1][b]).

[b] Investment Arbitrations

As previously stated, some predict that Mexico will lead the next wave of investment arbitrations due to the acts of the current administration against investors in the energy sector.[65] In our opinion; only time will tell if this wave occurs. However, a reality that we are currently facing in Mexico is that foreign investors are seeking legal advice to ensure that investment arbitration can be their last resort to receive compensation if their investments are frustrated.

This potential wave would come at a time when Mexico has concluded the USMCA, which entered into force on July 1, 2020, superseding NAFTA. The USMCA was concluded between Mexico and the U.S. and Canada, the two nations that have brought the majority of investment arbitrations against Mexico in the past (twenty-eight of the thirty-eight total).[66]

The USMCA, which may be considered a new generation treaty, "has far more limited investment protection than its predecessor"[67] which will have several implications for U.S. and Canadian investors. For instance, investment arbitration under USMCA is only accessible in investor-state disputes between the U.S. and Mexico. Therefore, if a Canadian investor wishes to initiate an investment arbitration against Mexico, it must do so under the Comprehensive and Progressive Agreement for Trans-Pacific Partnership (the "*CPTPP*"). The USMCA also contains a transitional regime extending the protections existing under NAFTA beyond its termination for a period of three years following the entry into force of the USMCA in specific circumstances.

As stated (section [C][1][a]), Mexico has a great track record in voluntarily complying with investment arbitration awards. As stated by Professor Emmanuel Galliard, "Mexico has had [38] arbitrations initiated against it, a majority of which arose under [NAFTA]. Of these, [ten] awarded damages to the investors.[68] Although in

65. Vallejo, D. "Will Mexico Lead the Next Wave of Investment Arbitration Claims?", Kluwer Arbitration Blog (2018); Flores Rueda, C., "Fact Summary: Legal Actions Taken by Mexico on the Energy Sector since 2018," Mealey's International Arbitration Report.
66. U.S. and Canadian investors have initiated twenty-six of the thirty-eight investment arbitrations that have taken place against Mexico.
67. Blackaby, N., "Populism and Investment Arbitration in Latin America" in International Arbitration in Times of Economic Nationalism, Kluwer Law International; Kluwer Law International, 17-38 (2022).
68. These are the awards in (i) *Abengoa, SA y COFIDES, SA v. United Mexican States*, ICSID Case No. ARB(AF)/09/2, Award (Apr. 18, 2013); (ii) *Cargill, Inc v. United Mexican States*, ICSID Case No. ARB(AF)/05/2, Award (Sep. 18, 2009); (iii) *Archer Daniels Midland and Tate & Lyle Ingredients Americas, Inc v. United Mexican States*, ICSID Case No. ARB(AF)/04/5, Award (Nov. 21, 2007); (iv) *Talsud, SA v. United Mexican States*, ICSID Case No. ARB(AF)/04/4, Award (Jun. 16, 2010); (v) *Gemplus, SA, SLP, SA, and Gemplus Industrial SA de CV v. United Mexican States*, ICSID Case No. ARB(AF)/04/3, Award (Jun. 16, 2010); (vi) *Corn Products International, Inc v. United Mexican States*, ICSID Case No. ARB(AF)/04/1, Award (Aug. 18, 2009); (vii) *Técnicas Medioambientales Tecmed v. United Mexican States*, ICSID Case No. ARB(AF)/00/2, Award (May 29, 2003); (viii) *Marvin Roy Feldman Karpa v. United Mexican States*, ICSID Case No.

some cases it initially pursued annulment, Mexico has voluntarily complied with the adverse awards, and often within a year of the final decision." However, this tendency could stop if the next administration keeps AMLO's tendencies.

[c] Consultations

We have also seen actions from the international community seeking to hold Mexico accountable for the acts of this administration.[69] For instance, the United States requested dispute settlement consultations under the USMCA against Mexico. Canada followed in the U.S.'s footsteps almost immediately.[70]

As reported by the U.S. Government "[t]he consultations relate to certain measures by Mexico that undermine American companies and U.S.-produced energy in favor of Mexico's state-owned electrical utility, the Comisión Federal de Electricidad (CFE), and state-owned oil and gas company, Petróleos Mexicanos (PEMEX)."[71]

As of today, the dispute has not reached the panel stage. But, if the case moves forward, and a panel decides that Mexico's actions are inconsistent with the USMCA, the U.S. and Canada would be permitted to suspend the application to Mexico of benefits "of equivalent effect to the non-conformity"[72] until the Parties agree on a settlement which "[ty]pically … involves the imposition of retaliatory tariffs on goods of the responding party." [73]

[2] Challenges Caused by the Mexican Judiciary

As already described above (section [A][1][b]), even if Mexican Courts have issued a wide array of pro-arbitration precedents, some threatening practices still make arbitration practice challenging in Mexico. Anti-arbitration injunctions that could lead to Mexican Courts ruling that arbitrators are in contempt are still issued by Mexican Courts. Arbitrators and arbitration institutions are still forced to litigate in set-aside proceedings. We still struggle with consistent denials of interim measure requests.

As described by renowned Mexican arbitration practitioners, Ruiz and Orta, "the reason behind the misapplication of the [*les arbitri*]'s core principles by the state Courts … should be understood as a consequence of the lack of exposure of state and federal Courts to arbitration-related cases, including Courts in Mexico City, which are, by far, the most experienced in the country, when it comes to arbitration."[74]

ARB(AF)/99/1, Award (Dec. 16, 2002); (ix) *Metalclad Corporation v. The United Mexican States*, ICSID Case No. ARB(AF)/97/1, Award (Aug. 30, 2000) and (x) *Lion Mexico Consolidated L.P. v. United Mexican States*, ICSID Case No. ARB(AF)/15/2), Award (Sep. 20, 2021).

69. Herrera, C., "Mexico Falls Further Behind on Climate at Leaders Summit," NRDC Expert Blog (2021).
70. *See* the statement of the Canadian Minister of International Trade.
71. *See* the press release issued by the Executive Office of the President of the United States.
72. USMCA, Art. 31.19.1.
73. *See* the press release issued by the Executive Office of the President of the United States.
74. Ruiz, V. & Orta, A., "The Arbitration Review of the Americas 2022: Mexico," Global Arbitration Review (2021).

We fully agree. The competent Mexican Courts to settle cases related to arbitration also have jurisdiction for a wide variety of civil and commercial cases (and until shortly, even bankruptcy proceedings). They have not received an exhaustive formation regarding arbitration and have a significant workload. These factors contribute to them sometimes issuing dangerous precedents for arbitration.

The problem with these practices is that they force arbitral tribunals and users of arbitration in Mexico to unnecessarily litigate; spending time and money. As stated above (section [A][1][b]), we have even observed how several foreign arbitrators add a section in their first procedural order of the arbitration including a waiver by the parties to sue arbitrators during the arbitration proceedings and when seeking to set aside the award.

[3] Challenges Caused by the Pandemic

The COVID-19 pandemic affected businesses all around the globe. Mexico was not the exception. Many companies were forced to close or were unable to comply with contractual commitments made before the pandemic. Due to this, we have observed several impacts in commercial arbitrations. For instance, we have observed that it has become extremely complicated to locate companies in order to notify the initiation of arbitration proceedings against them. Some companies seem to have vanished and cannot be notified. Also, we have observed that parties are struggling to pay the fees of arbitration institutions.

Even if arbitration in Mexico may face some challenges in the foreseeable future, we believe that our arbitration regime is strong enough to face the new demands that may come. As arbitration becomes more strategic in the country, which may contribute to further increasing its use, practitioners and local Courts may become even more acquainted with this dispute-resolution mechanism. We hope this can further contribute to the sophistication of arbitration practice in Mexico.

Part II Commercial Arbitration

CHAPTER 3

The Arbitration Agreement under Mexican Law

Elsa Ortega López

[A] INTRODUCTION

The drafting or review of an arbitration agreement under Mexican Law requires the analysis of two different sets of legal provisions. The first set is the Mexican Arbitration Law incorporated in Title IV, Book V of the Mexican Commerce Code (Articles 1415 to 1490) (Mexican Arbitration Law). This law was adopted in 1993 and is essentially the 1985 original version of the UNCITRAL Model Law on International Commercial Arbitration (UNCITRAL Model Law) with minor changes.[1] The incorporation of the UNCITRAL Model Law into Mexican legislation was an additional step toward Mexico's modernization of its legal framework to facilitate the resolution of disputes in commercial matters among domestic and international parties; the first move was the ratification of the Convention on the Recognition and Enforcement of Foreign Arbitral Awards (New York Convention) in 1971.

Although the Mexican Arbitration Law is located within the Mexican Commerce Code, the provisions of this Title IV, Book V should be interpreted separately from the rest of the stipulations within the code, as provided in Article 1051 of this statute.[2]

1. Mexico has a monism system, by which the same Arbitration Law applies to both domestic and international commercial arbitrations. Art. 1415 of the Mexican Commerce Code provides: "The provisions of this [Law] will be applicable to commercial arbitration both domestic, and international when the seat of the arbitration is in Mexican territory, except as provided in international treaties of which Mexico is a party or in other laws that establish a different procedure, or that provide that certain disputes are not susceptible to be solved in arbitration."
2. Paragraph four of Art. 1051 of the Mexican Commerce Code, located within Book V of the code, provides: "The conventional proceeding before the courts will be ruled by art. 1052 and 1053, while the arbitration proceeding will be ruled by the provisions in title fourth of this book."

The second set of norms that are relevant to analyzing an arbitration agreement under Mexican Law are the provisions of the Federal Civil Code. The reason is that under Mexican Law the provisions of this latter statute are applicable in all cases where there is no specific rule within the commercial legal framework.[3] Hence, for matters such as the capacity of the parties to arbitration agreements or the elements of validity of such agreements, the rules within the Federal Civil Code are of relevance.

Considering that an arbitration agreement is in essence a contract between two or more parties, two concepts are relevant for the analysis of arbitration agreements under Mexican Law. The first is the legal principle of party autonomy, which is the cornerstone of the regulation of contracts in Mexico. Pursuant to this principle, parties are free to enter or not enter into contracts, and when they decide to do so, they act on their free will and on a foot of equality.[4] Parties negotiate the terms of their contracts and are free to agree on their terms, provided these agreements are not against the public order.[5]

The second consideration is that because arbitration agreements are contracts, the Mexican legal framework that regulates contracts is applicable thereto. Among these provisions is the legal theory of the elements of the contract.

Pursuant to Mexican doctrine[6] and law, for a contract to exist, certain essential elements are required. These elements are: (a) the consent of the parties; and (b) the object, which is the subject matter of the contract. Without these elements, a contract is inexistent.[7]

In addition, Mexican law provides other elements that are necessary for the validity of a contract. These elements are: (i) that the parties that enter into the contract have legal capacity; (ii) that the agreement is entered without any defect in the consent of the parties (such as error, deceit or violence); (iii) that the object of the contract is lawful; and (iv) that the agreement of the parties complies with any formal requirements set by the law. The absence of any of these validity requirements results in the contract being null and void.[8]

---

3. Article 2 of the Mexican Commerce Code provides: "In the absence of provisions in this statute and other commercial laws, the provisions contained in the Civil Code for federal matters shall be applicable to commercial acts."
4. This principle is expressed for commercial transactions in Art. 78 of the Mexican Commerce Code, which provides: "In commercial contracts, each party commits itself in the manner and under the terms that the party appears to have wanted to undertake the obligation, without the validity of the commercial act depending on the fulfillment of specific formalities or requirements." However, under Art. 79 section I of the same code, certain commercial contracts do require the fulfilment of particular formalities: "Exceptions to the provision in the previous article are: I.—Those contracts that according to this Code or other laws must be entered into in a public deed or require formalities or solemnities for their effectiveness."
5. This limitation is established under Art. 6 of the Federal Civil Code which provides "The will of the parties does not release them from the obligation to comply with the law, nor allows them to alter it or modify it. Only private rights that do not directly affect public interest may be waived, when such waiver does not harm the rights of third parties."
6. Manuel Borja Soriano, Teoría General de las Obligaciones.
7. Article 1794 of the Federal Civil Code provides: "For the existence of a contract the following is required: I. Consent; II. Object that can be the subject matter of the contract."
8. Article 1795 of the Federal Civil Code provides: "The contract may be declared null and void for the following reasons: I. For the legal incapacity of the parties or one of them; II. For a defect in

[B] DEFINITION OF ARBITRATION AGREEMENT

Article 1416 of the Mexican Arbitration Law defines the term *arbitration agreement* as: "the agreement under which the parties decide to submit to arbitration all or certain differences that have arisen or may arise between them in respect to a certain legal relationship, whether contractual or not. The arbitration agreement may adopt the form of an arbitral clause in a contract or the form of an independent agreement."[9]

This definition helps clarify three main topics. The first is that in Mexico, the parties to an arbitration agreement may choose to submit to arbitration only some of the differences that arise from their legal relationship, and not all of them. Although this possibility exists in the law, I should clarify that in practice, it is not advisable to submit some portion of the dispute to arbitration and the rest to the jurisdiction of the courts, as this often results in parallel proceedings.

For example, due to a restriction on the arbitrability of the termination of administrative contracts set by certain laws in Mexico, a practice arose some years ago by which government-related entities such as Petróleos Mexicanos (Pemex) or Comisión Federal de Electricidad (CFE) included in some of their contracts a dispute resolution clause by which the administrative termination of the contract is submitted to the jurisdiction of the courts, while all other disputes that derive from the contract are submitted to arbitration. The outcome has been that most of these cases have been complicated by the possibility of making claims in two separate forums. The private party will claim in the arbitration that the government-related entity breached its obligations under the contract, while the latter will respond that it administratively terminated the contract because of the breaches of the private party. Often, the responding party will initiate a separate proceeding in the alternative forum, thereby significantly complicating and prolonging the resolution of the dispute and incorporating the additional risk of conflicting decisions.

The second clarification in this definition is that in Mexico, arbitration is possible not only for disputes in contractual matters but also for any controversy that derives from a non-contractual legal relationship. This clarification is important as often parties tend to argue that the portion of the dispute that does not directly derive from the contract, but is the result of an illicit act, escapes the arbitration agreement.

The third idea that is explained within the definition of arbitration agreement under the Mexican Arbitration Law is that the parties may submit to arbitration not only existing disputes but also potential disputes that may arise in the future provided that the parties establish within the arbitration agreement the delimitation of a certain legal relationship between them.

the consent of the parties; III. Because its object, motive or purpose is unlawful; IV. Because the consent was not expressed in the form provided by the law."

9. The text is almost identical to the one of Art. 7 of the UNCITRAL Model Law and Art. II, paragraphs 1 and 2 of the New York Convention.

[C] ELEMENTS OF THE ARBITRATION AGREEMENT

[1] Essential Elements

The definition of arbitration agreement contains the two essential elements that Mexican Law requires for the existence of any contract. First, the consent of the parties to submit a certain dispute to arbitration. In this context, consent may not be supposed, it must be explicit and clear. This is relevant because consent to submit a dispute to arbitration implies a waiver of the chance to appear before the courts. This waiver must be clear and explicit.[10] Mexican courts have confirmed this idea:

> [T]he clear and decisive statement by the parties to solve their disputes through arbitration, is the basis for the subsequent proceeding, the arbitration being carried out in the manner in which the parties wished for, nothing more. Hence, it is possible for the parties to substitute a judicial clause established in the initial contract for an arbitration agreement, by means of a subsequent contract, ad hoc or general, and it is also possible that the parties include in such new arbitration agreement the issues established in the original contract, provided that this is stated expressly and without doubt.[11,12]

And the second essential element of all contracts is the subject matter of such agreement or object of the contract. In the case of arbitration agreements, the subject matter consists of the already existing or future dispute that derives from a certain legal relationship whether contractual or not. The reference to a certain legal relationship between the parties must be specific. Hence, an arbitration agreement whereby the parties submit to arbitration any possible future dispute that arises between them (without reference to a specific legal relationship) would be considered invalid.

[2] Validity Elements

With respect to the requirements of validity, the Mexican Arbitration Law does not contain specific provisions. Hence, the general provisions in the Civil Federal Code are applicable. Pursuant to Article 1795 of the latter statute, the parties that enter into an arbitration agreement need to have legal capacity. In fact, the Mexican Arbitration Law provides that a cause for annulment of the arbitral award and/or for opposing its

10. Under Mexican Law, the waiver of a right must be carried out in a clear and precise manner, as provided in Art. 7 of the Federal Civil Code: "The waiver authorized in the preceding article does not produce legal effect if not carried out in clear and precise terms, so that there is no doubt of the right that is being waived."
11. Judicial precedent: ARBITRATION. THE WILL OF THE PARTIES TO SUBMIT MUST BE STATED EXPRESSLY AND WITHOUT DOUBT. Third Collegiate Court in Civil Matters of the First Circuit. Digital registration number 178812.
12. This and other single judicial precedents (*tesis aisladas*) referred to in this chapter are not binding under Mexican Law, but show the manner in which Mexican courts are interpreting a certain concept.

recognition and enforcement is that one of the parties to the arbitration agreement was affected by an incapacity.[13] [14]

In addition, although it is not expressly mentioned in the Mexican Arbitration Law, under the subsidiary provisions of the Federal Civil Code, no arbitration agreement would be valid if it was entered into under error, deceit or violence.

The civil legal framework also requires that the object of any contract or agreement be valid. In the case of arbitration, this question goes to the arbitrability of the subject matter contained in the arbitration agreement.

The last element established in Article 1795 of the Federal Civil Code for the validity of any contract under Mexican Law is the form. In this respect, the Mexican Arbitration Law does contain a specific provision as to the form that any arbitral agreement in Mexico should meet in order to be considered valid. This provision is Article 1423 of the Commerce Code, which reads as follows:[15]

> The arbitration agreement shall be in writing, and shall be recorded in a document signed by the parties o in an exchange of letters, telex, telegrams, fax or other means of telecommunication that prove the existence of the agreement, or in an exchange of a statement of claim and a statement of defense in which the existence of an arbitration agreement is maintained by one party without being denied by the other party. The reference made in a contract to a document that contains an arbitration clause, will constitute an arbitration agreement provided that the contract is in writing and the reference implies that the arbitration clause is a part thereof.

Under Article 1423 of the Commerce Code, there are four manners in which an arbitration agreement will be considered complying with the requirement of *in writing*.

The first of these manners is by having the arbitration agreement recorded in a document signed by the parties. This is the most common manner by which parties enter into arbitration agreements.

The second way is by having the arbitration agreement in an exchange of letters, telexes, telegrams, faxes or other means of telecommunication that prove the existence of the agreement. Although the Mexican Arbitration Law has not been updated to incorporate the more modern language contained in the 2006 amendments to the UNCITRAL Model Law, Mexican arbitration practitioners interpret the language "other means of telecommunications" to include emails.

In addition, since 2003 Mexico adopted within its Commerce Code the UNCITRAL Model Law on Electronic Commerce and the UNCITRAL Model Law on Electronic Signatures. The Mexican Commerce Code now incorporates provisions on the

13. Article 1457 of the Mexican Commerce Code: "Arbitral awards may only be declared null and void by the competent judge when: I. The party that is claiming the annulment proves that: a) One of the parties of the arbitration agreement was affected by an incapacity, …."
14. Article 1462 of the Mexican Commerce Code: "The recognition or enforcement of an arbitral award, regardless of the country in which it was rendered, may only be denied when: I. The party against which the award is being enforced, proves before the competent judge of the country in which the recognition or enforcement is being requested that: a) one of the parties of the arbitration agreement was affected by an incapacity, …."
15. This provision is almost identical to Art. 7.2 of the UNCITRAL Model Law, and inspired by Art. II, paragraph 1 of the New York Convention.

validity and enforceability of information contained in data messages[16] and the validity of electronic signatures.[17] With these amendments, parties may now argue under Mexican law that in the context of electronic commerce, an arbitration agreement will be considered to comply with the requirements of *in writing* and *signed* if these provisions are met.

The third manner is in an exchange of a statement of claim and a statement of defense in which the existence of an arbitration agreement is maintained by one party without being denied by the other.

The fourth and final manner established in Mexican law is the reference made in a contract to a document that contains an arbitration clause, provided that the contract is in writing and the reference implies that the arbitration clause is a part of the contract. This is used very often in trade transactions where the parties submit to the terms and conditions of one of them.

Mexican courts have recognized the different manners in which an arbitration agreement will be deemed in writing by using the concept of functional equivalence:

> Article 1423 of the Commerce Code provides that, as a general rule, the agreement must be in writing and recorded in a document signed by the parties. But this provision also states the applicability of the principle of functional equivalence, by recognizing this character to the exchange of letters, telex, telegrams, fax, and other means of telecommunications that prove the existence of the agreement; the exchange of a request for arbitration and its reply in which the existence of an arbitration agreement is maintained by one party without being denied by the other party; or else, by the reference made in a contract to a document that contains an arbitration clause, provided that the contract is in writing and the reference implies that that the arbitration clause is a part thereof.[18]

In those arbitration proceedings in which the rules of the institution provide for the execution of the Terms of Reference as part of the proceeding, such as the Rules of Arbitration of the International Chamber of Commerce (ICC Rules) or the Rules of Arbitration of the Centro de Arbitraje de México (CAM Rules), the Terms of Reference allows for the confirmation of the arbitration agreement. The foregoing, as the Terms of Reference, clearly identifies the dispute and its submission by the parties to the decision of the arbitral tribunal and is normally signed by the parties.

---

16. Article 89 bis of the Mexican Commerce Code: "The legal effects, validity and binding force of any type of information will not be denied by the sole reason that it is contained in a Data Message. Hence, such messages may be used as evidence in any kind of procedure before a legally recognized authority and shall produce the same legal effects that printed documents, provided that the data messages comply with the provisions of this Code and the corresponding legal rules."

    In addition, the first paragraph of Art. 93 provides: "When the law requires the written form for acts, agreements or contracts, this requirement will be considered fulfilled in Data Messages, as long as the information contained therein is maintained in its integrity and is accessible for ulterior use, regardless of its form or presentation."
17. Article 97 of the Mexican Commerce Code: "When the law requires or the parties agree the existence of a Signature in respect to a Data Message, this requirement will be considered as fulfilled if an Electronic Signature is used that is appropriate for the purpose for which that Data Message was generated or communicated."
18. Judicial precedent: ARBITRATION. FUNCTIONAL EQUIVALENCE AND WRITTEN FORM. Third Collegiate Court in Civil Matters of the First Circuit. Digital registration number 162222.

[D] EFFECTS OF THE ARBITRATION AGREEMENT

Mexican doctrine recognizes that an arbitration agreement has two main effects. The first effect is a positive one, consisting of binding the parties to their consent to solve any dispute in arbitration. The second effect is a negative one, by which the courts are excluded from solving the dispute.

These effects have been confirmed by Mexican courts, as expressed in the following language:

> [T]he arbitration agreement is the basis and cause of the [arbitration], because it compels the parties to submit to arbitration, and excludes the intervention of the State's judge to solve that particular dispute. In the existence of an arbitration agreement, both the parties and the courts must comply with it.[19]

In addition, Mexican courts have recognized the possibility that the arbitration agreement be extended to non-signatories, as stated as follows:

> [I]n principle, the effects of the arbitration agreement are only extended to those parties that entered into the agreement. However, there are certain cases in which non-signatories may be subject by the arbitration agreement. For example, in the case of a transfer to third parties ... Among the cases in which non-signatories may be involved by the effects of the arbitration agreement, is the assignment of rights ... Hence, the arbitration agreement does not lose its autonomy. It just happens that its effects can be extended to the connected commercial relationships, possibility that will be confirmed in each particular case, and only with respect to the arbitration agreement. The foregoing, because even in the presence of a contractual chain in which the contracts between the parties on primary obligations appear firmly related, it cannot be concluded that a transfer of the arbitration agreement has occurred if the clause does not appear expressly agreed throughout the successive contracts or if the transfer was not valid. This has the effect of setting a minimum requirement of certainty and effectiveness.[20]

[E] KINDS OF ARBITRATION AGREEMENT

The Mexican Arbitration Law provides for two types of arbitration agreements. The first type is referred to as an arbitration clause, and this is an arbitration agreement that is included in the contract. Under this type of agreement, the parties undertake to solve in arbitration any dispute that may arise in the future of their legal relationship.

The other kind of arbitration agreement is referred to as an independent arbitration agreement. Hence, it is not included in a contract. Normally the parties

19. Judicial precedent: ARBITRATION AGREEMENT. IT HAS ITS ORIGIN IN A CONTRACTUAL OR NON CONTRACTUAL LEGAL RELATIONSHIP (INTERPRETATION OF SECTION I OF ARTICLE 1416 OF THE COMMERCE CODE). Third Collegiate Court in Civil Matters of the First Circuit. Digital registration number 162237.
20. Judicial precedent: ARBITRATION. THE COURTS OR THE ARBITRATORS MUST ANALYZE THE EXISTENCE AND EFFECTIVENESS OF THE AGREEMENT TO TRANSFER TO THIRD PARTIES. Third Collegiate Court in Civil Matters for the First Circuit. Digital registration number: 178813.

enter into this kind of agreement to undertake to solve disputes that have already arisen between them. Therefore, in this kind of arbitration agreement, the parties decide to remove the dispute out of the sphere of the courts, so that it can be resolved by an arbitral tribunal.

Both types of arbitration agreements are recognized in section I of Article 1416 of the Mexican Arbitration Law.

[F] CONTENT OF AN ARBITRATION AGREEMENT

Besides the essential elements of an arbitration agreement explained in section [C] above, the Mexican Arbitration Law does not provide for additional elements that the parties need to include in their arbitration agreements.

Pursuant to the first paragraph of Article 1435 of the Mexican Arbitration Law, the parties are free to establish the rules of the arbitration:

> Subject to the provisions of this [Law], the parties will be free to agree on the procedure to be followed by the arbitral tribunal in conducting the proceedings.

In this sense, the Mexican Arbitration Law recognizes the existence of ad hoc arbitrations and of institutional arbitrations. Article 1417, sections I and II provide:

> When a provision in this [Law]:
>
> I. Allows the parties the authority to freely decide on a matter, such authority will comprise the right to authorize a third party, including an institution, to decide the matter at hand, except in those cases established in article 1445;[21]
>
> II. Refers to an agreement between the parties, it will be understood that all provisions of the rules of arbitration of an institution mentioned in such agreement will be comprised within such agreement;

It should be clarified that, as in other legislations, there are certain provisions in the Mexican Arbitration Law that are mandatory and that are limitations to the principle of party autonomy. One of these provisions is Article 1434 of the Mexican Arbitration Law which contemplates the principles of equality of the parties and due process:

> The parties should be treated with equality. Each of the parties should receive full opportunity to invoke its rights.[22]

These principles of equality and due process are relevant not only during the arbitration proceeding but also when entering into the arbitration agreement. For example, provisions within the arbitration agreement establishing that the selection of

21. Art. 1445 of the Mexican Arbitration Law refers to the decision by the arbitral tribunal of the applicable law, in the absence of selection by the parties.
22. Inspired in Art. 18 of the UNCITRAL Model Law.

the arbitrators will be carried out by only one of the parties or providing more prerogatives to one of them over the other could be considered invalid.[23]

When drafting their arbitration agreements, Mexican parties often use the standard arbitration clauses of the most commonly used arbitration institutions, both domestic and international. These institutions include the Centro de Arbitraje de México (CAM), the Cámara Nacional de Comercio de la Ciudad de México (CANACO), the International Chamber of Commerce (ICC), the International Centre for Dispute Resolution (ICDR) and the London Court of International Arbitration (LCIA).

The elements that the parties normally add to these standard clauses are: (i) the number of arbitrators (one or three); (ii) the place or seat of the arbitration; (iii) the language of the arbitration; and (iv) the applicable law.

In Mexico, parties often draft their arbitration agreements as multi-tiered clauses. In these clauses, the parties establish a series of consecutive dispute resolution methods before commencing arbitration. The most commonly used stages are: (i) an initial attempt at negotiation between high-level officers of the company; and (ii) a subsequent effort of mediation. In these cases, the consent of the parties to submit to arbitration, essential in an arbitration agreement, could be considered conditional on the exhaustion of the previous dispute resolution efforts agreed by the parties.

[G] APPLICABLE LAW TO THE ARBITRATION AGREEMENT

The Mexican Arbitration Law does not contain a specific provision stating the applicable law to the arbitration agreement. However, this situation is addressed in the provisions contained in the law in respect to the annulment of arbitral awards, and the recognition and enforcement of same.

In the first case, the Mexican Arbitration Law provides that the award may be declared null and void if the arbitration agreement is not valid under the law selected by the parties, or in the absence of such selection, under Mexican law.[24]

In the second case, the Mexican Arbitration Law provides that a judge may deny enforcement of an award if the arbitration agreement is not valid under the law selected by the parties, or in the absence of such selection, under the law of the seat of the arbitration.[25]

---

23. Mexican courts have confirmed the importance of these principles in the arbitration agreement: "[T]he arbitration proceeding is established in the [Mexican Arbitration Law] and three of the principles to be followed are: equality, due process, right to be heard and managing of the proceeding." Judicial precedent: ARBITRATION AWARD. AUTHENTICATION MENTIONED IN ARTICLE 1461 OF THE COMMERCE CODE FOR ENFORCEMENT OF. Fourth Collegiate Court in Civil Matters for the First Circuit. Digital registration number 2017915.
24. Art. 1457 of the Mexican Commerce Code: "Arbitral awards may only be declared null and void by the competent judge when: I. The party that is claiming the annulment proves that: ... a) ... the arbitration agreement is not valid under the law selected by the parties, or in the absence of such selection, under Mexican law."
25. Art. 1462 of the Mexican Commerce Code: "The recognition or enforcement of an arbitral award, regardless of the country in which it was rendered, may only be denied when: I. The party against which the award is being enforced, proves before the competent judge of the country in which the recognition or enforcement is being requested that: ... a) ... the arbitration agreement

Both instances refer to the possibility of the parties choosing the law applicable to the arbitration agreement, which does not necessarily need to correspond to the law of the seat of the arbitration.

[H] SCOPE OF THE ARBITRATION AGREEMENT

Under Mexican law, the scope of an arbitration agreement may freely be decided by the parties. Provided that the subject matter of such arbitration agreement is within the arbitrability established by the law, the parties to such agreement may decide whether they wish that all disputes be solved in arbitration, or only some of them.

The scope of the arbitration agreement is necessarily determined by the language of the agreement. If the language is restrictive, the field of action of the arbitral tribunal shall also be narrow. On the contrary, if the language is broad, the scope of the agreement shall be ample too.

The decision on the scope of the arbitration agreement and its correct drafting is relevant; this is because arbitration awards that exceed the scope of the arbitration agreement may be declared null and void or may not be enforced.[26]

[I] PATHOLOGICAL ARBITRATION AGREEMENTS

As in other jurisdictions, in Mexico, there are cases of pathological clauses. These defective arbitration agreements may have varying consequences, depending on the deficiency of the clause. If the essential consent of the parties to arbitrate is not clear and unequivocal, the arbitration agreement may end up being considered legally inexistent, ineffective, or of impossible enforcement. This would allow any of the parties to seek the resolution of the dispute before the Mexican courts.

However, the flaw of the arbitration agreement may be of a different kind. For example, the steps for the selection of the arbitral tribunal may be impractical, or there may be an error in the name of the arbitral institution selected by the parties. In these types of pathological arbitration agreements, the consequence may not be the hindrance to the arbitration taking place, but still quite harmful to the parties, such as the

is not valid under the law selected by the parties, or in the absence of such selection, under the law of the country in which the award was rendered."

26. Art. 1457 of the Mexican Commerce Code: "Arbitral awards may only be declared null and void by the competent judge when: I. The party that is claiming the annulment proves that: ... c) The award is about a dispute not included in the arbitration agreement or contains decisions that exceed the scope of the arbitration agreement. However, if the decisions in the award on the issues that were submitted to arbitration can be separated from those issues that were not, only the latter may be annulled; and Art. 1462 of the Mexican Commerce Code: "The recognition or enforcement of an arbitral award, regardless of the country in which it was rendered, may only be denied when: I. The party against which the award is being enforced, proves before the competent judge of the country in which the recognition or enforcement is being requested that: ... c) The award is about a dispute not included in the arbitration agreement or contains decisions that exceed the scope of the arbitration agreement. However, if the decisions in the award on the issues that were submitted to arbitration can be separated from those issues that were not, only the former ones may be recognized and enforced."

prolonging of the arbitration and the need for additional cost due to the need to go through further steps to solve the complications resulting from the inadequate language of the arbitration agreement.

CHAPTER 4

The Separability of the Arbitral Clause and the Competence of the Arbitral Tribunal in Mexico

Salvador Fonseca González

In Mexico, the genesis of the separability doctrine[1] and the principle of Competence-Competence have had their twists and turns.[2]

Arbitration in Mexico has a fairly long history and Mexican courts have been, for the most part, on the right side of things as long as arbitration is concerned. For instance, even before the country ratified the New York Convention[3] and adopted the UNCITRAL Model Law,[4] the Supreme Court of Mexico in a precedent dating back to 1933 clearly defined the nature of arbitration as an alternate means of dispute resolution, based on party autonomy, on which the arbitrators are not to be seen as authorities of the State that impart justice but simply as private individuals that resolve a controversy,[5] understanding that remains true to this date.

1. This doctrine, also known as the *autonomy of the arbitration clause*, means "that the arbitration clause in a contract is considered to be separate from the main contract of which it forms part and, as such, survives the termination of that contract" Alan Redfern et al., *Redfern and Hunter on International Arbitration* §3-60 (7th ed.).
2. This principle is understood as "a legal fiction granting arbitration tribunals the power to rule on their own jurisdiction" and as means to overcome "the conceptual problems arising out of any decision by the arbitrator on his own jurisdiction" Julian D. M. Lew et al., *Comparative International Commercial Arbitration* §14-13 and §14-16.
3. United Nations Convention on the Recognition and Enforcement of Foreign Arbitral Awards (New York, Jun. 10, 1958).
4. Model Law on International Commercial Arbitration of the United Nations Commission on International Trade Law (1985).
5. Civil Amparo under review (Amparo en Revisión) 4660/31. Compañía Mexicana de Petróleo El Aguila, S.A. May 26, 1933.

Mexico ratified the New York Convention in 1975 but it was not until after the country adopted the Model Law in 1993 as part of its Code of Commerce that more cases dealing with arbitration started to reach the courts and things started getting interesting.

As part of the adoption of the Model Law, the doctrine of separability of the arbitral clause and the principle of Competence-Competence were included, following Article 16 of the Model Law, in Article 1432 of the Code of Commerce, which reads:

> The arbitral tribunal may rule on its own jurisdiction, including any objections with respect to the existence or validity of the arbitration agreement.
>
> For that purpose, an arbitration clause which forms part of a contract shall be treated as an agreement independent of the other terms of the contract. A decision by the arbitral tribunal that the contract is null and void shall not entail ipso jure the invalidity of the arbitration clause.
>
> A plea that the arbitral tribunal does not have jurisdiction shall be raised not later than the submission of the statement of defense. A party is not precluded from raising such a plea by the fact that he has appointed, or participated in the appointment of, an arbitrator. A plea that the arbitral tribunal is exceeding the scope of its authority shall be raised as soon as the matter alleged to be beyond the scope of its authority is raised during the arbitral proceedings. The arbitral tribunal may, in either case, admit a later plea if it considers the delay justified.
>
> The arbitral tribunal may rule on a plea referred to in the preceding paragraph either as a preliminary question or in an award on the merits. If the arbitral tribunal rules as a preliminary question that it has jurisdiction, any party may request, within thirty days after having received notice of that ruling, the court to decide the matter, which decision shall be subject to no appeal; while such a request is pending, the arbitral tribunal may continue the arbitral proceedings and make an award.

Article 8 of the Model Law was also adopted in Article 1424 of the Code of Commerce in the following terms:

> A court before which an action is brought in a matter which is the subject of an arbitration agreement shall, if a party so requests, refer the parties to arbitration unless it finds that the agreement is null and void, inoperative or incapable of being performed.
>
> Where an action referred to in the preceding paragraph has been brought, arbitral proceedings may nevertheless be commenced or continued, and an award may be made, while the issue is pending before the court.
>
> ...

Not surprisingly, sooner than later court cases arose to test the limits of judicial intervention as to the competence of the arbitral tribunal to decide on its own competence and the validity of the arbitral clause.

In one of such cases, a Federal Circuit Court in Mexico City, in line with the generally accepted interpretation of Articles 8 and 16 of the UNCITRAL Model Law, ruled that the arbitration clause is independent of the other provisions of the contract to which it is a part and that the arbitral tribunal is empowered to rule on objections to the existence or validity of the arbitration agreement.[6]

In another case, a different Federal Circuit Court, departing from the mainstream international practice, held that despite Article 1432 of the Code of Commerce grants the arbitral tribunal the power to rule on its own jurisdiction, including any objections with respect to the existence or validity of the arbitration agreement, if a party requested the annulment of the arbitration agreement before the judge, then the judge (and not the arbitral tribunal) will be the competent to resolve such controversy.[7] The rationale of the court for this decision was that as Article 1,424 of the Commercial Code expressly establishes that the judge to whom a dispute is submitted on a matter that is the subject of an arbitration agreement, will refer the parties to arbitration *unless* it is proven that said agreement is null, ineffective or impossible to perform and given that the arbitral clause shall be understood as a separate agreement from the rest of the stipulations of the contract, the judge shall rule on the validity of the arbitral clause although the arbitral tribunal would remain competent to decide the merits of the case if ultimately the judiciary confirms the validity of the arbitral clause. This decision turned upside down the logic of the separability doctrine, which is normally used as the basis to conclude not that the judges are the ones to decide on the validity of the arbitral clause but, on the contrary, that arbitrators should have the authority to do so.

Given the contradiction, the matter was taken to the Supreme Court to rule on which of the interpretations should stand, and on January 2006, with the dissenting opinion of justices Olga Sánchez Cordero de García Villegas and José Ramón Cossío Díaz, the Supreme Court sided with the decision of the Tenth Civil Court for the First Circuit[8] and ruled that when an action is brought before a judge seeking to declare an arbitration clause null, ineffective or impossible to execute, the validity of the arbitral clause, given the principle of separability, must be previously resolved by the judge, despite the arbitral tribunal retains its competence to rule on the merits of the dispute and even in regards to any claims dealing with the existence and validity of the contract itself.[9]

This constituted a departure from the internationally accepted practice of giving the arbitral tribunal the *first shot* or opportunity to rule on the validity of the arbitral

6. Sixth Civil Circuit Court for the First Circuit, Amparo under Review (Amparo en Revisión) 3836/2004 (*LDC, S.A. de C.V. v. ADT Security Services, S.A., de C. V. and the Nacional Chamber of Commerce of Mexico City*).
7. Tenth Civil Circuit Court for the First Circuit, Amparo under Review (Amparo en Revisión) 31/2005 (*Servicio Electrónico Digital, S.A. de C.V. v. ADT Security Services, S.A., de C. V. and the Nacional Chamber of Commerce of Mexico City*).
8. A more detailed account of the competing cases and the Supreme Court decision can be found in Francisco González de Cossío's article *The Compétence-Compétence Principle, Revisited*, Journal of International Arbitration 24(3), 231-248 (2007) https://doi.org/10.54648/joia2007017.
9. Contradiction of thesis 51/2005-PS between the Sixth and the Tenth Circuit Courts for Civil Matters of the First Circuit. Jan. 11, 2006. By majority of three votes. Dissenting: Olga Sánchez: Cordero de García Villegas and José Ramón Cossío Díaz. Draftsman: Juan N. Silva Meza. Law Clerk: Eligio Nicolás Lerma Moreno. Jurisprudential Thesis 25/2006 approved by the First Chamber of the National Supreme Court of Justice on Mar. 29, 2006.

tribunal embedded in the competence-competence principle,[10] but it also showed a misunderstanding by the Mexican judiciary of the separability doctrine, because the Supreme Court apparently relied on this concept (e.g., that the arbitral clause is an agreement separate from the other provisions of the contract) to reach the (wrong) conclusion that the judicial courts are the ones to retain jurisdiction when the validity of the arbitral clause is disputed in a judicial matter despite that other contractual claims (e.g., those not related to the validity of the arbitral clause) could be referred to arbitration.

Another aspect that can be deduced from this case is that arbitration in Mexico was for long understood as a renunciation of the constitutional right to access justice by courts of the State and as such, courts in the country were traditionally reluctant to refer the parties to arbitration when one of them disputed the validity of the arbitral clause as this would carry the serious consequence of depriving said party of her day in court.

This case stirred the animosity of the arbitration community in the country and ultimately detonated a legislative reform that was passed in 2011 aimed at correcting this mistake and making the relationship between arbitration and the judiciary more efficient.[11]

As part of this reform, Articles 1464 and 1465 were added to the Code of Commerce to instruct judges how to proceed when faced with a request from a party to refer to arbitration. These articles read as follows:

> Article 1464. When a party request the referral to arbitration under Article 1424, the following shall be observed:
>
> I. The request shall be made in the first brief on the merits of the matter filed by that party.
> II. The court, after hearing the other parties, shall immediately resolve.
> III. If the court refers the parties to arbitration, it also shall order to suspend the proceedings before him.
> IV. Once the matter has been definitively resolved in arbitration, upon the petition of either party, the court shall declare the proceedings concluded.
> V. If in the arbitration it is found that the arbitral agreement is null and void or that the arbitral tribunal has no competence or if, in any case, the matter is not concluded in whole or in part in the arbitration, at the request of any of the parties, and after hearing all interested parties, the suspension referred in paragraph III of this article will be lifted.
> VI. There shall be no recourse against the order of the Court referring the parties to arbitration.

Article 1465. In the cases mentioned in the preceding article, the suspension of the proceeding and the referral of the parties to arbitration shall be done immediately. The referral to arbitration shall only be denied:

10. Gerold Herrmann, *The Arbitration Agreement as the Foundation of Arbitration and its Recognition by the Courts*, ICCA Bahrain Arbitration Conference, 48 (Kluwer Law and Taxation Publishers, 1993).
11. Published in the Federal Official Gazette on Jan. 27, 2011.

a) If in the reply to the request for referral to arbitration it is shown by means of a final resolution, either in the form of a judgment or an arbitral award, that the arbitral agreement was declared null and void, or
b) If the nullity, inoperativeness, or incapability of being performed of the arbitral agreement are notorious with the reply to the request for referral to arbitration. The court shall observe a rigorous criterion when determining this.

With this, the judicial error discussed above was corrected.

It is also worth noting that the constitutionality of this reform was put to the test in 2019 on an amparo that was filed in a matter on which the scope of the judge's discretion to refer the parties to arbitration was discussed.[12] The final decision on this case confirmed that the procedure established in Articles 1424, 1464 and 1465 of the Code of Commerce was constitutional as it allowed the party challenging the validity of the arbitral clause the opportunity to be heard before the issuance of a decision. This precedent also stressed the importance given by the law to preserve the effectiveness of the arbitral clause by restricting the arguments that can be made against the validity of the arbitral clause and by limiting the evidence that can be submitted in support of the same. In this regard, it clearly pointed out that the party trying to avoid the referral to arbitration could only rely in a firm resolution, be it in the form of a judgment or arbitration award, to prove that the arbitral clause has been set aside. In the same vein, it signaled that the legal requirements of notoriousness and the rigorous criteria that should be applied when analyzing these matters lead to the conclusion that only documentary evidence and arguments of a legal nature could be accepted from the party that alleges the ineffectiveness or impossible execution of the arbitration agreement as a reason to avoid the referral to arbitration.

With this, Mexico confirmed its alignment with the global mainstream view that the review by the judiciary should be prima facie to avoid dilatory tactics in arbitration proceedings.[13]

However, the most important pro-arbitration step was yet to be taken, this time not by the Congress but by the judiciary. In 2014, the Supreme Court of Mexico issued its ruling on the Amparo Directo 71/2014, the most important precedent dealing with arbitration to date in the country.[14]

Among many other features of arbitration, this precedent touched upon the nature of arbitration, the competence-competence principle and the *first shot* practice.

As to the nature of arbitration, in the Amparo Directo 71/2014 the Supreme Court departed from the notion that arbitration is a waiver of the right to justice by the state courts and following a legislative reform passed in 2008 that amended Article 17 of the

12. Second Circuit Court in Civil and Labor Matters of the 17th Circuit. Amparo under Review (Amparo en revision) 34/2019. Internacional de Cerámica, S.A.B. de C.V. August 15, 2019. Thesis: XVII.2o.C.T.12 C (10a). Federal Weekly Judiciary Gazette. Book 73, December 2019, Volume II, p. 1150.
13. E. Gaillard & J. Savage, Effects of the Arbitration Agreement, Part 2: Chapter III, Fouchard Gaillard Goldman on International Commercial Arbitration, pp. 411-412 (E. Gaillard & J. Savage eds., Kluwer Law International, Montreal, 1999).
14. Direct Amparo (Amparo Directo) 71/2014, May 18, 2016, First Chamber of the Nation's Supreme Court, Draftsman: Alfredo Gutiérez Ortiz Mena, Law Clerk: David García Sarubi (also known as the *AES Merida v. CFE* case).

Constitution[15] to mandate that the laws shall foresee alternative methods of dispute resolution, embraced the idea that instead of a renunciation to state justice, arbitration is an affirmative exercise of a constitutional right to accede to said alternate means of dispute resolution and that said right is relevant and should be protected.[16]

Regarding the competence-competence principle and the *first shot* practice, this precedent:

(1) Implicitly confirmed the idea that, in principle, the arbitrators are supposed to rule on any questions regarding their own jurisdiction and regarding the existence, validity and scope of the arbitral clause *before* the courts review their determinations either as part of an action under the fourth paragraph of Article 1432 of the Code of Commerce (Article 16 of the Model Law) or as part of a proceeding to set aside the arbitral award.

(2) Affirmed that both the arbitral tribunal and the judges, when dealing with issues regarding the existence, validity and scope of the arbitral clause, shall look at the language of the arbitral clause and if said language is clear, they have to simply apply it.

(3) Also stated that if, conversely, the language of the arbitral clause is ambiguous, not precise or vague, the arbitrators shall determine its meaning and the judges shall not impose their preferred interpretation, but simply verify if the interpretation of the arbitral tribunal is reasonable and only step-in if the arbitrators' ruling on their own competence or regarding the existence, validity or scope of the arbitral clause is capricious or arbitrary.

(4) In this vein, it established that when an arbitral tribunal interprets the terms of an arbitral agreement it should do it based on a reasonable interpretation. However, it should not feel compelled to follow the interpretation chosen by the judiciary, nor it should try to anticipate which of the interpretative options would be preferred by the judiciary.

(5) Finally, it clarified that a mere disagreement resulting from equally reasonable interpretations is not a basis for a judge to rule against an arbitral tribunal

15. Published in the Federal Official Gazette in June 2008.

16. The Supreme Court explained in this precedent that the constitutionalization of arbitration *a la Mexican* consist in that: (i) arbitration, while a private means of dispute resolution based on the free will of the parties, is constitutionally relevant and should be protected; (ii) arbitrators are not to be considered judges and they do not exercise any authority derived from the State; (iii) arbitration is not a means to impart *justice* as judges do, but simply a means to resolve a controversy. As such, in Mexico there is no room for amparo or constitutional actions against arbitral orders or awards, as such actions are reserved to challenge actions of judges and other State authorities; a view which is fundamentally different from the prevailing notion in other Latin American countries where arbitrators are formally and/or materially considered judges and understood to impart *justice* and where there is still the possibility to have arbitral orders and awards directly scrutinized by constitutional tribunals (this is the case of Colombia where Art. 116 of its Constitution expressly considers arbitrators as *temporary* judges and where they are understood to exercise a jurisdictional role [Sentencia de la Corte Constitucional, C-305/2013]; Peru, where arbitration is considered to have a jurisdictional essence subject to constitutional scrutiny [Cantuarias Salaverry, n° 6167-2005-PHC/ TC and Sociedad Minera de Responsabilidad Ltda. María Julia, n° 00142-2011-PA/TC]; among other countries).

determination as to his own jurisdiction or as to the existence, validity, and scope of an arbitral agreement.

This decision of the Supreme Court, even when it is not yet a mandatory precedent,[17] has proved to be sort of a *handbook* for judges and practitioners in Mexico when dealing with arbitration issues, one that particularly highlights the deference that judges shall grant to the arbitrators' determination regarding their own competence and the existence and validity of arbitral clauses. This is commendable and shows the commitment of Mexico and the Mexican judiciary to alternative dispute resolution in general and arbitration in particular.

17. In Mexico, subject to certain requirements -like the reiteration of judicial criteria or the resolution of conflicting criteria-, precedents of the Supreme Court and of the Federal Circuit Courts can become of a binding nature for future cases. While the Supreme Court decision on the Amparo Directo 71/2014 is not yet binding on lower courts, it does reflect the longstanding position of the Mexican judiciary in favor of arbitration, restating and building upon criteria favorable to arbitration set in earlier precedents including the judgment of Jun. 13, 2012 of the First Chamber of the Supreme Court in the notable Amparo en Revisión 755/2011 (also known as the *ADT Security Services* case) and the judgment of Jul. 13, 2012 issued by Fourth Federal Collegiate Circuit Court in Civil Matters in Mexico City in the Amparo Directo 4/2014 (also known as the *Conproca* case).

CHAPTER 5

Public Policy and Arbitrability in Mexico

Francisco González de Cossío

[A] INTRODUCTION

Public policy and arbitrability are the two ex officio grounds for setting aside awards or refusing their enforcement. This means that, in contrast to all other grounds, they need to be considered by courts irrespective of whether parties raise them. In and of itself, this is telling: that arbitration law asks that courts *always* evaluate these grounds necessarily means that there is something not only special but also important about these concepts. In this chapter, I shall canvas the Mexican experience with these grounds. To do so, I shall begin with public policy (*see* section [B] below) and then tackle arbitrability (*see* section [C] below). I will thereafter conclude with a comment which includes how Mexican arbitration law on point compares to internationally-accepted paradigms.

[B] PUBLIC POLICY

Public policy is the most interesting, problematic, and sought-after ground for setting aside and not enforcing arbitration awards. To describe the current black-letter rule on the matter I shall first start with an understanding as to how the concept is understood in Mexico. Thereafter I shall address how Mexican juridical actors have grappled with this (difficult and problem-prone) legal concept. The main argument put forward, is that the Mexican experience is in line with internationally-accepted standards. Albeit the experience is rich, is not free from vicissitudes; and the outcome is both interesting and laudable.

[1] Public Policy in the *Lex Scripta*

In line with modern arbitration regimes, the Mexican Arbitration statute envisages public policy as a ground for setting aside[1] and not enforcing arbitration awards.[2] Both provisions read as follows:

> Setting aside, 'if the court finds that ... the recognition or enforcement of the award would be contrary to public policy.
>
> Enforcement, 'if the court finds that, under Mexican law, ... the recognition or enforcement of the award would be contrary to public policy.

As may be observed, no definition of the concept exists, only its enunciation. Given that it is an open concept, delving into what the courts have said on the matter is in order. To do so, I shall divide the presentation into the early cases (*see* section [2] below), to then address the sensitive (*see* section [3] below) and seminal cases (*see* section [4] below), so as to then distill the black-letter law (*see* section [5] below).

[2] Early Cases

In 2010, in an appellate decision, the court conceived public policy as:

> Set of rules that according to a certain historical vision of society and relationships between people, are deemed necessary for the existence of the State and the individual's growth in harmony, balance and peace, concerning the defense of fundamental freedoms, rights or goods of human beings and the principles of their legal organization in order to fulfill their potential as members of a society.[3]

Later, in 2011, a first instance court defined public policy as follows:

> Set of rules on which the common good is based and before which individual rights cease to exist because it is in the interest of society as a whole rather than of individual rights to consider them in isolation.[4]

1. Commerce Code Art. 1457.II which in Spanish reads as follows: "El juez compruebe que según la legislación mexicana ... el laudo es contrario al orden público."
2. Commerce Code Art. 1462.II which in Spanish reads as follows: "El juez compruebe que, según la legislación mexicana ... el reconocimiento o la ejecución del laudo son contrarios al orden público."
3. *Amparo en Revisión* 195/2010, Maquinaria Igsa, Third Appellate Court in Civil Matters for the First Circuit, p. 151 which Spanish original reads as follows: "conjunto de reglas que según una determinada visión histórica de la vida social y de las relaciones entre los individuos, resulta necesaria para la existencia del Estado y el desarrollo del individuo en equilibrio, armonía y paz, lo que atañe a la defensa de las libertades, derechos o bienes fundamentales del hombre y de los principios de su organización jurídica para realizarse como miembro de una sociedad."
4. File 596/2011, 56th District Court for Civil Matters for Mexico City which in Spanish reads as follows: "conjunto de reglas en que reposa el bien común y ante los cuales ceden los derechos particulares porque interesan a la sociedad colectivamente más que a los ciudadanos aisladamente considerarlas." *Ibid.*, pp. 8-9.

Two other judgments defined public policy in the following manner:

> Public order determines a state of peaceful coexistence among the members of a community; this idea is associated with the notion of public peace, a specific objective of government measures.
>
> In a technical sense it refers to the set of legal institutions that identify or distinguish the law of a community; principles, norms and institutions that cannot be altered either by the will of individuals, (they are outside party autonomy) or by the application of foreign law.
>
> It follows that public policy laws do not necessarily refer to public law as opposed to private law. There are laws of public order that regulate institutions of private law which are fundamental social institutions such as kinship and marriage.[5]

A 2010 thesis is emblematic of this initial phase;[6] the thesis titled: "Public Policy. The Pro-arbitration Principle and Recognition of the Freedom of Contract in Assessing the Annulment of an Award."[7] The thrust of the *criteria* is found in the last sentence, which reads as follows:[8]

> The notion of public policy has as domestic and international backdrop, that arbitration may no frustrate, alter or obstacle in its mission. It requires precision as to its definition, scope and content since only by doing so can it be established under what cases and further to which conditions its application is apposite.

The thesis may be criticized and applauded at the same time. *Criticism* would be warranted in that the description is vague. It lacks precision. It is therefore a definition that does not define. More granularity was both needed and desired.

---

5. Both Judgments had the following identical language: "El orden público determina un estado de coexistencia pacífica entre los miembros de una comunidad; esta idea esta asociada con la noción de paz pública, objetivo específico de las medidas de gobierno. En sentido técnico se refiere al conjunto de instituciones jurídicas que identifican o distinguen el derecho de una comunidad; principios, normas e instituciones que no pueden ser alteradas ni por la voluntad de los individuos, (no está bajo el imperio de la autonomía de la voluntad) ni por la aplicación del derecho extranjero. De lo anterior se sigue que las leyes de orden público no se refieren necesariamente al derecho público como opuesto al derecho privado. Existen leyes de orden público que regulan instituciones del derecho privado la cuales son instituciones sociales fundamentales como el parentesco y el matrimonio." Cited in Francisco González de Cossío, *Arbitraje*, (5th edn, Porrúa 2018), p. 1040.
6. In Mexico, "Thesis" (*Tesis*) are summaries of the rule and rationale stemming from a judgment performed by the court itself. They distill the thought of Mexican courts. When a certain number of cases are found to exist with the same holding, they become binding precedents. Also, when they hail from higher courts (such as appellate (Collegiate) courts or the Supreme Court). Their ratio is often cited as criterio (literally, "criteria").
7. The Spanish original reads: ORDEN PÚBLICO. PRINCIPIO PROARBITRAJE Y RECONOCIMIENTO DE LA AUTONOMÍA DE LA VOLUNTAD PARA PONDERAR LA NULIDAD DEL LAUDO ARBITRAL (INTERPRETACIÓN DEL ARTÍCULO V, PUNTO 2, INCISO B), DE LA CONVENCIÓN SOBRE EL RECONOCIMIENTO Y EJECUCIÓN DE SENTENCIAS ARBITRALES EXTRANJERAS). Decision. Ninth Period. Appellate Courts. Judicial Weekly Gazette of the Federation. Volume: XXXIII, May 2011. Thesis: I.3o.C.953 C. p. 1241. Precedents.
8. Translation of: "La noción de orden público tiene como marco de referencia, nacional e internacional, la institución de arbitraje a la que no puede frustrar, alterar u obstaculizar en su misión y exige una precisión en cuanto a su definición, alcance y contenido, porque sólo de esa manera puede establecerse en qué casos y bajo qué condiciones resulta pertinente su aplicación."

It may nonetheless be praised in that, albeit abstract, what is noteworthy of the cited sentence is that it premises the understanding of the concept not only in a national but also an international understanding. It thereafter advances that said conception may not frustrate, alter or obstacle the goals of arbitration. A useful *dictum* given that often the vagueness of the legal concept lends itself to disruptive decisions—of the sort that hamper the purposes of arbitration. Hence, albeit vague, the *criterio* is teleologically commendable.

The same can be said of the observable experience for the first years of arbitration in Mexico. Albeit the descriptions in case law were nebulous, no mistaken or nefarious decisions existed. Therefore, even though they are abstract, the concepts were headed in the right direction. And as arbitration was fairly new (the statute embodying the modern Mexican law was adopted in December 1993), it stands to reason that both courts and practitioners were still grappling with its concepts. And public policy is unquestionably the most problematic.

Hence, a generalization that can be made of the first years of arbitration is that they displayed a good start.

[3] A Sensitive Case

In *Commisa v. PEP*, a public contract was administratively rescinded.[9] This rescission was concurrently challenged both by arbitration and constitutional (*amparo*) proceedings leading to an appellate court decision annulling the award on two independent grounds: public policy and arbitrability.[10] The analytical route assessed whether the fact that the applicable law included a *public* law regime qualified as "public policy" for annulment purposes. It concluded that it did: the award was found to be null as contrary to public policy given that administrative contracts: (i) are governed by administrative statutes and Article 134 of the Federal Constitution; and (ii) involve sensitive governmental needs that may not be adjudicated by a private tribunal.[11]

The matter was highly controversial and contentious. Nothing less than a great case that made (very) bad law.[12] The reason: it misconstrued and misapplied both grounds of annulment.

[4] Seminal Cases

A trilogy of cases is seminal on the matter. They shall be summarized.

9. *Corporación Mexicana de Mantenimiento Integral, S. de R.L. de C.V. v. Pemex-Exploración y Producción* ("*COMMISA v. PEP*"), ICC Case 13613, leading to a December 2009 award ordering Pemex to pay COMMISA more than USD 300 million.
10. *Amparo en Revisión* 358/2010, Eleventh Appellate Court for Civil Matters for the First Circuit. The analysis in this section focuses on the public policy prong of the decision. The arbitrability premise has been discussed in section [C] above.
11. This rationale summarizes a judgment of almost 500 pages.
12. As I posited in Francisco González de Cossío, "Mexico's Fantastic Three: A Pro-arbitration Trilogy" (2017), 33 Arbitration International 153, pp. 164-165 https://doi.org/10.1093/arbint/aiw038.

[a] Amparo en Revisión *755/2011*

In *Amparo en Revisión 755/2011*, the First Chamber of the Mexican Supreme Court exercised *certiorari*[13] to take cognizance of a case hinging on the notion of "public policy." The Supreme Court elaborated a comprehensive definition of the concept. The outcome was noteworthy, both in method and outcome. As to method, the Justice (*Ministro*) who penned the decision[14] guided his thinking by arbitration literature. The journal of the *Club Español del Arbitraje*, Spain Arbitration Review, was quoted to anchor the notion that, as with other legal concepts, "public policy" is an undetermined legal concept (*concepto jurídico indeterminado*) with a hard core and furry edges. It explained the concept thus:[15]

> The legal institutions of the State, principles, norms and institutions which conform it and transcend the community given how offensive and serious the mistake made in the decision is. The mechanism further to which the State avoids that certain acts of private individuals affect fundamental interests of the society.

After characterizing "public policy" as an open texture with furry edges, the Court determined that public policy is a legal concept having a hard core which should be understood as follows:[16]

> The legal principles, norms and institutions forming part of the State, which transcend to the legal community given the offensive and serious nature of the mistake committed in the award. It is the mechanism by which the State ensures that certain acts of private individuals do not impinge upon fundamental interests of society.[17]

---

13. Technically the Court "attracted" the case. *Atracción* is a procedural device having an equivalent outcome as the U.S.-*certiorary:* further to the same, the Supreme Court exercises its jurisdiction either to interpret a constitutional proviso or decide an important matter. It however differs in origin and function in that it constitutes the exercise of original jurisdiction vested upon the Mexican Supreme Court by the Constitution, and which was bestowed upon appellate courts for caseload expediency reasons.
14. A highly respected academic, judge and intellectual who has since left the bench upon expiry of his term, only to become a public intellectual, author and activist: Dr José Ramón Cossío Díaz.
15. *Amparo en Revisión* 755/2011, First Chamber of the Mexican Supreme Court, paras 69 and 70. Paragraph 81 reasons as follows: "un laudo arbitral es contrario al orden público y que, por ende, constituye una causa de nulidad, cuando la cuestión dilucidada se coloque más allá de los límites de dicho orden, es decir, más allá de las instituciones jurídicas del Estado, de los principios, normas e instituciones que lo conforman y que trasciende a la comunidad por lo ofensivo y grave del yerro cometido en la decisión. Un laudo de ese tipo estaría alterando el límite que marca el orden público, a saber, el mecanismo a través del cual el Estado impide que ciertos actos particulares afecten intereses fundamentales de la sociedad."
16. *Ibid.*, paras 69-70.
17. My translation of "las instituciones jurídicas del Estado, principios, normas e instituciones que lo conforman que trascienden a la comunidad por lo ofensivo y grave del yerro cometido en la decisión. El mecanismo a través del cual el Estado impide que ciertos actos particulares afecten intereses fundamentales de la sociedad." The context is the following *dicta*: "un laudo arbitral es contrario al orden público y que, por ende, constituye una causa de nulidad, cuando la cuestión dilucidada se coloque más allá de los límites de dicho orden, es decir, más allá de las instituciones jurídicas del Estado, de los principios, normas e instituciones que lo conforman y que trasciende a la comunidad por lo ofensivo y grave del yerro cometido en la decisión. Un

The decision was outstanding. To begin with, albeit couched in different words, its essence, in this author's opinion, comes very close to the most internationally-accepted definition of the concept, such as *Parsons & Whittemore's* "the most fundamental notions of morality and justice."[18]

Three aspects of the Supreme Court's analytical endeavor deserve underscoring:

(1) It adopted the "minimalist" approach of public policy. The Court's rationale is such that, put in the jargon of foreign and international law, particularly the debate on the minimalist/maximalist approach to public policy, Mexican courts have adopted the "minimalist" view of public policy.

(2) *Dicta* galore is provided which seeks to ensure that not just any mistake contained in the award deserves to be considered "public policy." The mistake must be "offensive" and "serious."

And it must impact the *fundamental* interests of society.

(3) That these adjectives were used shed the view that the Court considered that not just anything deserved to qualify as *public policy* for award setting aside or enforcement purposes; it must be serious in extreme.

The definition advanced by the decision was premised on salient international arbitration literature.[19] Hence, the decision is praiseworthy both for substantive and methodological reasons: it nurtured itself from the most internationally-accepted paradigms. Its progeny has followed closely said notion as we shall see.

[b] Conproca

One of Mexico's biggest and longest-standing cases involved the disputes stemming from the Cadereyta Project: the *Conproca* case.[20] 'The appellate-court judgment stemming from the award-challenge procedures addressed arbitration topics galore.[21] And it did so in a praiseworthy manner. I shall confine my comments to public policy.

The *Conproca* Judgment adopted a plausible definition of "public policy"; not only because of the (high) standard it used but also because of the method employed. It articulated the definition as follows:[22]

---

laudo de ese tipo estaría alterando el límite que marca el orden público, a saber, el mecanismo a través del cual el Estado impide que ciertos actos particulares afecten intereses fundamentales de la sociedad." *Ibid.*, para. 81.

18. United States Court of Appeals: *Parsons & Whittemore Overseas Company, Inc. v. Societe Generale de l'Industrie du Papier* (RAKTA), 508 F.2d 969, 974 (2d Cir. 1974).
19. The court cited an article contained in the *Spain Arbitration* journal of the Spanish Arbitration Club *(Club Español del Arbitraje)*. The said article addressed what should be understood as "public policy" further to internationally-accepted arbitration literature.
20. *Conproca* case (*Conproca, S.A. de C.V. v Petróleos Mexicanos and PEMEX Refinancion*) [2011] ICC case 11760/KGA.
21. Judgment of Fourth Civil Collegiate Court for Mexico City, Exp. D.C. 4/2014 ("*Conproca* Judgment").
22. My translation of "la violación a los principios esenciales del Estado, que trasciende a la comunidad por lo ofensivo y grave del yerro cometido en la decisión. ... el orden público se

> The breach of the essential principles of the State that impacts the community given the offensive and serious mistake made in the decision. Public policy is affected when the reason for the decision deprives the collectivity of a benefit granted by law.

As with the definition adopted in *Amparo in Revisión* 755/2011, this definition deserves applause in that, to be successful, a challenge to an award needs to be contrary to "essential" principles of the State. Also praiseworthy was that it plugged adjectives qualifying the type of mistake that the award needs to incur so as to warrant public policy concerns: they must be "offensive" and "serious." Said adjectives had the effect of *elevating* the standard and *narrowing* its scope. For instance, it said:

> Upon adopting a notion of public policy, it should be stressed that the violation must be *evident*. In other words, when said ground of annulment is invoked, the court must perform a *restrictive analysis* of the alleged violation and only if it is *patent* it may it order the annulment of the award.[23]
>
> The breach of public policy *must be evident*. The substance of the case must not be addressed in a manner similar to an appeal, where the legality of the reasons advanced by the tribunal is assessed.[24] (my emphasis)

The following words were employed to characterize the type of violations that must exist in order to determine the existence of a breach of public policy: "manifest,"[25] "patent,"[26] "notorious,"[27] and "truly serious."[28] Following the steps of the Supreme Court in *Amparo en Revisión* 755/2011,[29] the appellate court reasoned that:[30]

afecta cuando con motivo de la decisión se priva a la colectividad de un beneficio que le otorgan las leyes" (*Conproca* Judgment, pp. 65-66.) *Dicta* existed which was somewhat more nebulous. For instance, the appellate court also said: "An award will be contrary to public policy and therefore annullable when the decision exceeds the limits of the principles, norms and legal institutions composing the State in a manner that impacts the community given the offensive and serious mistake made in the decision. Such an award would alter the limits delineated by public policy, that is to say the mechanism by which the State impedes that certain acts of individuals affect fundamental interests of society." My translation of "un laudo arbitral es contrario al orden público y … por ende constituye una causal de nulidad, cuando la cuestión dilucidada se coloque más allá de los límites del dicho orden, es decir, más allá de las instituciones jurídicas del Estado, de los principios, normas e instituciones que lo conforman y que trasciende a la comunidad por lo ofensivo y grave del yerro cometido en la decisión. Un laudo de este tipo estaría alterando el límite que marca el orden público, a saber, el mecanismo a través del cual el Estado impide que ciertos actos particulares afecten intereses fundamentales de la sociedad."

23. *Conproca* Judgment, p. 66. My translation of "Una vez sentado lo que … debe entenderse por orden público, conviene decir además que la violación … debe ser evidente, es decir, cuando se invoque dicha causal, el tribunal deberá llevar a cabo un análisis restrictivo de la supuesta violación y sólo ante una patente violación podrá ordenar la nulidad."
24. *Conproca* Judgment, p. 80. My translation of "la violación al orden público debe ser evidente, no pueden analizarse las cuestiones de fondo como si se tratara de una apelación en la que se revisa la legalidad de los razonamientos del tribunal."
25. *Conproca* Judgment, p. 92.
26. *Ibid.*
27. *Ibid.*, p. 248.
28. *Ibid.* In its words: "verdaderamente grave."
29. Cited in section [I][D][1], above.

> An award is contrary to public policy and therefore may be annulled when the issue addressed exceeds the limits imposed by the principles, norms and institutions of the State and impacts the community given the offensive and serious mistake committed in the decision.

In doing so the appellate court stressed that the fact must be "evident" to justify the finding that a breach of public policy exists.[31] In its words:[32]

> Albeit the text of the law does not say so, the breach of public policy must be *evident, patent, serious* and *notorious* for the arbitral award to be considered as against public policy. And to do so, private acts must affect *fundamental interests of society*. (Emphasis added)

Premised on said high standard, the court concluded that:[33]

> The annulment of an award grounded on public policy must involve the *serious offense* impacting the domestic legal order of the country of issuance.
>
> An award will be contrary to public policy when the decision it adopts is so serious that it frontally collides with the respective legal order.[34] (Emphasis added)

The outcome was nothing less than outstanding.

The method followed by the appellate court is also noteworthy. It analyzed the text and *trabaux preparatoires* of the UNCITRAL Model Law on international commercial arbitration, its implementation guide, and digest of cases. Three international arbitration authors were cited (Dyalá Jimenez, Jan Paulsson and Francisco González de Cossío).[35] The fact that a Mexican appellate court nurtured its understanding of arbitration topics and premised its views on salient international literature is infrequent, plausible and noteworthy. But above all, it displays a pro-arbitration attitude.

---

30. *Conproca* Judgment, p. 298. My translation of "un laudo arbitral es contrario al orden público y por ende constituye causa de nulidad cuando la cuestión dilucidada se coloque más allá de los límites de dicho orden, es decir, más allá de las instituciones jurídicas del Estado, de los principios, normas e instituciones que lo conforman y que transciende a la comunidad por lo ofensivo y grave del yerro cometido en la decisión."
31. *Conproca* Judgment, p. 343.
32. *Ibid.* My translation of "Aunque el [texto legal] no lo dice la violación al orden público debe ser evidente, patente, grave y notoria ... para considerar que un laudo arbitral es contrario al orden público ... tiene que actualizarse una violación más allá de las instituciones jurídicas del Estado, de los principios, normas e instituciones que lo conforman y que trascienda a la comunidad por lo ofensivo y grave de la equivocación en lo decidido, por lo que un laudo de ese tipo estaría alterando el límite que marca el orden público, esto es, el mecanismo a través del cual el Estado impide que ciertos actos particulares afecten intereses fundamentales de la sociedad."
33. *Conproca* Judgment, p. 347. My translation of "para que se actualice la nulidad de laudo por una violación al orden público, dicha trasgresión debe ser de tal manera grave y trascendente que constituya una verdadera ofensa al orden jurídico interno del país en que se resuelve."
34. *Conproca* Judgment, p. 348. My translation of "un laudo será contrario al orden público cuando la decisión adoptada, como unidad, sea de tal manera grave y trascendente que choque frontalmente con el orden jurídico respectivo."
35. *Conproca* Judgment, pp. 295, 343 and 345. The last author was cited on the topic of public policy (Guido S. Tawil & Eduardo Zuleta eds, *Hacia una Definición Mexicana de orden público en el Arbitraje Comercial Internacional*, (Adeledo Perrot).

As a final comment, something else was added to this decision, however: the notion that public policy is affected when "the collectivity is deprived of a benefit granted by law." What exactly was meant by this was unclear. Definition eventually came from *AES Merida v. CFE*, to which I now turn.

[c] AES Mérida v. CFE

In August 2016, the Mexican Supreme Court issued a decision involving a challenge to an award flowing from an important energy case ("*AES Judgment*"). The case dealt with an award involving an electricity generation plant in the Yucatan Peninsula. It hailed from problems stemming from events that the contractor alleged constituted fortuitous events releasing it from liability vis-à-vis the Mexican Electricity utility (*Comisión Federal de Electricidad—"CFE"*[36]). The tribunal sided with the contractor. CFE challenged the award alleging public policy concerns.[37] The court of first instance rejected the setting aside request. Upon appeal, the Supreme Court exercised *certiorari*. The result was a judgment which made interesting contributions, *inter alia*, to the concept of public policy. To understand why, I shall briefly summarize what was argued, what was decided, and how it relates to the existing jurisprudential backdrop. In the arbitration, AES Mérida sued CFE asking that it recognize three force majeure events which it claimed impinged upon the generation of electricity in the Yucatan plant, further to an electricity purchase power agreement.[38] Upon receipt of the award, CFE sought to set it aside arguing that the award contained a restriction to the alternative dispatch which generated problems resulting in additional costs (unnecessary reserves) which jeopardized the functioning of the national electricity system. More importantly, it compromised the reliability of the electricity system in the Yucatan peninsula. In CFE's opinion, the award frustrated the public policy goals of the bid for the electricity plant which were to secure a generation plant with an alternative operation capacity of 484 MW when operating with gas, and 440 MW when operating with diesel. By failing to allow the achievement of said goal, CFE advanced the argument that the award diminished the reliability and security of the regional electric system of the Yucatan peninsula inasmuch as it resulted in a diminished operation in normal conditions. This impacted the collectivity, in CFE's view. It therefore actualized the public policy ground of annulment since it jeopardized the continuity, security and reliability of the electricity public service in the Yucatan peninsula.

The Supreme Court rejected the argument. In its view, accepting it would be an unwelcome invasion of the merits of the award, which is not legally possible. In doing

36. The CFE has been a constant and sophisticated user of arbitration. It habitually includes arbitration agreements in most all its dealings (and in all contracts having medium and higher importance). And it litigates them adroitly, making apposite use of arbitration law generally, and its remedies specifically. It is the poster child of adequate use of arbitration by public entities.
37. Namely, excess in mandate and jurisdictional questions.
38. "Contrato de compromiso de capacidad de generación de energía eléctrica y compraventa de energía eléctrica asociada y el contrato para el suministro de gas natural."

so, it cited precedents (including *Amparo en Revisión* 755/2011) which defined public policy as a "violation of the essential principles of the state which transcend to the community given the seriousness and offensiveness of the mistaken decision."[39] In discarding the argument the Court reasoned that:

(1) Public policy may be substantive or procedural.
(2) For public policy to exist the violation must be "evident." Public policy may be determined to exist only in "truly serious and notorious circumstances."[40]
(3) That a statute says it is a "public policy" statute is not a sufficient premise to conclude that *public policy* for award setting aside and enforcement purposes is actualized. Most Mexican laws use these words in one way or another. That the electricity law says so does not mean that disputes having to do with it involve "public policy" for award annulment or enforcement purposes.

Premised on the above, the Court rejected that the "weakening of the reliability and security of the electric system" arose to a violation of public policy for award-setting aside purposes.

The Court explained that *public policy* properly understood pertains to the legal principles that protect the essence of legal institutions. These include serious breaches of fundamental principles of procedural justice. It found that these were not extant in the case at hand. This determination is particularly interesting given CFE's (intelligently-posited) argument that the "weakening of the reliability and security of the electric system" triggered a public policy violation. As framed, the argument *could* have mustered acceptance; it *could* be interpreted as within the contours of the existing jurisprudence. That it nonetheless was found to *not* meet the public policy threshold is as telling as it is salutary. It meant that the Court, when faced with an intelligently-advanced argument which could arguably be accepted as falling within the scope of the thus far impressionistic notions shed by existing case law—and which would inure to the benefit of a public utility vis-á-vis a foreign investor—nonetheless stuck to the apposite construction and application of arbitration law: a higher standard. The case stands as a testimony of the Mexican judiciary's comprehension of the subject, as it is of its respect for awards. In a phrase, it is a pro-arbitration stance.

An additional aspect of the decision worth underscoring is that it addressed the loose end of *Amparo en Revisión 755/2011*[41] in an adroit manner. The Court held that the fact that the reliability and security of an electricity system affected an entire region of the country does not actualize the "collectivity deprived of a benefit granted by law" limb of the public policy definition adopted by the Court in *Amparo en Revisión* 755/2011. This puts to rest any concern that the amplitude of language used in *Amparo in Revision* 755/2011 could result in unjustifiably ample conceptions of public policy.

39. In its words "violación a los principios esenciales del estado que trascienda a la comunidad por lo ofensivo y grave de la equivocación en lo decidido."
40. "Circunstancias verdaderamente graves y notorias" were its exact words.
41. See s. II D. 1 *in fine*.

[d] Bilan

French doctrine uses a concept I avow to be fond of: a "*bilan*."[42] I offer a *bilan* on Mexican law on public policy as a ground to set aside or not enforce arbitration awards which consider not only the seminal cases described above but also lower-level decisions worth echoing, to provide a thorough picture of the topic. The judiciary has distilled the following black-letter rules:

- Public policy involves collective, not individual, interests.[43]
- Public goods (*bienes públicos*) are not "public policy."[44]
- Public interest (*interés público*) is not "public policy."[45]
- Public law (*derecho público*) is not "public policy."[46]
- Public procurement (*contratación pública*) is not "public policy."
- Public document (*documento público*) is not "public policy."[47]
- Public funds (*recursos públicos*) do not actualize *public policy*.[48]
- *Caducidad* is not "public policy."[49]

All of these conclusions are both praiseworthy and a step in the right direction.

[C] ARBITRABILITY

Arbitrability, properly understood, refers to the possibility that a dispute involving a certain subject matter may be solved through arbitration. It necessarily implies that certain subjects may *not* be solved by arbitration. In this section, I canvass the Mexican experience with arbitrability. To do so, I shall begin with the applicable legal provisions (*see* s. A below), so as to then address what courts have had to say on the matter (*see* s. B below) and offer a comment (*see* s. C below).

42. Literally "balance." French doctrine often uses the concept *bilan* so as to perform a summary of the status of the subject.
43. Civil Proceeding, File 596/2011, 56th Court for Civil Matters (Mexico City). *Amparo en Revisión* 195/2010, *supra* n. 3.
44. Civil Proceeding, 2006 Judgment in Award setting aside in case 213/2005-V, 12th Court for Civil Matters (First Circuit Mexico City).
45. *Contradicción de tesis* 2/89, Second and Third Collegiate Courts for Civil matters of the First Circuit, Third Chamber of the Supreme Court.
46. *Amparo en Revisión* 195/2010, *supra* n. 3. *Amparo en Revisión* 358/2010, *supra* n. 10. File 596/2011, 46th Court for Civil Matters for the First District, Third Collegiate Court on Civil Matters for the First Circuit.
47. In an (unreported) sports case an arbitral tribunal rejected evidence involving a notarial affidavit (*fe de hechos*) finding that it was untruthful, even apocryphal. In the annulment discussion, it was found that said finding by an arbitral tribunal did not actualize "public policy" for award setting aside proceedings further to Mexican law.
48. *Conproca* Judgment, p. 197.
49. *Amparo en Revisión* 527/2011, First Chamber of the Supreme Court.

[1] Legal Text and Doctrine Extant

Mexican arbitration law addresses the matter both as a ground to set aside an award and a reason to refuse enforcement of the award, thus:

Setting aside:

> If the court finds that the subject-matter of the dispute is *not capable of settlement by arbitration* under Mexican law.[50]

Non-enforcement:

> If the court finds that, under Mexican law, the subject-matter of the dispute is *not capable of settlement by arbitration.*[51]

Establishing when a matter may be solved by arbitration is often less than clear. A frequently-cited litmus test is that the matter: (1) is not expressly excluded by law; (2) not involve rights which may not be freely disposed of; (3) does not affect a public interest; or (4) does not involve third parties.[52]

As to (1), provisions impacting arbitrability are sprinkled all over the legal Mexican system. For instance, Article 615 of the Code of Civil Procedure for Mexico City provides that the following topics are not arbitrable: the right to alimony, divorce (except with regards to the separation of assets and monetary differences), matrimony annulment actions, the patrimonial regime of marriage, and disputes involving the civil state of persons.

Article 568 of the Federal Code of Civil Procedure provides that the following subject matters are within the exclusive jurisdiction of Mexican courts: matters involving land and water rights located in national territory, resources found in the maritime Economic Exclusive Zone, acts of authority, acts involving the internal regime of the State and instrumentalities both of the Federal Government and States, as well as the internal regime of Mexican embassies and consulates in foreign territory.

A treaty exists between Mexico and Spain involving the Recognition and Enforcement of Judgments and Arbitral Awards which includes a list of non-arbitrable matters.[53] The said list is question-begging. It is in fact quite bad. While some matters are mainstream, others are outright mistakes.[54] The list is so odd, and (fortunately)

50. Commerce Code Article 1457.II which provides: "El juez compruebe que según la legislación mexicana, el objeto de la controversia no es susceptible de arbitraje."
51. Commerce Code Article 1462.II which reads: "El juez compruebe que, según la legislación mexicana, el objeto de la controversia no es susceptible de arbitraje."
52. González de Cossío, *supra* n. 5, p. 1611.
53. Agreement between the United Mexican States and the Kingdom of Spain on the Recognition and Enforcement of Judgments and Arbitration Awards in Civil and Commercial Matters of May 3, 1992.
54. *See, e.g.*, Matters involving tax, customs, civil state and capacity of persons, divorce, marriage annulment, bankruptcies, labor matter, social security, nuclear damages. F or instance, administrative matters (even though plenty of administrative laws expressly provide for arbitration), patrimonial regime of marriages (which Article 615 of the Code of Civil Procedure for Mexico City adroitly and expressly authorizes it), wills (even though the matter may in fact be arbitrated), liquidation of companies (albeit some disagree), liability for tort (a matter of accepted arbitrability), and maritime and air disputes (topics often arbitrated).

ignored in practice, that I have proposed denouncing the Treaty lest it cause mischief.[55] To understand how courts have understood and applied the concept as reflected in the cited regime, looking at what courts have said on the matter is of use.

[2] Case Law

Case law on the matter has been scarce. Jurisprudence exists establishing general guidance (*see* section [a] below) as well as case law on the arbitrability of public contracts (*see* section [b] below), from which rules of thumb may be distilled (*see* section [c] below).

[a] General Case Law

Mexican jurisprudence has issued a series of decisions embodying legal criteria (*criterios*) shedding light as to how arbitrability matters will be conceived. The most salient are:

[i] Matters for Arbitration: Intrinsic and Extrinsic Limits to Contractual Freedom

The thesis provides as follows:[56]

> Freedom of contract and its relation to matters of free disposition which may be subject to arbitration confined within certain intrinsic and extrinsic limits.
>
> The extrinsic limits come from the outside the will of the individual and are usually embodied in a legal rule, such as those relating to morality, good customs and public order. The latter include mandatory rules and prohibitions.
>
> the subject matter of the dispute is not subject to arbitration when the law stipulates it or when it concerns matters regulated by mandatory rules or prohibitions, because it constitutes a limitation to contractual freedom.
>
> ... the award as an expression of the power of disposition of the parties ... the expression of the intangibility of private rights. It is subject to the respect of the

55. González de Cossío, *supra* n. 5, p. 414.

56. MATERIA DE ARBITRAJE. LÍMITES INTRÍNSECOS Y EXTRÍNSECOS A LA AUTONOMÍA PRIVADA PARA ESTABLECERLA. Decision, Ninth Period. Appellate Courts. Judicial Weekly Gazette of the Federation. Volume: XXXIII, May 2011. Thesis: I.3o.C.950 C. Page 1217. Precedents (The pertinent parts reads as follows: "La autonomía privada de los particulares y su relación con las materias de libre disposición susceptibles de arbitraje se encuentra supeditada a ciertos límites intrínsecos y extrínsecos ... Los límites extrínsecos provienen del exterior, actúan fuera de la voluntad del individuo y se plasman, por regla general, en una norma jurídica, como las que se refieren a la moralidad, como las buenas costumbres y el orden público, por ejemplo, y las atinentes a la legalidad, como son las normas imperativas y prohibitivas ... el objeto de la controversia no es susceptible de arbitraje cuando así lo dispone la ley o se trata de cuestiones reguladas por normas imperativas o prohibitivas, porque constituye un límite al ejercicio de la autonomía privada ... el laudo como expresión de la potestad de disposición de las partes ... es la expresión de la intangibilidad de los derechos privados pero sujeta al respeto del orden público del Estado Mexicano, como lo previene el artículo 1457, fracción II, del Código de Comercio." (Complete text annexed to this article).

public order of the Mexican State, as provided in Article 1457, section II, of the Commercial Code.

The above decision is plausible in that it explains that arbitration is a by-product of contractual liberty. Moreover, contractual freedom is limited by what this decision defines as "intrinsic" and "extrinsic" limitations. The latter include limitations on contractual freedom further to the applicable law, namely, limitations found in mandatory provisions.

[ii] *Subject Matter of Arbitration: Fixed by Contractual Freedom When Not Contrary to the Law*

A similar view is echoed in this thesis where the Court said that:[57]

> Individuals are recognized as being free to contract.
> the nature of the arbitration clause or independent agreement.
> the protected legal interest concerns the fact that arbitration may only deal with matters which, as a general rule, have a commercial connotation deriving from the law governing the subject matter of the arbitration.
> the lawfulness of the subject matter of the arbitration agreement; ... the arbitrators jurisdiction does not exceed these limits and that the award deals with a subject matter that is arbitrable.

This precedent echoes the principle that freedom of contract is the lodestar of arbitrability. It exemplifies the assertion by citing commercial law matters.

[iii] *Public Policy as a Limit on Freedom of Contract and the Setting Aside Ground*

The same rationale is voiced in the following thesis, albeit its heading (*rubro*) refers to "public policy," the reasoning relates to arbitrability. It said:[58]

57. MATERIA DE ARBITRAJE. ES FIJADA POR LIBRE VOLUNTAD DE LAS PARTES CUANDO NO ES CONTRARIA A LA LEY. Decision. Ninth Period. Judicial Weekly Gazette of the Federation. Volume: XXXIII, May 2011. Thesis: I.3o.C.947 C. Page 1216. Pecedents. The cited relevant portions of the Thesis read as follows "Se les reconoce a los particulares la libertad de contratar ... la naturaleza de la cláusula arbitral o convenio independiente ... el bien jurídico que se tutela atañe a que el arbitraje sólo puede versar sobre materias disponibles con arreglo a derecho y que en el caso de que se trate tengan, por regla general, una connotación mercantil derivada del ordenamiento en que se regula la cuestión del arbitraje ... licitud del objeto del convenio arbitral; que los árbitros tengan competencia objetiva y que no excedan esos límites así como que el laudo verse sobre una materia arbitrable." (Complete text annexed to this article).
58. ORDEN PÚBLICO COMO LÍMITE A LA AUTONOMÍA DE LA VOLUNTAD Y CAUSA DE NULIDAD DEL LAUDO ARBITRAL. Decision. Ninth Period. Judicial Weekly Gazette of the Federation. Volume: XXXIII, May 2011. Thesis: I.3o.C.948 C. Page 1239. Precedents. Relevant translated text reads in Spanish as follows: "sólo pueden ser sometidas al arbitraje las cuestiones que sean de libre disposición para las partes ... legitimación para disponer del derecho sujeto al arbitraje, como una expresión de su capacidad general para emprender negocios jurídicos ... poder de disposición ... la materia de libre disposición susceptible de arbitraje debe ser entendida como aquella regulada por el ordenamiento jurídico que puede ser sustituida por el poder de la autonomía de la voluntad de las partes porque no tiene un carácter imperativo

> Only matters that are freely disposable by the parties may be submitted to arbitration.
>
> legitimacy to dispose of the right subject to arbitration, as an expression of their general capacity to undertake legal transactions.
>
> right of disposition ... the matter of free disposition subject to arbitration must be understood as that regulated by the legal system that can be substituted by the power of party autonomy because it does not have an absolute imperative character but authorizes individuals to exercise their freedom to do or omit what is not prohibited or commanded.
>
> the power to create individualized rules which discipline private actions is recognized as well as arbitration as the ideal procedure or alternative mechanism resolve disputes that may arise, provided it is lawful and recognized by the law as worthy of protection.

In this decision, the concept of free disposition (*cuestiones de libre disposición*) was hailed as the lodestar of what matters may be subject to arbitration.

[iv] Judgment in (Accumulated) Cases 242/2015-II, 302/2017-II and 317/2017-II

A recent (unreported) 370+ page judgment issued an explanation on arbitrability which is worthy of citation *ad extenso*:

> When the matter resolved in the corresponding award is not subject to arbitration, the lawfulness of the arbitration agreement is in question. The subject matter of the arbitration has already been decided in a final and definitive decision or its subject matter is inseparably linked to others over which the parties have no power of disposition revealing that the arbitrator lacks objective jurisdiction.[59]

absoluto sino que se autoriza a los particulares a ejercer su libertad para hacer u omitir lo que no está prohibido ni mandado ... Se reconoce a favor de los particulares el poder creador de las normas individualizadas que deben disciplinar su actuación y al arbitraje como procedimiento idóneo o mecanismo alternativo por el que pueden solucionar las posibles controversias que surjan, siempre y cuando sea lícito y reconocido por el ordenamiento como digno de protección." (Complete text annexed to this article).

59. Judgment in (accumulated) cases 242/2015-II, 302/2017-II and 317/2017-II of 4 October 2022, issued by the Twelfth District Court Judge for Civil Matters for Mexico City, declared res judicata on 18 May 2023. Its description of arbitration in Spanish is the following "cuando la materia resuelta en el laudo correspondiente, no es susceptible de arbitraje, lo que en realidad se cuestiona es la licitud del objeto del convenio arbitral, porque la materia de ese arbitraje, por vía ejemplificativa, ya haya sido decidida en resolución definitiva y firme o se encuentre su materia inseparablemente unida a otras sobre las que las partes no tienen poder de disposición y revela que existe una falta de competencia objetiva del árbitro ... Entonces, la materia de libre disposición susceptible de arbitraje, debe ser entendida como aquella regulada por el ordenamiento jurídico que pueden ser sustituida por el poder de la autonomía de la voluntad de las partes porque no tienen un carácter imperativo absoluto, sino que se autoriza a los particulares a ejercer su libertad para hacer u omitir lo que no está prohibido ni mandado ... Es decir, se reconoce a favor de los particulares el poder creador de las normas individualizadas que deben disciplinar su actuación, y al arbitraje como procedimiento idóneo o mecanismo alternativo por el que pueden solucionar las posibles controversias que surjan, siempre y cuando sea lícito y reconocido por el ordenamiento como digno de protección ... El bien jurídico que se tutela ... el arbitraje sólo puede versar sobre materias disponibles la autonomía privada de los particulares y su relación con las materias de libre disposición susceptibles de arbitraje se encuentra supeditada a ciertos límites intrínsecos y extrínsecos. Los límites intrínsecos se refieren al

Therefore, the matter of free disposition susceptible of arbitration must be understood as that which the legal system allows freedom of contract to regulate matters not prohibited not mandated.

That is to say, the power to create individualized norms that discipline their actions is recognized in favor of individuals, and arbitration is recognized as the ideal procedure or alternative mechanism by which they can resolve any disputes that may arise, provided that the subject matter is lawful and recognized by the law as worthy of protection.

The protected legal interest ... arbitration may only deal with matters within the freedom to contract. Its relationship with matters of free disposition which may be resolved through arbitration is subject to intrinsic and extrinsic limits. The intrinsic limits refer to the recognition that private autonomy in the measure of the interest that is intended to be exercised or realized through the rules that individuals set to obtain a specific objective; it is the limitation of conduct to make it compatible with others.

Extrinsic limits, however, come from the outside, the will of the individual and are generally embodied in a legal rule.

Thus, the extrinsic limits refer to morality, such as good morals and public order, for example, and to legality, i.e., imperative and prohibitive norms. The subject matter of the dispute is therefore not subject to arbitration when the law so provides or when it concerns matters regulated by mandatory or prohibitive rules, because it constitutes a limit to the exercise of private autonomy. Consequently, it should not be ignored that the award as an expression of the power of disposition of the parties over a right and the way in which any controversy related to the same is resolved by the will of the parties, is the expression of the intangibility of private rights but subject to the respect of the public order of the Mexican State, as provided in Article 1457, section II, of the Code of Commerce.

[b] *Arbitrability of Public Contracts*

The amplest judicial discussion on arbitrability flowed from public contracts. In *Commisa*, an appellate court held that the award was null as it involved non-arbitrable topics. Three premises supported said conclusion:[60]

reconocimiento de que la autonomía privada en la medida del interés que pretende ejercerse o realizarse a través de las normas que los particulares fijan para obtener un objetivo concreto; es la limitación de la conducta para hacerla compatible con las demás ... En tanto que los límites extrínsecos provienen del exterior, actúan fuera de la voluntad del individuo y se plasman, por regla general, en una norma jurídica ... Así, encontramos aquellos que se refieren a la moralidad, como las buenas costumbres y el orden público, por ejemplo, y las atinentes a la legalidad, como son las normas imperativas y prohibitivas. De esa manera, el objeto de la controversia no es susceptible de arbitraje cuando así lo dispone la ley o se trata de cuestiones reguladas por normas imperativas o prohibitivas, porque constituye un límite al ejercicio de la autonomía privada. Entonces, no debe desconocerse que el laudo como expresión de la potestad de disposición de las partes sobre un derecho y la forma en que cualquier controversia relacionada con el mismo se resuelve por voluntad de aquellas, es la expresión de la intangibilidad de los derechos privados pero sujeta al respeto del orden público del Estado Mexicano, como lo previene el artículo 1457, fracción II, del Código de Comercio."

60. *Amparo en Revisión* 358/2010, *supra* n. 10.

(1) *Acts of authority*: although the arbitration agreement was broad, the appellate court determined that it could not include disputes involving administrative rescissions given that these were considered acts of authority.[61]
(2) *Exclusive jurisdiction*: was found to exist on administrative tribunals to take cognizance of challenges to acts of authority (including administrative rescissions).
(3) *Res judicata* (*Cosa juzgada refleja*): inasmuch as a decision by a competent court existed which had upheld the rescission, the court reasoned that said determination was "reflective res judicata" (*cosa juzgada refleja*) vis-à-vis the arbitral tribunal. To the extent the arbitral tribunal made determinations involving the rescission which act had already been adjudicated by a Mexican *amparo* court, the appellate court concluded that the arbitral tribunal exceeded its mandate when it took cognizance of the issue, as the matter had become non-arbitrable.

The said conclusions are worthy of criticism, both in premise and in conclusion. I shall succinctly address each.

(1) *Acts of authority*: The characterization of a contractual rescission as an act of authority is eyebrow-raising. A contractual termination is an often-seen *private* act which can scarcely be found to have a public component in its legal DNA. That the appellate court so found is questionable—but admittedly not without support. It is *questionable* as Mexican law includes in its corpus the *iure gestionis v iure imperii* distinction of governmental action. Case law however does exist qualifying certain administrative law cases as *acta iure imperi*. And the decision cited a 1995 Supreme Court ruling supporting said rationale.[62] Hence, the criticism could (should) not only be directed at the decision but also at the status of the matter under Mexican administrative law.
(2) *Exclusive jurisdiction*: At the time when the contract was entered into, no provision existed which established that the matter was not subject to arbitration or that exclusive jurisdiction existed. The law changed in May 2009 to provide that administrative rescissions and early terminations are not arbitrable. Hence, the finding of exclusive jurisdiction is questionable both substantively and temporally. Substantively, given that the finding that the subject matter was entrusted exclusively to courts lacked a source of authority. Temporally, the source of authority which eventually came to exist, came

61. The conclusion was anchored in a 1995 binding precedent of the Supreme Court. Some have read the decision to find that an ex post facto application of a public procurement statute existed. Said reading is mistaken.
62. Said binding precedent provided as follows: CONTRATO DE OBRA PÚBLICA. LA COMPETENCIA PARA CONOCER DEL CONFLICTO SUSCITADO POR SU RESCISIÓN, PROVENIENTE DE UN ACTO ADMINISTRATIVO DE AUTORIDAD, CORRESPONDE A UN JUZGADO DE DISTRITO EN MATERIA ADMINISTRATIVA. Eighth Period. En banc Court. Judicial Weekly Gazette of the Federation. Volume: X, Junio 1994. Thesis: P./J. 20/94. Page 18, Precedents cited in the judgment in *Amparo en Revisión* 358/2010, *supra* n. 10, p. 349.

after. (And the theory is in itself questionable: a wrinkle in Mexican law in need of ironing out.)

(3) *Res judicata*: The notion that once an *in casu* subject has been decided by one court should bind one arbitral tribunal seems questionable. It runs afoul of the simple notion that should jurisdiction exist, the tribunal vested with it can and should decide all aspects of said case. The record or mission of one should not be amputated because of overlap with another. The fact that other tribunals or courts exist with overlapping jurisdiction should not diminish jurisdiction. It only means that *both* will be vested with jurisdiction in performing *their* respective task. Should an issue (factual or legal) be comprehended by both, this means that *each* organ will need to come up with *its* respective view as to the matter, which admittedly may or may not coincide. Should different outcomes hail from two or more tribunals or courts, it will be the result of the simple fact that *parties have so contracted*. Taking the view that consistency dictates attaching more weight to one opinion simply because it came to be at an earlier time is not the best view of the matter: *ex hypothesi*, if two organs exist with jurisdiction to take cognizance of the matter, it means that something is occurring that lends itself to lack of consistency. And this is not as serious as some posit. It is a fact of life that different laws and tribunals exist further to different regimes. Admittedly, this could trigger overlap. But the outcome however need not be one taking precedence over another. Rather, if parties (purposefully or inadvertently) choose to have a plurality, they are entitled (or should be held) to what they bargained for, including the possibility of different results. And calls to arms because of the existence of different results are both exaggerated and insufficient to justify some sort of correction: plurality exists for the simple reason that we live in a plural and complex world. And parties often bring about such outcomes in their contracting.

The matter has never come up again. And the theory is contradicted by practice galore: not only do public contracts, works and infrastructure projects habitually envisage arbitration as the method of resolution of disputes, but Mexican arbitration practice also often sees disputes stemming from public contracts as being subject to arbitration. The theories evinced in *Commisa* have never been echoed again. *Commisa* is therefore best understood as more of an *anomaly* than reflective of a trend or the current status of the law.

[c] *Bilan*

The black-letter rules to be distilled from the above-cited case law are the following:

(1) *Rule:* Arbitration is understood to be the product of contractual freedom. Parties are vested with the right to choose which problems they wish to

channel through arbitration as a result of their liberty to contract. Matters of "free disposition" are therefore the core realm within which arbitration may be used.

(2) *Exception:* Arbitration is limited by "extrinsic" limits. That is to say, limitations provided by the legal system in norms of mandatory application.

(3) *Public contracts:* Agreements with public entities are a specialized field with specialized rules, which may not be generalized. A case-by-case analysis is required.

[D] CONCLUSION

The Mexican experience with the concepts of public policy and arbitrability has been interesting. Sensitive cases involving these topics triggered the risk that the outcome would be affected by idiosyncratic views or stances convenient to powerful parties (particularly public entities), instead of good law stemming from cool-headed intelligent reflection. In contrast, what one observes is good law. Decisions displaying arbitration acumen, independence of the Judiciary and a favorable disposition vis-à-vis arbitration.

In contrast to other jurisdictions where *public policy* has been the *enfant terrible* engendering much mischief, in Mexico, albeit sensitive cases have existed with implications of such magnitude that the fear of bad law was a real and present danger, the aggregate outcome has been good law. Put under the lens of the most accepted international arbitration theory, Mexican law, and practice is consistent with internationally-accepted arbitration law concepts. The current blackletter definition of public policy is, in its content, if not in its words, coincidental with what this author considers to be the definition of the concept: that of *Parsons & Whittemore*: the "most basic notions of morality and justice."[63] The difficult scenarios that have been addressed are also in line with international experience. In and of itself, this is noteworthy, as given their difficulty, they could have easily provoked a mistake—after all, as the commonly cited proverb warns, *great cases make bad law.*

Something similar, but with a caveat, can be said about *arbitrability*. The law extant is by and large adroit. Mexican law on arbitrability follows the internationally accepted canons of what may or may not be subject to arbitration. The exception is the administrative law concepts of administrative rescissions and early terminations in public procurement contracts—by-products of the French *droit administratif* tradition which Mexico (and a good part of Latin America) follows. This is a wrinkle that needs to be ironed out. It however is not the rule of the matter, but rather more aptly understood as an exception.

63. United States Court of Appeals: *Parsons & Whittemore Overseas Company, Inc. v. Societe Generale de l'Industrie du Papier* (RAKTA), *supra* n. 18.

ANNEX: FULL TEXT OF CITED THESIS

Public Policy

ORDEN PÚBLICO. PRINCIPIO PROARBITRAJE Y RECONOCIMIENTO DE LA AUTONOMÍA DE LA VOLUNTAD PARA PONDERAR LA NULIDAD DEL LAUDO ARBITRAL (INTERPRETACIÓN DEL ARTÍCULO V, PUNTO 2, INCISO B), DE LA CONVENCIÓN SOBRE EL RECONOCIMIENTO Y EJECUCIÓN DE SENTENCIAS ARBITRALES EXTRANJERAS). La noción de orden público de que trata la institución de nulidad de laudo arbitral está determinada en el contexto de la reforma al Código de Comercio que reguló aquélla. Con arreglo a lo previsto en el artículo V, punto 2, inciso b), de la Convención sobre el Reconocimiento y Ejecución de Sentencias Arbitrales Extranjeras, celebrada en Nueva York, de mil novecientos cincuenta y ocho, publicada en el Diario Oficial de la Federación, el veintidós de junio de mil novecientos setenta y uno, se puede denegar el reconocimiento y la ejecución de una sentencia arbitral si la autoridad competente del país en que se pide el reconocimiento y la ejecución, comprueba que el reconocimiento o la ejecución de la sentencia serían contrarios al orden público de ese país, en razón de las leyes y convenios y tratados celebrados por el Estado Mexicano. La noción de orden público tiene como marco de referencia, nacional e internacional, la institución de arbitraje a la que no puede frustrar, alterar u obstaculizar en su misión y exige una precisión en cuanto a su definición, alcance y contenido, porque sólo de esa manera puede establecerse en qué casos y bajo qué condiciones resulta pertinente su aplicación.[64]

[PUBLIC POLICY. PRO-ARBITRATION PRINCIPLE AND RECOGNITION OF THE INDIVIDUAL'S AUTONOMY TO CONSIDER THE NULLITY OF THE ARBITRAL AWARD (INTERPRETATION OF ARTICLE V, POINT 2, PARAGRAPH B), OF THE CONVENTION ON THE RECOGNITION AND ENFORCEMENT OF FOREIGN ARBITRAL AWARDS. The notion of public policy that deals with the institution of nullity of the arbitral award is determined in the context of the reform of the Commercial Code that regulated it. Pursuant to the provisions of Article V, point 2, paragraph b, of the Convention on the Recognition and Enforcement of Foreign Arbitral Awards, celebrated in New York in 1958, published in the Official Gazette of the Federation on June 22, 1971, the recognition and enforcement of an arbitral award may be denied if the competent authority of the country where the recognition and enforcement is requested, proves that the recognition or enforcement of the award would be contrary to the public order of such country, by reason of the laws and conventions and treaties entered into by the Mexican State. The notion of public policy has as its frame of reference, national and international, the institution of arbitration which cannot be

64. ORDEN PÚBLICO. PRINCIPIO PROARBITRAJE Y RECONOCIMIENTO DE LA AUTONOMÍA DE LA VOLUNTAD PARA PONDERAR LA NULIDAD DEL LAUDO ARBITRAL (INTERPRETACIÓN DEL ARTÍCULO V, PUNTO 2, INCISO B), DE LA CONVENCIÓN SOBRE EL RECONOCIMIENTO Y EJECUCIÓN DE SENTENCIAS ARBITRALES EXTRANJERAS). Tesis. Novena Época, Tribunales Colegiados de Circuito. Semanario Judicial de la Federación y su Gaceta. Tomo XXXIII, mayo 2011. Tesis: I.3o.C.953 C. Página: 1241. Precedentes.

frustrated, altered or hindered in its mission and requires precision as to its definition, scope and content, because only in this way can it be established in which cases and under what conditions its application is pertinent.]

"**Arbitrability**

MATERIA DE ARBITRAJE. LÍMITES INTRÍNSECOS Y EXTRÍNSECOS A LA AUTONOMÍA PRIVADA PARA ESTABLECERLA. La autonomía privada de los particulares y su relación con las materias de libre disposición susceptibles de arbitraje se encuentra supeditada a ciertos límites intrínsecos y extrínsecos. Los intrínsecos se refieren al reconocimiento de que la autonomía privada en la medida del interés que pretende ejercerse o realizarse a través de las normas que los particulares fijan para obtener un objetivo concreto se limita para hacerla compatible con las demás. Los límites extrínsecos provienen del exterior, actúan fuera de la voluntad del individuo y se plasman, por regla general, en una norma jurídica, como las que se refieren a la moralidad, como las buenas costumbres y el orden público, por ejemplo, y las atinentes a la legalidad, como son las normas imperativas y prohibitivas. Además, debe destacarse que el legislador de modo ordinario establece las normas con arreglo a las cuales los individuos crean y disciplinan las relaciones y situaciones jurídicas que les interesan, a fin de garantizar certeza jurídica y paz social. Estas normas pueden tener el carácter de derogables o supletorias o bien, son inderogables. Las normas derogables o supletorias sirven y auxilian a los particulares para que un determinado negocio sea efectivo y estén conscientes de que una vez realizados los supuestos que las mismas prevén sus consecuencias se apliquen, como lo prevé el mismo ordenamiento. Las normas inderogables se refieren a aquellas que tienen la naturaleza de imperativas y las prohibitivas, que se establecen por el legislador para tutelar intereses públicos y son un límite a la autonomía privada y, cuando se inobservan, con arreglo a lo dispuesto por el artículo 8o. del Código Civil Federal, de aplicación supletoria al Código de Comercio, son nulas, salvo cuando la ley ordene lo contrario. De esa manera el objeto de la controversia no es susceptible de arbitraje cuando así lo dispone la ley o se trata de cuestiones reguladas por normas imperativas o prohibitivas, porque constituye un límite al ejercicio de la autonomía privada. Entonces, no debe desconocerse que el laudo como expresión de la potestad de disposición de las partes sobre un derecho y la forma en que cualquier controversia relacionada con el mismo se resuelve por voluntad de aquéllas, es la expresión de la intangibilidad de los derechos privados pero sujeta al respeto del orden público del Estado Mexicano, como lo previene el artículo 1457, fracción II, del Código de Comercio."[65]

ARBITRATION. INTRINSIC AND EXTRINSIC LIMITS FOR THE ESTABLISHMENT OF PRIVATE AUTONOMY. The private autonomy of individuals and their relationship with matters of free disposition susceptible to arbitration is subject to certain intrinsic and extrinsic limits. The intrinsic limits refer to the recognition that private autonomy,

65. MATERIA DE ARBITRAJE. LÍMITES INTRÍNSECOS Y EXTRÍNSECOS A LA AUTONOMÍA PRIVADA PARA ESTABLECERLA. Tesis. Novena Época, Tribunales Colegiados de Circuito. Semanario Judicial de la Federación y su Gaceta. Tomo XXXIII, mayo 2011. Tesis: I.3o.C.950 C. Página: 1217. Precedente.

to the extent of the interest to be exercised or realized through the rules that individuals set to obtain a specific objective, is limited in order to make it compatible with the others. The extrinsic limits come from outside, they act outside the will of the individual and are embodied, as a general rule, in a legal rule, such as those referring to morality, such as good customs and public order, for example, and those relating to legality, such as the imperative and prohibitive rules. In addition, it should be noted that the legislator ordinarily establishes the rules according to which individuals create and discipline the legal relationships and situations that interest them, in order to ensure legal certainty and social peace. These rules may have the character of derogable or supplementary, or they may be non-derogable. The repealable or supplementary rules serve and assist the individuals so that a certain business is effective and they are aware that once the assumptions that they foresee are made, their consequences will be applied, as provided by the same ordinance. The non-derogable rules refer to those that are imperative in nature and the prohibitive ones, which are established by the legislator to protect public interests and are a limit to private autonomy and, when they are not observed, in accordance with the provisions of article 8 of the Federal Civil Code, of supplementary application to the Code of Commerce, they are null and void, except when the law orders otherwise. Thus, the subject matter of the controversy is not subject to arbitration when so provided by law or when it concerns matters regulated by mandatory or prohibitive rules, because it constitutes a limit to the exercise of private autonomy. Therefore, it should not be ignored that the award as an expression of the power of disposition of the parties over a right and the way in which any controversy related thereto is resolved by the will of the parties, is the expression of the intangibility of private rights but subject to the respect of the public order of the Mexican State, as provided in Article 1457, section II, of the Code of Commerce.

MATERIA DE ARBITRAJE. ES FIJADA POR LIBRE VOLUNTAD DE LAS PARTES CUANDO NO ES CONTRARIA A LA LEY. Se les reconoce a los particulares la libertad de contratar como facultad que tienen para decidir si se vinculan o no con otras personas en una relación jurídica y la libertad contractual, con arreglo a la cual pueden trazar el alcance y contenido del negocio jurídico que se crea, de modo que se regula no sólo el nacimiento de la relación jurídica sino los efectos de la misma. El artículo 1416, fracción II, del Código de Comercio es el que establece de modo expreso qué materias son susceptibles de arbitraje y a la vez reconoce el derecho subjetivo de los particulares de actualizar o dar existencia al supuesto de hecho que refiere esa norma, porque sólo la autonomía de la voluntad puede dar lugar a la cláusula arbitral o al convenio, pero que puede ser configurada libremente en sus efectos por aquéllos limitada únicamente por el propio ordenamiento jurídico. Esto último también tiene una consecuencia jurídica práctica fundamental porque atendiendo a la naturaleza de la cláusula arbitral o convenio independiente, ésta conserva su eficacia aunque uno de los sujetos que intervino en ella ya no la quiera o acepte, pues una vez que ha nacido adquiere una existencia propia y separada de los sujetos y de su voluntad conforme a lo cual sus efectos no son atribuidos a los sujetos mismos sino a la voluntad que aquéllos plasmaron en esa cláusula arbitral o convenio independiente. Es decir, el bien jurídico que se tutela atañe a que el arbitraje sólo puede versar sobre materias disponibles con arreglo a derecho y que en el caso de que se trate tengan, por regla general, una connotación mercantil derivada del ordenamiento en que se regula la cuestión del arbitraje, según se advierte de la norma citada y los convenios que el Estado Mexicano ha suscrito sobre ese tema, pero colmando siempre la licitud del objeto del convenio arbitral; que los árbitros tengan competencia objetiva y que no excedan esos límites así como que el laudo verse sobre una materia arbitrable.[66]

[**ARBITRATION. IS FIXED BY THE WILL OF THE PARTIES WHEN IT IS NOT CONTRARY TO THE LAW.** Individuals are recognized the freedom to contract as the power they have to decide whether or not to enter into a legal relationship with other persons and the freedom of contract, under which they can determine the scope and content of the legal business that is created, so that not only the birth of the legal relationship is regulated but also its effects. Article 1416, section II, of the Code of Commerce, expressly establishes which matters are subject to arbitration and at the same time recognizes the subjective right of individuals to actualize or give existence to the factual assumption referred to in that provision, because only the autonomy of the will can give rise to the arbitration clause or the agreement, but it can be freely configured in its effects by the former, limited only by the legal system itself. The latter also has a fundamental practical legal consequence because, in view of the nature of the independent arbitration clause or agreement, it retains its effectiveness even if one of the parties that intervened in it no longer wants or accepts it, since once it has come into being it acquires an existence of its own and separate from the parties and their will, according to which its effects are not attributed to the parties themselves but to the will that they expressed in that independent arbitration clause or agreement. In other words, the legal right that is protected is that the arbitration may only deal with matters available under the law and that in the case in question have, as a general rule, a commercial connotation derived from the law regulating the arbitration matter, as can be seen in the aforementioned rule and the agreements that the Mexican State has signed on this subject, but always fulfilling the lawfulness of the object of the arbitration agreement; that the arbitrators have objective competence and that they do not exceed those limits, as well as that the award be on an arbitrable matter.]

ORDEN PÚBLICO COMO LÍMITE A LA AUTONOMÍA DE LA VOLUNTAD Y CAUSA DE NULIDAD DEL LAUDO ARBITRAL. El artículo 1457, fracción II, del Código de Comercio, señala que es nulo el laudo cuando el Juez compruebe que el objeto de la controversia no es susceptible de arbitraje, según la ley mexicana. Los supuestos de anulabilidad deben enmarcarse dentro de la pretensión del legislador de hacer operativa la institución arbitral y los resultados que se esperan de ella, ya sea que se trate de una controversia que no es susceptible de arbitraje o bien que el laudo sea contrario al orden público. Se trata de una regulación implícita de que sólo pueden ser sometidas

66. MATERIA DE ARBITRAJE. ES FIJADA POR LIBRE VOLUNTAD DE LAS PARTES CUANDO NO ES CONTRARIA A LA LEY, Tesis. Novena Época, Tribunales Colegiados de Circuito. Semanario Judicial de la Federación y su Gaceta. Tomo XXXIII, mayo 2011. Tesis: I.3o.C.947 C. Página: 1216. Precedente.

al arbitraje las cuestiones que sean de libre disposición para las partes, como reflejo del principio proveniente del artículo 1798 del Código Civil Federal, de aplicación supletoria al Código de Comercio, relativo a que "Son hábiles para contratar todas las personas no exceptuadas por la ley," y que en tratándose de la materia de arbitraje, implica que tienen la legitimación para disponer del derecho sujeto al arbitraje, como una expresión de su capacidad general para emprender negocios jurídicos. Cuando la materia resuelta en el laudo correspondiente no es susceptible de arbitraje, lo que en realidad se cuestiona es la licitud del objeto del convenio arbitral, porque la materia de ese arbitraje, por vía ejemplificativa, ya haya sido decidida en resolución definitiva y firme o se encuentre su materia inseparablemente unida a otras sobre las que las partes no tienen poder de disposición y revela que existe una falta de competencia objetiva del árbitro. Entonces, la materia de libre disposición susceptible de arbitraje debe ser entendida como aquella regulada por el ordenamiento jurídico que puede ser sustituida por el poder de la autonomía de la voluntad de las partes porque no tiene un carácter imperativo absoluto, sino que se autoriza a los particulares a ejercer su libertad para hacer u omitir lo que no está prohibido ni mandado. Se reconoce a favor de los particulares el poder creador de las normas individualizadas que deben disciplinar su actuación y al arbitraje como procedimiento idóneo o mecanismo alternativo por el que pueden solucionar las posibles controversias que surjan, siempre y cuando sea lícito y reconocido por el ordenamiento como digno de protección.[67]

[**PUBLIC POLICY AS A LIMIT TO PARTY AUTONOMY AND CAUSE FOR ANNULMENT OF THE ARBITRATION AWARD.** Article 1457, section II, of the Code of Commerce, states that the award is null and void when the judge finds that the subject matter of the dispute is not susceptible to arbitration, according to Mexican law. The assumptions of nullity must be framed within the legislator's intention to make the arbitration institution and the results expected from it operative, whether it is a dispute that is not susceptible to arbitration or the award is contrary to public order. This is an implicit regulation that only matters that are freely disposable by the parties may be submitted to arbitration, as a reflection of the principle derived from Article 1798 of the Federal Civil Code, of supplementary application to the Code of Commerce, which states that "All persons are capable of contracting, unless otherwise exempted by law," and that in the case of arbitration, this implies that they have the legal standing to dispose of the right subject to arbitration, as an expression of their general capacity to undertake legal business. When the matter resolved in the corresponding award is not subject to arbitration, what is really in question is the lawfulness of the subject matter of the arbitration agreement, because the subject matter of such arbitration, by way of example, has already been decided in a final and firm resolution or its subject matter is inseparably linked to others over which the parties have no power of disposition and reveals that there is a lack of objective competence of the arbitrator. Therefore, the matter of free disposition susceptible to arbitration must be understood as that

67. ORDEN PÚBLICO COMO LÍMITE A LA AUTONOMÍA DE LA VOLUNTAD Y CAUSA DE NULIDAD DEL LAUDO ARBITRAL. Tesis. Novena Época. Tribunales Colegiados de Circuito. Semanario Judicial de la Federación y su Gaceta. Tomo XXXIII, mayo 2011. Tesis: I.3o.C.948 C. Página: 1239. Precedente.

regulated by the legal system that can be substituted by the power of the autonomy of the will of the parties because it does not have an absolute imperative character, but it authorizes individuals to exercise their freedom to do or omit what is not forbidden or commanded. It is recognized in favor of individuals the power to create individualized rules that should discipline their actions and arbitration as a suitable procedure or alternative mechanism by which they can resolve any disputes that may arise, provided it is lawful and recognized by the law as worthy of protection.]

ÁRBITROS, NULIDAD Y CADUCIDAD DEL COMPROMISO EN. El artículo 620 del Código de Procedimientos Civiles vigente en el Distrito Federal, dispone que el compromiso arbitral produce la excepción de incompetencia, y aun cuando en rigor podría decirse que incumbe, en términos generales, al Juez que está conociendo de la materia sometida al compromiso, el resolver sobre su nulidad, sino en todo caso, a los árbitros, de acuerdo con el artículo 630 del propio ordenamiento, interpretado en sus alcances por el tenor del 1245 del anterior Código de Procedimientos Civiles, o a la autoridad judicial ante quien se proponga un juicio especial para alcanzar tal declaración de nulidad, también debe tenerse en cuenta que esta regla no es absoluta, sino que requiere determinadas excepciones aconsejadas por una recta interpretación. Así por ejemplo, cuando se hubiese sometido al compromiso arbitral una materia no compromisoria, como la relativa al divorcio o a la nulidad del matrimonio, sería contrario a una recta interpretación y a la eficacia de una cumplida administración de justicia, el que el tribunal que estuviese conociendo del juicio de divorcio, declarara su incompetencia, por el solo hecho de existir el compromiso, alegando tener incapacidad absoluta para declarar la nulidad del mismo, o más bien su inexistencia, por contraerse a materia prohibida por la ley, siendo más lógico considerar que el tribunal está capacitado para estudiar el punto de incompetencia, con el objeto de declarar si la misma existe, o no, y estudiar si en realidad existe el compromiso que verse sobre materia permitida por la ley; por lo que cuando se alega que el compromiso ya no puede tener eficacia jurídica o ser imposible de realizarse, por haber caducado la relación jurídica, como consecuencia de la imposibilidad del nombramiento de árbitro, es notorio que ésta cuestión tiene que analizarla la autoridad estimada incompetente, para el efecto de resolver si las cosas son realmente como se afirman, pues si el compromiso es imposible de llevarse a término, no existe causa que obligue a declarar la incompetencia, a pesar del compromiso pactado, porque por la imposibilidad del nombramiento de árbitros puede llegar a considerarse aquél como borrado o inexistente, puesto que a tal cosa equivale la imposibilidad de su ejecución.[68]

[**ARBITRATORS, NULLITY AND EXPIRATION OF THE ARBITRATION AGREEMENT.** Article 620 of the Code of Civil Procedures in force in the Federal District, provides that the arbitration agreement produces the exception of incompetence, and even though strictly speaking it could be said that it is incumbent, in general terms, on the Judge who is hearing the matter subject to the agreement, to decide on its nullity,

68. Arbitros, Nulidad y Caducidad del Compromiso En. Tesis. Quinta Época Época. Tercera Sala. Semanario Judicial de la Federación y su Gaceta. Tomo LVII, septiembre de 1938. Registro digital: 356622. Página 2770. Precedente.

but in any case, on the arbitrators, in accordance with Article 630 of the same law, interpreted in its scope by the wording of 1245 of the former Code of Civil Procedures, or to the judicial authority before whom a special trial is proposed to reach such declaration of nullity, it must also be taken into account that this rule is not absolute but requires certain exceptions advised by a correct interpretation. Thus, for example, when a non-compulsory matter, such as divorce or nullity of marriage, has been submitted to arbitration, it would be contrary to a correct interpretation and to the efficiency of the administration of justice if the court hearing the divorce proceeding were to declare its incompetence, by the mere fact of the existence of the arbitration agreement, claiming to have absolute incapacity to declare the nullity of the same, or rather its non-existence, for contracting a matter prohibited by law, being more logical to consider that the court is qualified to study the point of incompetence, with the purpose of declaring if the same exists, or not, and to study if in reality the commitment exists that deals with a matter permitted by law; Therefore, when it is alleged that the commitment can no longer have legal effectiveness or be impossible to be carried out, because the legal relationship has expired, as a consequence of the impossibility of appointing an arbitrator, it is notorious that this issue must be analyzed by the authority deemed incompetent, for the purpose of resolving whether things are really as alleged, because if the commitment is impossible to be carried to term, there is no cause to declare the incompetence, in spite of the agreed commitment, because due to the impossibility of the appointment of arbitrators, it can be considered erased or non-existent, since the impossibility of its execution is equivalent to such a thing.]

CHAPTER 6
Arbitrators and Arbitral Tribunals

Eduardo Siqueiros T.

[A] INTRODUCTION

The purpose of this chapter is to examine the role of arbitrators in the resolution of disputes in Mexico and to address the principles under Mexican law regarding their appointment, duties and rights, as well as the experience in the application of such law by the local judiciary.

Mexico adopted in 1993 the UNCITRAL Model Law practically *ad verbatim* with respect to the composition of an arbitral tribunal and duties of an arbitrator, and therefore this chapter does not purport to examine in a detailed manner the requirements for the appointment, qualifications, duties or the responsibilities of an arbitrator, but rather how these aspects are addressed in Mexico:

> The first question is therefore, why would an arbitrator or arbitral tribunal be treated differently under Mexican law and practice as done in other jurisdictions? The answer is, simply, that there is no such reason generally, but there are certain subtle adaptations to local reality. Either by the Mexican legislature or the manner in which the rule has been identified to be applied by the judiciary. On occasions, local arbitral institutional rules will apply, and they have specific rules that differ from the rest.

This chapter will include not only an analysis of the Mexican law on commercial arbitration[1] but also the rules of the two major arbitration centers in Mexico—Centro de Arbitraje de México (CAM)[2] and the National Chamber of Commerce (CANACO) since

1. Commercial Code, Title Fourth (*Código de Comercio, Título Cuarto*).
2. The Rules have been recently been updated to become effective as of Dec. 1, 2022, and can be found at https://camex.com.mx/wp/wp-content/uploads/2022/12/Reglas-de-Arbitraje-del-CAM-2022.pdf. An English version is pending to be uploaded.

they are frequently used in domestic arbitrations.[3] Since a large number of local and international arbitration disputes involving substantial financial consequences—including but not limited to large contracts with the two major State-owned enterprises (*Petróleos Mexicanos* PEMEX) and the Federal Electricity Commission (*Comisión Federal de Electricidad* or CFE) are commonly submitted to the ICC Rules[4] or the LCIA Rules,[5] references to these may also be made, when appropriate.

Contrary to other jurisdictions, Mexico does not have an arbitration legislation that is applicable to domestic legislation while another to international arbitration proceedings. The rules are the same.

[B] LEGAL NATURE OF THE ROLE OF AN ARBITRATOR

Mexican courts have defined the arbitrator as a person providing a service, a "professional services provider" who acquires obligations (such as performing and deciding the dispute in accordance with the applicable rules), and the right to be compensated.

A recent decision by Mexican federal courts provides ample description of the duties and rights of an arbitrator:

> an arbitrator is a professional services provider; a private individual who renders her/his services to resolve a dispute in an impartial manner, and if the award is rendered null as a consequence of the absence thereof, then the arbitrator may be sued for professional malpractice, given the breach to her/his obligations, along with indemnification of damages arising from the corresponding liability; this, regardless of the fact that the lack of impartiality of the arbitrator affects the standing and reputation of the arbitrator, as this may be affected if his professionalism to carry out his work is placed into doubt. Likewise, as a consequence of such rendering or services [certain] rights are also acquired, such as the right to receive compensation for such services, which would be affected with the impediment insofar as the consequence is the need to cease examining and deciding on the case submitted by the parties.[6]

3. The most recent version of the Rules was approved in August 2007 and are available at https://arbitrajecanaco.com.mx/wp-content/uploads/2022/04/REGLAMENTODEARBITRAJECANACO.pdf.
4. The January 2021 Rules Arbitration of the International Court of Arbitration can be found at https://iccwbo.org/dispute-resolution-services/arbitration/rules-of-arbitration/.
5. The October 2022 Rules Arbitration of the London Court of International Arbitration can be found at https://www.lcia.org/DisputeResolutionServices/lcia-arbitration-rules-2020.aspx.
6. "... el árbitro es un prestador de servicios profesionales, un particular que presta sus servicios para dirimir una controversia de manera imparcial y, de declararse la nulidad del laudo por falta de ésta, el árbitro puede ser sujeto de demanda por responsabilidad profesional, dado el incumplimiento de sus deberes, así como el consecuente reclamo de la indemnización correspondiente por dicha responsabilidad; ello con independencia de que la declaración de parcialidad del árbitro afecta su reputación como prestador de servicios, pues puede verse mermada al poner en duda su profesionalismo al realizar las actividades a las que se dedica; de igual manera, en virtud de esa prestación del servicio de arbitraje también adquiere derechos, como el de recibir una remuneración por la prestación de sus servicios, que se verá afectada con la declaración de impedimento, dado que su consecuencia es dejar de conocer y resolver el arbitraje que le fue encomendado por las partes." Digital registry: 2023673, Eleventh Collegiate Circuit Court for Civil Matters of the First Circuit. Amparo en revisión 406/2018. Víctor Manuel Ruiz Barboza. Aug. 28, 2019. Unanimity. Proponent: Irma Rodríguez Franco. Secretary: Maricela Nieto Vargas.

As the decision indicates, the arbitrator is a services provider and, as such, has duties arising thereunder—some of which shall be examined below, which may trigger liability on account of malpractice.

[1] Appointment of an Arbitrator

Parties are free to select whether they desire a sole arbitrator or a tribunal, and in the latter case the number of arbitrators, and this selection can be made: (i) in the arbitration clause itself, whether this is prior to the occurrence of a dispute; or (ii) at the time the parties submit to arbitration to settle an existing dispute. However, Mexico departs the UNCITRAL Model Law with respect to the default selection. Failure of the parties to determine the number of arbitrators means that it shall be a sole arbitrator that shall be appointed (Article 1426), whereas the former provides for three.[7]

In dealing with an arbitral tribunal, the general rule is that each of the parties shall have the right to appoint an arbitrator. If such party has not been afforded the right, it may challenge the award issued for lack of proper notification of the process, making reference to Articles 1457, section I, subsection b) of the Commercial Code—equivalent to Article 36(a) of the UNCITRAL Model Law and Article V.1.b). of the New York Convention.[8]

The third arbitrator—who shall act as the presiding arbitrator—shall be appointed by the two party-appointed arbitrators. This process can be modified by agreement among the parties, whether at the time the arbitration clause is executed or at a later time.[9] But if the two arbitrators fail to agree on the presiding arbitrator, such appointment shall be made by the local court of the site of arbitration, assuming it is an ad hoc arbitration and not subject to the rules of a specific institution. Indeed, failure to reach such an agreement will be that the local first instance judge of the site of arbitration shall make such an appointment through a procedure established in the chapter dealing with judiciary support of arbitration.[10] In the appointment of an arbitrator, and unless the parties select another system, the court shall be required[11] to:

(1) hear both parties and if it deems advisable, hold a hearing to address oral arguments; and
(2) consult, *inter alia*, with one or more arbitral institutions or chambers of commerce and industry.

Once the court has this information, it will prepare a list of no less than three candidates which the court will share with the parties, who will then have an

7. The same rule applies under the CAM Rules, Art. 14.2. Under CANACO Rules, the institution shall decide on the number, Art. 7.
8. Registry: 162,067, Third Collegiate Circuit Court for Civil Matters of the First Circuit, *Amparo en revisión* 195/2010. Maquinaria Igsa, S.A. de C.V. y otra. 7 de octubre de 2010. Unanimity. Proponent: Neófito López Ramos. Secretary: José Luis Evaristo Villegas.
9. And this right is acknowledged under Art. 1426 of the Commercial Code.
10. Chapter X, Arts. 1466 of the Commercial Code, et seq.
11. Article 1467 of the Commercial Code.

opportunity to grade—as well as to strike out any candidates they refuse and return the list for the court to make the designation. Upon completion of the process, the court shall make the appointment.

Both CAM and CANACO can also act as appointing authority in cases that are not being administered by such institutions, whether at the request of the parties themselves or at the request of a domestic court. In this connection, CAM has issued Guidelines for the appointment of arbitrators, in force as of June 1, 2010, although these deal with administrative procedures as to their appointment, rather than attributes of the arbitrators to be selected.[12]

Mexican courts can also become involved in the event one of the parties fails to appoint an arbitrator in accordance with the terms of the arbitration agreement. As in the case of the UNCITRAL Model Law, the courts shall consider (but shall not be required to do so) the appointment of an arbitrator with a nationality different than that of the parties. Obviously, the provision intends to eliminate one of the reasons for lack of impartiality of the designated arbitrator but since nationality does not trigger necessarily a lack of impartiality, it will be up to the court to decide.

Once an arbitrator is selected by a Mexican court, the court shall ensure to have statements as to impartiality and independence from the selected individual before her/his designation is confirmed.[13]

Having a tribunal with three arbitrators is not always desired. It may be a burden in cost and time to ensure a swift solution for a decision. That is why recent amendments to institutional rules favor the appointment of a single arbitrator for disputes involving a reduced amount of controversy. This, in addition to streamlining the proceedings to make them shorter and without the need for an evidentiary hearing will seek efficiencies in cost and time.[14] In dealing with streamlined or simplified arbitration, the rule is that a sole arbitrator is to be appointed.[15]

[2] Multiparty Cases

Contrary to institutional laws commonly used in Mexico (CAM, CANACO, ICC and LCIA) Mexican law does not contemplate multiparty appointments. Under the four institutional rules mentioned, such appointment shall be attempted to be made jointly

12. They can be consulted at: https://camex.com.mx/nombramiento-de-arbitros/. CAM has also issued guidelines for the appointment of secretaries of arbitral tribunals. https://camex.com.mx/wp/wp-content/uploads/2017/11/lineamientos-del-cam-para-el-nombramiento-de-arbitros.pdf.
13. Article 1467, section IV of the Commercial Code.
14. The ICC Rules provide for accelerated arbitration in those cases involving less that the U.S. Dollar equivalent of USD XX. CAM has also recently amended its rules to establish the threshold at MX 3 million pesos (approximately USD 167,000 as of June 2023), and CANACO set the threshold at a multiple of 124,860 inflation denominated index (UDIS) (equal to approximately USD 54,000 as of June 2023).
15. Under Art. 4(1) CAM Simplified Rules (*Reglas de Arbitraje Simplificado y de Baja Cuantía*), found as Appendix III of the CAM Rules, and Art. 6 of the CANACO Rules (*Reglamento para Arbitrajes de Baja Cuantía*), which can be consulted at https://ccmexico.com.mx/documentos/legislacion/arbitrajeabc/reglamentoabc.pdf.

among the claimants, and jointly by the respondents, but failure to reach an agreement shall trigger the appointment of the three arbitrators by the relevant institution.[16] It is uncertain how the issue would be addressed by the Mexican judiciary if this issue was to be submitted to local courts, although it is quite possible that the same principle would be followed.

[3] Emergency Arbitrator

Although most rules arbitral institutions commonly used in Mexico allow for the appointment and functions of an emergency arbitrator to decide on emergency measures prior to the establishment of the arbitral tribunal,[17] Mexican law does not, albeit grants the parties access to courts to examine and issue *interim* measures.[18]

[4] Requirements/Qualifications

There are no mandatory requirements for an individual to be appointed as an arbitrator, such as being an attorney, having prior experience of acting as such or any other occupation, unless the parties themselves establish in the arbitration agreement such a requirement or condition. Different cases have had engineers, accountants or businesspeople acting as arbitrators, but in such cases, they are normally designated as sole arbitrators and commonly assisted by a legal expert. Nonetheless, nothing prevents the parties from establishing particular requirements to be met depending on the nature of the contact of the claim (assuming one has commenced), although these are not common. Despite the infrequency, disputes are likely to arise from the alleged failure of one or more of the arbitrators to meet the prerequisites. This will trigger the procedure for challenging the arbitrator examined below. In a high-profile case submitted to Mexican courts, the annulment of the award was sought under the challenge that the members of the Tribunal were not "experts in the matter in dispute"—as the arbitral clause established—but the challenge was dismissed, among other reasons, for the challenging party having participated in the appointment and failure to timely challenge.

Nonetheless, it would not be uncommon for a Mexican court who is to make the appointment of an arbitrator to examine not only the issue of nationality but also the expertise required (assuming a specific degree of experience is required) and experience as an arbitrator of the relevant individual. As indicated above, on occasions national courts consult with arbitral institutions whether they have a list of individuals from which they could choose.[19]

16. Articles 16(2) CAM Rules, 10 CANACO Rules, 12(6) ICC Rules, and 8 LCIA Rules.
17. Articles 30 Bis CAM Rules, and 13(1) CANACO Rules and 29(2) as well as Appendix V of the ICC Rules, 9B LCIA Rules.
18. Articles 1470 and 1478, Commercial Code.
19. It is common for national courts in Mexico to rely on lists of experts that are acknowledged, and event registered as such in various specialties after completion of a registration process (e.g., engineering—and various engineering specialties or other occupations).

Despite that, there is no requirement under law for a party to appoint an arbitrator who speaks and can understand and read the language of a case which is not her/his own, the failure to have the capability could trigger a challenge or increase the costs of arbitration to permit such an arbitrator to become fully involved. It is possible that the tribunal will consider this issue at the time of deciding on the costs of arbitration, even with the opposition of such an arbitrator.

Mexican courts have confirmed that a tribunal that is not integrated as per the terms of the arbitration agreement is not only subject to challenge but will also be in peril of annulment of the award, whether the fault is on one of the parties, the arbitrator or the nominating institution as well.[20]

Despite the challenge and the duration it may take for a final result, Mexican law confirms the terms of the UNCITRAL Model Law in providing that, while the challenge is being reconsidered, both during the internal process within the tribunal and while in national courts, the tribunal may continue to act as such and even render its award.[21]

[5] Independence/Impartiality

It is to be expected that the key attribute to be met by an arbitrator, whether this be a sole arbitrator or a member of the tribunal, and whether she/he be party appointed or court appointed or even one appointed by the other two arbitrators, is to be independent and impartial.

But Mexican law does not impose such a requirement, but rather only requires that the appointed or proposed arbitrator disclose any facts or circumstances to the parties that could justifiably doubt her/his independence and/or impartiality.[22] It is up to the parties to decide whether, despite such failure to meet the independence and impartiality threshold, they elect no to challenge.

Mexican law does not provide elements to discern the concepts of independence and impartiality, and therefore principles to be found in treatises and references would apply, including the IBA Guidelines on Conflicts of Interest in International Arbitration.[23]

However, federal courts in Mexico have tied the concept of impartiality to the subject matter of the dispute[24] and acknowledged that the tribunal must resolve with

20. Registry:162,070 Third Collegiate Circuit Court for Civil Matters of the First Circuit. Amparo en revisión 195/2010. Maquinaria Igsa, S.A. de C.V. y otra. 7 de octubre de 2010. Unanimidad de votos. Proponent: Neófito López Ramos. Secretary: José Luis Evaristo Villegas.
21. Article 1429, Commercial Code.
22. Article 1428, Commercial Code, Arts. 13(1) and (2) CAM Rules, 12(1) and (2) CANACO Rules, 11(1)(2) and (3) ICC Rules, and 5(4) and (6) LCIA Rules.
23. The latest Guidelines, approved by the IBA Council in October 2014, may be found at https://www.ibanet.org/MediaHandler?id=e2fe5e72-eb14-4bba-b10d-d33dafee8918.
24. Registry 166506, First Chamber, Novena Época. Semanario Judicial de la Federación y su Gaceta, Tomo XXX, September 2009, p. 432. Tesis: 1ª. CLXVII/2009. Amparo en revisión 131/2009. Talent Agency Unlimited, S.A. de C.V. 27 de mayo de 2009. Unanimity. Proponent: Olga Sánchez Cordero de García Villegas. Secretary: Emmanuel G. Rosales Guerrero.

impartiality[25] This means that, even though the parties decide not to object to an arbitrator who disclosed issues of failure of independence and impartiality, this does not release the arbitrator from her/his obligation to decide with impartiality.

The Supreme Court of Mexico interpreted the requirement of impartiality not only to exclude influence from one but also to further extend to any common influence or instruction from the parties in deciding the case:

> It is important to also mention that arbitrators must decide those matters submitted to their jurisdiction with impartiality, and they may not derive nor orient their functions or their decisions by common consent of the parties (except in the case it is a consent award through a settlement reached to conclude the proceedings), because such consent only operates at the commencement of the arbitration, through the arbitration agreement, but then becomes irrelevant; this is so given that the proceedings may be reviewed subsequently by the judiciary to corroborate the arbitrator's impartiality.[26]

Making reference to Article 1427, section V of the Commercial Code, the Supreme Court has stated that the court entrusted with the appointment of an arbitrator shall take into account all conditions to ensure the appointment of an *independent* arbitrator, together with the advisability of an arbitrator with a nationality different than that of the parties.[27]

The First Chamber of the Supreme Court has confirmed that local courts can *verify* the arbitrator's impartiality.[28]

[6] Duty of Disclosure

An arbitrator who is to be appointed or has been appointed must disclose any circumstances which, in the perception of the parties, may give justified doubts as to her/his independence and or impartiality.[29] The duty is present not only at the time of

25. "el árbitro adquiere obligaciones derivadas de su encargo, como resolver la controversia con imparcialidad." *See*, Digital Registry: 2023673, Eleventh Collegiate Circuit Court for Civil Matters of the First Circuit. *Amparo en revisión* 406/2018. Víctor Manuel Ruiz Barboza. Aug. 28, 2019. Unanimity. Proponent: Irma Rodríguez Franco. Secretary: Maricela Nieto Vargas.
26. First Chamber of the Supreme Court of Justice, *Amparo en Revision* 131/2009. Talent Agency Unlimited, S.A. de C.V. 27 de mayo de 2009. Proponent: Olga Sánchez Cordero de García Villegas. Secretary: Emmanuel G. Rosales Guerrero. "Resulta importante señalar también que los árbitros deben resolver imparcialmente las cuestiones sometidas a su potestad y no deben derivar u orientar sus funciones ni sus decisiones por el común consentimiento de las partes (salvo que se exprese como transacción para finiquitar el proceso arbitral), porque dicho consentimiento sólo opera en el momento inicial del arbitraje -que es el compromiso- pero después será irrelevante; tan es así que incluso el procedimiento puede ser revisado posteriormente por la autoridad jurisdiccional a fin de corroborar la imparcialidad del árbitro."
27. Amparo en Revisión 755/2011, ADT Security Services, 2012.
28. "puede ser revisado posteriormente por la autoridad jurisdiccional a fin de corroborar la imparcialidad del árbitro." Registry 166501, First Chamber, Ninth Epoch. Semanario Judicial de la Federación y su Gaceta, Tomo XXX, September 2009, p. 435. Tesis: 1ª. CLXVI/2009. Amparo en revisión 131/2009. Talent Agency Unlimited, S.A. de C.V. May 27, 2009. Unanimity. Proponent: Olga Sánchez Cordero de García Villegas. Secretary: Emmanuel G. Rosales Guerrero
29. Article 1428 Commercial Code. Also, Art. 15(2) CAM Rules, and Art. 11(2) ICC Rules and 5(4) LCIA Rules.

appointment or acceptance but also remains in force throughout the proceedings. If any circumstance should arise, she/he must disclose to the parties. If the parties have concerns over such circumstances, they may seek a challenge of the arbitrator.

These circumstances could encompass, for example, new appointments, or situations that are similar to those under merits, or any others that may be found in the IBA Guidelines on Conflicts of Interest in International Arbitration[30]

This does not mean that the disclosure will disqualify her/him from acting as an arbitrator, of course, and it will be subject to the parties' decision whether or not to challenge the appointment. If any of the parties do, however, the decision as to the challenge shall be decided by the tribunal itself, although such decision is subject to an appeal before national courts, which decision shall be final. Such a decision by the national court may be, however, subject to appeal within the judiciary under Mexican law under the regular process of judicial appeals. This may take months to complete, if not longer.

In the case of administered arbitration, the decision is expedited and remains in the institution itself, applying the relevant arbitration rules. This is one of the reasons administered arbitration is favored. The challenge is ultimately decided by the relevant institution.[31]

Recalling a case[32] the Supreme Court confirmed that an arbitrator shall at all times during the course of the arbitration the duty to disclose any impediments and "reasons" (*motivos*) that may generate a justifiable doubt with respect to her/his impartiality or independence and that the arbitrator shall communicate to the parties during the course of the arbitral proceedings:[33]

> the arbitral tribunal or sole arbitrator, as may be the case, shall decide the conflict in accordance with the law elected by the parties. Unless otherwise agreed, it shall be deemed that all indication or law or legal provisions of a specific country shall refer to substantive law [of that jurisdiction] and if the parties do not agree on a law that is to apply to the merits, the arbitral tribunal, taking into account the characteristics and contacts or connections to the case, shall determine the applicable to case. Likewise, the sole arbitrator or arbitral tribunal may decide the dispute as 'amiable compositeur' or 'ex aequo et bono' (in conscience) but only if the parties have expressly authorized him to that end (article 1445, third paragraph), provided that resolving as 'amicable compositeur' or 'ex aequo et bono' implies a procedure which is eminently contractual where the solution to the controversy is presented as a more fair and good solution in contrast to the dispute than legal, or strictly in the terms of law, and is based on the will of the parties in dispute, which presents itself as a transfer of consent.[34]

30. The latest Guidelines, approved by the IBA Council in October 2014, may be found at https://www.ibanet.org/MediaHandler?id=e2fe5e72-eb14-4bba-b10d-d33dafee8918.
31. Articles 13(1) and (2) CAM Rules, 14 and 16 CANACO Rules, 14 ICC Rules, and 10 LCIA Rules.
32. Amparo en Revisión 755/2011, ADT Security Services, 2012.
33. "el deber de manifestar sus impedimentos y motivos que puedan generar duda justificada sobre su imparcialidad o independencia, lo cual deberá comunicar en todo momento durante el curso del procedimiento arbitral a las partes."
34. "el tribunal arbitral o el árbitro único, según sea el caso, decidirá el litigio conforme con las normas elegidas por las partes; salvo acuerdo en contrario, se entenderá que toda indicación del derecho u ordenamiento jurídico de un país determinado se refiere al derecho sustantivo, y si las

[7] Confirmation of Arbitrators

The Commercial Code does not require confirmation of arbitrators by any authority, but institutional rules do.[35] Unless challenged as per the above, once an arbitrator is appointed by the party (or the third arbitrator by her/his peers in the tribunal) her/his duties shall commence.

[8] Duties of Arbitrators

Mexican law does not address the duties or arbitrators in a consolidated manner, although these arise from the provisions in the law. These obligations include, but are not limited to:

(a) *Disclosure*. As previously examined, the duty to disclose any facts or circumstance could give rise to justified doubts, in the view of any of the parties, as to their independence and impartiality—not only at the time of their appointment but also at any time during proceedings, promptly after they learn or become aware of such fact or circumstance.[36]
(b) *Decide on their own Jurisdiction*. The principle of *competenz-competenz* also previously examined which deals with the authority to rule on their own ability to act as an arbitrator in the case in accordance with the arbitral agreement.[37]
(c) *Fair and Equitable Treatment*. This duty is expressly established in Mexican law and provides that the tribunal shall have the duty to act fairly and treat the parties equally and grant each full opportunity to present their case.[38]
(d) *Care and Diligence*. In this connection, the tribunal not only has the right—but also the duty—to determine the manner in which the proceedings shall be handled,[39] which broadly includes issues of the procedure, the language of the arbitration, together items that deal with the timing of the

partes no acuerdan la norma que debe regir el fondo, el tribunal arbitral, tomando en cuenta las características y conexiones del caso, determinará el derecho aplicable. Asimismo, el árbitro o tribunal arbitral podrá decidir la contienda como 'amigable componedor' y/o 'en conciencia', pero sólo si las partes lo han autorizado expresamente para ello (artículo 1445, párrafo tercero), en el entendido de que resolver en 'amigable composición' y/o 'en conciencia' implica un procedimiento eminentemente contractual donde la solución a la controversia se presenta mediante una decisión más equitativa y justa que jurídica, o estrictamente apegada al derecho aplicable y que está fundada en la propia voluntad de las partes en disenso, lo que se presenta por una transmisión de la voluntad." Tesis Aislada CLXXI/2009. First Chamber. Sep. 9, 2009. *Amparo en revisión* 131/2009, May 27, 2009. 5 votos. Proponent: Olga Sánchez Cordero de García Villegas. Secretary: Emmanuel G. Rosales Guerrero.

35. Article 15(2) CAM Rules, and Art. 13(1) CANACO Rules and Art. 13(2) ICC Rules.
36. Article 1428 of the Commercial Code.
37. Article 1432 of the Commercial Code. Also, Art. 15(2) CAM Rules, and Art. 26(1) CANACO Rules, Arts. 6(5) ICC Rules and 23(1) LCIA Rules.
38. Article 1434 of the Commercial Code. Also, Arts. 21(2) CAM Rules, 20(1) CANACO Rules, 22(4) ICC Rules and 14(1) and 14(5) LCIA Rules.
39. Article 1435 of the Commercial Code. Also, Arts. 21(1) CAM Rules, 20(1) CANACO Rules, Art. 19 ICC Rules and 14(1) and (2) LCIA Rules.

submissions, manner in which these are to be filed, place and timing of any hearings, submissions on witness and experts' statements[40] The power of the tribunal to make all of these determinations shall be subject, however, to any specific agreement reached by the parties. This is under the premise that the parties are enabled to establish the terms of the arbitration in the arbitration agreement but keeping also under consideration that the tribunal will have authority as to the manner in which the arbitration will be managed.

This duty also entails the obligation on the arbitrator to be available to carry out her/his duties. It is not infrequent that arbitrators take on the responsibility to act as such with little time available to perform, or small windows of availability to fix times for the holding of key events during the proceedings, such as the first hearing to discuss the procedural calendar, to decide on procedural issues, to hold the evidentiary hearing and, lastly but most importantly, to deliberate and prepare the award. It is common that primary responsibility for drafting the award, or at least drafts for discussion among the arbitrators after deliberations is placed on the president of the tribunal, and the president must have time availability to carry out such duty.

The tribunal will need to be diligent in not only carrying out the proceedings with efficiency with respect to time and cost but also timely communicating with the parties in connection with, *inter alia*, the terms for the submissions, notifying them of the time and place of any evidentiary or other hearing to take place.

(e) *Confidentiality*. The arbitrator or tribunal needs to respect the duty of confidentiality regarding the facts, the allegations and, in general, every aspect of the case, the only exceptions being when there is a legal duty to disclose as would occur, for example, if and when required by a competent court.

(f) *Decide*. The key duty of the tribunal is, ultimately, to decide the issues that are brought by the parties under dispute. Not only procedural matters, but importantly, also those of merit. Mexican law does not establish the need for the parties to execute at the start of the proceedings a document establishing the issues under dispute, such as the Terms of Reference which some institutional rules contemplate[41] but the arbitrators must finally decide the different claims (and counterclaims, if this were the case) that are brought to the proceedings by the parties. The decision must address the parties' case in its entirety. No more; no less. Just as the tribunal must resolve all issues presented, and avoid leaving out any (known as *infra petita*), it likewise may not decide on issues that have not been presented for resolution (known as *ultra petita*). In the first case, any one of the parties may request the issuance

40. Article 1438 of the Commercial Code. Also, Arts. 26 CAM Rules, 20(2) CANACO Rules, 22 ICC Rules and 14(6) LCIA Rules.
41. Articles 23 ICC Rules, and 24 CAM Rules.

on an additional award.[42] In the second, however, it may risk the annulment of the award.[43]

Mexican courts have confirmed that, unless the parties expressly authorized the arbitrator to decide otherwise, the arbitrator shall be required to decide and issue the award in accordance with applicable law, which in regard to commercial law needs to take into account commercial practices to the case:[44]

> the tribunal shall decide on the basis of the terms agreed and take into account commercial practices applicable to the case (article 1445, last paragraph); and if there is no agreement [among the parties] to the contrary, the award must be rendered as a general rule in writing, reasoned and signed.

Article 1445 of the Commercial Code requires indeed the arbitrator to decide "... in accordance with the terms of the agreement and shall take into account applicable commercial practices."[45] It does not identify guidelines on how these are to be evidenced, so it will be up to the parties to submit and for the arbitrator to determine the manner in which they are.

There are no differences in the duties or powers of party appointed or arbitral institution or court-appointed arbitrators, nor in their right to compensation, but the parties may grant authority to the arbitrator appointed as president to adopt procedural decisions during the arbitration. The other members of the tribunal may likewise authorize expressly the president upon the parties' omission.[46] Arbitral institution rules commonly grant such authority as well, upon agreement by the parties or the other members of the tribunal.[47]

[9] How Does a Tribunal Work?

Mexican law does not establish any particular rules for the process of deliberation and decision of tribunals, except to provide, as the UNCITRAL Model Law, that the

42. Article 1451 of the Commercial Code. Also, Arts. 36(1) CAM Rules, 44(1) CANACO Rules, Art. 36(3) ICC Rules and 14(1) and 27(3) LCIA Rules.
43. Article 1462, section I.(e). of the Commercial Code, which is equivalent to Art. 36(1)(a)(iii) of the UNCITRAL Model Arbitration Law and Art. V.1.c) of the New York Convention on the Recognition and Enforcement of Foreign Arbitral Awards.
44. "el tribunal arbitral debe decidir con base en las estipulaciones del convenio y tener en cuenta los usos mercantiles aplicables al caso (artículo 1445, último párrafo); y si no existe pacto en contrario, por regla general el laudo deberá dictarse por escrito, motivado y firmado." Register 166511, First Chamber, Ninth Epoch. Federal Judicial Bulletin (Semanario Judicial de la Federación y su Gaceta), Volume XXX, September 2009, p. 426. Tesis: 1ª. CLXXI/2009. *Amparo en revisión* 131/2009. Talent Agency Unlimited, S.A. de C.V. May 27, 2009. Unanimity. Proponent: Olga Sánchez Cordero de García Villegas. Secretary: Emmanuel G. Rosales Guerrero.
45. Article 1445, fourth paragraph provides: "En todos los casos, el tribunal arbitral decidirá con arreglo a las estipulaciones del convenio y tendrá en cuenta los usos mercantiles aplicables al caso."
46. Article 1446 of the Commercial Code.
47. However, Art. 38(2) CANACO Rules requires a decision made by the president to be subsequently confirmed by the tribunal. Art. 26(5) LCIA Rules.

decisions are to be adopted by majority vote.[48] No unanimity is required for either procedural decisions or the award itself, and even the decision or award may lack the signature of the other arbitrator, but in that case, the decision or award shall express the reasons for the reasons therefor.[49]

Some institutional rules also grant the president of the tribunal the power to issue the award upon failure to reach a majority in the decision.[50]

[10] Compensation

In exchange for the responsibilities to be undertaken and the work to be performed, the arbitrator has the right to be compensated. This principle is recognized expressly by Mexican law and courts, with the Supreme Court acknowledging that, as the relationship is one of rendering a service:[51]

> Likewise, as a consequence of such rendering or services [certain] rights are also acquired, such as the right to receive compensation for such services, … .[52]

Interestingly, federal courts in Mexico have further indicated that the services should be deemed to carry duties of "means" (*medios*) rather than duties of "results" (*resultados*) to the arbitrator, which implies that the content of the obligations is to carry them out in a diligent manner, without expecting a specific result. In such a case,

48. Article 1448 of the Commercial Code. Also, Arts. 32(1) CAM Rules, 38(1) CANACO Rules, 32(1) ICC Rules, and 26(5) LCIA Rules.
49. Article 1448 of the Commercial Code. Also, Arts. 39(4) CANACO Rules, and 26(6) LCIA Rules
50. Article 1446 of the Commercial Code and Arts. 32(1) CAM Rules, and 38(1) CANACO Rules, 32(1) ICC Rules, and 26(5) LCIA Rules.
51. "En ese orden de ideas, el árbitro adquiere obligaciones derivadas de su encargo, como resolver la controversia con imparcialidad, pero también adquiere derechos, como recibir una remuneración por sus servicios; además, al ser el árbitro un particular que realiza funciones jurisdiccionales pero sin imperio, en sus actividades profesionales debe responder por las afectaciones que ocasione, derivadas de un actuar parcial, aunado a que puede dar lugar a la nulidad del laudo que dicte o a que se decrete su inejecutabilidad, en razón de no cumplir con los requisitos para la designación del árbitro, entre ellos que sea independiente e imparcial. Así, dichos efectos sólo dejarán de afectar al árbitro si se revoca por los medios de impugnación previstos en la ley, y no por la emisión del laudo arbitral, ya que éste sólo rige para la situación jurídica de las partes en el arbitraje y no tiene jurisdicción sobre las decisiones del Juez que declara la recusación." Digital Registry: 2023673, Eleventh Collegiate Circuit Court of the First Circuit. Amparo en revisión 406/2018. Víctor Manuel Ruiz Barboza. Aug. 28, 2019. Unanimity. Proponent: Irma Rodríguez Franco. Secretary: Maricela Nieto Vargas.
52. "el árbitro es un prestador de servicios profesionales, un particular que presta sus servicios para dirimir una controversia de manera imparcial y, de declararse la nulidad del laudo por falta de ésta, el árbitro puede ser sujeto de demanda por responsabilidad profesional, dado el incumplimiento de sus deberes, así como el consecuente reclamo de la indemnización correspondiente por dicha responsabilidad; ello con independencia de que la declaración de parcialidad del árbitro afecta su reputación como prestador de servicios, pues puede verse mermada al poner en duda su profesionalismo al realizar las actividades a las que se dedica; de igual manera, en virtud de esa prestación del servicio de arbitraje también adquiere derechos, como el de recibir una remuneración por la prestación de sus servicios, que se verá afectada con la declaración de impedimento, dado que su consecuencia es dejar de conocer y resolver el arbitraje que le fue encomendado por las partes." Digital registry: 2023673, Eleventh Collegiate Circuit Court of the First Circuit. Amparo en revisión 406/2018. Víctor Manuel Ruiz Barboza. Aug. 28, 2019. Unanimity. Proponent: Irma Rodríguez Franco. Secretary: Maricela Nieto Vargas.

the fees earned cannot be expected to be reimbursed by the fact that the award is subsequently annulled. The decision is quite direct:

> In the case of an arbitrator, his function is reduced to diligently place his knowledge, through the issuance of an award or judgment, without the expectation that he can warranty that his decisions cannot be revoked or annulled, because the law is not an exact science and the appreciation of facts, circumstances and legal provisions is always subject to considerations that may be more or less variable, this is, his obligation is one of means, and therefore he has the right to receive compensation once the service has been provided, without the possibility of requiring him to reimburse the relevant amount on account of the award having been annulled.[53]

The Commercial Code, in line with the UNCITRAL Model Law, provides that the right to be compensated includes not only the fees of the arbitrator but also expenses incurred by the arbitrators, such as travel expenses and the cost of expert advice, or any other assistance required by the arbitrator.[54]

When there is administered arbitration, it is the institution itself which deals with the determination, collection and disbursement of compensation to the arbitrators. This method makes it easier for the arbitrators to concentrate on the case and avoid determination of their own fees and potential disagreements with the parties or one of the parties. Both on determination and collection of the fees. In this respect, the parties normally can anticipate the amount of arbitration costs(inclusive of arbitrator fees) that will be payable under a table that is generally established and publicized by the relevant institution.[55] Institutions will require from the parties advances toward fees at the commencement of the arbitration, typically before the file is delivered to the arbitrator.

In dealing with administered arbitration, one of the difficult issues in the collection of advances toward the fees and other expenses is dealing with the institution itself.

---

53. "Tratándose de un árbitro, su función se reduce a poner diligentemente sus conocimientos para la composición del litigio, a través del pronunciamiento de una sentencia o laudo, sin que pueda exigírsele que garantice que sus determinaciones no podrán ser revocadas o nulificadas, porque el derecho no es ciencia exacta y la apreciación de hechos, circunstancias y normas está siempre sujeta a criterios que pueden ser más o menos variables, esto es, su obligación es de medios y, por ello, se hace acreedor a la contraprestación correspondiente una vez prestado el servicio, sin que pueda obligársele a restituir el importe respectivo por el hecho de haberse declarado la nulidad del laudo." Annulment of an Arbitral Award. As a consequence of it declaration, it is not viable to order the arbitrators to restitute their fees. Eighth Collegiate Circuit Court of the First Circuit. Amparo directo 960/2019. Rodrigo Zamora Etcharren. Sep. 3, 2020. Unanimity. Proponent: Abraham S. Marcos Valdés. Secretary: Miriam Marcela Punzo Bravo. Amparo directo 961/2019. Héctor Gerónimo Calatayud Izquierdo. 3 de septiembre de 2020. Unanimity. Proponent: Abraham S. Marcos Valdés. Secretary: Miriam Marcela Punzo Bravo. Amparo directo 963/2019. Centro de Arbitraje de México, S.A. de C.V. 3 de septiembre de 2020. Unanimity. Proponent: Abraham S. Marcos Valdés. Secretary: Miriam Marcela Punzo Bravo.
54. Article 1416, section IV of the Commercial Code. Also, Arts. 2 ICC Rules, 28 LCIA Rules (referred in general as "Arbitration Costs"), Art. 40 CAM Rules and Art. 45 CANACO Rules.
55. For example, *see* Appendix I to CAM Rules (*Arancel para el cálculo de gastos del arbitraje*), Anexo CANACO Rules (*Arancel para el cálculo de cuotas administrativas y honorarios de los Árbitros*), Appendix III ICC Rules (*Arancel de gastos administrativos y de honorarios del árbitro*). The LCIA Rules generally contemplate fees based on an hourly rate for the work undertaken by the arbitrators.

Failure of one of the parties to make the advance will suspend the arbitration or terminate it unless the other covers that portion that has been unpaid. The institution may require additional advances during the proceedings by reason of the complexity of the case or the value of the dispute increasing, or both.[56] If the parties fail to make payment of the additional advance, the same principle is applied. Either payment is made by both or one in default of the other, or the case shall be suspended or terminated by reason of the claim being deemed to have been withdrawn.

This benefit is not available in ad hoc arbitration. Following the principles of the UNCITRAL Model Law, the Mexican Commercial Code provides that the tribunal may determine its own fees and require the parties to make advances toward thereto. Absent special arrangements, it would be under the responsibility of the arbitrator/tribunal to hold in deposit the amount of fees and advances toward costs. This may present challenges as Mexican law does not easily support having trust accounts or a special regime for the holding of money in instances such as these. Current anti-money-laundering and tax regulations require strict compliance with reporting which may be a legitimate reason for an arbitrator to avoid the responsibility for holding funds.

If any one of the parties to the arbitration desires court support in the determination of the reasonableness of the fees to be established, such party may petition the local court, which may comment on the proposal.[57] The same can be petitioned with respect to additional requests for advances toward fees and arbitration expenses.[58] Only after there has been a petition for advances that remain unpaid for more than thirty days (and one party has not covered the portion of the other defaulting party) may the tribunal suspend the arbitration or terminate the proceedings.[59]

At the end of the proceedings, the tribunal shall deliver a statement of account to the parties and reimburse any remaining sums in deposit.

As one can expect, one of the decisions of a tribunal in the arbitration is to determine which of the parties shall bear the costs of arbitration. Both the costs of arbitration (understood as the arbitrator's fees and expenses, and other costs, such as the administrative fees of the administering institution). Mexican law and the institutions commonly utilized acknowledge the duty and right of the tribunal to make this determination.[60]

[11] Immunity

Although a provision is normally incorporated into the rules of major arbitral institutions establishing a general principle of exoneration or limitation of liability of an arbitrator, this is not found in Mexican law.

56. Articles 38 CAM Rules, 48 CANACO Rules, and 37 ICC Rules.
57. Article 1444 of the Commercial Code.
58. Article 1456 of the Commercial Code.
59. Article 1456, fourth paragraph of the Commercial Code.
60. Article 1455 of the Commercial Code. Also, Arts. 40.3(c) CAM Rules, 45 CANACO Rules, 38 ICC Rules, and 28(2) LCIA Rules.

A typical clause is found in Article 43 of the CAM Rules, which provides:

> Neither the arbitrators, CAM, its General Council, its Secretary General nor the members of its Secretariat shall be liable for any act or omission in connection with an arbitration proceeding conducted under its auspices.

The CANACO Rules establish a similar principle of exoneration.[61] The ICC Rules ICC Rules,[62] however, recognize the limitation of liability, but cautiously limit such exclusion where prohibited by law.

> The arbitrators, any person appointed by the arbitral tribunal, the emergency arbitrator, the Court and its members, ICC and its employees, and the ICC National Committees and Groups and their employees and representatives shall not be liable to any person for any act or omission in connection with the arbitration, except to the extent such limitation of liability is prohibited by applicable law.

Naturally, any exclusion contemplated under the rules of a local or international institution would be restricted if it is prohibited under applicable law, despite the inexistence of such a legend.

The Commercial Code, which incorporated the UNCITRAL Model Law, subsequently adopted a chapter in 2011 to deal with the intervention of the Mexican judiciary in arbitration. This chapter includes, *inter alia*, the recognition of interim measures ordered by arbitral tribunals, which was a step in the right direction; however, the relevant provision contains an onerous risk for the members of the tribunal, since it provides that the relevant parties requesting the interim measures, as well as the arbitral tribunal ordering them, shall become liable for any damages and lost profits caused.[63] There is no qualification as to whether the measures ordered were adopted, for example, under deceit, in bad faith or without legal support.

[12] Is an Arbitrator an Authority for Judicial Challenge?

The issue of whether an arbitrator is or not an "authority" resides on whether the parties have recourse to a judicial review of the award. As one can expect, it has been the party who has not been favored with the award who has typically taken the position that the arbitrator(s) should be deemed to be such to seek the recourse of "amparo." There were conflicting decisions in the past, and changes to relevant laws caused

61. Article 6 CANACO Rules, "Queda expresamente establecido que ni la Cámara Nacional de Comercio de la Ciudad de México, ni los miembros de la Comisión, ni la Secretaría General, ni los miembros de la Secretaría General, ni los árbitros, serán responsables, frente a persona alguna, de hechos, actos u omisiones relacionadas con el arbitraje."
62. Article 41 ICC Rules. A similar provision is to be found in Art. 31. of the LCIA Rules, but with a further caveat: "(i) where the act or omission is shown by that party to constitute conscious and deliberate wrongdoing committed by the body or person alleged to be liable to that party; or (ii) to the extent that any part of this provision is shown to be prohibited by any applicable law."
63. Article 1480 Commercial Code, last paragraph, "De toda medida cautelar queda responsable el que la pide, así como el Tribunal Arbitral que la dicta, por consiguiente son de su cargo los daños y perjuicios que se causen."

uncertainty which has now been essentially removed. Fortunately, the federal courts have ruled that they are not.

Indeed, federal courts have confirmed the lack of *imperium* of the arbitrator or arbitral tribunal, acknowledging that the arbitrator cannot therefore be deemed to be an "authority" for purposes of an amparo challenge:[64]

> Therefore, an award is a decision that has the attributes of being unchallengeable, unchangeable, and coercibility, but only the concrete efficacy and enforcement of the order are always left to the competent court designated by the parties or that of the site of the arbitration. The arbitrator lacks jurisdictional powers [imperium] which is one of the attributed of the jurisdiction that is inherent to the State jurisdictional bodies. This implies that the arbitrator lacks the force of the State to enforce the order, although the award itself does not lack the attributes of finality [cosa juzgada], since the power to decide the dispute is a delegation made by the State through the legal provision, and only reserves the right to enforce.

This does not, in any manner reduce the nature of a final decision of the award rendered. A key element that federal courts in Mexico have found to determine that an arbitrator is not an authority for purposes of the *amparo* challenge is that they do not hold standing (*legitimación pasiva*) in the challenge of the annulment of the award that has been filed. The function entrusted to the arbitrators is to apply their knowledge to the resolution of the dispute submitted by the parties, and they lack interest of their own to be sought or defended. At the time of his appointment, there is no conflict between the parties and the arbitrator. The decision provides:

> In this sense, arbitrators lack standing [legitimación pasiva] to defend the legality of their intervention in an arbitration proceeding, nor of the award itself rendered upon conclusion, and therefore they cannot be the passive subject of an annulment proceeding, because, given their involvement as a neutral and impartial person to decide an arbitral dispute, they lack interest and standing for the award to subsist or be annulled since the nature of their involvement cannot be validly placed against the interest that the parties defend in the proceedings where the validity of the award that was rendered by them is being challenged.[65]

64. "Por lo tanto, el laudo es una resolución que tiene los atributos de inimpugnabilidad, inmutabilidad y coercibilidad, sólo que la eficacia y realización concreta de lo condenado quedan siempre al Juez competente designado por las partes o el del lugar del juicio. El árbitro carece de la facultad de hacer cumplir, ante sí, el laudo que emitió, porque no tiene la potestad o imperium, que es uno de los atributos de la jurisdicción y que es inherente a los órganos jurisdiccionales del Estado. Ello implica que el árbitro carece de la fuerza del Estado para hacer efectiva la condena, pero el laudo en sí mismo no está despojado de los atributos de la cosa juzgada, puesto que la facultad de decidir la controversia es una delegación hecha por el Estado a través de la norma jurídica, y sólo se reserva la facultad de ejecutar…." Registry 189345, Tesis: I.3o.C.231 C, Third Collegiate Court for Civil Matters in the First Circuit, Amparo directo 1303/2001. Constructora Aboumrad Amodio Berho, S.A. de C.V. Mar. 8, 2001. Unanimity. Proponent: Neófito López Ramos. Secretaria: Lina Sharai González Juárez.
65. "En ese sentido, los árbitros no tienen la legitimación necesaria para defender la legalidad de su intervención en un procedimiento arbitral, ni la del laudo con que éste culmine y, por lo mismo, no pueden ser sujetos pasivos de una pretensión de nulidad, en razón de que al intervenir como órgano neutral e imparcial resolviendo el conflicto arbitral, carecen de interés y legitimación para que el laudo subsista o deje de subsistir, ya que por la naturaleza misma de su actuación no pueden válidamente contraponerse al interés que defienden las partes en el juicio en el que se cuestiona la validez del laudo por ellos pronunciado." Annulment of an Arbitral Award. As a

Likewise, another decision makes the distinction of an arbitrator, where his powers and duties arise from the agreement reached among private parties:

> even though Private arbitrators have the authority to decide legal disputes which the parties may submit to their attention, and since this is sourced from an agreement reached among private parties, the function of arbitrators is a private nature and the same character applies to all of the activities they undertake to decide the relevant controversy, i.e., they are not State officials nor do they have their own or delegated jurisdiction, since their authority does not emanate from a legal provision but from the consent of the parties which is expressed in the agreement that the law acknowledges, and since those who appoint arbitrators and establish limits to their function do not act ¡in the public interest, this is in a capacity of a State body, but rather in private interest, logically the functions of these arbitrators are nor public but private, which means they lack imperium, and hence the arbitrators themselves cannot deem themselves to be State authorities nor their actions equivalent to those of an authority, for which reason the challenge of amparo filed against such actions is denied.[66]

Another more recent decision addresses the same principles:

> the arbitrator does not meet the requirements of article 5, section II; second paragraph of the Amparo Law, since the actions that the arbitrator undertakes do not equal to those of an authority for purposes of the challenge of amparo, given that she/he does not make them in an unilateral and obligatory manner, as they lack the power of imperium to enforce, because the intervention of an judicial authority is required for this purpose, aside from the fact that their functions are not determined by a general provision of la, since there is no legislation of such nature that deals with their existence and undertakings, given that their actions are ruled by the agreement among the parties.[67]

---

consequence of it declaration, it is not viable to order the arbitrators to restitute their fees. Annulment of an Arbitral Award. Arbitrators lack standing in the proceedings where this claim has been filed. Eighth Collegiate Circuit Court of the First Circuit. Amparo directo 960/2019. Rodrigo Zamora Etcharren. 3 de septiembre de 2020. Unanimity. Proponent: Abraham S. Marcos Valdés. Secretary: Miriam Marcela Punzo Bravo. Amparo directo 961/2019. Héctor Gerónimo Calatayud Izquierdo. 3 de septiembre de 2020. Unanimity. Proponent: Abraham S. Marcos Valdés. Secretary: Miriam Marcela Punzo Bravo. Amparo directo 963/2019. Centro de Arbitraje de México, S.A. de C.V. 3 de septiembre de 2020. Unanimity. Proponent: Abraham S. Marcos Valdés. Secretary: Miriam Marcela Punzo Bravo.

66. "aunque los árbitros privados tienen la facultad de resolver los conflictos jurídicos que las partes sometan a su consideración, como ello emana de un compromiso formado entre particulares, la función de los árbitros es privada e igual carácter tienen todas las actividades que desarrollan a fin de resolver la controversia de que se trate, esto es, no son funcionarios del Estado ni tienen jurisdicción propia o delegada, dado que sus facultades derivan no de una norma general, sino de la voluntad de los contratantes expresada en el acuerdo que la ley reconoce, y como quien nombra a los árbitros y determina los límites de su oficio no obra en interés público, o sea, en calidad de órgano del Estado, sino en interés privado, lógicamente las funciones de esos árbitros no son públicas, sino privadas, lo que significa que carecen de imperio, de suerte que no pueden los mismos árbitros conceptuarse como autoridades del Estado ni sus actos son equivalentes a los de autoridad, por lo que resulta improcedente el juicio de amparo promovido en su contra." Digital Registry: 2009139, Collegiate Circuit Courts; Queja 195/2014. Cecilia Flores Rueda y otros. Oct. 29, 2014. Unanimity. Proponent: Abraham S. Marcos Valdés. Secretaria: Patricia Villa Rodríguez.
67. "el árbitro no cumple con los requisitos derivados del artículo 5o., fracción II, segundo párrafo, de la Ley de Amparo, ya que los actos que realiza no equivalen a los de una autoridad para los

Yet two other decisions of the Supreme Court distinguish the powers of the arbitrator versus those of the judiciary:

> it is valid to state that arbitrators possess "authority" but lack jurisdictional power, which is an exclusive attribute of the State, and therefore are only enabled to undertake all those actions for which their authority simply allow, and will be required to request the cooperation of courts in respect other that may require jurisdictional power, as is the case, for example, of provisional and enforcement measures, where the assistance of the State judiciary is required to achieve such measures through proceedings that shall be contentious (by reason of the manner in which interests shall be debated).[68]
>
> all actions taken by an arbitrator or arbitral tribunal, while there is a possibility of deciding a specific or determinable dispute – and exercise certain jurisdictional authority, does not equal, at all, to the jurisdictional powers of the State, since in the latter the authority arise from the [Constitution] and is therefore generic and permanent, while arbitral jurisdiction is subject to, without doubt, to the consent of the parties, and consequently is always specific and temporary … . It is therefore without challenge that an arbitrator or arbitral tribunal cannot in any manner decide with respect to those matters that have not been expressly agreed to among the parties or are otherwise a matter of public order.[69]

efectos del juicio de amparo, porque no los efectúa en forma unilateral y obligatoria, al carecer de la facultad de imperio para ejecutarlos, pues requiere de la intervención de una autoridad judicial para ese efecto, además de que sus funciones no están determinadas en una norma general, pues carece de una legislación de ese carácter que lo rija en su existencia y actuación, pues sus actos se regulan por lo pactado entre las partes." Arbitrators and Appointed Secretary in the Arbitration Proceedings. They are not to be deemed authorities for purposes of the Amparo Challenge. Digital Registry: 2018229; Amparo en revisión 197/2018. Aug. 9, 2018. Twelfth Collegiate Circuit Court for Civil Matters of the First Circuit. Majority of votes; unanimity on the content of this precedent. Disidente: Adalberto Eduardo Herrera González. Proponent: Neófito López Ramos. Secretaria: Angélica Rivera Chávez.

68. "de ahí que sea válido afirmar que los árbitros poseen 'autoridad' pero les falta 'potestad', la cual es atributo exclusivo del Estado y por ello podrán realizar todos aquellos actos para los que baste la simple autoridad, y deberán solicitar la cooperación de los tribunales respecto de aquellos otros que requieran la potestad, como ocurre por ejemplo en materia de medidas o providencias cautelares y de ejecución en donde se requiere del auxilio de la jurisdicción estatal para lograr dichas medidas mediante procedimientos que (por la forma como se debatirán los intereses) serán contenciosos." Registry 166501, First Chamber, Novena Época. Semanario Judicial de la Federación y su Gaceta, Tomo XXX, septiembre de 2009, p. 435. Tesis: 1ª.CLXVI/2009. Amparo en revisión 131/2009. Talent Agency Unlimited, S.A. de C.V. May 27, 2009. Unanimity. Proponent: Olga Sánchez Cordero de García Villegas. Secretary: Emmanuel G. Rosales Guerrero.
69. "Los árbitros reciben sus facultades directamente de las partes; sólo con relación a éstas reciben el carácter de jueces, y no pueden pronunciarse más que sobre las cuestiones que ellas les propongan. … toda actuación del árbitro o tribunal arbitral en tanto existe la posibilidad de que resuelva determinado o determinable conflicto, es decir, ejerza una cierta jurisdicción, no se equipara, en lo absoluto, a la función jurisdiccional del Estado, puesto *que* ésta última surge de lo acogido por nuestra Ley Suprema y, por consiguiente, es genérica y permanente; en cambio, la jurisdicción arbitral se supedita, indiscutiblemente, a la voluntad de los particulares, consecuentemente, ésta es siempre determinada y temporal; lo dicho, pues, la jurisdicción arbitral, no es posible sustanciarse si la expresión de la voluntad de las partes, esto es, la manifestación de las mismas de someter determinada o determinable disputa, mediante pacto expreso, al poderío arbitral. De ahí que sea inconcuso que un árbitro o tribunal arbitral de ningún modo podrá pronunciarse respecto de aquellas cuestiones que no hayan sido estrictamente convenidas por las partes o que sean propiamente de orden o de interés público. …." Amparo en Revisión 2160/2009, First Chamber, Supreme Court of Justice. Sep. 8, 2010, Unanimity Grupo Radio Centro, S.A. de C.V., pp. 35-38.

CHAPTER 7

Document Production

*Carlos Manuel Loperena Ruiz & Alejandro Flores Patiño**

[A] INTRODUCTION

The value and weight of the documents are key in any method of dispute resolution. Either because of its nature or because of the drawbacks of other evidence means, documentary evidence is well appreciated when it comes to resolving a dispute. Moreover, currently, the most relevant evidence in international arbitration and even in domestic arbitration is documentary evidence, since most of the commercial transactions are entered in writing, although Mexican law does not provide for the written formality in commercial transactions.[1] Most business people prefer to have their rights well defined in writing than leave it to the memory of the other party or to other kinds of evidence. Their attorneys are hired for that purpose. Notwithstanding the foregoing, while it is true to say that the production of any document should be simple, it might become complex depending on different circumstances touching an arbitration procedure.

Witness evidence has been proven not to be 100% trustable as we wish it should be. The ICC task force regarding this evidence has made quite clear that memory betrays people too often.[2] The main rule in Mexican law regarding the interpretation and construction of contracts is that if the words are clear and leave no room for doubt,

* This chapter reflects the thoughts, knowledge and experience of the authors at the time when it was created. The chapter does not refer to any particular case and its application may be subject to the particular conditions and circumstances of every case.

1. Article 78 of the Code of Commerce.
2. International Chamber of Commerce (ICC), ICC Arbitration and ADR Commission Report on the *Accuracy of Fact Witness Memory in International Arbitration: Current Issues and Possible Solutions* (Nov. 30, 2020).

the interpreter should stick to the literal meaning of the words,[3] which is not easy to do when there is no written evidence regarding the agreement of the parties.

The document is a universal piece of evidence which is widely produced in the field of arbitration.[4] However, as widely known, while UNCITRAL Model Law on International Commercial Arbitration (UNCITRAL Model Law) has been extensively incorporated in an important number of countries all over the world, such an incorporation may vary from one country to another, not to mention the fact that the interpretation of the same text by different courts may lead to different conclusions. Thus, for example, the disclosure of documents under the counterparty's control will take place in arbitration proceedings and the scope of such disclosure may depend on how the *lex arbitri* (or the legal framework applicable to the place where the production of documents is sought) rules this issue.

Additionally, and most importantly, the practitioner shall consider the parties' arbitration agreement (or any other agreement on procedural matters). Indeed, while the applicable legal framework may be relevant (especially if there might be a mandatory provision restricting document production), the agreement in this respect is a key factor.

Last but not least, when practitioners have permissive tools (legal framework and agreement of the Parties on document production), the legal background of the arbitrators might play a relevant role in document production. Here, we hold that the local legal framework of the practitioners has had an influence over the production of documents in international arbitration, and Mexico is not an exception. In that sense, as pointed out by Fry, the production of documents is a feature common in both civil and common-law systems, "where practices diverge is with respect to the right to compel the disclosure of documents and, in particular, those documents that may be adverse to the party's position."[5]

All the above points considered, it is clear that the flexibility, as well as the international character of the arbitration, may lead to a wide range of possibilities when it comes to the production of documents. Then, in this chapter, the authors will attempt to provide a perspective of the document production in arbitration under Mexican law. For those purposes, the authors will develop the notion of the document and the arbitral tribunal's power on the production of documents both under Mexican legislation and considering some institutional local rules of arbitration.

Next, the chapter will provide some thoughts on the production of documents considering the possessor: (1) the Party producing the documents; (2) the counterparty; and (3) a third party.

3. Article 1851 of the Federal Civil Code.
4. Jason Fry, *Evidence in International Arbitration The IBA Rules on the Taking of Evidence in International Commercial Arbitration*, in *El Contrato de Arbitraje*, 643 (Eduardo Silva Romero dir., Fabricio Mantilla Espinosa coord. 2005).
5. *Ibid.*

Then, we will provide a perspective, under Mexican law, of the court's assistance to the production of documents. There, the authors will treat the procedural regulation, particularly the procedure set forth for production of evidence in commercial arbitration.

Finally, the authors will provide their perspective regarding sanctions when a party is reluctant to provide a document during the arbitration proceedings and will reflect whether the production of documents may be grounds to challenge an award under Mexican law.

It is worth considering that the practice of commercial arbitration in Mexico, as abroad, is private and usually confidential. Consequently, except for those cases which are resolved by the courts and, prior consent of the parties, become public, there is little written information about the topic; legislation and some local authorities become the main sources. Such information is usually complemented by practice and experience by the authors and third parties shared in congresses, seminars or specialized forums. Such sources were considered when this chapter was written.

[B] DOCUMENT (MEANING AND SCOPE)

The authors of Civil Procedure works in Mexico have been discussing the definition of a document for many years, without reaching an agreement. More precisely, Mexican *lex arbitri* does not provide any definition of document. Lacking a legal source, practitioners are expected to rely on either authorities or the so-called *soft-law*. Regarding the latter, in arbitration, this problem has been solved by the IBA Rules on the Taking of Evidence in International Arbitration (IBA Rules) which contains the definition of document that is widely accepted by arbitration practitioners: *Document* means a "writing, communication, picture, drawing, program or data of any kind, whether recorded or maintained on paper or by electronic, audio, visual or any other means."[6] That is to say, a document is any tangible or intangible good. While the definition does not provide more detail, the authors conclude that regarding intangible goods the accessibility to the relevant information is a key factor. In any case, the characteristics of such intangible goods must be sufficient to prove a fact.

By taking such definition, an arbitral tribunal avoids doctrinal dilemmas and idiosyncratic bias which may lead to incertitude when a *lex arbitri* is applied. In the authors' perspective, the wideness of the definition provides enough room for the arbitrators to admit a broad number of pieces of evidence and obtain the facts to resolve a case; probative value will always depend on the piece of evidence itself as well as its relationship with other evidence though.

6. *IBA Rules on the Taking of Evidence in International Arbitration*, Definitions section (International Bar Association 2010).

[C] DOCUMENT PRODUCTION

[1] Arbitral Tribunal Discretionary Powers

[a] Under Mexican Legislation

Mexico is a civil-law country and, as in any other, the disclosure of all documents, useful and useless to the party's case, is not encouraged, nor accepted. Thus, automatic discoveries (that might become expensive) are rejected. Notwithstanding the foregoing, that does not mean that the production of documents, particularly those under counterparty's, even third parties, control is not feasible. As discussed further below, the Mexican legal framework is permissive for the parties to take control of the production of documents in commercial arbitration.

While it is true to say that Mexico has a vigorous number of legislations ruling the arbitration, the core related to commercial arbitration is: (i) The Convention on the Recognition and Enforcement of Foreign Arbitral Awards (New York Convention); (ii) the Inter-American Convention on International Commercial Arbitration (Inter-American Convention); and (iii) the Code of Commerce (particularly, Articles 1415 to 1480).

Both the New York Convention and the Inter-American Convention do not set forth a specific provision governing the discretionary powers of the arbitral tribunals. As in most countries, the local legislation rules the particularities of the proceedings, including the arbitral tribunals' powers. Indeed, Mexican statute establishes that the parties are free to agree upon the procedure that they and the arbitrators shall observe; lacking such an agreement that the arbitrators are free to conduct as we mentioned in the following paragraphs.

[i] Arbitration Legislation

Mexico, as an adopter of the UNCITRAL Model Law, has a general provision stating the arbitrator's power to conduct the proceedings. However, there is not a specific article ruling the arbitral tribunal's powers to produce documents. So, Article 1435 of the Code of Commerce provides as follows:

> Article 1435. Subject to the provisions of this title, the parties are free to agree on the procedure to be followed by the arbitral tribunal in conducting the proceedings.
>
> Failing such agreement, the arbitral tribunal may, subject to the provisions of this title, conduct the arbitration in such manner as it considers appropriate. The power conferred upon the arbitral tribunal includes the power to determine the admissibility, relevance and weight of any evidence.

In the absence of a specific provision on the production of documents in the Mexican *lex arbitri*, the authors hold that, in order to have a better understanding of how the production of documents is locally seen, it is convenient to take a look at the spirit of the procedural civil local provisions. It does not mean that in Mexico the local civil-procedural perspective is retaken into the arbitration, but rather why a full-automatic-thorough disclosure is not practiced before courts nor arbitral tribunals in Mexico.

[ii] A Reference to Local Civil Procedures Codes

Most of the local civil procedure codes provide that when a party refuses to produce a document or a good requested by the counterparty for inspection of the court, it would be presumed that the facts intended to prove those documents or goods are true. Then, this presumption reverses the burden of proof to the other party, and therefore the facts are considered true unless otherwise proven.

Despite the existence of these provisions, it is very rare that one party requests the production of a document from the other party since in Mexican judicial litigation a party goes to court when the evidence already in its possession is not enough to demonstrate and to present its case. Otherwise, trial lawyers do not go into the venture of starting a litigation with not enough evidence already in hand.

In Mexican procedural law, the complaint cannot be amended but in very limited circumstances and not in all state jurisdictions. That is why production of documents is rarely used in Mexico in spite of the existence of some provisions regarding the consequences of the rejection of a party to produce a document.

[iii] Under Local Institutional Arbitration Rules

The authors believe it is important to provide a perspective of local rules of arbitration. For those purposes, we will provide a reference to the relevant provisions of three local institutional arbitration rules:

> CANACO
>
> The National Chamber of Commerce of Mexico City has the Commission of ADR and Arbitration which administrates arbitration proceedings where the parties have chosen to go to arbitration under its rules. The *CANACO* Rules of Arbitration are inspired on the UNCITRAL Arbitration Rules and, consequently, in Article 29(3) of said Arbitration Rules we find the following provision:
>
> > 3. At any time during the arbitral proceedings the arbitral tribunal may require the parties to produce documents or other evidence within such a period of time as the arbitral tribunal shall determine.
>
> CAM
>
> Inspired by the ICC Arbitration Rules, the Arbitration Rules of the Arbitration Center of Mexico (CAM), into rule 26(4), state as follows:
>
> > (4) At any time during the proceedings, the arbitral tribunal may summon any party to provide clarifications or additional evidence.

CAIC

With respect to the Rules of Arbitration of the Arbitration Center of the Construction Industry, Article 37(2) provides as follows:

> 2. At any time during the proceedings, the Arbitral Tribunal may demand, within the term it determines is reasonable, that the parties submit documents or other evidence; in the event that they do not, it can make the inferences that it considers justified.

Considering the above, we can conclude that Mexican arbitration rules follow the current formulae provided by either ICC arbitration rules or the UNCITRAL arbitration rules. That is, arbitral tribunals are granted general powers to conduct the proceedings, though with no specific or special provision regarding the production of documents. An important fact to highlight is that CAIC arbitration rules set forth a consequence in the event one party does not submit the relevant evidence as required. Such provision may lead us to reflect whether the parties shall agree (directly or indirectly -by selecting arbitration rules providing so) on the arbitral tribunal's power on drawing inferences (to consider that such power has been granted) or is rather an implicit power of the arbitrators. The authors will go into more detail in the sanctions section of this article.

[b] Documents under Party's Possession, Custody or Control and Objection of the Documents

One of the multiple categories of documents states that they may be classified as: (i) those which are produced voluntarily to the arbitration (usually to support the party's allegation which is producing the evidence); and (ii) those which are produced under compulsion.

[i] Under the Party's Possession, Custody or Control Providing the Evidence

Apart from those cases where the document is alleged to be forged, altered or falsified, documents produced voluntarily are really not a source of procedural problems. The party having the document under its possession has a natural incentive to produce such evidence. In general terms, either because of the *lex arbitri* or the arbitration rules selected by the parties, each party has the burden of proof of their claims or defenses. Consequently, if each party does not produce the evidence during the proceedings, the relevant party may not be successful in presenting their case. For those reasons, in the authors' view, the issues to take care of are when and how to produce such documents.

In memorials or in witness statement

Considering the lack of legal provisions: (i) the agreement of the Parties and, in the absence of it; (ii) clarification by the arbitral tribunal and the Parties are key elements on how documents are to be produced.

As regards the agreement of the parties, they can obviously rule such an issue directly into the arbitration agreement. They can indirectly do it by selecting arbitration rules governing this issue too. In this respect, it is worth mentioning that local arbitration rules and procedural orders tend to provide that the parties shall produce the documents giving rise to, or related to, the dispute[7] with the request for arbitration and the answer to the request. Therefore, any other document, in the absence of the parties' agreement, shall be produced when the arbitral tribunal orders so. It is usually established in procedural order number one that provides for the formalities to be followed with the memorial of complaint and the memorial of answer and the exhibits attached thereto.

Under Mexican law, in principle, the production of documents in witness statements is not forbidden. Thus, practically speaking, as with any other procedural matter, such possibility is under the parties' agreement and, failing such agreement, it will be up to the arbitrators' decision. However, in the authors' opinion, the parties and the arbitral tribunal must pay attention to the fact that such production observes the minimal procedural guarantees: the equal treatment of the parties as well as the full opportunity to present their case (Article 1434 of the Mexican Commerce Code[8]).

As regards equal treatment, the arbitral tribunal would have to consider that the production of documents in witness statements does not mean to breach the procedural timetable set forth by it. That is, the production of documents in witness statements should not be a way to circumvent the procedural timetable by producing a document at a later stage. In the authors' view, it is worth considering whether: (i) the relevant document is under the party's control or possession and, if so, it was produced at the right stage; and (ii) the production of the relevant document in the witness statement is justified.

Talking about the consequences if a document is not produced as agreed by the parties or -failing such agreement- determined by the arbitral tribunal, it is worth highlighting a particular provision existing under *CANACO* Arbitration Rules: Article 2(4). Such article—as in other provisions from different arbitration rules—sets forth that all written communications submitted by any party, as well as all documents annexed thereto, shall be sent to each party, each arbitrator, and the ADR and Arbitration Commission of CANACO. However, the particularity is on the consequences: a written communication will not take effect unless such a requirement is fulfilled. That is to say that if, when producing one document, one of the parties, one of the arbitrators or the ADR and the Arbitration Commission of CANACO do not receive such document, the consequence is that such document is not considered produced according to the procedural timetable and will not be considered by the arbitral tribunal when deciding the case. While the arbitral tribunal is entitled to decide whether the delay or impediment is justified, the hard consequence is notable.

7. Article 9, section (3), subsection d) (Arbitration rules of CAIC). CAM Arbitration Rules: Art. 6(4). CANACO Arbitration Rules: Art. 23.
8. Article 1434 of the Code of Commerce. The parties shall be treated with equality and each party shall be given a full opportunity of presenting his case.

Documents in foreign language and voluminous documents (summary, table, graphics, extracts, or samples)

Under Mexican law, following the rule set forth by the UNCITRAL Model law, "the arbitral tribunal may order that the documentary evidence shall be accompanied by a translation into the language or languages agreed upon by the parties or determined by the arbitral tribunal."[9] It is a discretionary power of the arbitral tribunal. The legal provision does not set forth the consequence if the relevant party does not accompany the translation of a document. For such a reason, it is advisable that, when ordered, the arbitral tribunal sets forth the consequence if the translation is not accompanied, for example, the determination of the relevance and weight of the documentary evidence not accompanied by the relevant translation shall be affected or the relevant document shall not take effect.

As regards the production of voluminous documents, under Mexican law, there is not a specific provision ruling this issue. Thus, the will of the parties will prevail and, in the absence of such an agreement, the arbitral tribunal will rule the production of this kind of documents. As far as the authors are concerned, according to their experience, it is not possible to set a preference for handling voluminous documents in Mexican practice. Apparently, it will depend on the legal background and experience of the parties and the members of the arbitral tribunal.

Anyway, the authors believe that summaries may be helpful as the party producing the documents indirectly ends up highlighting the relevant section, they pretend the arbitral tribunal to take into account. A risk of using such summaries, however, might be that important sections of the document might be not included misleading the arbitral tribunal's perspective.

Tables or lists of documents might be another important tool to handle massive documents. By using such a tool, the arbitrators and the other parties would easily be aware of the universe of evidence produced by counterparties. Once again, the success of the tool might depend on the information used to create such lists and/or tables. For such reasons, the authors point out that the arbitral tribunal plays a definitive role when they set forth the requirements to observe during the production of such tables or lists.

While useful, extracts and samples might be difficult to handle during proceedings since, in the authors' view, setting forth the requirements may vary considerably from one arbitrator to another, not to mention the fact that observing such requirements may lead to biased results. It seems to us that, by choosing certain samples, the party producing the documents ends up discarding others; thus, subjectivity might be a constant element.

[ii] Under the Counterparty's Possession, Custody or Control

In common-law countries, prior to any court proceeding, parties are required to make disclosure of documents. In case of failure to produce them, the court may draw

9. Article 1438 of the Code of Commerce. Similarly, CANACO Arbitration Rules, Art. 22(2).

adverse inferences. In civil law countries, the approach is different. The parties are usually entitled to require the court for an order that the other party produce specific and identified documents, which have not been previously produced. Consequently, the proceedings are less costly and a party is only compelled to produce such documents specified by the counterparty.[10]

Considering that, under Mexican law, in commercial arbitration, the parties are free to choose the procedure, resulting in the most efficient way to conduct the arbitration, the parties are entitled to decide whether disclosure is appropriate and, if so, whether it should be limited to specific documents. Failing such an agreement, the arbitrator will make a discretionary decision on that matter.

If the parties agreed on having a disclosure, except for those agreements breaching the minimal procedural guarantees, the arbitral tribunal shall follow such agreement. The parties may agree directly to the arbitration agreement or by selecting arbitration rules where the disclosure is ruled. Concerning the arbitration rules, take the CAIC Arbitration Rules, for example. As mentioned before, Article 37 expressly grants the power to the arbitral tribunal to require the parties to produce pieces of evidence. It is a general provision which is not as specific as the IBA Rules on document production. However, in the authors' opinion, it is wide enough to require the disclosure of documents. Moreover, on the basis of the arbitral tribunal's freedom to conduct the proceedings, it could implement similar provisions to those of the IBA Rules.

Now, if the parties do not, partially or completely, agree on the disclosure stage, the decision will be taken by the arbitral tribunal. As far as the authors are concerned, the general power to conduct the proceedings includes the arbitral tribunal's power to handle a disclosure stage. At the end of the day, the disclosure is the request by the arbitral tribunal for one party to produce certain evidence under its possession, custody or control. Indeed, it is our belief that said general power is broad enough to order the disclosure of a piece of evidence. The relevant issues might be whether, considering: (i) the (inherent conditions of the) evidence; (ii) the law; or (iii) the addressee of the request, such request is enforceable.

With respect to the inherent conditions of the piece of evidence to be produced, it is relevant (and logical) that such a piece of evidence should be under the addressee's possession, custody or control. In other words, the (direct or indirect) physical access to such a document is a key factor. It is not just the absence of physical barriers, but an entitlement over such a piece of evidence. If such a condition is fulfilled the arbitral tribunal will still have to verify the other two conditions: (i) absence of any legal interdiction; and (ii) confirm whether the addressee is party to the arbitration agreement.

Redfern schedule

Aiming at offering a view on the use of this schedule in Mexico, bearing in mind that, under Mexican law, the proceedings will be handled as agreed by the parties or, lacking

10. Capper Phillip, *International Arbitration: A Handbook* 211 (2004).

such agreement, as decided by the arbitral tribunal, the well-known Redfern schedule[11] is widely used in Mexican arbitration, including domestic arbitration. It is due to the influence of common-law arbitrators and party attorneys who have been in touch with Mexican arbitrators and Mexican practitioners who have learned about discovery and the limited discovery provided for in arbitration procedures of an international nature.

Moreover, many Mexican arbitrators usually try to include the IBA Rules as a source of soft law, these being inspiring principles for the reception of evidence in arbitration cases, including the domestic ones, given the effectiveness of these provisions considering that civil-law countries do not have discovery rules for the civil procedure and that full discovery is unknown to most civil law attorneys.

In any case, practitioners are encouraged to be careful when adopting a specific procedure to produce documents during arbitration proceedings. Even if the parties agree to adopt the *Discovery* as a tool to handle such a stage, it is strongly recommended to narrow the scope of the *Disclosure* and consider the application of tools such as sanctions; in sum, it is not to adopt an outside institution but to adapt it.[12]

Fishing expeditions

By fishing expeditions, a party pretends to obtain as many pieces of information as possible to put them together and "create" its case. We all know that discovery may be used as sufficient expedition to obtain more information from the other party than that which is necessary to present the case. Such kind of practice is not popular in commercial arbitration in Mexico. That is why, by using the Redfern schedule, arbitrators are entitled to resolve which documents can be requested from each party after the petition of the counterparty. Arbitral tribunals must have the prudence and the wisdom to understand the intention of the requesting party and avoid any intent of fishing expeditions with the excuse of the Redfern schedule or the production of documents stage in an arbitration proceeding.

[iii] Under Third Party's Possession, Custody or Control

Another scenario is when third parties have a relevant document under their possession, custody or control. Taking into account that a third party is not a party to the arbitration agreement nor to the arbitration procedure, and providing unless otherwise set forth by the applicable law, an arbitral tribunal does not have powers to compel a

11. Traditional scheme is normally used: (i) first column: Identification of the documents or the category of the documents required by one party (and under the other party's possession, custody or control); (ii) second column: reason justifying the request of the relevant document; (iii) third column: space where the other party will provide its comments about or objection to the other party's request of documents; and (iv) fourth column: space where the arbitral tribunal will write down its decision on each case, if necessary. So, in the absence of objection by the respondent party, the document shall be produced. Otherwise, the arbitral tribunal shall decide considering the arguments put forward by both parties.

    However, we must acknowledge that if, in the first column, the requesting party point out a category of the documents, the arbitral tribunal must carefully handle the production of documents. Otherwise, there is a risk such production becomes a kind of fishing expedition.
12. Miguel Gómez Jene, *Arbitraje Comercial Internacional* 312 (2018).

party to produce a document. In such a scenario, so long as the applicable law provides so, the tool is to file the request before the courts of the state where the documents are to be found. The authors will develop this topic further below.

[iv] Objection of the Documents

Under Mexican law, before a court, a document can be subject to an objection because of: (i) its authenticity; and (ii) its probative value. In other words, a document is objected to because it is fake or, even if it is authentic, the party objecting to the document states that such document does not prove what the party producing the piece of evidence pretends.

In commercial arbitration in Mexico, the objection of documents is not ruled; consequently, there are no specific procedures for such a purpose. Grounds for the objection of documents as well as steps and stages used before civil courts are helpful to commercial arbitration in Mexico.

Regarding the grounds for objection, authenticity and probative value are retaken and used before arbitral tribunals whose place of arbitration is in Mexico. Now, particularity on the ground of the authenticity of the document has to do with how a document is originally produced during the proceedings. While it is not a "written rule," in commercial arbitration in Mexico, a document, except for very few cases, is produced in copy.[13] Moreover, prior to an agreement by the parties (or even the sole direction of the arbitral tribunal), on the grounds of ecological reasons, now it is quite often that the parties produce the documents only in digital copies.

Procedural timetables issued under Mexican *lex arbitri* usually state that, either in hard copies or in digital ones, when one party pretends to object to a document produced by another party, the objecting party shall require the other party to produce the original document. Once this document is produced, the arbitral tribunal shall issue its decision considering both parties' arguments and the original document.

It is worth mentioning that some practitioners point out that the objection of the probative value is rather an allegation and as a such it does not deserve a particular stage, thus, any challenge to the probative value of a piece of evidence should be made when final allegations are made (prior to the issuance of the final award).

With respect to the procedures to object to a document, the arbitral tribunals usually set forth into the procedural timetable two terms: (i) those documents produced before the procedural timetable shall be objected (if there is any ground for it) within a certain number of days following the issuance of such timetable and (ii) those produced afterward shall be objected within a certain number of days following the production of each document.

In general terms, when it comes to the objection of documents, as in any other stage of the proceedings, the arbitral tribunal shall observe the equal treatment of parties and the full opportunity to present their case. Therefore, once one of the parties

13. Francisco González Cossio, *Arbitraje* 641 (2018).

object a document produced by its counterparty, the latter will be given a term to put forward its arguments. Next, the arbitral tribunal shall issue its decision. The arbitral tribunal might decide to make a decision on the objection at a later stage though.

Finally, another reason to object to a document has to do with its origin. In connection with the source of the documents and their legal origin, there is no civil nor commercial legislation regarding it but in Mexico, there is a general rule in the civil procedure codes that forbid evidence that is against the law or the morals. Such criteria may be used in commercial arbitration to determine whether a document could be objected to. In the authors' view, two key issues might play a relevant role: public policy and *lex arbitri*. The former has to do with the frequent question: what is public policy? And the latter has to do with the common debate of to what extent an arbitrator is compelled to observe the law of the seat of arbitration.

[c] Court's Assistance

In commercial arbitration, under Mexican law, arbitrators do not have any kind of public authority to compel or subpoena third parties to provide documents or information or even to appear as witnesses in an arbitral procedure. So, Mexico, as an adopter of the UNCITRAL Model Law, follows the same criterion as many other countries: the courts of the place of arbitration provide assistance in the taking of evidence. More precisely, Article 1444 of the Code of Commerce states as follows:

> The arbitral tribunal or a party with the approval of the arbitral tribunal may request the assistance of the court in taking evidence.

Then, such provision implicitly states that, when the assistance of the court is pretended under such provision, it is not only enough that the proceedings had started but it is also necessary that the arbitral tribunal was already appointed. Besides, only the arbitral tribunal or the relevant party (seeking such assistance)—with the arbitral tribunal's approval—is entitled to require such assistance. As any other adopter of the UNCITRAL Model Law, the Code of Commerce is committed with the minimal intervention of courts during the proceedings and, as a consequence, the approval of the arbitral tribunal is required to trigger the court assistance.

For many years, Mexican *lex arbitri* just ruled court assistance in the taking of evidence in commercial arbitration based on such article. As in many other jurisdictions, this not only could raise questions but also lead to problems. With no procedural rules, practitioners and judges could take ways and measures which results might vary from case to case. Incertitude and frustration could have been common denominators in each experience.

Fortunately, on January 27, 2011, the Code of Commerce was amended, and Chapter X (of the Title Fourth) was added. Chapter X rules the courts' assistance in commercial settlements and into the arbitration. In broad terms, such chapter rules three sorts of proceedings: (i) one procedure related to the referral of the parties to arbitration; (ii) the special trial on commercial settlement agreements and arbitration applicable for certain topics;[14] and (iii) the voluntary jurisdiction applicable to other topics.[15]

The Mexican lawmakers set forth that the court assistance into arbitration shall take place under the voluntary jurisdiction procedure. Indeed, Article 1466 of the Code of Commerce sets forth that the request for assistance in taking evidence provided for in Article 1444 of such code shall be processed by means of voluntary jurisdiction.

In Mexico, voluntary jurisdiction is a procedure where, by law or because of a party's request, court assistance is required, but no contentious issue is at stake. The Code of Commerce sets forth that such voluntary jurisdiction shall be conducted in accordance with Articles 530 to 532 and 534 to 537 of the Federal Code of Civil Procedures. In our opinion, it is relevant to point out that the judge is authorized to amend the measures issued during the voluntary jurisdiction.

Such procedure may be used not only to obtain a piece of evidence under the possession, custody or control of a third party but also to obtain a piece of evidence under the possession, custody or control of a party to the arbitration.

Notwithstanding those provisions, we have no knowledge of any case where arbitrators and or parties have requested the assistance of a court to obtain evidence for an arbitration procedure and what was the outcome of such request. Thus, while Mexico possesses a modern legal framework ruling the court assistance in taking evidence in commercial arbitration, nowadays it is expected a lack of experience by the courts to put into practice such provisions.

An important remark to make is the scope of application of such provisions. As stated before, Mexico follows the UNCITRAL Model Law and, consequently, the place of arbitration is relevant to determine whether the provisions of the Title Fourth (related to commercial arbitration) are applicable. As in the UNCITRAL Model Law, the Code of Commerce rules certain exceptions in which the place of arbitration is not relevant and, even if such place is abroad, the Mexican provisions on commercial arbitration are still applicable. Such exceptions are related to: (i) referral of the parties to arbitration; (ii) interim measures of protection; and (iii) recognition and enforcement of arbitration.

However, as we can see, the provisions related to the court's assistance in taking evidence are not considered. In consequence, if an arbitral tribunal or a party to an arbitration, whose place of arbitration is abroad in Mexico, intends to obtain the assistance of a Mexican court to take some evidence in Mexico, they will not be able to go directly to the Mexican court to require such assistance. Such arbitral tribunal or relevant party will have to require such assistance to the court of the seat of arbitration and such court will have to transfer such request to the Mexican court. International cooperation may not be the quickest option to take evidence in an arbitration procedure though.

14. The decision on challenge of an arbitrator, the decision on the jurisdiction of the arbitral tribunal, the taking of interim measures, the recognition and enforcement of interim measures, the setting aside of commercial settlement agreements and arbitral awards.
15. Besides the court assistance, the request for appointment of arbitrators and the consultation on the fees of the arbitral tribunal.

[d] *Sanctions*

[i] *Adverse Inferences*

Under Mexican law, there is no specific provision ruling such power, nor a provision interdicting the existence of such power. In the absence of rules, as mentioned all over this chapter, the agreement of the parties is a key element that puts away any incertitude on this subject.

It is widely spread that the adverse inferences are sanctions that are announced by arbitrators in the case of the rejection of the production of documents following the Redfern schedule or any other means of document production that the arbitrators or the parties have established in a given procedure. It is often said that adverse inferences are the sole tool the arbitrators possess to "enforce" their decisions.

Notwithstanding the above, it is worth considering several issues related to such topic: (i) whether the agreement of the parties on adverse inferences is required to the arbitral tribunal be granted such power; (ii) the scope of such power; (iii) whether a methodology is necessary to apply such power (for example, whether the arbitral tribunal must announce such sanction prior to its application, which elements the arbitral tribunal must consider to apply such sanction and which consequence the arbitral tribunal can reach). There is no unanimous consensus for each of the points above. However, provisions such as Article 37(2) of the CAIC Arbitration Rules (quoted above), which sets forth that if the parties do not submit documents or other evidence required by the arbitral tribunal, the latter is entitled to make the inferences that it considers justified, leads us to assert that agreement of the parties (to grant such power) might be, at least, suitable (otherwise, such arbitration rules could have been silent on this respect).

In our experience, it is very rare that arbitrators, at the moment of rendering their award, invoke adverse inferences against the party who was reluctant to produce documents at that stage in the arbitral procedure. We are of the idea that, prior to a methodology communicated to the parties in advance, arbitrators must follow the warning already given to the parties and make adverse inferences at the time of considering the evidence and the legal arguments of the party who has been reluctant to produce documents although the order of the arbitral tribunal.

[ii] *Allocation of Costs*

Contrary to the topic of adverse inferences, on the topic of allocation costs, under Mexican law, there are provisions ruling such power. The Code of Commerce, following the spirit of the UNCITRAL Model Law, defers to the parties the ruling of the costs of arbitration; failing such agreement, the provisions of such code apply.

With respect to this subject, on the one hand, the CAIC Arbitration Rules[16] and CANACO Arbitration Rules[17] set forth that the costs of arbitration shall be borne by the unsuccessful party. However, said rules also state that the arbitral tribunal is entitled to apportion each of such costs between the parties if it determines that apportionment is reasonable, taking into account the circumstances of the case. On the other hand, CAM Arbitration Rules[18] grant discretionary power to the arbitral tribunal to allocate the costs of arbitration.

So, while two of said sets of rules, in principle, adopt the principle *costs follow the event*, all those rules end up granting discretionary power to the arbitral tribunal to allocate costs. In the authors' opinion, such discretionary power encompasses the possibility of allocating the costs considering the parties' behavior during the arbitration proceedings (including the non-production of documents when required by the arbitral tribunal). In any case, the authors' hold that it is suitable that the arbitral tribunal, prior to the demand of production of documents, announce to the parties the consequence if they do not produce the relevant document.

Regarding the Code of Commerce, failing the agreement of the parties also sets forth the principle "costs follow the event," but, similar to CAIC and CANACO Arbitration Rules, the code grants discretionary power to the arbitral tribunal to allocate the costs of arbitration. The reasoning produced above is also applicable to the Code of Commerce.

[D] CONCLUSIONS

Mexico possesses a friendly legal framework that not only allows but also encourages document production. However, the parties are strongly encouraged to adopt rules, provisions or measures that ease such production. Take IBA Rules or arbitration rules containing provisions on consequences if one of the parties fails to produce some evidence, for example. As regards the court's assistance, even if we believe Mexico is at the forefront of legal framework on this topic, the lack of experience of the courts to apply such provisions may lead to practical problems, not to mention the fact that such provisions are only applicable provided the seat of arbitration is in Mexico. In sum, if the seat of arbitration is in Mexico, the experience of the parties and the arbitral tribunal on this subject will be relevant to obtain a good result.

16. Article 63.
17. Article 47.
18. Article 40(3).

CHAPTER 8

The Measure of Damages in Mexico and Their Quantification

Herfried Wöss & Adriana San Román Rivera

[A] INTRODUCTION

Mexican damages law has until recently been characterized by being rudimentary and tied to a literal interpretation of the *damnum emergens* and *lucrum cessans* measure of damages with little development through jurisprudence, as well as a notorious tendency to under-compensation. Since 2015, things have changed through jurisprudence at creating a strong notion of moral damages, including punitive damages subject to a high level of culpability, leading to considerable amounts of compensation being awarded. This is due to changes in the Mexican Federal Constitution in 2011 incorporating human rights treaties as part of the constitutional order and the confirmation of the obligation of total reparation or 'integral reparation' by the Mexican Supreme Court. However, more important than the contractual and extra-contractual notion of moral damages is the transformation from international customary law into Mexican civil law of the *Factory at Chorzów dictum* through the application of the American Convention on Human Rights and the jurisprudence of the Inter-American Court of Human Rights of which Mexico is a party. This transformation introduced the modern measure of *expectation interest* into Mexican law, which went largely unnoticed.

Mexican damages law is largely based on French law and is characterized by the traditional distinction between *damnum emergens* and *lucrum cessans*, which has now been overcome by jurisprudence as has happened in France and other civil countries.[1]

1. Herfried Wöss et al., *Damages in International Arbitration under Complex Long-Term Contracts*, 78-184, Ch. 4 (Oxford University Press, Oxford International Arbitration Series, 2014).

[B] MEXICAN DAMAGES LAW: AN OVERVIEW

Mexican damages law is found in Articles 1910 to 1934 bis on the *Liability for Illicit Acts* and Articles 2104 to 2118 on the *Consequences of the Non-Performance of Obligations* of the Mexican Federal Civil Code and the civil codes of the Mexican federal entities. The Federal Civil Code is applicable as a supplemental source of law in commercial matters according to Article 2 of the Mexican Commercial Code. As in France, both provisions on extra-contractual and contractual liability are used for contractual claims as the non-performance of a contract may also be considered an illicit act.

Article 1910 of the Federal Civil Code reads: 'Anyone who acting illegally or against good faith causes damage to another, is obliged to repair it, ...' According to Article 1915 of the Federal Civil Code, the primary remedy is the re-establishment of the situation before the illicit act or the payment of damages and loss of profits if such reparation is not possible. Damages under Mexican civil law derive from the principle of *pacta sunt servanda.* Article 1796 of the Federal Civil Code establishes that '[f]rom the moment of their perfection, contracts are mandatory for the parties, not just for the terms expressly signed upon, but also for the consequences that, according to their nature, are applicable according to good faith, usage or law'.

The starting point for a damages claim under Mexican law is a breach of contract. According to Article 2104 of the Federal Civil Code, '[w]hoever is obligated to perform an act and does not do it according to the agreement, shall be responsible for losses and gains deprived ...'. Article 2028 of the Federal Civil Code reads that '[w]hoever is obligated to refrain from an act, shall be liable to pay damages and loss of income in case of contravention'. These articles refer to an obligation to do or to forebear. Fault is presumed in any act contrary to an obligation.[2] Liability may be excused if the breach of contract was due to force majeure according to Article 2111 of the Federal Civil Code.

Article 2108 of the Federal Civil Code defines *damnum emergens* as 'the patrimonial loss or detriment suffered as a consequence of non-performance of an obligation'. *Lucrum cessans* or loss of profit established in Article 2109 of the Federal Civil Code is 'the deprivation of any legal gain that should have been obtained through the performance of an obligation'. This follows the classical distinction between *damnum emergens* and *lucrum cessans,* whereby the former consists of a reduction of the claimant's patrimony and the latter in the lack of increase of such patrimony due to the breach. Both are a classical measure of damages.

The causality requirement is found in Article 2110 of the Federal Civil Code according to which 'damages and loss profit must be a direct and immediate consequence of the non-performance of an obligation, whether caused or necessarily will be caused'. The reference to 'direct and immediate consequence' refers precisely to causality. This formula contemplates two situations, damages that have been caused and loss of profits that necessarily will be caused.

This causation formula may cause difficulties with respect to loss profit claims which are often consequential damages, i.e., result from subsequent contractual

2. Joaquín Martínez Alfaro, *Teoría de las Obligaciones* 190 (Editorial Porrúa 8th ed. 2001).

relationships where a buyer receives defective goods and cannot resell them for a profit. In this case, the damages may be determined as the cost of reparation of the defective goods (concrete valuation) or the difference between the value of the defective good and the market value of conforming goods (abstract valuation) and the lost profits that were not made due to the impossibility to re-sell them. The re-sale of the goods is normally through subsequent contracts, i.e., lost profits are normally consequential damages which could be considered indirect damages. Under French law, this issue is solved through the foreseeability test under Article 1231-3 of the reformed French Civil Code. Damages that are foreseeable are considered direct damages. Foreseeability is not required under French law in case of bad faith or intentional causation of damages. Mexican law does not contain a reference to foreseeability which gives rise to mis-interpretation of the causality test, which should not be applied literally. The aforementioned situation could also be analysed in a more straightforward manner by comparing the economic situation of the injured party caused by the breach of contract, to the hypothetical economic situation but-for the breach which leads to the expectation interest.

Relevant judicial precedents seem to part from a liberal approach to causality. In its non-binding dictum with the register 813305, the Third Chamber of the Mexican Supreme Court stated with respect to 'Direct and Immediate Cause' that 'cause must be understood as efficient cause, this means, the determining factor, in order to understand that because of the non-performance, damages and loss profit are necessarily caused. If non-performance is solely a secondary factor subordinate to other factors, it cannot be concluded that it is the direct and immediate cause for damages and loss of profit'.[3] There is not much indication in Mexican damages law and jurisprudence about the applicable theory of causation,[4] but there is an indication that Mexican law follows the theory of the normal course of events whereby extraordinary events or causes are being ignored.[5]

Whereas Mexican law does not contain an express duty of mitigation, the duty of mitigation applies as a general principle of law according to Article 19 of the Federal Civil Code. Contributory negligence as another causality-related limitation of damages is governed by Article 1910 of the Federal Civil Code, which adds to the general obligation of the tortfeasor to compensate damages caused by an illegal act or by a violation of the good faith principle, 'unless he proves that the damage was caused as a consequence of the inexcusable fault or negligence of the victim'.

Other elements that affect the damages to be awarded and which are considered together with the applicable causation theory, mitigation and contributory negligence

3. Tercera Sala de la Suprema Corte de la Nación, Sexta Época, informe 1958, tesis aislada, materia civil, registro no. 813305, p. 28.
4. Herfried Wöss, *Assessment of Damages in Commercial Arbitration after Covid-19: The Relevance of the Applicable Causation Theory*, 1-14, Journal of Damages in International Arbitration 1 (2023).
5. Primera Sala de la Suprema Corte de la Nación, Semanario Judicial de la Federación LXXII, Quinta Época, tesis aislada, materia civil, registro no. 362771, p. 5877, https://sjf2.scjn.gob.mx/detalle/tesis/362771.

as part of the measure of damages in its wide sense, are the date of the determination of damages and the burden and the standard of proof.

With respect to the date of the determination of damages, Mexican law and jurisprudence do not provide indications. As regards the burden of proof, the principle *actori incumbit probatio* applies, which means that it is upon the claimant to prove damages. For the standard of proof, the Mexican Supreme Court established the following non-binding criteria distinguishing between past damages and future losses under the heading of 'Damages and Loss of Profits. Proof of': 'The evidence required in order to prove the existence of damage is radically different to that which must be met in order to prove loss of profits, so that it cannot be analysed with one and the same criterion. When dealing with proof of damage, concrete facts have been realised in the past; it is about proving the extent of the patrimonial detriment caused by the damages event, and therefore the exact mathematical proof of that detriment is possible. ... When dealing with loss of profits, we are faced with future facts that were not realised. ... Experience and good sense teach us that in most cases loss of profits is not subject to demonstration with direct and rigorous evidence that may produce absolute certainty of its existence, and in the majority of cases we must accept relative certainty. ... Commentators, when explaining the German Civil Code dispositions on this matter, state that the absolute certainty of future profit cannot be demanded, and that only the objective possibility of profit in the *normal course of events* and special circumstances is enough.'[6] (Emphasis added)

This means that the Mexican Supreme Court established a different standard of proof for past damages as compared with future lost profits and requires certainty for past damages and probability for lost profits. It also indicates the application of the hypothetical normal course of events causation theory by citing German law commentators.

The aforementioned judicial precedent 'Damages and Loss of Profits. Proof of.' refers to the before- and after-method when stating that the damages result from a comparison between the injured party's patrimony before and after suffering the loss. As evidenced by leading economists, the 'before and after' method leads to distortions when determining damages. The difference between the *before versus after* approach and the premise of a *but-for* value is that in the former, damages most probably would not 'wipe out all the consequences of the breach', while in the latter they would.[7]

[C] THE MEASURE OF DAMAGES UNDER MEXICAN AND COMPARATIVE LAW

The measure of damages is what the law allows to be compensated and is a normative notion. Mexican damages law used to be characterized by a strict adherence to the *damnum emergens* and *lucrum cessans* measure of damages. The distinction between loss and lost profits is difficult to apply and requires adjustments in order to avoid

6. *Ibid.*
7. Prof. Pablo T. Spiller and Santiago Dellepiane, in Herfried Wöss et al., *Damages in International Arbitration*, *supra* n. 1, para. 6.33.

under- and overcompensation. It also leads to under-compensation in countries where lost profits claims are rejected due to legal policy concerns, which is different from the situation in the US where pure lost profits claims are common.[8] As mentioned by Mommsen, the author of *The Doctrine of Interest* (1855), the distinction between *damnum emergens* and *lucrum cessans* is not more than an indication of possible damages.[9]

The measure of damages *damnum emergens* and *lucrum cessans* was known in Roman law but not further developed.[10] It was actually introduced at the end of the Middle Ages and the beginning of the Modern Age as a consequence of the prohibition of interest, which was considered usury and a sin by the catholic church under canonical law. Due to pressure from the 'Italian' (Medici) and 'German' banks (Fugger and Welser) it was necessary to introduce substitute remedies in their favour in case of loans that were not duly paid back. Under the heading of *damnum emergens*, the banker could claim the capital and under the heading *lucrum cessans*, the lost profits or quasi-interest. With these headings, the catholic church avoided granting an exception from the prohibition of interest but met the needs of the upcoming banking industry by granting alternative remedies.[11]

The difficulty of using the *damnum emergens* and *lucrum cessans* measure of damages may be illustrated by the carton freezer arbitration whereby the Mexican producer of high-quality pork meat, a client of the authors, signed an EPC contract for the engineering, procurement and construction (FIDIC silver book for EPC turnkey contracts) of a carton freezer plant for its slaughterhouse in Merida, Yucatán, with a New Zealand company that supposedly had developed a new state-of-the-art freezing technology. For whatever reason, the contract was signed with the Brazilian subsidiary of the New Zealand freezing equipment firm. The performance requirements for the carton freezer plant was a certain amount of different size boxes that had to be frozen to -18°C within twenty-four hours. Once the plant had been constructed and operations began, it turned out that the output did not seem to comply with the specifications. In order to secure evidence, the client organized testing with professional measuring equipment and before a notary public, which proved that only 12% of the boxes achieved the required temperature within the established freezing time. This output rate meant a total failure of the carton freezer plant, as the operation did not allow to determine which meat boxes complied with the freezing temperature.

8. Robert L. Dunn, *Recovery of Damages for Lost Profits*, Vol. 1 (Lawpress 6th ed., 2005); Nancy J. Fannon and Jonathan Dunitz (eds), *The Comprehensive Guide to Economic Damages* (Business Valuation Resources 6th ed. 2020).
9. Friedrich Mommsen, *Beiträge zum Obligationenrecht: Abth. Zur Lehre von dem Interesse* 11-12 (E.U. Schwetschke und Sohn 1855).
10. Reinhard Zimmermann, *The Law of Obligations: Roman Foundations of the Civilian Tradition* 826-827 (Oxford University Press 1996).
11. Herfried Wöss and Adriana San Román Rivera, *Damages in International Commercial Arbitration*, in *International Arbitration and EU Law* paras 7.49-55 (José Rafael Mata Dona and Nikos Lavranos eds, Edward Elgar Publishing 2021); Max Neumann, *Geschichte des Wuchers in Deutschland bis zum Jahre 1654* 49-50 (Zeitschrift für Kirchenrecht, V Jahrgang, Laupp & Siebeck 1865); AWB Simpson, *The History of the Common Law of Contract: The Rise of the Question of Assumpsit* 144 (Oxford University Press 1975).

The pork meat was for export to Japan and subject to stringent phytosanitary requirements controlled by a Japanese inspector based in Merida. Prices for top-quality pork meat are considerably higher in Japan than in Mexico. In order to obtain the required phytosanitary certificates for export to Japan from the Japanese inspector, the freezing specifications were essential. The capacity of the external freezing site in lieu of the in-house carton freezer, was limited.

Without going into the details of the structuring of the corresponding damages claim,[12] the dispute was about the total loss of the investment in the carton freezer plant and the cost of its demolition as it was built within the slaughterhouse's premises and took valuable space that was needed for a new freezer facility. Apart from that, due to the limited capacity of the external facility, additional sales both contracted and expected, were lost.

This means that in order to determine the damages in the carton-freezer arbitration, the actual economic situation of the business unit with a non-performing carton freezer (that is considering the cost of the non-performing carton freezer, its demolition and cost of external freezing services) would have to be compared with the hypothetical economic situation of the business unit considering a well-functioning carton freezer meeting specifications. The compensation of the economic difference between both economic situations is equivalent to total compensation or total reparation.[13]

Under the *damnum emergens* and *lucrum cessans* measure of damages, the loss of the investment in the carton freezer would be *damnum emergens*, and the profits lost from future and additional sales that would have been made with a performing carton freezer would be the *lucrum cessans*. If *damnum emergens* and *lucrum cessans* are added, it would result in double counting, that is overcompensation. In order to avoid that, adjustments will have to be made. It must be kept in mind, that future sales would serve to recover the investment in the carton freezer, that is why asking for losses and lost profits would lead to double counting.

This unnecessary complication leads to the modern measure of damages in the form of *expectation interest*, which may be formulated as follows: 'What would be the economic situation of the injured party if the contract had not been violated?' The expectation interest has been developed both in England as well as on the European continent in the mid-nineteenth century. In 1948, the leading English case *Robinson v. Harman* established that the aim of damages is to give the injured party the necessary amount of money to put him 'so far as money can do it, in the same position as he would have been in had the contract been performed'.[14] In 1855, Mommsen developed his *'Doctrine of Interest'* which states that the interest to be compensated is the economic difference between two situations: the actual situation affected by the breach of contract or violation of an international law standard, and the hypothetical situation

12. Herfried Wöss and Adrian San Román Rivera, *Advanced Seminars on Damages in International Arbitration©*, https://woessetpartners.com/467/.
13. Herfried Wöss and Adriana San Román Rivera, *Damages in International Commercial Arbitration* paras 7.14-7.17, *supra* n. 11.
14. *Robinson v. Harman* (1848) 13 P.D. 191 (CA), p. 200.

but-for the breach or illegal act, which is the so-called expectation interest. This doctrine spread through Europe and was also adopted in the United States where modern methods of damages valuation were developed in the context of antitrust damages claims.[15] The application of the differential hypothesis or but-for premise is the means to achieve full compensation or total reparation.[16] This means that the hypothetical (normal) course of events has to be reconstructed, which is the situation of the injured party had the breach of contract not occurred.

[D] LEADING CASE: THE FRUSTRATED TURN-KEY CONSTRUCTION OF A HOSPITAL IN CHIHUAHUA

In its jurisprudential ruling VII-J-SS-31 as of 8 March 2012, the plenary of the Superior Chamber of the Federal Tribunal of Fiscal and Administrative Justice established in its 'Declaration of Absolute Nullity of the Official Communication of Rescission of a Public Works Contract, its Scope'[17] that 'the circumstances of the execution of the contract have to be pulled back to the state in which they were at the moment when the official communication of rescission was made. That means that the contract is considered in execution and, therefore, taking into account this situation, the contracting authority has to come to consider the conclusion of the works from the stage in which it was, taking into consideration the legal situation of the injured contractor, in order to proceed with the execution of the said works, as if the rescission order had not existed'.

This jurisprudential ruling of a tribunal specialized in public works contracts is a landmark decision as it marks the transition from the *before-and-after* approach to the *but-for* premise and the expectation interest in Mexican damages law.

This ruling was successfully invoked by the authors of this chapter as damages counsel in the administrative litigation *Servicios Profesionales Encha (Encha) v. Instituto Mexicano de Seguro Social*: In 2005, the Mexican Social Security Institute adjudicated a contract for the construction of a hospital to Encha. The Mexican Social Security Institute rescinded the contract on 15 July 2007 when 50% of the works were already executed. The outstanding works were then awarded to a third-party contractor who executed a significantly larger project.

In light of the impossibility that Encha continue with the project and the impossibility of *restitutio in integrum*, after several rounds of *amparos*, the tribunal ordered in 2015 the substitute performance of the contract in the form of the compensation of the damages suffered by Encha, which would be determined in an incidental procedure under Article 58, section II, paragraph (f) of the Federal Law for

15. American Bar Association (ABA) *Proving Antitrust Damages: Legal and Economic Issues* (American Bar Association 3rd ed. 2017).
16. Friedrich Mommsen, *Zur Lehre von dem Interesse* 27, *supra* n. 9: 'Das Interesse ist allerdings ein Schadenersatz; und sofern man den Ausdruck Schadenersatz allein auf die vollständige Entschädigung bezieht, treffen beide Ausdrücke in ihrer Bedeutung zusammen' ('Interest means, however, damages; and if the expression damages is exclusively understood as full compensation, both terms coincide in their meaning.').
17. https://www.tfja.gob.mx/aps-tfja/sctj/tesis-pdf-detalle/38337/.

Administrative Litigation Procedure and Articles 358 to 364 of the Federal Code of Civil Procedure.

According to the jurisprudential ruling VII-J-SS-31, we argued that the administrative tribunal had to reconstruct the normal course of events with respect to the construction of the hospital taking into consideration any additions to its scope as Encha would have constructed the same hospital as the third-party constructor. In the incidental procedure, we presented an expert opinion containing a financial model taking into consideration certain costs that had to be reimbursed as updated with the legal interest rate of 9 % applicable to public works to the date of the expert opinion, as well as the profits established in the contract (18.02 %) albeit for non-executed works for the same scope of project, also updated to the date of the expert opinion. The standard of proof argued and accepted by the Magistrate was the one cited before of Damages and Loss of Profits, Proof of.

The incidental judgment of 4 March 2019 of the Fifth Regional Metropolitan Chamber followed the measure of damages formulated by the authors and led to an award of significant damages.

The jurisprudential ruling of the specialized Federal Tribunal of Fiscal and Administrative Justice and the leading case of *Encha v. the Mexican Social Insurance Institute* paved the way to the principle of total reparation and the application of the differential hypothesis or *but-for* premise, that is, the *expectation interest*, in Mexican law.

[E] THE MODERNIZATION OF MEXICAN DAMAGES LAW: THE TRANSFORMATION OF THE *FACTORY AT CHORZÓW* FORMULA INTO MEXICAN CIVIL LAW

The modernization of Mexican damages law commenced with the incorporation into the Mexican federal constitution of human rights and human rights treaties through the reform of Article 1 of the Mexican Federal Constitution[18] and the dictum of the First Chamber of the Mexican Supreme Court on 19 October 2011, referring to full compensation or 'integral reparation or fair compensation'. This dictum reads:[19]

> Integral Reparation of the Damage or Fair Compensation. This fundamental right was incorporated in this legal system through the reform of Article 1 of the Constitution published on June 10, 2011.
>
> The decree of reforms to the Political Constitution of the United Mexican States, ... aimed at amplifying the legal framework of the protection of fundamental rights, ... which made it necessary to incorporate into this Fundamental Law human rights established in international treaties entered into by the Mexican State, ... incorporating in Article 1 of the Constitution the human rights principles known as pro personae or pro homine .... In this respect, it is up to the State to take all necessary measures to assure that any violation of fundamental rights of its

18. Reform of the Mexican Federal Constitution as of 20 Jun. 2011, https://www.diputados.gob.mx/LeyesBiblio/pdf/CPEUM.pdf.
19. Tesis 1ª. CXCIV/2012 (10ª.) en Materia Constitucional, Tesis Aislada, Semanario Judicial de la Federación y su Gaceta, Libro XII, Septiembre de 2012, Tomo 1, p. 522, registro digital: 2001744.

people, caused by persons, be repaired by the person who caused it. As from the entry into force of the said constitutional reform, the right to an integral reparation or just compensation ... established in Article 63 of the American Convention on Human Rights, may be considered incorporated into the Mexican legal order.

On 5 April 2017, the First Chamber of the Mexican Supreme Court rendered a fundamental jurisprudential ruling with the title *Fundamental Right to an Integral Reparation or Just Compensation. Its Concept and Scope.*[20] This so-called *jurisprudential thesis* is binding and refers to the right to integral reparation:

> taking into consideration the criteria established by the Inter-American Court of Human Rights, the right to integral reparation permits, as far as possible, to annul all consequences of the illicit act and to re-establish the situation which would have existed in all probability if the act had not been committed, and if that is possible, to proceed with the payment of a just indemnification as compensatory means for the loss caused, which shall not generate a profit to the victim, but award an adequate compensation. In this sense, the modern law of damages looks at the nature and extension of the damage to its victims and not at the victimizer. That is, the damage caused is which determines the nature and the amount of the indemnification, so that the compensation may not imply an enrichment nor an impoverishment for the victim or its successors; moreover, it is not pretended that the responsibility be excessive, as it is subdued to qualitative requirements. ... .

The wording of the aforementioned ruling quotes the dictum of the Permanent Court of Justice in the *Factory at Chorzów* case in 1927[21] which confirms the international customary law measure of damages:

> [R]eparation must, so far as possible, wipe out all the consequences of the illegal act and re-establish the situation which would, in all probability, have existed if that act had not been committed. ... .

The reference to 'wipe out all consequences of the illegal act' establishes the total reparation principle in international law and resembles Mommsen's but-for premise, which aims 'to place the injured in the position it would be for the breach'.[22] It aims to avoid both over- and under-compensation and establishes a standard of proof in the form of 'all probability' which is a rather high threshold. Apart from that, it confirms the Roman law approach that damages law focuses on the position of the victim and not of the aggressor.[23]

The adoption of the *Factory at Chorzów* dictum and the principle of full or integral compensation through the Inter-American human rights mechanism has been confirmed in a commented edition of the American Convention of Human Rights which states that the Inter-American Court of Human Rights (Court) has developed a vast jurisprudence of the right to reparation, in particular, based on the responsibility of

20. Primera Sala de la Suprema Corte de la Nación, Seminario Judicial de la Federación, Jurisprudencia, Tesis 1ª./J. 31/2017 (10ª.), registro digital: 2014098, https://sjf2.scjn.gob.mx/detalle/tesis/2014098.
21. 1928 PCIJ Services A, No. 17, p. 47.
22. Herfried Wöss et al., *Damages in International Arbitration*, paras 5.180-183, *supra* n. 1.
23. Christian Schieder, *Interesse und Sachwert, zur Konkurrenz zweier Grundbegriffe des römischen Rechts* 23 (Wallstein 2011).

States for internationally wrongful acts. Article 63.1 of the American Convention on Human Rights (Pact of San José, Costa Rica) is considered a fundamental principle of the law of Nations, which has been defined, among others, through the Permanent Court of Justice judgment in the case *Factory at Chorzów.* Accordingly, the Member States of the Convention are obliged to implement mechanisms that aim to apply the criteria and principles established by the Court.[24] Article 63.1 of the Convention refers to the payment of fair compensation to be paid to the injured party for the consequences of the measure or situation that constitutes a violation of a right or freedom protected by the Convention.

With respect to compensation, according to the jurisprudence of the Court, *restitutio in integrum* means the re-establishment of the situation before the damaging event as well as the reparation of the consequences produced by the violation, as well as the payment of an indemnification as compensation for patrimonial and extra-patrimonial damages including moral damages. If restitution of the prior situation is not possible, then all consequences of the damaging event have to be compensated as established in the *Factory at Chorzów* case. On that basis, the Court developed the notion of *integral reparation* which may consist of a conjunction of different measures of reparation, in order to compensate the damages. In particular, the Court refers to the preventive effect of integral reparation, in the form of the compensation of the damages caused (compensatory principle) and rejects punitive damages.[25] The reference to 'fair indemnification' used in Article 63.1 of the Convention is compensatory and not sanctioning. Exemplary or dissuasive damages are not admitted.[26]

This landmark judgment of the Mexican Supreme Court is in essence the transformation of international customary damages law confirmed by the *Factory at Chorzów* judgment, into Mexican civil law through jurisprudence of the Mexican Supreme Court. In a series of judicial precedents, the Mexican Supreme Court further established the notion of *integral reparation* and *fair compensation* both with respect to the responsibility for damages of the Mexican State, as well as in the area of private law, both of which have their origin in Article 63.1 of the Convention and the jurisprudence of the Court. Its incorporation into Mexican law results from the so-called objective function of human rights established in the judgment Amparo Directo 1621-2010,[27] also known as the third-party effect of fundamental rights in continental Europe, which means that the new law to damages is not only applicable to illegal measures of the State but also applies between legal and natural persons.[28]

24. *Convención Americana sobre Derechos Humanos Comentada* 824-825 y nota al pie no. 9 (Suprema Corte de Justicia de la Nación y Konrad Adenauer Stiftung, Programa Estado de Derecho para Latinoamérica, primera edición, 2014), https://www.corteidh.or.cr/tablas/30237.pdf.
25. *Ibid.*, 837; Inter-American Court of Human Rights: Case *Atala Riffo and daughters v. Chile.* Reparations and costs, para. 241 (Judgment of 24 Feb. 2022, Serie C No. 239).
26. *Ibid.*, 838; Inter-American Court of Human Rights: Case *Godínez Cruz v. Honduras.*, para. 36 (Reparations and costs. Serie C. No. 8. Judgment of 21 July 1989).
27. https://arturozaldivar.com/wp-content/uploads/2020/09/ADR-1621-2010.pdf.
28. Edgardo Muñoz, Rodolfo Vázquez Cabello, *Elementos, umbral y quantum de los daños punitivos en el derecho mexicano* 9-10, 37, con referencias añadidas, en *Derecho de Daños – Ideas para iniciar el Diálogo* (Suprema Corte de Justicia de la Nación, octubre de 2021).

The *Factory at Chorzów* dictum is cited in nearly all leading investment arbitration cases. As stated in the investment arbitration award *Burlington v. Ecuador*,[29] wiping out all the consequences of the illegal act 'involves the obligation to restore the undertaking and, if this be not possible, to be its value at the time of the indemnification, which value is to take the place instead of restitution which has become impossible'.[30] The arbitral tribunal stated that its task is to place Burlington in the situation it would have been had Ecuador not expropriated the investment, which is also referred to as the but-for premise.[31]

As the authors of this chapter have shown elsewhere in detail,[32] the full or integral reparation principle derives from Greek philosophy and the works of scholastics such as Saint Thomas Aquinas (1225-1275). Hugo Grotius (1583-1645) established the leading damages doctrine in Chapter 17 of his masterwork *De iure bellis ac pacis* based on total reparation and the compensation of damages and lost profits, which comprises the violation of legal positions including property, contract and the law. Grotius' doctrine was further developed by another natural law scholar, Samuel Pufendorf (1632-1694) who was heavily influenced by Thomas Hobbes. Damages law was understood as a defence based on the absolute prohibition of 'neminem laedere' (not to hurt anybody).

The application of the but-for premise is the means to achieve full or integral compensation or total reparation. The *Factory at Chorzów* formula replicates the but-for premise already recognized in private law by stating that *'reparation must, as far as possible wipe out all the consequences of the illegal act and re-establish the situation which would, in all probability, have existed if that act had not been committed'*. As already observed by Prof. Hersch Lauterpacht, private law sources and analogies are found in international law, in particular in the areas of the measure of damages.[33]

The transformation of the *Chorzów* formula into Mexican civil law leads to the expectation interest measure of damages as the ideal measure in order to achieve the compensatory and preventions principles of damages law. The expectation interest leads to the following key question: 'What would be the economic situation of the injured party but-for the breach?' The *differential hypothesis* or *but-for* premise would also provide for the reliance interest measure of damages, which leads to the question of: 'Which would be the economic situation of the injured party had it not entered into the contract or suffered the illegal act?' The reliance interest leads to the compensation of the wasted expenses or sunk investment.[34]

---

29. *Burlington Resources Inc. v. Republic of Ecuador* (ICSID Case No. ARB/08/5, Decision on Reconsideration and Award, 7 Feb. 2017).
30. *Ibid.*, paras 326 and 327.
31. *Ibid.*, paras 332 and 337.
32. Herfried Wöss and Adriana San Román Rivera, *Damages in Investment Treaty Arbitration* paras 17-09-17.16 in *International Arbitration and EU Law* (José Rafael Mata Dona and Nikos Lavranos eds, Edward Elgar Publishing 2021).
33. Hersch Lauterpacht, *Private Law Sources and Analogies of Law* 6 (Longmanns, Green & Co. Ltd. 1927) 6; Hersch Lauterpacht, *The Development of International Law by the International Court* 32 (Cambridge University Press 1958).
34. For example, *Bear Creek Mining Corporation v. Republic of Peru*, paras 595-604, 738 (ICSID Case No. ARB/14/21, Award, 30 Nov. 2017).

Furthermore, the differential hypothesis contemplates the following causality question: 'Would the damage have occurred without the breach of contract or the illegal act?' If the answer is yes, there might be a concurring causation which has or has not been taken into consideration according to the applicable causation theory. As stated by the Mexican Supreme Court in its dictum *Damages and Loss of Profits. Proof of*, the reference to German law appears as choice of the hypothetical normal course of events causation theory which normally excludes concurring or alternative causes.[35]

The introduction of the measure of damages of expectation and reliance interest opened the door to substantial damages claims corresponding to integral reparation and the compensatory principle. It may also remedy the situation of imperfect obligations, that is obligations that are not being observed without any further consequence which is one of the shortcomings of the Mexican legal system, and provides the injured party with an effective remedy.

[F] QUANTIFICATION

There is no further reference to the quantification of damages in Mexican law apart from the reference to expert evidence[36] and with respect to moral damages albeit in a general manner.[37] Comparative law refers to the abstract and concrete valuation of damages.[38] Abstract valuation refers to market values ('difference in value') and is the preferred method in commercial transactions where time is of the essence. It is often easier to refer to market values than to make an analysis of the individual situation of the injured party. Abstract valuation is normally measured at the moment of the damaging event or the moment performance is due and is the applicable method under UN-Sales Law (CISG)[39] and many commercial laws.[40]

Concrete valuation refers to the precise situation of the injured party and how to restore it to the position it would have been in had the breach of contract not occurred ('cost of cure'). The difference in the amount of compensation between abstract and concrete valuation may be significant as explained by the authors with respect to the English law case *Ruxley Electronics & Construction v. Forsyth*[41] where the application of

35. Herfried Wöss, *Assessment of Damages in Commercial Arbitration after Covid-19: The Relevance of the Applicable Causation Theory*, *supra* n. 4.
36. Daños y Perjuicios. Incidente Previsto en el Artículo 129 de la Ley de Amparo. La Prueba Pericial es la Idónea para calcular el Monto Económico que dejó de percibir el Incidentista (Tercero Perjudicado) al prolongarse la Suspensión del Acto Reclamado, por no tener la Posesión del Inmueble Controvertido. Primer Tribunal Colegiado en Materia Civil del Cuarto Circuito, Seminario Judicial de la Federación y su Gaceta, Tomo XXX, Julio de 2009, p. 1909, Registro 166980, https://sjf2.scjn.gob.mx/detalle/tesis/166980.
37. https://sjf2.scjn.gob.mx/detalle/tesis/2023165.
38. Herfried Wöss and Adriana San Román Rivera, *Damages in International Commercial Arbitration* paras 7.62-7.73, *supra* n. 11.
39. Irmgard Schwenzer, *Commentary to the UN Convention on the International Sale of Goods* Art. 74, para. 43 (Oxford University Press 4th ed. 2016); §376 Austrian UGB (Unternehmensgesetzbuch).
40. Herfried Wöss, *Schadenersatz* 751, para. 9 in *Handbuch Schiedsgerichtsbarkeit und ADR* (Michael Nueber ed., LexisNexis Orac, 2021).
41. *Ruxley Electronics and Construction Ltd. v. Forsyth* [1996] 1 AC 344.

English or French law would lead to significantly different results, whereby the difference-in-value approach of English law (abstract valuation) would not give rise to damages, because of a swimming pool constructed not in conformity with the specifications, as the market value of the house and the swimming would not change if the specifications had been met. Under the *pacta sunt servanda* approach of French law and the resulting concrete valuation, the swimming pool would have to be reconstructed at perhaps exorbitant cost.[42]

[G] MORAL AND PUNITIVE DAMAGES

The influence of international human rights law in Mexico has brought significant development in the area of moral and also punitive damages.[43] This development has been rather impressive and mainly refers to accidents or mistreatment of individuals caused by grossly negligent or reckless conduct or omission.

Article 1916 of the Mexican Civil Code reads:

> Moral damage is every affectation suffered by a person in its feelings, affections, creeds, decor, honour, reputation, private live, physical configuration or aspect, or with respect to the consideration it has with others.

When an illicit conduct or omission produces moral damage, the responsible for such damage has the obligation to repair it through compensation in money, without prejudice to having caused material damage, both with respect to contractual and extra-contractual liability.

The amount of compensation is determined by the judge taking into account the rights violated, the grade of culpability, the economic situation of the tortfeasor, and of the victim, as well as all other circumstances of the case.

This provision includes a non-limited list of situations which lead to moral damages, including defamation and the violation of personality rights, including liberty, and physical and psychological integrity. The Mexican Supreme Court confirmed in a jurisprudential ruling in 2005, that legal entities are entitled to claim moral damages.[44]

The Mexican Supreme Court has rendered some high-profile judgments under this heading starting with the *Mayan Palace* case, where damages exceeding USD 1 million were awarded.[45] Recently, Google Inc. was sentenced to pay moral damages in

42. *See* Herfried Wöss and Adriana San Román Rivera, *Damages in International Commercial Arbitration*, paras 7.62-7.73, *supra* n. 11.
43. Edgardo Muñoz, *El renacimiento del derecho de daños en México. Un análisis comparativo* (Tirant México 2019).
44. Primera Sala de la Suprema Corte de la Nación, Semanario Judicial de la Federación y su Gaceta, Tomo XXI, Abril de 2006, p. 155, Registro 178767, https://sjf2.scjn.gob.mx/detalle/tesis/178767.
45. Amparo directo en revisión 593/2015, https://www.scjn.gob.mx/sites/default/files/listas/documento_dos/2017-04/ADR-593-2015-170425.pdf; Amparo directo 30/2014, Daño Moral Indemnización y Daños Punitivos por la negligencia de un Prestador del Servicio de Hospedaje, https://www.scjn.gob.mx/derechos-humanos/sites/default/files/sentencias-emblematicas/resumen/2022-02/Resumen%20AD30-2013%20DGDH.pdf.

the amount of USD 250 million in favour of a Mexican couple and their company, for having permitted the creation and publication by a third party of a defamatory blog which was not erased in spite of a judicial request.[46] The appeal judgment is still pending.

This development has to be seen in light of the lamentable fact that until recently personal injuries caused by negligent behaviour rarely led to damages awards. The Mexican Federal Labour Law prices the loss of limbs and parts of the human body with rather ridiculous indemnifications. The Mexican Supreme Court sought to compensate for this lack of proper compensation through moral damages which is certainly an encomendable undertaking.

Moral damages under the new doctrine are characterized by an emphasis on the violation of the different grounds established in Article 1916 of the Mexican Civil Code and the requirement of a high standard of culpability. In contrast with the high requirement of culpability, there is a rather low standard of proof with respect to the quantification of damages and a high level of discretion of the judge.[47]

The tendency of the Mexican Supreme Court to award moral damages as punitive damages is, however, questionable. According to a leading commentary on the American Convention of Human Rights, the Inter-American Court of Human Rights has rejected the award of punitive damages and underlined the compensatory principle of damages.[48] Punitive damages lead to overcompensation and are considered unfair. Where moral damages are arbitrable, that is within the scope of the arbitration clause and contract-related, awards granting punitive moral damages would normally not be subject to execution due to grounds of violation of public policy, at least in civil law countries.[49]

It is the opinion of the authors that the application of modern damages law in the form of the expectation interest and the differential hypothesis or but-for premise, as introduced into Mexican civil law through the transformation of international customary law, could lead to similar damages awards as many of the recent moral and punitive damages judgments. Damages under the compensatory principle or the measure of expectation interest are based on principles of fairness and the avoidance of under- and overcompensation and are grounded on evidence, though judicial discretion is certainly justified with respect to moral damages where quantification is always a challenge.

46. https://www.eleconomista.com.mx/opinion/Richter-vs.-Google-danos-por-250-millones-de-dolares-20220619-0013.html.
47. With respect to the possible quantification of moral and punitive damages, see: Edgardo Muñoz and Rodolfo Vázquez Cabello, *Elementos, umbral y quantum de los daños punitivos en el derecho mexicano*, en Derecho *de Daños – Ideas para iniciar el diálogo* (Suprema Corte de Justicia de la Nación, octubre de 2021).
48. *Convención Americana sobre Derechos Humanos Comentada* 837, *supra* n. 24.
49. Markus A. Petsche, *Punitive Damages in International Commercial Arbitration: Much Ado about Nothing?* 89-104, 29 Arbitration International 1 (2013) https://doi.org/10.1093/arbint/29.1.89.

[H] CONCLUSIONS

The headlines of the modern Mexican damages law refer to substantial awards of moral and punitive damages which may be explained by centuries of under- or no compensation of damages and *lex imperfecta* with regards to contractual and public obligations. The turn toward moral damages is justified where there is a substantial degree of suffering that may not be easily quantified. In other cases, the expectation interest measure of damages introduced by the Mexican Supreme Court is a still more revolutionary development that paves the way to the compensatory principle and *integral reparation* with respect to both contractual liability and tort.

It is, therefore, of utmost importance for party counsel to learn how to formulate damages claims and, for judges and arbitrators, to analyse and decide claims under the expectation and reliance interest measures of damages.

PART III Judicial Intervention in Support of International Arbitration

CHAPTER 9

Judicial Aid to International Arbitration in Mexico

Carlos Alvarado

[A] INTRODUCTION

Arbitration and court proceedings before national courts coexist. They not only coexist but interact in an often-complex relationship. Lord Mustill said:

> there is a plainly tension here. On the one hand the concept of arbitration as a consensual process reinforced by the ideas of transnationalism leans against the involvement of mechanism of state through the medium of a municipal court. On the other side there is the plain fact, palatable or not, that it is only a Court possessing coercive powers which could rescue the arbitration if it is in danger of foundering.[1]

This is not a minor issue. Both, the excessive intervention, and the insufficient participation of national courts could lead to a futile arbitration. Therefore, to find the equilibrium between these two forces, national legislations need to carefully design their own systems of court intervention, and national courts must self-restrict to act within said system.

This chapter addresses the interaction between international arbitration and the Mexican courts. From the judicial non-interference principle to the cases where the judicial aid or control is either available or required, from the Constitutional regulation of arbitration to the Mexican Commercial Code which contains the *lex arbitri*, from the competent courts to the rules of procedure.

1. Lord Mustill of House of Lords in the case *Coppée Levalin S.A./NV v. Ken-Ren Chemicals and Fertilizers LTD* [1994] in Alan Redfern & Martin Hunter, *Law and Practice of International Commercial Arbitration* 328 (2004).

It is not the chapter's intention to deepen in each of the cases where judicial intervention is required, but to provide an overview of the interaction between courts and arbitration. In this book, there are chapters specifically addressing each of those topics.[2]

[B] JUDICIAL NON-INTERFERENCE IN ARBITRATION

The principle of judicial non-interference in international arbitration is fundamentally important to the arbitration efficacy. It ensures that an arbitration can proceed "without the delays, second- guessing, and other problems associated with interlocutory judicial review of procedural decisions."[3] This principle can be recognized either directly or indirectly by international treaties and national legislation.

Mexico adopted this principle from the UNCITRAL Model Law. Article 1421 of the Mexican Commercial Code provides that: "Unless provided otherwise, in the matters governed by this Title [the *lex arbitri*[4]], no judicial intervention will be required."[5] The Courts will only intervene in those specific cases established in the Commercial Code.[6]

The Mexican Courts have addressed the non-interference principle in some precedents. The Supreme Court's First Chamber concluded that one of the most important principles of the *lex arbitri* is the judicial intervention only *as an exception*[7] and that such intervention must take place in accordance with the rules of the arbitral legislation.[8] It also ruled that the parties choose the judicial non-intervention seeking celerity, pragmatism, and procedural speed.[9] Other Federal Courts have concluded that by submitting to arbitration, the parties opt for the judicial non-intervention;[10] that by

2. For instance: Arbitrators and arbitral tribunals (Siqueiros); Recognition and enforcement of awards (Manzano and Magallanes); Interim measures (Ruiz and Orta); Challenge of arbitration awards (Bañuelos); etc.
3. Gary Born, *Principle of Judicial Non-interference in International Arbitral Proceedings: The Anniversary Contributions—International Litigation & Arbitration*, 1000 (2009).
4. The Mexican *lex arbitri* is contained in Title IV, Fifth Book, of the Commercial Code.
5. Although the principle remains the same, the wording of Art. 5 of the UNCITRAL Model Law (both in English and Spanish) is slightly different from this article. "In matters governed by this Law, no court shall intervene except where so provided in this Law."
6. *See* section [C] Judicial intervention.
7. *Intervención judicial excepcional.*
8. 1a. CLXX/2009. *Commercial Arbitration. Relevant Aspects and Principles Governing Title Four of Book Five of the Commercial Code.* (*ARBITRAJE COMERCIAL. ASPECTOS RELEVANTES Y PRINCIPIOS QUE RIGEN EL TÍTULO CUARTO DEL LIBRO QUINTO DEL CÓDIGO DE COMERCIO*).
9. 1a. CCLVIII/2007. *Arbitral Award. Article 1460 of the Commercial Code, by Providing That the Resolution of Set Aside Ancillary Proceeding Is Not Subject to Appeal, Does Not Violate the Guarantee of Access to Judicial Protection.* (*LAUDO ARBITRAL. EL ARTÍCULO 1460 DEL CÓDIGO DE COMERCIO, AL DISPONER QUE LA RESOLUCIÓN DEL INCIDENTE DE NULIDAD RELATIVO ES IRRECURRIBLE, NO VIOLA LA GARANTÍA DE ACCESO A LA TUTELA JURISDICCIONAL*).
10. I.7o.C.26 C (10a.) *Arbitral Award. Denial of Enforcement. Analysis of the Scenario Outlined in Section c) of Fraction I of Article 1462 of the Commercial Code.* (*LAUDO ARBITRAL. DENEGACIÓN DE SU EJECUCIÓN. ANÁLISIS SOBRE LA ACTUALIZACIÓN DE LA HIPÓTESIS SEÑALADA EN EL INCISO C) DE LA FRACCIÓN I DEL ARTÍCULO 1462 DEL CÓDIGO DE COMERCIO*).

the incorporation of the *lex arbitri* the legislative sought to govern the arbitration by the judicial non-intervention principle, or minimum intervention of the judicial bodies, giving priority to the parties' will, and; that allowing the judicial intervention to review each of the arbitrator's decisions would abolish arbitration as dispute settlement mechanism.[11]

Additionally, in 2008 the Mexican Constitution was amended to establish that the Mexican laws must provide alternative dispute resolution mechanisms.[12] By interpreting such amendment, the Supreme Court ruled that the submission to arbitration represents the exercise of constitutional freedoms that must be protected by the Courts.[13] In other words, the Mexican Courts not only have the obligation not to interfere with the arbitration but to protect it.

[C] JUDICIAL INTERVENTION

The Mexican Courts cannot intervene in arbitration unless specifically provided by the Mexican *lex arbitri*. Pursuant to the Commercial Code, judicial intervention is required or allowed in the following cases:[14]

[1] Challenge of Arbitrators

Article 1429 of the Commercial Code contains Article 13 of the UNCITRAL Model Law. The parties may agree on the procedure for challenging arbitrators, and failing such agreement the challenge will be heard by the arbitral tribunal. Should the challenge be not successful, the decision might be reviewed by the Mexican Courts.

Within thirty days following the decision that rejected the challenge, the challenging party may request the Court to decide on the challenge. The Court will hear the challenge pursuant to the Special Proceedings for Arbitration[15] explained below.[16] Article 1429 of the Commercial Code states that the Court's decision is not subject to appeal.[17] However, it might be challenged via *amparo*, a constitutional trial.[18]

---

11. I.3o.C.566 C *Nullity of Resolutions Within Commercial Arbitration Proceedings. National Courts Lack of Jurisdiction to Hear Them. (NULIDAD DE ACTOS DENTRO DEL PROCEDIMIENTO ARBITRAL MERCANTIL. NO CORRESPONDE SU CONOCIMIENTO A UN TRIBUNAL JUDICIAL).*
12. *See* Art. 17 fifth paragraph of the Mexican Constitution.
13. 1a. XXXVI/2017 (10a.). *Arbitration. Normative Implications Arising from Its Constitutionalization since the June 2008 Reform. (ARBITRAJE. IMPLICACIONES NORMATIVAS DERIVADAS DE SU CONSTITUCIONALIZACIÓN A PARTIR DE LA REFORMA DE JUNIO DE 2008).*
14. This chapter does not seek to address thoroughly all the scenarios for judicial intervention, but only to make a brief reference. For further details, please go to the specific chapter of this book.
15. *See* Art. 1470.I of the Commercial Code.
16. *See* section [E] Judicial proceedings.
17. This prohibition to appeal was included prior to the inclusion of the Special Proceedings for Arbitration in 2011. Nowadays it could be redundant, since all resolutions issued in the Special Proceedings for Arbitration are no subject to appeal or any other ordinary challenge.
18. *See* section [E] Judicial proceedings.

[2] Arbitral Tribunal's Competence

Article 1432 of the Commercial Code contains the *kompetenz-kompetenz* principle. The arbitral tribunal may rule on its own jurisdiction, including any objections with respect to the existence or validity of the arbitration agreement. The arbitral Tribunal may decide on its jurisdiction either within the final award or in a preliminary award or decision. In both cases, this decision might be reviewed by the Courts.

When the arbitral tribunal rules on its own jurisdiction in a preliminary decision the parties will have thirty days to request before a Mexican Court the revision of this decision.[19] This revision will be conducted under the Special Proceedings for Arbitration.[20] Article 1432 of the Commercial Code provides that the Court's decision will not be subject to appeal, however, it could be subject to be challenged via *amparo*.

[3] Interim Measures Issued by the Courts

Pursuant to Article 1425[21] of the Commercial Code even when there is an arbitration agreement, the parties may request interim measures to the National Courts before or during arbitral proceedings. This applies regardless of whether the seat of the arbitration is in Mexico or abroad.[22] The request for interim measures before a Court will be conducted under the Special Proceedings for Arbitration.[23]

The Mexican *lex arbitri* gives the Courts *full discretion* in the granting of interim measures. In a non-binding precedent, a Federal Court has confirmed that the Judges have full discretion in the issuance of interim measures, but they must follow the standards of rationality and coherence, and apply the rules of logic, experience and proportionality.[24]

[4] Recognition and Enforcement of Interim Measures Granted by the Arbitral Tribunal

Unless provided otherwise, the arbitral tribunals have the power to issue interim measures.[25] Pursuant to Article 1479 of the Commercial Code, the interim measures granted by the arbitrators will be binding and the Courts will enforce them upon a party request, unless the arbitral tribunal provided otherwise. The recognition and enforcement of interim measures will be conducted under the Special Proceedings for

19. Should the decision be taken in the final award, the arbitral tribunal's jurisdiction might be reviewed by the Court in the proceedings for the recognition and enforcement, or set-aside of the arbitration award.
20. *See* Art. 1470.II of the Commercial Code.
21. Taken from Art. 9 of the UNCITRAL Model Law on International Commercial Arbitration.
22. *See* Art. 1415 second paragraph of the Commercial Code.
23. *See* Art. 1470.III of the Commercial Code.
24. I.4o.C.34 C (10a.). *Judicial Procedure to Adopt Interim Measures Related to Arbitration. It Is Subject to the Court's Broad Discretion.* (*PROCEDIMIENTO PARA LA ADOPCIÓN JUDICIAL DE MEDIDAS CAUTELARES VINCULADAS AL ARBITRAJE. ESTÁ SUJETO A DISCRECIÓN AMPLIA DEL JUZGADOR*).
25. *See* Art. 1433 of the Commercial Code.

Arbitration.[26] Article 1480 of the Commercial Code (based on Article 17 I of the UNCITRAL Model Law) lists those limited cases for which the recognition and enforcement of the interim measure may be refused.

It is arguable that the Mexican Courts will recognize and enforce the interim measures, even when issued by an arbitral tribunal seated abroad. Although Article 1415 of the Commercial Code (which lists the articles applicable when the arbitration is abroad) does not include Article 1433 (the Arbitrator's powers to grant interim measures), Article 1480 of the Commercial Code provides that the interim measures granted by an arbitral tribunal will be recognized and enforced regardless of the *State* where they were issued. We believe that using *country* (as in the UNCITRAL Model Law[27]) rather than *State* would have provided more clarity. State could be used either for a country or for each of the thirty-two Federal Entities (states) that integrate Mexico as a country. However, based on a comprehensive interpretation of the Mexican *lex arbitri*, on Article 17(H) of the UNCITRAL Model Law, and on the Explanatory Note by the UNCITRAL secretariat on the 1985 UNCITRAL Model Law on International Commercial Arbitration as amended in 2006,[28] it could be claimed that the Mexican Courts shall recognize and enforce interim measures granted by arbitral tribunals, regardless of whether the arbitration takes place in Mexico or elsewhere.[29]

[5] Setting-Aside of Arbitration Awards

Arbitration awards rendered in Mexico[30] are subject to be set aside by the Mexican Courts. Article 1457 of the Commercial Code provides the grounds for which an arbitration award might be set aside. These grounds are those contained in Article 34 of the UNCITRAL Model Law.

Pursuant to Article 1458 of the Commercial Code, the request to set aside an arbitration award shall be filed within three months of the notification of the award, or the additional award for its correction or interpretation. The Special Proceedings for

26. *See* Art. 1470.IV of the Commercial Code.
27. Article 17(H)(1) of the UNCITRAL Model Law on International Commercial Arbitration: "An interim measure issued by an arbitral tribunal shall be recognized as binding and, unless otherwise provided by the arbitral tribunal, enforced upon application to the competent court, irrespective of the *country* in which it was issued, subject to the provisions of article 17 I."
28. "13. Another aspect of applicability is the territorial scope of application. The principle embodied in article 1 (2) is that the Model Law as enacted in a given State applies only if the place of arbitration is in the territory of that State. However, article 1 (2) also contains important exceptions to that principle, to the effect that certain articles apply, *irrespective of whether the place of arbitration is in the enacting State or elsewhere* (or, as the case may be, even before the place of arbitration is determined). These articles are the following ... *articles 17 H* and 17 I on *the recognition and enforcement of interim measures ordered by an arbitral tribunal,* and articles 35 and 36 on the recognition and enforcement of arbitral awards."
29. In a recent judgment, the First Chamber of the Mexican Supreme Court expressly recognized that the UNCITRAL Model Law works as a guiding criterion to interpret the Mexican *lex arbitri*. (Primera Sala, Amparo Directo en Revisión 7790/2019, para. 99).
30. Mexican Courts lack jurisdiction to set-aside arbitration awards rendered abroad. *See* section [D] Competent Courts.

Arbitration apply to the request to set aside arbitration awards.[31] Upon a party's request, the Court might suspend the proceedings for a period of time to give the arbitral tribunal an opportunity to resume the arbitral proceedings or to take such other action as in the arbitral tribunal's opinion will eliminate the grounds for setting aside.[32]

[6] Recognition and Enforcement of Arbitration Awards

Mexico is a signatory of the New York Convention, the Inter-American Convention on International Commercial Arbitration, and other conventions containing the obligation of recognizing and enforcing arbitration awards. Additionally, pursuant to the Commercial Code, Mexican Courts shall recognize and enforce arbitration awards regardless of whether they were issued in Mexico or abroad.[33]

The recognition and enforcement of an arbitration award may be refused only under the grounds listed in Article 1462 of the Commercial Code (same grounds as Article 36 of the UNCITRAL Model Law and the New York Convention). The recognition and enforcement of the arbitration award will be conducted under the Special Proceedings for Arbitration,[34] and the requesting party shall submit the original or certified copy of the arbitration award duly authenticated, the original or certified copy of the arbitration agreement and, if applicable, an official translation of both.[35]

[7] Other Judicial Aid

Article 1466 of the Commercial Code provides that the Mexican Courts might also aid with: (1) appointing arbitrators; (2) taking evidence; and (3) consultation of the tribunal's fees.

When the parties did not agree on the mechanism to select arbitrators (either within the arbitration agreement or by the selection of arbitration rules), and it is a sole arbitrator proceeding, the Court will appoint the arbitrator should the parties be unable to agree on the arbitrator. In arbitrations with three arbitrators, each party shall appoint one arbitrator, and the two arbitrators thus appointed shall appoint the third arbitrator; if a party fails to appoint the arbitrator within thirty days of receipt of a request to do so from the other party, or if the two arbitrators fail to agree on the third arbitrator within thirty days of their appointment, the appointment shall be made by the court. Court appointments are upon a party's request.[36]

The arbitral tribunal or the parties (with the tribunal's approval) might ask the Court to assist with the taking of evidence, pursuant to Article 1444 of the Commercial

31. *See* Art. 1470.V of the Commercial Code.
32. *See* Art. 1459 of the Commercial Code, taken from Art. 34(4) of the UNCITRAL Model Law.
33. *See* Art. 1461 of the Commercial Code.
34. *See* Art. 1471 of the Commercial Code.
35. *See* Art. 1461 of the Commercial Code.
36. *See* Art. 1427 of the Commercial Code.

Code.[37] To the author's knowledge, there are no precedents whereby the Mexican Courts analyze the scope of this article of the Commercial Code.

Upon a party's request and subject to the Court's consent, the arbitral tribunal can consult with the Court the amount of its fees. The Court might make suggestions to the arbitral tribunal in that regard.[38] The author is not aware of the existence of judicial precedents addressing consultations regarding the tribunals' fees.

These three judicial interventions are conducted under the non-contentious proceedings regulated by Articles 530 to 532 and 434 to 537 of the Federal Code of Civil Procedure.[39] In essence, once the request is submitted before the Court, the other party will have three business days to review the request, and then a hearing will take place and the Court will issue its determination. The Court's determination might be modified, and it is not subject to appeal. However, on June 7, 2023, the new National Code for Civil and Family Proceedings was enacted, and the Federal Code of Civil Procedure will no longer be in force.[40] Therefore, Article 1466 of the Commercial Code might be reformed to reflect the change.

Table 9.1 Judicial Intervention in Mexico

Judicial Intervention	*Proceedings*	*Applicable when the Seat of the Arbitration Is Abroad*	*Relevant Articles (Commercial Code)*	*Time Frame*
		Jurisdiction and tribunal		
Remission to arbitration	Procedure established in Article 1464 of the Commercial Code	Yes	1415, 1424, 1464, 1465	The request must be made in the first submission on the merits before the Court (*See explanation regarding the non-binding precedent*)
Aid to appointing arbitrators	Non-contentious proceedings under the Federal Code of Civil Procedure	No	1427, 1466(I), 1467, 1468	

37. Based in Art. 27 first paragraph of the UNCITRAL Model Law.
38. Article 1454 third para. of the Commercial Code.
39. *See* Art. 1466 of the Commercial Code.
40. The new National Code for Civil and Family Proceedings will replace the Federal Code of Civil Procedure, and the local codes of civil procedure. Its applicability at the Federal level will start when Congress so determines it upon the Judiciary's request, but no later than Apr. 1, 2027.

Judicial Intervention	*Proceedings*	*Applicable when the Seat of the Arbitration Is Abroad*	*Relevant Articles (Commercial Code)*	*Time Frame*
Consultation of the Tribunal's fees	Non-contentious proceedings under the Federal Code of Civil Procedure	No	1454, 1466(III)	
Challenge of arbitrators	Special Proceedings	No	1429, 1470(I)	30 days after the decision that denied the challenge
Revision of the Arbitral Tribunal's competence (when in a preliminary award)	Special Proceedings	No	1432, 1470(II)	30 days after the Tribunal's decision
		Interim measures and evidence		
Interim measures issued by the Courts	Special Proceedings	Yes	1415, 1425, 1470(III)	Prior or during the arbitration proceedings
Enforcement of interim measures granted by the Arbitral Tribunal	Special Proceedings	Yes (*See explanation*)	1433, 1479, 1480, 1470(IV)	
Aid for the taking of evidence	Non-contentious proceedings under the Federal Code of Civil Procedure	No	1444, 1466(II), 1469	
		Award		
Recognition and enforcement of arbitration awards	Special Proceedings	Yes	1415, 1461, 1462, 1463, 1471	
Setting-aside of arbitration awards	Special Proceedings	No	1457, 1458, 1459 1470(V)	3 months following the notification of the award

Source: Table created by author.

[D] JUDICIARY STRUCTURE IN MEXICO AND COMPETENT COURTS

Mexico is a federation formed by thirty-two federal entities or States,[41] and each State has its own judicial branch.[42] Therefore, there is a Federal Judicial branch and thirty-two local (i.e., state-based) judicial branches. Each State has its own constitution and decides the integration and organization of its judiciary. The Federal Judiciary branch is integrated by the Supreme Court of Justice, the Electoral Court, Regional Plenary Sessions, Collegiate Circuit Courts, Collegiate Courts of Appeal and District Courts,[43] and it is divided into thirty-two circuits.[44]

Commercial matters are subject to the principle of concurrent jurisdiction.[45] Pursuant to this principle, both Federal and Local Courts have jurisdiction to hear commercial disputes. It is up to the claimant whether to file their claim before the Federal or local Courts.

The Special Proceedings have a commercial nature, and therefore the principle of concurrent jurisdiction applies. Additionally, the Mexican *lex arbitri* makes clear the application of this principle. Section 1422 of the Commercial Code provides:

> When judicial intervention is required, the first instance federal or local judge of the place where the arbitration takes place shall have jurisdiction.
>
> If the place of arbitration is outside the national territory, the recognition and enforcement of the award shall be heard by the first instance federal or local judge of the domicile of the executed party or, failing that, of the location of the assets.

Consequently, when the seat of the arbitration is in Mexico, the party seeking judicial aid can decide whether to file its claim before the local or Federal Courts of the seat of the arbitration. Different drivers may impact this decision (e.g., potential timing of resolution, the Court's familiarization with arbitration, etc.).

When the seat of the arbitration is abroad, then the competent Courts to recognize and enforce the award will be those of the defendant's domicile or, failing those, the Courts of the place where the assets are located. Section 1422 says nothing about the competent Courts for other judicial aid to arbitration when the seat of the arbitration is abroad (e.g., interim measures, assistance with evidence, etc.). However, some Courts have accepted to apply the same rule applicable to the recognition and enforcement of awards, which could also be similar to the jurisdiction rules contained in section 1104[46] of the Commercial Code.[47]

41. Thirty-one States and Mexico City. *See* Arts. 40 and 43 of the Mexican Constitution.
42. *See* Art. 116 of the Mexican Constitution.
43. *See* Art. 94 of the Mexican Constitution.
44. General Resolution 3/2013 of the Council of the Federal Judicature.
45. This principle is contained in Arts. 104.I of the Mexican Constitution, and 53.I of the Federal Judiciary's Organic Act.
46. Article 1104 of the Commercial Code states that "Except for what is stipulated in Article 1093, regardless of the nature of the legal proceeding, the competent judge shall be, in the following order: I. The one in the place designated by the defendant to be judicially summoned for payment; II. The one in the place designated in the contract for the fulfillment of the obligation. III. The one in the domicile of the defendant. If the defendant has several domiciles, the

In a non-binding precedent, the Supreme Court ruled that the Courts of the seat of the arbitration have exclusive jurisdiction to hear about the set aside of arbitration awards.[48] Therefore, Mexican Courts lack jurisdiction to set aside arbitration awards when the arbitration took place abroad.

[E] JUDICIAL PROCEEDINGS

When Mexico adopted the UNCITRAL Model Law in 1993 in the Commercial Code, it did not include specific proceedings for the judicial aid to arbitration. Sections 1460 and 1463 of the Commercial Code established that to seek the set aside or the recognition and enforcement, respectively, of an arbitration award, the rules for the ancillary proceedings of the Federal Civil Code would apply.

In 2011, there was a major reform to the Commercial Code, including the addition of a chapter named *Judicial Intervention in Commercial Settlements and Arbitration*[49] to the Mexican arbitral legislation (the 2011-Reform).[50] With the 2011-Reform it was incorporated in the Mexican *lex arbitri* the Special Proceedings for Commercial Transactions and Arbitration (Special Proceedings for Arbitration). The Special Proceedings to Arbitration applies for: (1) challenges against arbitrators; (2) the revision of the arbitration tribunal's jurisdiction, when the decision was not taken in the final award; (3) issuance of interim measures by the Courts; (4) recognition and enforcement of interim measures ordered by an arbitral tribunal;(5) set aside of arbitration awards;[51] and (6) the recognition and enforcement of the arbitration awards.[52]

The Special Proceedings for Arbitration is a once instance and (aimed to be a) summary trial. Once served, the defendant will have fifteen business days to file its defense submission. Should the parties and the Judge do not need additional evidence, the hearing for conclusions shall be scheduled within the following three days. If additional evidence is required, there will be a ten-day probatory term. The judgment shall be issued after the hearing, and no ordinary challenge can be filed against the final judgment nor intra-procedural resolutions.

The final judgment, however, can be challenged through a constitutional trial, the *amparo* trial. There are two kinds of *amparo*: direct (once-instance, heard by a

---

competent judge shall be the one chosen by the claimant. In the case of legal entities, for the purposes of this section, their domicile shall be considered as the location of their administration."

47. The applicability of this Section is not uniformly accepted. Some practitioners and authors claim that other provisions of the Commercial Code different from Title IV, Chapter V, do not apply to arbitration.
48. 1a. CLXXIII/2011. International Commercial Arbitration. The Judge of the Seat Is Competent to Rule on the Setting Aside of the Arbitral Award (*ARBITRAJE COMERCIAL INTERNACIONAL. ES COMPETENTE EL JUEZ DEL LUGAR DONDE ÉSTE SE LLEVÓ A CABO PARA CONOCER DE LA NULIDAD DEL LAUDO ARBITRAL*).
49. Chapter X, of Title IV, Fifth Book, of the Commercial Code.
50. Published in the Federal Official Gazette (*Diario Oficial de la Federación*) on Jan. 27, 2011.
51. All these subsections referred to in section 1470 of the Commercial Code.
52. *See* Art. 1471 of the Commercial Code.

Collegiate Tribunal[53]), and indirect (two-instances, heard by a Federal Judge and then by the Collegiate Tribunal). The time difference in obtaining a final and binding judgment between these two kinds of *amparo* is considerable, and it could be argued that an *amparo indirecto* will last at least twice as the *amparo directo*.

With the inclusion of the Special Proceedings for Arbitration, many litigators and Courts considered that the applicable *amparo* against the Special Proceedings for Arbitration's final judgment was the direct one, and others considered that it was the indirect *amparo*. This debate arose in the First Chamber of the Mexican Supreme Court, which in 2019 issued a binding precedent stating that final judgments issued in the setting aside or recognition and enforcement of arbitral awards, must be challenged through indirect *amparo*.[54] This criterion is mandatory for all Courts.

Although the Special Proceedings for Arbitration is aimed to be an expeditious trial, in some cases it could be not as expeditious as it seems. This is due to different factors: (1) the Court's workload; (2) the incorporation of stages not specifically provided in the Special Proceedings for Arbitration (e.g., the claimant's chance to make a statement on the defense submissions, ancillary proceedings arising from procedural defenses like lack of representation, etc.); (3) delays in the evidentiary stage; and (4) *amparo* trials against intra-procedural resolutions,[55] etc.

[F] REMISSION TO ARBITRATION (*KOMPETENZ-KOMPETENZ*'S NEGATIVE EFFECT)

The history of the remission to arbitration in Mexico has two periods: pre-2011 Reform and post-2011 Reform.

[1] Remission to Arbitration Pre-2011 Reform

When Mexico embraced the UNCITRAL Model Law in 1993, Articles 1424 and 1432 of the Commercial Code incorporated Articles 8[56] and 16, respectively, of the UNCITRAL Model Law.

Article 1432 of the Commercial Code contains the *kompetenz-kompetenz* principle: the arbitral tribunal may rule on its own jurisdiction, including any objections regarding the existence or validity of the arbitration agreement. Under Article 1424, when a dispute containing an arbitration agreement is before a Court, the Court shall, upon a party's request, refer the parties to arbitration unless it finds that the agreement

53. In exceptional cases, it can be heard by the Mexican Supreme Court.
54. 1a./J. 87/2019 (10a.). *Arbitral Award. Against the Judgment Issued in the Special Proceeding for Its Setting Aside, or Its Recognition and Enforcement, The* AMPARO INDIRECTO *[Two Instances Constitutional Trial] Proceeding is Admissible* (*LAUDO ARBITRAL. EN CONTRA DE LA SENTENCIA EMITIDA EN EL JUICIO ESPECIAL EN QUE SE DILUCIDE SU NULIDAD, O BIEN, SU RECONOCIMIENTO Y EJECUCIÓN, PROCEDE EL JUICIO* DE AMPARO INDIRECTO).
55. The general rule is that indirect *amparos* cannot be filed against intra-procedural resolutions, but there are exceptions.
56. The requirement of requesting the remission to arbitration "no later than when submitting his first statement on the substance of the dispute" was not included.

is null and void, inoperative or incapable of being performed. This Article is also in line with Article II.3 of the New York Convention.

The question then arises, who will have the first shot to rule over the arbitration agreement's validity? In other words, by interpreting the above-mentioned articles, the Mexican Judiciary had to decide which approach of the negative effect of the *kompetenz-kompetnz* would adopt: the French (give the arbitral tribunal the first shot), or the American one (give it to the Courts).

In 2004, a Federal Collegiate Court found that the arbitral tribunal had the authority to hear in the first place over the validity of the arbitration agreement.[57] In contrast, in 2005, another Federal Collegiate Court ruled that when the nullity of the arbitration agreement is claimed, the first short to rule over the arbitration agreement's validity belongs to the Courts. A clear contradiction of criteria.[58]

The issue arrived at the Mexican Supreme Court's First Chamber, which, when ruling the criteria contradiction (*contradicción de tesis*) 51/2055-PS, concluded that when a dispute subject to an arbitration agreement is brought before a Court and the claimant is seeking the nullity of such arbitration agreement, then it is necessary that, before sending the parties to arbitration, the Court rules over the arbitration agreement's validity. This ruling constituted a binding precedent.[59]

[2] Remission to Arbitration Post-2011 Reform

The 2011 Reform left no room for doubt, and Mexico adopted the French approach to the *kompetenz-kompetenz* negative effect. Should a dispute subject to an arbitration agreement be brought before a National Court, the Court must refer the parties to arbitration.

Articles 1424 and 1432 of the Commercial Code remained the same,[60] but two new Articles 1464 and 1465 were added within a new chapter regulating judicial aid to arbitration. Similar to Article 1448[61] of the French Procedural Civil Code, when a party requests the remission to arbitration, the Court must immediately refer the parties to arbitration, unless the arbitration agreement: (1) has been voided through binding

57. Sixth Federal Court for Civil Matters of the First District, *revision* challenge 3836/2004.
58. Sixth Federal Court for Civil Matters of the First District, *revision* challenge 31/2005.
59. 1a./J. 25/2006. *Commercial Arbitration. The Competence to Rule on the Setting Aside of the Arbitration Agreement, as Provided in the First Paragraph of Article 1424 of the Commercial Code, Lies with the Judge and Not the Arbitral Tribunal.* (*ARBITRAJE COMERCIAL. COMPETENCIA PARA CONOCER DE LA ACCIÓN DE NULIDAD DEL ACUERDO DE ARBITRAJE PREVISTA EN EL PRIMER PÁRRAFO DEL ARTÍCULO 1424 DEL CÓDIGO DE COMERCIO, CORRESPONDE AL JUEZ Y NO AL TRIBUNAL ARBITRAL*).
60. Article 1424 of the Commercial Code was later amended on Jun. 6, 2022. A third paragraph was included: "Without prejudice to what is established in the first paragraph of this article, when a resident abroad has expressly submitted to arbitration and attempts individual or collective litigation, the judge will refer the parties to arbitration. If the judge denies the recognition of the arbitral award under the terms of article 1462 of this Code, the rights of the claimant to promote the appropriate action will be preserved."
61. When a dispute subject to an arbitration agreement is brought before a court, such court shall decline jurisdiction, except if an arbitral tribunal has not yet been seized of the dispute and if the arbitration agreement is manifestly void or manifestly not applicable.

judgment or arbitral award; or (2) it is manifestly null or impossible of being performed.[62] Interestingly, the Mexican *lex arbitri* did not adopt as an exception that the arbitral tribunal has not yet been appointed.

When a party seeks the remission to arbitration:[63] (1) the request must be done in the first submission on the merits;[64] (2) the Court shall hear the other party; (3) should the Court remit to arbitration, the judicial proceedings will be suspended; and (4) the Court's decision cannot be challenged through ordinary[65] means. Nevertheless, in some cases, this decision might be challenged through *amparo indirecto*.

[G] CONCLUSION

Mexico has a strong legal framework regulating the interaction between international arbitration and the judiciary. The Constitution specifically refers to the alternative dispute resolution mechanisms, and the Commercial Code incorporated the UNCITRAL Model Law with some improvements that many could consider pro-arbitration (e.g., the French approach of the *kompetenz-kompetenz's* negative effect).

The principle of non-judicial intervention has been expressly recognized, and the cases where the Courts must or may intervene are well identified in the Mexican *lex arbitri*. In general, judicial precedents have correctly interpreted the arbitration principles and legislation, establishing clear boundaries to the judicial aid or control to commercial arbitration.

---

62. Article 1464 of the Commercial Code states that: "When a party requests a remission to arbitration under the terms of Article 1424, the following shall be observed: I. The request must be made in the first pleading addressing the substance of the matter submitted by the applicant. II. The judge, after hearing the other parties, shall promptly rule on the matter. III. If the judge orders remission to arbitration, the judge shall also order the suspension of the proceedings. IV. Once the matter has been finally resolved in arbitration, at the request of any party, the judge shall terminate the legal proceeding. V. If the set aside of the arbitration agreement is resolved, the incompetence of the Arbitral Tribunal is established, or in any way the matter is not concluded, in whole or in part, through arbitration, at the request of any party and after a hearing with all interested parties, the suspension referred to in section III of this article shall be lifted. VI. There shall be no appeal against the resolution deciding on the remission to arbitration."
63. Article 1465 of the Commercial Code states that: "In cases referred to in the preceding article, the stay of judicial proceedings and remission to arbitration shall occur immediately. Remission to arbitration shall only be denied: a) If, during the hearing held with the request for remission to arbitration, it is demonstrated by means of a final resolution, whether in the form of a judgment or arbitral award, that the arbitration agreement was declared null and void; or b) If the nullity, ineffectiveness, or impossible execution of the arbitration agreement is evident from the hearing held with the request for referral to arbitration. In making this determination, the judge must adhere to a rigorous standard."
64. There is a non-binding precedent from the First Circuit stating that this request can be done at any time prior to the judgment. I.3o.C.425 C (10a.) *Remission to Arbitration. It May Be Requested at Any Stage of the Proceedings, up Until Before the Issuance of the Final Judgment (Scope of the Non-binding Legal Precedents I.3o.C.503 C AND I.3o.C.504 C)* (*REMISIÓN AL ARBITRAJE. PUEDE SOLICITARSE EN CUALQUIER ETAPA DEL PROCEDIMIENTO, HASTA ANTES DEL DICTADO DE LA SENTENCIA DEFINITIVA (ALCANCE DE LAS TESIS AISLADAS I.3o.C.503 C Y I.3o.C.504 C)*).
65. In some cases, this decision could be challenged through a two instances constitutional trial (*amparo indirecto*).

CHAPTER 10

Interim Measures under the Mexican *Lex Arbitri*

Víctor M. Ruiz & Andrea Orta

[A] INTRODUCTION

Mexico adopted the 1985 version of the UNCITRAL Model Law on International Commercial Arbitration (UNCITRAL Model Law) in 1993 by adding a new section to its, by then, hundred-year-old Code of Commerce. While the rationale behind the addition of *Titulo Cuarto* was to provide Mexico with a legal framework that catered to the requirements of international trade,[1] the adoption of the Model Law was, in fact, required by the U.S. and Canadian governments as a condition to enter into the NAFTA, to afford their constituents a neutral forum to resolve their business disputes in connection with their investments in Mexico.[2]

Like many jurisdictions at the time, Mexico adopted the Model Law almost in its entirety and is the *lex arbitri* in domestic and international arbitrations seated within Mexican territory since July 23, 1993. Aside from including provisions that allowed the adaptation of the Model Law to the Mexican legal framework, the only significant changes to the original 1985 text, were those introduced by the Mexican Congress to Articles 10[3] and 28.3[4] of the Model Law, which deals with the number of arbitrators and the determination of the applicable law, in lieu of an agreement of the parties.

1. Opinion of the legislative process of the amendment to the Commerce Code, Legislative Decree for the amendment of the Commerce Code (1993).
2. Otherwise, Mexico ratified both the 1958 New York Convention (1971), and the 1975 Panama Convention (1978).
3. Article 10 of the Model Law: "(1) The parties are free to determine the number of arbitrators. (2) Failing such determination, the number of arbitrators shall be three."
4. Article 28.3 of the Model Law: "... Failing any designation by the parties [of the applicable law], the arbitral tribunal shall apply the law determined by the conflict of laws rules which it considers applicable. ...."

According to Articles 1426 and 1445 of the Code of Commerce, the parties are free to choose the number of arbitrators and the law that shall be applied to the merits of the dispute, respectively; however, in the absence of an agreement by the parties in both scenarios: (1) the case shall be decided by a sole arbitrator—instead of a three-member tribunal; and (2) the arbitrator or arbitrators shall determine the applicable law considering the characteristics and relevant connections of the case—as opposed to following a set of conflict of law rules for such purpose.[5]

Otherwise, Mexico adhered to the *compétênce-compétênce* and *separability* doctrines fostered by the UNCITRAL Model Law in Article 1432 of the Code of Commerce. Likewise, Mexico adopted Article 17 of the UNCITRAL Model Law[6] *verbatim* in Article 1433 of the Code of Commerce,[7] with respect to the power of arbitral tribunal to adopt interim measures.

While the UNCITRAL Model Law was amended in 2006 to clarify that the tribunal's power to adopt provisional measures included temporary order aimed at: (1) maintaining or restoring the status quo; (2) causing a party to take action to prevent, or refrain from taking action likely to cause harm to the proceedings; (3) preserving assets to satisfy an award and/or evidence considered relevant and material to the outcome of the dispute,[8] as well as other important provisions related to the (4) standards required for the adoption of interim measures;[9] (5) adoption of preliminary orders;[10] and (6) enforcement of interim measures adopted by arbitral tribunals,[11] Mexico did not amend its *lex arbitri* to reflect these changes.

---

5. Otherwise, Mexico added Arts. 1452 to 1456 to the Code of Commerce with respect to the costs of arbitration (arbitrators' fees and expenses and other legal costs), basically following the provisions set out in the 1976 UNCITRAL Arbitration Rules (Arts. 38 to 40).
6. Article 17 of the Model Law: "Unless otherwise agreed by the parties, the arbitral tribunal may, at the request of a party, order any party to take such interim measure of protection as the arbitral tribunal may consider necessary in respect of the subject matter of the dispute. The arbitral tribunal may require a party to provide appropriate security in connection with such measure."
7. Article 1433 of the Code of Commerce: "Unless otherwise agreed by the parties, the arbitral tribunal may, at the request of one of them, order the taking of the necessary precautionary measures in respect of the subject matter of the dispute. The arbitral tribunal may require sufficient security from any party in connection with such measures."
8. Article 17 (Power of arbitral tribunal to order interim measures) of the Model Law states:

   (1) Unless otherwise agreed by the parties, the arbitral tribunal may, at the request of a party, grant interim measures.
   (2) An interim measure is any temporary measure, whether in the form of an award or in another form, by which, at any time prior to the issuance of the award by which the dispute is finally decided, the arbitral tribunal orders a party to:
      (a) maintain or restore the status quo pending determination of the dispute;
      (b) take action that would prevent, or refrain from taking action that is likely to cause, current or imminent harm or prejudice to the arbitral process itself;
      (c) provide a means of preserving assets out of which a subsequent award may be satisfied; or
      (d) preserve evidence that may be relevant and material to the resolution of the dispute.

9. Article 17 A (Conditions for granting interim measures) of the Model Law.
10. Article 17 B (Applications for preliminary orders and conditions for granting preliminary orders) and Art. 17 C (Specific regime for preliminary orders) of the Model Law.
11. Article 17 H (Recognition and enforcement) of the Model Law.

[B] INTERIM MEASURES IN ARBITRATION

[1] Interim Measures Granted by States Courts

Mexican *lex arbitri* is incorporated in the Commerce Code[12] and it is applicable only if the seat of arbitration is Mexico. However, Mexican *lex arbitri* will also apply in cases where the arbitration is seated elsewhere (i.e., in a different jurisdiction),[13] and: (1) court intervention whenever an action is brought in a case which is subject to an arbitration agreement;[14] (2) interim measures;[15] and (3) enforcement and recognition of awards.[16]

In line with the Model Law,[17] Article 1421 of the Mexican *lex arbitri* recognizes the international principle of no court intervention, except in the matters provided by the law.[18] A Mexican court can only intervene in the cases foreseen in the *lex arbitri*, one of these cases is related to interim measure. Where a court intervention is required, the competent court to perform functions of arbitration assistance is the first-instance court at the federal or local level.[19]

Arbitration is designed so that courts have minimal involvement. However, such intervention is necessary given that arbitrators lack the imperium to enforce their decisions, which leads to the need for judicial assistance in arbitration matters. A court's intervention may be requested for the adoption of interim measures in aid of arbitration. Although arbitrators themselves have the power to grant interim measures, Article 1425 of the Mexican *lex arbitri* provides that interim measures can be requested by state courts. This provision establishes that interim measures can be requested even before the commencement of the arbitral proceedings or during the proceedings.

[a] Types of Interim Measures That Can Be Granted by States Courts

Interim measures that can be granted as part of the assistance in arbitration matters are not the same measures issued in commercial procedures.

12. Specifically Mexican *lex arbitri* is contained in Title IV of Book Five of the Commerce Code.
13. Article 1415 of the Commerce Code.
14. Article 1424 of the Commerce Code.
15. Article 1425 of the Commerce Code.
16. Articles 1461, 1462 and 1463 of the Commerce Code.
17. Article 5 of the Model Law states: "In matters governed by this Law, no court shall intervene except where so provided in this Law."
18. Article 1421 of the Commerce Code states: "Unless otherwise provided, in the matters governed by this section, no judicial intervention will be required."
19. Article 1422 of the Commerce Codes states: "When judicial intervention is required, the judge of the first federal instance or of the common order of the place where the arbitration takes place shall be competent to hear the case. When the place of arbitration is outside the national territory, the judge of the first federal instance or of the common order of the domicile of the defendant or, in the absence thereof, the judge of the location of the assets, shall be competent to hear the recognition and enforcement of the award."

Article 1425 of the Mexican *lex arbitri* provides that interim measures can be requested to state courts and Article 1478[20] provides that courts have full discretion whenever adopting interim measures. Nonetheless, Mexican *lex arbitri* does not clarify what is to be understood by interim measures or what types of interim measures can be granted.

Article 1168 of the Commerce Code[21] foresees that in a commercial proceeding, only the following precautionary measures may be granted: (1) placement of a person in custody; and (2) withholding of assets. However, the First Chamber of the Mexican Supreme Court of Justice, through a binding criterion,[22] established that precautionary measures of security foreseen in Articles 384 to 388[23] of the Federal Code of Civil Procedures[24] are also applicable to commercial matters.

In this regard, the Mexican Supreme Court of Justice has issued a criterion recognizing that the arbitration regulation contained in the Mexican *lex arbitri* is a complete regulation.[25] Furthermore, the Seventh Collegiate Court in Civil Matters of the

20. Article 1478 of the Commerce Code states: "The judge shall enjoy full discretion in the adoption of interim measures referred to in Article 1425."
21. Article 1168 of the Commerce Code states:

> In commercial proceedings only the precautionary measures or precautionary measures provided for in this Code may be ordered, which are the following:
>
> I. Placement of a person in custody, when there is a well-founded fear that the person against whom a suit is to be brought or has been brought is absent or concealed. Such a measure shall have only the effects provided for in Article 1173 of this Code;
> II. Withholding of property, in any of the following cases:
> (a) Where there is a well-founded fear that the property pledged as security or in respect of which an action in rem is to be brought will be disposed of, concealed, dilapidated, disposed of or insufficient, and
> (b) in the case of personal actions, provided that the person against whom the action is brought has no property other than that on which the proceeding is to be conducted, and there is a well-founded fear that he will dispose of, conceal, dilapidate or dispose of it. In the cases referred to in this section, if the property consists of cash or money on deposit in credit institutions, or other fungible property, it shall be presumed, for the purposes of this Article, that there is a risk that it will be disposed of, concealed or squandered, unless the person affected by the measure guarantees the amount of the debt. In the case of the withholding of property whose title or ownership is subject to registration in any public registry, the judge shall order that the annotation be made thereon.

22. Tesis: 1a./J. 27/2013 (10a.), *PRECAUTIONARY MEASURES IN COMMERCIAL MATTERS. WHEN THE REQUEST FOR THE MEASURE IS NOT BASED ON THE CASES PROVIDED FOR IN ARTICLE 1168 OF THE COMMERCE CODE, THE RESTRICTION CONTAINED IN ARTICLE 1171 OF THE SAME LAW TO ISSUE THEM, DOES NOT PREVENT THE SUPPLEMENTARY APPLICATION OF THE SECURITY MEASURES PROVIDED FOR IN NUMERALS 384 TO 388 OF THE FEDERAL CODE OF CIVIL PROCEDURES (PARTIAL ABANDONMENT OF THE TESIS 1a. LXXIX/2007 and 1a. LXXXI/2007)* [2013] Federal Weekly Judiciary Gazette, 552.
23. Articles 417 to 423 of the National Code of Civil and Family Proceedings govern the measures of security.
24. The Federal Code of Civil Procedure was abrogated by decree published in the Official Gazette of the Federation on Jun. 7, 2023. Pursuant to the Third Transitory Article, the Federal Code of Civil Procedure was abrogated, as well as the civil and family procedural legislation of the States.
25. Tesis 1a. CLXX/2009, *COMMERCIAL ARBITRATION. RELEVANT ASPECTS AND PRINCIPLES GOVERNING TITLE FOUR OF BOOK FIVE OF THE CODE OF COMMERCE* [2009] Federal Weekly Judiciary Gazette, 427.

First Circuit established that the rules applicable to arbitration are specialized and exclude general rules of the Commerce Code.[26] Hence, provisions on precautionary measures for commercial matters do not apply supplementarily in arbitration.

Moreover, there is an express rule in the Mexican *lex arbitri* that grants the court full discretion in the adoption of interim measures in support of arbitration. This specific rule is contained in Article 1478 of the Commerce Code and trumps the application of the general provision set forth in Article 1168 of the Commerce Code.

The Fourth Collegiate Court in Civil Matters of the First Circuit has held a criterion sustaining that courts have full discretion in granting interim measures in assistance of arbitration but in no way this broad discretion can be interpreted as a *carte blanche* for the judge to subjectively decide whatever but that the judge "must be subject to standards of rationality and coherence, in accordance with the prevailing system of sources, the main rules of logic, experience and proportionality, constant in the decision, through a discourse of justification presented under the same parameters, which serve as a counterbalance to the excess of that discretionary power."[27]

In support of a court's broad discretion to adopt provisional measures in aid of arbitration, it should first be noted that Mexico recognizes the right to access alternative dispute resolution mechanisms,[28] and judges are to abide by the will of the parties to resort to them;[29] accordingly, any interim measure ordered by a state court must be in support of arbitration and thus cannot be aimed at preventing the parties from being afforded their right to resolve their disputes in arbitration or otherwise from interfering and/or hindering its development.

The Amparo on review 2160/2019 of the First Chamber of the Supreme Court of Justice of the Nation, established the idea of arbitration in Mexico by determining that the will of the parties is the substantial expression that admits the jurisdiction of the Arbitral Tribunal and demonstrates its intention to dispense with states courts.[30]

---

26. Tesis I.7o.C.150 C, *COMMERCIAL ARBITRATION. ITS LEGISLATION IS SPECIALIZED AND THEREFORE, EXCLUSIVE OF GENERAL RULES* [2010] Federal Weekly Judiciary Gazette, 1734.
27. Tesis: I.4o.C.34 C (10a.), *PROCEDURE FOR THE JUDICIAL ADOPTION OF INTERIM MEASURES RELATED TO ARBITRATION. IS SUBJECT TO THE BROAD DISCRETION OF THE JUDGE.* [2016] Federal Weekly Judiciary Gazette, 2878.
28. Tesis: I.3o.C.427 C (10a.) *ALTERNATIVE DISPUTE RESOLUTION MECHANISMS IN CIVIL MATTERS. IF A PARTY DOES NOT RESORT TO THEM IN SPITE OF HAVING BEEN NOTIFIED OF THEIR INITIATION, THIS DOES NOT INITIATION, THIS DOES NOT MEAN THE LOSS OF THE RIGHT TO RESORT TO FORMAL JUSTICE,* [2020] Federal Weekly Judiciary Gazette, 2607.

    Tesis: I.3o.C.426 C (10a.), *ALTERNATIVE DISPUTE RESOLUTION MECHANISMS IN CONSUMER PROTECTION MATTERS. IF THE PARTIES AGREE THAT THEY MUST BE EXHAUSTED BEFORE GOING TO THE BEFORE GOING TO THE COMPETENT COURTS, THE AGREEMENT OF WILLS MUST PREVAIL.* [2020] Federal Weekly Judiciary Gazette, 2608.
29. Tesis: I.3o.C.6 CS (11a.), *ALTERNATIVE MEANS OF DISPUTE RESOLUTION. IN ACCORDANCE WITH ARTICLE 17 OF THE GENERAL CONSTITUTION, THE WILL OF THE PARTIES TO RESORT TO THEM MUST BE PRIVILEGED, WITHOUT TO RESORT TO THEM, WITHOUT THIS IMPLYING THE WAIVER OF THE STATE'S JURISDICTION,* [2023] Federal Weekly Judiciary Gazette, 3918.

    Tesis: I.3o.C.81 C (11a.), *MENTAL SUFFERING. IS NOT CONFIGURED WITHIN A JURISDICTIONAL PROCEEDING, DUE TO THE FACT THAT THE PARTIES HAVE NOT REACHED A SATISFACTORY AGREEMENT THROUGH THE USE OF ALTERNATIVE MEANS OF DISPUTE RESOLUTION,* [2023] Federal Weekly Judiciary Gazette, 3839.
30. Amparo on review 2160/2009, 2160/2019 of the First Chamber of the Supreme Court of Justice of the Nation, Sep. 8, 2010, Unanimity of four votes.

However, some judges have incorrectly interpreted the *compétènce-compétènce* principle established in Article 1432 of the Code of Commerce due to an unfortunate precedent of the Mexican Supreme Court that has been displaced by 2011 amendments to the *lex arbitri* that empowered state courts to adjudicate a case albeit an arbitration clause, ineffectiveness, or unenforceability of an arbitration agreement and under that incorrect interpretation some judges have suppressed the arbitrator in his powers conferred by the parties.[31]

Finally, the arbitral system contains the checks and balances necessary to achieve its effectiveness, but for the arbitral system to function, such understanding and respect must come with special emphasis from the judges. In that sense, any interim measures granted by Mexican state courts in assistance to the arbitration must be aimed at preserving the object of the arbitration or the evidence of the proceeding that is essential for the resolution of the dispute but may not be aimed at interrupting the arbitration proceedings.

As Mexican *lex arbitri* should be understood as an independent law, it should be understood that the judge has no limitation when granting interim measures in assistance to arbitration.

[2] Substantive Requirements for the Adoption of Interim Measures

Like most arbitration laws and rules, the Mexican *lex arbitri* does not specify the standards that must be applied by arbitral tribunals to order interim measures. To determine these standards, arbitrators in Mexico generally look at international arbitration practice, the law of the place of arbitration and scholarly writings. Some commentators suggest that absent an agreement by the parties, arbitrators are also likely to turn to the Model Law as revised in 2006, for guidance.[32]

In this regard, it is generally accepted that a party applying for emergency measures must show that the measures requested are urgent and that substantial harm is likely to occur if such measures are not immediately granted—*periculum in mora*—that such harm substantially outweighs the harm that is likely to result to the party against whom the measure is directed, if the measure is granted—*balance of interests*—and that there is a reasonable possibility that the requesting party may succeed on the merits—*fumus boni iuris*.[33]

In addition to the above standards, some scholars and practitioners suggest that in granting urgent relief the arbitrator must not be required to pre-judge the merits of

31. Tesis: 1a./J. 25/2006, *COMMERCIAL ARBITRATION. JURISDICTION TO HEAR THE ACTION FOR NULLITY OF THE ARBITRATION AGREEMENT PROVIDED FOR IN THE FIRST PARAGRAPH OF ARTICLE 1424 OF THE COMMERCIAL CODE, CORRESPONDS TO THE JUDGE AND NOT TO THE ARBITRAL TRIBUNAL, [2005]* Federal Weekly Judiciary Gazette, 1416.
32. N. Voser and C. Boog. *ICC Emergency Arbitrator Proceedings: An Overview*, in *Interim, Conservatory and Emergency Measures in ICC Arbitration*, ICC International Court of Arbitration Bulletin, Special Supplement 81 (2011).
33. B. Ehle. *Emergency Arbitration in Practice*, in *New Developments in International Commercial Arbitration 2013* 96 (2013).

the dispute between the parties.[34] In fact, in ICC Case No. 12040, the Arbitral Tribunal noted that there is a trend in ICC arbitral practice according to which the following standards have to be met for the granting of interim relief: no pre-judgment of a case, urgency and irreparable or substantial harm.[35]

The revisions to the UNCITRAL Model Law (2006) and Arbitration Rules (2010) followed a somewhat similar approach. While they do not make any reference to urgency as a pre-requisite for granting interim relief, they do require a showing that harm is likely to result that cannot be adequately reparable by a damages award if the relief is not granted (*periculum in mora*), that such harm outweighs the harm likely to result to the respondent if the order is granted (*balance of interests*) and that there is a reasonable possibility that the applicant will succeed on the merits of the relevant claim (*fumus boni iuris*).

[a] *Urgency* (Periculum in Mora)

The standard of *urgency* is sometimes (rightly) held to be included within the much broader standard of *periculum in mora*—if there is no danger in the delay there is obviously no urgency. While many courts and tribunals have laid down several definitions, an Arbitral Tribunal acting under the ICC Rules set forth the classic formulation that defined urgency as arising where there is "a risk of serious and irreparable harm, present or future...that would render indispensable the taking of an immediate decision such as to eliminate, avoid or reduce such harm."[36]

In the same vein, another ICC Tribunal held that "a situation has an urgent character when it requires that measure be taken in order to avoid that the legitimate rights of a party are not placed in peril."[37]

Urgency is one of the most well-established requirements for granting interim relief. However, it must not be interpreted literally to require that an arbitral tribunal establish serious damage in the near future. Instead, it must be analyzed on a case-by-case basis and within the context of the dispute between the parties.[38] In a case

34. In accordance with the Arbitral Tribunal in ICC case 13194 indicated that "a party seeking interim relief must demonstrate urgency and that irreparable harm and *that no pre-judgment of the merits of the dispute is involved in order to warrant relief* before a final award is granted" in A. Yelşilirmak, *Interim and Conservatory Measures in ICC Arbitral Practice, 1999-2008,* in *Interim, Conservatory and Emergency Measures in ICC Arbitration*, ICC International Court of Arbitration Bulletin, Special Supplement (2011).
35. A. Yelşilirmak, *Interim and Conservatory Measures in ICC Arbitral Practice, 1999-2008, in Interim, Conservatory and Emergency Measures in ICC Arbitration*, ICC International Court of Arbitration Bulletin, Special Supplement (2011).
36. E. Schwartz, *The Practices and Experience of the ICC Court,* in International Chamber of Commerce, *Conservatory and Provisional Measures in Arbitration,* ICC International Court of Arbitration Bulletin 60 (1993).
37. *Ibid.*
38. O. Rydén, *On the Legal Frameworks and Substantive Standards Governing the Granting of Interim Measures in International Commercial Arbitration*, LLM Thesis, Faculty of Law, Lund University (Fall 2011).

such as this one, where the parties have ongoing obligations vis-à-vis each other, the severity of the breaches of contract by one of the parties naturally increases with time, making urgency a reality. Accordingly, international arbitration practice has turned to a broader definition of the standard that is more aptly for international business relations, such as the one proposed by the Arbitral Tribunal in ICC Case No. 10596 which held that in order to prove that the measures requested are urgent—and cannot await the constitution of the Arbitral Tribunal—it was sufficient to establish that "a party's potential losses are likely to increase with the mere passing of time and that it would be unreasonable to expect a party to wait for the final award ..." for interim relief to be granted.[39]

In fact, most decisions which state that the damage must be irreparable in the end, only require that there be a material risk of serious damage to the applicant in order to grant the measures requested.[40] Following this approach, learned commentators have also noted that there is a tendency to consider that the standard of *urgency* also justifies interim measures designed to avoid the aggravation of the dispute that is the subject of the arbitration and not so much as to prevent irreparable harm from occurring.[41]

[b] Balance of Interests

The balance of interest or balance of equities theory translates into the idea that the adoption of an interim measure should not cause prejudice that would be more significant or serious than the prejudice that the interim measure aims to prevent.

This theory has been held to be implicit in the proper application of the standard of *periculum in mora* as the urgency to prevent a prejudice cannot be properly considered if the requested measure would cause equal or greater prejudice.

In applying the balance of interest theory, for interim measures to be granted, the applicant must satisfactorily establish that the harm caused to it if the requested measures are not granted substantially outweighs the harm that is likely to result to the party against whom the measures are requested. In this regard, Arbitral Tribunals have been prone to order interim measures if the requesting party shows a possibility of harm and the respondent is unlikely to suffer damage because of the measure, especially when the respondent's actions appear destructive with regard to the parties' relationship or dispute.[42]

39. Award in ICC Case 10596 (unpublished). Referred to in A. Yelşilirmak, *Provisional Measures in International Commercial Arbitration* (Kluwer Law International, 2005) 179.
40. G. Born, *International Arbitration: Law and Practice* (Kluwer Law International, 2012) 207.
41. E. Schwartz, *The Practices and Experience of the ICC Court,* in International Chamber of Commerce, *Conservatory and Provisional Measures in Arbitration* (1993) ICC International Court of Arbitration Bulletin 61.
42. O. Rydén, *On the Legal Frameworks and Substantive Standards Governing the Granting of Interim Measures in International Commercial Arbitration*, LLM Thesis, Faculty of Law, Lund University (Fall 2011).

[c] *No Pre-judgment of the Merits*

In the process of granting interim measures, the arbitrators must not prejudge the merits of the dispute between the parties. Otherwise, to the extent that the measures requested require the arbitrator to consider the merits of the dispute, the arbitrator must refrain from granting the requested relief.

[d] **Fumus Boni Iuris** *(Prima Facie Case on the Merits)*

To grant interim or conservatory measures, the standard of *fumus boni iuris* requires that the applicant establish a sufficient likelihood that it will prevail on the merits. The rationale behind this standard is to ensure that the requesting party actually has a right that is justified to protect by way of interim relief, or that the request is not merely frivolous. However, to the extent that this condition may be inconsistent with the requirement that forbids an arbitrator to prejudge the merits of the case, this standard can only be properly applied through a prima facie analysis. In this regard, Gary Born has suggested that establishing a prima facie case does not prejudge the merits as it is an inherently provisional assessment that is subject to review.

[3] Recognition of Interim Measures Granted by Arbitral Tribunals

In relation to interim measures granted by the arbitral tribunal, as noted previously, Mexico departed from the text of the Model Law but did establish the power of the arbitral tribunal to grant interim measures[43] and the obligation to recognize any interim measure granted by an arbitral tribunal and to enforce such measure.[44]

Article 1479 of the Commerce Code recognizes that any interim measure granted by an arbitral tribunal must be recognized as binding and that the interim measure must be enforced upon request. In the event that an interim measure granted by the arbitral tribunal is not voluntarily complied with, a judge may be seized. As mentioned above, the assistance of a judge is required since the arbitrator lacks imperium and has no power to enforce the interim measures they granted.

43. Article 1433 of the Code of Commerce.
44. Article 1479 of the Commerce Code states:

> Any interim measure of protection ordered by an Arbitral Tribunal shall be recognized as binding and, unless otherwise ordered by the Arbitral Tribunal, shall be enforced upon application for such enforcement before the competent court, irrespective of the state in which it was ordered, and subject to the provisions of Article 1480.
>
> The party seeking or having obtained recognition or enforcement of an interim measure shall promptly inform the judge of any revocation, suspension or modification of that measure.
>
> The judge before whom recognition or enforcement of an interim measure is sought may, if he considers it appropriate, require the requesting party to provide adequate security, where the Arbitral Tribunal has not yet ruled on such security or where such security is necessary to protect the rights of third parties.

The party that has requested and obtained recognition or enforcement of the interim measure granted by the arbitral tribunal must inform the judge when the interim measure has been revoked, suspended, or modified. Likewise, in the case of an application for recognition or enforcement of an interim measure, the judge may require the applicant to provide security.

Following the Model Law,[45] Article 1480 of the Commerce Code foresees the grounds for refusing recognition and enforcement of an interim measure granted by an arbitral tribunal. Recognition and enforcement of an interim measure granted by an arbitral tribunal may be refused only: (a) upon request by a party, the court is satisfied that (1) the refusal is warranted on any of the grounds set forth in subsections (a), (b), (c), or (d) of section I of Article 1462 which refers to the ground for refusing recognition or enforcement of the award,[46] (2) the arbitral tribunal's decision regarding the provision of security in connection to the interim measure granted by the arbitral tribunal has not been complied with, and (3) the interim measure has been revoked or suspended by the arbitral tribunal or by a state court, whenever the court is empowered to do so; or (b) the judge determines that (1) the interim measure is incompatible with the powers conferred to the judge, (2) one of the grounds for refusal set forth in section II of Article 1462[47] applies to the recognition or enforcement of the interim measure.[48]

45. Article 17 H (Recognition and enforcement) of the Model Law.
46. Article 1462 of the Commerce Code states:

> The recognition or enforcement of an arbitral award, irrespective of the country in which it was made, may be refused only when:
>
> I. – The party against whom the award is invoked proves before the competent judge of the country where recognition or enforcement is sought that:
> (a) A party to the arbitration agreement was under some incapacity, or that the arbitration agreement is invalid under the law to which the parties have subjected it, or, if nothing has been commenced in this respect, under the law of the country where the award was made;
> (b) Was not given proper notice of the appointment of an arbitrator or of the arbitral proceedings, or was otherwise unable to assert his or her rights;
> (c) The award deals with a dispute not contemplated by the arbitration agreement or contains decisions that exceed the terms of the arbitration agreement. However, if the provisions of the award which relate to matters submitted to arbitration can be separated from those which are not, the former may be recognized and enforced;
> (d) The composition of the arbitral tribunal or the arbitral proceedings were not in accordance with the parties' agreement or, in the absence of such an agreement, were not in accordance with the law of the country where the arbitration took place; or
> (e) The award is not yet binding on the parties or has been set aside or suspended by the judge of the country in which, or under the law of which, the award was made; or
>
> II. – The judge proves that, under Mexican law, the subject matter of the dispute is not arbitrable; or that the recognition or enforcement of the award is contrary to public policy.

47. *Ibid.*
48. Article 1480 of the Commerce Code states:

> Recognition or enforcement of an interim measure may be refused only:

Pursuant to Article 1480 of the Commerce Code: (1) when a judge intervenes with respect to interim measures in arbitration assistance, the judge cannot review the content of the interim measure granted by the arbitral tribunal; and (2) the party requesting the interim measure is responsible for the interim measure, as well as the arbitral tribunal that issues it, and therefore any damages caused are their responsibility.[49]

[4] Requirements to Grant an Interim Measure

It can be considered that the degree of substantiation and motivation in the granting of interim measures by a judge and an arbitrator are similar, but not the same. According to the Mexican *Lex Arbitri*, the Arbitrator at the moment of granting an interim measure is responsible for the effects it may have, unlike those issued by a judge.[50]

Derived from this, although the arbitrator is not obliged to give reasons and grounds for his decisions,[51] in the case of precautionary measures, the arbitrator must be very careful with the reasons for granting them, that is to say, he must justify the granting of such measures to the parties in a correctly.

I. At the request of the party against whom it is invoked if the judge is satisfied that:
   a) Such refusal is warranted on the grounds set forth in subsection a), b), c) or d) of section I of Article 1462, or
   b) The arbitral tribunal's decision with respect to the provision of security in connection with the interim measure issued by the arbitral tribunal has not been complied with, or
   c) The interim measure has been revoked or suspended by the arbitral tribunal or, where so empowered, by the court of the State in which the arbitration takes place or under the law of which that interim measure was granted, or

II If the judge finds that:
   a) The interim measure is incompatible with the powers conferred upon the judge unless the judge decides to reformulate the interim measure to adjust to its own powers and procedures for the purposes of enforcing that interim measure without modifying its substance, or
   b) Any of the grounds set forth in section II of Article 1462 is applicable to recognition and enforcement of the interim measure.

Any determination made by the judge with respect to any ground set forth in section I of this article shall apply only for the purposes of the application for recognition and enforcement of the interim measure. The judge to whom recognition or enforcement is sought may not, in the exercise of that duty, undertake a review of the content of the interim measure.

The party requesting the interim measure is liable for all interim measures, as well as the Arbitral Tribunal that issues it, and therefore the damages caused shall be borne by them.

49. The obligation of the arbitral tribunal to respond for damages caused by the issuance of an interim measure was a modification incorporated into the Commerce Code in the amendment published in the Official Gazette of the Federation on Jan. 27, 2011.
50. Article 1480 of the Commerce Code states: "... The party requesting the interim measure is liable for all interim measures, as well as the Arbitral Tribunal that issues it, and therefore the damages caused shall be borne by them."
51. Amparo on review 7790/202019 of the First Chamber of the Supreme Court of Justice of the Nation, Aug. 5, 2020, Unanimity of four votes.

Article 17(G) of the Model Law[52] imposes the liability for any costs and damages caused by the measure or the order requested and empowers the Arbitral Tribunal to award such costs and damages, however under the Mexican *Lex Arbitri* the liability is shared between the party who requested the interim measure and the Arbitral Tribunal who granted,[53] thus generating a well-founded fear in arbitrators at the time of granting interim measures. At this time, there is no known judgment imposing liability on an arbitrator for the granting of an interim measure, although Article 1480 of the Commerce Code states there is a tangible possibility.

Specifically, Article 17(a) of the Model Law establishes[54] the requirements that the Arbitral Tribunal has to satisfy at the moment of granting an interim measure: (1) a balance of convenience; and (2) an interim measure being a reasonable possibility, although the Mexican *Lex Arbitri* does not establish any requirements and consequently can be interpreted that the Arbitral Tribunal has to follow the same rule of the Article 1478 explained above.

It is preferable that in the absence of requirements for the granting of interim measures, the arbitrators under the Mexican *Lex Arbitri*, to avoid any affectation by a liability action satisfy the requirement of: (1) a balance of convenience; (2) appearance of good faith (*fumus boni iuris*); and (3) the danger of delay and urgency (*periculum in mora*) as a criterion of reasonableness.

52. Article 17 G of the Model Law:

> Costs and damages The party requesting an interim measure or applying for a preliminary order shall be liable for any costs and damages caused by the measure or the order to any party if the arbitral tribunal later determines that, in the circumstances, the measure or the order should not have been granted. The arbitral tribunal may award such costs and damages at any point during the proceedings.

53. Article 1480 of the Commerce Code states:

> The party requesting the interim measure is liable for all interim measures, as well as the Arbitral Tribunal that issues it, and therefore the damages caused shall be borne by them.

54. Article 17 A. Conditions for granting interim measures:

> The party requesting an interim measure under article 17(2)(a), (b) and (c) shall satisfy the arbitral tribunal that:
>
> (a) Harm not adequately reparable by an award of damages is likely to result if the measure is not ordered, and such harm substantially outweighs the harm that is likely to result to the party against whom the measure is directed if the measure is granted; and
> (b) There is a reasonable possibility that the requesting party will succeed on the merits of the claim. The determination on this possibility shall not affect the discretion of the arbitral tribunal in making any subsequent determination.
>
> (2) With regard to a request for an interim measure under article 17(2)(d), the requirements in paragraphs (1)(a) and (b) of this article shall apply only to the extent the arbitral tribunal considers appropriate.

[5] Proceedings Relating to Interim Measures

The Commerce Code provides for the possibility that interim measures may be granted directly by the arbitral tribunal or by the judge.

Pursuant to the provisions of sections III and IV of Article 1470 of the Commerce Code,[55] both the adoption of interim measures by a judge and the recognition and enforcement of interim measures ordered by an arbitral tribunal are processed in accordance with a special procedure set forth in Articles 1472 to 1476.[56]

The procedure for adopting interim measures issued by a court in assistance of arbitration and the recognition and enforcement of interim measures granted by the arbitral tribunal are subject to a special procedure[57] consisting of the following stages. First, with the lawsuit filed, the judge orders the defendant to be summoned. The defendant has fifteen days to answer the complaint.[58] If no evidence is presented or if the judge does not consider that it is necessary, a hearing will be held within three days to hear the pleadings.[59] If evidence has been presented, there will be an evidentiary period of ten days.[60] Once the plea hearing has been held, the judge will summon to sentence.[61]

---

55. Article 1470 of the Commerce Code states:

    They shall be processed in accordance with the procedure set forth in Arts 1472 to 1476:

    I. The decision on the challenge of an arbitrator referred to in the third paragraph of section 1429.
    II. The decision on the jurisdiction of the Arbitral Tribunal, when it is determined in a decision which is not an award on the merits of the case, as provided for in section 1432, third paragraph.
    III. The adoption of the interim measures referred to in Article 1425.
    IV. The recognition and enforcement of interim measures ordered by an Arbitral Tribunal.
    V. The nullity of commercial transactions and arbitral awards.

56. These articles are contained in Chapter X (On Judicial Intervention in Commercial Transactions and Arbitration) of Title Four (Commercial Arbitration) of Book V (Commercial Lawsuits) of the Commerce Code.
57. Article 1472 of the Commerce Code states: "The special procedure on commercial transactions and arbitration, referred to in Arts. 1470 and 1471, shall be processed in accordance with the following articles."
58. Article 1473 of the Commerce Code states: "Once the lawsuit is admitted, the judge shall order the defendants to be summoned, giving them fifteen days to answer."
59. Article 1474 of the Commerce Code states: "Once the term to answer the claim has elapsed, without the need for a default notice, if the parties do not present evidence and the judge does not deem it necessary, a hearing will be held within the following three days, which will take place whether or not the parties attend."
60. Article 1475 of the Commerce Code states: "If evidence is offered or the judge deems it necessary prior to the holding of the hearing, a ten-day evidentiary delay shall be opened."
61. Article 1476 of the Commerce Code states: "Once the hearing has been held, the judge shall summon the parties to hear the judgment. The intermediate resolutions dictated in this special trial and the sentence that resolves it will not be appealable."

Unlike what happens in other types of proceedings,[62] in the case of a request for interim measures to a judge in arbitration assistance, there are no ex parte interim measures. This is contrary to other proceedings in which there is an application for interim measures in which, according to case law,[63] is understood not to constitute a privative act and therefore the guarantee of prior hearing does not apply, so that in those proceedings there are ex parte interim measures.

In terms of Article 1473 of the Commerce Code, the opposing party must be summoned so that it can submit its response. After analyzing the request and the corresponding response, the judge will determine whether or not to grant the requested interim measure or to recognize and enforce the interim measures granted by the arbitral tribunal. The fact that there are no ex parte interim measures has been widely debated and, in some cases, criticized because it is not advantageous in comparison with other proceedings in which interim measures are granted ex parte.

In relation to the rules regarding the interim measures, in an isolated criterion,[64] the Second Collegiate Court in Civil Matters of the Third Circuit identified that there is a normative antinomy because for this court there are two groups of provisions. On the one hand, Articles 1470 to 1476 of the Commerce Code require that for the recognition and enforcement of interim measures granted by the arbitral tribunal, a trial procedure must be followed and, on the other hand, Articles 1470 and 1480 of the Commerce Code indicate that the interim measures granted by an arbitral tribunal is binding and must be enforced when the enforcement is requested before the judge unless there is an assumption for the denial of the recognition and enforcement of the interim measure. In view of this situation, the Second Collegiate Court in Civil Matters of the Third Circuit, considering on the one hand, the guarantee of a hearing and, on the other hand, the effectiveness of the interim measure, proposes as a criterion to be followed that the judge should give greater weight to the rule underlying Articles 1479 and 1480 as it is consistent with the system of interim measures in general and with this solution the maintenance of the factual situation is guaranteed.

[6] Anti-arbitration Measures

Following the principle of minimal judicial intervention, judges may only intervene in those cases that are expressly contemplated in the Mexican *lex arbitri* and which were generally described in [B][1] of this chapter. None of these cases provides for judicial

62. Within the rules applicable to precautionary measures in commercial proceedings, Article 1177 of the Commerce Code disposes that in case of precautionary measures granted as prejudicial acts, the measures may be granted outright, without summoning the person against whom it is requested.
63. Tesis P./J. 21/98, *PRECAUTIONARY MEASURES. DO NOT CONSTITUTE PRIVATIVE ACTS, AND THEREFORE THE GUARANTEE OF PRIOR HEARING DOES NOT APPLY TO THEIR IMPOSITION* [1998] Federal Weekly Judiciary Gazette, 18.
64. Tesis: III.2o.C.8 C (10a.), *PRECAUTIONARY MEASURES. FOR THEIR ADOPTION, RECOGNITION AND ENFORCEMENT IN ARBITRATION PROCEEDINGS, THE GUARANTEE OF PRIOR HEARING IN FAVOR OF THE AFFECTED PARTY DOES NOT APPLY IN ORDER TO PRESERVE THE RIGHT OF THE PARTY REQUESTING THEM AND IN COMPLIANCE WITH JURISPRUDENCE P./J. 21/98* [2013] Federal Weekly Judiciary Gazette, 1385.

intervention to decree judicial measures aimed at suspending the arbitration proceedings or, as they are called, anti-arbitration measures. In fact, this type of measure goes against the will of the parties who, through an arbitration agreement, agreed that their disputes would be resolved by arbitration, being a more flexible process in which, in principle, there is no judicial intervention.

Judicial measures tending to suspend an arbitration proceeding are a clear interference in the arbitration, thus moving away from the spirit of the Model Law reflected in the Mexican *lex arbitri* and even from the spirit of the different international treaties that Mexico has entered into in the field of arbitration.

This type of measure contravenes the provisions of Article 1424 of the Commerce Code[65] which expressly authorizes the continuation of an arbitration despite the existence of a parallel action in court. In terms of this Article, if an action is brought before a judge on a matter in respect of which there is an arbitration agreement, the judge must refer the parties to arbitration, at the time it is requested by any of them unless it is proven that the arbitration agreement is null, ineffective or of impossible execution. Furthermore, this provision textually states that "If the action referred to in the preceding paragraph has been brought, arbitral proceedings may nevertheless be commenced or continued and an award made while the matter is pending before the judge."[66] Thus, it is clear that the commencement of court proceedings does not imply the suspension of arbitration; on the contrary, the law authorizes the pursuit of arbitral proceedings.

Furthermore, Article 1421 of the Commerce Code limits judicial intervention in arbitration to those cases expressly indicated in the Mexican *lex arbitri*. In other words, no Article contained in Title IV of Book Five of the Commerce Code authorizes the intervention of a judge for the granting of judicial measures that suspend or prevent the commencement of an arbitration proceeding.

A court order preventing a party from initiating arbitration pursuant to a valid and enforceable arbitration agreement is not only unlawful but should also be unenforceable and unconstitutional. Under the Mexican *lex arbitri*, judicial intervention in arbitration is limited to acts in aid of arbitral proceedings whether initiated or not. The intervention of a state court in aid of arbitration certainly does not include the possibility of affecting the autonomy of a party to resort to this mechanism for the

---

65. Article 1424 of the Commerce Code states:

> The judge to whom a dispute is submitted concerning a matter which is the subject of an arbitration agreement shall refer the parties to arbitration at the time it is requested by either of them, unless it is established that such agreement is null and void, ineffective or of impossible execution.
>
> If the action referred to in the preceding paragraph has been brought, arbitral proceedings may nevertheless be commenced or continued, and an award may be rendered while the matter is pending before the court.
>
> Without prejudice to the provisions of the first paragraph of this Article, where a resident abroad has expressly submitted to arbitration and is seeking an individual or collective dispute, the judge shall refer the parties to arbitration. If the judge denies recognition of the arbitration award under the terms of Article 1462 of this Code, the rights of the plaintiff to bring the appropriate action shall remain unaffected.

66. *Ibid.*

resolution of disputes. Moreover, anti-arbitration measures may constitute a violation of Article II of the New York Convention[67] which expressly obliges state courts of the contracting parties to recognize and enforce arbitration agreements.

The Mexican Arbitration Institute filed a position stating that: (1) the Mexican *lex arbitri* does not authorize judges to suspend arbitrations; (2) the Mexican Supreme Court has confirmed that judicial intervention in arbitration is exceptional and is limited to assisting arbitration in the cases expressly provided for in Mexican arbitration law; (3) the purpose of interim measures adopted by courts in assistance of arbitration are intended to preserve or protect the subject matter of the dispute to be heard or submitted to arbitration; and (4) injunctions or judicial measures tending to suspend arbitral proceedings are not only illegal but also violate the principle of competence-competence which empowers arbitrators to decide on their own competence and on the validity and existence of an arbitration agreement.[68]

However, there have been cases in which judges have granted injunctive relief to stay arbitration. In one case where an arbitration had already been initiated, the defendant filed a lawsuit in a local court alleging the nullity of the contract which was the basis of the action, and which contained the arbitration agreement. It also requested an ex parte injunction to suspend the arbitration until the nullity action was resolved. The Second Judge of First Instance of Commercial Matters of the Judicial District of Hermosillo, Sonora, heard the legal action and granted the measure in order for the arbitration to be suspended, basing his decision on the jurisprudence 25/2006[69] of the First Chamber of the Supreme Court of Justice. It is important to note that the measure granted was not individualized and only ordered "the suspension of the arbitration" to avoid "a damage to the plaintiffs of difficult repair, to the extent that the central point on which rests this private heterocomposite figure, is labeled ineffective in the lawsuit in question." Moreover, when the stay of arbitration was granted, the sole arbitrator in this case had not been appointed.

Once the corresponding arbitration institution appointed the sole arbitrator, he decided to continue the arbitration based on Articles 1424 and 1432 of the Commerce

67. Article II of the Commerce Code states:

    1. Each Contracting State shall recognize an agreement in writing under which the parties undertake to submit to arbitration all or any differences which have arisen, or which may arise between them in respect of a defined legal relationship, whether contractual or not, concerning a subject matter capable of settlement by arbitration.
    2. The term 'agreement in writing' shall include an arbitral clause in a contract or an arbitration agreement, signed by the parties or contained in an exchange of letters or telegrams.
    3. The court of a Contracting State, when seized of an action in a matter in respect of which the parties have made an agreement within the meaning of this Article, shall, at the request of one of the parties, refer the parties to arbitration, unless it finds that the said agreement is null and void, inoperative or incapable of being performed.

68. Mexican Institute of Arbitration, *Posture illegality of judicial measures to suspend arbitral proceedings* (2018).
69. Tesis 1a./J.25/2006, *COMMERCIAL ARBITRATION. COMPETENCE TO HEAR THE ACTION FOR NULLITY OF THE ARBITRATION AGREEMENT PROVIDED FOR IN THE FIRST PARAGRAPH OF ARTICLE 1424 OF THE COMMERCIAL CODE, CORRESPONDS TO THE JUDGE AND NOT TO THE ARBITRAL TRIBUNAL* [2006] Federal Weekly Judiciary Gazette, 5.

Code. In view of this, the judge who granted the anti-arbitration measure, individualized the same and ordered the sole arbitrator to refrain from continuing to hear the arbitration, warning him of a fine if he did not comply with the order, in addition to administrative arrest and a hearing before the Public Prosecutor's Office for contempt of a court order. The sole arbitrator continued to hear the arbitration and was fined. There was a second injunction to refrain from hearing the arbitration.

The sole arbitrator filed an indirect amparo against the anti-arbitration measure and the two injunctions, which were heard by the First District Court in Civil Matters in Mexico City.[70] The arbitrator was granted the definitive suspension of the challenged acts. The indirect amparo trial concluded with a judgment that dismissed the amparo trial and denied the protection of Federal Justice to the arbitrator.

In parallel to the indirect injunction, a party to the arbitration filed an appeal to fight the suspension of the arbitration before an appellate court in Hermosillo, which declared the arbitration suspension measure illegal and revoked it. The Hermosillo appellate court's reasons for declaring the anti-arbitration measure illegal were: (1) that the injunction contravened Article 1424 of the Commerce Code, which expressly authorizes the continuation of the arbitration in case of parallel action before the courts; and (2) that the continuation of the arbitration did not imply an unremedied injury to the parties.

The arbitrator filed an appeal for review against the judgment issued in the indirect amparo proceeding, which was heard by the Eleventh Collegiate Court in Civil Matters of the First Circuit,[71] which concluded with a judgment in which the challenged judgment was modified, and the arbitrator was granted the amparo and the protection of Federal Justice.

Courts have no jurisdiction to suspend arbitrations and any judicial measure to this end is unlawful. As for the arbitrators, when there is an anti-arbitration measure, they are faced with the choice between complying with the court order or continuing the arbitration. Ideally, the arbitrators should continue with the arbitration proceedings. However, this is not a foolproof solution applicable to all cases. On the contrary, it is a casuistic situation and should depend on the court's motivation for ordering the anti-arbitration measure.

Likewise, arbitrators may challenge anti-arbitration measures since arbitrators have a legal interest in challenging the power of the judge who ordered an anti-arbitration measure, which is illegal, and provided that such measure may have a direct effect on their assets and freedom.

[C] CONCLUSION

In conclusion, judicial intervention in assistance of arbitration should be minimal and only in those cases expressly provided for in the Mexican *lex arbitri*.

70. First District Court in Civil Matters in Mexico City: Amparo Indirecto 138/2017.
71. Eleventh Collegiate Court in Civil Matters of the First Circuit, Appeal of Review 351/2017.

State courts can grant interim measures in assistance of arbitration and have full discretion whenever granting such measures. Also, judges can intervene when recognizing and enforcing interim measures ordered by an arbitral tribunal.

Cases of judicial intervention in assistance of arbitration do not contemplate the possibility of a judge granting an interim injunction to suspend an arbitration proceeding. This type of judicial measure, commonly called anti-arbitration measures, is illegal.

CHAPTER 11

Recognition and Enforcement of Arbitration Awards in Mexico

Montserrat Manzano & Adrián Magallanes

[A] INTRODUCTION

One of the distinguishing features of international commercial arbitration in most jurisdictions is that, in contrast to commercial litigation, once the arbitral tribunal renders its award on the merits the parties may not appeal against the arbitral tribunal's application of questions of law. This construct may give rise to the false impression that upon the receipt of the arbitral award, the disputing parties will necessarily comply with its terms, culminate their dispute, and move on.

Often, however, notwithstanding the possibility that award debtors may well comply in good faith with the award rendered against them, they may alternatively look to resist the recognition and enforcement of those arbitral awards rendered against them. In such circumstances, the award creditor will have to resort to appearing before the courts of the jurisdictions in which they believe the award debtor holds assets and seeking a judicially-ordered recognition and enforcement of the arbitral award.

In this chapter, we set out the framework for recognizing and enforcing arbitral awards in Mexico.

[B] CONCEPTUALIZING RECOGNITION AND ENFORCEMENT

The recognition and the enforcement of awards are terms that are commonly, but erroneously, used interchangeably. However, the two concepts are intertwined, and it is common to refer to both simultaneously, as the New York Convention does.

While generally, if an award is enforced, it is also recognized, there may be cases in which a recognized award is not enforced. The recognition of an award occurs through a national court proceeding that leads to a judicial decision, known as "*exequatur*," in which the court acknowledges the existence of the arbitration and the decision of the tribunal.[1] Enforcement, on the one hand, is the judicial process, usually carried out simultaneously and in some cases following the recognition proceeding of an award, that gives effect to the mandate of the award.[2] The enforcement of an award allows the application of legal sanctions should the award debtor fail or refuse to comply with the award voluntarily.

Certain authors have conceptualized recognition as a defensive process, and enforcement as an offensive one. For these authors, recognition may be requested "when a court is asked to grant a remedy in respect of a dispute that has been the subject of previous arbitral proceedings."[3] On the other hand, enforcement acts as a sword to compel the party against whom the award was made to carry it out.[4]

Mexican law follows the rules set forth in the New York Convention and the UNCITRAL Model Law. As such, there is no codified legal distinction between the terms "recognition" and "enforcement."

Nonetheless, in a 2009 non-binding precedent, the First Chamber of the Mexican Supreme Court set forth its understanding of these concepts. The court defined the recognition of an arbitral award as "the formal act carried out by the judicial authority that declares it as final and binding on the disputed points between the parties."[5] Consequently, the effect of this recognition "is to give legal effects to the resolutions of an award."[6] The Mexican Supreme Court therefore acknowledged that the recognition of an award does not necessarily convey its enforcement, since the recognition could be requested as a defense to raise a res judicata argument or to be used as evidence to set off.

Conversely, the Mexican Supreme Court ruled that enforcing an award "means to materialize the effects of the decision, even coercively and even against the will of the parties committed to complying with it."[7] As such, it considered that in an enforcement judgment, "the effects of the arbitral decision are ordered to be materialized and consummated to their ultimate consequences"[8] even with the possibility of using public force.

1. Julian DM Lew et al., Comparative International Commercial Arbitration (Kluwer Law International, 2003), p. 690.
2. *Ibid.*, p. 691.
3. "Chapter 11. Recognition and Enforcement of Arbitral Awards," in Nigel Blackaby, Constantine Partasides, et al., Redfern and Hunter on International Arbitration (Sixth Edition), 6th edition (© Kluwer Law International; Oxford University Press 2015) p. 610.
4. *Ibid.*, p. 612.
5. Non-binding precedent 1a. CLXXIII/2009, under registration number 166508, First Chamber of the Supreme Court of Justice, Ninth Period, Civil Matters, Federal Official Weekly and its Gazette, Volume XXX, September 2009, p. 430, under heading "*COMMERCIAL ARBITRATION. NULLITY, RECOGNITION AND ENFORCEMENT ARE JUDICIAL PROCEEDINGS RELATED TO ARBITRAL AWARDS (INTERPRETATION OF ARTICLES 1422, 1457 TO 1462 OF THE COMMERCE CODE).*"
6. *Ibid.*
7. *Ibid.*
8. *Ibid.*

[C] APPLICABLE PROCEDURAL LAW FOR RECOGNITION AND ENFORCEMENT OF AWARDS

[1] International Treaties

To facilitate the process of recognizing and enforcing arbitral awards, in 1958 the United Nations Conference on International Commercial Arbitration ("UNCITRAL") published the Convention on the Recognition and Enforcement of Foreign Arbitral Awards, better known as the "New York Convention," which at the time of writing has been ratified by 171 States.

Similarly, in 1985 UNCITRAL published the first version of its Model Law on International Commercial Arbitration, which, *inter alia*, sets forth corresponding proposals for provisions of domestic law in relation to the recognition and enforcement of arbitral awards.

In Latin America, rules on recognition and enforcement were also later harmonized under the Inter-American Convention on International Commercial Arbitration 1975 (known as the "Panama Convention"). Additionally, two other Latin American conventions also deal with the recognition and enforcement of judgments and awards, the Inter-American Convention on Extraterritorial Validity of Foreign Judgments and Arbitral Awards (the Montevideo Convention) and, for the Mercosur States (of which Mexico is not part), the Protocol of Las Leñas. This parallelism may be considered a distinctive feature of the recognition and enforcement of arbitral awards in Latin America.

Mexico was one of the first Latin American States to adopt such international and domestic laws with respect to the recognition and enforcement of foreign arbitral awards. Mexico ratified the New York Convention in 1971 and adopted the UNCITRAL Model Law (with certain modifications) into its Commerce Code in 1993, while also adopting the Panama and Montevideo Conventions in 1978 and 1987, respectively.

[a] New York Convention

Mexico ratified the New York Convention without limitations or reservations on April 14, 1971. It applies to the recognition and enforcement of foreign arbitral awards, as opposed to awards rendered within Mexico. In the latter case, pursuant to a judicial precedent issued by the Seventh Collegiate Circuit Court in Civil Matters in the First Circuit, the provisions of the Commerce Code apply.[9]

The New York Convention was intended to build a normative framework to facilitate the recognition and enforcement of both foreign arbitral awards and arbitration agreements. In essence, pursuant to this convention, foreign arbitral awards

9. Non-binding precedent, under registration number 2001130, issued by the Seventh Collegiate Circuit Court in Civil Matters in the First Circuit, Tenth Period, Civil Matters, Federal Official Weekly and its Gazette, Book X, July 2012, p. 1877, under heading "*ARBITRAL AWARD. WHEN THE CONVENTION ON THE RECOGNITION AND ENFORCEMENT OF FOREIGN ARBITRAL AWARDS IS NOT APPLICABLE.*"

should be recognized and enforced in the courts of states that have adopted it, subject to only a handful of narrow procedural and substantive grounds for objecting to enforcement. The Convention is broadly celebrated, in particular as having found an appropriate balance between setting international substantive rules where necessary and deferring to domestic law where harmonization is not necessary.

The New York Convention establishes, in its Article V, seven exhaustive grounds on which a party against whom an arbitral award was rendered might object to the recognition and enforcement of it. In the case of the first five, the burden of proof lies with the party opposing enforcement. The latter two may be relied upon by the enforcement court on its own motion. These are as follows:

(1) Where the parties to the arbitration agreement were "under the law applicable to them, under some incapacity" or where "the said agreement is not valid under the law to which the parties have subjected it or, failing any indication thereon, under the law of the country where the award was made" (Article V(1)(a)).
(2) Where the party against whom the award is invoked "was not given proper notice of the appointment of the arbitrator or of the arbitration proceedings or was otherwise unable to present his case" (Article V(1)(b)).
(3) Where "the award deals with a difference not contemplated by or not falling within the terms of the submission to arbitration, or it contains decisions on matters beyond the scope of the submission to arbitration, provided that, if the decisions on matters submitted to arbitration can be separated from those not so submitted, that part of the award which contains decisions or matters submitted to arbitration may be recognized and enforced" (Article V(1)(c)).
(4) Where "the composition of the arbitral authority or the arbitral procedure was not in accordance with the agreement of the parties, or, failing such agreement, was not in accordance with the law of the country where the arbitration took place" (Article V(1)(d)).
(5) Where "the award has not yet become binding on the parties or has been set aside or suspended by a competent authority of the country in which, or under the law of which, that award was made" (Article V(1)(e)).
(6) Where the "subject matter of the difference is not capable of settlement by arbitration under the law" of the country where recognition and enforcement are sought (Article V(2)(a)).
(7) Where the recognition and enforcement of the award "would be contrary to the public policy" of the country where recognition or enforcement is sought (Article V(2)(b)).

In the case of the first five of these grounds, the burden of proof is transferred to the party opposing a request for enforcement. This transfer is one of the most important characteristics of the New York Convention and is one of the key factors underpinning the "pro-enforcement bias" that it generates.[10]

Following Mexico's subscription to the New York Convention, the Mexican courts quickly incorporated the overarching principles of it. Four publicly available decisions were issued by Mexican courts, interpreting the New York Convention in the years before Mexico adopted the UNCITRAL Model Law as part of its Commerce Code. Two of them expressly addressed the recognition and enforcement of arbitral awards.

First, in 1977, a first-instance court of the Superior Court of Justice of Mexico City held that concerning foreign arbitral awards, there is no need for Mexican courts to perform an *exequatur,* nor for an award creditor to send the arbitral award to Mexican courts through a letter rogatory.[11] This decision is now codified in Article 1471 of the Commerce Code.[12]

Second, also in 1977, the Court of Appeals of the Superior Court of Justice of Mexico City ruled that there was no need to summon a party to the arbitral proceeding under the requirements of the Federal Code of Civil Procedure. According to this ruling, as long as the defendant was summoned to the arbitral proceeding under the conditions set forth in the arbitration agreement itself and the New York Convention, the summons to the proceeding is valid and does not require any additional formalities.[13]

The Mexican courts issued both decisions before July 1993, when the Mexican Federal Congress approved the introduction of Title IV to the Fifth Book of the Mexican Commerce Code. In that Title, Mexico adopted the UNCITRAL Model Law and, by extension, the New York Convention grounds to refuse the recognition and enforcement of arbitral awards.

[b] Panama Convention

In addition to the New York Convention, since March 27, 1978, Mexico has been a party to the Interamerican Convention on International Commercial Arbitration, also

10. Cf. Montevideo Treaties of international Procedural Law of 1889 (Art. 5) and of 1940 (Art. 6) and the Bustamante Code of 1928 (Art. 423), which place the burden of proof on the requesting party to prove that enforcement proceeds under those laws. *See* Horacio Grigera Naon, *Países de América Latina como Sede de Arbitrajes Comerciales Internacionales* 48 (ICC Special Supplement 1995).
11. *See*: "Mexico No. 1, Presse Office S.A. v. Centro Editorial Hoy S.A., Tribunal Superior De Justicia, Eighteenth Civil Court of First Instance for the Federal District of Mexico, 24 February 1977," in Pieter Sanders (ed.), Yearbook Commercial Arbitration 1979—Volume IV, Yearbook Commercial Arbitration, Volume 4 (© Kluwer Law International; ICCA & Kluwer Law International 1979) pp. 301-301 (https://www.kluwerarbitration.com/document/ipn874).
12. *Article 1471:* For the recognition and enforcement of the awards referred to in Articles 1461 to 1463 of this Code, exequatur is not required. Except when recognition and enforcement is requested as a defense in a lawsuit or other proceeding, recognition and enforcement shall be promoted in the special lawsuit referred to in Articles 1472 to 1476.
13. "Mexico No. 2, Malden Mills Inc. v. Hilaturas Lourdes S.A., Tribunal Superior De Justicia, Court Of Appeals (Fifth Chamber) For The Federal District Of Mexico, 1 August 1977," in Pieter Sanders (ed.), Yearbook Commercial Arbitration 1979—Volume IV, Yearbook Commercial Arbitration, Volume 4 (© Kluwer Law International; ICCA & Kluwer Law International 1979) pp. 302-304 (https://www.kluwerarbitration.com/document/ipn876).

known as the Panama Convention.[14] Nineteen countries of the Americas are party to this treaty. Articles 4, 5, and 6 of the Convention govern the setting aside, recognition, and enforcement of arbitral awards.[15]

The Panama Convention's provisions on recognition and enforcement are highly similar to those set out in the New York Convention. It in fact adopted either *verbatim* or very minorly modified, many provisions of the New York Convention.[16]

In particular, the two Conventions include essentially the same list of grounds for refusing the recognition and enforcement of awards, listed above,[17] and both conventions establish the transfer of the burden of proof to the party resisting the recognition and enforcement of the award. That is, both Article 5(1) of the Panama Convention and Article V.1 of the New York Convention provide that an enforcement request may only be refused if the party opposing the request is able to show the existence of one of the grounds established therein.

Given the intentional similarity of the two Conventions and the fact that both regulate the same subject matter, it has long since been questioned why the Panama Convention was necessary in the first place.[18] In reality, the reasons were probably more political than legal.

Notwithstanding the compatibility of the Conventions, the Panama Convention—*unlike the New York Convention*—does not establish its relationship to other treaties. The New York Convention establishes in its Article VII.1 that it does not exclude the application of a more favorable law, treaty or convention. Accordingly, to the extent that the application of the Panama Convention would lead to a result more favorable toward enforcement than the New York Convention, the Panama Convention would prevail, provided there exists an irrevocable normative conflict between the Conventions.[19]

Such normative conflicts between the two Conventions appear to not have arisen in practice, and the two Conventions tend to be applied harmoniously in enforcement proceedings. Nonetheless, the existence of two Conventions governing largely the same subject matter raises the potential for treaty conflict.[20]

---

14. *See*: Organization of American States database, B-35: Convención Interamericana sobre Arbitraje Comercial Internacional (https://www.oas.org/juridico/spanish/firmas/b-35.html).
15. *Ibid.*
16. One of the delegates who participated in drafting the Panama Convention, Charles Norberg of the U.S., once said that the convention "was carefully drawn up to as to be fully compatible with the New York Convention"—Charles Robert Norberg, *Inter-American Commercial Arbitration: Unicorn or Beast of Burden*, 5 Pace Law Review 607 (1985) https://doi.org/10.58948/2331-3528.1588.
17. Panama Convention, Art 5.1; New York Convention, Art. V.1.
18. Albert Jan Van Den Berg, *The New York Convention of 1958 and the Panama Convention of 1975: Redundancy or Compatibility?*, 5 Arbitration International 228 (1989) https://doi.org/10.1093/arbitration/5.3.214.
19. The same result would likely arise pursuant to Article 30 of the Vienna Convention on the Law of Treaties (1969), which, in the case of the application of successive treaties in respect of the same subject matter, establishes that the earlier treaty (i.e., the New York Convention) applies only to the extent that its provisions are compatible with those of the later treaty (i.e., the Panama Convention).
20. The subject matter of the Panama Convention is broader than the subject matter of the New York Convention. The latter applies to the recognition and enforcement of foreign arbitral awards, subject to the reciprocity and commercial reservations that can be submitted pursuant to Art.

[c] Domestic Law

The Mexican Commerce Code governs the recognition and enforcement of arbitral awards in Mexico. Title IV (Commercial Arbitration) of its Fifth Book (Commercial Proceedings) contains the relevant provisions concerning arbitral proceedings seated in Mexico and the intervention of the Mexican judiciary in relation to commercial arbitrations. Through Title IV, Mexico adopted, with certain amendments, the UNCITRAL Model Law of 1985, and thus by extension the limited grounds to resist recognition and enforcement set out in the New York Convention.[21]

Title IV contains the only domestic provisions applicable to requests for the recognition and enforcement of arbitral awards in Mexico, whether they be final, interim, or partial awards. Nonetheless, according to Article 2 of the Mexican Commerce Code, the Federal Civil Code may apply in the event the Commerce Code fails to regulate any matter. At the time of writing, there is an ongoing debate within the Mexican judiciary regarding whether Title IV is hermetic and self-contained, or whether the rest of the provisions of the Commerce Code and by consequence the Federal Civil Code too, apply alternatively for all matters that are not regulated within Title IV.

In 2010, the Seventh Collegiate Circuit Court in Civil Matters in the First Circuit issued a non-binding precedent that held that the Mexican arbitration law was designed under the principle of non-intervention (or at least minimum intervention) of a juridical body, privileging the will of individuals to opt for arbitration. Accordingly, the court held that the arbitration laws contained in the Commerce Code were specifically chosen to be hermetic, restrictive, self-contained, constituting a body that contains all its parts without needing to rely on other laws through supplementary provisions. Thus, the court excluded the possibility of applying common civil and commercial legislation and even went so far as to exclude the suppletory application of general rules.[22]

However, various other courts have held to the contrary, and have applied legal provisions contained either in the general part of the Commerce Code, in the Federal Code of Civil Procedure, the Mexican Constitution, and general principles of law. The reason behind this is that while Title IV of the Commerce Code is indeed a specialized regulation, it does not exist independently of the general provisions that govern all

---

I(3). The Panama Convention, by contrast, does not specify its scope of application, but its title suggests that its recognition and enforcement provisions apply to awards issued in international commercial arbitrations. However, since these terms (international and commercial) are not defined, the scope is ambiguous. What is clear is that it covers matters not covered by the New York Convention, such as the applicable procedural rules in the absence of party agreement (Art. 3).

21. As of the time of writing, Mexico has not yet adopted in its Commerce Code, the 2006 amendments to the UNCITRAL Model Law. However, certain judicial non-binding precedents have reaffirmed some of the 2006 amendments.
22. Non-binding precedent, I.7o.C.150 C under registration number 163413, issued by the Seventh Collegiate Circuit Court in Civil Matters in the First Circuit, Ninth Period, Civil Matters, Federal Official Weekly and its Gazette, Volume XXXII, December 2010, p. 17, under heading "*COMMERCIAL ARBITRATION. ITS LEGISLATION IS SPECIALIZED AND, THEREFORE, EXCLUDES GENERAL RULES.*"

proceedings, and to have incorporated each general procedural rule into Title IV would have been excessively burdensome and inefficient, given that all such rules are already contained elsewhere in the Commerce Code or in the Federal Code of Civil Procedure.

Whereas this contradiction is not a settled matter, it may be problematic to assume that every single possible controversy arising from an arbitration proceeding can be resolved without reference to other general provisions and principles of law.

[D] STATUTE OF LIMITATIONS TO REQUEST THE RECOGNITION AND ENFORCEMENT OF AWARDS

The Mexican Commerce Code does not establish a specific statute of limitations to request the recognition and enforcement of arbitral awards, whether they be domestic or international. Instead, parties must apply the general rules established in the code, which pursuant to its Article 1047, is ten years.

In the case of the recognition and enforcement of an arbitral award, the clock starts to run from the day after the award is notified. Although there is no legal precedent explicitly addressing this issue, this has been tacitly recognized by the Collegiate Circuit Courts in non-binding precedents.[23] Such an approach gives credence to the view that the Commerce Code as a whole and the Federal Code of Civil Procedure apply in the event of lacunae in Title IV of the Commerce Code.[24]

[E] JURISDICTION OF THE COURTS

[1] The Competent Courts

Under Mexican law, federal and local first-instance civil courts have joint jurisdiction over judicial proceedings related to commercial arbitration proceedings. This derives from Article 1422 of the Commerce Code, which states that when judicial intervention is required, the competent court will be either the state or federal first instance court of the seat of the arbitration.[25] As such, both courts could be competent to order the recognition and enforcement of an arbitral award, and it is up to the applicant to choose between the two courts.

23. Non-binding precedent, under registration number 176595, Ninth Period, Civil Matters, Federal Official Weekly and its Gazette, Volume XXII, December 2005, p. 2623, under heading *"COMMERCIAL ARBITRATION. CRITERIA FOR DETERMINING THE INEFFECTIVENESS OF THE ARBITRATION AGREEMENT."*
24. This is a clear example of a court holding that the general provisions of the Commerce Code are alternatively applicable to Title IV when a specific matter is not regulated within the specialized legislation.
25. *Article 1422*: When judicial intervention is required, the federal court of first instance or the ordinary court of the place where the arbitration takes place shall be competent to hear the case.

    When the place of arbitration is outside the national territory, the judge of first instance, federal or common law, of the domicile of the defendant or, in the absence thereof, the judge of the location of the assets, shall be competent to hear the recognition and enforcement of the award.

Both federal and local first-instance civil courts also have joint jurisdiction over recognition and enforcement proceedings for foreign awards. Pursuant to the second paragraph of Article 1422, the competent court to recognize and enforce an award is either the state or federal court of the place in which the domicile of the party against whom the award is going to be enforced is located, or, subsidiarily, of the place where the assets that are going to be seized are located.

[2] Required Documentation

The award creditor seeking the recognition and enforcement of the award must file an application in writing. Pursuant to Article 1461 of the Commerce Code, the only required additional documentation to request the recognition and enforcement of an award is: (i) the original authenticated award or a certified copy of it; and (ii) the original or certified copy of the arbitration agreement.

In a non-binding precedent, a Collegiate Circuit Court held that this requirement implies that the requesting party must furnish a copy of the award, authenticated by the personnel of the arbitral institution that administered the proceedings or a certified copy issued by a Notary Public or a Public Commercial Attestor.[26]

Pursuant to Article 1055, sections I and II of the Mexican Commerce Code, parties must submit all documents in Spanish, and the courts must perform all judicial acts in the same language. Hence, parties must provide a certified translation of all the original documents that were not prepared in Spanish.[27] This means that in the context of the request for recognition and enforcement of awards, if the award itself, or the arbitration agreement, were executed in a foreign language, the applicant shall also attach translations issued by a certified translator.

There is no other documentary requirement to request the recognition and enforcement of an award. However, it may be advisable for the party seeking the enforcement to also attach relevant documentation of the arbitral proceeding, e.g., the terms of reference, procedural orders, or the briefs submitted by the parties. Nonetheless, this is not mandatory.

---

26. Non-binding precedent I.14o.C.26 C (10a.), under registration number 2017915, issued by the Fourteenth Collegiate Circuit Court in Civil Matters in the First Circuit, Tenth Period, Gazette of the Federal Official Weekly, Book 58, September 2018, Volume III, p. 2389, under heading "*ARBITRATION AWARD. AUTHENTICATION REFERRED TO IN ARTICLE 1461 OF THE CODE OF COMMERCE FOR ITS ENFORCEMENT.*"
27. Commerce Code *Article 1055*: Commercial trials are ordinary, oral, executive or special trials regulated by any law of a commercial nature. All commercial trials, with the exception of oral trials which have special rules, shall be subject to the following:

    I. All pleadings of the parties and judicial proceedings must be written in Spanish, easily legible to the naked eye, and must be signed by those who intervene in them. When any of the parties does not know how or is unable to sign, he shall impose his fingerprint, and another person shall sign on his behalf and at his request, indicating these circumstances;
    II. Documents drafted in a foreign language must be accompanied by the corresponding Spanish translation; ... .

[3] The Recognition and Enforcement Process

The recognition and enforcement of awards in Mexico is an adversarial proceeding. This means that the applicant must file a claim against the losing party of the arbitration, who will have the opportunity to respond and object to the petition.

Article 1471 of the Mexican Commerce Code establishes that the proceeding for recognizing and enforcing an award is a special proceeding named "special trial on commercial transactions and arbitration" unless the recognition and execution of the award is being raised in court as a defense in another proceeding. Article 1471 of the Mexican Commerce Code as well as the special trial, is a Mexican creation that does not derive from either the New York Convention or the UNCITRAL Model Law.

Once the court has acknowledged receipt of the request to recognize and enforce an award, the court will summon the respondent to the proceeding. The respondent, in turn, will have a fifteen-day period to file its answer.[28] As a standardized practice, this period is deemed to refer to fifteen business days, as this is the general rule for all judicial proceedings in Mexico. However, in a recent non-binding decision, the Twelfth District Court in Civil Matters in Mexico City held that this time frame shall be counted as calendar days.[29]

In this respect, while Article 1419 of the Commerce Code (which that court applied) states that the statute of limitations shall comprise all days, various legal authorities have acknowledged that this provision refers to terms within the arbitration proceeding, not to those within judicial proceedings related to an arbitration proceeding.[30] Indeed, such an article is similar to Article 2.6 of the 2010 UNCITRAL Arbitration Rules,[31] which only regulates the arbitral proceeding itself and cannot comprise related judicial proceedings. Consequently, the fifteen-day period should be seen as excluding non-business days. Otherwise, the courts would be forced to issue orders on days that are officially non-working days. This would also make it the only proceeding in Mexico

28. Commerce Code *Article 1473*: Once the claim has been admitted, the judge shall order the defendants to be summoned, granting them a term of fifteen days to answer.
29. Special trial on commercial transactions and arbitration 132/2020. According to this District Court, judicial proceedings related to arbitration are governed by Art. 1419 of the Mexican Commerce Code. This article expressly states that non-working days and holidays shall be counted in the statute of limitations concerning judicial proceedings on arbitration.
30. Instituto Mexicano de Arbitraje, Legislación Mexicana de Arbitraje Comercial (Porrúa, 2015), p. 39. "Finally, it is important to clarify that the rule contained in this article is only applicable with respect to the computation of time periods in an arbitration proceeding and not with respect to the computation of time periods provided or granted in a special or voluntary jurisdiction proceeding that is processed to invoke judicial support to arbitration or any other proceeding before state courts. In other words, there is a clear distinction between the computation of time limits in arbitration AND the computation of time limits in a jurisdictional proceeding before a State court."
31. Article 2. Notice and calculation of periods of time. …

    6. For the purpose of calculating a period of time under these Rules, such period shall begin to run on the day following the day when a notice is received. If the last day of such period is an official holiday or a non-business day at the residence or place of business of the addressee, the period is extended until the first business day which follows. Official holidays or nonbusiness days occurring during the running of the period of time are included in calculating the period.

regulated under this rule, contrary to the fact the five-day working week of the courts is not only customary but also enshrined in legislation.

After this fifteen-day period to respond to the statement of claim, there is an additional period to submit evidence. There is no statutory period in the Mexican Commerce Code for this procedural stage. Furthermore, Article 1474 of the Commerce Code states that when there is no evidence, or the court deems it unnecessary, the court will schedule a closing hearing to take place within the following three days.[32]

If evidence is indeed offered or the court deems it necessary, the court may establish an additional ten-day period for presenting evidence.[33] This generally pertains to evidence other than documents that are analyzed by means of their own content without requiring any additional steps to be presented in court.

After the closing hearing, the court will issue its ruling.[34] The waiting period for the court's ruling will depend on the court's workload. However, it usually takes around two months to issue the final ruling from the closure of the hearing.

Incidentally, in Mexico, the recognition and enforcement of an award can be raised as a counterclaim in a nullity proceeding regarding the same award, under Article 1417(III) of the Commerce Code.[35] However, nullity and recognition and enforcement proceedings can also take place separately, and can even be heard by different courts, but be subjected to consolidation in terms of Article 1477 of the Commerce Code.[36] Nevertheless, the proceedings cannot be consolidated if they are being heard in different territorial jurisdictions or if one is being processed in a federal court and the other in a state court.

Accordingly, it is advisable to have appropriate legal assistance when filing either a nullity or a recognition and enforcement proceeding, and it may be recommendable to attempt to avoid separate proceedings to avoid contradictory decisions.

32. Commerce Code *Article 1474.*: Once the term for answering the claim has elapsed, without the need for a default notice, if the parties do not present evidence and the judge does not consider it necessary, a hearing for pleadings shall be summoned within the following three days, which shall be held whether or not the parties are present or not.
33. Commerce Code *Article 1475.*: If evidence is offered or the judge deems it necessary prior to the holding of the hearing, an evidentiary delay of ten days shall be opened.
34. Commerce Code *Article 1476.*: Once the hearing has been held, the judge shall summon the parties to hear the decision. The intermediate resolutions issued in this special trial and the decision that resolves it will not be appealable.
35. Non-binding precedent I.3o.C.729 C, under registration number 167398, issued by the Third Collegiate Court in Civil Matters of the First Circuit, Ninth Period, Civil Matters, Federal Official Weekly and its Gazette, Volume XXIX, April 2009, page 1955., under heading "*COUNTERCLAIM FOR RECOGNITION AND ENFORCEMENT IN THE INCIDENT OF NULLITY OF THE ARBITRATION AWARD. ITS PROCEDURE IS NOT PROHIBITED BY THE CODE OF COMMERCE CODE AND IS CONSISTENT WITH THE PURPOSE OF THE INSTITUTION.*"
36. Commerce Code Article 1477.: Special proceedings concerning nullity or recognition and enforcement of commercial awards may be consolidated. In order for the consolidation to proceed, it is necessary that the hearing of pleadings has not been held. The consolidation shall be made in favor of the judge who has issued the notice. The joinder does not proceed with respect to proceedings that are heard in different territorial jurisdictions or abroad, nor between federal courts and those of the states. The joinder will be processed in accordance with Arts. 73 to 75 of the Federal Code of Civil Procedures. The resolution that resolves on the consolidation cannot be appealed.

[4] Procedure for Service Outside the Jurisdiction

There is no procedure for carrying out the service of process outside the jurisdiction of the court for proceedings related to arbitration. The service of process therefore must follow the standard practice for all judicial proceedings if there is a need to serve to process to someone outside the court's jurisdiction. Accordingly, if the domicile in which to serve process is located within Mexico but outside the court's jurisdiction, the competent court of the place of the domicile will be in need of a letter of request issued by the court hearing out the proceeding to be able to carry out the service of process. In contrast, if the domicile is outside of Mexico, the Ministry of Foreign Affairs will intervene and serve the process through a rogatory letter.

In practice, it is unusual to serve process outside the court's jurisdiction, given the amount of time it would take to do so. Notifying the losing party of the arbitration through a letter of request or through a rogatory letter could take months.

Since recognizing and enforcing awards is expected to be a quick procedure, requesting such a petition to a court that will not have territorial jurisdiction over the defendant or the assets is rarely advisable.

[F] GROUNDS TO REFUSE THE RECOGNITION AND ENFORCEMENT OF ARBITRAL AWARDS

Article 1462 of the Mexican Commerce Code sets forth the New York Convention and UNCITRAL Model Law grounds on which a Court may refuse the recognition and enforcement of an award:

> **Article 1462.**—Recognition or enforcement of an arbitral award may only be refused, regardless of the country in which it was rendered, when:
>
> I. —The party against whom the award is invoked proves before the competent court of the country where recognition or enforcement is sought that:
> (a) One of the parties to the arbitration agreement was affected by some incapacity, or that such agreement is invalid under the law to which the parties have subjected it, or if nothing has been initiated in this respect, under the law of the country in which the award was made;
> (b) It was not duly notified of the appointment of an arbitrator or of the arbitral proceedings, or was otherwise unable to assert its rights;
> (c) The award relates to a dispute not comprised by the arbitration agreement or contains decisions that exceed the terms of the arbitration agreement. However, if the provisions of the award which relate to matters submitted to arbitration can be separated from those which are not, the former may be recognized and enforced;
> (d) The composition of the arbitral tribunal or the arbitral proceedings did not conform to the agreement of the parties or, failing such agreement, did not conform to the law of the country where the arbitration took place; or
> (e) The award is not yet binding on the parties or has been annulled or suspended by the court of the country in which, or under the law of which, the award was made; or

II. —The court finds that, under Mexican law, the subject matter of the dispute is not arbitrable; or that the recognition or enforcement of the award is contrary to public policy.

This article refers to two principal scenarios. The first regulates the five grounds for refusal to recognize and enforce an award in which the burden of proof lies with the respondent. The second scenario refers to the two cases in which the court could refuse the recognition and enforcement of an award ex officio.

Mexican courts have acknowledged that these scenarios are limited,[37] and should be applied restrictively, without allowing for new grounds for refusal through precedents and legal interpretations.

Article 1462 was adopted from Article 36 of the Model Law, Article V of the New York Convention and Article 5 of the Panama Convention. It is closely related to Article 1457 of the Commerce Code, which establishes the grounds for seeking the annulment of an award, given that the grounds for nullity and for resisting enforcement are similar. Most judicial precedents issued by Mexican courts refer to the setting aside of an award. Nonetheless, these precedents are applicable *mutatis mutandis* to the recognition and enforcement of an award given the similarities between Articles 1457 and 1462.

Having this in mind, the Third Collegiate Circuit Court in Civil Matters in the First Circuit resolved constitutional appeal 195/2010 and issued several non-binding precedents interpreting Article 1457 of the Mexican Commerce Code that may be applicable to the recognition and enforcement of awards.

The first ground to set aside an award (Article 1457(I)(a)) refers to the case in which one of the parties lacked the capacity to execute the arbitration agreement, or where the arbitration agreement is invalid. According to a non-binding precedent issued by this Circuit Court, this section focuses on the subjective aspect of the arbitration agreement, i.e., the legal capacity of the parties. Additionally, it establishes that if the arbitration agreement is not valid under the applicable law, or subsidiarily under Mexican law, it will be null and void.[38] This ground for nullity corresponds to the first ground for denying the recognition and enforcement of an award, in terms of Article 1462(I)(a), transcribed above.

The second ground to set aside an award, (Article 1457(I)(b)), is that one of the parties was not duly notified of the appointment of an arbitrator. The notification of the appointment of an arbitrator is necessary to guarantee the right of the party to

37. Non-binding precedent 1a./J. 87/2019 (10a.), under registration number 2021235, issued by the First Chamber of the Supreme Court, Tenth Period, Civil Matters, Gazette of the Federal Official Weekly, Book 73, December 2019, Volume I, p. 253, under heading "*ARBITRATION AWARD. AGAINST THE JUDGMENT ISSUED IN THE SPECIAL TRIAL IN WHICH ITS NULLITY, OR ITS RECOGNITION AND ENFORCEMENT, IS BEING ELUCIDATED, AN INDIRECT AMPARO PROCEEDING MAY BE FILED.*"

38. Non-binding precedent I.3o.C.943 C, under registration number 162072, issued by the Third Collegiate Circuit Court in Civil Matters in the First Circuit, Ninth Period, Civil Matters, Federal Official Weekly and its Gazette, Volume XXXIII, May 2011, p. 1228, under heading "*NULLITY OF THE ARBITRATION AWARD DUE TO THE INCAPACITY OF ONE OF THE PARTIES OR BECAUSE THE AGREEMENT IS CONTRARY TO THE LAW (SECTION I OF SUBSECTION A) OF ARTICLE 1457 OF THE COMMERCE CODE).*"

challenge the appointment, and thus ensure that the arbitral tribunal is impartial and independent. Similarly, this subsection comprises the right of the parties to be notified of the arbitral acts since it underlies the arbitral duty to treat the parties fairly. The last clause similarly refers to the parties' right to present their case and accordingly reflects the right to due process.[39] This ground for nullity corresponds to the second ground for denying the recognition and enforcement of an award, in terms of Article 1462(I)(b), transcribed above.

The third ground to annul an award, set forth in Article 1457(I)(c), refers to cases in which the arbitral tribunal resolved a matter beyond its remit. The federal courts have acknowledged that this provision sanctions the lack of legitimacy of the arbitral tribunal to resolve a matter that the parties did not wish to submit before it.[40] This ground for nullity corresponds almost identically to the third ground for denying the recognition and enforcement of an award, in terms of Article 1462(I)(a), transcribed above.

The fourth ground to set aside an award, set forth in Article 1457(I)(d), is that the composition of the arbitral tribunal or the arbitration proceeding was not held in accordance with the parties' agreement.[41] This ground for nullity corresponds almost identically to the fourth ground for denying the recognition and enforcement of an award, in terms of Article 1462(I)(d), transcribed above.

There are two other grounds to set aside an award, established in section II of Article 1457 of the Commerce Code. The first one refers to the arbitrability of the dispute, legal authorities have recognized that there are some subject matters under Mexican law that are not arbitrable, such as civil status, and the validity of marriage.[42] The second one relates to public policy. In this regard, the First Chamber of the Supreme Court has held that it will only apply when an award directly violates fundamental legal principles or institutions.[43]

39. Non-binding precedent I.3o.C.944 C, under registration number 162067, issued by the Third Collegiate Circuit Court in Civil Matters in the First Circuit, Ninth Period, Civil Matters, Federal Official Weekly and its Gazette, Volume XXXIII, May 2011, p. 1231, under heading "*NULLITY OF THE ARBITRATION AWARD DUE TO IMPROPER NOTIFICATION OR SERIOUS LACK OF DEFENSE (SECTION I, SUBSECTION B) OF ARTICLE 1457 OF THE COMMERCE CODE).*"
40. Non-binding precedent I.3o.C.945 C, under registration number 162071, issued by the Third Collegiate Circuit Court in Civil Matters in the First Circuit, Ninth Period, Civil Matters, Federal Official Weekly and its Gazette, Volume XXXIII, May 2011, p. 1229, under heading "*NULLITY OF THE ARBITRATION AWARD FOR INCONSISTENCY IN EXCEEDING THE SUBJECT MATTER OF THE CONTROVERSY (SECTION I, SUBSECTION C) OF ARTICLE 1457 OF THE COMMERCE CODE).*"
41. Non-binding precedent I.3o.C.9466 C, under registration number 162070, issued by the Third Collegiate Circuit Court in Civil Matters in the First Circuit, Ninth Period, Civil Matters, Federal Official Weekly and its Gazette, Volume XXXIII, May 2011, p. 1230, under heading "*NULLITY OF THE ARBITRATION AWARD DUE TO IMPROPER COMPOSITION OF THE ARBITRAL TRIBUNAL (SECTION I, SUBSECTION D) OF ARTICLE 1457 OF THE COMMERCE CODE).*"
42. Francisco González de Cossío, Arbitraje, (Porrúa, 2018), pp. 266-272.
43. Non-binding precedent, under registration number, issued by the First Chamber of the Supreme Court, Tenth Period, Civil Matters, Gazette of the Federal Official Weekly, Book 40, March 2017, Volume I, p. 442, under heading "*JUSTICIABILITY OF ARBITRATION AWARDS WHEN A SUBJECT OF THE PARASTATAL PUBLIC ADMINISTRATION CLAIMS THAT PUBLIC ORDER IS VIOLATED (INTERPRETATION OF ARTICLE 1457, SECTION II, OF THE COMMERCE CODE).*"

One of the main differences between Article 1457 and Article 1462 of the Commerce Code is that the latter establishes an additional ground to refuse the recognition and enforcement of an award: that it is not yet binding upon the parties or that it had been suspended or annulled by a court at the seat of the arbitration.

Pursuant to Article 1463 of the Commerce Code, if a party seeks the recognition and enforcement of an award and there is a pending judicial decision—*before the court of the seat of the arbitration or before the court of the country under whose laws the award was rendered*—concerning the suspension or annulment of said award, the court may adjourn its decision if the opposing party provides sufficient guarantees. It is noteworthy that this article states that the court "may" adjourn its decision and, hence, it is not bound to do so. Legal authorities have held that the court "has therefore, according to the referred article, the option to adjourn its decision."[44] This power seeks to avoid unnecessary suspensions and, ultimately, ensure that the outcome of the process will be sufficiently guaranteed so as to not affect the party.[45] The provisions of Article 1463 are applicable to proceedings related to arbitrations seated in Mexico as well as abroad.[46]

In a recent decision, the Eleventh Federal District Court in Civil Matters in Mexico City decided to proceed with the recognition and enforcement of an award notwithstanding that it had been challenged and the decision on annulment not yet res judicata.[47] In our opinion, this approach is compatible with the pro-arbitration bias that all courts should adopt pursuant to Article 17 of the Mexican Constitution.[48] However, the circumstances of the specific case play a pivotal role in this kind of resolution, which is why a case-by-case analysis is recommendable.

If a Mexican court recognizes an arbitral award and orders its enforcement, it acknowledges that the arbitration agreement is valid, that the parties were afforded the opportunity to present their case, and that the arbitral tribunal did not exceed its competence. The consequence of the acknowledgment of these points is that the award is binding upon the parties. Additionally, through its decision to recognize and enforce an award, the court is necessarily declaring that the subject matter of the dispute is arbitrable, and does not violate Mexican public policy.

Once the decision regarding the recognition and enforcement of the award becomes res judicata,[49] the winning party can file a motion to enforce the award through which the court may grant the use of public force to seize assets to ensure the payment of any amount due under the award.

44. Instituto Mexicano de Arbitraje, *supra*, p. 286.
45. *Ibid.*, pp. 286-287.
46. *Ibid.*
47. Special trial on commercial transactions and arbitration 73/2022.
48. *Article 17.* ... The laws shall provide for alternative dispute resolution mechanisms. ... .
49. *See* next section on the available remedies against the court decision issued in an award recognition and enforcement proceeding, and the moment in which the ruling becomes final.

[G] AVAILABLE REMEDIES AGAINST THE RECOGNITION AND ENFORCEMENT OF AN ARBITRAL AWARD

Pursuant to Article 1476 of the Mexican Commerce Code, the parties cannot appeal the decision issued in the special process to request the recognition and enforcement of an award.[50] Nonetheless, the court decision that recognizes and orders the enforcement of the award is not final, since the losing party can file a constitutional proceeding named "*amparo*" against the ruling.

In *amparo* proceedings, the parties can raise arguments concerning the violation of their fundamental rights, such as due process or fair and equal treatment. *Amparo* claims are filed before Federal Courts, which are the only Mexican courts authorized to decide on the unconstitutionality of acts of the State. There are two different types of *amparo* proceedings to raise constitutional claims: the direct *amparo* claim, and the indirect *amparo* claim.

A direct *amparo* claim allows the plaintiff to raise arguments concerning the constitutionality of rulings that are final, and arguments challenging the constitutionality of the decisions issued in proceedings that are carried out in the same form as a trial. An indirect *amparo* claim allows the plaintiff to raise arguments concerning the unconstitutionality of acts of the State other than final rulings.

Another difference is that for indirect *amparo* claims, there is always the possibility of filing a constitutional appeal that reviews the decision issued in the *amparo* proceeding. In other words, unless the parties decide against filing an appeal, an indirect *amparo* claim is always a two-instance proceeding. In contrast, a direct *amparo* proceeding only admits a constitutional appeal under specific circumstances determined by law and the resolutions of the Supreme Court, such as the societal interest of a specific case, the transcendence of the case, or the novelty of the analysis required to resolve the case.

There was a judicial debate derived from contradicting precedents regarding the available remedy against a judicial decision on the recognition and enforcement of an arbitral award. The Plenary on Civil Matters of the First Circuit held that the legal remedy was the direct *amparo*,[51] whereas the Third Collegiate Circuit Court of Civil Matters in the Sixth Circuit held it was indirect *amparo*.[52] The differing stances were reached based on contradicting criteria regarding whether the resolution issued in recognition and enforcement proceedings can be considered rulings that "put an end" to a trial or not.

50. Commerce Code *Article 1476.*: Once the hearing has been held, the judge shall summon the parties to hear the decision. The intermediate resolutions The intermediate resolutions dictated in this special trial and the decision that resolves it will not be appealable.
51. Binding Precedent PC.I.C. J/23 C (10a.), under registration number 2010812, issued by the Plenary on Civil Matters of the First Circuit, Tenth Period, Civil and Common Matters, Gazette of the Federal Official Weekly, Book 26, Volume III, p. 2214, January 2006, under heading: "*ARBITRATION AWARD. THE TERMINAL RESOLUTION ON ITS NULLITY OR RECOGNITION AND ENFORCEMENT ISSUED IN THE SPECIAL PROCEEDING CAN BE CHALLENGED VIA DIRECT AMPARO.*"
52. *See*: Ruling on the Direct Amparo 505/2018 issued by the Third Collegiate Circuit Court on Civil Matters of the Sixth Circuit.

In December 2019, the First Chamber of the Supreme Court analyzed these contradictory criteria and issued a binding precedent stating that the available legal remedy is the indirect *amparo*.[53] According to this precedent, judicial proceedings related to the setting aside or recognition and enforcement of awards do not constitute final rulings that trigger the use of direct *amparo*, since they do not resolve the merits of the dispute (which were resolved through the award).

This decision has been the subject of criticism.[54] An indirect *amparo* claim will always entail the possibility of challenging the ruling through a constitutional appeal. Accordingly, a party who refuses to comply voluntarily with an award will have two opportunities to challenge the recognition and enforcement of the award, necessarily extending the timeframe for the award creditor to finally obtain the judicial recognition and enforcement of it. The result is contrary to the principle of celerity of arbitral proceedings.

[H] AVAILABLE INTERIM MEASURES

According to Article 1425 of the Commerce Code, parties can seek interim measures before Mexican courts before the commencement of the arbitration proceeding or during the arbitration.[55] However, this code is silent concerning the possibility of obtaining interim relief once the arbitral tribunal issues its award, and while it is pending recognition and enforcement.

This silence could be interpreted as an impediment to obtaining interim relief to ensure the recognition and enforcement of an arbitral award, given that Title IV to the Fifth Book of the Mexican Commerce Code contains the regulation related to arbitration proceedings and the judicial intervention in such proceedings, including the recognition and enforcement of an award.

However, others could argue that it is possible to obtain interim measures to guarantee that the losing party would be capable of fulfilling the award since the Plenary on Civil Matters of the First Circuit issued a binding precedent stating that interim measures are inherent to the right of access to justice; hence, the possibility to adopt injunctive relief and the nature of the relief that may be granted must be analyzed on a case-by-case scenario.[56]

---

53. Binding Precedent 1a./J. 87/2019 (10a.), under registration number 2010812, issued by the First Chamber of the Supreme Court of Justice, Tenth Period, Civil and Common Matters, Gazette of the Federal Official Weekly, Book 26, Volume III, p. 2214, January 2006, under heading: "*ARBITRATION AWARD. THE TERMINAL RESOLUTION ON ITS NULLITY OR RECOGNITION AND ENFORCEMENT ISSUED IN THE SPECIAL PROCEEDING CAN BE CHALLENGED VIA DIRECT AMPARO.*"
54. *See*: Asociación Latinoamericana de Arbitraje, Revista ALARB. Arbitraje y Constitución, Volumen I (2020) (https://arbitrajeccc.org/wp-content/uploads/2021/02/Volumen-1-2020-Arbitraje-y-Constitucion.pdf).
55. *Article 1425.:* Even if there is an arbitration agreement, the parties may, prior to the arbitration proceedings or during their arbitration proceedings or during the course thereof, request the judge to order interim injunctive relief, interim measures.
56. Binding Precedent PC.I.C. J/94 C (10a.), under registration number 2020903, issued by the Plenary on Civil Matters of the First Circuit, Tenth Period, Constitutional and Civil Matters,

Since Article 1425 of the Commerce Code does not establish a specific procedure to obtain interim relief once an award has been issued, this second position would rely on the general provisions of this code.

In this vein, Article 1168 of the Commerce Code refers to the possibility of obtaining interim measures in commercial judicial proceedings. Further, Article 1177 of this code establishes that a party to a commercial proceeding can request interim measures before or after the claims have been filed.[57] In the first scenario, i.e., before the commencement of a trial, the interim measures requested can be granted ex parte.

The possibility to grant interim measures ex parte, or without prior hearing, has been sustained by the Plenary and the First Chamber of the Supreme Court, which have issued non-binding precedents confirming the foregoing, both in the case of interim measures in general, as well as specifically in the case of seizure of assets, which is one of the most common means to guarantee the enforcement of an award. [58]

Further, the Collegiate Circuit Courts have interpreted Article 1478 of the Commerce Code. According to a non-binding precedent issued by the Fourth Collegiate Circuit Court in Civil Matters of the First Circuit, Article 1478 provides for the complete discretion of judges when granting interim measures. The court ruled that this procedure shall have maximum flexibility in light of the unforeseeable situations that may arise in any specific case.[59]

In other jurisdictions, it is not uncommon for a party seeking the annulment of an award to also file an anti-suit injunction to avoid the winning party from seeking the recognition and held that any interim relief that orders a party to refrain from

---

Gazette of the Federal Official Weekly, Book 71, October 2019, Volume III, p. 2979, under heading "*PRECAUTIONARY MEASURES OR PRECAUTIONARY MEASURES IN COMMERCIAL LAWSUITS. THEY ARE INHERENT TO THE RIGHT TO JURISDICTION, THEREFORE THE LIMITATION OF THEIR GRANTING MUST FOLLOW A FUNCTIONAL INTERPRETATION IN ACCORDANCE WITH ARTICLE 1168 OF THE COMMERCE CODE AND ARTICLES 1 AND 17 OF THE CONSTITUTION.*"

57. *Article 1177.:* The provisional injunctions established by this Code may be decreed, both as pre-judicial acts, as well as after the initiation of any of the lawsuits provided for therein. In the first of the cases, the order will be decreed outright, without summoning the person against whom it is requested, once the requirements set forth in this ordinance have been met. In the second case, the order shall be substantiated in an incident, by a separate docket of the case file, and shall be heard by the judge or court which, at the time the request is filed, is hearing the case.
58. Non-binding precedent P. IX/97, under registration number 199503, issued by The Plenary of the Supreme Court. Tenth Period, Civil matters, Judicial Weekly of the Federation and its Gazette. Volume V, January 1997, p. 115, under heading "*INTERIM MEASURE. ITS DECREE OR LIFTING DOES NOT REQUIRE A PRIOR HEARING.*" and Non-binding precedent 1a. CCXLII/2018 (10a.), under registration number 2018656, issued by the first chamber of the Supreme Court, Tenth Period, Constitutional and Civil Matters, Gazette of the Judicial Weekly of the Federation. Book 61, December 2018, Volume I, p. 316, under heading "*SEIZURE IN COMMERCIAL PROCEEDINGS. IN ITS ISSUANCE, LIFTING OR SUBSTITUTION, THE RIGHT TO A PRIOR HEARING DOES NOT APPLY.*"
59. Non-binding precedent I.4o.C.34 C (10a.), under registration number 2012480, issued by the Fourth Collegiate Circuit Court in Civil Matters in the First Circuit, Tenth Period, Civil Matters, Gazette of the Federal Official Weekly of the Federation, book 34, September 2016, Volume IV, p. 2878, under heading "*PROCEDURE FOR THE JUDICIAL ADOPTION OF INTERIM MEASURES RELATED TO ARBITRATION. IS SUBJECT TO THE BROAD DISCRETION OF THE JUDGE.*"

submitting a dispute before courts violates the fundamental right of access to justice and is contrary to Article 17 of the Mexican Constitution.[60]

This matter is not settled. Even if there are some arguments to support the possibility of obtaining interim relief to ensure the recognition and enforcement of an award, it is also reasonable to argue that the Commerce Code does not regulate these requests and, therefore, the courts cannot grant these types of injunctions. At the time of writing, Mexican Courts have not addressed this issue. Until there is a binding precedent on this matter, it would depend on a case-by-case scenario to determine whether it is possible to obtain interim relief once the arbitral tribunal issues its award, while it is pending recognition and enforcement.

[I] CONCLUSION

Like many other countries, Mexico follows the tradition of adopting the UNCITRAL Model Law into its legislation for regulating arbitral proceedings in general and specifically, the recognition and enforcement of arbitral awards. The incorporation of the provisions of the Model Law into the Mexican Commerce Code alongside the necessary special rules to ensure the efficacy of the regulation within the Mexican legal system has led to a modern legislation that is up to date with the highest international standards.

This combination has strengthened the arbitration arena in Mexico and has positioned the country as a trustworthy and solid choice for carrying out arbitration proceedings, particularly given that the pro-arbitration principle is not only codified in law but also enshrined in the Mexican constitution.

A lot of the credit for the development of the regulation of arbitration proceedings has come from both binding and non-binding precedents issued by the judiciary. The criteria adopted by the tribunals of the State have deepened the understanding of the legal provisions and principles that regulate arbitration in Mexico through the various interpretations of the scope of the different legal figures encompassed by the regulatory framework.

Moreover, the judicial precedents have also solidified the harmonious interaction between the specific Mexican law and the provisions of both the Model Law and international treaties on the subject and have gradually perfected an already forefront legislation. In turn, Mexico has become a strong choice of arbitral seat and has the

60. *See*: Non-binding precedent I.15o.C.3 C (11a.), under registration number 2024663, issued by the Fifteenth Collegiate Circuit Court in Civil Matters in the First Circuit, Eleventh Period, Constitutional and Civil Matters, Gazette of the Federal Official Journal, Book 13, May 2022, Volume V, p. 4679, under heading "*PRECAUTIONARY MEASURES IN COMMERCIAL MATTERS. IT IS IMPROPER TO DECREE THEM IF THEIR PURPOSE IS TO INHIBIT OR PREVENT A PERSON FROM EXERCISING THE CORRESPONDING ACTIONS BEFORE THE COURTS, SINCE THIS IMPLIES VIOLATING THE RIGHT OF ACCESS TO JURISDICTION.*"; *See also*: Non-binding precedent, under registration number, issued by the Fifteenth Collegiate Circuit in Civil Matters in the First Circuit, Tenth Period, Common Matter, Gazette of the Federal Official Weekly, Book 72, November 2019, Volume III, p. 2520, under heading "*PROVISIONAL STAY OF EXECUTION. IT IS APPROPRIATE TO GRANT IT AGAINST A PRECAUTIONARY MEASURE THAT RESTRICTS THE FUNDAMENTAL RIGHT OF ACCESS TO JUSTICE.*"

necessary legal engineering to ensure that both national and foreign arbitral awards are truly enforceable.

Despite these advances, there is still room for improvement and further development of the legal framework surrounding arbitration, and concretely, in matters related to the recognition and enforcement of arbitral awards. Courts have hindered the celerity and efficiency of the enforcement proceeding by incorrectly determining that the legal remedy against the resolution issued in the special trial is an indirect *amparo* claim given that this ruling is not a final decision that puts an end to a trial, thus allowing the possibility of more judicial revisions to this decision and deferring the actual materialization of the effects of the award. If possible, it would be beneficial to reconsider this decision and emit a new precedent on the subject.

Nonetheless, Mexico has a pro-enforcement bias and its courts have adopted corresponding practices that go beyond the Model Law's provisions. This includes the possibility of obtaining interim measures specifically aimed at guaranteeing the enforcement of awards, such as the seizure of assets, which can even be granted ex parte.

In any case, the very clear pro-arbitration stance that has been embraced by Mexican law, and the commitment of both congress and the judiciary to ensure that this principle is effectively applied, has placed Mexico as a significant player within the international arbitration forum.

CHAPTER 12

Setting Aside Arbitration Awards in Mexico

Vicente Bañuelos Rizo

[A] LEGAL FRAMEWORK AND TREATY PROVISIONS

As a UNCITRAL Model Law (Model Law) jurisdiction,[1] Mexico strongly favors national and international arbitration, and the thresholds for setting aside an award—the same as the Model Law's, mimic those of the New York Convention and the Panama Convention. In Mexico, the criteria for setting aside awards have been consistently interpreted in favor of the validity and enforcement of awards.

As mentioned in previous chapters of this book, Commercial Law in Mexico, both substantive and procedural, is Federal and applicable to all of the thirty-one states and the Capital (Mexico City) that comprise the Mexican Republic.[2] Commercial arbitration is organized by the Commercial Federal Code, namely the Title IV of the Fifth Book.

The Model Law was incorporated into the Commercial Code in 1993,[3] extending its scope not only to international arbitrations but also to national arbitrations.[4] This

1. The 1985 version of the UNCITRAL Model Law on International Commercial Arbitration was enacted in Mexico in the year 1993 (Federal Official Gazette, Jul. 22, 1993), by amending Section Fourth, "Commercial Arbitration" of the last and Fifth Book of the Commercial Code). In 2011, some articles of this section were amended and added, with the intention to regulate the specific proceedings that apply to the judicial supervision and assistance to arbitration proceedings.
2. The Mexican Republic is comprised of thirty-one States and the capital, Mexico City, all of which have their own Executive, Legislative and Judicial Branches.
3. Although some provisions of the Model Law were incorporated in 1989 (Federal Official Gazette, Jan. 4, 1989), the "tropicalization" made by the Mexican Legislature was substantial, and therefore, it was not until 1993 that the 1985 version of the UNCITRAL Model Law was adopted.
4. The motivation of the Legislative Branch was:

> The main virtue of the Model Law is its international recognition. If, when negotiating a contract or the settlement of a dispute, the national law is proposed and assimilated to the UNCITRAL Model Law, there would be no need to consider a specific national law, thus eliminating fears and suspicions. One of the issues that most interest the

approach, taken by many other jurisdictions, enhances the uniformity sought by the Model Law and has substantially increased the set of cases that interpret it.

Mexico is also a signatory state to the New York[5] and Panama Conventions,[6] which together with its extensive pro-arbitration case law, makes it an arbitration-friendly jurisdiction.

[B] THE ACTION TO SET ASIDE AN AWARD AS THE ONLY AVAILABLE RECOURSE

According to the Model Law, the only recourse available against an award is an application for setting it aside.[7] When enacting the Model Law, Mexico redrafted the Spanish version of the Model Law, and applied the adverb "only" to the annulment,

parties when determining the place of arbitration is precisely the law applicable to the arbitration trial; therefore, the proposed reform would promote Mexico as a venue for international commercial arbitrations, whether they involve issues in which a Mexican party is interested or arbitration between foreign parties. Although of recent date, the following countries have enacted laws based on the UNCITRAL Model Law: Australia, Bulgaria, Canada, Cyprus, Hong Kong, Nigeria, Peru, Scotland, United States of America, which confirms its adaptation to the political, legal, and economic systems of the various regions of the world. However, it is considered that at present, in light of the increasing globalization of world markets, there is no justification for differentiating, in commercial matters, between domestic and international commercial arbitration, which is why both domestic and international commercial arbitration would be maintained as the scope of application, as had already been established in the legal reforms of 1988. (translated by the author).

The original Spanish text reads:

La principal virtud de la Ley Modelo es su reconocimiento internacional. Si al negociarse un contrato o la solución de una controversia, se propone la ley nacional, y ésta se asimila a la Ley Modelo de la CNUDMI, no se tendría que estudiar una ley nacional específica, eliminándose así temores y suspicacias. Una de las cuestiones que más interesa a las partes cuando determinan el lugar del arbitraje, es precisamente la ley aplicable al juicio arbitral; de modo que la reforma que se propone, promovería que México fuera sede de arbitrajes comerciales internacionales, ya sea que se trate de cuestiones en las que una parte mexicana esté interesada, o que se trate de arbitraje entre partes extranjeras. No obstante ser de fecha reciente, han promulgado leyes basadas en la Ley Modelo de la CNUDMI: Australia, Bulgaria, Canadá, Chipre, Escocia, Estados Unidos de América, Hong Kong, Nigeria, Perú; lo que confirma su adecuación a los sistemas políticos, jurídicos y económicos de las diversas regiones del globo. Por otro lado, se considera que en la actualidad, a la luz de la cada vez mayor globalización de los mercados mundiales, no se justifica la diferenciación, en materia comercial, entre el arbitraje comercial interno y el internacional; razón por la cual se mantendría como ámbito de aplicación tanto el arbitraje comercial nacional como el internacional, como ya se había establecido en las reformas legales de 1988.

5. Mexico is a party to the Convention on the Recognition and Enforcement of Foreign Arbitral Awards, also known as *New York Convention*, since 1971 (Federal Official Gazette, Jun. 22, 1971).
6. Mexico is a party to the Inter-American Convention on International Commercial Arbitration, also known as *Panama Convention*, since 1978 (Federal Official Gazette, Apr. 27, 1978).
7. Article 34 of the Model Law.

rather than stressing—as intended by the drafters of the Model Law[8]—that the only available recourse against an award is an application or action[9] to set it aside:

> Article 1457.—Arbitral awards may only be annulled by the competent judge when:
>
> I. —The party bringing the action proves that:
> a) One of the parties to the arbitration agreement was affected by any incapacity, or that such agreement is not valid under the law to which the parties have subjected it, or failing any indication thereon, under the Mexican legislation;
> b) It was not duly notified of the appointment of an arbitrator or the arbitral proceedings, or was unable, for any other reason, to assert its rights;
> c) The award deals with a dispute not provided for in the arbitration agreement or contains decisions that exceed the terms of the arbitration agreement. However, if the decisions on matters submitted to arbitration can be separated from those not submitted to arbitration, only the latter may be annulled; or
> d) The composition of the arbitral tribunal or the arbitral procedure were not in accordance with the agreement of the parties, unless such agreement was in conflict with a provision of this Section from which the parties cannot derogate, or, failing such agreement, did not comply with this Section; or
>
> II. —The judge finds that, according to Mexican legislation, the subject-matter of the dispute is not susceptible of being settled by arbitration, or that the award is contrary to public policy.[10]

---

8. The original text of the proposed article reads: "Article 34. Application for setting aside as *exclusive* recourse against tribunal award," as shown in the *Travaux préparatoires* of the Model Law, while the Explanatory Note further explains: "The first measure of improvement is to allow only one type of recourse, to the exclusion of any other means of recourse regulated in another procedural law of the State in question."

   Yearbook of the United Nations Comission on International Trade Law, 317th Meeting (Jun. 11, 1985) https://uncitral.un.org/en/texts/arbitration/modellaw/commercial_arbitration/travaux.

   Explanatory Note by the UNCITRAL Secretariat on the Model Law in International Commercial Arbitration (Jun. 21, 1994), https://uncitral.un.org/en/texts/arbitration/modellaw/commercial_arbitration.
9. The Mexican Legislature substituted the word "application" and used "action," in order to make it consistent with Mexican procedural practice, and more importantly, to some provisions—such as the those organizing the burden of proof—that refer to action. We refer to the burden of proving in sub-section [E][1][a] of this chapter.
10. Translated by the author. The original Spanish text reads:

> Artículo 1457.—Los laudos arbitrales sólo podrán ser anulados por el juez competente cuando:
>
> I. —La parte que intente la acción pruebe que:
> a) Una de las partes en el acuerdo de arbitraje estaba afectada por alguna incapacidad, o que dicho acuerdo no es válido en virtud de la ley a que las partes lo han sometido, o si nada se hubiese indicado a ese respecto en virtud de la legislación mexicana;
> b) No fue debidamente notificada de la designación de un árbitro o de las actuaciones arbitrales, o no hubiere podido, por cualquier otra razón, hacer valer sus derechos;

Even with this amended drafting, Article 1421 of the Commercial Code—inspired by Article 5 of the Model Law, which adopts the non-intervention principle applicable to Courts—prevents other actions or recourses against the award:

> Article 1421.—Unless otherwise provided, in matters governed by this title, judicial intervention shall not be required.[11]

The criterion that the only recourse against an award is the application to set it aside, which excludes recourses against provisional orders issued by arbitrators or an action to annul the arbitration proceeding, has been confirmed in at least two Federal precedents:

(1) The Third Collegiate Court in Civil Matters of the First Circuit (Case 172973) ruled that any act or procedural order that takes place or is issued within the arbitration procedure, may not be subject to a judicial recourse, because the arbitration agreement has the effect of barring any judicial action or recourse, except in those cases where the judicial supervision and control is expressly required by the Commercial Code, referring to the application to set aside an award as one of the cases where judicial intervention is permitted. This Collegiate Court stressed that arbitration would not be efficient if Courts were indiscriminately allowed to intervene in arbitrations.[12]

(2) The Seventh Collegiate Court in Civil Matters of the First Circuit (Case 163414) ruled that once an award has been rendered, it may only be reviewed by a Court if there is an application to set it aside under Articles 1457 and 1458 or a recognition and enforcement petition under Articles 1460, 1461 and 1462 of the Commercial Code,[13] stressing that the "arbitration procedure" itself may not be subject to an annulment action, because such an action is not provided for in the Commercial Code, and a Court does not have the power to create actions not statutorily regulated.

---

c) El laudo se refiere a una controversia no prevista en el acuerdo de arbitraje o contiene decisiones que exceden los términos del acuerdo de arbitraje. No obstante, si las disposiciones del laudo que se refieren a las cuestiones sometidas al arbitraje pueden separarse de las que no lo están, sólo se podrán anular estas últimas; o

d) La composición del tribunal arbitral o el procedimiento arbitral no se ajustaron en el acuerdo celebrado entre las partes, salvo que dicho acuerdo estuviera en conflicto con una disposición del presente título de la que las partes no pudieran apartarse o, a falta de dicho acuerdo, que no se ajustaron al presente título; o

II. —El juez compruebe que según la legislación mexicana, el objeto de la controversia no es susceptible de arbitraje, o que el laudo es contrario al orden público.

11. Translated by the author. The original Spanish text reads: "Artículo 1421.—Salvo disposición en contrario, en los asuntos que se rijan por el presente título, no se requerirá intervención judicial."
12. *Collegiate Circuit Courts* (Mexico), Case 172973, I.3o.C.566 C; TA.
13. *Collegiate Circuit Courts* (Mexico), Case 63414, I.7o.C.151 C; TA.

In conclusion, Mexican Case Law makes it clear that the only possible recourse against an award is the "action" to set it aside, although a defendant may resist the recognition and enforcement of an award, based on almost identical causes, per Article 1462 of the Commercial Code.

[C] STATUTE OF LIMITATION

The Commercial Code adopted the three-month statute of limitation to file a petition to annul the award, contained in paragraph 3 of Article 34 of the Model Law:

> Article 1458.—The petition for annulment must be submitted within a period of three months from the date of notification of the award, or if the request has been made in accordance with Articles 1450 and 1451, from the date on which that request has been resolved by the arbitral tribunal.[14]

According to Article 1419 of the Commercial Code, the three-month period starts running the next day the award is notified and if the deadline falls on a non-working day, it is extended until the next working day when the Courts resume.[15]

Generally, an award is notified by electronic means and later hand-served or received via courier. Even though an argument can be made that the original award is required to file it as the basis of the application, a cautious litigant should consider the first notification, generally the electronic notification, for purposes of calculating the deadline to file the petition.

In the case one of the parties has requested a correction, interpretation or an additional award, the statute of limitation starts to run after such application has been resolved and notified by the Tribunal. Although the extension of the time limit for these reasons is prone to delaying tactics, the Working Group in charge of drafting the Model Law decided to retain this extension as it was a reasonable consequence of the possibility of making such requests.[16]

14. Translated by the author. The original Spanish text reads: "Artículo 1458.—La petición de nulidad deberá formularse dentro de un plazo de tres meses contado a partir de la fecha de la notificación del laudo o, si la petición se ha hecho con arreglo a los artículos 1450 y 1451 desde la fecha en que esa petición haya sido resuelta por el tribunal arbitral."
15. Article 1419 has no counterpart in the Model Law, but its drafting is similar to that of Art. 2 of the UNCITRAL Arbitration Rules: "Article 1419.—For the purposes of calculating the time-limits provided for in this Section, such time-limits shall begin to run from the day following that on which a notification, note, communication, or proposal is received. If the last day of that period is an official holiday or non-working day at the place of residence or business establishment of the recipient, this period will be extended until the next working day. All other official holidays or non-working days that occur during the course of the period shall be included in the calculation of the period." (translated by the author). The original Spanish text reads: "Artículo 1419.—Para los fines del cómputo de plazos establecidos en el presente título, dichos plazos comenzarán a correr desde el día siguiente a aquél en que se reciba una notificación, nota, comunicación o propuesta. Si el último día de ese plazo es feriado oficial o no laborable en el lugar de residencia o establecimiento de los negocios del destinatario, dicho plazo se prorrogará hasta el primer día laborable siguiente. Los demás días feriados oficiales o no laborables que ocurran durante el transcurso del plazo se incluirán en el cómputo del plazo."
16. A/CN.9/246, para. 138.

[D] PROCEDURE TO FILE AN APPLICATION TO SET ASIDE AN AWARD

[1] Competent Court

Article 1422 of the Commercial Code provides that whenever judicial intervention is required, the Court with jurisdiction shall be that of the place of arbitration:

> Article 1422.—When judicial intervention is required, the Federal Court of first instance or the State Court of the place where the arbitration takes place shall have jurisdiction to hear the matter.
>
> When the place of arbitration is outside of the national territory, the Federal Court of first instance or the State Court with jurisdiction in the domicile of the party against whom enforcement is sought, or alternatively, the location of the assets, shall have jurisdiction to handle the recognition and enforcement of the award.[17]

When the place of arbitration is abroad, the Commercial Code clearly provides that no action to set aside the award may be brought before the Mexican Courts. Article 1415 of the Commercial Code, interpreted *a contrario sensu,* excludes the Articles of the code that organize the recourse to set the award aside—that is, Articles 1457, 1458 and 1459 of the Commercial Code—by providing which are the only Articles of the code that apply to arbitrations that take place abroad:

> Article 1415.—... The provisions of Articles 1424, 1425, 1461, 1462, and 1463 shall apply even when the place of arbitration is outside the national territory.[18]

The Supreme Court has already resolved this matter in a non-binding but very persuasive precedent.[19] The case refers to a joint venture agreement executed between U.S. and Mexican companies, whose purpose was to open convenience stores within the northern part of Mexico. The agreement provided that a new Mexican company would be incorporated and that any dispute under the agreement would be resolved through arbitration, under the ICC arbitration rules, with San Diego as the place of arbitration. The U.S. investor commenced arbitration against the Mexican company, claiming the restitution of profits that were unduly distributed, and an order to

17. Translated by the author. The original Spanish text reads: "Artículo 1422.—Cuando se requiera la intervención judicial será competente para conocer el juez de primera instancia federal o del orden común del lugar donde se lleve a cabo el arbitraje. ... Cuando el lugar del arbitraje se encuentre fuera del territorio nacional, conocerá del reconocimiento y de la ejecución del laudo el juez de primera instancia federal o del orden común competente, del domicilio del ejecutado o, en su defecto, el de la ubicación de los bienes."
18. Translated by the author. The original Spanish text reads: "Artículo 1415.—... Lo dispuesto en los artículos 1424, 1425, 1461, 1462 y 1463, se aplicará aún cuando el lugar del arbitraje se encuentre fuera del territorio nacional."
19. At the time this judgment was issued, the Law provided for additional requirements for decisions from the Supreme Court of Justice to become a binding precedent. Nevertheless, all precedents from the Supreme Court of Justice that are not binding, become a very persuasive authority that is normally followed by the Courts of the country.

reinstate officers that were removed in violation of the agreement. A panel of three arbitrators found in favor of the U.S. investor, and the Mexican company filed an action to set aside the award before the Tijuana Courts (Baja California). The U.S. investor objected to the jurisdiction of the Tijuana Courts, and the Court of Appeals of Baja California ruled that the Tijuana Court lacked jurisdiction to resolve an action to set aside the award.

The Mexican company filed a constitutional appeal (Amparo Directo 8/2011), and the Supreme Court of Justice upheld the decision issued by the Court of Appeals. The Court found that according to Articles 1415, 1422 and 1457 of the Commercial Code, together with Articles I, V and VI of the New York Convention, and 5 of the Panama Convention, when an international arbitration takes place outside of Mexico, no action to set aside the award may be brought before a Mexican Court. The synthesis published by the Court is the following:

> INTERNATIONAL COMMERCIAL ARBITRATION. THE COURT OF THE PLACE WHERE IT TOOK PLACE IS COMPETENT TO RULE ON THE SETTING ASIDE OF THE AWARD. From the combined interpretation of Articles 1422, 1457, 1461, and 1462 of the Commercial Code, as well as the Convention on the Recognition and Enforcement of Foreign Arbitral Awards (New York Convention), adopted on 10 June 1958, and published in the Official Gazette of the Federation on 22 June 1971, and the Inter-American Convention on International Commercial Arbitration (Panama Convention), signed on 30 January 1975, and published in the same official publication on 27 April 1978, one must conclude that only the Court of the place where the international arbitration proceedings were conducted may rule on the nullity of an international arbitral award. This is in accordance with the rules adopted by the Commercial Code, which enjoy international consensus aimed at ensuring the effectiveness of awards issued in international arbitration proceedings, providing legal certainty, and avoiding that parties in conflict resort to their domestic courts to request the nullity of an award when it is not in their favor; a different solution would cause the jurisdiction of national judges to be exceeded by allowing them to annul resolutions issued abroad according to foreign law.[20]

It is remarkable that the Supreme Court of Justice also applied Article 1422 in a similar but vice-versa manner, depriving effects to a foreign judgment that ordered the recognition and enforcement of an award. In a dispute between a foreign reinsurance company and a Mexican insurance company (Aseguradora Interacciones, S.A.), the former obtained from the High Court of Justice of the United Kingdom a judgment recognizing the award issued in that country. The foreign reinsurer brought an action to enforce the UK judgment—which had already recognized the UK award—instead of an action to recognize and enforce that foreign award. This action was brought before

20. Translated by the author. *Supreme Court of Justice* (Mexico), Case 161136; 1a. CLXXIII/2011, TA. The public version of the judgment is accessible at www.newyorkconvention1958.org, and is referred as: Mexico/Jun. 29, 2011/Mexico, Primera Sala de la Suprema Corte de Justicia de la Nación (First Chamber of the Supreme Court of Justice of the Nation)/Amparo directo 8/2011. The synthesis quoted above does not refer to Art. 1415, but the judgment repeatedly refers to said legal provision.

a Mexico City District Court which granted enforcement. After several appeals, the Mexican Supreme Court of Justice attracted the matter. On the ground that, pursuant to the New York Convention, the High Court of Justice of the United Kingdom lacked jurisdiction to recognize and enforce an award that would have effects in Mexico (even if it had jurisdiction within its own country):

> Article 1422.—... When the place of arbitration is outside of the national territory, the Federal Court of first instance or the State Court with jurisdiction in the domicile of the party against whom enforcement is sought, or alternatively, the location of the assets, shall have jurisdiction to handle the recognition and enforcement of the award
>
> From the above, it can be inferred that the issue of jurisdiction is fundamental to determine whether foreign judgments and rulings are enforceable. For the recognition and enforcement of an award (when the place of arbitration is outside the national territory), the judge with jurisdiction is that of the domicile of the party against whom enforcement is sought or, alternatively, the location of the assets, has jurisdiction.
>
> In the same provision cited above, it is established that, to resolve matters related to jurisdiction, the recognized rules of international law must be taken into account. Article III of the Convention on the Recognition and Enforcement of Foreign Arbitral Awards, of which Mexico and the United Kingdom are parties, provides the following:
>
>> Each Contracting State shall recognize arbitral awards as binding and enforce them in accordance with the rules of procedure of the territory where the award is relied upon, under the conditions laid down in the following Articles. There shall not be imposed substantially more onerous conditions or higher fees or charges on the recognition or enforcement of arbitral awards to which this Convention applies than are imposed on the recognition or enforcement of domestic arbitral awards.
>
> Therefore, this Court concludes that pursuant to Articles 1347-A,[21] paragraph III, and 1422 of the Commercial Code, in relation to the transcribed provision of the Convention on the Recognition and Enforcement of Foreign Arbitral Awards, the High Court of Justice of the United Kingdom lacked the legal power to homologate an arbitral award rendered in that country because it is intended to be enforced in Mexico.[22]

This precedent bars the enforcement of foreign judgments that recognize the validity of domestic awards, that may be used to bypass the national recognition and enforcement proceedings applicable under the Commercial Code, as well as the provisions of the New York and Panama Conventions.

21. Article 1347-A, para. III of the Commercial Code, provides that a foreign judgment may only be enforce if the foreign Court has jurisdiction to resolve the matter "under the rules recognized by international law."
22. Translated by the author. This precedent was downloaded from https://bj.scjn.gob.mx/doc/sentencias_pub/9jMu3ngB_UqKst8omxLw/%22Carta%20rogatoria%22 on Jul. 24, 2023. Mexico/Apr. 6, 2011/Mexico, Primera Sala de la Suprema Corte de Justicia de la Nación (First Chamber of the Supreme Court of Justice of the Nation)/Amparo en Revisión 371/2010.

[2] Procedure and Recourses

The current proceeding to set aside an award was amended in 2011,[23] and is provided for in Articles 1470 to 1477 of the Commercial Code:

> Article 1470.—The following petitions shall be processed in accordance with Articles 1472 to 1476: ... V. The setting aside of commercial transactions and arbitral awards.
>
> Article 1471.—For the recognition and enforcement of awards referred to in Articles 1461 to 1463 of this Code, no homologation procedure is required. Except when recognition and enforcement are requested as a defense in a lawsuit or another proceeding, the recognition and enforcement shall be pursued through the special trial referred to in Articles 1472 to 1476.
>
> Article 1472.—The special trial related to commercial transactions and arbitration, referred to in Articles 1470 and 1471, shall be conducted in accordance with the following Articles.
>
> Article 1473.—Once the lawsuit is admitted, the judge shall order the defendants to be summoned, granting them a term of fifteen days to respond.
>
> Article 1474.—Once the term to respond the lawsuit has elapsed, without the need for a default petition, if the parties do not submit evidence, or the judge does not consider it necessary, a hearing for closing arguments will be scheduled within the following three days, regardless of whether the parties attend.
>
> Article 1475.—If evidence is offered or deemed necessary by the judge prior to the hearing, a ten-day period for presenting evidence will be granted.
>
> Article 1476.—After the hearing, the judge will summon the parties to hear the judgment. Interim rulings issued within this special trial and the judgment resolving it are not subject to recourse.
>
> Article 1477.—Special trials related to the setting aside or recognition and enforcement of commercial awards may be joined together. For this consolidation to take place, the closing arguments hearing must not have taken place. The joinder shall be made in favor of the Court that heard the case first. Consolidation is not permissible under cases tried between different territorial jurisdictions or foreign jurisdictions, nor between Federal and State Courts. The consolidation process is subject to the provisions of Articles 73 to 75 of the Federal Code of Civil Procedures. The resolution regarding the consolidation is not subject to recourse.[24]

Once the lawsuit is filed, the Court issues an initial ruling, and if the lawsuit and its exhibits are in order, it will admit the lawsuit and order its summoning through the Court clerk, or if national or international cooperation is required, through requesting assistance to a national or international Court with jurisdiction in the place where the defendants reside. When the Court finds the lawsuit is deficient, it should give the plaintiff an opportunity to correct, amend or complement the lawsuit, or accompany certain documents.[25] If the plaintiff fails to comply, then the lawsuit is rejected.

---

23. Federal Official Gazette, Jan. 27, 2011.
24. Translated by the author. The original Spanish version may be accessed at http://www.ordenjuridico.gob.mx.
25. Although there is no specific legal provision ordering a Court to grant the plaintiff an opportunity to correct, amend or supplement the lawsuit, there are at least two precedents applicable by analogy, that support this conclusion: (1) *Circuit Plenary* (Mexico), Case 2021427, PC.VII.C. J/9 C (10a.); (2) *Supreme Court of Justice* (Mexico), Case 167733,1a./J. 126/2008. In a very recent case, the Eight Collegiate Court for Civil Matters of Mexico City (docket 196/2023), ruled that the

According to Articles 1473 and 1474 of the Commercial Code, the parties may only file one brief—the plaintiff its lawsuit and the defendant its response. In practice, it is common for trial courts to permit a third exchange of briefs, permitting the plaintiff to reply to the defenses contained in the response. This second opportunity in favor of the plaintiff is expressly regulated with respect to procedural defenses (i.e., lack of jurisdiction, improper venue, lack of procedural standing, lis pendens, etc.).[26] In our experience, trial courts generally grant this opportunity—applying the general three-day rule to set the deadline—as it is normally understood to be procedurally unfair for the plaintiff not to be heard with respect to defenses that it could not have anticipated, and for which, it could have not otherwise argued or offered evidence.

These Articles do not set an express time frame for offering evidence. Nevertheless, under regular rules of procedure, documents must be offered and accompanied by the lawsuit and the response to the lawsuit.[27] In addition, in the cases where the plaintiff chooses to offer witness or expert witness testimony or other evidence, they must be offered with the initial briefs. We reach this conclusion by interpreting Articles 1473 and 1475, that provide that a hearing will be held if evidence is offered, and therefore, the only chance to offer evidence is with the initial briefs. This has also been the rule in more than thirty special trials in which the undersigned has participated.

It is important to stress that the plaintiff has the burden to prove the causes for annulling an award, and therefore, if the plaintiff fails to offer the relevant evidence in the lawsuit, it is very likely that its action to set the award aside will fail.

[3] *Lex Specialis*

As explained above, the procedure to annul an award is organized by Articles 1470 to 1477 of the Commercial Code. There is a precedent that clarifies that other sections of the Commercial Code are not to be applied to the annulment and enforcement of the award proceedings.

For instance, if the party against whom the setting aside of the award is sought counterclaims the enforcement of the award, such party may not obtain an attachment of assets until the judgment is enforceable, even though there are certain legal provisions outside the "Commercial Arbitration" section of the Commercial Code, that could be read as favoring such petition.[28]

[4] Representation Through a Power of Attorney

The plaintiff must be represented by an attorney-in-fact. The respective power of attorney (POA) is generally granted to an attorney, although general powers of

Court's duty to provide an opportunity to the plaintiff to correct any irregularity of the lawsuit or exhibits, also applies to a special arbitration procedure where an application to set an award aside is made.

26. Procedural defenses are resolved through a summary proceeding in which the plaintiff is heard and a hearing is later set. Art. 1129 of the Commercial Code.
27. Article 1061 of the Commercial Code.
28. *Collegiate Circuit Courts* (Mexico), Case 2009520; I.11°.C.77 C (10ª.).

attorneys may also be granted to non-attorneys, who then authorize an attorney within the respective trial.

The first choice should be to use the services of a Mexican notary public for the granting of the POA. If that is not possible, because the POA needs to be granted abroad, then it can be granted before the respective Mexican Consulate, and in the alternative, before a local notary public; in this case, the form of the power of attorney must be reviewed by a Mexican attorney, and once the power of attorney is granted it must be stamped with an *apostille* (The Hague Convention) and in some cases further notarized in Mexico. If no *apostille* is available it can also be legalized at the respective Mexican Consulate.

[5] Confidentiality

Unlike other jurisdictions, the docket of a Mexican judicial proceeding may only be consulted by the parties, and the most relevant documents are kept in a secure location within the Court. In some Courts, such as Federal Courts, the rulings are published omitting the names of the parties. By searching in databases, one may find out the names of the parties involved in each case. This also applies to special arbitration trials.

[6] Possibility of Counterclaiming the Enforcement of the Award

Article 1477 of the Commercial Code permits the defendant of an action to set aside, to counterclaim the enforcement and recognition of the award. The joinder of these two actions avoids contradictory resolutions, and more importantly, expedites the resolution on the validity of the award.

[7] Award of Attorneys' Fees

When the proceeding to annul and enforce an award was subject to an ancillary proceeding (*incidente*), a precedent clarified that attorneys' fees could not be awarded, as such a proceeding was not considered an ancillary proceeding.[29]

But now that the annulment proceeding has a more detailed regulation and is named a "special arbitration trial," a more appropriate interpretation is that the rules for awarding attorneys' fees, regulated in Article 1084 of the Commercial Code are to be applied.[30] Because an annulment action is a declaratory action, the way to quantify attorneys' fees is by applying the rules for these types of actions which in Mexico City and most entities, result in amounts that are very low for international standards.

[8] Lack of Ordinary Recourses: The *Amparo* as the Only Recourse

Article 1476 of the Commercial Code expressly excludes recourses within the proceeding and expressly forbids any recourse against the final judgment deciding on the

29. *Collegiate Circuit Courts* (Mexico), Case 190832, IX.1o.39 C.
30. *Collegiate Circuit Courts* (Mexico), Case 2010767, I I.6o.C.28 C.

action to set the award aside. This regulation, forbidding any ordinary recourse, has been considered constitutional by the Mexican Supreme Court of Justice.[31]

The Mexican legal system, like some other Latin-American systems, has the peculiarity that acts of authorities, including those of the Judiciary, are subject to a constitutionality review. In a special arbitration trial, the type of constitutional recourse that the parties may file is a two-instance constitutional appeal, called *amparo indirecto*. The first instance is resolved by a District Court and the second instance by a Collegiate Court. In very few cases, the Supreme Court of Justice may decide to attract certain cases.

[E] CAUSES TO SET ASIDE AN AWARD

As previously explained, the causes for the denial of recognition and enforcement of an arbitral award in Mexico are provided for in Article 1457 of the Commercial Code, and these may be summarized in the following manner.

Causes that require proof by the plaintiff, as provided for in section I of Article 1457:

(3) Incapacity of the parties (subparagraph a),
(4) Invalidity of the arbitration agreement (subparagraph a),
(5) Defective notification on the appointment of an arbitrator or the proceedings (subparagraph b),
(6) Inability of one of the parties to assert its defense rights (subparagraph b),
(7) The award exceeds the scope of the Arbitration Agreement (subparagraph c),
(8) Defects in the constitution of the Arbitral Tribunal (subparagraph d), and
(9) Violation to the Arbitration Agreement (subparagraph d).

Causes that the Court must review ex officio, as provided for in section II of Article 1457:

(1) The subject-matter of the dispute is not susceptible of being settled by arbitration, and
(2) The award is contrary to public policy.

[1] General Annulment Causes

[a] Burden of Proof

The Commercial Code adopted the same rules of the burden of proof set out in the UNCITRAL Model Law and the New York and Panama Conventions. Most of the causes to set aside an award need to be proven by the plaintiff; only in extreme circumstances—where it is evident that the award is contrary to public policy or the dispute was not susceptible to being settled by arbitration—may the Judge act ex officio and annul the award without the plaintiff having to prove the annulment cause.

31. *Collegiate Circuit Courts* (Mexico), Cases 170493, 170494 and 170495.

There is a precedent that interprets Article 1197 of the Commercial Code that clarifies that when the annulment cause is based on foreign law, then the plaintiff has the burden of proving such law.[32] Because foreign statutes and precedents are regularly available through the internet, or an internet-based service, the plaintiff may opt to have the relevant statutes or precedents certified by a notary public with the respective official translation (if required). Nevertheless, when the amount at stake permits so, it is also prudent to offer an expert report on foreign law, explaining to the Mexican Court the correct interpretation of the respective statute or precedent.

[b] Due Process

Specifically with regards to subparagraph b) of section I, the Supreme Court of Mexico concluded that said provision relates to Article 1434 which seeks to safeguard equal treatment for the parties and a full opportunity for them to assert their rights in the proceedings.[33]

By applying this due process rules, annulment may be granted if the seeking party is able to prove that at any given point during the proceedings, it was deprived of a reasonable opportunity to defend its interests. Whether evidence or arguments put forth were not considered by the arbitrator or when there was an unequal treatment in contrast with the party looking to enforce the award, these must necessarily translate into actual procedural violations depriving one party of equal treatment or the opportunity to fully assert its rights.

In cases in which the respondent of an arbitration does not appear before the arbitrators, it is advisable for the claimant to use the services of a notary public to certify the delivery of the request of arbitration and, in some cases, the first procedural order.[34] This may either cause the respondent to finally appear before the arbitrator, or in the alternative, may serve as a "vaccine" against an action to set the award aside.

[c] Standard of Review

While minimal judicial intervention is desirable and, in theory, a Court is not empowered to analyze the merits of the dispute, the judge must also ensure that due process, as provided by the applicable *lex arbitri*, is respected. Rather than looking at the merits of the award, the review which the Judge must carry out has to do with a revision of the proceedings themselves.

32. *Collegiate Circuit Courts* (Mexico), Case 2024059, I.3o.C.121 K (10a.).
33. *Supreme Court of Justice* (Mexico), Case 2025648, 1a. XXX/2022 (10a.); *Supreme Court of Justice* (Mexico), Case 2025652, 1a. XXX/2022 (10a.).
34. The first notification in a judicial proceeding is highly regulated and protected by the Law. Even though arbitration legislation does not require the use of notaries to serve a request for arbitration, one must consider that Courts are used to rigorously protect the first notification. In a recent case, an award was declared invalid because there was insufficient evidence that the respondent was properly notified.

[d] *The Court Must Not Re-analyze the Merits of the Dispute*

Case law has consistently prevented Courts from re-analyzing the merits of the dispute while resolving on the validity of the award:

(1) "However, Judges are not authorized to conduct a comprehensive review of arbitral awards since doing so could lead to their nullification, even on substantive grounds."[35]
(2) While reviewing if the award exceeded the scope of the arbitration agreement, the 7th. Collegiate Court on Civil Matters in Mexico City resolved: "Judges are not authorized to conduct a comprehensive review of arbitral awards since doing so could lead to their nullification, even on substantive grounds. For this, it would be necessary for the parties to appear before the Judge to present their arguments in advance."[36]
(3) "So, the judgment in the special proceeding, whose scope is limited to procedural matters and not substantive issues, which are specifically defined and do not aim to resolve the merits of the dispute raised by the parties."[37]
(4) "The fact that commercial legislation does not provide for judicial control over the decision that constitutes the merits of the arbitral award through ordinary recourses is in line with the nature and purposes of arbitration as a constitutionally recognized alternative dispute resolution method."[38]

In my experience, this standard of review is consistently applied by Courts, not only because the annulment causes were drafted in a restrictive manner but also because, from a practical standpoint, it is easier for a Court to review the possible procedural faults committed during an arbitration, than re-analyzing a case that was not tried before the Court.

[e] *Standard of Review with Respect to the Jurisdiction of the Arbitral Tribunal*

When it comes to deciding on the jurisdiction of the Arbitral Tribunal, the Mexican standard of review is pro-arbitrator. The Mexican Supreme Court of Justice has set the following two-pronged test. A review of the arbitration agreement, and when said agreement is ambiguous, to defer to the arbitrators' interpretation, provided it is reasonable:

> In this way, Judges must exercise self-restraint and not scrutinize the interpretative decisions of arbitrators with the same scope as when reviewing a lower court's decision. Therefore, they must evaluate the validity of arbitral awards using a two-step standard. First, the judicial authority must refer to the text of the

35. *Collegiate Circuit Courts* (Mexico), Case 186229, XV.1o.50 C.
36. *Collegiate Circuit Courts* (Mexico), Case 2002333, I.7o.C.26 C (10a.).
37. *Supreme Court of Justice* (Mexico), Case 2021235, 1a./J. 87/2019 (10a.).
38. *Supreme Court of Justice* (Mexico), Case 2025648, 1a. XXX/2022 (10a.).

arbitration agreement or arbitration clause and determine if the terms used by the parties are clear and precise, in which case the Judge must apply it. If the contractual stipulation is not clear, judges must proceed to the second step, which is when it is evident that the language of the arbitration agreement is ambiguous, inadequately specified by the parties, or vague. In such cases, the power of the arbitrators to determine its meaning should be given precedence. Here, judges should not impose their preferred interpretation but rather verify if the arbitral tribunal's interpretation is reasonable and only declare its invalidity if the arbitral decision is capricious or arbitrary, with it being sufficient to establish the use of a reasonable interpretative method.[39]

[2] Ex Officio Causes for Annulment

[a] The Dispute Is Not Susceptible to Being Settled by Arbitration

Unlike some other UNCITRAL Model Law jurisdictions—for example, Spain, Guatemala, Nicaragua, Perú and Paraguay—Mexico has no express provision specifying which disputes may or not be settled through arbitration, and following the UNCITRAL text, recognizes that other statutes may provide that certain disputes are not susceptible of arbitration.[40]

Generally speaking, "arbitration can only refer to matters that are legally available to the parties according to the law,"[41] and therefore, all commercial disputes are subject to arbitration, except for specific matters that the law expressly reserves to Courts, such as insolvency matters,[42] liability derived from anti-trust violations[43] and unfair competition,[44] the rescission and early termination of public contracts,[45] enforcement of certain guarantee trusts and pledges,[46] sanctions of a punitive nature,[47] etc.

While resolving an action to set aside an award, the Mexican Court must analyze ex officio if the matters resolved in the award were susceptible to arbitration. But what happens when only part of an award is resolving matters not susceptible to arbitration? Could the Court apply the same principle as that contained in paragraph c), section I of Article 1457 of the Commercial Code? There is still no case law resolving this issue, but

39. *Supreme Court of Justice* (Mexico), Case 2025648,1a. XXX/2022 (10a.); *Supreme Court of Justice* (Mexico), Case 2014012, 1a. XXXVII/2017 (10a.).
40. Article 1415 of the Commercial Code, which corresponds to Art. 1 of the UNCITRAL Model Law, provides that the Arbitration Section of the code regulates arbitration, except for "other laws that provide for a different procedure or determine that certain disputes are not subject to arbitration."
41. *Collegiate Circuit Courts* (Mexico), Cases 162087 and 162088, I.3o.C.947 C and I.3o.C.950 C.
42. Article 17 of the Mexican Bankruptcy Law (*Ley de Concursos Mercantiles*).
43. Article 134 of the Mexican Anti-Trust Law (*Ley Federal de Competencia Económica*).
44. Article 6 bis of the Mexican Commercial Code (*Código de Comercio*).
45. Article 98 of the General Law for Public Works and related Services (*Ley de Obras Públicas y Servicios Relacionados con las Mismas*).
46. According to Art. 1414 bis 2, guarantee trusts and non-possessory pledges, may only be enforced by a Court when one of the parties opposes the agreed upon procedure.
47. Mexican Law only allows compensatory damages and with some restrictions, penalty clauses. Sanctions of a punitive nature can only be imposed by an authority, not a private arbitrator.

if only part of the award deals with matters not susceptible of arbitration, and such part is separable from the other, it could be argued that only the infringing part should be set aside, by applying the contractual principle of conservation (*principio de conservación del contrato*).[48]

[b] The Award Is Contrary to Public Policy

In all jurisdictions, public order in arbitration is a controversial topic; Mexico is not the exception. Because arbitration was conceived with an international commercial mindset, public order should also be analyzed under a different lens than the one we may use when applying other National Laws. Applying this line of thought, the Third Collegiate Court in Civil Matters of Mexico City resolved: "The concept of public policy, both nationally and internationally, serves as a framework for the institution of arbitration that it should not thwart, alter, or obstruct in its mission."[49]

In 2017, in a public contract dispute involving a State-owned company, the Mexican Supreme Court of Justice ruled that an award may only be annulled for infringing public order when "it directly violates fundamental legal principles or institutions."[50]

[F] CONCLUSION

In practice, Mexico's setting aside proceeding is pro-arbitration in the sense that, generally speaking, awards are respected. The main area of opportunity is that we have a two-instance recourse against the judgment resolving the annulment recourse, which in addition to the fact that the enforcement of the award may be stayed because of an annulment proceeding, could cost a substantial delay in enforcing an award. The best way to avoid having two successive proceedings is by counterclaiming the enforcement of the award within the annulment proceeding filed by the defendant.

48. Article 2238 of the Mexican Federal Civil Code.
49. *Collegiate Circuit Courts* (Mexico), Case 162053, I.3o.C.953 C.
50. *Supreme Court of Justice* (Mexico), Case 2014011,1a. XXXVIII/2017 (10a.).

Part IV Investment Arbitration

CHAPTER 13

Mexico's International Investment Law Framework: Bilateral and Multilateral Investment Treaties

Alan Bonfiglio Ríos & Jorge Escalona Gálvez[*]

[A] INTRODUCTION

A diverse number of international treaties form international investment law. These treaties take the shape of bilateral investment treaties (BITs), free trade agreements (FTAs), and regional free trade agreements such as the expired North American Free Trade Agreement (NAFTA), the United States-Mexico-Canada Agreement (USMCA), and the Comprehensive and Progressive Agreement for Trans-Pacific Partnership (CPTPP). These treaties either often include an investment chapter or at least encompass specific investment promotion and protection provisions.

For instance, investment treaties usually contain an investment chapter divided into two sections. First, a section that pertains to the investment itself, which mainly includes standards of protection granted to foreign investors who are nationals of the Parties of the treaty. Some of these standards include the obligation to provide fair and equitable treatment (FET), full protection and security (FPS), the prohibition against arbitrary or discriminatory measures, national treatment (NT), most-favored-nation treatment (MFN), transfer of funds, and protection against unlawful expropriation. To enforce these protections, treaties typically include a second section providing an international dispute settlement mechanism between the State Party to the treaty and the foreign investor of the other State Party. This mechanism has been chiefly investor-State arbitration.

* The views and opinions expressed in this article pertain exclusively to the authors and do not reflect those of the Secretariat of Economy nor the Mexican State.

In most scenarios, investor-State arbitration is given through an offer to arbitrate by the State, providing for arbitration under one of these alternatives: (i) The ICSID Convention[1] and ICSID's Arbitration Rules; (ii) the ICSID Additional Facility Rules; (iii) the UNCITRAL Arbitration Rules and on some occasions; (iv) other arbitration rules agreed upon by the parties to the dispute.[2]

Accordingly, this chapter illustrates how Mexico's history in the early investment protection regimes dates back to the establishment of mixed claims commissions in the late nineteenth and early twentieth centuries. For instance, the Mexico-U.S. Claims Commission was created under the General Claims Convention in 1923 between Mexico and the U.S. These mixed claims commissions were the predecessors of international investment arbitration tribunals.[3]

This chapter also details Mexico's trade liberalization that helped achieve a more robust investment protection framework, including investor-State dispute settlement mechanisms (ISDS) in NAFTA, BITs, and FTAs. Further, it explains the new regime for investment protection and dispute settlement agreed upon in new-era treaties, as the one in the USMCA.

[B] THE OLD DAYS: EARLY INVESTMENT PROTECTION REGIMES

In the origins of investment protection and international investment law, foreign investment disputes were resolved through diplomatic protection, ad hoc arbitration, and mixed claims commissions.

Diplomatic protection derives from a State's right to protect one of its national property. As Dolzer describes, "an injury to the property of a foreigner was an injury to the foreigner's home State which obtained the right to exercise protection over that property, known as diplomatic protection."[4] At its core, diplomatic protection enabled the State of nationality or home State to endorse a national's claim against a host State. Consequently, it translated the claim and dispute to an inter-State level.

For instance, in its Draft Articles on Diplomatic Protection, the International Law Commission (ILC) defined it as:

> For the purposes of the present draft articles, diplomatic protection consists of the invocation by a State, through diplomatic action or other means of peaceful settlement, of the responsibility of another State for an injury caused by an internationally wrongful act of that State to a natural or legal person that is a

1. The Convention on the Settlement of Investment Disputes between States and Nationals of Other States (ICSID Convention, or Washington Convention).
2. Among the arbitral institutions that generally handle investor-State arbitration cases different from the International Centre for Settlement of Investment Disputes (ICSID), are the Permanent Court of Arbitration (PCA), the International Chamber of Commerce (ICC), and the Stockholm Chamber of Commerce (SCC).
3. *See* Antonio Gómez Robledo, *México y el Arbitraje Internacional* XIII-XIV (2nd ed. Editorial Porrúa 1994). We point out that in Mexico's history, three notable arbitration cases (*Fondo Piadoso de las Californias*, *La Isla de la Pasión*, and *El Chamizal*) are commonly highlighted in its diplomatic history and have been of significant historical resonance.
4. Rudolf Dolzer, Ursula Kriebaum & Christoph Schreuer, *Principles of International Investment Law* 2 (3rd ed. Oxford University Press 2022).

national of the former State with a view to the implementation of such responsibility.[5]

Despite its use, diplomatic protection had drawbacks for nationals and investors.[6] To set some examples: (i) the State of nationality had no obligation to initiate or exercise diplomatic protection; (ii) the claimant State had no obligation to transfer any monetary compensation paid to the nationals related to the dispute; and (iii) States also used military means (besides economic and political) to exercise it, leading to several conflicts and even military interventions by the practice of *Gunboat Diplomacy*.[7] Notably, this was problematic for investors, and in replacement, other mechanisms surged for solving international investment disputes.

The second mechanism involved ad hoc arbitration, where ad hoc tribunals or "umpires" solved disputes concerning violations of foreigners that arose in the nineteenth and early twentieth centuries.[8] However, these arbitrations worked without a practical procedural framework, rules, or basis for jurisdiction and faced many challenges to render awards efficiently, consistently, and coherently.[9]

The third mechanism consisted of mixed claims commissions with jurisdiction over a broad category of disputes. They consisted of a mixed dispute settlement mechanism where States selected commissioners of mixed nationalities. This system was flexible and designed to resolve claims: (i) between citizens of different States; (ii) between citizens of one State versus another State; and (iii) between the States themselves.[10] In most cases, an international treaty established these commissions.[11]

5. *Draft articles on Diplomatic Protection*, International Law Commission (2006).
6. C.L. Lim., Jean Ho & Martins Paparinskis, *International Investment Law and Arbitration* 5-6 (2nd ed. Cambridge University Press 2021). Scholars C.L. Lim, Jean Ho, and Martins Paparinskis refer to the Don Pacifico incident, where a British national whose house was mobbed, obtained a British espousal for pursuing his claim for the losses and injuries sustained to him and his family. In such a diplomatic protection case, the judges ruled that the host State (Greece) had breached "the duty of every civilized Government to protect Persons and Property within its jurisdiction."
7. *See* Miller Scott & Gregory N. Hicks, *Investor-State Dispute Settlement A Reality Check*, Center for Strategic & International Studies (January 2015). Miller Scott & Gregory N. Hicks cite examples of gunboat diplomacy by the U.S., its military intervention in foreign countries to defend Americans' private international commercial interests. For example, they describe former President *Theodore Roosevelt's Corollary* to the Monroe Doctrine that declared a U.S. right to militarily intervene in Central American and Caribbean countries to preserve their economies if they could not satisfy their international debts.
8. Borzu Sabahi, Noah Rubins & Don Wallace Jr, *Investor-State Arbitration* 38 (2nd ed. Oxford University Press 2019). Borzu Sabahi, Noah Rubins & Don Wallace Jr. refer to the *Gentini* case as an example of procedural and substantive ambiguity inherent in ad hoc tribunals.
9. *Ibid.*
10. C.L. Lim et al., *supra* n. 6, at 5.
11. *See* Willem Theus, *Chapter 1; There and Back Again: From Consular Courts Through Mixed Arbitral Tribunals to International Commercial Courts, in the Mixed Arbitral Tribunals* 41, 1919-1939 (Hélène Ruiz Fabri, Studies of the Max Planck Institute Luxembourg for International, European and Regulatory Procedural Law, 2013). *See also* Borzu Sabahi et al., *supra* n. 8, at 36. An early example is the arbitration mechanism established by the Jay Treaty of 1794 between the U.S. and the UK. Under that treaty, the mixed commission established was meant to settle the diverse number of disputes between the States and between their nationals, such as matters of outstanding pre-peace debts owed by U.S. citizens or residents to British creditors.

These commissions were most prominent in the nineteenth century and lasted well until the 1930s when about eighty mixed international commissions replaced the single arbitrator tribunals of the earlier era.[12]

Despite the amplified use of mixed claims commissions, Lillich describes, "the success of a mixed commission depended to a disproportionate degree upon the ability of its commissioners."[13] Lillich explains that if the commissioners chosen by the States executed their duties with speed and impartiality, the mixed commissions would help settle international claims and develop customary international law. However, "too often this was not the case."[14] Despite their ability or inability to handle claims, mixed international claims commissions did serve as a substitute for diplomatic espousal.

By way of illustration, Mexico and the U.S. established one of the most prominent mixed claims commissions just before World War II to settle Mexican agrarian expropriations.[15] Under President Alvaro Obregon's administration in the 1920s, Mexico took on a mission of negotiating a formula that José Prieto describes "would allow Mexico to solve its disputes with foreigners, acquire recognition for his government, and at the same time avoid any perception within Mexico that the new government had bowed to the will of the Americans and European."[16]

The background behind its creation is that the U.S. and some European nations had refused to recognize any Mexican government that was hesitant to repair damages caused by foreign nationals during the years of the Mexican Revolution.[17] According to José Prieto, the result of those negotiations led to agreements with the U.S.—known as the "Bucareli Agreements"—and the European States, which constituted one of the most "innovative adjudicatory experiments of the 20th century."[18] Among them, it included the Mexican Claims Commissions, which consisted of eight adjudicative bodies based on similar international agreements and rules of procedure mutually established between Mexico and seven different countries in the wake of the Mexican Revolution.[19]

12. C.L. Lim et al., *supra* n. 6, at 6.
13. William L. Griffin, *International Claims: Their Adjudication by National Commissions, in Buffalo Law Review* 11, 685 (Richard B. Lillich, 1962).
14. *Ibid.*
15. C.L. Lim et al., *supra* n. 6, at 6.
16. José Gustavo Prieto Muñoz, *Chapter 3: The Mexican Claims Commissions and the Mixed Arbitral Tribunals in the 1920s: Lessons on Legitimacy and Legacy in International Adjudication, in the Mixed Arbitral Tribunals* 91, 1919-1939 (Hélène Ruiz Fabri, Studies of the Max Planck Institute Luxembourg for International, European and Regulatory Procedural Law, 2013).
17. *Ibid.*
18. *Ibid.*
19. *Ibid.*, at 91-92. The seven Commissions were: The Mexico-U.S. General Claims Commission; the Mexico-U.S. Special Claims Commission; the France-Mexico Special Claims Commission under the Convention between France and Mexico of Sep. 25, 1924; the Germany-Mexico Special Claims Commission under the Arrangement between Germany and Mexico of Mar. 16, 1925; the Spain-Mexico Special Claims Commission under the *Convención que crea una Comision especial de Reclamaciones entre los Estados Unidos Mexicanos y España* of Nov. 25, 1925; the Great Britain-Mexico Special Claims Commission under the Convention between his Majesty and the President of the United Mexican States of Nov. 19, 1926; the Italy-Mexico Special Claims Commission under the *Convención de Reclamaciones celebrada entre los Estados Unidos*

The General Claims Convention between the United Mexican States and the United States of America established the Mexico-U.S. General Claims Commission on September 8, 1923.[20] This Convention took effect in 1924 to enhance the Mexico-U.S. relationships to form a "quasi-judicial" organ for settling claims arising after July 4, 1868. Most cases of the commission derived from claims due to wrongful killing, denial of justice, seizure of property, unlawful arrest and detention, breach of contract, and disputes over taxes.[21]

Three members composed the commission and applied international law principles when resolving disputes.[22] It worked from 1924 to 1931 with various meetings in Washington, DC, and Mexico City. In numbers, it received 3,617 claims, dismissed 54 cases, awarded 94, and had 3,469 pending claims. In 1941, all pending claims were terminated with an *en bloc* agreement between Mexico and the U.S.[23]

Years later, Mexico and the U.S. established a special commission to settle claims arising from Mexico's Revolution. The special commission resolved claims brought by private citizens against Mexico for damages suffered due to violence during the Mexican Revolution from 1910-1920. It rendered decisions based on principles of equity instead of applying international law principles.[24]

Nonetheless, as Cline describes, "neither the General Claims Commission nor the Special Claims Commission ... were successful, in part due to differing estimates of damage and culpability, but also because political posturing made individual claims cause for the defense of national honor on both sides."[25] Nonetheless, although it was ad hoc in nature, the structure of the General Claims Commission reflects many current elements in the investment treaty regime of today.[26]

Assuredly, mixed claims commissions were predecessors of new dispute settlement mechanisms established by the mid-twentieth century. To illustrate one's point, other contemporary examples of dispute settlement mechanisms and investment protection regimes inspired by the mixed claims commissions include the United Nations Compensation Commission, the Friendship Commerce and Navigation treaties, lump sum settlement agreements,[27] and investment guarantee programs,[28] among others.[29]

Mexicanos y el Gobierno de Italia; and the Belgium-Mexico Administrative Arbitration Tribunal under the *Convenio celebrado entre los Gobiernos de los Estados Unidos Mexicanos y el Reino de Bélgica* of May 20, 1927.

20. Borzu Sabahi et al., *supra* n. 8, at 38.
21. *Ibid.*, at 39. *See also* Howard F. Cline, *The United States and Mexico* 322 (Cambridge: Harvard University Press 1961).
22. One member of the U.S., one from Mexico, and one from a neutral country. Borzu Sabahi et al., *supra* n. 8, at 39.
23. José Gustavo Prieto Muñoz, *supra* n. 16, at 92.
24. *Ibid.*
25. Howard F. Cline, *supra* n. 21, at 208.
26. Borzu Sabahi et al., *supra* n. 8, at 39. *See also* Christian Tietje & Freya Baetens, *The Impact of Investor-State-Dispute Settlement (ISDS) in the Transatlantic Trade and Investment Partnership* (Jun. 24, 2014). Mixed claims commissions had jurisdiction to decide both State-to-State disputes and controversies between States and individuals.
27. Borzu Sabahi et al., *supra* n. 8, at 40. These agreements relegated large classes of complex, individual claims to adjudication by an administrative tribunal inside the home State of the

Nonetheless, the most important legacy is how diplomatic espousal had evolved into mixed claims commissions. These commissions established through States' agreements allowed for a dispute settlement mechanism in which claimants could pursue their claims directly against the host State, a development that at the time constituted a substantial procedural innovation.[30]

Indeed, the Mexican Claims Commissions had an important substantive legacy since they provided a body of precedents for the standards of treatment of aliens and international responsibility for States cited in several international instruments in the past century.[31] As José Prieto describes, the Mexican Claims Commissions' decisions provided "argumentative choices" for drafting the Articles on the Responsibility of States for Internationally Wrongful Acts (ARSIWA) and have been used by twenty-first-century lawyers advocating cases before investment tribunals. For example, the *Neer* case,[32] decided by the Mexico-U.S. Claims Commission has been cited multiple times in investor-State arbitration cases and is considered "the formulation of the minimum standard" under customary international law.[33]

Overall, the continuing and evolving arbitration and dispute resolution practice through mixed claims commissions eventually channelled the establishment of institutions and new international treaties.[34] Not surprisingly, Tietje highlights that investment protection after 1959 transitioned to more specific protections toward foreign investors since they become more detailed and built in a way to facilitate "changing economic relationships," giving more efficient means for the settlement of disputes and treatment protections in line with "global needs."[35]

[C] MEXICO'S TRADE LIBERALIZATION: NAFTA, BITS, FTAs, USMCA AND INVESTOR-STATE ARBITRATION

In the aftermath of World War II, most nations started to liberalize their economic relations by agreeing to international treaties that locked reciprocal market access, rights, and concessions, while securing the protection of their nationals abroad.[36]

injured parties, permitting the States to resolve complex outstanding legal issues and enhance diplomatic relations more generally.

28. For example, the Multilateral Investment Guarantee Agency (MIGA) was created under the World Bank.
29. *See* C.L. Lim et al., *supra* n. 6, at 8. The best-known modern successor of the mixed claims commissions of old is the Iran-U.S. Claims Tribunal, which contributed significantly to the creation of investment arbitration.
30. Borzu Sabahi et al., *supra* n. 8, at 11.
31. José Gustavo Prieto Muñoz, *supra* n. 16, at 105.
32. *L.F.H. Neer & Pauline E. Neer v. Mexico*.
33. Borzu Sabahi et al., *supra* n. 8, at 639. *See also* Yannick Radi, *Rules and Practice of International Investment Law and Arbitration*, 6 (Cambridge University Press 2020). Dr. Radi explains that the decision of the Mexico-U.S. Claims Commission in *Neer* is "often considered having played a major role in consolidating the customary status of the minimum standard of treatment."
34. William Theus, *supra* n. 11, at 41.
35. Christian Tietje & Freya Baetens, *supra* n. 26, at. 19.
36. Sergio Puig & Meg Kinnear, *NAFTA Chapter Eleven at Fifteen: Contributions to a Systemic Approach in Investment Arbitration*, ICSID Review - Foreign Investment Law Journal, Vol. 25, No. 2 (Jun. 8, 2011).

Mexico was not foreign to that, from the beginning, trade policies have safeguarded local producers and industries through imposed import licensing requirements, elevated tariffs, and official import reference prices.[37] Such measures motivated foreign companies to build industries in Mexico rather than export, and, therefore, did not create nor stimulate sufficient development of Mexico's raw materials and agriculture.[38]

However, trade liberalization and foreign direct investment (FDI) promotion were fostered during Mexico's 1980s economic landscape.[39] By late 1987, a new framework agreement between Mexico and the U.S. was entered to smooth trade and investment between the two countries.[40] This framework agreement contained a mechanism for Mexico and the U.S. to consult on trade matters, solve disputes, and negotiate to remove or reduce trade barriers.[41]

From 1980 to 1989, Mexico pursued a strategy of trade liberalization and FDI promotion with aims of internalization based on a bilateral relationship with the U.S. along with multilateral relationships through the GATT to unlock foreign markets and reach reciprocity for its trade liberalization.[42] It was clear that strengthening its relationship with the U.S. through a free trade agreement reflected a way to lock in the reforms of its market-opening measures of the mid-1980s.[43] Afterward, what inevitably turned a reality with negotiations between Mexico, Canada, and the U.S. in the early 1990s was NAFTA in 1994. The Mexican government's point of view of the significant function of NAFTA was to "embody the newly liberalized trade regime (since 1985) into a comprehensive international treaty to lock-in free market policies against future changes of government."[44]

[1] The NAFTA

The NAFTA negotiations were an important example of international trade negotiations, especially when it was built on the Canada-U.S. Free Trade Agreement of 1988 to reduce trade barriers between the three countries.[45]

37. Leonard P. Feldman, *U.S.-Mexico Free Trade Agreement*, Global Business & Development Law Journal, Vol. 4 Issue 2 (1991).
38. *Ibid.*
39. Sergio Puig & Meg Kinnear, *supra* n. 36, at 228. Experts in the field acknowledge that President Salinas' administration took many steps to liberalize the Mexican economy, install broader access to markets on trade and investment, ease the State's role in the economy, and provide more favorable conditions for business. *See also* Penélope Pacheco-López, & Anthony P. Thirlwall, *Trade Liberalisation in Mexico: Rhetoric and Reality*, Department of Economics Discussion Paper, No. 04, 03 (2004). For example, in 1986, Mexico became a member of the General Agreement on Tariffs and Trade (GATT). As a condition of becoming a GATT member, Mexico agreed to lower its maximum tariff rates to 50%.
40. *NAFTA and the Mexican Economy*, Congressional Research Archive (Jun. 3, 2010).
41. Leonard P. Feldman, *supra* n. 37, at 566.
42. Penélope Pacheco-López & Anthony P. Thirlwall., *supra* n. 39, at 12.
43. *See* Gary Clyde Hufbauer & Jeffrey J. Schott, *NAFTA Revisited: Achievements and Challenges*, Institute for International Economics (October 2005).
44. Penélope Pacheco-López & Anthony P. Thirlwall., *supra* n. 39, at 12.
45. *See* Francisco García Hernández & Niall M. Fraser, *Conflict Analysis of the NAFTA Negotiations*, Cuadernos del Centro de Estudios Estratégicos, ITESM (June 1992).

In the context of the NAFTA negotiations, Mexico sought new market access to the rest of North America. At the same time, Canada and the U.S. took the occasion to enhance their existing bilateral framework.[46] As reported by those involved, the NAFTA negotiations were incredibly complex. The techniques used in many parts of the agreement proved "transformative" and "enduring."[47] Nonetheless, the three countries reached a deal in principle in August 1992 and signed a final accord in December 1992. After clearing major political hurdles from all sides, NAFTA finally entered into force on January 1, 1994, and expired on June 30, 2020, replaced by the USMCA, which entered into force on July 1, 2020.

NAFTA Chapter XI was one of the most debatable sections of the treaty from the start of the negotiations. The parties' positions changed radically.[48] On the one hand, the U.S. wanted to bargain with its BIT model treaty, which encompassed some of the most far-reaching investment protection commitments at that time and was mainly intended to strict Mexico. On the other hand, Mexico had been an ardent supporter of the *Calvo Doctrine*.[49] At last, Canada wanted to keep the investment rules it had bargained under the 1988 treaty with the U.S., a treaty that excluded investor-State arbitration. In sum, the NAFTA negotiations drafts of Chapter XI display the particularities of a controversial aspect: foreign investment protection.

Pertaining to NAFTA Chapter XI provisions on investment, it is of utmost importance to understand that it relied on arbitration as a critical tool to support FDI. Chapter XI provided substantive provisions (section A) and a dispute settlement mechanism (section B). Concerning the first item, it contained several protections that obliged the States to accord certain types of treatment for investment.[50]

Various arbitral tribunals from the investor-State arbitration cases that have arisen under Chapter XI have examined the specifics of these provisions. Similarly, these substantive provisions have been tested through the years by "imaginative claimants who seek to stretch its intended interpretations to afford ever greater protections for investors."[51]

Concerning the investor-State dispute settlement mechanism, NAFTA Chapter XI allowed private parties (foreign investors, both natural and legal persons) to initiate

46. *See* Eric Miller, *Remaking NAFTA: Its Origin, Impact and Future*, Canadian Global Affairs Institute (August 2017).
47. *Ibid.*
48. *See* Wolfgang Alschner, Rama Panford-Walsh & Dmitriy Skougarevskiy, *What Can the Negotiations of NAFTA 1.0 Teach Us about the Fate of NAFTA 2.0?*, Ottawa Faculty of Law Working Paper No. 2018-05 (Jan. 29, 2018). Remarkably, in one investor-State arbitration case, the tribunal requested the release of the negotiations drafts of Chapter XI, which were made available in April 2002. *See Pope & Talbot Inc. v. The Government of Canada*, UNCITRAL, Award in Respect of Damages, May 31, 2002, paras. 37-38.
49. Argentine diplomat and legal scholar Carlos Calvo elaborated this doctrine in his International Law of Europe and America in Theory and Practice (1868). It asserted that rules governing the jurisdiction of a country over aliens and the collection of indemnities should be bid equally to all nations, regardless of size. It further affirmed that foreigners who held property in Latin American countries and had claims against such States' governments should forward to the courts within such nations for redress instead of pursuing diplomatic intervention.
50. Aaron Cosbey, *Chapter 6 The Road to Hell? Investor Protections in NAFTA's Chapter 11, in International Investment for Sustainable Development* (Lyuba Zarsky 2004).
51. *Ibid.*

arbitration directly against NAFTA Parties. Therefore, it allowed arbitrating cases under three pre-established mechanisms through the ICSID Convention, ICSID's Additional Facility Rules, and UNCITRAL Rules. As of June 2024, eighteen cases brought before ICSID against Mexico under NAFTA Chapter XI have concluded.[52]

Notably, some criticisms and controversies have arisen concerning different topics of NAFTA. Still, there can be small doubt that one of the most debatable has been Chapter XI.[53] Eventually, as with all things, NAFTA Chapter XI drew concerns about its scope, operation, and investor-State arbitration mechanism to solve disputes.[54] Some debate that investment arbitration has had a broadly protective regime for foreign investors and, consequently, has inappropriately transgressed the State's ability to regulate investment within its territory.[55] Yet, others have argued that it has had a beneficial effect and influence on international investment law and ISDS, including transparent arbitration proceedings.[56]

---

52. *B-Mex, LLC and others v. United Mexican States* (ICSID Case No. ARB(AF)/16/3); *Enerflex US Holdings Inc. and Exterran Energy Solutions, L.P. v. United Mexican States* (ICSID Case No. ARB/23/22); *Sepadeve International LLC v. United Mexican States* (ICSID Case No. ARB/23/6) *Sastre and others v. United Mexican States* (ICSID Case No. UNCT/20/2); *Lion Mexico Consolidated L.P. v. United Mexican States* (ICSID Case No. ARB(AF)/15/2); *L1bre Holding, LLC v. United Mexican States* (ICSID Case No. ARB/21/55); *Vento Motorcycles, Inc. v. United Mexican States* (ICSID Case No. ARB(AF)/17/3); *Joshua Dean Nelson v. United Mexican States* (ICSID Case No. UNCT/17/1); *KBR, Inc. v. United Mexican States* (ICSID Case No. UNCT/14/1); *Cargill, Incorporated v. United Mexican States* (ICSID Case No. ARB(AF)/05/2); *Corn Products International, Inc. v. United Mexican States* (ICSID Case No. ARB(AF)/04/1); *Archer Daniels Midland Company and Tate & Lyle Ingredients Americas, Inc. v. United Mexican States* (ICSID Case No. ARB(AF)/04/5); *Bayview Irrigation District and others v. United Mexican States* (ICSID Case No. ARB(AF)/05/1); *Waste Management, Inc. v. United Mexican States* (ICSID Case No. ARB(AF)/00/3); *Marvin Roy Feldman Karpa v. United Mexican States* (ICSID Case No. ARB(AF)/99/1); *International Thunderbird Gaming Corporation v. The United Mexican States*, UNCITRAL; *Gami Investments Inc. v. Mexico*, UNCITRAL; *Fireman's Fund Insurance Company v. United Mexican States* (ICSID Case No. ARB(AF)/02/1); *Metalclad Corporation v. United Mexican States* (ICSID Case No. ARB(AF)/97/1); *Waste Management, Inc. v. United Mexican States* (ICSID Case No. ARB(AF)/98/2); and *Robert Azinian and others v. United Mexican States* (ICSID Case No. ARB(AF)/97/2).
53. Elizabeth Whitsitt, *NAFTA Fifteen Years Later: The Successes, Failures and Future Prospects of Chapter 11*, Investment Treaty News (Feb. 17, 2009).
54. To the point that Canada is not a party to the USMCA's investor-State dispute settlement mechanism (Annexes 14-D and 14-E). The new treaty limits investor-State arbitration between the U.S. and Mexico.
55. *See* Vera Korzun, *The Right to Regulate in Investor-State Arbitration: Slicing and Dicing Regulatory Carve-Outs*, 50 Vanderbilt Journal of Transnational Law 2 (2017). Korzun describes that commentators note concerns toward investor-State arbitrations that combat State measures lead to a "regulatory chill," which is amply defined as "less-than optimal regulation that would be introduced by the governments because of fear of investor–state claims by foreign investors".
56. Elizabeth Whitsitt. *supra* n. 53. As one expert describes when asked about the positive influence of Chapter XI on international investment law, she described: "Firstly, it can be said that the early NAFTA cases in the 1998-2002 period ... raised awareness of the investor-state dispute mechanism to such an extent that it spurred its wide use and application around the world ... Secondly, because of the transparency of the NAFTA dispute settlement process, investor-state arbitration has moved out of the exclusive domain of a select few Washington and London firms to being a world-wide phenomenon ... The influence of NAFTA has had a positive impact on opening up ICSID and WTO arbitration processes because of its example. Thirdly, NAFTA tribunals have dealt with some of the most contentious substantive issues in international law, such as the construction of the Fair and Equitable Treatment obligation and National Treatment.

Despite encountering ourselves in the post-NAFTA era, the treaty uplifted the regional economy between the U.S., Mexico, and Canada. When the three countries signed it, it was agreed to grant each other MFN status in trading, eliminate tariffs on imports and exports, protect each other's investments, and decide on procedural rules to settle disputes. Overall, these commitments were intended to generate more cross-border and multinational investment possibilities through FDI, which is now an achieved objective and designed to continue with the USMCA.

[2] The BITs

States enter into BITs and other investment agreements to provide security, and attract, and protect foreign investment.[57] Overall, BITs provide substantive protections for foreign investors. In addition, they incorporate ISDS mechanisms enabling foreign investors to bring claims against States due to violations of investment protection standards.

Notably, Mexico has entered more than thirty BITs with different countries, including both developed and developing.[58] If one reviews the language of these BITs, one can encounter different investment standards of protection such as fair and

Fourthly, it has encouraged respect for the international rule of law. The example set by the NAFTA parties visibly and tangibly supports the international rule of law in ways that other conventions and treaties do not."

57. Borzu Sabahi et al., *supra* n. 8, at 4.
58. BIT Mexico-Switzerland signed on Jul. 10, 1995 and entered into force on Mar. 14, 1996; BIT Mexico-Argentina signed on Nov. 13, 1996 and entered into force on Jul. 22, 1998; BIT Mexico-Netherlands signed on May 13, 1998 and entered into force on Oct. 1, 1999; BIT Mexico-Austria signed on Jun. 29, 1998 and entered into force on Mar. 23, 2001; BIT Mexico-Germany signed on Aug. 25, 1998 and entered into force on Feb. 23, 2001; BIT Mexico-Belgium-Luxembourg Economic Union signed on Aug. 27, 1998 and entered into force on Mar. 18, 2003; BIT Mexico-France signed on Nov. 12, 1998 and entered into force on Oct. 11, 2000; BIT Mexico-Finland signed on Feb. 22, 1999 and entered into force on Aug. 20, 2000; BIT Mexico-Uruguay signed on Jun. 30, 1999 and entered into force on Jul. 1, 2002; BIT Mexico-Portugal signed on Nov. 11, 1999 and entered into force on Sep. 4, 2000; BIT Mexico-Italy signed on Nov. 24, 1999 and entered into force on Dec. 4, 2002; BIT Mexico-Denmark signed on Apr. 13, 2000 and entered into force on Sep. 24, 2000; BIT Mexico-Sweden signed on Oct. 3, 2000 and entered into force on Jul. 1, 2001; BIT Mexico-Republic of Korea signed on Nov. 14, 2000 and entered into force on Jul. 6, 2002; BIT Mexico-Greece signed Nov. 30, 2000 and entered into force Sep. 27, 2002; BIT Mexico-Cuba signed on May 30, 2001 and entered into force on Mar. 29, 2002; BIT Mexico-Czech Republic signed on Apr. 4, 2002 and entered into force on Mar. 14, 2004; BIT Mexico-Iceland signed on Jun. 24, 2005 and entered into force April 28, 2006; Mexico-Australia BIT signed on Aug. 23, 2005 and entered into force on Jul. 18, 2007; BIT Mexico-Panama signed on Oct. 11, 2005 and entered into force on Dec. 14, 2006; BIT Mexico-United Kingdom signed on May 12, 2006 and entered into force on Jul. 25, 2007; BIT Mexico-Trinidad and Tobago signed on Oct. 3, 2006 and entered into force on Sep. 16, 2007; BIT Mexico-Spain (renegotiated) signed on Oct. 10, 2006 and entered into force on April 3, 2008; BIT Mexico-India signed on May 21, 2007 and entered into force on Feb. 23, 2008; BIT Mexico-Slovakia signed on Oct. 26, 2007 and entered into force on Apr. 8, 2009; BIT Mexico-China signed on Jul. 11, 2008 and entered into force on Jun. 6, 2009; BIT Mexico-Belarus signed on Sep. 4, 2008 and entered into force on Aug. 27, 2009; Mexico-Singapore BIT signed on Nov. 12, 2009 and entered into force on Apr. 3, 2011; BIT Mexico-Bahrain signed on Nov. 29, 2012 and entered into force on Jul. 30, 2014; BIT Mexico-Kuwait signed on Feb. 22, 2013 and entered into force on Apr. 28, 2016; BIT Mexico-Turkey signed on Dec. 17, 2013 and entered into force on Dec. 17, 2017; BIT Mexico-Brazil signed on May 26, 2015 and entered into force on Oct. 7, 2018; BIT

equitable treatment, protection against unlawful expropriation, national treatment, most favored nation treatment, full protection, and security, among others.

In essence, there are groups of BITs based on proposals from Mexico's trading partners; based on Chapter XI of NAFTA, and based on both NAFTA Chapter XI and recent aspects reflected in the latest generation of international investment agreements.[59] Nevertheless, most of the BITs entered by Mexico have been directly influenced by NAFTA. Despite these three groups of BITs, each treaty contains the characteristics that reflect the product of several rounds of negotiation before the signing of the treaty itself.

In the majority of the BITs entered by Mexico, the Contracting Parties include investment arbitration as the primary mechanism for settling disputes, offering submission of an arbitration claim under ICSID (both under the ICSID Convention and the Additional Facility Rules), UNCITRAL Arbitration rules, or any other arbitration rules that the disputing parties may agree.[60] Interestingly, other relevant characteristics include six months' notice of intent requirement[61] and fork-in-the-road clauses.[62]

Despite the considerable number of BITs entered by Mexico, the reality is that most investor-State arbitration cases initiated against it have NAFTA Chapter XI as the instrument for the basis for consent and not so many other BITs. Just eleven cases faced by Mexico have been resolved under BITs, specifically under the treaties concluded with Argentina, France, Portugal, Singapore, the Netherlands and Spain.[63]

Even with the current tendency of denouncing the ICSID Convention, withdrawing consent for arbitration, and/or terminating IIAs by States as a reaction to the latest criticism of the investor-State arbitration regime, Mexico has refrained from doing so.

Mexico-United Arab Emirates, signed on Jan. 19, 2016 and entered into force on Jan. 25, 2018; and BIT Mexico-Hong Kong signed on Jan. 23, 2020 and entered into force on Jun. 16, 2021.

59. For example, the BIT Mexico entered with Hong Kong.
60. For instance, the BIT concluded between Mexico and Sweden establishes that the investor may choose to submit the dispute for resolution to the International Chamber of Commerce by an ad hoc tribunal under its arbitration rules.
61. *See* BIT Mexico-Slovakia, Art. 12 Notice of Intent and Consultations ("2. With the objective of resolving the dispute amicably, the disputing investor shall notify in writing to the disputing contracting party its intention to submit a claim to arbitration at least six months before the claim is submitted ...").
62. *See* BIT Mexico-Netherlands, Art. Two Settlement of Disputes between a Contracting Party and a national of the other Contracting Party ("6. If a national of a Contracting Party submits a claim to arbitration, neither the national, nor its enterprise, may initiate or continue proceedings before a national tribunal").
63. *Consolidated Water Coöperatief, U.A. v. United Mexican States* (ICSID Case No. ARB/22/6); *Sastre and others v. United Mexican States* (ICSID Case No. UNCT/20/2); *PACC Offshore Services Holdings Ltd v. United Mexican States* (ICSID Case No. UNCT/18/5); *Coöperatieve Rabobank U.A. v. United Mexican States* (ICSID Case No. ARB/20/23); *Eutelsat S.A. v. United Mexican States* (ICSID Case No. ARB(AF)/17/2); *Telefónica S.A. v. United Mexican States* (ICSID Case No. ARB(AF)/12/4); *Cemusa - Corporación Europea de Mobiliario Urbano, S.A. and Corporación Americana de Equipamientos Urbanos, S.L. v. United Mexican States* (ICSID Case No. ARB(AF)/13/2); *Abengoa, S.A. y COFIDES, S.A. v. United Mexican States* (ICSID Case No. ARB(AF)/09/2); *Talsud, S.A. v. United Mexican States* (ICSID Case No. ARB(AF)/04/4); *Gemplus, S.A., SLP, S.A. and Gemplus Industrial, S.A. de C.V. v. United Mexican States* (ICSID Case No. ARB(AF)/04/3); and *Técnicas Medioambientales Tecmed, S.A. v. United Mexican States* (ICSID Case No. ARB(AF)/00/2).

As one example shows, to counterbalance and safeguard the State's interest, in its latest BIT with Hong Kong, it did safeguard and emphasize both Contracting States' right to regulate when protecting specific public interests by adopting measures to protect the environment, health, and other regulatory objectives. It demonstrated that despite the importance of promoting and protecting foreign investments, Contracting Parties do have an inherent right to regulate the protection of public interests.[64]

[3] Not Everything Is NAFTA and BITs: FTAs Concluded by Mexico

Considering the importance of NAFTA Chapter XI on investment, the new investment regime of Chapter 14 of the USMCA, and over thirty BITs entered by Mexico granting investment protection; Mexico has other investment protection provisions in its FTAs.[65]

To cite one example, the CPTPP established an international trade agreement between Mexico, Australia, Brunei, Canada, Chile, Japan, New Zealand, Malaysia, Peru, Singapore, and Vietnam. Mexico ratified the CPTPP in 2018. It contains an investment chapter (Chapter 9) divided into two sections, one substantive (section A) and one procedural (section B).[66]

Section A includes provisions to encourage investors to voluntarily incorporate into their internal policies those internationally recognized standards, guidelines, and principles of corporate social responsibility.[67] In addition, it considers each Contracting Party's right to regulate in public interest areas such as the protection of the environment, health or other regulatory objectives.[68]

What is particular about section B of the CPTPP is the fact that it expressly allows respondent States to make a counterclaim in connection with the factual and legal basis of the claim brought by the claimant investor or rely on a claim for the set-off against the claimant investor.[69]

To provide another example, in 1997, Mexico was the first Latin American country to conclude an Economic Partnership, Political Coordination, and Cooperation

64. Eckhard Janeba, *Regulatory Chill and the Effect of Investor State Dispute Settlements*, CESIFO Working Paper No. 6188 (Nov. 2016).
65. Among them: FTA Mexico-Costa Rica, which entered into force on Jan. 1, 1995; FTA Mexico-Colombia-Venezuela which entered into force on Jan. 1, 1995; FTA Mexico-Chile, which entered into force on Aug. 1, 1999; FTA Mexico-EU which entered into force on Oct. 1, 2000; FTA Mexico-Liechtenstein Principality which entered into force on Jul. 1, 2001; FTA Mexico-Japan which entered into force on Apr. 1, 2005; FTA Mexico-Costa Rica-El Salvador-Honduras-Nicaragua which entered into on Jul. 1, 2013, for Costa Rica, Jan. 1, 2013, for Honduras, Sep. 1, 2012, for Nicaragua and Sep. 1, 2013, for Guatemala; FTA Mexico-Panama which entered into force on Jul. 1, 2015; the *Protocolo Adicional al Acuerdo Marco de la Alianza del Pacífico* which entered into force on May 1, 2016; and the *Tratado Integral y Progresista de Asociación Transpacífico* (TIPAT or CPTPP) which entered into force on Dec. 30, 2018.
66. Accessible at: www.sice.oas.org/Trade/TPP_Final_Texts/English/Chapter9.pdf.
67. CPTPP, Art. 9.17 Corporate Social Responsibility.
68. CPTPP, Art. 9.16 Investment and Environmental, Health and other Regulatory Objectives.
69. CPTPP, Art. 9.19 Submission of a Claim to Arbitration. Interestingly, counterclaims in investor-State arbitration are debated even when almost all arbitration rules provide the right to assert them. *See also* Yaraslau Kryvoi, *Counterclaims in Investor-State Arbitration*, Minnesota Journal of International Law, (2012).

Agreement with the European Union (EU-Mexico Global Agreement). The agreement encompassed trade provisions developed in a Free Trade Agreement that entered into force in October 2000 for the part related to trade in goods and in 2001 for the aspects related to trade in services.[70] Curiously, the original EU-Mexico Global Agreement did not contain an investor-State dispute settlement mechanism. A topic that is now incorporated into the modernized EU-Mexico Global Agreement through a chapter on liberalization and investment protection, including the new Investment Court System mechanism.[71] On April 21, 2018, the EU and Mexico reached an agreement in principle and finalized it in 2020. However, to this day, as occurs with CETA and the FTAs with Vietnam and Singapore, the FTA negotiated between Mexico and the EU has yet to be finalized.

Another example is the Free Trade Agreement between Mexico and Central American countries. In 2008, Mexico had three FTAs with Central American countries, which included the Mexico-Costa Rica FTA, the Mexico-Nicaragua FTA, and the Mexico-El Salvador-Guatemala, and Honduras FTA.[72]

After a series of negotiations between 2010 and 2011, a single Free Trade Agreement between Central America and Mexico was reached and signed on November 22, 2011, under the name of *Tratado de Libre Comercio entre los Estados Unidos Mexicanos y las Repúblicas de Costa Rica, El Salvador, Guatemala, Honduras y Nicaragua*. This FTA includes an investment Chapter XI,[73] which among other things, provides investment protections and a dispute settlement mechanism of investor-State arbitration. For instance, Article 11.19 provides an obligation for both Parties to try

70. *See* Enriqueta Serrano Caballero, *The modernization of the European Union-Mexico Association Agreement: between change and continuity*, Occasional paper FC/EU-LAC (2022). The countries that entered the EU-Mexico Global Agreement with Mexico include Belgium, Denmark, Germany, Greece, Spain, France, Ireland, Italy, Luxembourg, the Netherlands, Austria, Portugal, Finland, Sweden, and the United Kingdom.
71. In parallel to the negotiation of the modernization of the EU-Mexico Global Agreement, the European Commission conducted negotiations with Canada, Singapore, and Vietnam, which included the creation of an Investment Court System. In essence, the new Investment Court System in the modernized agreement is a meaningful change considering the future of investor-State dispute settlement and the criticism of the arbitration system, representing a new dispute settlement mechanism conceived as being a permanent court replacing *ad hoc* arbitration tribunals. *See* Daniel Behn, Ole Kristian Fauchald & Malcom Langford, *The Legitimacy of Investment Arbitration:* Empirical Perspectives (Cambridge University Press 2022); David. A Ma, *BIT Unfair: An Illustration of the Backlash against International Arbitration in Latin America*, Journal of Dispute Resolution, (2012); Michael Waibel et al., *The backlash against investment arbitration: perceptions and reality*, The Hague: Kluwer Law International (March 2010); and Susan D. Franck, *The Legitimacy Crisis in Investment Treaty Arbitration: Privatizing Public International Law through Inconsistent Decisions*. Fordham Law Review, n. 4, (2005). *See also* Milcar Jeff Dorce, *Le Mexique et l'Arbitrage International d'Investissement: Un Paysage Pluraliste*, RBA N° 77, Doutrina Internacional, Jan-Mar/2023.
72. The Mexico-Costa Rica FTA was signed on Apr. 5, 1994 and entered into force on Jan. 1, 1995; the Mexico-Nicaragua FTA was signed on Dec. 1997 and entered into force on Jul. 1, 1998 and the Mexico-El Salvador Guatemala and Honduras was signed on Jun. 29, 2000 and entered into force on Mar. 15, 2001. *See* Background and Negotiations: http://www.sice.oas.org/tpd/CACM_MEX/CACM_MEX_e.asp.
73. Accessible at: http://www.sice.oas.org/Trade/CACM_MEX_FTA/Text_s.asp#Cap%C3%ADtuloXI.

settling the dispute through consultations and negotiation, which can encompass the use of non-binding third-party procedures, such as conciliation and mediation.

In summary, even when NAFTA and now the USMCA might steal the entire spotlight regarding Mexico's FTAs, Mexico has many FTAs with countries where investment promotion and protection provisions are in place.

[4] The USMCA

In December 2018, the United States, Mexico, and Canada entered a new FTA to replace NAFTA. As with the NAFTA and other BITs entered by Mexico, the USMCA includes a new Chapter 14 on Investment containing substantive investment protections and investor-State dispute settlement provisions.

First, concerning investor protections under the USMCA, it contains core investment provisions of NAFTA Chapter XI. For example, similar to NAFTA, the text of the USMCA requires all Parties to "accord to covered investments treatment by customary international law, including fair and equitable treatment and full protection and security."[74] Nonetheless, Article 14.6 does contain new clarifications by stating that the concepts of "fair and equitable treatment" and "full protection and security" do not require treatment in addition to or beyond the minimum standard treatment of aliens under customary international law.[75]

In addition, Article 14.6 provides elements of what entails both of those standards. For instance, it describes that the FET standard "includes the obligation not to deny justice in criminal, civil, or administrative adjudicatory proceedings under the principle of due process embodied in the principal legal systems of the world." In contrast, FPS describes that each Party must provide the police protection required under customary international law. Further, Article 14.6 expressly excludes the investor's expectations from the scope of breach of the MST, "even if there is loss or damage to the covered investment as a result."

In a similar vein to NAFTA, Articles 14.4 and 14.5 include non-discrimination provisions, requiring that each country accord the investors and investments of another country treatment no less favorable than that it accords, in like circumstances, to its investors or the investors of any other country throughout the lifecycle of the investment.[76] However, this new provision does give more clarity to interpret "in like circumstances," meaning "the totality of the circumstances, including whether the relevant treatment distinguishes between investors or investments based on legitimate public welfare objectives."[77]

74. Article 14.6 Minimum Standard of Treatment.
75. A clarification initially carved out by the NAFTA Notes of Interpretation of Certain Chapter 11 Provisions published on Jul. 31, 2001. Accessible at: http://www.sice.oas.org/tpd/nafta/commission/ch11understanding_e.asp.
76. Articles 14.4(1) National Treatment and 14.5(1) Most-Favored-Nation Treatment. This entails the establishment, acquisition, expansion, management, conduct, operation, and sale or other disposition of investments.
77. Articles 14.4(4) National Treatment and 14.5(4) Most-Favored-Nation Treatment.

Like NAFTA, the USMCA prohibits any party from expropriating or nationalizing a covered investment either directly or indirectly through measures equivalent to expropriation or nationalization except for: (i) a public purpose; (ii) in a non-discriminatory manner; (iii) on payment of prompt, adequate, and effective compensation; and (iv) in accordance with due process of law.[78] Of interest, the USMCA contains an independent Annex 14-B on expropriation, which explains that Article 14.8.1 addresses both direct and indirect expropriation. For the first one, Annex 14-B describes that it occurs when an investment is nationalized or otherwise directly expropriated through formal transfer of title or outright seizure.[79] While for indirect expropriation occurs when a party's action or series of actions has an effect equivalent to direct expropriation without formal transfer of title or outright seizure.[80]

Furthermore, Annex 14-B affirms that non-discriminatory regulatory actions designed to protect legitimate public welfare objectives would not constitute indirect expropriation except in "rare circumstances."[81] In addition, the USMCA places new limits on the enforceability of this provision through its Annex 14-D (Mexico-U.S. investment disputes).

Second, regarding ISDS provisions, the USMCA implements Annex 14-D and keeps the investor-State arbitration mechanism under the ICSID Convention, the ICSID's Additional Facility Rules, UNCITRAL Arbitration Rules, or any other arbitration rules agreed by the parties.[82] Nonetheless, investor-State arbitration under the USMCA is mainly limited between the U.S. and Mexico.

Third, the USMCA includes other features in its investor-State dispute settlement provisions. For government contracts in "Covered Sectors," Annex 14-E of the USMCA provides that a privileged regime applies to foreign investors that are "party to a covered government contract" and engaged in activities in the same "covered sectors," which include: (i) oil and gas; (ii) power generation; (iii) telecommunications; (iv) transportation; and (v) infrastructure.

These investors can only access Annex 14-D for enforcing claims on direct expropriation and national treatment and most favored nation treatment, with the broad exception of claims on "the establishment or acquisition of an investment."[83] Consequently, submitting claims for indirect expropriation and the minimum standard of treatment—which includes FET and FPS—need to be espoused by the investor's home State using the USMCA's State-to-State dispute settlement mechanism[84] or directly brought by the investor before the host State's courts.

In contrast with Chapter XI of the NAFTA, Chapter 14 of the USMCA requires investors to exhaust local remedies before commencing arbitration, except where

78. Article 14.8 Expropriation and Compensation. Notably, this article shall be interpreted in accordance with Annex 14-B (Expropriation).
79. Annex 14-B(2) Expropriation.
80. Annex 14-B(3) Expropriation.
81. Annex 14-B(3)(b) Expropriation.
82. Article 14.D.3: Submission of a Claim to Arbitration.
83. Article 14.D.3: Submission of a Claim to Arbitration (1)(a)(i)(A).
84. Chapter 31 Dispute Settlement of the USMCA.

"recourse to domestic remedies was obviously futile."[85] In the same vein, Chapter 14 requires investors, before pursuing arbitration, to receive a final decision from a court of last resort of the host State or that at least thirty months have elapsed from the date court proceedings were initiated.[86]

Each regime of protection concedes different time limits for submitting disputes to arbitration. In the non-privileged regime, investors must submit disputes to arbitration up to four yours from the date on which the claimant first acquired, or should have first acquired, knowledge of the breach.[87] In contrast, under the privileged regime, no claims shall be submitted to arbitration if less than six months have elapsed from the events giving rise to the claim and more than three years have elapsed from the date on which the claimant learned of the breach.[88]

Primarily, two particular procedural aspects are relevant. On the one hand, the USMCA includes renewed provisions on panel selection and transparency.[89] On the other hand, Article 14.D.6 (5) requests arbitrators to comply with the International Bar Association Guidelines on Conflicts of Interest in International Arbitration, including guidelines regarding direct or indirect conflicts of interest. As well as refraining from taking instructions from any organization or government regarding the dispute, nor acting as counsel or as party-appointed expert or witness in any pending arbitration under the annexes to that chapter (i.e., avoid double-hatting practices).

As with NAFTA, arbitral tribunals will take some time to interpret these new provisions and for parties to adapt and make them into a testable set of rules. Overall, the USMCA contains a modernized investment chapter with substantive protections and a dispute settlement mechanism of investor-State arbitration to enforce those investment protections.

[5] The Brazilian Model: The Economic Cooperation Agreement Between Mexico and Brazil

Another highlighting treaty with investment promotion and protection provisions is the Cooperation and Investment Facilitation Agreement between the United States of Mexico and the Federative Republic of Brazil, signed in 2015 and entered into force on

85. Article 14.D.5: Conditions and Limitations on Consent, fn. 25.
86. Article 14.D.5: Conditions and Limitations on Consent (1)(b).
87. Article 14.D.5: Conditions and Limitations on Consent (1)(c).
88. Annex 14-E (4)(a) and (b).
89. On July 1, 2022, ICSID's new rules for arbitration proceedings came into effect and apply to all ICSID arbitrations commenced from that date onward. The new set of rules aim to "streamline procedures to enable greater access and speed, increase transparency, and enhance disclosures, with the ultimate goal of facilitating foreign investment for economic growth." One of the main topics addressed by the new arbitration rules is transparency and the mechanisms by which ICSID arbitrations—traditionally confidential—may be "opened" to the public. *See ICSID Administrative Council Approves Amendment of ICSID Rules*, ICSID News Releases (Mar. 21, 2022). *See also* Gary J Shaw, *The 2022 ICSID Rules: A Leap Toward Greater Transparency in ICSID Arbitration*, ICSID Review, Vol. 00, No. 0 at 1, (2022).

October 7, 2018.[90] Within its goals and objectives, this agreement sought to promote cooperation between the Parties to facilitate and promote mutual investment, along with establishing an institutional framework for facilitating investments, establishing mechanisms for risk mitigation and conflict prevention, and for the management of a cooperation agenda, among other instruments mutually agreed.

Within its provisions, both Parties included investment protections on discrimination, expropriation, compensation for losses, transfers, and corporate social responsibility.[91] In contrast to other BITs, this agreement encompasses State-to-State arbitration for violations under the treaty once consultations and negotiations between the Parties are conducted and previously examined by a "Joint Committee."[92]

This type of dispute settlement provisions of State-to-State arbitrations offered by Brazil is no surprise, as the country has departed from the current system by setting aside investor-State arbitration. In other words, the Brazilian model and practice regarding BITs or FTAs provide that disputes shall be settled through State-to-State arbitration.[93] This seems to replicate the traditional rule of diplomatic protection.

[6] Active Voice in Investor-State Forums

In today's criticism of the current investor-State arbitration regime, various forums have been gaining importance in discussing, proposing, and eventually implementing reforms to address the concerns of all parties involved, mainly the users, which are States and investors. One of these forums has been Working Group III of the UNCITRAL on Investor-State Dispute Settlement Reform,[94] and ICSID's process of consultations when amending its Rules and Regulations for 2022.[95] Mexico has actively participated in these matters.

Top it off, Mexico's actions on ratifying the ICSID and New York Conventions, promoting the permanence of the investor-State dispute settlement mechanism in the

90. Accessible at: https://investmentpolicy.unctad.org/international-investment-agreements/treaty-files/4718/download.
91. Articles 4-13 of the Agreement.
92. For major context, the Brazilian BITs do not permit the foreign investor to bring arbitration directly. Those treaties foresee the establishment of a joint committee to impulse investment cooperation and nominate ombudspersons within each country's administration to give official support to investment. Only then, a mechanism of State-to-State arbitration can initiate, which can be brought by the signatory States in case an investment dispute cannot be resolved through the intergovernmental channels. *See* Milcar Jeff Dorce, *supra* n. 71; and Geraldo Vidigal & Beatriz Stevens., *Brazil's New Model of Dispute Settlement for Investment: Return to the Past or Alternative for the Future?* The Journal of World Investment & Trade, 19(3), at 488 (May 2018).
93. Geraldo Vidigal & Beatriz Stevens, *supra* n. 92, at 475 and 487.
94. *See Working Group III: Investor-State Dispute Settlement Reform*, United Nations Commission On International Trade Law (UNCITRAL).
95. *See ICSID Releases 2022 Versions of its Rules and Regulations*, ICSID News Releases (Jun. 22, 2022), https://icsid.worldbank.org/news-and-events/news-releases/icsid-releases-2022-versions-its-rules-and-regulations.

USMCA, and entering the various BITs and FTAs described, do show a coherent and consistent posture of promoting and protecting foreign investment.[96]

[D] CONCLUSIONS

The current investor protection regime and practice of investor-State arbitration have their foundations in the old international treaties, ad hoc arbitration cases, mixed claims commissions, the ICSID Convention, and many other bodies encompassing both the protection of foreign investors' rights and dispute settlement mechanisms for investment claims resolution.

As this chapter described, Mexico has been part of this history of creation and evolution of international investment law and ISDS mechanisms by entering into various FTAs, BITs, and, most importantly, NAFTA Chapter XI. For good reason, when it comes to the system of international arbitration, Mexico has chosen the path of "flexibility or pluralism," by adopting various investment arbitration options in its international investment agreements.[97]

In fine, Mexico's degree of foreign investment protection displays a wide array of BITs, FTAs with investment chapters, and the USMCA, a treaty that still preserves the foundational aspects of investment treaty protection of NAFTA Chapter XI but introduces new substantive and procedural innovations along with a reflection of the newest practices employed in investment treaty practice. As with everything else, the immediate future will show how Mexico keeps developing its investment law framework amid the concerns from States and investors toward the reform of the current system of investor-State dispute settlement.

96. *See* Orlando Federico Cabrera Colorado, *Mexico Joins ICSID: A Coherent and Consistent History Underpinning the Rule of Law but not Investment*, World Arbitration and Mediation Review (WAMR) Vol. 11 No. 4, at 529-530, (2017).
97. Milcar Jeff Dorce, *supra* n. 71.

CHAPTER 14

Mexico's Legacy in the Investment Treaty Practice

Orlando Federico Cabrera Colorado[*]

[A] INTRODUCTION

According to the *Oxford Learner's Dictionary*, legacy means 'money or property that is given to you by somebody when they die; a situation that exists now because of events, actions, etc., that took place in the past; something that somebody has done successfully and that has positive effects even after they retire or die'.[1] This chapter briefly explains the evolution of Mexico's investment treaty practice. Particularly, the focus will be discussing how Mexico's foundation in the past has led to the doctrines of legitimate expectations, the Calvo doctrine and the early notions of the minimum standard of treatment as set by the *Neer* case, as well as the *Hull Formula*.

This chapter postulates that Mexico has been successful at managing dispute resolution of foreign investment claims. This successful management has positive effects and echoes in many other types of cases because, in the process, these foreign investment disputes developed case law, international customary law, and overall international law. The current foreign investment protection had its origin in many violent events that started out of gunboat diplomacy. However, from 1897 to 1911, President Porfirio Díaz understood foreign investment's relevance and used three types of investors to develop his economic policy and the country: British and US nationals

* The author wishes to thank Eduardo Siqueiros T. (Arbinter) and Daria Pietropaolo (University of Miami School of Law) for helpful comments and observations on an earlier version of the article. All errors and ideas remain the author's own.

1. *Oxford Learner's Dictionaries* https://www.oxfordlearnersdictionaries.com/us/definition/english/legacy_1?q=legacy.

invested in commodities; foreign investors purchased Mexican bonds that financed infrastructure projects; English, French, German, and Spanish investors developed local industries including textile factories, breweries, cotton, sugar and tobacco plantations.[2] Subsequent administrations realised foreign investors' need to keep industrialising the country,[3] and in 1992, when Mexico was negotiating the North America Free Trade Agreement (NAFTA), leaders perceived the need to grant wider protection through many investment treaties. Since then, Mexico's responsible attitude toward the management of investment disputes has avoided draining public finances. Mexico's unsuccessful cases do not compare by far with the immense damages awarded to foreign investors resulting from treaty claims against Russia, Pakistan, Ecuador, or India.

This chapter briefly showcases Mexico's past and current accomplishments in managing foreign investment disputes. As will be discussed further, foreign investors used gunboat diplomacy as a point of departure for dispute management. Over time, states have shifted toward a more sophisticated system of dispute resolution in the form of mixed claims commissions where sovereigns have delegated to a tribunal the responsibility to decide a case. This chapter explores old cases of mixed claims commissions and investment tribunals cases and compares the results of other cases. Certainly, Mexico's acceptance to protect foreign investments as it commits to in international investment agreements underpins modern investment treaty practice and gives way to the modern system of Investor-State Dispute Settlement (ISDS).

This chapter addresses the following questions: What is Mexico's legacy in investment arbitration and investment treaties? How has Mexico contributed to the prevalent state of affairs in investment arbitration and investment treaties? What decisions of modern dispute resolution deserve recognition and should serve as models for the future? Which of Mexico's victories have had positive effects after the end of the case?

This chapter starts with a brief review of gunboat diplomacy applied to Mexico, then it moves to discuss the US-Mexico Mixed Claims Commission set by the Bucareli Treaties. After a discussion of the Calvo Doctrine that was held by this Mixed Claims Commission, this chapter explains the minimum standard of treatment as developed in the *Neer* case by the Commission. Then, it touches upon the Hull Formula and the legitimate expectations' origin. Later, the chapter addresses Mexico's commitment to protect foreign investment and Mexico's handling of disputes. Lastly, we explore the last salient pyrrhic victory of PACC Offshore against Mexico because the arbitration community praised this case as a victory for the State due to the damages that were awarded.

2. Alexander Bohrisch and Wolfgang Köning, *La política Mexicana sobre inversiones extranjeras* 12-14 (El Colegio de México 1968).
3. *Ibid.*, 16-18.

[B] A SITUATION THAT EXISTS NOW BECAUSE OF EVENTS, ACTIONS, ETC., THAT TOOK PLACE IN THE PAST

[1] Gunboat Diplomacy Applied to Mexico

Gunboat diplomacy and Mexico's sovereign indebtedness produced a shocking foreign investment dispute.[4] On 31 October 1861, France, Great Britain, and Spain concluded the London Convention to intervene in Mexico's coastal fortresses toward obtaining loan repayments from Mexico.[5] To this intervention for the collection of public debt, the French Emperor Napoleon III added an objective, and manoeuvred to establish a French client state in Mexico, and eventually installed Maximilian of Habsburg, Archduke of Austria, as Emperor of Mexico.[6] Certainly, this dispute represented a major lesson for a nascent independent country. Mexico learned the prowess of French imperialism that put an end to an infant democracy and set in place a Second Mexican Empire. Through the years, disputes with foreigners evolved into more sophisticated dispute settlements by mixed claims commissions.

[2] Mixed Claims Commission: Bucareli Treaties

In the face of war-like circumstances, diplomatic protection gave rise to more reasoned mechanisms against armed intervention through the establishment of claims commissions in international treaties. Between 1923 and 1924, the United States and Mexico reached the adoption of the so-called Bucareli Conventions, which consist of two international treaties to resolve claims for damages suffered by US citizens during the Mexican Revolution (Special Convention) and by nationals of both countries for losses or damages (General Convention).[7] In the Special Convention, Mexico, ex gratia, felt morally obligated to provide full compensation. As such, the Bucareli treaties set the US-Mexico Claims Commission.

Three aspects of these treaties merit a comment because they set some foundations of the current ISDS system. *First*, both instruments established State-to-State arbitration before an ad hoc binational Commission.[8] Claims, therefore, had to be filed by the government of each country on behalf of the affected nationals. *Second*, the

4. Indirect foreign investment consists of capital inflows in two ways: (1) foreign indebtedness, i.e., foreign loans; and (2) the acquisition of stock shares. At this point, I refer to the first meaning of the terms, i.e., Mexico's indebtedness through foreign loans. *See* Gloria M. Delgado de Cantú, *México, estructuras política, económica y social* 263 (Pearson Prentice Hall 2d. ed. 2003).
5. Mexico's debt, denominated in pesos, was as follows: 68,994,542.54 to England, 2,800,762.03 to France and 9,460,986.29 to Spain. 8 José Rogelio Alvarez, *Enciclopedia de México* 4328-4329 (World Colour, Massachusetts 1998).
6. Office of the Historian, *French Intervention in Mexico and the American Civil War, 1862–1867*, US Department Justice (14 Dec. 2022), https://history.state.gov/milestones/1861-1865/french-intervention.
7. Convención Especial de Reclamaciones (Special Convention), DOF 26 Feb. 1924, y Convención General de Reclamaciones (General Convention) DOF 2 Apr. 1924.
8. Special Convention, Art. I; General Convention, Art. I. Alberto J. Pani *Las Conferencias de Bucareli* (Jus México 1953).

Commission was constituted by one member appointed by the US President, one by the Mexican President and the third one by mutual agreement between two Governments; if Mexico and the US failed to reach an agreement, the President of the Permanent Administrative Council of the Permanent Court of Arbitration had to designate the third member.[9] *Third*, both instruments established that it was unnecessary to exhaust legal remedies as a condition precedent to the validity or admissibility of any claim.[10]

The above provisions contrast in part with the current ISDS. These provisions also reveal ISDS's past, present and future. First, the current ISDS system allows investors to bring a claim without the need for diplomatic intervention. Presently, the selection of arbitrators remains the same in the United States-Mexico-Canada Agreement (USMCA), Mexico's most recent treaty.[11] Contrary to the Bucareli treaties, the USMCA now requires that certain types of investors initiate a proceeding before a local court for at least thirty months prior to submitting a claim to arbitration, with some exceptions.[12]

The case law developed by this US-Mexico Claims Commission merits attention because it sets the foundations for the Calvo Clause's validity, and the Minimum Standard of Treatment's recognition that this chapter now turns to explore.

[3] The Calvo Doctrine Limits Privileges for Foreigners

Two centuries ago, Latin American states found in the Calvo Doctrine the possibility of restricting or eliminating the danger of foreign interventions, and the foreigners' demands for a privileged treatment. Today, the doctrine still appears in several bodies of Mexican law, but investment treaties and Mexico's inclusion of arbitration clauses in state contracts have substantially reduced its vigour. Mexico continues to include components of the Calvo Clause, like waivers of diplomatic protections, in companies' deeds of incorporation and contracts.

[a] The Notions of the Calvo Doctrine

The Calvo Doctrine encompasses three main foundations: national sovereignty, territorial jurisdiction, and equality between nationals and foreigners.[13] In this sense, states, being free, independent, and sovereign, should not suffer any type of interference by third states. Consequently, foreigners should not have access to privileged judicial or arbitral international forums, but rather only to the national State courts.[14]

9. *Ibid.*
10. General Convention, Art. V; Special Convention, Art. VI.
11. USMCA, Art. 14.D.6.1.
12. USCMA, Art. 14.D.5.1.d.
13. Francesco Tamburini, *Historia y Destino de la "Doctrina Calvo": ¿Actualidad u obsolescencia del pensamiento de Carlos Calvo?* 24 *Revista de estudios históricos – jurídicos* 81-101 (2002) https://www.scielo.cl/scielo.php?script=sci_arttext&pid=S0716-54552002002400005.
14. Vol. A-C Alonso Gómez-Robledo Verduzco, 'Cláusula Calvo' *Diccionario Jurídico Mexicano* 559-561 (Raúl Márquez Romero ed., Porrúa México 2007).

At its core, the Calvo Doctrine seeks equality between foreigners and nationals. This equality incorporates two aspects. First, foreigners must receive the same treatment as nationals; this entails that foreigners can only enjoy the rights granted to nationals in the judicial courts. Second, foreigners can only benefit from national treatment and not from a privileged regime with greater rights than locals in which foreigners claim to have other remedies or means of defence than those offered by the local authorities.[15]

[b] *The History of the Calvo Clause*

The first case on record using the Calvo Doctrine dates back to 1873 when in a note addressed to the US Ambassador Foster, the Mexican Minister of Foreign Affairs José María Lafragua, citing Calvo, asserted that the Mexican State was not compelled to protect more US citizens than Mexicans. Thus, there was no need to grant privileges. Foster responded that the author on which Lafragua relied was not internationally accepted.[16]

Despite this first unsuccessful result with the Calvo Clause, more than fifty years later the US-Mexico Claims Commission favourably upheld its validity. The US-Mexico General Claims Commission rendered one of the most celebrated awards for both the history of the Calvo Clause and international foreign investment law. In *North American Dredging Company of Texas (USA) v. United Mexican States,*[17] the Commission enforced the Calvo Clause.

The US brought a claim on behalf of the North American Dredging Company of Texas, a US corporation, to recover losses and damages allegedly suffered for contract breaches for dredging at the port of Salina Cruz. The company and the Mexican government entered into a contract, which included a Calvo Clause as 'an indispensable provision' subscribed to secure the contract's award.[18]

The Calvo Clause provided that the contractor shall be considered Mexican in all matters concerning the execution of the work. The contractor shall not claim, nor shall it have, any other rights or means to enforce the contract than those granted by Mexican law, nor shall it 'enjoy any other rights than those established in favour of Mexicans'.[19] Consequently, the clause deprived the contractor of any additional rights as non-Mexicans, and it prohibited the intervention of foreign diplomatic agents.[20]

Based on the clause above, Mexico challenged the Commission's jurisdiction, asserting that the Calvo Clause deprived the company of the right to submit any contractual claims to the Commission.[21]

15. *Ibid.* Santiago Montt, *State Liability in Investment Treaty Arbitration, Global Constitutional and Administrative Law in the BIT Generation* 39-40 (Hart 2012).
16. Tamburini, *supra* n. 13.
17. *North American Dredging Company of Texas (U.S.A.) v. United Mexican States,* 31 Mar. 1926, pp. 26-35 https://legal.un.org/riaa/cases/vol_IV/26-35.pdf.
18. *Ibid.*, paras 26-27.
19. *Ibid.*, citing the Calvo Clause of the contract contained in Art. 18.
20. *Ibid.*, p. 27.
21. *Ibid.*, para. 1.

The Commission found no international rule prohibiting a limitation on the sovereign right of a nation to protect its citizens abroad.[22] Mexico asked the investor 'as a condition for awarding it the contract' to 'promise not to call directly upon [its] own Government to intervene in your behalf in connection with any controversy', but rather to seek redress under Mexican law before Mexican courts, 'and claimant by subscribing to this contract … has answered, "I promise"'.[23] Moreover, the Commission did not find 'any generally recognized rule of positive international law which would give to [an alien's] Government the right to intervene to strike down a lawful contract' including the Calvo Clause.[24]

Further, the Commission interpreted that the Calvo clause's 'purpose was to bind the claimant to be governed by' Mexican law and 'to use the remedies existing under such' law.[25] The Commission found that the claimant agreed not to invoke its Government's assistance regarding the contract as a condition for Mexico to award him the contract.[26]

The Commission observed that the claimant promised in writing to abide by local laws, remedies, and authorities, but it behaved as if the Calvo Clause were non-existent. It accepted the Calvo Clause to procure the contract but had no intention of ever observing its provisions because it never sought any redress before local authorities.[27]

The Treaty required: (1) a citizen to submit a claim to his Government; and (2) the claim's espousal by that Government.[28] The Calvo Clause precluded the claimant from presenting to the US Government any contract claim, except for denial of justice. The Commission found that the claimant did not rightfully present the claim to its Government for espousal; thus, the Commission could not know it and had no jurisdiction.[29]

To summarise, under the General Convention, for a claim to fall within the Commission's jurisdiction, it had to be brought by a citizen of one Government against the other Government and the claimant had to present the claim for its 'interposition' before its Government. The claimant agreed to the Calvo Clause, to be bound and governed by Mexican law administered by Mexican courts, and not to invoke or accept its Government's assistance, but it did not bind itself to the contract. Moreover, the claimant accepted the Calvo Clause as a condition to win the contract. The claimant did not pretend that it made any attempt to comply with the Calvo Clause, by which it was bound. Therefore, the claimant was not able to rightfully present this claim to the US Government for its interposition. The Commission found that the claimant could not bind the US Government with respect to remedies for international law violations except for denial of justice. But the claimant voluntarily entered into a contract binding itself not to call its Government to intervene on its behalf regarding the contract. Given

22. *Ibid.*, para. 9.
23. *Ibid.*, para. 10.
24. *Ibid.*, para. 11.
25. *Ibid.*, para. 14.
26. *Ibid.*, para. 15.
27. *Ibid.*, para. 18.
28. *Ibid.*, para. 19.
29. *Ibid.*, para. 20.

that its claim related to this contract, it could not present its claim to its Government for interposition or espousal before the Commission.[30] As a result, the Commission decided that the case was not within its jurisdiction and dismissed the case.

This award echoed as it was recognised by other arbitration tribunals in foreign investment matters, including the subsequent 1930s cases: *Mexican Union Railway, International Fishers Company, Interoceanic Railway of Mexico*, and *MacNeill*.[31] In this way, Mexico contributed to the development of the development of the Calvo Doctrine in international investment matters.

[c] The Present Practice of the Calvo Clause in Mexico and the EU

In Mexico, the Calvo Doctrine appears even today in numerous contracts between States and foreigners through the famous 'Calvo Clause'. It usually consists of: (1) an obligation to submit disputes arising from the contract to local jurisdiction and the application of domestic law; as well as (2) the waiver by the foreigner to the diplomatic protection of his home State and the entire claim itself.[32] Nonetheless, despite Mexico's frequent application of the Calvo Clause in many state contracts, Mexico today frequently accepts international arbitration.

First, the Mexican Constitution states today: 'The State may grant the same right to foreigners' 'to acquire the domain of lands, waters and their accessions or to obtain concessions for the exploitation of mines or waters,' 'provided that they agree before the Ministry of Foreign Affairs to consider themselves as nationals with respect to such property and not to invoke the protection of their governments with respect to such property; under penalty, in case of failure to comply with the agreement, of losing the property they have acquired for the benefit of the Nation'.[33] Besides, the same agreement must appear in the companies' deeds incorporated under Mexican law that admit foreigners.[34] And even in the oil contracts granted by the Mexican State, there is a waiver to invoke diplomatic protection.[35]

30. *Ibid.*, para. 24.
31. Gómez-Robledo Verduzco, *supra* n. 14, at 561.
32. *Ibid.*, at 559.
33. Mexican Political Constitution, Art. 27, I.
34. Article 14 of the Regulations of the Foreign Investment Law states:

> ARTICLE 14.—When the articles of incorporation do not include a clause excluding foreigners, an express agreement or covenant must be executed that forms an integral part of the articles of incorporation, whereby the foreign partners, current or future of the company, are obligated before the Ministry of Foreign Affairs to be considered as nationals with respect to:
>
> I. The shares, equity interest or rights that they acquire from such companies;
> II. The goods, rights, concessions, participations or interests owned by such companies, and
> III. The rights and obligations deriving from the contracts to which the companies themselves are a party.

Second, on the other side of the Atlantic, in the intra-EU investment context, Ludic and Lindinger observe that the Calvo Clause has been resuscitated. They argue that the *PL Holdings* judgment endorses the EU Commission's anti-arbitration policy because, in 2021, the Court of Justice of the European Union (CJEU) held that an ad hoc arbitration agreement between a Member State and an investor of another Member State is incompatible with EU law if this agreement is identical to the content of the arbitration clause at issue in the case which gave rise to the *Achmea* judgment.[36] They observe that intra-EU Bilateral Investment Treaties (BITs) confer rights only to investors from one of the two Member States, and for the EU Commission, this discriminates among EU nationals. Thus, investment disputes must be prosecuted in domestic litigation; 'an absolute local remedies requirement irreconcilable with the arbitration facility commonly embodied in intra-EU BITS'.[37] In *PL Holdings*, the CJEU interprets the Treaty on the EU (TEU) requiring Member States not to remove disputes from the jurisdiction of their own courts because they would remove them from the judicial remedies TEU requires them to provide in areas subject to EU law. For Ludic and Lindinger, the EU treaties share traits with the Calvo Clause.[38]

Under Mexican law, the Calvo Clause requires foreigners to waive diplomatic protection but not to international arbitration as it occurs today in the intra-EU investment context, as Ludic and Lindinger underscore. In contrast to the EU's approach and despite the Mexican Constitution's provisions, Mexico's position toward the Calvo Clause's application is moderate because it regularly accepts international arbitration in state contracts and even with a seat abroad, for example, in The Hague, Kingdom of the Netherlands.[39] Additionally, today, in practice, the effects of the Calvo Clause appear to be unknown or ineffective. News frequently reports diplomatic interventions, but it does not report sanctions imposed by Mexico against foreign investors depriving them of their property after invoking diplomatic protection.

> The aforementioned agreement or pact must include the waiver to invoke the protection of their governments under penalty, otherwise, of forfeiting to the benefit of the Nation the rights and assets they may have acquired.

35. Contrato para la Exploración y Extracción de Hidrocarburos bajo la Modalidad de Producción Compartida entre Comisión Nacional de Hidrocarburos y Sierra O&G Exploración y Producción, S. de R.L. de C.V.; Talos Energy Offshore Mexico 2, S. de R.L. de C.V. y Premier Oil Exploration and Production Mexico, S.A. de C.V. (4 Sep. 2015) https://www.gob.mx/cms/uploads/attachment/file/117310/CNH-R01-L01-A2-2015.pdf.
36. Sebastian Ludic and Christophn Lindinger, *The Renaissance of the Calvo Clause in EU Law,* JUS MUNDI Blog (14 Dec. 2022) https://blog.jusmundi.com/the-renaissance-of-the-calvo-clause-in-eu-law/. Citing *PL Holdings S.a.r.l. v. Poland,* SCC Case No. V 2014/163, Judgment of the Grand Chamber of the European Court of Justice, 26 Oct. 2021 para. 46.
37. *Ibid.*
38. *Ibid.*
39. Public Works and Related Services Law, Art. 98; Acquisitions, Leases and Public Services Law, Art. 80; Public Private Partnerships Law, Art. 139; Hydrocarbons Law, Art. 21; PEMEX Law, Art. 115; CFE Law, Art. 118; Electric Power Industry Law, Art. 96.

[4] The Minimum Standard of Treatment as Envisioned in the *Neer* Case

In the early twentieth century, jurists in Europe and the US argued that there was a standard of fairness in foreign investors treatment.[40] This idea began in various trade treaties, as well as decisions of claims commissions.[41] In particular, the US-Mexico General Claims Commission upheld the idea of a minimum standard of treatment.[42] The first and often one of the most cited cases in the current era of investment arbitration is *Neer*, which we refer to in the relevant part:

> it is in the opinion of the Commission ... to hold ... that the treatment of an alien, in order to constitute an international delinquency, should amount to an outrage, to bad faith, to wilful neglect of duty, or to an insufficiency of governmental action so far short of international standards that every reasonable and impartial man would readily recognize its insufficiency. Whether the insufficiency proceeds from deficient execution of an intelligent law or from the fact that the laws of the country do not empower the authorities to measure up to international standards is immaterial.[43]

Under this standard, the Commission judged Mexico favourably for alleged acts of denial of justice. It is a three-page decision, but it outlines issues of denial of justice, fair and equitable treatment, as well as the minimum standard of treatment in international law. This case has been cited in recent investment arbitration awards such as *Pope & Talbot v. Canada, LG&E v. Argentina, Thunderbird v. Mexico, Waste Management II v. Mexico, GAMI v. Mexico, Mondev v. United States, ADF v. United States, Glamis Gold v. United States, and Merrill & Ring Forestry v. Canada.*[44] In this way, Mexico has contributed to case law development on minimum standard of treatment in investment arbitration.

[5] Hull Formula

Between 1915 and 1940, the Mexican government expropriated several agrarian and oil properties, the ownership of which included some US nationals. Given numerous nationalisations carried out by the Mexican President Lázaro Cárdenas, the US replied with the Hull Rule. In 1938, in a note, the US Secretary of State, Cordell Hull, created the rule that bears his name and is recognised by customary international law. Secretary Hull's words represent the position that 'full compensation' for the property

40. Ian Brownlie, *System of the Law of Nations, State Responsibility – Part I* 7 (Oxford University Press 1986).
41. Hans Neufeld, *The International Protection of Private Creditors from the Treaties of Westphalia to the Congress of Vienna (1648-1815): A Contribution to the History of the Law of Nations* 47-55 (Stijthoff Leiden 1971).
42. Five cases are typically cited to support the existence of the standard of minimum standard of treatment: *Neer* (1926) IV RIAA 60, *Faulkener* (1927) 21 AJIL 349, *Harry Roberts* (1927) 21 AJIL 357, *Hopkins* (1927) 21 AJIL 160 and *Way* (1929) 23 AJIL 466.
43. *Neer and Neer (U.S.A.) v. United Mexican States*, Decision, 15 Oct. 1926 para. 4.
44. Maria Kostytska and Ignacio Torterola, *L. Fay H. Neer and Pauline Neer (USA) v. United Mexican States*, IACL https://www.transnational-dispute-management.com/legal-and-regulatory-detail.asp?key=27819.

of aliens requires *prompt, adequate and effective compensation.*[45] Prompt meaning without delays; adequate, i.e., proportional to the nationalised asset; and effective in convertible currency, US dollars.[46]

In response, the Mexican Government replied that it did not reject the principle of compensation but maintained that the measure of compensation must depend on the ability of the nationalising State to pay; otherwise, the obligation to pay 'immediately the value of private property' would deny the State the right to restructure its economy and reduce economic reforms. Although Mexico had proceeded with oil nationalisation, the US reversed the Hull Doctrine. The US implemented the Good Neighbor Policy, as it had legitimate concerns about Mexico selling oil to Nazi Germany. In November 1941, the Roosevelt Administration decided to enter into an agreement with Mexico to combine compensation for expropriated land and oil nationalisation.[47]

Mexico's contribution to international law echoed in other latitudes. For example, Hersch Lauterpacht asserted that States should compensate based on payments gradually determined over a long period and calculated with reference to the State's economic position.[48] In nationalisation cases, Eduardo Jiménez de Aréchaga observed that custom confirms that States have accepted deferred compensation, even those that defend the Hull Formula. To illustrate, Britain and France have paid compensation for the nationalisation of banks, airlines, insurance companies, transportation, steel, and coal industries in the form of interest-bearing long-term bonds. Belgium, the US, and Switzerland accepted this formula, even though the measures affected their nationals.[49]

Despite the deferred compensation, the Hull Formula remains in full effect. It appears in treaties like NAFTA,[50] the Comprehensive and Progressive Agreement for Trans-Pacific Partnership (CPTPP),[51] and USMCA.[52] To illustrate, Mexico has honoured and paid in full all ISDS arbitration awards entered against it.

[6] Early Development of Legitimate Expectations due to Mexico's Past Cases

Mexico's investment arbitration contributions to international law expand on many topics, and this chapter will focus on analysing the early developments of legitimate

45. Andrew T. Guzmán, *Why LDCs Sing Treaties that Hurt Them: Explaining the Popularity of Bilateral Investment Treaties* [1997-1998] 38 Virginia Journal of International Law 639 http://scholarship.law.berkeley.edu/cgi/viewcontent.cgi?article=1903&context=facpubs.
46. Tamburini, *supra* n. 13.
47. O Thomas Johnson Jr and Jonathan Gimblett, *From Gunboats to BITS: The Evolution of Modern International Investment Law* in Karl Sauvant ed., *Yearbook of International Investment Law and Policy 2010-2011* 656 (Oxford University Press New York 2012).
48. 255 Ian Brownlie, *General Course on Public International Law* 144 (Recueil des cours de l'Académie de droit International Martinus Nijhoff Publishers 1995).
49. *Ibid.*, 146-147.
50. NAFTA, Art. 1110.3.
51. CPTPP, Art. 9.8.1 (c).
52. USCMA, Art. 14.8.1 (c).

expectations given that several tribunals have found legitimate expectations as Fair and Equitable Treatment's (FET) dominant element.[53] Of course, some dissidents do not concur.[54] Be as it may, Mexico's legacy set the foundations of the legitimate expectations doctrine.

Bonnitcha observes that the doctrine of legitimate expectations recently appeared as an FET element.[55] Although Dolzer found some foundations in comments made in the early arbitral awards of the twenty-first century,[56] Mexico made substantial contributions in several cases.

In 2000, the *Metalclad* tribunal noted that 'Metalclad was led to believe, and did believe, that the federal and state permits allowed for the construction and operation of the landfill.'[57] The tribunal found that '[r]elying on the representations of the federal government, Metalclad started constructing the landfill'[58] and 'Metalclad was entitled to rely on the representations of federal officials and to believe that it was entitled to continue its construction of the landfill.'[59] These and other actions against transparency halting the landfill's construction led the tribunal to conclude that Metalclad was not treated fairly or equitably, and Metalclad succeeded in its claim under NAFTA Article 1105.[60] Nevertheless, one year later, the Supreme Court of British Columbia partially set aside the award albeit on transparency.[61]

In 2003, for the first time, the *Tecmed* tribunal instituted the protection of an investor's expectations in general terms,[62] by providing that under NAFTA, the FET standard requires treatment 'that does not affect the basic expectations that were taken into account by the foreign investor to make the investment'.[63]

In 2004, the *Waste Management II* tribunal bridled its decision regarding legitimate expectations after introducing FET's notions. The Tribunal held:

> [The] minimum standard of treatment of [FET] is infringed ... if the conduct is arbitrary, grossly unfair, unjust or idiosyncratic, is discriminatory and exposes the

53. *Saluka Investments BV v. the Czech Republic*, UNCITRAL, Partial Award (17 Mar. 2006), para. 302 ('the standard of "fair and equitable treatment" is therefore closely tied to the notion of legitimate expectations which is the dominant element of that standard'.); *EDF (Services) Ltd. v. Romania*, ICSID Case No. ARB/05/13, Award (8 Oct. 2009) para. 216; *GPF GP S.à.r.l v. Poland*, SCC Case No. 2014/168, Final Award, (29 Apr. 2020), para. 543 ('a consensus emerges about the core components of FET, which include the protection of legitimate expectations').
54. *Cairn Energy PLC and Cairn UK Holdings Limited v. The Republic of India*, PCA Case No. 2016-07, Final Award (21 Dec. 2020), para. 1723.
55. Jonathan Bonnitcha, *Substantive Protection under Investment Treaties: A Legal and Economic Analysis* 167 (Cambridge, 2014).
56. *Ibid.* citing Dolzer and Schreuer, *Principles of International Investment Law* (2nd ed.) 146-147.
57. *Metalclad Corporation v. The United Mexican States*, ICSID Case No. ARB(AF)/97/1, Award (30 Aug. 2000) para. 850.
58. *Ibid.*, para. 87.
59. *Ibid.*, para. 89.
60. *Ibid.*, paras 97-101.
61. *Metalclad Corporation v. The United Mexican States*, ICSID Case No. ARB(AF)/97/1, Decision of the Supreme Court of British Columbia on the challenge by the Petitioner 2001 BCSC 664 (2 May 2001), paras 72-76.
62. Bonnitcha, *supra* n. 55, at 167.
63. *Técnicas Medioambientales Tecmed, S.A. v. United Mexican States*, ICSID Case No. ARB(AF)/00/2, Award (29 May 2003) para. 154.

> claimant to sectional or racial prejudice, or involves a lack of due process leading to an outcome which offends judicial propriety—as might be the case with a manifest failure of natural justice in judicial proceedings or a complete lack of transparency and candour in an administrative process. In applying this standard it is relevant that the treatment is in breach of representations made by the host State which were reasonably relied on by the claimant.

In 2006, however, the *Thunderbird* tribunal invoked for the first time the 'legitimate expectations' syntagma.[64] Thunderbird, the investor, argued that 'if an investor or investment reasonably relies on the representations of government officials and suffers damages because of such reliance, the responsibility of the State is engaged under international law'.[65] Thunderbird contended that through NAFTA's ratification, 'Mexico authored a set of legitimate expectations upon which an investor or investment could reasonably rely.'[66] The *Thunderbird* tribunal found that:

> the concept of 'legitimate expectations' relates, within the context of the NAFTA framework, to a situation where a Contracting Party's conduct creates reasonable and justifiable expectations on the part of an investor (or investment) to act in reliance on said conduct, such that a failure by the NAFTA Party to honour those expectations could cause the investor (or investment) to suffer damages.[67]

Despite the above principle, the tribunal found that the official letter at issue did not generate legitimate expectations for the investor.[68]

Subsequent case law has modelled the concept of legitimate expectations by describing those situations giving rise to legitimate expectations such as contractual arrangements between the investor and the States;[69] formal and informal representations made to investors,[70] as well a more elaborated methodology of arbitral tribunals in appreciating a breach of legitimate expectations.[71] But Mexico's early case law set the foundations.

[C] MEXICO'S ACCEPTANCE OF FOREIGN INVESTMENT

Mexico's modern acceptance of foreign investments started with the signature of NAFTA and entry into force in 1994. Thereafter, Mexico continued to conclude other

64. Bonnitcha *supra* n. 55 p. 167.
65. *International Thunderbird Gaming Corporation v. The United Mexican States*, Arbitral Award (26 Jan. 2006) para. 138.
66. *Ibid.*
67. *Ibid.*, para. 147.
68. *Ibid.*, para. 148.
69. *Glamis Gold v. USA*, Ad hoc Arbitration, Award (8 Jun. 2009) paras 766, 813.
70. *Etrak v. Libya*, ICC, Final Award (22 Jul. 2019) para. 315.
71. *Ioannis Kardassopoulos v. The Republic of Georgia*, ICSID Case No. ARB/05/18, Award (3 Mar. 2010) ('the fact that it was after the investment was made that specific assurances of compensation were given, which assurances gave rise to a specific expectation of compensation, does not preclude Mr. Fuchs from holding throughout the term of his investment the legitimate expectation that Georgia would conduct itself vis-à-vis his investment in a manner that was reasonably justifiable and did not manifestly violate basic requirements of consistency, transparency, even-handedness and nondiscrimination'.).

FTAs with identical or closely similar provisions to NAFTA and incorporated NAFTA jurisprudence in subsequent treaties. Mexico has ten Free Trade Agreements containing an investment chapter with the following States: CPTPP (Australia, Brunei Darussalam, Canada, Chile, Japan, Malaysia, New Zealand, Peru, Singapore, Vietnam); Chile; Pacific Alliance (Chile, Colombia and Perú); Colombia; Central America (Costa Rica, El Salvador, Guatemala, Honduras and Nicaragua); USMCA (US and Canada); Japan; Panama; Perú; and Uruguay.[72]

To supplement foreigners' protection, Mexico has concluded thirty BITs in force with Argentina, Austria, Bahrein, Belarus, Belgium and Luxembourg, Check Republic, China, Cuba, Denmark, Finland, France, Germany, Greece, Hong Kong, Iceland, Italy, Korea, Kuwait, the Netherlands, Portugal, Singapore, Slovakia, Spain, Sweden, Switzerland, Trinidad and Tobago, Turkey, United Arab Emirates, United Kingdom, and Uruguay.[73]

Mexico's legacy remains unaltered. Mexican policies show consistency and coherence despite changes in administration. Mexico and the US negotiated and concluded the USMCA even when the past and present administrations involved have different policies. Mexico keeps protecting foreign investment with the network of treaties described above. Mexico's steadfastness and consistency stand out given that some defectors like Bolivia, Canada, the EU, India, and Venezuela have lost faith in the investment arbitration system. Moreover, Mexico actively participated in the ICSID rules amendments and continues to participate in the debate at UNCITRAL Group III on ISDS Reform.

[D] DAMAGES AWARDED: AN APPROPRIATE DEFENCE

Mexico has created a legacy for the international community not only by developing case law but also by efficiently managing claims, particularly those that avoided drains to Mexican finances, and represent savings for Mexican's taxes.

The following chart describes the total number of cases where Mexico was a Respondent and the current outcome.

Table 14.1 Mexico as a Respondent State in ISDS Cases

Outcome of the Case	*No.*
Discontinued	5
Pending	16
Settled	1

72. Gobierno de México, *Comercio Exterior, Países con Tratados y Acuerdos firmados con México*, (14 Dec. 2022) https://www.gob.mx/se/acciones-y-programas/comercio-exterior-paises-con-tratados-y-acuerdos-firmados-con-mexico.
73. *Ibid.*

Outcome of the Case	*No.*
Decided in favour of the State	12
Decided in favour of the Investor	11
Total number of cases where Mexico was a Respondent	**45**

Source: Chart prepared with information from the Investment Dispute Settlement Navigator of UNCTAD Investment Policy Hub: https://investmentpolicy.unctad.org/investment-dispute-settlement.

Reviewing the total number of cases decided in favour of the investor we find the following:

Table 14.2 Cases Decided in Favour of the Investor, Amounts Claimed and Awarded

No.	*Cases Decided in Favour of the Investor*	*Amount Claimed Millions of USD*	*Amount Awarded Millions of USD*	*Percentages of Amounts Claimed*
1	*Abengoa*	70	40.3	57.57%
2	*ADM*	100	33.5	33.5%
3	*Cargill*	123.8	77.3	62.43%
4	*CPI*	325	58	17.84%
5	*Feldman*	30.3	0.74	2.44%
6	*Gemplus*	37	4.5	12.16%
7	*Lion*	99	49.2	49.69%
8	*Metalclad*	90	16.7	18.55%
9	*PACC Offshore*	227.1	6.7	2.95%
10	*Talsud*	37	6.4	17.29%
11	*Tecmed*	52	5.5	10.57%
	Total	**1,191.2**	**298.84**	**25.08%**

Source: Chart jointly prepared by Carlos Alvarado and the author with information taken from each award. Please note that, at the time of the elaboration of the present chapter, Lion is subject to a set aside proceeding.

As we can see from the chart above, so far, investment arbitral tribunals have ordered Mexico to pay in damages a total of USD 292 million.[74] This heavily contrasts with the amounts of compensation awarded in:

74. If we remove *Lion*, which Mexico is seeking to set aside in the US District Court for the District of Columbia, so far Mexico has lost USD 242.94 million. 1:21-cv-03185, 2022, *United Mexican States v. Lion Mexico Consolidated L.P.*, [2021] US Dist. Of Columbia Dist. Ct.

(1) other major ISDS cases, like Russia that lost USD 50 billion in the *Yukos*[75] saga, or Pakistan that lost USD 4.09 billion in *Tethyan Copper*,[76] or India that lost USD 1.4 billion in *Carin*.[77] Although past decided cases against Mexico have not dealt with similar amounts claimed, now Mexico encounters major risks arising out of *Odyssey* where the claimant demands payment of USD 3.5 billion[78] and NAFTA legacy claims;[79] and
(2) other commercial arbitrations where Petróleos Mexicanos (PEMEX) and Comisión Federal de Electricidad (CFE), Mexico's state-owned enterprises, were involved. PEMEX paid USD 435 million to settle a thirteen-year-old dispute with US engineering company KBR, ending the *COMMISA v. PEMEX* saga regarding the enforcement of an ICC award set aside in Mexico and upheld in New York[80] and CFE paid USD 270 million to a Chinese-Mexican consortium to settle an LCIA award over a hydroelectric project disrupted by local protests.[81]

The causes that led to Mexico's success in defeating investors and being awarded those relatively small awards may be speculative, however, the author observes the following facts:

(1) Mexico holds a specialised office, *Dirección General de Consultoría Jurídica de Comercio Internacional*, with around twenty-two lawyers devoted to coordinating Mexico's defence in dispute resolution procedures under international

75. *Yukos Capital SARL v. The Russian Federation*, PCA Case No. 2005-04AA227, Final Award (18 Jul. 2014); *Hulley Enterprises Ltd. v. Russian Federation*, PCA Case No. 2005-03/AA226, Final Award (18 Jul. 2014); *Veteran Petroleum Limited v. The Russian Federation*, PCA Case No. 2005-05/AA228, Final Award (18 Jul. 2014).
76. *Tethyan Copper Company Pty Limited v. Islamic Republic of Pakistan*, ICSID Case No. ARB/12/1, Award, (12 Jul. 2019).
77. *Cairn Energy PLC and Cairn UK Holdings Limited v. The Republic of India*, PCA Case No. 2016-07, Final Award (21 Dec. 2020).
78. *Odyssey Marine Exploration, Inc. v. United Mexican States* (ICSID Case No. UNCT/20/1) Notice of Arbitration (5 Apr. 2019) para. 134.
79. USMCA, Annex 14-C provides that a protected 'legacy investment' is an investment of a US investor in Mexico established or acquired before NAFTA's termination that was already in existence on the date of USMCA's entry in force on 1 Jul. 2020.
80. *See* KBR, *KBR Recovers Almost Half Billion Dollar Judgment, Resolves Lengthy Commercial Dispute* (Press Release, 10 Apr. 2017) https://seekingalpha.com/filing/3499833, accessed 4 Dec. 2022. *See* also the judgment rendered by the US Second Circuit Court of Appeals *Corporacion Mexicana De Mantenimiento Integral, S De RL De CV v. Pemex-Exploracion y Producción*, Docket No 13-4022 (2d Cir 2016), and the award rendered in *Corporación Mexicana de Mantenimiento Integral, S de RL de CV v. Pemex Exploración y Producción*, ICC Case No 13613/CCO/JRF.
81. Cosmo Sanderson, *Mexican State Utility Pays Hydro Award*, GAR (7 Jul. 2021) https://globalarbitrationreview.com/article/mexican-state-utility-pays-hydro-award; *Omega Construcciones Industriales, S.A. de C.V., Sinohydro Costa Rica, S.A., Desarrollo y Construcciones Urbanas, S.A. de C.V., and CAABSA Infraestructura, S.A. de C.V., v. Comisión Federal de Electricidad (CFE)*, Case No. 1:20-cv-05787, US District Court Southern District of New York; *Omega Construcciones Industriales, S.A. de C.V., Sinohydro Costa Rica, S.A., Desarrollo y Construcciones Urbanas, S.A. de C.V., and CAABSA Infraestructura, S.A. de C.V., v. Comisión Federal de Electricidad (CFE)*, LCIA Case No. 163471, Final Award (22 Jun. 2020).

treaties.[82] Although other countries, like Argentina or Spain, have similar teams, in 2003, Mexico established the Professional Career Service system. This is a public policy grounded in a special law[83] aiming at the professionalisation of public officers, promoting efficiency in public management. This translates into an improvement in the services offered.[84]

(2) Mexico has retained the same two counsellors, Cameron Mowatt and Stephan E. Becker, since the very first cases in 1997, *Metalclad*[85] and *Robert Azinian*,[86] to the most recent ones registered before ICSID in 2021 like *Nelson*[87] and *Fineley Resources*.[88] Although Mexico has sought additional help to handle new cases.[89]

Mexico stands out for its good track record of paying all ISDS awards against it.[90] This contrasts with Venezuela, Spain, Russia, Ukraine and Argentina, which, according to Lavranos, are the top five most delinquent respondents in the world when it comes to the refusal to pay ISDS awards.[91] Thus, Mexico not only accepts and protects foreign investments but its commitments are also real given that Mexico has paid all awards entered against it. Mexico stands by its principles.

[E] MEXICO'S SUCCESS AND POSITIVE EFFECTS IN *PACC OFFSHORE*

From the list of Mexico's adverse awards, a recent pyrrhic investor's victory merits analysis: *PACC Offshore Services Holding LTD*. In this case, even though the investor

82. Reglamento Interior de la Secretaría de Economía (17 Oct. 2019) Art. 48.
83. *Ley del Servicio Profesional de Carrera en la Administración Pública Federal*, 10 Apr. 2003, last amendment on 9 Jan. 2006.
84. Gobierno de México, Servicio Profesional de Carrera (29 Jan. 2023) https://www.gob.mx/conapo/acciones-y-programas/servicio-profesional-de-carrera-26349#:~:text=%C2%BFQu%C3%A9%20es%20el%20Servicio%20Profesional,se%20ofrecen%20a%20la%20ciudadan%C3%ADa.
85. *Metalclad Corporation v. United Mexican States*, ICSID Case No. ARB(AF)/97/1, Respondent's Counter-Memorial (17 May 1998).
86. *Robert Azinian, Kenneth Davitian, & Ellen Baca v. United Mexican States*, ICSID Case No. ARB(AF)/97/2, Respondent's Counter-Memorial (5 Oct. 1998).
87. *Joshua Dean Nelson v. United Mexican States* (ICSID Case No. UNCT/17/1) Final Award (5 Jun. 2020).
88. *Finley Resources Inc., MWS Management Inc., and Prize Permanent Holdings, LLC v. United Mexican States* (ICSID Case No. ARB/21/25) Procedural Order No. 1 (17 Dec. 2021).
89. Given that Mexico is presently handling thirteen cases, it has brought Curtis Mallet Prevost Colt & Mosle's assistance to advise it on three pending investment treaty arbitrations. Cosmo Sanderson, *Curtis wins bid to advise Mexico in 13 disputes*, GAR (7 Oct. 2022) https://globalarbitrationreview.com/article/curtis-wins-bid-advise-mexico-in-13-disputes; Secretaría de Economía, Acta Correspondiente a la Celebración del Acto de Fallo de la Licitación Pública internacional LA-010000999-E79-2022 (28 Jul. 2022).
90. Secretaría de Economía, Comercio Exterior, Solución de Controversias, https://www.gob.mx/se/acciones-y-programas/comercio-exterior-solucion-de-controversias; Nikos Lavranos, Report on Compliance with Investment Treaty Arbitration Awards 2022, International Law Compliance, p. 11 https://www.internationallawcompliance.com/wp-content/uploads/2022/10/Compliance-with-Investment-Treaty-Arbitration-Awards-FINAL-updated-REPORT-18-10.pdf.
91. *Ibid.*, p.2. Lavranos has found that so far, Spain has not paid a single ISDS award since the Maffezini Award issued in 2000.

prevailed, it did so at such an expensive cost. The claimant is a Singaporean investor who brought its claim under the Mexico-Singapore BIT. The dispute related to the bareboat charter services that the claimant provided to Oceanografía (OSA), a private company, who in turn sub-chartered them to PEMEX.

In 2011, PEMEX needed additional offshore support vessels for expansion plans. The claimant believed that it could meet PEMEX's demand, and it would charter vessels through a Joint Venture to OSA so that OSA could sub-charter them to PEMEX after bidding in PEMEX's public tenders.[92]

The Tribunal found that OSA was not an investment or investor as defined by the BIT, and the claimant had no stake in OSA's ownership. The connection with OSA was purely contractual. Therefore, the Tribunal separated Mexico's actions attributed to the claimant in connection with OSA from acts allegedly taken against the claimant and the subsidiaries.[93]

This case helps to better understand the definition and scope of an investor. Based on the language in the BIT, the Tribunal observed that the claimant and its investment were entirely the consequence of the claimant's contractual relationship with OSA. The Claimant was affected by most measures only secondarily and indirectly, through OSA, and not primarily. In other words, if the claimant had not contracted with OSA, it would be unaffected by the measures.[94] As a result, the tribunal found that since the claimant did not suffer direct harm, the claimant was insufficiently proximate to be considered an investor under the BIT.[95] However, the Tribunal did find a significant relationship resulting in jurisdiction regarding three measures: (1) a diversion court order requesting PEMEX to make payments to an authority managing assets (SAE) instead to the Invex Trust Fund;[96] (2) the attachment's extension to a subsidiary's vessels; and (3) an order blocking claimant's subsidiaries from contracting directly with PEMEX.[97] The claimant did not prevail on these issues but did succeed in establishing that Mexico breached its fair and equitable treatment obligation under the BIT.

Regarding the first measure, the Tribunal found that judicial expropriation is possible but 'under the presence of unusual circumstances, situations of "clear evidence of egregious and shocking conduct" by courts'.[98] The claimant did not succeed in establishing the direct expropriation of payments owned by OSA to POSH via the Invex Trust because it did not[99] show the courts acted in an egregious or shocking manner.[100]

92. *PACC Offshore Services Holdings Ltd v. United Mexican States*, ICSID Case No. UNCT/18/5, Award (11 Jan. 2022) paras 51-52.
93. *Ibid.*, para. 128.
94. *Ibid.*, para. 147.
95. The BIT provided that an investor of a Contracting Party may submit to arbitration a claim that the enterprise has incurred loss or damage by reason of, or arising out of, that breach.
96. *Ibid.*, para. 97.
97. *Ibid.*, para. 149.
98. *Ibid.*, para. 229.
99. The BIT provided that an investor of a Contracting Party may submit to arbitration a claim that the enterprise has incurred loss or damage by reason of, or arising out of, that breach.
100. *Ibid.*, para. 243.

Second, the Tribunal found that a detention order deprived the claimant of some vessels for a four-to-five-month period, and no evidence showed that Mexico ever intended a permanent deprivation. In the end, the claimant recovered the vessels. Therefore, the tribunal dismissed the expropriation claim.

Third, concerning the Blocking Order the tribunal found that PEMEX did not give the claimant or its subsidiaries promises to enter into new and future contracts, once the OSA contracts were terminated.[101] Therefore, the tribunal concluded that the claimant did not show that it had a right to new contracts.

The claimant did prevail on the issue of fair and equitable treatment. In its award, the tribunal further develops 'fair and equitable treatment' when the BIT 'links it to the minimum standard of treatment'.[102] The tribunal found that the detention order's actual reason for attachment was to ensure service of OSA to PEMEX, not uncertainty as to title to the vessels. The subsidiaries retained the vessel's ownership but not their benefit. The measure deprived the owners of the income generated by the vessels during the detention periods. And, Mexico did not compensate the owners. As a result, the tribunal found the detention order arbitrary, grossly unfair and unjust, and it breached the FET standard.[103]

Naturally, liability was limited to damages resulting from the detention order.[104] The tribunal found that the damage to the vessel's detention amounted to USD 6,712,226[105] plus interest.[106] Each party had to bear its own costs and USD 342,144.59 concerning 50% of the Tribunal's and the ICSID Secretariat's costs.[107] This case underscores the relevance of having a direct relationship with the government, most especially to be sufficiently proximate to be considered an investor under the treaty. In this way, Mexico keeps developing its legacy, but now to interpret the meaning and scope of an investor under the BIT's wording.

[F] FINAL COMMENT

Mexico's legacy in investment treaty practice is vast. This chapter has highlighted some aspects of Mexico's influence on forging several foundations, including the Calvo clause, the Hull Formula, the minimum standard of treatment and the notion of legitimate expectations. These accomplishments echo not only in the current development of case law but also in the text of USMCA, CPTPP and its predecessor, NAFTA.

Mexico accepts and protects foreign investment, and it stands by its principles. Mexico has complied with the investment awards ordering it to pay damages. As discussed, the damages paid arising out of all the awards entered against Mexico are far less than those entered against other states or Mexican state-owned enterprises. By

101. New contracts would have had to be subject to public bidding with the consequential uncertainty that a bid for them would be successful.
102. *Ibid.*, para. 255.
103. *Ibid.*, para. 259.
104. *Ibid.*, para. 271.
105. *Ibid.*, para. 274.
106. *Ibid.*, para. 278.
107. *Ibid.*, paras 279-282.

paying those damages, Mexico has honoured its treaty obligations. This gives investors an assurance that despite treaty violations that may occur, Mexico's commitments are real. Only time will tell whether the strategies of the past will serve to defend Mexico from current and future investor's claims. Meanwhile, the world will watch Mexico continue to contribute to the world's legacy of investment arbitration.

Part V Particular Issues and Players in Mexican Arbitration

CHAPTER 15
Commercial Arbitration and State Entities

Marco Tulio Venegas & Michelle Carrillo

[A] INTRODUCTION

Currently, in Mexico, there is a legal system of collision between public and private law. Global free market economic trends have put many activities that were previously reserved as strategic sectors of the Mexican state into private investors' hands, thus generating a conflict between private and public law. The new market dynamics have exponentially increased the execution of contracts that allow for private investors to fund and participate in the development of essential infrastructure projects—particularly in the oil and energy sectors—from which they were excluded as recently as three decades ago.

Commercial arbitration has been caught in the middle of this private versus public law struggle in public-private partnership transactions, giving rise to a paradigm shift when it comes to arbitration proceedings that involve the State and its instrumentalities. Arbitration with public entities has rekindled the issue of the so-called *double personality* of state-owned entities, forcing us to reexamine the implications of arbitrating disputes that involve them. Mexican administrative law is ambivalent with respect to the role that government agencies play during the contracting, execution and termination stages of a public works or public procurement contract. Such ambivalence manifests itself in different ways, but without a doubt, the most complex consists of the state entities' power to mutate the legal nature in which they participate as parties to a contract: in the event of administrative rescission, Mexican state-owned entities and companies are legally capable of transforming themselves from private entities into governmental authorities, thereby unilaterally modifying the rights, obligation and legal status of a given public contract.[1]

The possibility of submitting certain disputes to arbitration with state-owned entities in Mexico is, undoubtedly, a result of the commercial arbitration evolution in the region. This is historically tied to the policies and dominant ideologies behind the country's economic model since the ratification of NAFTA.

Mexico's legislation has only—relatively—recently allowed for arbitration agreements to be incorporated into public contracts.[2] Traditionally, Mexican law did not provide for the possibility of arbitrating disputes arising from public contracts. Mexico's gradual transition toward a free market has also affected the dispute resolution regulations concerning public contracts laws, thus opening the door—albeit not completely—for commercial arbitration involving state-owned entities.

As a matter of principle, the Mexican government is composed of centralized and decentralized entities. Although they are both state-controlled instrumentalities, the main difference between them is the ability to make decisions independently, as well as to own and manage their own assets. Whereas there are also some autonomous governmental bodies, they are not relevant for the purposes of commercial arbitration, given their specific functions and regulations.

Pursuant to the fundamental principle of legality, Mexican authorities are only permitted to act and render decisions—including the execution of contracts—on the basis of specific legal provisions to that effect. Accordingly, the ability of a state-owned entity to enter into an agreement and to incorporate an arbitration clause to resolve any disputes arising therefrom must be expressly established in a legal provision.

The possibility of arbitrating contractual disputes with state-owned entities in Mexico is tied to the evolution of the country's commercial arbitration regime during the last years of the twentieth century. An adequate understanding of this evolution requires the identification of different periods, marked by the government policies implemented throughout them:

(1) the initial legislative and implementation period started at the beginning of the 1990s and concluded in the year 2000;
(2) the *try-out* period from the year 2000 to the year 2013, in which actual and important disputes between state-owned entities and national and international private entities were submitted to arbitration;
(3) the energy reform period from 2013 to 2018; and
(4) the *restraining period*, from 2018 to date.

1. For instance, according to Arts. 61 and 26 of the Public Works Law (*Ley de Obras Públicas y Servicios Relacionados con las Mismas*), public entities are entitled to administratively rescind public contracts. Pursuant to Art. 98 of the same Law such rescission could not be subject to arbitration.
2. In 2009 the Public Works Law allowed the possibility of including arbitration clauses in public contracts by amending the content of Arts. 98 and 99.

[1] The Initial Period

Originally, the Mexican constitution of 1917 provided that any contract entered into by the government for the development of public works or the procurement of goods and services was to be awarded through public bidding. However, public works continued to be regulated through several secondary laws and regulations, causing public procurement schemes to be intricate and practically incomprehensible.

At the time, the Mexican approach to the state's sovereignty remained highly traditional and formalistic. The possibility of having a public entity submit to the decision of a private arbitration tribunal on issues related to strategic industries seemed challenging, if not disputable. Pursuant to the traditional viewpoint under the Mexican legal system—which was heavily influenced by the French conception of the state's administrative activity—the contracts executed by public entities with private companies were *administrative contracts*. The sui generis nature of administrative contracts blended commercial covenants with *exorbitant clauses*, which, for instance, authorized public entities to terminate the agreement without cause and for public policy reasons.

Notwithstanding the Mexican state's growing presence in the economy through public procurement, the relationship between state-owned and private entities was not always harmonious. Indeed, more often than not, disputes between government entities and the contracting private parties arose, either during the performance of the public works or after they had been finalized and delivered.

Typically, disputes arising from public contracts deal with issues ranging from claims for delays in finalizing the works, or for quality of the works performed, of the services rendered or of the goods delivered, to claims regarding contract interpretation.

Historically, any disputes arising from public contracts were submitted to the Mexican federal courts, which had exclusive jurisdiction *ratione materiae* to hear them.

Within this theoretical framework, the possibility of including arbitration clauses in administrative contracts was admitted into practice in the early 1990s, as the Mexican economy started opening to foreign investment in the strategic sectors of infrastructure, oil and gas. However, the arbitrability of these disputes was more based on a seemingly theoretical approach—and on the implementation of certain governmental policies—rather than on a clear and structured legal system. As a result, the judicial precedents rendered throughout this period reflected the possibility of including arbitration clauses in some contracts executed by *Petróleos Mexicanos* (Pemex)—the Mexican state-owned oil company—and CFE—the utility company of the Mexican State.

In this context, and as part of the process of globalization, which was heavily implemented in Mexican policies and laws during the 1990s and particularly with the adoption of NAFTA, Mexico agreed under Article 2022 to "provide appropriate procedures to ensure observance of agreements to arbitrate and for the recognition and enforcement of arbitral awards."[3]

3. Pursuant to NAFTA Art. 2022(3), Mexico shall be deemed to be in compliance with this obligation if it is a party to and is in compliance with the New York Convention and the Panama Convention.

Consistent with the obligations undertaken in NAFTA, Mexico adopted the UNCITRAL Model Law in 1993, upgrading its Arbitration Law to reflect the worldwide consensus of the best international arbitration practices.[4] This reform marked the start of the modern legislative era of commercial arbitration in Mexico.

Additionally, in 1994 the Mexican government also enacted a new Public Procurement and Public Works Law, which authorized the incorporation of arbitration clauses in those contracts that the Ministry of the Treasury through general rules, and subject to the prior opinion of the Ministry of Commerce and Industrial Development, authorizes.[5]

Consistent with the above, the Organic Laws of Pemex and CFE allowed them to enter into contracts with private individuals and companies, to the extent that the ownership of the oil and gas, and the production, transmission or distribution of electricity was not assigned to them. In other words, such public entities were free to enter into contracts for the construction of refineries, lease and construction of exploration and production platforms, hydroelectric, thermoelectric and any other plants for the production of electricity, etc., as well as for the acquisition of machinery and equipment related to said type of projects.

The new legislative framework provided national and foreign investors with a friendlier and more certain environment to participate in large infrastructure projects as contractors, not only with the oil and electricity companies of the government but also with the Ministry of Communications and Transportation. Hand in hand came a strong policy in favor of development through infrastructure projects, successfully leading to the expansion of the works performed to the building of dams, offshore oil rigs, oil refineries, gas pipelines, wind energy parks, hydroelectric plants, electricity generation agreements, fuel supply agreements, among others.

Ultimately, this was a targeted legal reform designed to entice investors into the infrastructure sector to trigger its growth, modernize the country's connectivity system, and facilitate the exchange of goods and services within the NAFTA region.

Along with the modernization of the economic landscape and as a result of these new policies, between 1994 and 2000 two other phenomena were unchained, namely: (1) public entities increasingly included arbitration clauses in contracts related to major infrastructure projects; and (2) commercial arbitration between private and state-owned companies started to grow at an important pace. Eventually—during the decade of the 2000s—this led to relevant disputes that changed once again Mexico's regulatory landscape of arbitration.

---

4. Presidential statement of legislative intent (Federal Official Gazette of July 27, 1993) presented to the Mexican Congress so that it would enact Mexico's Arbitration Law in the Commercial Code: "The Model Law constitutes a solid and encouraging basis for the harmonization and perfecting desired for the national laws. It regulates all the procedural stages of the arbitral procedure, from the arbitration agreement to the recognition and enforcement of the arbitration award, and reflects the worldwide consensus on the principles and most important aspects of international arbitration practice ...."
5. Now called the Ministry of Economy.

Specifically, in the energy sector—including electricity, oil, and gas—CFE and Pemex entered into contracts for hundreds of millions of dollars not only with U.S. investors but also with large Mexican construction companies, in which they submitted their disputes to arbitration. Notably, the ICC model clause became the most common arbitration agreement incorporated by state-owned entities at the time. First, because of the preeminent promotion of international arbitration by the International Chamber of Commerce since the beginning of the 1990s. Second, and more importantly, because of the ICC's image of independence before the Mexican authorities, resulting from its international vocation and French origins, which contributed to it being perceived as a civil law-oriented institution and, thus not akin to common law principles or ideologies.

[2] The Try-Out Period

During the first years of the decade of the 2000s some judicial precedents were issued by Mexican courts, confirming that public contracts entered into by state-owned entities—such as Pemex—should be considered contracts executed and performed in a status of "equality" vis-à-vis the private contractor.

These precedents[6] led to the confirmation of the *contractual* nature of the decisions made by state-owned entities in the context of and for the purposes of public contracts, while at the same time upholding the arbitrability of any disputes arising therefrom, particularly in connection with the rescission or early termination. Accordingly, some disputes to which Pemex and CFE were parties, and which dealt, among other topics, with the rescission of the contracts and the contractors' subsequent claim for damages and lost profits, were subject to arbitration without any restriction on arbitrability.

During this period, and in an effort to separate the features regarding public works from those related to governmental procurement, the Mexican Congress enacted two separate laws in order to differentiate the particularities of the two aspects of public procurement. Thus, on January 4, 2000, both the Public Works Law (*Ley de Obras Públicas y Servicios Relacionados con las Mismas*) and the Public Procurement Law (*Ley de Adquisiciones, Arrendamientos y Servicios del Sector Público*) were published in the Federal Official Gazette.

Both laws maintained the same language as the former *Ley de Adquisiciones y Obras Públicas* with respect to arbitration. Therefore, as a general rule, disputes arising from public contracts would continue to be resolved by federal courts, whereas only the disputes expressly authorized by the government through general rules would exceptionally be submitted to arbitration.

6. Digital Registration: 189920, Instance: Circuit Collegiate Courts, Ninth Epoch, Matter(s): Administrative, Thesis: VI.3o.A.12 A, Source: Judicial Weekly Gazette. Volume XIII, April 2001, p. 1100. Type: Isolated. Pemex-Refinación. Franchise and Supply Agreements: Its Rescission Is Not a Sovereign Act for Purposes of the Amparo Lawsuit.

During this period, some court precedents were issued with conflicting interpretations as to the nature of the contractual activities conducted by Pemex[7] and CFE. One position held that in the execution of a public contract, Pemex and CFE were acting as "private contractors" and not as public entities with governmental authority.[8] However, the opposite position was also held by other court precedents at the time.[9] Nevertheless, with the exception of the *COMMISA* case—as explained below—neither Pemex nor CFE ever argued that the rescission of a public contract should be deemed as a sovereign decision, nor challenged its arbitrability on that basis. In fact, in arbitration proceedings dealing with the validity of the administrative rescission by Pemex, the latter never argued that the dispute was inarbitrable. In summary, the existing *status quo* and the law—although not entirely clear—never impacted the validity or enforceability of the arbitration clauses contained in the agreements executed by Pemex or CFE with private contractors, nor restricted the arbitrability of the disputes arising therefrom.

Moreover, the common understanding that the public entities' activities were performed within a context of contractual equality—rather than as an exercise of sovereign authority—effectively excluded the possibility of challenging their decisions through the *amparo* proceeding.

The *amparo* is a constitutional procedure against violations of human rights stemming from "acts of authority"—including laws or decisions enacted by government authorities. The characterization of a decision or resolution as an "act of authority" for purposes of the Amparo Law (*Ley de Amparo*) depends on the acts' intrinsic attributes. The Mexican jurisprudence has defined the term "act of authority," for *amparo* protection purposes, as the intentional act of a governmental authority, which affects specific legal relationships and which is enforced upon the individual in an imperative, unilateral and enforceable manner, without the need of a judicial order.

Accordingly, the *amparo* is an extraordinary procedure, independent from the proceedings that gave rise to the resolution or act of authority that is being challenged.

7. Pemex or *Petróleos Mexicanos* is a fully-owned state entity with its own patrimony and full capacity to act on its own behalf, in charge of all Mexican oil related activities. Through *Petróleos Mexicanos*. the Mexican State managed the monopolistic control on the hydrocarbons owned by the nation.
8. There are two specific precedents as follows: Digital Registration: 165726 Instance: Second Chamber of The Supreme Court of Justice, Ninth Epoch, Matter(s): Administrative, Thesis: 2a./J.210/2009, *Source*: Judicial Weekly Gazette. Volume XXX, December 2009, p. 306, Type: Jurisprudence Pemex-Refinación. It Is Not an Authority for Purposes of the Amparo Lawsuit When It Rescinds Franchise Agreements Entered into with Individuals or Entities for the Supply of Fuel in Station Services and Digital Registration: 187602, Instance Circuit Collegiate Courts, Ninth Epoch; Matter(s): Administrative; Thesis: X.3o. J/2 Source: Judicial Weekly Gazette, Volume XV, March 2002, p. 1147, Type: Jurisprudence. Federal Commission of Electricity. When It Performs Conducts Related to the Provision of the Service of Electric Energy Is Not Deemed as an Authority for Purposes of the Amparo Lawsuit.
9. Digital Registration: 2007153 Instance: Circuit Collegiate Courts, Tenth Epoch Matter(s): Civil, Administrative, Thesis: IV.2o.A.88 A (10a.) *Source*: Judicial Weekly Gazette. Book 9, August 2014, Volume III, p. 1712, Type: Isolated Precedent. Franchise and Supply Agreement of Fuel and Other Liquid Combustibles Resulting from Oil Refinement Executed Between Private Parties and Pemex-Refinación. Because Its Subject Matter Is of Public Policy, the Injunction Against Its Rescission in an Amparo Lawsuit Against Its Rescission Must Be Denied.

The *amparo* proceeding is not an appeal, nor can it be considered a second or third instance of the original proceedings in which the act of authority was issued. In *amparo,* the plaintiff is the party that considers its civil or constitutional rights to have been violated by a certain act of an authority—as defined above. Hence, the defendant is always an authority (authority or defendant authority).[10] There is also a third party who generally supports the validity of the acts of the authorities, and whose interests are that such acts be upheld. Finally, there is an additional party, a representative of the attorney general in charge of supporting the upholding of the public interest.

For purposes of this chapter, it should be noted that in recent years there has been a trend within the judicial and legislative branches to expand the concept of "act of authority" in order to make the *amparo* procedure available for private individuals and companies, as much as possible, against decisions that were not traditionally or formally deemed "acts of authorities," because the use of *imperium* (or "state power of enforcement") was not clearly present. In this regard, the analysis of the exercise of the *imperative* powers of the public entity is not as strict as it has been in the past. Based precisely on this positive trend—that allows individuals further standing against potentially unconstitutional acts of power—some contractors have initiated and succeeded in challenging through *amparo* trials, certain decisions rendered by state-owned entities in the context of public contracts, which could be considered a "gray area" as to whether or not they constitute acts of authority.

Paradoxically, whereas making *amparo* available to challenge non-traditional acts of authority may seem very positive at first glance, it has led to a clash with arbitration as a means to resolve disputes arising from public contracts. As a result of this trend, contractual conducts of state-owned entities may now be deemed as "acts of authority" for the purposes of challenging them through *amparo*, which effectively makes them—and any consequences arising therefrom—inarbitrable. Unfortunately, the evolution of public and private law in the same direction, to grant individuals options to assert their rights, has provoked an incompatibility that is threatening the evolution of the Mexican Legal System into the twenty-first century.

During the renowned *COMMISA* case, the matter of arbitrability of the administrative rescission was put to the test. The contractor filed for arbitration against Pemex, essentially claiming the damages and losses it suffered as a result of Pemex's rescission of a public contract, while simultaneously challenging the rescission itself through an *amparo* lawsuit. In the first instance, the Federal Courts dismissed the *amparo* reasoning that the rescission could not be deemed as a sovereign decision ("act of authority"). Thereafter, COMMISA challenged the first-instance ruling and the dismissal was lifted, which effectively led to the acknowledgment that the rescission of the contract by Pemex constituted a sovereign act of authority. However, while resolving the merits of the challenge against the administrative rescission, the Federal Courts confirmed its validity. In parallel, COMMISA obtained a favorable award for damages and losses in the arbitration, which implicitly meant that, for the Arbitral Tribunal, the administrative rescission ordered by PEMEX was not valid. After the arbitral award

10. Article 5 of the *Amparo* Law (*Ley de Amparo*).

was rendered, a complex dispute before Mexican and NY Courts ensued, in which the parties sought—respectively—the setting aside and the recognition and enforcement thereof. At some point during this process, settlement discussions were held with the Federal Comptroller Office, which among other topics of the dispute, analyzed the prior decision rendered in the *amparo* proceedings in connection with the validity of the administrative rescission. In the end, after conflicting decisions were rendered by the U.S. Courts (ordering the recognition and enforcement of the award) and by the Mexican Courts (ordering the setting aside of the award), the dispute was settled amicably.

This case had a lasting impact on the Mexican legal system in connection with the arbitrability of the early termination and administrative rescission of public contracts. Specifically, on May 28, 2009, the Mexican Congress published new reforms to both the Public Works Law and the Public Procurement Law, which entered into force thirty days after their publication in the Official Federal Gazette.

Both reforms brought significant changes to Mexican government procurement, such as novel provisions regulating open international public biddings, new classifications for public biddings according to their source (i.e., domestic, international, and open international biddings), the establishment of procedures to guarantee better quality, price and financing opportunities for the public works or services, among others.

Expectedly, they also entailed relevant amendments to the provisions governing the resolution of disputes arising out of public contracts. Both laws now provide for the possibility of submitting certain disputes to arbitration and to other alternative dispute resolution mechanisms.

Specifically, the 2009 amendments—still in force—provide that disputes regarding contract interpretation and performance may be submitted to arbitration, with the following caveat: whereas the Public Works Law authorizes arbitration as a possible method for the resolution of any such disputes arising from of all public works contracts, the Public Procurement Law restricts the use of arbitration to long term service contracts.

Indeed, both Article 98, paragraph 1, of the Public Works Law and Article 80, paragraph 1, of the Public Procurement Law, provide—in identical terms—that "an arbitration agreement may be entered with respect to those disputes between the parties, that arise from the interpretation of the contractual clauses or issues related to the performance thereof, under the terms of Title Four of Book Five of the Commerce Code."[11]

11. Article 98 of the Public Works Law provides: "An arbitration agreement can be contracted with respect to those controversies that arise between the parties regarding interpretation of the clauses of the contracts or for questions arising from their execution, according to the terms of Title Four of the Fifth Book of the Commercial Code."

Article 80 of the Public Procurement Law (*Ley de Adquisiciones, Arrendamientos y Servicios del Sector Público*) provides: "An arbitration agreement can be contracted with respect to those controversies that arise between the parties regarding interpretation of the clauses of the contracts or for questions arising from their execution, according to the terms of Title Four of the Fifth Book of the Commercial Code."

Nevertheless, this apparent legislative evolution had a poison pill provision: both the Public Works Law and the Public Procurement Law restrict the arbitrability of certain disputes, providing that the administrative rescission of public contracts, the early termination thereof, as well as any other matters provided by such laws, shall be non-arbitrable.[12]

The aforementioned restriction materialized the position that the administrative rescission of a public contract, as well as the early termination thereof, constitutes an administrative resolution, which should be deemed as a governmental decision, rather than a merely contractual one. Therefore, pursuant to the current legislation, in the event a private party is not satisfied with the administrative rescission or early termination of the contract, it must challenge any such decision through an administrative procedure, either before the relevant government entity, before the federal administrative courts, or—ultimately—before a federal court in an *amparo* procedure. Naturally, the interaction between these judicial or administrative proceedings before national courts and the existing arbitration clauses is unclear and has led to scenarios of parallel litigations. Unfortunately, after almost fifteen years, these provisions remain in force and even influenced the content of Mexico's 2013 energy reform.

Finally, it is worth mentioning that during this period, specifically in 2008, Article 17 of the Mexican Constitution was amended to include a provision recognizing that legislation can allow for specific alternative dispute resolution mechanisms. The Mexican forum considers this provision as the constitutional recognition of arbitration as a valid method to resolve disputes, even between private and public entities.

[a] The Energy Reform Period: 2013 Through 2018

After the Mexican government nationalized the oil and gas industries and for almost seventy-five years the direct participation of private companies in the activities of exploration and extraction of oil was not only impermissible but also considered somewhat of a taboo. However, an alliance of political forces that seemingly overpowered the main left-wing opposition, was able to pass a legislative reform in the Mexican Congress, essentially providing for the transformation of the operation, nature and purpose of Pemex and the CFE[13] into "productive enterprises of the State." The reform provided these entities with total freedom to include any alternative dispute resolution method in the contracts they executed with private companies or individuals.[14]

12. Both Articles 98 and 80 provide that the administrative rescission and the early termination of the contract as well as any other matter determined by the Regulations of both laws shall be non-arbitrable: "The administrative rescission, the early termination of the contracts and those cases set forth in the Regulations of this Act will not be arbitrable."
13. The *Comisión Federal de Electricidad* (Federal Agency of Electric Power) was the state-owned company through which the Mexican State focused its policy of control of production and supply of electric power.
14. Article 81 of the Law of *Petróleos Mexicanos* and Art. 83 of the Law of the Federal Agency of Electric Power. Prior to this reform CFE and PEMEX could agree to arbitration, but not necessarily to any other alternative dispute resolution method. Furthermore, there were restrictions on the arbitration of certain disputes such as those related to the validity of the administrative rescission.

Therefore, any contract executed by them for the performance of public works, or the procurement of public goods and services could be submitted not only to arbitration but also to any other alternative dispute resolution method, such as mediation, expert testimony, dispute boards, etc.

Notably, as a consequence of the 2008 amendment to Article 17 of the Mexican Constitution (as outlined in section [A][2] *supra*), alternative dispute resolution methods were introduced as permissible modalities to the human right of access to justice. Whereas the Organic Laws of Pemex and CFE do not specifically list or regulate in detail the alternative dispute resolution methods that they can include in their contracts, a systematic interpretation thereof, in light of Article 17, leads to the conclusion that both Pemex and CFE are free to agree on any available dispute resolution method, as they see fit and according to their specific needs in each contract.[15]

This conclusion is also supported by the fact that their Organic Laws clearly provide that contracts entered into by the productive enterprises of the State, once executed, would be deemed of a private nature and governed by the applicable commercial or civil law.[16] Additionally, in connection with their internal regime, these laws provided that Pemex and CFE shall be governed in a supplementary manner by the applicable commercial or civil legislation.[17] With this new legal regime, the dichotomy—often contradictory—between Administrative Law and Commercial Law at the time of solving the disputes between Pemex and CFE and their contractors,[18] was eliminated. As a result, disputes submitted by the productive enterprises of the State to the competence of an arbitral tribunal, mediator, or expert, have a clear legal framework: the content of the corresponding contract and the applicable commercial and civil legislation,[19] without having to resort to administrative laws, which recurrently contradicted the principles of contract and/or commercial law.

This change was an important vertex targeted by the Mexican government to entice private national and foreign investors.

Furthermore, Pemex and CFE were authorized to agree to be submitted to foreign laws and tribunals for the purposes of contracts executed by them outside of Mexico, or performed abroad, as well as to arbitration.

In addition to the new legal regime of Pemex, the Hydrocarbons Law authorized the National Commission of Hydrocarbons—in its capacity as an agency of the Mexican government—to award and execute contracts for the exploration and extraction of

15. Article 7 of the Law of *Petróleos Mexicanos* and the Law of the Federal Agency of Electric Power clearly provide that the agreements and other legal acts executed by such companies may include any of the terms permitted by the commercial and civil legislation.
16. Expressly excluding the Laws on Procurement of the Public Sector and the one on Public Works and Related Services (Art. 75 of the Pemex Law and Art. 77 of the CFE Law).
17. Article 3 of the Pemex Law and the Law of the Federal Agency of Electric Power.
18. As of today, there are relevant cases pending before arbitral tribunals and foreign courts regarding this topic in which PEMEX has mainly argued to have exorbitant powers over private companies in contractual relationships giving rise to situations of inequality and uncertainty.
19. With this reform, the restriction previously imposed on the arbitrability of the administrative rescission or early termination of the agreements entered into by PEMEX and CFE was eliminated. Likewise, the need to conciliate or solve potential contradictions between the administrative legislation of public law character and the commercial and civil legislation of private law nature was abolished de facto.

hydrocarbons with private national and foreign companies. These contracts could be referred to any alternative dispute resolution method, including arbitration in law, governed by Mexican law and conducted in the Spanish language.

Notwithstanding the above, and in tune with the previous conception of administrative rescission and early termination as sovereign decisions or acts of authority, the Hydrocarbons Law unequivocally provided the inarbitrability thereof regarding contracts for the exploration and extraction of hydrocarbons.[20]

The rationale behind this inarbitrability stems from the fact that, in accordance with the energy reform, hydrocarbons continued to be exclusively and strategically owned by the Mexican state. Consequently, the administrative rescission of a contract for the exploration and extraction of hydrocarbons had the purpose of rescuing the contractual areas awarded to the private company in favor of the State. In this context, allowing arbitration as a valid method to challenge the administrative rescission amounted to admitting that the immediate recovery of the contractual area awarded was not necessarily guaranteed. For this reason, and consistent with the principle of exclusive national ownership of hydrocarbons, the immediate recovery, which is an effect inherent to administrative rescission, constituted a matter of public policy, inarbitrable by nature.

Unfortunately, allowing for general disputes arising from a contract of exploration and extraction of hydrocarbons to be submitted to arbitration, while simultaneously excluding the arbitrability of the administrative rescission (and the early termination) generated undesired effects that have already materialized in the past. As explained in section [A][2] *supra*, with respect to Pemex and CFE's previous legal regime, the inarbitrability of the administrative rescission of a contract generated uncertainty and an undesired scenario of parallel litigation (simultaneous arbitration and judicial litigation on interconnected causes and effects). In this sense, the inarbitrability in the context of exploration and extraction contracts represented in itself a high component of risk—consisting of potential parallel and contradictory litigation—which was ultimately counterproductive for the potential of investment intended with the energy reform.

During this limited period of five years, very few disputes led to actual commercial arbitration proceedings involving Pemex, CFE or the National Commission of Hydrocarbons as parties. However, at the same time, the implementation of the energy reform was slow and did not bring the immediate economic results that the Mexican government expected.

In any event, within the limited disputes that involved CFE, the Supreme Court of Justice issued a relevant precedent in connection with the scope of public policy (for purposes of setting aside an award) in contracts related to the generation of electricity by a private company.[21] Specifically, the Supreme Court determined that, when agreeing to submit to arbitration a dispute that arises from this type of contract, the public entity in question—in this case CFE—implements an institutional design that assumes the risks of having an arbitral tribunal giving a contractual interpretation

20. Article 21 of the Hydrocarbons Law.
21. Direct Amparo 71/2014 ruled by the First Chamber of the Supreme Court of Justice.

contrary to the position of the CFE. At the time, such a decision reflected a clear-cut pro-arbitration stance of the Mexican judiciary, which empowered arbitral tribunals to directly interpret contracts related to the generation and supply of electricity.

Furthermore, this decision also provided that an award can validly order a state-owned entity to pay damages and losses, even if it adversely affects the state. In this regard, it was established that the budget of state-owned entities must recognize the payment obligations arising from contractual relationships, according to the principles of honesty and transparency in the exercise of the public budget, provided under Article 134 of the Mexican Constitution.

[b] The "Restraining Period": 2018 up to the Present Times

With the arrival of a new left-wing party into the Presidency and Congress of Mexico, the energy reform objectives have been paralyzed de facto. Moreover, the government has aggressively pursued the renegotiation of contracts with national and foreign investors, implementing targeted legislative amendments to limit the projected profits of renewable energy projects and to strengthen the commercial and operative position of Mexico's core instrumentalities: PEMEX and CFE. The aim of the government has been to "*rescue*" both entities and to recover the sovereignty over the strategic sectors of oil, gas, and electricity.

The new policies and direction of the Mexican government have taken their toll on arbitration involving state-owned entities. Particularly, the government has refused to continue including arbitration clauses in the contracts executed by Pemex and CFE. Although the pre-existing contracts with arbitration clauses continue to be in force, the government has used other means to effectively change the legal landscape and reclaim the security and sovereignty over the energy sector. In this regard, new laws and regulations have been enacted, which can only be challenged through *amparo* proceedings or which in some specific scenarios, can lead to potential investor-state claims.

This new trend of public policies against globalization and ideologically intended to strengthen the role of the State and its instrumentalities will undoubtedly affect and diminish the role of commercial arbitration in disputes involving public entities. In the meantime, however, it is also foreseeable that the existing contracts with arbitration clauses will likely trigger an important number of arbitrations. This, in the understanding, however, that the ultimate fate of the awards rendered in any such arbitration proceedings will depend on the way in which the Supreme Court of Justice and the Federal Courts reevaluate and re-conceive the concept of public policy under a more sovereign and state-oriented approach.

[i] The Boom of Commercial Arbitrations Involving State-Owned Entities

Paradoxically—and perhaps as a result of the current political and economic landscape—commercial arbitration involving Mexican state-owned entities has boomed when it comes to contracts signed by previous presidential administrations.

Thus, while Mexico may be taking steps toward reclaiming its sovereign control over the so-called strategic sectors and strengthening its main instrumentalities, commercial arbitrations between private parties and these public entities have never been more common.

This phenomenon is hardly coincidental. Mexico's targeted legislative amendments since 2018 are part of a discourse that ultimately aims to shift the country's paradigm on many fronts. Regardless of any political views, it is unquestionable that the government's efforts to "strengthen" the position of state-owned entities in the energy sector have led to unrest among domestic and foreign investors, who relied on the previous political and legislative landscape to either partner with the former or pursue an enterprise in Mexico. Beyond purely legislative reforms, Mexico's changing paradigm also encompassed the enactment of various internal policies and austerity measures that have effectively impacted the way in which state-owned entities operate and conduct themselves vis-à-vis their pre-existing contractual relationships.

In parallel, the COVID-19 pandemic led to a historic drop in Mexico's GDP, which added to the drop in international oil prices, and soon challenged the government's transformative agenda. Whereas the government's nationalistic project was rooted in the idea of positioning Pemex as one of the main economic engines of the country, the company reported significant net losses during the fourth quarter of 2019.[22]

Although no specific statistics are publicly available, it is safe to say that commercial arbitration involving Mexican state-owned entities has significantly increased in recent years—presumably as a result of the combination of the aforementioned factors. By 2020—solely in the context of ICC Arbitration—19.8% of newly registered cases worldwide involved a state or a state-owned entity as parties to the dispute,[23] whereby 10% to 15% originated from the Latin-American region, including Mexico.[24]

More than ever, commercial arbitration is an essential and legitimate way of resolving disputes that involve state-controlled entities in Mexico. This has undoubtedly contributed to creating a better and more uniform understanding of the arbitral procedure, as well as maximizing its benefits and features for these types of disputes. Arbitral institutions, such as the International Chamber of Commerce, have made significant efforts toward facilitating and furthering the participation of states and state entities as parties to arbitration proceedings. During the past decade, and as part of these efforts, the ICC issued a report on Arbitration Involving States and State Entities under the ICC Rules of Arbitration, based on the general recognition that "[c]laims arising from commercial contracts constitute the largest category of cases involving states or state entities" and that "[t]he most frequent kinds of contracts are

22. Financial Statements of PEMEX for the 4th Quarter of 2019 (December 31, 2019), https://www.pemex.com/en/investors/financial-information/Reporte%20de%20Resultados%20no%20Dictaminados%20%20Archivos/Annex%204Q19.pdf.
23. In addition to investor-state disputes that were either administered by the ICC or in which the ICC acted as appointing authority.
24. International Chamber of Commerce, *2020 ICC Dispute Resolution Statistics* 11, 26 (2021), https://iccwbo.org/news-publications/arbitration-adr-rules-and-tools/icc-dispute-resolution-statistics-2020/.

those relating to construction, maintenance and the operation of facilities or systems."[25]

To the extent that there are no separate sets of rules for arbitrating these types of disputes, the ICC Report has proved to be a useful tool when it comes to maximizing the benefits of the existing rules for cases involving states or state entities. In recognition of the special features of these disputes, the ICC Report provides guidance for the drafting of arbitration agreements applicable to contracts entered into by states or state entities, as well as insight into matters of procedure and generalized practices.

Regarding the drafting of arbitration clauses, the ICC Report recommends that parties separate from the standard ICC arbitration clause, in order to take into account the specific needs and traits of disputes involving states and state-owned entities, such as the following:

(1) the size of the arbitral tribunal, given that more than 85% of ICC cases involving states or state entities were referred to three-member tribunals;[26]
(2) the arbitrator nomination system and applicable time period;[27]
(3) the exclusion or opt out of the Emergency Arbitrator Provisions;
(4) confidentiality of the arbitration proceedings;[28]
(5) the inclusion of enhanced transparency provisions;[29] and
(6) specific provisions on the state's immunity from enforcement.

---

25. International Chamber of Commerce, *Arbitration Involving States and State Entities under the ICC Rules of Arbitration: Report of the ICC Commission on Arbitration and ADR. Task Force on Arbitration Involving States or State Entities* (November 11, 2016), https://iccwbo.org/news-publications/arbitration-adr-rules-and-tools/icc-arbitration-commission-report-on-arbitration-involving-states-and-state-entities-under-the-icc-rules-of-arbitration/.
26. The ICC Report recommends for states wishing to submit their disputes to a three-member tribunal, to amend the standard ICC model clause as follows: "All disputes arising out of or in connection with the present contract shall be finally settled under the Rules of Arbitration of the International Chamber of Commerce by *three* arbitrators appointed in accordance with the said Rules." International Chamber of Commerce, *Arbitration Involving States and State Entities under the ICC Rules of Arbitration: Report of the ICC Commission on Arbitration and ADR. Task Force on Arbitration Involving States or State Entities* (November 11, 2016), https://iccwbo.org/news-publications/arbitration-adr-rules-and-tools/icc-arbitration-commission-report-on-arbitration-involving-states-and-state-entities-under-the-icc-rules-of-arbitration/.
27. "States and state entities wishing to have the president of a three-member tribunal nominated by the party-nominated arbitrators or by the parties themselves should accordingly add the following to the standard ICC arbitration clause: The third arbitrator, who shall act as president of the arbitral tribunal, shall be jointly nominated by [the other two arbitrators/the parties] within [30] days from the [confirmation/appointment] of the second arbitrator. If the president of the arbitral tribunal is not nominated within this time period, the Court shall appoint such arbitrator." *Ibid.*
28. Provided that ICC arbitration is not confidential *per se*, the ICC Report suggests that states and their private counterparties make the following additions to the arbitration clause: "The parties agree to keep confidential the existence of the arbitration, the arbitral proceedings, the submissions made by the parties and the decisions made by the arbitral tribunal, including its awards, except as required by applicable law and o the extent not already in the public domain." *Ibid.*
29. "states/state entities and their private contractual counterparties can agree on greater transparency, for example by providing for the award, proceedings or submissions of the parties to be made public..." *Ibid.*

The Report also identified certain practices developed by the ICC Court in arbitrations involving states or state entities, regarding the role of the Court and the ICC National Committees,[30] the prima facie assessment of the arbitration agreement and its extension to a non-signatory state or state entity,[31] the constitution of the arbitral tribunal,[32] and the scrutiny of draft awards.[33]

[B] FINAL REMARKS

Although in the last thirty years, arbitrating contractual disputes with public entities has become common and acceptable, the results have not been completely satisfactory to either the private sector or the Mexican government. On the side of the private sector, the certainty and predictability of the regulatory landscape have not been completely achieved. In addition, the judiciary's ability to adapt to the paradigm of international arbitration has been slow, and just when it appeared that a friendly arbitration stance had been finally adopted, the new trend of the current governmental policies is threatening to backlash and call for more aggressive enforcement of the concept of public policy in favor of the government.

However, the results obtained by the Mexican government in the arbitrations involving public entities have been far from satisfactory. Many relevant awards for hundreds of millions of dollars have been rendered and ultimately paid, either directly or through settlements. The source of a significant portion of these adverse awards is rooted in several factors. The management of the contracts during their performance is far from ideal. Due to the manner in which the personal and administrative responsibility of public officers is regulated, important decisions are delayed, and the bureaucracy often causes contractual breaches and losses that otherwise could have been avoided. In addition, once the dispute is triggered, the defense of the legal position of the state entities is hindered by the small size and lack of material resources of the internal legal departments. Although the ability and efforts of the members of such legal departments are remarkable considering the circumstances, the lack of a unified defense of all the governmental agencies in one single department reduces the possibility of exchanging experiences to improve the overall likelihood of success in disputes. At the same time, arbitral tribunals are often integrated by national or

30. As a result of concerns raised by states and state entities regarding the role of the Court and the ICC National Committees, the Report restates the independence of the Court's members, while also noting that "during the scrutiny of a draft award by the Court, the Court's long-standing practice is to exclude from the session any Court member who may be interested in the case, including, for example, the Court member proposed by the ICC National Committee in any state involved in the case." *Ibid.*
31. "Evidence suggests that the Court was always more restrictive in applying Art 6(2) of the 1998 ICC Rules where one of the parties sought the extension of the arbitration agreement to a non-signatory state or state entity." *Ibid.*
32. Pursuant to the Report, "[i]t is the Court's practice to submit disputes involving states and state entities to a three-member arbitral tribunal," given states' and state entities' preference, and unless they specifically request for the dispute to be submitted to a sole arbitrator. *Ibid.*
33. The scrutiny of draft awards is strengthened in cases where states or state entities are involved, given that the Court's practice is to scrutinize them at its plenary sessions. *Ibid.*

international arbitrators who are unfamiliar with the logic and complexity of Mexico's administrative laws, public law regime, and public contracts, and who mistakenly approach these types of disputes as mere commercial controversies.

All the above factors weigh in and lead to unfavorable results, ultimately creating a false perception of mistrust in arbitration among government officials. Instead of adopting measures to strengthen their internal legal departments, state-owned entities follow the easy route of blaming the "arbitration" or the international institutions themselves. In this context, it would be desirable for the Mexican government to create and invest in a special agency of highly prepared professionals in charge of managing and leading the arbitration disputes involving state-controlled entities—and potentially the investor-state cases as well. In addition, it would also be advisable to amend the laws necessary to change the attitude and the way in which public officers manage public contracts and assume their responsibilities, leading them to become more efficient in performing their duties.

CHAPTER 16

Arbitration in the Mexican Power Sector

René Irra de la Cruz & Elisa Legorreta Pastor[*]

[A] INTRODUCTION

The power sector involves an extensive range of complexities that should be considered when assessing the risks to which investors could be exposed, including technical, political, and regulatory risks.

By its nature, the intervention of governments in the power market is key when it comes to the types of disputes investors could potentially face. Throughout the years, public policy has naturally tended to change depending on the administration in charge. This tendency creates an expected clash between the government's autonomy to establish the rules governing the power sector and the certainty that investors should be granted when deciding to participate in such a market. However, governments should not have a free pass to change the established electricity regime.

This back-and-forth tendency is particularly true for Mexico. As we will further develop, in the first half of the twentieth century, Mexico had an open-market framework nationalized in the second half of the same century. The market was *reopened* once again in the 1990s, which led to a paradigm change in 2013, in which private actors could have a very relevant participation in the generation and distribution of electricity. However, since 2018, the current administration has imposed a legal and de facto governance to dismantle the energy sector's liberalization, contradicting the Mexican Constitution and international treaties.

To better understand arbitration in the Mexican Power Sector and the typical type of disputes that are brought to arbitration, first, we will briefly explain the evolution

* The authors would like to thank the invaluable contribution of María Fernanda Gaminio and Genoveva Silva, associates of the international arbitration team of Cuatrecasas.

and latest developments of the legal framework (section [B]). Second, we will refer to the typical disputes brought to arbitration in the sector (section [C]). Third, we will address recurrent procedural issues that arbitral tribunals face in disputes concerning the power sector (section [D]). Finally, we will elaborate on future challenges for the Mexican Power Sector (section [E]).

[B] LEGAL FRAMEWORK

[1] Evolution of the Legal Framework

[a] Framework Before the Energy Reform of 2013

Before 1960, Mexico had an open-market framework in the power sector. However, alongside the nationalization of the Mexican power sector led by former President Adolfo López Mateos, the Mexican Constitution provided that the generation, transmission, distribution, and supply of electricity is a *strategic activity* exclusively reserved to Federal Power Commission (*Comisión Federal de Electricidad* or CFE for its Spanish acronym) as a state-owned enterprise.[1] Therefore, the new framework implemented the model of vertical integration or monopoly of CFE by controlling all links in the electricity value chain.

In 1992, the Mexican Congress approved the amendment to the Public Service Electricity Law (*Ley del Servicio Público de Energía Eléctrica* or LSPPE for its Spanish acronym) allowing private sector participation in the generation of electricity through limited schemes that were not considered public services. These schemes included the generation of electric energy through self-supply, cogeneration, and small production, as well as the electric energy carried out by independent producers for sale to CFE.[2] With these exceptions, the State controlled all the sector's activities.

At the beginning of 2000, Mexico had an installed generation power capacity of 35,385 MW and a transmission and distribution network of 614,653 km, equivalent to more than fifteen complete circles of the Earth.[3] A million users were incorporated into the electricity network yearly.[4] The need to acquire private investment became crucial due to the fast-growing market.

By that time, Mexico had acquired relevant international commitments. With the entry into force of the Kyoto Protocol in February 2005,[5] Mexico was obliged to

1. Official Gazette of the Federation, *Decreto que reforma los párrafos cuarto, quinto, sexto y séptimo, fracción I, del artículo 27 y los artículos 42 y 48 de la Constitución Política de los Estados Unidos Mexicanos* (Jan. 20, 1960), https://www.diputados.gob.mx/LeyesBiblio/ref/dof/CPEUM_ref_054_20ene60_ima.pdf.
2. Article 3 of *Ley del Servicio Público de Energía Eléctrica* (2012), https://www.senado.gob.mx/comisiones/energia/docs/marco_LSPEE.pdf.
3. *Historia de la CFE, Comisión Federal de Electricidad*, https://www.cfe.mx/nuestraempresa/pages/historia.aspx.
4. *Ibid.*
5. *Kyoto Protocol to the United Nations Framework Convention on Climate Change* (1997), https://www.gob.mx/semarnat/articulos/protocolo-de-kioto-sobre-cambio-climatico.

drastically reduce greenhouse effect emissions, joining the global wave against climate change.[6] Foreign pressure played an extremely relevant role in reactivating the discussion of a structural energy reform that aimed to open the market to the private sector and introduce renewable energy sources.

In June 2012, the Mexican Congress approved the General Law on Climate Change (*Ley General de Cambio Climático*), whereby Mexico assumed *aspirational goals* to reduce greenhouse effect emissions by 30% by 2020 and 50% by 2050.[7] Also, under this law, Mexico committed to an unconditional reduction of 22% of its greenhouse emissions and 51% of its carbon emissions by 2030.[8] To achieve these goals and others, the Mexican State, through the Ministry of Energy (*Secretaría de Energía* or SENER for its Spanish acronym), in coordination with CFE and the Regulatory Commission of Energy (*Comisión Reguladora de Energía* or CRE for its Spanish acronym), committed to promoting the generation of electricity from clean energy sources to reach at least 35% by 2024.[9]

[b] A Change of Paradigm: The Energy Reform of 2013

In 2013, the Mexican government headed by former President Enrique Peña Nieto promoted the political agreement known as the *Pact for Mexico*,[10] which enacted seven structural reforms to the Mexican Constitution. Among them, is the energy reform.

The energy reform proposal created a regime of laws that completely changed the policy of the Mexican power sector, amending Articles 25, 27 and 28 of the Mexican Constitution. After approval, the constitutional reform became effective on December 21, 2013 (the Constitutional Energy Reform).[11] This reform entitled the promulgation of a set of federal laws to regulate the energy market explicitly.

The main axes of this reform involved: (1) the change in the nature and regulation of state agencies, such as the CFE to state-owned productive companies; (2) the opening of the energy market to private entities, both local and foreign, promoting competition in the market; (3) the use of best practices to privilege sustainability and investment in renewable energies; and (4) the implementation of electricity auctions to ensure long-term contractual relationships with investors.[12]

6. *Ibid.*
7. *Ley General de Cambio Climático, Art. Second Transitional* (2012), https://www.diputados.gob.mx/LeyesBiblio/pdf/LGCC.pdf.
8. *Ibid.*
9. Article Third Transitional of *Ley General de Cambio Climático* (2012).
10. *Secretaría de Relaciones Exteriores, Resumen del Pacto por México* (2012), https://consulmex.sre.gob.mx/calexico/index.php/component/content/article/4-articulos/58-pacto-por-mexico.
11. Official Gazette of the Federation, *Decreto por el que se reforman y adicionan diversas disposiciones de la Constitución Política de los Estados Unidos Mexicanos,* in *Materia de Energía* (Dec. 20, 2013), https://dof.gob.mx/nota_detalle.php?codigo=5327463&fecha=20/12/2013#gsc.tab=0.
12. Articles 25, 27 and 28 of *Constitución Política de los Estados Unidos Mexicanos* (2022), https://www.diputados.gob.mx/LeyesBiblio/pdf/CPEUM.pdf.

Aligned with the Constitutional Energy Reform, in August 2014, the Mexican Congress approved the Power Industry Law (la *Ley de la Industria Eléctrica* or LIE).[13] The purpose of the LIE was to promote the sustainable development of the power industry and guarantee its continuous, efficient, and safe operation for the benefit of users, as well as to comply with the obligations of public and universal service, clean energy, and the reduction of polluting emissions.[14] To that end, the law provided that the generation and commercialization of power are rendered under a regime of *free competition*.[15]

The new energy legal framework immediately attracted local and foreign investment in the Mexican energy sector. The market was encouraged by large-scale auctions organized by the National Center of Power Control (*Centro Nacional de Control de Energía* or CENACE for its acronym in Spanish), conducted in 2015, 2016 and 2017. The auctions were designed to introduce new competitors in the power generation arena. The auction mechanism obliged basic service suppliers to purchase the cheapest products in auctions.

The above meant that the electricity dispatch, which is the mechanism whereby CENACE decides the order in which each power plant injects its energy into the grid in a given period, was based on economic merits, i.e., the products with the lowest prices entered the transmission, and distribution interconnections first.

Auctions also encouraged clean energy power generators through investments in new clean power plants in the Mexican power market by introducing the clean energy certificates (*certificados de energía limpia* or CELs for its acronym in Spanish). For the clean energy market to grow, only renewable energy plants established after August 2014 were qualified to obtain CELs. Therefore, unqualified plants had to purchase CELs from qualifying generators to comply with annual requirements, creating a CEL trade market achieved through long-term auctions and/or bilateral contracts known as Power Purchase Agreements (PPAs).

During the implementation of the new energy policy that favored clean energy sources, on September 14, 2016, Mexico ratified the Paris Agreement, joining the twenty-nine countries that had already taken this step, which together accounted for 42.96% of global emissions.[16] In essence, the Paris Agreement sought to: (1) limit the average temperature increase to below 2°C above pre-industrial levels and continue efforts to limit 1 to 1.5°C; (2) improve global adaptive capacity, strengthen resilience, and reduce and reduce vulnerability to climate change; and (3) increase the flow of

13. Official Gazette of the Federation, *Decreto por el que se expiden la Ley de la Industria Eléctrica, la Ley de Energía Geotérmica y se adicionan y reforman diversas disposiciones de la Ley de Aguas Nacionales* (Aug. 11, 2014), https://www.dof.gob.mx/nota_detalle.php?codigo=5355986&fecha=11/08/2014#gsc.tab=0.
14. *Ibid.*
15. Article 4 of *Ley de la Industria Eléctrica* (2014), https://www.diputados.gob.mx/LeyesBiblio/pdf/LIElec.pdf.
16. Secretaría de Medio Ambiente y Recursos Naturales, *Mexico delivers to the UN the ratification of the Paris Agreement* (Sep. 21, 2016), https://www.gob.mx/semarnat/prensa/mexico-entrego-a-la-onu-la-ratificacion-del-acuerdo-de-paris.

financial resources to support the transformation to resilient societies and low-carbon economies.[17]

[c] A Setback to the Energy Reform of 2013

Since 2018, under the umbrella that the planning and control of the energy sector is constitutionally reserved to the Mexican government,[18] the current administration headed by Andrés Manuel López Obrador attempted to reverse the 2013 energy policy through administrative acts. Specifically, the new administration seeks to return the State's dominance in Mexico's energy sector, privileging state-owned companies.

During the pick of the pandemic of COVID-19 in 2020, the Federal Executive Branch (*Ejecutivo Federal*) issued various administrative acts through SENER, the Regulatory Commission of Energy (*Comisión Reguladora de Energía* or CRE), and CENACE, which directly impacted the conditions of the open power market.

By way of example, SENER issued the modification of the Guidelines for the Acquisition of the clean Energy Certificates (*la modificación de los Lineamientos para la Adquisición de Certificados de Energía Limpia*),[19] CENACE issued the Agreement of April 29, 2020,[20] which was followed by the issuing of the Reliability Policy (*Política de Confiabilidad*) of May 15, 2020,[21] by SENER. The Federal Administration justified such acts on the grounds that they were issued to guarantee the reliability and safety of the National Electric System (*Sistema Eléctrico Nacional* or SEN for its acronym in Spanish), as well as to strengthen the CFE as the State company responsible for the transmission and distribution of electric energy, during the pandemic caused by COVID-2019.

It was only natural that the private sector reacted to these acts of authority. Therefore, national and foreign investors challenged these acts through Amparos (constitutional appeals or challenges), which resulted in their suspension. The Second Chamber of the Mexican Supreme Court of Justice (*Suprema Corte the Justicia de la Nación* or SCJN for its acronym in Spanish) in file CC 89/2020 resolved that CENACE's Agreement was unconstitutional. The SCJN found that the reliability policy impacted the principles of competition and free access to the National Electric System (SEN), as

17. *Ibid.*
18. Article 25 of *Constitución Política de los Estados Unidos Mexicanos*.
19. Official Gazette of the Federation, *Lineamientos que establecen los criterios para el otorgamiento de Certificados de Energías Limpias y los requisitos para su adquisición* (Oct. 31, 2014), https://dof.gob.mx/nota_detalle.php?codigo=5366674&fecha=31/10/2014#gsc.tab=0.
20. *Acuerdo para garantizar la eficiencia, calidad, confiabilidad, continuidad y seguridad del Sistema Eléctrico Nacional, con motivo del reconocimiento de la epidemia de la enfermedad por el virus SARS-CoV2 (Covid-19) CENACE* (Apr. 29, 2020), https://www.cenace.gob.mx/Docs/16_MARCOREGULATORIO/SENyMEM/(Acuerdo%202020-05-01%20CENACE)%20Acuerdo%20para%20garantizar%20la%20eficiencia,%20Calidad,%20Confiabilidad,%20Continuidad%20y%20seguridad.pdf.
21. Official Gazette of the Federation, *Acuerdo por el que se emite la Política de Confiabilidad, Seguridad, Continuidad y Calidad en el Sistema Eléctrico Nacional* (May 15, 2020), https://dof.gob.mx/nota_detalle.php?codigo=5593425&fecha=15/05/2020#gsc.tab=0.

well as the guarantee of environmental protection and sustainability in the development of the electric industry, giving an advantage to CFE beyond certain constitutional rights.[22]

As a response to these challenges, on February 1, 2021, President López Obrador submitted a decree to reform the LIE. Both legislative chambers (the Deputies Chamber and the Mexican Senate) approved the reform on February 23, 2021, and March 2, 2021, respectively. The reform was published in Mexico's Official Gazette on March 9, 2021 (the Amended LIE).[23]

The Amended LIE drastically amends Mexico's electricity sector with wide-ranging consequences. The proposed amendments provide CFE with new attributions and more favorable conditions for its participation in the electricity market. To that end, the amendments limit the competitive participation of private companies in the sector, which will entail the perpetration of acquired rights.

In sum, the Amended LIE makes four substantial amendments: (1) modifies the economic dispatch method by prioritizing the injection of electricity into the grid by plants owned by CFE, regardless of cost-efficiency and sustainability consequences; (2) states that all clean generation plants will be qualified to obtain CELs regardless of the date the power facilities began operating and their ownership, which inhibits the country's transition to a sustainable electricity sector; (3) provides that CRE shall review existing permits granted under the self-supply scheme and revoke those that the said authority considers that they were granted in *fraud of the law*; and (4) limits the conditions for competition in the sector by adding subjective additional requirements for power generation permits, causing legal uncertainty for those seeking to invest in Mexico, in violation of the Constitution and international treaties and agreements.[24]

At the moment of writing this chapter, several judicial proceedings challenging the constitutionality of the Amended LIE are pending. In that respect, it is expected that the judiciary will decide soon the future of the power legal framework, at least, until subsequent amendments are enacted.

[2] Dispute Resolution Mechanisms

[a] Legal Sources for Arbitration in the Mexican Power Sector

Arbitration finds its legal basis and recognition at all levels of Mexican Law. At a constitutional level, arbitration has been recognized by Article 17 of the Mexican Constitution by an amendment introduced in 2017, guaranteeing that the laws shall provide for alternative dispute resolution mechanisms. Consequently, there is a

22. CC 89/2020. Resolution issued by the Second Chamber of the Supreme Court of Justice of the Nation (Feb. 3, 2021), https://www2.scjn.gob.mx/juridica/votos/2020/13835.docx.
23. Official Gazette of the Federation, *Decreto por el que se reforman y adicionan diversas disposiciones de la Ley de la Industria Eléctrica* (Mar. 9, 2021), https://dof.gob.mx/nota_detalle.php?codigo=5613245&fecha=09/03/2021#gsc.tab=0.
24. *Ibid.*

constitutional recognition and protection of arbitration as a dispute resolution mechanism.

The Mexican Arbitration Act is included in the last part of the Mexican Commercial Code,[25] which was first included in 1989. In 1993, said Chapter was renamed *Commercial Arbitration,* and its last amendment was included in 2012. Mexican Arbitration provisions are a transposition of UNCITRAL Model Law on International Commercial Arbitration with certain additions, particularly when it comes to the judicial intervention in support of arbitration.

Although there is a specific chapter dedicated to the general legal framework of arbitration in Mexico, we will only highlight the most relevant aspects for the sake of this chapter.

Monism approach

Article 1415 of the Commercial Code provides that this set of rules shall apply to domestic arbitrations and to international arbitrations sitting in Mexico.[26] Therefore, Mexico has adopted the monism approach to arbitration, establishing the same set of rules for domestic and international arbitrations as opposed to the dualism approach, which establishes a set of rules for domestic arbitrations and a different set of rules for international arbitrations.[27]

Arbitral Tribunal Competence

Arbitral tribunals are entitled to decide upon their own jurisdiction even when faced with allegations of nullity of the arbitration agreement.[28] In this respect, Mexican law recognizes the *competence-competence* principle giving the arbitrators the power to decide upon their own jurisdiction before any decision of any national court. Articles 1424[29] and 1464 of the Commercial Code contain provisions that avoid parallel litigations when it comes to claims relating to the nullity of the arbitration agreement and the jurisdiction of national courts to hear any given matter. Mexican judges receiving a dispute that could fall within the scope of an arbitration agreement shall refer the parties to arbitration for the arbitrators to decide upon their jurisdiction on the matter.

25. Fifth Book, Ch. Fourth of the Mexican Commercial Code, Arts. 1415 and ff.
26. "Art. 1415.—The provisions of this Title shall apply to domestic commercial arbitration, and to international arbitration when the place of arbitration is in the national territory, except as provided for in international treaties to which Mexico is a party or in other laws that international treaties to which Mexico is a party or in other laws that establish a different procedure or provide that certain procedure or provide that certain disputes are not subject to arbitration."
27. *See, e.g., Chile, Colombia, Cuba, Ecuador and Uruguay in Cristián Conejero, El arbitraje comercial internacional en Iberoamérica. Marco legal y jurisprudencial* (1st ed. La Ley. 2009).
28. Article 1432 of the Commercial Code.
29. "Art. 1424.—The judge to whom a dispute is submitted concerning a matter which falls within the scope of an arbitration agreement shall refer the parties to arbitration at the time it is requested by any of them, unless the judge finds that such agreement is null and void, ineffective or impossible to execute."

Enforcement and nullity of arbitral awards

Recognition and enforcement of arbitral awards can be refused by national courts under the same grounds contained in Article V of the New York Convention.[30] The same is true for the grounds to obtain the nullity of the arbitral award when the seat of the arbitration is located in Mexico. Undoubtedly, the fact that the enforcement and nullity grounds are exactly the same as those contained in the New York Convention shows that Mexico has been willing to adopt the international standards of arbitration and has taken strong steps to provide a solid legal background for arbitration as a dispute resolution mechanism.

Judicial intervention

In 2011 and 2012, the Mexican Arbitration Act was amended to include specific provisions for judicial intervention in support of arbitration. Among the most relevant provisions we can cite:

(a) Recognition of the *competence-competence* principle imposing national courts to refer parties to arbitration when receiving a dispute that falls within the scope of an arbitration agreement.[31]
(b) Non-contentious procedures for appointment of arbitrators, assistance in the taking of evidence and certain consultations on arbitrator's fees.[32]
(c) Specific procedures for arbitrators' challenges, challenges of jurisdictional decisions issued by arbitral tribunals, judicial interim measures in support of arbitration, enforcement of interim measures granted by arbitral tribunals and nullity of arbitral awards.[33]

In this last respect, the Mexican Arbitration Act has gone one step beyond when it comes to the enforcement of interim measures granted by arbitral tribunals. It is not uncommon that arbitral tribunals grant interim measures through an order and not through an award. Depending on the seat of the arbitration and or the place where the interim measure is to be enforced, procedural issues concerning enforcement could be faced. Article I of the New York Convention expressly provides that:

> Article I. This Convention shall apply to the recognition and enforcement of arbitral awards made in the territory of a State other than the State where the recognition and enforcement of such awards are sought, and arising out of differences between persons, whether physical or legal. It shall also apply to arbitral awards not considered as domestic awards in the State where their recognition and enforcement are sought. (Emphasis added).

The fact that the New York Convention only applies to the enforcement of arbitral awards may invite national courts to refuse recognition of interim measures granted by

30. United Nations Convention on the Recognition and Enforcement of Foreign Arbitral Awards (Jun. 10, 1958).
31. Article 1464 of the Commercial Code.
32. Article 1466 of the Commercial Code.
33. Article 1470 of the Commercial Code.

arbitral tribunals by means of an order under the ground that they only are entitled to recognize and enforce awards if the applicable law does not provide otherwise. With the inclusion of Article 1470 of the Mexican Arbitration Act, national courts can enforce interim measures granted by arbitral tribunals by means of an order as there is now a specific provision entitling judges to do so.

Arbitrability of disputes in the Power Sector

Concerning subjective arbitrability, i.e., that the relevant entities are allowed to submit their disputes to arbitration, the new Law of the Federal Electricity Commission, enacted in 2014, provides in Article 7 that "The contracts, and all the legal acts, in general, in which CFE participates, can include any provision allowed by commercial and civil laws..."

In this regard, Article 118 of said law provides that:

> Article 118. National disputes involving the Federal Electricity Commission and any of its subsidiaries, whatever their nature may be, shall be decided by federal courts...
>
> However, the Federal Electricity Commission and any of its subsidiaries *may agree on alternative dispute resolutions mechanisms and arbitration agreements pursuant commercial laws and international treaties to which Mexico is a party.*

Concerning other relevant participants of the Power Sector, the Bases for the Electricity Market, more specifically Base 19.3 contemplates the mechanism for dispute resolution and distinguishes, on the one hand, disputes between the CENACE and market participants and, on the other hand, disputes among market participants.

In 2016, the Ministry of Energy issued a Manual for Dispute Resolution which develops on the procedure already established under Base 19.3. The Manual foresees the possibility that the CENACE and the market participants, as well as market participants among themselves, include arbitration agreements in their contracts to resolve the disputes that arise in the Wholesale Electricity Market. As such, it is relevant to note that the Manual for Dispute Resolution establishes that the rules that apply in case of any arbitration are those of the International Center for Dispute Resolution (ICDR).[34]

For objective arbitrability, i.e., the matters that can be submitted to arbitration, the disputes in the power sector follow the general rule of arbitrability in Mexico. In this regard, the requirements to submit a dispute to arbitration are: (1) that the subject matter of the dispute is not expressly excluded from the possibility of being arbitrated; (2) the dispute relates to rights that can be waived; (3) certain issues of public policy; and (4) that the dispute does not relate to third parties rights.[35]

Consequently, Mexican law provides for a solid legal background for submitting to arbitration disputes relating to, or arising from, the Mexican power sector.

34. Official Gazette of the Federation, *Manual para la Solución de Controversias* (Mar. 6, 2016), https://www.dof.gob.mx/nota_detalle.php?codigo=5430145&fecha=16/03/2016#gsc.tab=0.
35. Francisco González de Cossío, *Arbitrabilidad de controversias en materia de sociedad mercantiles*, http://gdca.com.mx/PDF/arbitraje/ARBITRABILIDAD%20CONTROVERSIAS.pdf.

[b] Contractual Sources for Dispute Resolution Mechanisms

To address the risks and complexities inherent to the value chain of electricity, contracts foresee multi-tiered dispute resolution clauses.

In most contracts related to the generation, transmission, and distribution of electricity that CFE celebrates with private entities, the dispute resolution clause contemplates a dispute resolution system that differentiates the treatment of technical controversies from those that are not technical.

As a first step, the contracts usually contain the obligation for the parties to attempt to resolve their disputes through common agreements and negotiations by officers of certain corporate level.

If the parties were to not reach an agreement, the contracts foresee the submission of technical and administrative matters to the analysis of an independent expert, whose findings are final and binding not only for all parties but, in most cases, also for an arbitral tribunal. Under this contractual scheme, experts could be allowed to analyze, among others: (1) technical and administrative matters; (2) the fulfillment of specifications contained in the contract; (3) if a delay in construction is attributable to force majeure or a fortuitous event; and (4) issues pertaining to the costs of finalizing a project. Nonetheless, the line that differentiates the catalog of possible technical disputes (expert's jurisdiction) from a legal dispute (arbitral tribunal's jurisdiction) is paper thin. These issues may arise from the same cause and their separation may not be possible, leading to countless procedural complexities.

All controversies that are not technical—and thus are not under the expert's jurisdiction—must be resolved through arbitration. Certain contracts provide for an ICC arbitration clause and some others provide for an LCIA arbitration clause.

However, the contracts celebrated between the entities and/ or private operators within the value chain of electricity are also frequently submitted to a multi-tiered dispute resolution clause providing for negotiation, a technical expert and arbitration. For the latter, it is common to find that parties submit their disputes to the ICC Arbitration Rules.

[C] TYPICAL DISPUTES IN THE MEXICAN POWER SECTOR

As previously mentioned, the value chain of electricity is vast and presents countless complexities, which in turn defines the types of disputes that might result in arbitration. For reasons of length, it would be impossible to list all the controversies susceptible to arbitration in the electricity sector.

For this chapter, we will explore the most common controversies that we have been confronted with and that have been submitted to arbitration,[36] grouping them into two segments: (1) controversies between private participants and CFE; and (2) controversies among private operators themselves. The possible controversies and

36. For confidentiality issues, we will only refer to the types of disputes in general, without referring to the case identification details.

disputes that might result in an arbitration between the CENACE and the individuals in the Wholesale Electricity Market are excluded from this analysis as they are merely casuistic.

[1] Typical Disputes Between Private Participants and CFE

The electricity industry in Mexico features a bundled scheme in which CFE is not only involved in the generation of electricity but is also the utility responsible for distributing and transmitting the power that is produced and sold by other private participants.

[a] Generation

Pursuant to the actual legal and regulatory scheme, CFE participates as the *off-taker* (with the Power Purchase Agreements scheme or PPAs) or as the generator. In the first case, the private participants own the power facilities and are responsible for the project development and the sale of electricity to CFE subsidiaries. In the latter case, CFE owns the power plant facilities, and the private participant is responsible for the construction and procurement of the project.

[i] PPAS with Independent Power Producers (IPPs)

Under this scheme, the IPP oversees the design, construction, and operation of the power generating plant. Therefore, the project is frequently divided into: (1) the design, engineering, equipment supply, construction, starting, and pre-operational tests of the generation facility; and (2) the commercial operation period.

Alongside the contract for electricity capacity, the IPP also celebrates a series of related contracts that guarantee the project's viability. These agreements include financing contracts, contracts for the purchase of the plant's side, contracts for transportation services, and contracts for the supply of fuel to obtain enough base fuel (usually gas) and alternative fuel (usually diesel) to run the facility in the operation phase, and electricity supply contracts for each required phase of the project (construction of the facility, performance testing, and commercial operation). From these references, it is simple to deduce the types of disputes that arise from the execution of these contracts.

During the initial stage of the project, disputes related to the date of initiation could occur. The date of commencement of the works could be affected further by a delay in the acquisition of the licenses,[37] the assignment by CFE to the IPP of the real estate rights of the site of the works,[38] the lack/delay of the supply and service contract

37. CFE's Risk.
38. *Ibid.*

for transportation of fuel,[39] the delay in celebrating the agreement for the supply of electricity required for the construction of the plant,[40] among others.

During the facility construction stage, the following disputes could arise:

- time and delays, including the costs associated with said delays;
- disruptions;
- environmental issues;
- additional costs related to errors and/or changes in design.

During the stage of operational testing, before the commercial operation, the IPP can face claims from CFE related to the guaranteed values. A common dispute arises when the net demonstrated capacity of the facility[41] is less than the net guaranteed capacity. In this case, the IPP must pay liquidated damages under a penalty clause for not reaching the net guaranteed capacity. Other guaranteed values include the net heat rate or the net production of energy.

During the commercial operation phase, the disputes that can arise include compliance with fuel gas specifications for the gas turbines according to industry standards under Mexican regulation (*Normas Oficiales Mexicanas*); compliance with the agreed Power outages, liability derived from full-forced outages and load loss due to technical issues (i.e., auto-ignition and flashbacks), Force Majeure linked to the lack of fuel supply in agreed conditions, fuel supply pricing mechanisms and Capacity and Energy pricing mechanisms.

Other types of disputes include the availability of the plant to operate and generate electricity, the plant outages, and the difference between the consumption of the nominated electricity in the Day-Ahead Electricity Market (MDA) and the electricity effectively acquired.

[ii] PPAs (Hedge) with Generators

Under this contractual scheme, aside from the abovementioned issues, we can also find disputes related to Time and Delays, Liquidated Damages derived from the failure to comply with the provisional acceptance date, and Contractual termination due to Generator's failure to comply with the commercial operation date.

[iii] Construction and Procurement of CFE Power Plants

In the case of the construction and procurement of electricity plants by CFE, in addition to the disputes mentioned earlier, we can also face the following disputes and heads of claim:

39. IPP's Risk.
40. Shared Risk.
41. *Capacidad neta demostrada.*

- Force Majeure or Breach of Contract linked to land titles or collective forms of land tenure.
- Compliance with fuel, energy, or water supply specifications under contractual provisions.
- Compliance with the supply of parts under contractual specifications.
- Liquidated Damages derived from underperformance during the testing period.
- Compliance with completion of the Punch List before the commercial operation date.

[b] Transmission and Distribution

As stated above, CFE is responsible for the transmission and distribution of electricity. To comply with this obligation, CFE often celebrates construction agreements with private entities under several contractual schemes to ensure the construction and procurement of transmission lines and electrical substations.

The frequent disputes arbitral tribunals are faced with under the schemes of construction transmission and distribution infrastructure include:

- Availability of the sites for the contractor where the electrical substation and/or the transmission line will be constructed, as well as the impacts on time and cost this delay may cause. Access to the site is a risk inherent to CFE. Therefore, the contractor must be compensated for any delay caused by this.
- The definition of the line's trajectory and its physical indication on site is an exclusive competence of CFE. Therefore, the contractor should be compensated for any delays in this matter. Changes can occur concerning the definition of the line, whether it is an aerial line or an underground line.
- Delays in completing crucial events regarding the engineering, procurement of equipment and construction.
- Costs overrun arising from changes and errors in the design or any other cause attributable to CFE.
- Quality and completion claims regarding CFE engineering specifications.

[2] Typical Disputes Between Private Entities

In contractual schemes concluded between private parties, the disputes that may be encountered are similar to those listed above. However, the differentiating element will be the distribution of risks negotiated in each case. We will briefly refer to disputes arising from: (1) the construction of electrical facilities; (2) energy price disputes; and (3) disputes related to renewable energy that we frequently encounter to be submitted to arbitration.

[a] *Design and Construction of Power Facilities Disputes*

Aside from the disputes mentioned above relating to the construction of the plants, there is another group of recurrent claims relating to the principal equipment of the energy facilities.

Equipment plays a significant role in the performance and fit for purpose of facilities for the generation of electricity. For example, in a cogeneration plant where the system simultaneously produces heat and electricity from a single source of energy (usually gas), the gas and vapor turbines are critical for the correct facility's functioning.

In that respect, the power plants' main equipment, for both conventional and renewable generation, must be designed to have a lasting service life given the nature of the project and the extreme functioning conditions with which such main components are faced.

Among the central claims related to equipment and facility components; we can find the reduction of the useful lifespan due to premature corrosion due to climatic conditions in which the plant operates. In this sense, the operating conditions of the rotor and blades of a gas turbine in a cogeneration plant in the north of the country, with a dry environment, are not the same as in the same plant operating in the southeast, with a humid and saline climate.

An additional factor that can cause premature wear and reduced service lifespan can be the overheating of the metallic structures, that could be caused by a problem in the design or maintenance of the equipment. The root cause analysis (RCA) will be the basis to determine that the party could eventually assume this risk pursuant to the contract.

In the case of renewable energy projects, the lifespan of the photovoltaic systems can reach thirty years, which is why the equipment and structures in these systems should be designed to meet this criterion.[42] One example is that international industry standards provide that the designs of the structures on which the photovoltaic panels are mounted must comply with quality certifications that include corrosion prevention,[43] quality of aluminum and steel components,[44] wind resistance of the structures, verification of the soil conditions on which they will be installed and the quality of cables and connectors,[45] among others.

In the case of wind power projects, the analysis of the quality and service life is similar to that of major components. The industry standards of certification[46] provide that the components must be designed to have a service life of at least twenty years, including the blades, blade bearings, main shafts and bearings, gearbox, generator, converters, and the tower.

A recurrent issue is that the agreements for the procurement of equipment usually contain a limitation of liability clauses for the equipment manufacturers,

42. Solar Power Europe, *Engineering & Construction Procurement Best Practice Guidelines Version 2.0*.
43. EN ISO 1461 and EN 10346.
44. DIN EN 1090.1.
45. IEC 62930:2017.
46. IEC 61400, including IEC 61400-1/A1 Wind Turbines – Part 1: Design requirements.

limiting the liability to a certain amount and time. The issue is that certain design failures of the equipment only become noticeable after the equipment has been in operation for a longer period than the warranty period established in the agreements. The Contractor or Owner of the project finds themselves in a situation where the equipment loses its operational ability without being able to generate energy under an expired warranty period. In this case, the damages to be claimed could include reparation and/or equipment substitution costs and the losses incurred because of the outage of the generation facility.

In this case, the text of the contracts, the contractual risk allocation, and the factual background must be analyzed on a case-by-case basis to determine the type of actions that could be filed to claim the manufacturer the damages caused by the appearance of such defects and/or the enforceability of the warranty and limitation of liability clauses.

[b] Energy Price Disputes

In Power Purchase Agreements concluded among private entities, the price of electricity is usually defined by different variables that can include: (1) a fixed fee considering the capacity agreed upon; (2) a fee for the fuel used in the power plant to generate the electricity; (3) a fee for the transportation of said fuel; (4) a variable fee for the operation and maintenance of the facility; (5) a fee for the operation and maintenance of the power plant; and (6) a deviation charge for deviation of the electricity consumed in respect of the minimal agreed consumption if that is the case.

Thus, different variables determine the price of electricity, whose interpretation and application can potentially create disputes between the parties to the contract. By way of example, circumstances affecting the price and/or availability of the base fuel and the dependency on alternative fuel can affect the formula for the price of electricity. Essentially the base fuel is usually gas, which is less expensive at a higher efficiency. In the absence of the availability of base fuel, the power plants are designed to function with alternative fuel (diesel), which is more expensive at a lower efficiency.

Depending on the formula in each case, the availability of fuel could have a direct impact on the price of electricity as the formula would have variables to adjust the fuel that is used in each relevant period and adjust the price of the electricity for a specific period.

[c] Renewable Energy Disputes

[i] General Contractual Schemes

Frequently, renewable energy projects (wind and photovoltaic) are implemented through specific purpose vehicles (SPVs) that enter financing contracts (including trusts with lenders), EPC contracts for the design, procurement, and construction of the facility, O&M contracts for the commercial operation phase and the subsequent contracts that derive from the operation stage including but not limited to interconnection agreements, coverage and capacity agreements, among others. It is expected that whoever designs and builds the facility for the Client, will later operate the plant on behalf of the Owner.

Commonly, the dispute resolution clauses contained in these types of schemes are the same as those mentioned earlier: multi-tiered clauses including: (1) a negotiation phase at a certain level of corporation officers; (2) an independent expert for certain disputes; and (3) arbitration.

[ii] Examples of Typical Disputes

National Electric System Regulatory bodies intervention

Upon the date of elaboration of this chapter, the intervention of operators in the market has generated certain disputes in the electric power value chain. The inactivity of the CRE and CENACE has translated into the denial of granting and/or modifications of interconnection permits and the denial of granting pre-operational testing permits for the commercial operation of certain generation projects.

This inactivity has produced countless delays in initiating projects that are linked to Project finance schemes, which, in turn, are linked to the revenue arising from the sale of electricity. These delays could generate breaches and disputes in the contract chain. Generally, the financing, EPC, and the O&M contracts contain an arbitration clause.

Another impact generated by the intervention of regulatory bodies due to the change in the public energy policy is the prioritization changes in the dispatch order of the generators. This change has particularly affected renewable generators since dispatch restrictions have been imposed on them, generating contractual claims as will develop in the following section.

Performance disputes

In renewable energy projects, particularly in photovoltaic facilities, claims concerning performance guarantees are common. These guarantees ensure a certain amount of electric power generation. The amount of power produced by a power plant can be determined by two factors: (1) the Performance Ratio (PR); and (2) the facility Availability.

The PR consists of a methodology to measure a photovoltaic plant's performance. In other words, it is the power plant's capacity to convert solar irradiation into electricity. The PR is a quotient between the actual production of a photovoltaic system and the theoretical production if the system does not suffer any loss.[47] These contracts contain a guaranteed PR, which the contractor must reach in both, the design construction phase and operation phase of the plant.

47. Section 10.3.1 IEC 61724-1 Ed. 1.0 2017-03.

The concept of Availability—as its name indicates—responds to the availability of the power plant to generate electricity with the available solar resources. This value can be impacted by: (1) unavailability produced by the facility components; or (2) unavailability of the electrical grid.

The fulfillment of the guaranteed values can be affected by defects in the design, defects in the construction, maintenance issues, or circumstances not attributable to the contractor, such as exclusion events or impacts generated by the dispatch of the operators in the electricity market. Depending on the specific formula for each case, the y associated penalty will be calculated as liquidated damages that will compensate the Client for the energy that will not be produced because the guaranteed threshold has not been reached during the expected years of the plant's commercial operation.

The wording in the EPC and O&M contracts and the formulas established therein will define the calculation, methodologies and risks inherent to the facility's PR and Availability. However, we will describe some of the challenges and disputes that arbitral tribunals have been faced with.

Verification Year for the PR

Depending on the calculation formula contained in the contract, the year or period in which the PR is measured for penalty purposes may be decisive. It is common that in the first year of operation errors and contingencies occur, such as, defects in certain equipment, and potentially impact the PR. In the first year, the contractor assumes the repairs within its contractual scope to reach the guaranteed value. In this curve, likely, the first year's PR will not reach the guaranteed value, but it will be met in the second year of operation when the contractor has been able to have the plant up and running. For this reason, it is common for warranty periods under EPC to be extended for twenty-four months. The risk that exists is that, if the guaranteed PR under the EPC is calculated according to year 1 in these circumstances, which would no longer be present in year 2 and subsequent years, the contractor could face penalties for a PR not met for events that are no longer present in the remaining twenty-four years of plant operation.

Double Penalty: interrelation between PR and Availability

The measurement of the PR becomes relevant during two specific moments: (1) during the provisional acceptance; and (2) when the Final Acceptance Certificate is issued (CAD). If the PR does not reach the guaranteed value, the contractor will be penalized for the differential. In the commercial operation phase, the measurable factors that could generate penalties for the operator for not reaching the guaranteed values or given the case, create a bonus for exceeding the expected power generation values can include the PR, the Availability of the power plant, and the real production of electricity.

If the EPC and O&M contracts are unclear as to the interrelation of the penalty for the PR in the construction phase and the PR and/or Availability during the O&M stage, there is a risk that the operator will be penalized during the operational phase for values that have already been penalized during the EPC phase.

In other words, and at the risk of oversimplifying, if the plant had a guaranteed PR of 100% and during the EPC phase reached 98%, the contractor would be penalized for that 2%. During the commercial operation phase, the guaranteed theoretical value from which the performance will be evaluated cannot be 100%, but rather the 98% that was verified at the time of the emission of the CAD. If not, there would be a risk that the operator would be penalized based on a parameter that has already been penalized.

Similarly, it is essential that the contract establishes the excluded events related to measuring the PR and the Availability. If not, there is a risk that the same event could be penalized in the PR measurement formula and in the measurement methodology for the Availability.

Dispatch Restrictions (curtailments)

Dispatch decisions by electricity market operators and regulators may also negatively impact the measurement of the guaranteed values. Subject to the interpretation of the Exclusion Events contained in the relevant contracts it is unreasonable to assume that the unavailability of the power grid caused by the regulators and dispatch priorities is within the scope of the plant operator's risk.[48] Even international industry standards foresee that the unavailability generated by dispatch restrictions should be excluded from the PR calculation.[49]

Among these events, we can find Force Majeure situations, damages caused by the power grid due to external reasons or dispatch decisions that imply that the plant cannot deliver to the grid all the energy it can generate at a specific time.

[D] RECURRENT PROCEDURAL ISSUES

The complexity of power projects requires the involvement of multiple parties, which results in projects being implemented through various interrelated contracts. This reality can create procedural challenges in disputes brought to arbitration depending on how the contractual framework is designed.

A traditional contractual scheme in a renewable energy project between corporate group A (as the project owner) and corporate group B (as the project contractor) can result in the following complexities:

(1) A financing contract between A and banks (lenders) with their own guarantees.
(2) A trust[50] where A1 (owner subsidiary) has contributed the rights to the project contracts from which the banks will recover their financing.
(3) A signed EPC agreement between A1 (owner subsidiary) and B1 (subsidiary contractor of B), with an arbitration clause.

48. Section 9.4 of the Solar Power Europe, *Engineering & Construction Procurement Best Practice Guidelines Version 2.0.*
49. IEC 61724-1 Ed.1.0 2017-03.
50. Under Mexican law, trusts have assets and legal personality.

(4) A Parent Company Guarantee (PCG) agreement signed between A and B to guarantee B1's obligations, with an arbitration clause.
(5) An O&M agreement to operate the plant signed between A1 and B2 (subsidiary of B).
(6) Major equipment supply contracts between B and C (supplier) implemented as follows:
- equipment purchase agreement between B1 and C1 (subsidiary of C);
- transportation and installation agreement between B1 and C2 (subsidiary of C2);
- service and maintenance agreement of the equipment between B1 and C3 (a subsidiary of C).

[1] Incompatibility of Multiple Arbitration Clauses

In a recent ICC case, a dispute arose from a renewable project that was already in operation, involving all the parties from Groups A and B. B1 and B2 initiated an arbitration against A1 based on the EPC and O&M contracts. A1 filed a counterclaim under the same contracts and requested the joinder of B to respond to the obligations of its subsidiaries based on the PCG contract.

B1 and B2 contested the joinder request of B based on the incompatibility of the arbitration agreements contained in the EPC and O&M contract, on the one hand, and the PCG contract, on the other hand, raising an objection based on Article 6(3) and 6(4) of the ICC Rules. In this regard, the EPC and O&M contracts provided for ICC arbitration, with a three-member tribunal, with Mexico City as the seat of the arbitration and Mexican law as the applicable law. However, the PCG contract provided for ICC arbitration, with a tribunal composed of one member under a different applicable law and a different seat for the arbitration.

The ICC Court decided upon the objection and determined that the arbitration should proceed under the EPC and O&M contracts, including the additional parties, but excluding the PCG contract. This decision is per the established practice that a difference in the number of arbitrators or the arbitration set constitutes an irremediable incompatibility of the arbitration agreements.[51]

[2] Non-signatories

In another recent ICC case and under a similar contractual scheme, A1 brought a claim against B1, B2, and B for breaches relating to the construction of a renewable facility and the non-performance of the guaranteed values, including the guaranteed PR. The arbitration was initiated based on the EPC, O&M, and PCG contracts. A1 claimed that B, having participated directly in the negotiations and the execution of the EPC and O&M contracts, was bound by the arbitration agreements and should have been considered a party to said contracts.

51. Fry et al., *The Secretariat's Guide to ICC Arbitration* 3-243.

The tribunal resolved that the fact that the parties had established under the EPC contract that B would later surrender a corporate warranty (through the PCG contract) revealed that the true intention of the parties was for B not to be considered a party to the contract and denied having jurisdiction over B.

[3] Legal Standing to Claim

The issue relating to the legal standing to claim derives from the fact that, under Mexican Law, the trust figure has its own legal standing. In this sense, pursuant to the same contractual scheme mentioned above, if A1 contributes its rights of the project contracts to the trust as part of the project finance, the holder of such rights ceases to be an A1 and becomes the trust. Therefore, any claim against B and its subsidiaries should be brought by the trust as the holder of the rights.

As a result, it is expected that for the proper exercise of the rights that have been contributed to the trust, powers of attorney and waivers are granted among the trust and the A1, since issues of legal standing to claim may arise not only in the arbitration but also in the award enforcement proceedings before national courts, if the party seeking to enforce the award is not the holder of the rights under the contracts that gave rise to the award.

[4] Multi-tiered Dispute Resolution Clauses

As referred to in previous sections, multi-tiered dispute resolution clauses have been commonplace. Particularly, since energy contracts have a highly technical component, it is usual to find a clause that holds that an expert in the field should finally resolve technical issues, leaving the legal disputes to an arbitral tribunal. Moreover, specific clauses provide that the decisions rendered by the independent expert shall be binding not only for the parties but also for subsequent arbitral tribunals.

These clauses have apparent benefits, such as allowing for the continuation of a project through intermediate technical resolutions and debugging a potential arbitration contingency, leaving the arbitration either for: (1) disputes other than technical ones; or (2) the enforcement of the expert decision.

However, in practice, these types of clauses may also give rise to drawbacks as there can be cases in which the technical and legal issues of a dispute are so inextricable intertwined that an independent expert may be confronted to decide upon legal issues and/or the arbitral tribunal may be faced to decide on technical issues against the wording of the relevant clauses. This could give rise to jurisdictional challenges and jeopardize the outcome of the dispute.

[E] FUTURE CHALLENGES

The Mexican power sector faces several challenges on at least two levels: domestic and international.

At the domestic level, the change in the game's rules will necessarily shift the participation of private entities. It will put more pressure on public entities to fulfill the growing need for electricity. However, the definitive legal framework still depends judiciary's decision when deciding the multiple constitutional challenges filed against the Amended LIE.

At the international level, the amendments have also generated reactions. In this regard, on July 20, 2022, the Office of the United States Trade Representative (USTR) announced the request for state-to-state consultations under Chapter 31 of the T-MEC (*Tratado entre México, Estados Unidos y Canada,* also known as USMCA). The U.S. stated that the Mexican Government's public policy and regulatory actions have negatively impacted U.S. companies in the energy sector to benefit CFE and *Petroleos Mexicanos* (PEMEX). Canada later joined the consultation process.

The U.S. is challenging: (1) the Amended LIE 2021 that prioritizes CFE-produced electricity over electricity generated by all private competitors; (2) Mexico's inaction, delays, denials, and revocations of private companies' abilities to operate in Mexico's energy sector; and (3) a June 2022 action that advantages PEMEX, CFE, and their products in the use of Mexico's natural gas transportation network.[52] The U.S. states that these measures are inconsistent with several of Mexico's T-MEC obligations, including under the Market Access, Investment, and State-Owned Enterprises chapters.[53]

U.S. and Canada decided to continue negotiations with Mexico after the seventy-five-day period provided on Article 31.6.1 of the T-MEC and have not yet submitted the dispute to a panel.

Apart from the Mexico and U.S. relationships, the Amendments could also be incompatible with Mexico's international commitments, such as the Transpacific Economic Cooperation Agreement and Bilateral Investment Treaties (BITs) to which Mexico is a signatory. Under these international instruments, the change of the public energy policy could be deemed as a breach of the fair and equitable treatment protection of international investors, as the changes would affect the investor's legitimate expectations and could imply an arbitrary and discriminatory treatment.

[F] CONCLUDING REMARKS

Arbitration has undoubtedly served as an efficient and effective dispute-resolution mechanism for a vast majority of controversies in the Mexican power sector.

From a regulatory perspective, the Mexican power sector's certainty and the definitive legal framework are the main concerns that will define future developments.

The regulatory setback, if confirmed once the constitutional challenges are decided, will undoubtedly impact the capacity to fulfill the constant and growing need to generate, distribute and transmit electricity in the country and will discourage new

52. U.S. USMCA, *Consultation against Mexico,* https://ustr.gov/sites/default/files/US%20Cons%20Req%20Mexico%20energy_072022.pdf.
53. *Ibid.*

investments in this sector. However, the reality imposes the need for new investments to meet the country's power requirements.

The intervention of governments and the changes in the power market public policies are a constant that can be evidenced throughout history. As a recent example, Spain amended its regulatory framework for electricity and renewables between 2010 and 2015. Essentially, the Spanish government imposed certain cuts to renewable projects, rendering them unfeasible. Those regulatory changes generated a wave of international investment claims in which international investors have been granted the relief sought as the tribunals consistently have found that Spain breached the investors' legitimate expectations.[54]

As George Santayana once said, "Those who cannot remember the past are condemned to repeat it."[55]

54. For example, *see InfraRed Environmental Infrastructure GP Limited and others v. Kingdom of Spain*, ICSID Case No. ARB/14/12; *RENERGY S.à.r.l. v. Kingdom of Spain*, ICSID Case No. ARB/14/18; *NextEra Energy Global Holdings B.V. and NextEra Energy Spain Holdings B.V. v. Kingdom of Spain*, ICSID Case No. ARB/14/11; *OperaFund Eco-Invest SICAV PLC and Schwab Holding AG v. Kingdom of Spain*, ICSID Case No. ARB/15/36; *JGC Holdings Corporation (formerly JGC Corporation) v. Kingdom of Spain*, ICSID Case No. ARB/15/27.
55. George Santayana, *The Life of Reason or the Phases of Human Progress* 284 (1920).

CHAPTER 17

The Rise in Mexico's Energy Disputes: A Focus on Oil and Gas Cases

Diana María Pineda Esteban & Julia González Romero

Mexico has seen a boom of energy—related to arbitration cases—due to a reverse opening of markets and industries. The stakeholders have been directly attacked by President Lopez Obrador's administration since 2018, through the enactment of policies, regulations and statutes, and the arbitrary decisions made in specific cases, that prevent private investors from obtaining the benefits of their millionaire ventures in Mexico. These factors have challenged the status of the Rule of Law in Mexico. As reported by the International Chamber of Commerce, in 2021 Mexico became the fifth most sued country by foreign investors. The fossil-fuel reliance of Mexico makes this industry especially relevant for local growth, foreign investment attraction and, hence, new, and other potential arbitration cases.

[A] FOSTERING FDI: MEXICO'S INSTITUTIONAL ARRANGEMENT AND INVESTMENT TREATIES

To become a more attractive country for foreign investors, during the 1990s Mexico made two significant changes to its legal and structural arrangement: the first one in its internal framework and governmental composition, while the second one followed the wave of bilateral investment treaty (BIT) negotiations.[1]

In its structure, Mexico created independent institutions and agencies to oversee diverse matters, from the national economy—through the central bank, Banco de México—to energy—through the Energy Regulatory Commission (CRE). The logic

1. Kenneth J. Vandevelde, *U.S. Bilteral Investment Treaties, The Second Wave*, Michigan Journal of International Law, (1993), https://repository.law.umich.edu/cgi/viewcontent.cgi?article=1601&context=mjil.

behind the new institutional arrangement was the same in all cases: to consolidate public agencies of a technical nature, with highly specialized personnel, and impartial decisions, "isolated from any political influence or private interest."[2]

This institutional assembly divided two public functions: the public policy-making and the regulatory powers. The regulatory autonomy in energy initiated the opening of markets through regulations that years later promoted and guaranteed open access to the electric grid and fossil fuels facilities and leveled the dominant power that the State companies—Petróleos Mexicanos (Pemex) and Comisión Federal de Electricidad (CFE)—had through its previously integrated models.[3] Moreover, these institutions invested in their human resources, who became highly specialized and independent from political shifts.[4]

Mexico signed its first BIT in 1995 and produced a wide network of investment treaties, considering that international flows, especially those coming from foreign direct investments (FDI), play a fundamental role in economic development, technology transfer and job creation. These BITs contain measures and clauses intended to protect, at the international law level, the investments made by investors of each State Party in the Mexican territory.

Mexico's BITs favor an equitable floor for competition, establish a minimum standard for FDI protection, and provide an investor-State dispute settlement mechanism (ISDS) for those cases in which the BIT is violated by the Mexican State and the investor suffers damages in its investments.[5] Currently, Mexico has thirty-six BITs[6] and twelve free trade agreements with investment protection provisions.

Those two measures placed Mexico as one of the emerging countries most open to FDI and the ninth-largest recipient of FDI in the world. Nonetheless, according to the United Nations Conference on Trade and Development's (UNCTAD) World Investment Report 2021,[7] FDI inflows fell to USD 29 billion in 2020, from USD 34 billion the previous year (-15%). The first quarter of the year received 60% of those entries when reinvested profits are usually recorded. Currently, FDI in Mexico comes mainly from the United States, Spain, Canada, and Germany.

---

2. Guillermo García Alcocer, *CRE: 25 years stengthening, Regulatory Autonomy (CRE: 25 años fortaleciendo, Autonomía Regulatoria)*, Milenio, (Oct. 29, 2018), https://www.milenio.com/opinion/guillermo-garcia-alcocer/columna-guillermo-garcia-alcocer/cre-25-anos-fortaleciendo-autonomia-regulatoria.
3. In 1992, the first steps to open the energy sector were undertaken, when private investment in power generation was allowed under the self-supply, cogeneration and independent power producers. In October 1993, the CRE was created exclusively to regulate the electricity sector. Two years later, the reform of the natural gas market opened it to private participation, with the exception of production, which was reserved to the State via Pemex.
4. Alcocer, *supra* n. 2.
5. *See, What are the Reciprocal Investment Promotion and Protection Agreements (Que son los Acuerdos de Promoción y Protección Recíproca de las Inversiones)*, Gobierno de México, (Apr. 5, 2018), https://www.gob.mx/se/articulos/que-son-los-acuerdos-de-promocion-y-proteccion-reciproca-de-las-inversiones-appris.
6. *See, Investment Policy Hub-International Investment Agreements Navigator, Mexico*, UNCTAD (2022). https://investmentpolicy.unctad.org/international-investment-agreements/countries/136/mexico.
7. UNCTAD, *supra* n. 6.

As further explained below, the decrease is correlational to multiple factors of political nature and legal and economic impact, including persistent concerns about President Andrés Manuel López Obrador's (AMLO) critical stance on public-private partnerships, the role of the private sector in key industries—like oil and gas—changes in the energy sector's legal framework, along with the financial situation of the State oil company Pemex, the massive aid the latter receives from the government (valued at USD 3.5 billion), and investments with low economic and social impact—such as the Dos Bocas refinery.[8]

One of the key targets of AMLO's administration has been to unwind the energy reform that opened the industries to private participation and foreign direct investment in December 2013.

[1] New Rules, New Opportunities: The Energy Overhaul of 2013

After nearly eight decades of exclusive national development, Mexico received an energy boost with the 2013 structural and legal reform (Energy Reform) that ended most State monopolies in oil, gas, and power industries and opened opportunities for new business ventures that attracted the attention of local and foreign investment. The Energy Reform resulted in relevant new projects, despite volatile market conditions.

[B] UPSTREAM OPPORTUNITIES: ATTRACTING THE MAJORS INTO EXPLORATION VENTURES

Although the Mexican State—through Pemex—retained 83% of proven and probable reserves and 21% of prospective resources, several international oil companies (IOCs) ventured into Mexico's upstream industry via Exploration and Extraction Contracts (E&E Contracts) with the National Hydrocarbons Commission (CNH).

To this date, there are 109 E&E Contracts, mostly for offshore developments, with investors from twenty different countries. As of June 2022, E&E Contracts had paid revenues to the Mexican State in USD 5,701 and represented USD 12,272 of accumulated investment.[9]

Offshore developments have resulted in some very attractive discoveries. In 2017, the American firm Talos Energy (Talos) announced the discovery of 735-950

8. *See, Mexico: Foreign Investment (México: Inversión Extranjera), Santander* (December 2022), https://santandertrade.com/es/portal/establecerse-extranjero/mexico/inversion-extranjera. *See, Foreign Direct Investment in Mexico (Inversión Extranjera Directa en México)*, IMCO, (Aug. 18, 2021), https://imco.org.mx/datos-del-primer-semestre-de-2021-de-la-inversion-extranjera-directa/.
9. *See, Relevant Figures of Oil Rounds in Mexico* (Cifras Relevantes de Rondas Petroleras en México), Gobierno de Mexico-Rondas Petroleras, (Nov. 30, 2022), https://rondasmexico.gob.mx/esp/cifras-relevantes/?tab= (the authors note that the number of E&E Contracts could be higher should the AMLO administration had not cancelled the upcoming bidding rounds).

million barrels of oil equivalent (Mboe) in the Zama basin,[10] while the Spanish Repsol announced two significant deep-water discoveries for a total sum of 650 Mboe in its Mexican upstream assets.[11] In 2021, the Russian Lukoil started drilling its first exploration well, while the Italian Eni announced a discovery of 150-200 Mboe. That same year, the Malaysian Petronas announced to spud its exploration well in Mexico's Block 12.[12]

Mexico also witnessed various investments in the form of mergers and acquisitions in hydrocarbon production. For instance, in July 2021, Lukoil agreed to pay USD 435 million to acquire a 50% operating stake in two Mexican shallow-water blocks from Fieldwood Energy.

E&E Contracts have been key to increasing oil and gas production since they extract 176 Mb of oil and 244.3 million cubic meters of natural gas. Considering that some of those private investments will reach a production phase, the upstream segment is expected to witness significant growth during the following periods.[13]

But even if the IOCs have continued to enlarge their business in Mexico, State-owned companies Pemex and CFE suffered an inter-annual contraction of 16.7% in the first four months of 2022. Funds for such companies amounted to MXN 81.851 billion (USD 4.04 billion), down from MXN 91.558 billion in the same period of 2021.[14] Also, Pemex's expenses in construction, maintenance and acquisition of capital goods decreased by 18.1% to MXN 75.794 billion.[15]

Physical investment in Pemex and CFE in April reached MXN 25.87 billion, which, considering inflation, translated into a 10.3% drop compared to the same month of 2021. Pemex allocated MXN 24.12 billion to physical investment, a year-on-year decrease of 8.5% in real terms.

CFE allocated MXN 6.057 billion to the construction, maintenance, and acquisition of capital goods, 4.2% more than in the first four months of 2021. Meanwhile, April's investment contracted 29.8% in real terms, to MXN 1,749 million.

10. *Andrew Baker, Mexico's Pemex to Operate Zama Oil Discovery Made By "Disappointed" Talos Energy*, Natural Gas Intelligence, *(March 28, 2022)*, https://www.naturalgasintel.com/mexicos-pemex-to-operate-zama-oil-discovery-made-by-disappointed-talos-energy/
11. *See, Repsol makes two significant deepwater oil discoveries in Mexican waters*, Repsol, (May 04, 2020, 12:00 PM CEST). https://www.repsol.com/en/press-room/press-releases/2020/repsol-makes-two-significant-deepwater-oil-discoveries-in-mexican-waters/index.cshtml
12. Antonio Trujillo, *Russian Oil Company Starts Drilling in Mexico*, Mexico Business News, (August 18, 2021, 13:17 PM ST), https://mexicobusiness.news/oilandgas/news/russian-oil-company-starts-drilling-mexico
13. *See*, Mordor Intelligence, *Mexico Oil & Gas Market – Growth, Trends, Covid-19, Impact and Forecast (2022-2027)*, (2021), https://www.mordorintelligence.com/industry-reports/mexico-oil-and-gas-market?gclid=EAIaIQobChMIz-im_Oqh-wIV0g-tBh3F5QfiEAAYAiAAEgKwMPD_BwE.
14. Julio Gutiérrez, *Pemex Reports Losses of 224 thousand 363 billion pesos in 2021 (Reporta Pemex Pérdidas por 224 mil 363mdp en 2021)*, La Jornada, (February 28, 2022, 18:20 PM ST), https://www.jornada.com.mx/notas/2022/02/28/economia/reporta-pemex-perdidas-por-224-mil-363-mdp-en-2021/.
15. *See, Mexico's 2023 Budget: PEMEX and CFE Investments (Presupuesto 2023 de México: inversiones de PEMEX y CFE)*, BNAMERICAS, (2022), https://app.bnamericas.com/article/section/all/content/xvyc7tv1x-investment-watch-pemex-cfe-capex-down-17-mexinols-us460mn-methanol-plant.

[C] FOSSIL FUELS IN MEXICO: IMPORTS RELIABILITY

The renewed paradigm also opened the gasoline and diesel markets and further refined the natural gas industry.[16] CENAGAS, an independent system operator (ISO), manages the national gas pipeline system and the State utility company, CFE, increased the national pipeline system by approximately 5,000 kms. Those pipelines are owned and operated by private companies, including subsidiaries of Sempra Energy and TC Energy. In 2019, the government estimated that the increase in natural gas pipeline kilometers was 66% compared to 2012.[17]

Since April 2016, any company with a permit may import fuel and private companies can operate all kinds of midstream facilities, which are available to all interested users through an open non-discriminatory access. Before the Energy Reform, the transport and storage of refined products were carried out exclusively through Pemex, therefore, all infrastructure was owned by the State, which, upon the opening of the marketing industry, had little incentives to provide logistics services to competitors of Pemex.[18] To this date, the main storage capacity is still controlled by the combined presence of both Pemex and CFE with over 17.3 Mboe.

Mexico, with its large population and fuels market of 800,000 barrels per day, represents the fourth-largest gasoline market in the world and the sixth-largest in automotive fuels (gasoline and diesel). This, in turn, represents conditions of vulnerability, due to the high dependence on imported fuels, especially from the United States.[19]

Therefore, opportunities translated into new fuels storage projects and the establishment of new import strategies by major traders, such as Trafigura and Glencore; the IOCs—Shell, Chevron, BP, and Total; and major refiners, such as Marathon Petroleum Corp. and Valero. These foreign traders and marketers sponsored storage projects by the Dutch Royal Vopak, the world's leading independent tank storage company, and the American firms Sempra Energy and Monterra Energy (Monterra), among other foreign investors.

All the new ventures attracted by the Energy Reform were then challenged by President AMLO's political views, the COVID-19 pandemic and the worldwide slowdown, and an administrative paralysis that froze all permitting in energy matters. In

16. The natural industry began in 1995. The Energy Reform of 2013 added additional levels of openness as its secondary regulation further defined the open/non-discriminatory access to infrastructure and strengthened the autonomous regulator, the CRE.
17. *See, Status of Natural Gas Infrastructure (Estatus de la Infraestructura de Gas Natural), SENER*, (October 2019), https://www.gob.mx/cms/uploads/attachment/file/497827/Estatus_de_gasoductos_octubre_2019.pdf.
18. *See, Transition to Competitive Gasoline and Diesel Markets (Transición Hacia Mercados Competidos de Gasolinas y Diesel)*, COFECE (2018), https://www.cofece.mx/wp-content/uploads/2018/01/DOC-GASOLINAS-FINAL.pdf.
19. *See, ibid.* COFECE states that "Mexico has inventories to cover approximately 12 days of gasoline and diesel. This is low compared to other countries... which could be less in some regions of the country. This means that the supply chain, through imports and refineries, must be kept operating continuously, since any interruption of the supply greater than 12 days, on average, would cause shortages."

sum, around 1,000 permits were awaiting approval by the CRE, 50% of which correspond to gas stations.[20]

Although the pandemic has ceased to be a determining factor, the opportunities of storage companies teamed up with big off-takers continue to be very attractive, should the openness introduced by the Energy Reform have prevailed and if Mexico was not under a Rule of Law crisis.[21]

[1] Unwinding the Energy Reform: AMLO's Political Commitment

Mexico was starting to see the benefits of the 2013 Energy Reform when AMLO, as presidential candidate, announced his intention to upend the Mexican energy sector and restore the dominance of Pemex and the CFE.[22]

In sum, AMLO claims that the Energy Reform caused significant damage to Mexico's national energy security. Since he took office in December 2018, his administration has intended to materialize the campaign discourse to revert the Energy Reform via several legislative initiatives and regulatory amendments, as well as direct measures against targeted investments, and a general battle against the renewable power industry. All these actions, whether of general application or direct acts of authority, may be analyzed under the standards of investment protection treaties.

The measures taken by the AMLO administration have led to differences with its main trade and investment partners, the United States and Canada, among other individual proceedings initiated by specific foreign investors. Although several of the government's amendments and actions have been blocked in the federal courts, last April the National Supreme Court failed to reach a qualified majority necessary to block with general effects some unconstitutional amendments made to the Electric Industry Statute.[23] In sum, the judicial proceedings shall continue and each of their resolutions will be one of high relevance to define future potential claims by countries or investors against the Mexican State.

Different from what is seen in the power industry, where the attacks became frontal since the very first actions of the AMLO administration, the attacks on the oil and gas industry came in the form of isolated acts. One of the very first was the imposition of tougher conditions to secure and maintain import permits for fuels,[24]

20. Patricia Tapia Cervantes, *Oil Projects Halted by the CRE Amount to 100 Million Dollars* (*Proyectos petrolíferos detenidos por la CRE ascienden a 100mdd)*, Forbes (Nov. 18, 2021, 14:44 PM ST), https://www.forbes.com.mx/negocios-proyectos-petroliferos-detenidos-por-la-cre-ascienden-a-100-mdd/.
21. The authors adopt the thesis that concludes a crisis in Mexico's rule of law, based on the arbitrary exercise of discretionary powers; the default under the investors' legitimate expectations, which are protected at a constitutional level; the over-extended governmental paralysis, under the COVID-19 flag, which froze all permitting in the oil and gas industry; among other factors.
22. *See*, Electric Power Outlook 2023, BNAMERICAS, (2022), https://app.bnamericas.com/report/section/all/content/xjryvcsdq-electric-power-outlook-2023.
23. *Ibid.*
24. *See, Ruling that establishes the goods whose import and export is subject to regulation by the Ministry of Energy (Acuerdo que ruling that establece las mercancías cuya importación y*

which was accompanied by a delay in the processing of all governmental authorizations, from a change of brand in a gas retail station to the issuance of new permits to operate terminals and pipelines.[25]

The permitting delays started when almost all Commissioners of the CRE resigned due to pressure from the AMLO administration to impose a new paradigm.[26] Furthermore, during the first half of 2019, the CRE's governing body ran out of quorum, which translated into several unattended requests (i.e., permit applications) and no new regulation.[27]

Following the lack of quorum, in 2019 the energy regulator suffered a substantial decrease in its budget with a 28% drop—close to MXN 100 million—which caused the reduction of more than three hundred members of its staff.[28]

[D] LEGISLATIVE AND REGULATORY COUNTERMEASURES: A POTENTIAL WAVE OF INVESTMENT-TREATY CASES

On May 5, 2021, the Mexican government enacted a decree that amended the Hydrocarbons Statute (HS Amendment), with controversial aspects that include SENER's power to suspend or revoke hydrocarbon permits if there is "imminent danger to national security, energy security, or the national economy," with no objective standards to trigger such measure, creating room for discretionary (and potentially, arbitrary) use of such power.

The HS Amendment also provides that the government can temporarily occupy the private facilities—i.e., terminals or pipelines—"to safeguard the national interest" and can transfer its operation to State-owned entities, Pemex and CFE. Although such a provision has not been yet enforced, its inclusion in the legal system has raised the political risk of direct investments in infrastructure, which precisely were the most attractive opportunities posed by the Energy Reform.[29]

---

exportación está sujeta a regulación por parte de la Secretaría de Energía), Diario Oficial de la Federación, (Dec. 26, 2020), https://www.dof.gob.mx/nota_detalle.php?codigo=5608832&fecha=26/12/2020#gsc.tab=0.

25. Karol García, *CRE Unlocks Procedures for 150 Gas Station Permits* (CRE destraba trámites de 150 permisos gasolineros), El Economista, (Sep. 30, 2022, 13:50 PM ST), https://www.eleconomista.com.mx/empresas/CRE-destraba-tramites-de-150-permisos-gasolineros-20220930-0030.html.
26. *See, Head of Mexican Energy Regulatory Commission resigns,* Noé Cruz Serrano, El Universal (Jun. 4, 2019, 12:38 PM ST) https://www.eluniversal.com.mx/english/head-mexican-energy-regulatory-commission-resigns and *Due to Lack of Quorum in the CRE There Are Dozens of Permits Stuck*, Arturo Solís, Forbes (Apr. 8, 2019, 6:37 AM ST) https://www.forbes.com.mx/por-falta-de-quorum-en-la-cre-hay-docenas-de-permisos-atorados/.
27. García, *supra* n. 25.
28. Diana Nava, *A Weakened Regulator: This Is How the CRE Has Lost Strength This Six-Year Oeriod (Un regulador debilitado: así es como la CRE ha perdido fuerza este sexenio)*, Expansión, (Jan. 15, 2021, 05:00 AM ST), https://expansion.mx/empresas/2021/01/15/un-regulador-debilitado-asi-es-como-la-cre-ha-perdido-fuerza-este-sexenio.
29. *See, Global Energy: Official Gazette publishes decree reforming the Hydrocarbons Law; enters into force May 5, Global Energy, 2021 (Global Energy: DOF publica un decreto que reforma la Ley de Hidrocarburos; entra en vigor el 5 de mayo)*, Global Energy, (May 4, 2021), https://globalenergy.mx/noticias/hidrocarburos/publica-dof-decreto-que-reforma-la-ley-de-hidrocarburos-entra-en-vigor-el-miercoles-5-de-mayo/.

Other measures introduced by the HS Amendment and secondary regulation directly benefit Pemex, since import, marketing, and distribution companies—the IOCs, traders, and mid-sized firms—heavily depend on the fuels' storage infrastructure provided by Pemex. These companies had an obligation to establish a safety inventory by 2019, in response to Mexico's reliability on imports, unless their storage commitments implied the construction of a new terminal, in which case the obligation would become enforceable when such new facilities became operational.

Thousands of constitutional reliefs (*amparos*) were filed against the HS Amendment. In response, Federal Judges granted injunctions that prevented the authorities from enacting the HS Amendment. The final ruling will eventually be issued by the Mexican Supreme Court of Justice.

Notwithstanding, these amendments eliminated the extension right, which translated into: (i) a loss of interest in the construction of new terminals, primarily supported by private investors; (ii) a complete reliance on existing facilities, majorly dominated by Pemex, with very few private terminals; (iii) little interest by Pemex to rent storage capacity to third-party traders and marketers; (iv) unequitable conditions to compete, due to Pemex's vertical integration; (v) a reverse in open access and non-discriminatory policy;[30] (vi) increased risk in the fuels markets; and (vii) loss of interest of downstream players to increase their volumes of fuels in Mexico.

Other key actions and omissions that the AMLO administration has enacted to harm private participation in energy, which could result in violations of the protection granted by investment protection treaties, are:

(1) Massive closure of privately-operated terminals.
(2) Reduction of permittees, through the permit freeze and revocation of existing permits, which benefits the dominant players, Pemex and CFE.
(3) Deleting long-term permits for imports of fuels, deterring long-term commitments and new infrastructure investments in fuels.
(4) Toughening permitting requirements.[31]
(5) Certain obligations in matters of volumetric control were introduced. Such obligations were impossible to meet, and permit-holders were—and continue to be—at risk of losing their permits.
(6) SENER issued a ruling by which all users of Mexico's Natural Gas Transportation Service system—the biggest and most crucial pipeline system in Mexico—should acquire natural gas from CFE or PEMEX to continue using such a system.

30. Although the framework still provides for open/non-discriminatory access, Pemex has not opened its terminals for third-party use since 2018, when the last open season procedure took place. Pemex is obligated by statute to develop such open seasons, however, there has been no enforcement of such obligation.

31. The new framework applicable to permit applications for marketing or imports, require the applicant to have secured storage. As mentioned before, there are very few options other than Pemex, who has not tendered new contracts to rent capacity to parties other than Pemex. Additionally, terminal developers may have less incentives to build terminals with a party that has not secured an import and marketing permit and who may not be able to use its capacity.

(7) Ninety-two companies that imported hydrocarbons or refined products were suspended from the importers' registry, including Kansas City Southern de México, as well as the IOCs Repsol and Total.[32]
(8) Separately, the CRE revoked 139 marketing permits on the basis that the permits had not been used for over a year.
(9) CRE conducted verification inspections and closed several petroleum products' transloading and storage facilities.[33]
(10) One of the most damaging decisions made by the AMLO administration was to suspend for nearly three years all rulings and regulations from energy regulators—CRE, SENER—under the argument of the COVID-19 pandemic.

These regulatory measures have caused legal certainty in Mexico to be questioned and have raised speculation on possible commercial and investment treaty arbitrations.

Domestic tribunals have stopped several regulatory changes from being implemented and in some cases, have made energy authorities uplift their deadlines suspensions. In addition, these decisions have slowed the expected avalanche of arbitrations. Currently, both investment and commercial arbitrations seem to be on the rise.

[E] FROM THE ENERGY REFORM TO THE COUNTER-REFORM: OIL AND GAS IN A NUTSHELL

According to UNCTAD's report of 2021,[34] Mexico's FDI inflow fell 15% to USD 29 billion with respect to the previous year, which follows a recession that started in 2019. Specifically in the oil and gas industries, FDI in the sector dropped 63% in the first six months of this year to USD 278 million.[35]

Mexico's energy mix continues to be heavily reliant on fossil fuels, with little incentive to focus on other sources of energy. In sum, the Mexican oil and gas downstream market is expected to register a compound annual growth rate of less than 1.43% during the forecast period of 2016-2026. Factors to be highlighted are the increasing demand for natural gas and rising investment in refineries and liquified natural gas (LNG) terminals.

32. Currently, only eighty-six companies have valid registration as importers to import fuels. This means that the suspension of ninety-two companies represented more than half of the total permitted firms. In addition to such registry, SENER has to grant an import permit. Fifty-eight of the current permits are expiring throughout 2022. Previous experience suggests they are unlikely to be renewed by SENER.
33. Nayeli González, *CRE Suspends Fuel Transportation due to Audits (Por auditorías CRE suspende transporte de combustibles)*, Onexpo Nacional, (Jul. 20, 2021), https://www.onexpo.com.mx/NOTICIAS/POR-AUDITORIAS-CRE-SUSPENDE-TRANSPORTE-DE-COMBUSTI_3fmqS/.
34. *See*, James X. Zhan & James X. Zhan team, *World Investment Report 2021: Investing in Sustainable Recovery*, UNCTAD (2021), https://unctad.org/system/files/official-document/wir2021_en.pdf.
35. Arturo Solís, *Foreign Investment in Mexico's Oil and Gas Sector Plummets in First-Half*, Bloomberg, (Aug. 25, 2022), https://www.bloomberglinea.com/english/foreign-investment-in-mexicos-oil-and-gas-sector-plummets-in-first-half/.

The major nationalities represented in these industries are the United States of America, Spain, Canada, the United Kingdom, China, Germany, France, and Italy. Nevertheless, Pemex, Royal Dutch Shell PLC, TC Energy Corporation, BP PLC, and ExxonMobil Corporation are the major companies operating in Mexico's Oil and Gas Market.

The government highlighted the investment of USD 40 billion for the energy sector. It will be applied by United States companies—from now until 2024—in pipelines, liquefaction plants and fertilizers. Also, in crude oil extraction in partnership with Pemex, in accordance with existing contracts.[36]

[F] CURRENT STATUS OF MEXICO'S FDI IN-FLOWS

FDI comes mainly from the United States, Spain, the United Kingdom, Germany, and Luxemburg.[37] Historically, the major foreign investors in Mexico have been the United States, Spain, Canada, Japan, and Germany. All such countries have negotiated investment-protection agreements with Mexico.

Mexico and Spain signed a treaty on energy cooperation, known as the Agreement on Industrial, Energy and Mining Cooperation. It includes the energy sector; some interesting aspects are that to International Centre for Settlement of Investment Disputes (ICSID), they provide deemed expropriation, and include "fair and equitable treatment" or "national treatment" clauses, and "most-favored-nation" clauses.

Subsequently, to protect the investors, they signed a BIT, known as the Agreement for the reciprocal promotion and protection of investments between the Kingdom of Spain and the United Mexican States, done in Mexico on October 10, 2006.

Although Mexico and the United Kingdom do not have a specific treaty for the energy field, British companies operate in the Mexican energy sector and, like Spain, are protected by the BIT signed on July 25, 2007. Same scenario between Mexico and Italy, China, Germany, and France, they did sign an energy cooperation treaty, but it does not seem to be in force today.

As mentioned above, Canada is not a party to the ISDS provisions under USMCA, however, Canadian investors have access to the protection and mechanisms granted in the CPTPP.[38]

In sum, common rights granted to foreign investors in terms of the BITs adopted by Mexico include, among others, fair and equitable treatment, non-discrimination, and minimum level of treatment. With regards to expropriation, nearly all treaties protect investments from direct expropriation and—in less cases—indirect expropriation. Regarding the most favored nation and national treatment, most BITs contain a

36. *See, Mexico Agrees to $40 Billion Dollars in Private U.S. Investment in Energy Sector* (*México pacta inversión privada estadounidense por 40mil mdd en sector energético*), Energía Hoy (Jul. 14, 2022), https://energiahoy.com/2022/07/18/mexico-pacta-inversion-privada-estadouniden se-por-40-mil-mdd-en-sector-energetico/#: ~ :text = %2D%20Al%20informar%20los%20resul tados%20de,plantas%20de%20licuefacci%C3%B3n%20y%20fertilizantes.

37. Santander, *supra* n. 8.

38. Since the CPTPP includes several signatories, protection granted by the multilateral treaty may overlap with the corresponding BITs.

reservation on tax matters. Few BITs include umbrella clauses. All BITs contain cooling-off period provisions. All cases shall analyze the role of local courts, whether the BIT requires exhaustion of national remedies before Mexican courts, has a permissive approach to allow disputes to be heard before courts or through arbitration, or contains fork-in-the-road provisions.

Also, in July 2018, Mexico ratified the Convention on the Settlement of Investment Disputes between States and Nationals of Other States with the World Bank (ICSID Convention),[39] which entered into force for Mexico on August 26, 2018. Thirty-two of Mexico's BITs refer to the ICSID Convention.[40] Mexico is participating in at least three arbitrations in the ICSID. One is a group of U.S. investors in an oil and gas project, as described below.

Mexico is a signatory to fourteen free trade agreements and thirty-six bilateral investment agreements (BITs).[41] BITs provide qualifying investors and investments with substantive and procedural rights. If the host country (in this case, Mexico) violates such rights, they grant the possibility to sue Mexico directly.

Lastly, Mexico has a robust arbitration legal framework. It has ratified the Convention on the Recognition and Enforcement of Foreign Arbitral Awards and the Inter-American Convention on International Commercial Arbitration.

[G] NAFTA SUNSET CLAUSE

The North American Free Trade (NAFTA), in force since 1994, was replaced by the United States-Mexico-Canada Agreement (USMCA) on July 1, 2020. A sunset period for claims under NAFTA was provided and will end on June 30, 2023.

To date, over seventy-six claims have been filed under NAFTA: thirty against Canada, twenty-seven against Mexico and nineteen against the United States.[42]

As detailed below, USMCA is less protective of foreign investment so considering its sunset clause, we expect to see a rise of claims under USMCA in December 2022 and January 2023, especially from Canadian investors.

[H] NAFTA VERSUS USMCA

One of the major changes introduced by the USMCA is that Canada is not a party to the ISDS mechanism. Therefore, only Mexico and the United States may have access to such measures.

---

39. *See, Database of ICSID Member States*, ICSID, 2022, https://icsid.worldbank.org/about/member-states/database-of-member-states/member-state-details?state=ST195.
40. Cosmo Sanderson, *Curtis Wins Bid to Advise Mexico in 13 Disputes*, Global Arbitration Review (Oct. 7, 2022), https://globalarbitrationreview.com/article/curtis-wins-bid-advise-mexico-in-13-disputes.
41. *See, Investment Policy Hub-International Investment Agreements Navigator, Mexico, UNCTAD* (2022), https://investmentpolicy.unctad.org/international-investment-agreements/countries/136/mexico.
42. *See, Investment Policy Hub-Investment Dispute Settlement Navigator,* UNCTAD (2022), https://investmentpolicy.unctad.org/investment-dispute-settlement.

Chapter 14 of the USMCA deals with investor protection mechanisms, which are significantly reduced from those contained in the NAFTA. Nonetheless, investors can file their NAFTA claims before July 1, 2023, provided that the dispute arises out of investments made when NAFTA was still in force and remained in existence as of July 1, 2020.

According to USMCA, an investment is every asset that an investor owns or controls, directly or indirectly, that has: i) commitment of capital; ii) the expectation of gain profit; or iii) the assumption of risk. Additionally, an investment that is covered under the USMCA is defined as an investment of a Party, in the territory of another Party (in this case, Mexico) in the existence of the USMCA.

The rights and protections of the United States and Mexican investors are governed by Annex 14-D of the USMCA. According to this Annex, in the event of a qualifying investment dispute, the claimant must first fulfill procedural prerequisites by:

(a) seeking to resolve the dispute, first through consultation and negotiation, which may include the use of non-binding, third-party procedures, such as good offices, conciliation, or mediation. If the dispute cannot be settled, the claimant may submit a claim to arbitration; and
(b) exhausting local remedies by filing a proceeding before a competent court or administrative tribunal in Mexico and obtaining a final decision from a court of last resort or arguing that thirty months have elapsed from the date the proceeding was initiated. The exception to this requirement would exist if the remedies were obviously futile or ineffective. The USMCA does not define "futile or ineffective remedies" and this standard has not yet been defined by investment tribunals.

Likewise, Mexico-United States investment disputes related to covered government contracts are regulated by Annex 14-E. However, in this annex, the exhaustion of the local remedies clause does not apply to covered government contracts in oil and gas, power generation, and infrastructure, among other sectors. However, not all investments made in oil and gas derive from a contract with the government.[43]

All other investors may only be able to claim direct expropriation and national treatment and most-favored-nation treatment. Claims for indirect expropriation and minimum standard of treatment—including fair and equitable treatment—would have to be argued in a State-to-State dispute settlement mechanism or directly brought by the investor before local courts.

In this regard, the local remedies rule in international investment arbitration finds its application when it is specifically required in the investment agreement, as it is in Annex 14-D of the USMCA. Also, the "Convention on the Settlement of Investment Dispute Between States and Nationals of other States" confirms that a contracting State

43. E&E Contracts would fall under the privileged regime. A different scenario will be available to permit-holders for import, marketing, transport (i.e., pipelines), storage, distribution, liquefaction (i.e., LNG), regasification, among other midstream and downstream activities.

may require the exhaustion of local administrative or judicial remedies as a condition of its consent to arbitration under this Convention. Even though this requirement has been ignored in several arbitration cases; the clear trend in the ICSID is to require compliance with exhaustion of domestic remedies prerequisite to consider the investments covered.

An investor may lose the benefits of Chapter 14 if the enterprise is owned or controlled by a person of a non-Party or has no substantial business activities in the territory (in this case, Mexico). Also, if a Party (in this case, Mexico) makes a payment to an investor in the form of indemnity with respect to a covered investment, the Parties (State and investor) shall recognize the transfer of any right the investor would have possessed.

Concerning the features of the investments, the USMCA recognizes that nothing in Chapter 14 shall prevent a Party (in this case, Mexico) from endorsing a measure appropriate to ensure that investment is undertaken in a manner sensitive to the environment, health, safety, and other regulatory objectives. Moreover, Article 14.17 establishes that enterprises that invest in Mexico shall voluntarily incorporate into their internal policies the internationally recognized standards in areas such as labor, environment, gender equality, human rights, indigenous and aboriginal people's rights, and corruption.

[I] CURRENT OIL AND GAS ARBITRATION CASES VERSUS MEXICO: TALOS AND MONTERRA

Talos Energy (Talos) became an oil operator in 2015, when CNH awarded it, jointly with its partners Premier Oil and Sierra Oil (owned by Wintershall DEA), an E&E Contract in shallow waters of the Gulf of Mexico. As previously mentioned, in 2017 Talos announced the discovery of the most promising oil field discovered by a private operator in Mexico since the exploration and production sector was opened to private participation in 2014.[44]

After Talos' announcement of the Zama discovery, in 2019 Pemex announced that Talos' area intersected with an entitlement assigned to Pemex by the Mexican government, which led to protracted discussions about a unitization agreement, which would set out the operation and the rules for how the resources would be divided. After both companies failed to reach an agreement in March 2021, the decision was left in the hands of SENER, which in July of that year made Pemex the Zama operator, with a stake of 82.65%. The 17.35% awarded to Talos by SENER is below the percentage of resources estimated to be in Talos' block, much closer to 50%.

The analysis on which SENER based its decision to favor the State company was based on twenty criteria, seventeen of which were met by Talos, while Pemex

44. *See, Mexican Zama Field Plan Presented and Production Projected for 2024 (Presentan plan de campo mexicano Zama y proyectan producción para 2024)*, BNAMERICAS (2022), https://www.bnamericas.com/es/noticias/presentan-plan-de-campo-mexicano-zama-y-proyectan-produccion-para2024#:~:text=Zama%20es%20el%20yacimiento%20petrol%C3%ADfero,la%20participaci%C3%B3n%20privada%20en%202014.

accredited all of them. Three criteria that took advantage of the private player were aimed, from the beginning, to favor the Mexican state company: a minimum production of 10,000 barrels of crude oil within Mexico; installed transportation and marketing capacity; and national development projects.[45]

In September 2021, Talos filed a Dispute Notice over Zama based on the BIT between Luxembourg and Mexico.[46] In 2022, it was announced this dispute was temporarily paused.[47]

Monterra's case derived from the federal government's aggressive inspections of storage facilities owned and operated by private companies during 2021, which led to several closures, including Monterra's.[48] The firm argues that it operated with all permits required for such a facility.

Monterra notified the Mexican Government of its intentions to launch international arbitration under the North American Free Trade Agreement for suspending the operations of its storage terminal,[49] claiming damages for USD 667 million.[50]

45. Diana Nava, *The 3 Impossible Factors for Talos to Meet That Gave Zama to Pemex (Los 3 factores imposibles de cumplir para Talos que dieron Zama a Pemex)*, Expansión, (Jul. 9, 2021, 05:00 AM ST), https://expansion.mx/empresas/2021/07/09/pemex-zama-talos-factores-sener-operacion.
    It was impossible for a private operator to meet the local presence standards, since the upstream industry was barely open to private participation in 2014 and most of the contracts awarded to private operators required exploration, meaning that there was no guarantee over the commerciality of the hydrocarbons in a specific block. As a matter of fact, the Zama discovery was the first discovery made by a private operator in Mexico. Furthermore, midstream development of transportation continues to be in progress, with several delays caused by the COVID-19 pandemic and, especially, the slow-down in the processing and granting of permits by the governmental agencies. Therefore, only the State company, who before the Energy Reform operated vertically integrated, had the possibility to meet those discretionary standards of local presence.
46. Max de Haldevang, *Talos Files Dispute Notice Against Mexico over Zama*, Bloomberg (Sep. 3, 2021, 20:32 PM CDT), https://www.bloomberg.com/news/articles/2021-09-03/talos-files-usmca-dispute-notice-against-mexico-over-zama-field.
47. Mariana Parraga, Dave Graham & Adriana Barrera, *EXCLUSIVE Talos Energy pauses Mexico Oil Arbitration Bid amid High-Level Talks*, Reuters (May 22, 2022, 06:00 AM CDT), https://www.reuters.com/business/energy/exclusive-talos-energy-pauses-mexico-oil-arbitration-bid-amid-high-level-talks-2022-05-18/.
48. Mary Anastasia O'Gardy, *Mexico Moves to Seize American Assets*, WSJ Opinion (Oct. 17, 2021, 14:41 PM ET), https://www.wsj.com/articles/mexico-american-assets-obrador-amlo-energy-11634496785.
    As reported by the Wall Street Journal, "Mexican National Guard troops sealed the front gates of the Monterra Energy fuel terminal in Tuxpan, Veracruz, last month. The facility was closed by order of Mexico's energy regulator… Monterra told [the author] it has complied with all regulations but that the energy regulator isn't answering its calls and the terminal remains closed."
49. *See*, *Monterra Energy Takes Legal Action Against Closure of its Tuxpan Facility by Submitting to the Government of Mexico a Notice of Intent under NAFTA*, Monterra Energy (Feb. 22, 2022), http://monterraenergy.com/wp-content/uploads/2022/02/220220-Monterra-NAFTA-NoD-press-release-ENG-final.pdf.
50. *See*, *Mexico Sanctions Monterra Amid Negotiation to Avoid Arbitration (México sanciona a Monterra en Medio de Negociación para evitar Arbitraje)*, Ciar Global, (May 30, 2022), https://ciarglobal.com/mexico-sanciona-a-monterra-en-medio-de-negociacion-para-evitar-arbitraje/.

[J] RISE IN COMMERCIAL ARBITRATION: CASES VERSUS STATE-OWNED COMPANIES AND AGENCIES

In October 2022, the Mexican Ministry of Economy awarded a bid to an international law firm to represent Mexico in three arbitrations already being held at ICSID. One of those cases has been brought by oil and gas investors from the United States. This firm will also handle ten matters still under the notice of dispute stage (one of them being *Monterra's* case).[51]

Also, in October, two awards against the CFE were made public. The first is a claim brought up by ATCO (a Canadian company) concerning a natural gas pipeline and concluded with a sentence to CFE to pay USD 100 million.[52] The second one was brought up by the Spanish company Duro Felguera about the generation plant Empalme II. In this case, CFE was sentenced to pay USD 20 million.[53]

In addition to those adverse awards, CFE is involved in more than twenty arbitrations brought up by private companies against the Mexican-owned company.[54]

Likewise, Pemex has been part of different commercial arbitrations. One of the essential precedents is the *Commisa v. Pemex* case, formally known as *Corporación Mexicana de Mantenimiento Integral, S. De R.L. de C.V.* (COMMISA) *v. Pemex-Exploración y Producción*, was a significant international arbitration dispute between a subsidiary of KBR, an American engineering and construction firm, and *Pemex-Exploración y Producción*, a subsidiary of Pemex. The dispute arose in 2004 when Pemex terminated two contracts with COMMISA for the construction of oil platforms in the Gulf of Mexico, claiming that COMMISA had not fulfilled its contractual obligations. COMMISA challenged the termination, and the parties agreed to resolve the matter through arbitration. In 2009, the arbitration panel, held under the International Chamber of Commerce rules, favored COMMISA. Pemex appealed the decision, and in 2011, a Mexican court nullified the award, stating that the arbitration panel exceeded its authority by considering a dispute involving public contracts.

COMMISA then sought to enforce the arbitration award in the United States. In 2013, a U.S. district court upheld the arbitration award, finding that the Mexican court's decision to nullify the award was contrary to public policy. Pemex appealed this decision to the United States Court of Appeals for the Second Circuit. In 2016, the Second Circuit affirmed the lower court's decision, upholding the arbitration award in favor of COMMISA.[55]

---

51. Sanderson, *supra* n. 40.
52. Diana Gante, *The Arbitrations Faced by the CFE (Los arbitrajes que enfrenta la CFE)*, Reforma, (May 30, 2022), https://www.reforma.com/aplicacioneslibre/preacceso/articulo/default.aspx?__rval=1&urlredirect=/los-arbitrajes-que-enfrenta-la-cfe/ar2484068.
53. *See, CFE Loses Another Arbitration, Will Now Pay 22 Million Dollars (CFE Pierde Otro Arbitraje, Ahora pagará 22 Millones de Dólares)*, Encuentro Internacional de Energía México (Oct. 7, 2022), https://encuentroenergia.mx/energia-electrica/cfe-pierde-otro-arbitraje-ahora-pagara-22-millones-de-dolares/.
54. Gante, *supra* n. 52.
55. United States Court of Appeals: *Corporación Mexicana De Mantenimiento Integral, S. De R.L. De C.V. v. Pemex-Exploración Y Producción*, 832 F.3d 92 (2nd Cir. 2014).

In conclusion, the ongoing arbitrations involving Mexican companies such as Pemex and CFE with international investors and companies and the recent awards made against CFE highlight the importance of ensuring fair and equitable dispute resolution mechanisms in international business transactions. In addition, the *Commisa v. Pemex* case serves as a reminder of the challenges involved in enforcing international arbitration awards and the role of national courts in recognizing or annulling them.

CHAPTER 18
Shareholders and M&A Disputes

Rodrigo Zamora Etcharren & Ana María Castro Dosal

There seems to be a growing momentum in Mexico's M&A market, as evidenced by the increase in the number of M&A deals reported in 2022.[1] Moreover, the COVID-19 pandemic had an impact on shareholder legislation in Mexico.

As to M&A transactions, according to Ignacio Pesqueira Taunton, activity is very high in Mexico. Mexican companies and high-net-worth individuals capitalizing through private equity funds, and large corporations are trying to buy into the market.[2]

Relevant transactions are happening in Mexico, for example, 2022 culminated with the sale by Grupo Bimbo, the world's largest bakery, of Ricolino, its confectionary business, to Mondelēz International, for approximately USD 1.3 billion.[3]

In terms of shareholder legislation, it appears that the pandemic has compelled Mexican legislators toward modernization. This has resulted in the initiative to reform the General Law of Business Entities (LGSM) to regulate the virtual or remote presence of shareholders at corporate meetings. The aim is to grant equal legal validity to both remote and physical attendance. The initiative emphasizes the importance of avoiding economic stagnation during pandemic times. Moreover, it acknowledges that the rapid pace of technological advancements and constant scientific discoveries surpass the

1. According to the Transactional Track Record, 85 transactions occurred in the first quarter of 2022, 191 in the second quarter, and 310 in the third quarter. *Transactional Track Record*, (1Q 2022) https://www.ttrecord.com/en/publications/market-reports/monthly-report-mexico/Mexico-1Q-2022/2087/, (2Q 2022) https://www.ttrecord.com/en/publications/market-reports/monthly-report-mexico/Mexico-2Q-2022/2106/, (3Q 2022) https://www.ttrecord.com/en/publications/market-reports/monthly-report-mexico/Mexico-3Q-2022/2127/.
2. *Roundtable: The Impact of Political Instability and Social Unrest on Dealmaking in Latin America, in The Guide to Mergers and Acquisitions*, 11-19 (Paola Lozano and Daniel Hernández eds., 2d. ed., 2021).
3. *Mondelez International Agrees to Acquire Ricolino, Mexico's Leading Confectionery Company, from Grupo Bimbo* (April 2021) https://ir.mondelezinternational.com/news-releases/news-release-details/mondelez-international-agrees-acquire-ricolino-mexicos-leading.

speed at which Mexican laws are created. Therefore, it is crucial to provide society with elements of certainty.[4]

While the future of M&A transactions appears promising, it is expected that the increase in transactions will also lead to a proportional rise in controversies related to M&A, including potential shareholder disputes. In this chapter, we will examine the Mexican legal framework, the typical types of shareholder and M&A disputes, and important considerations for dispute resolution in these areas.

[A] LEGAL FRAMEWORK

Private commercial entities are mainly regulated through the General Law of Business Entities (*Ley General de Sociedades Mercantiles*), the General Law of Negotiable Instruments and Credit Operations (*Ley de Títulos y Operaciones de Crédito*), the Foreign Investment Law (*Ley de Inversión Extranjera*) and the Commerce Code (*Código de Comercio*). In addition, public entities must comply with the Stock Markets Law (*Ley del Mercado de Valores*), the Economic Competition Law (*Ley Federal de Competencia Económica*), as well as specific regulations issued by the National Banking and Securities Commission (*Comisión Nacional Bancaria y de Valores*), and internal regulations issued by the Mexican Stock Exchange.

Under Mexican Law, there are four primary forms of entities commonly incorporated or established: (1) *Sociedad Anónima de Capital Variable (S.A. de C.V.)*,[5] comparable to a corporation in the U.S.; (2) *Sociedad de Responsabilidad Limitada de Capital Variable (S. de R.L. de C.V.)*,[6] similar to an LLC in the U.S.; (3) *Sociedad Anónima Promotora de Inversión de Capital Variable (S.A.P.I. de C.V)*, a subtype of S.A. de C.V., regulated under the Stock Markets Law;[7] and (4) *Sociedad Anónima Bursátil de Capital Variable (S.A.B. de C.V.)*, also regulated under the Stock Markets Law.[8]

The General Law of Business Entities serves as the primary regulation governing shareholder's agreements, the rights and obligations of the partners, as well as the structure and operation of various types of companies. Additionally, it establishes the fundamental aspects of mergers and corporate divestitures in Mexico, with only eight articles specifically addressing the merger,[9] and spin-off of companies.[10]

4. *Initiative to reform several provisions of the General Law of Business Entities (LGSM) to regulate the presence of shareholders remotely* (February 2021) http://sil.gobernacion.gob.mx/Archivos/Documentos/2021/02/asun_4141859_20210223_1614156700.pdf.
5. Articles 87-206 and 213-221 of the General Law of Business Entities.
6. *Ibid.*, Arts. 58-86.
7. Articles 12-13 of the Stock Markets Law.
8. *Ibid.*, Art. 22.
9. Under Mexican Law, both a merger agreement between the merging entities and the corresponding corporate resolutions are needed for a corporate merger to take place. Global Law and Business, *Arbitration of M&A Transactions, a Practical Global Guide* 160 (2013). *See also supra* n. 5, Arts. 222-228.
10. *Ibid.*, 161. A spin-off occurs when part of a company is divested to form a new entity.

[B] COMMON M&A DISPUTES

There is a wealth of literature, including books, articles, and publications, that extensively cover the potential disputes arising from an M&A transaction. Generally, authors categorize M&A transaction disputes into those that may occur before the deal's closing and those that arise after the agreement's completion. The doctrine uniformly addresses the various challenges that may arise depending on the stage of the transaction.

Below, we will briefly analyze some of the issues that can arise at each stage of an M&A transaction, focusing on specific aspects that may be of interest in the Mexican context.

M&A follow a similar structure worldwide, aiming to achieve agreements that reflect increasing levels of understanding and commitment throughout the negotiation process.[11]

The initial stages of the transactions focus on ensuring confidentiality and governing the exchange of information:

> In the preparatory phase of an M&A transaction, the basic terms and conditions, the deal structure and/or procedural matters are regularly recorded in the form of a letter of intent (LoI), a memorandum of understanding (MoU) or a term sheet. In the advanced stages of the transaction, information and documents relating to the target company are usually exchanged only based on and subject to a non-disclosure agreement (NDA).[12]
>
> Disputes arising in the preliminary stage of a transaction often result in the abortion of the contemplated transaction.[13]

Disputes that arise during the pre-signing or pre-closing stages of an M&A transaction are often related to the abandonment of negotiations by one of the parties. However, they can also involve the breach of a specific clause of a preliminary agreement. Examples of such clauses include confidentiality, exclusivity, or conditions that require reporting, assessing, and considering a superior offer from a third party, or obligations to provide all agreed-upon documents within a specified time frame.[14]

In 2020, a major entertainment company filed a request for arbitration before the International Chamber of Commerce (ICC) against two other entertainment corporations concerning the cancellation of the planned acquisition of a prominent entertainment company specializing in concerts and live events. The acquisition had been publicly announced in 2019. The purchasing company

11. *See ibid.*, 166.
12. Eliane Fischer & Michael Walbert, *The Arbitration Agreement and Arbitrability, Efficient and Expeditious Dispute Resolution in M&A Transactions*, Austrian Yearbook on International Arbitration 2017 (Christian Klausegger, Peter Klein et al. eds., January 2017) https://www.kluwerarbitration.com/document/kli-ka-austrianyb-2017004-n?q=M%26A%20transactions.
13. *Ibid.*
14. *See supra* n. 9, 304.

unilaterally terminated the share purchase agreement alleging it needed to assess the potential impact of COVID-19 on the target entertainment company's concert and live events business and operations in Mexico and Latin America.[15]

After the purchaser's notification of termination, one of the seller corporations issued a statement to the Mexican Stock Exchange, announcing the suspension of the arbitration. This happened because the purchaser company decided to proceed with the acquisition of the target entertainment company. The agreement stipulates that the purchaser company will acquire a 51 % stake in the target entertainment company, with 11 % coming from one of the other entertainment corporations and 40 % from the remaining entertainment company, as originally announced back in July 2019.[16]

Following the completion of an M&A transaction, disputes can arise due to two main reasons:

Disagreement over the purchase price adjustment post-closing. Purchase price adjustments are commonly included in M&A transactions because it is often not feasible to determine the net working capital on the closing date itself. Sufficient time is required for the entity to complete the "closing of the books."[17]

As a result, the parties establish a preliminary price at closing and agree to a subsequent price adjustment once all the information becomes available. In the event of a disagreement and failed negotiation, the contract typically includes provisions for submitting the dispute to be resolved by an accounting firm to determine the net working capital.[18]

Perceived defects in the equivalence of performance and counter-performance. This arises when one party believes there are deficiencies in the performance and counter-performance equivalence of the transaction. Such defects can be attributed to erroneous assumptions or expectations regarding the subject of the transaction. These errors may result from incorrect assumptions made by the buyer or inappropriate information (knowingly or unknowingly) provided by the seller.[19] Claims in this category often fall into two general types: claims for breach of representations and warranties and claims for breach of indemnities, which will be addressed below.

15. *Live Nation Reaches Agreement in Mexico Ending ICC Arbitration* (*Live Nation llega a acuerdo en México poniendo fin a Arbitraje CCI*) (September 2021) https://ciarglobal.com/live-nation-llega-a-acuerdo-en-mexico-poniendo-fin-a-arbitraje-cci/.
16. *Ibid.*
17. A. Vincent Biemans & Gerald M. Hamsen, *M&A Disputes: A Professional Guide to Accounting Arbitrations* 5 (2017).
18. *Ibid.*
19. *Tactics in M&A Arbitrations* 5 (Dr. Karl J.T. Wach & Frank Meckes eds., 2008).

[1] Claims for Breach of Representations and Warranties

In an M&A context, a representation is understood as:

> an assertion of a past or existing fact, given by one party to induce another party to enter into an agreement. A warranty is a promise that the assertion of existing facts or future facts are or will be true, along with an implied promise of indemnity if the assertion is false. The distinction is important as it leads to different remedies. Whereas misrepresentation may allow the buyer to rescind the contract and claim damages on the grounds that it entered into the agreement without having had a clear representation of reality, a breach of warranty would allow the buyer to claim damages, but not to rescind the contract.[20]

Mexican legislation is consistent with the effects described in the preceding paragraph. As to misrepresentation, the legislation provides for the rescission of a contract where there was an error regarding the determining motive of the parties to the agreement (known as "error de nulidad").[21]

As for breaches of warranty, it is possible to argue the applicability of calculation errors (referred to as "error de cálculo") set forth in the code. Because the violation is not enough to rescind the contract, there can be a proportional adjustment through damages.[22] Here, it is important to point out that Mexican Law does not provide for any consequential damages.

[2] Claims for Breach of Indemnities

In an M&A context, indemnities are understood as:

> either stand-alone agreements or contractual stipulations whereby a party accepts in advance to be liable for another person's loss or to hold a person harmless of potential claims that may be brought against third parties'.[23] 'The incorporation of an indemnity takes place at the end of a due diligence process, when the buyer has had an opportunity to identify the potential liabilities of losses which the target company may incur in relation to events that are outside the buyers' control.[24]

While our courts have not specifically addressed claims for breach of indemnities in M&A transactions, it may be interesting to consider a precedent from the *Mayan Palace* case to anticipate how courts could interpret the concept of holding an entity harmless from potential claims by third parties.

The *Mayan Palace* case involves a tragic incident where a young man died from electrocution after his kayak tipped over in a negligently electrified artificial

20. Gauthier Vannieuwenhuyse, *The Rise of M&A Arbitration* (April 2021) http://arbitrationblog.kluwerarbitration.com/2021/04/06/the-rise-of-ma-arbitration/.
21. Article 1813 of the Federal Civil Code.
22. Article 1814 of the Federal Civil Code.
23. *See supra* n. 9, 343.
24. *Ibid.*

lake at a hotel. His parents sued the hotel company, seeking compensation for moral damages, civil liability, and court expenses. This case is noteworthy because it marks the first time the Mexican Supreme Court granted punitive damages to the family.[25]

Considering the novelty of awarding punitive damages, there is a somewhat unnoticed precedent that could apply to indemnities. In analyzing the validity of the release contracts signed by the guests at the start of their stay, the Supreme Court emphasized that such contracts can only waive private rights that do not directly affect the public interest or affect third parties.[26]

When taken out of its original context (i.e., tort liability for the hotel's negligence), the aforementioned precedent could have an impact on the interpretation of claims brought by third parties.

[C] COMMON SHAREHOLDER'S DISPUTES

Governance claims may arise concerning shareholder's meetings, surveillance rights (such as the request for information, reviewing the company's operations, and approving financial statements), the exercise of minority rights depending on the entity type, as well as opposition and nullity claims.[27]

A family member of a person with a disability filed a request before court (known as "jurisdicción voluntaria") to have their relative declared as being in a state of interdiction. Given that this person was a shareholder in a company, the family member petitioned the judge to request information from the company regarding the person's rights to dividends under the shareholder's agreement to calculate his living expenses based on the income of those dividends.[28]

The court determined it appropriate to require the company to provide information concerning the person's corporate rights, as a measure of protection of its assets, pursuant to Article 12, numeral 5 of the Convention on the Rights of Persons with Disabilities.[29]

Regarding opposition claims, the LGSM provides that resolutions passed by shareholders' meetings are binding even for absent or dissenting shareholders, except

25. Mexican Supreme Court of Justice, Center for Constitutional Studies of Mexico's Supreme Court of Justice, *Excerpt of the Amparo Directo 30/2013* (2014) https://www.scjn.gob.mx/derechos-humanos/sites/default/files/sentencias-emblematicas/summary/2022-02/Summary%20AD 30-2013%20HRO.pdf.
26. Mexican Supreme Court of Justice, *Amparo Directo 30/2013* (2014).
27. Alejandro García González et al., *The Mergers and Acquisitions Litigation Review*, 3rd edn, p. 117 (Roger A Cooper (ed.), October 2022).
28. Tesis aislada I.3o.C.6 CS (10a.), digital registry: 2023789 (2021).
29. *Ibid. See also* Art. 12 of the Convention on the Rights of Persons with Disabilities.

for the right of opposition. According to the LGSM, shareholders representing 25% of the capital have the right to oppose such resolutions and request an injunction to suspend its effects while the procedure takes place. The claimants must fulfill the following requirements:[30]

(1) File the opposition claim within fifteen days following the shareholder's meeting.
(2) Have voted against the resolution or not attended the meeting.
(3) Specify the violation of the bylaws or legal provisions.
(4) Deposit their shares until the trial finishes.
(5) Post a bond to cover the possible damages from the non-execution of the resolutions if the court determines the opposition claim to be without merit.

However, the purpose of the action of nullity is to render the shareholder's meeting null and void. This can occur for several reasons, such as:

(1) Lack of notice of meeting.
(2) Failure to meet the requirements for proper notice (i.e., lack of capacity of the person issuing the notice, or failure to include date and agenda).
(3) Inadequate publicity of the meeting.
(4) The meeting taking place in a location or on a date different from what was indicated in the notice, or in a place other than the corporate domicile.
(5) Insufficient representation of shareholders with the required amounts of capital needed to establish a quorum.

Unlike an opposition claim which challenges a specific agreement or act, a nullity claim challenges the entire meeting. The objection in a nullity claim is that the requirements for the meeting were not fulfilled.

Courts grant injunctions to preserve rights rather than constitute them. It is possible to seek an injunction under Mexican Law, provided the requesting party demonstrates a substantial likelihood of success on the merits and proof of irreparable harm if there is no grant for relief. Mexican courts require evidence of a preexisting right to justify the granting of an injunction. If granted, the judge will request the posting of a bond, the amount of which is determined at the court's discretion.[31]

Regarding nullity claims, Mexican courts have determined that due to their distinct nature from opposition claims, the regulations pertaining to opposition claims cannot be applied by analogy to nullity claims. Therefore, in a nullity claim, claimants are unable to seek an injunction to suspend the agreements

30. *Supra* n. 5, Arts. 200-205.
31. Tesis jurisprudencial IIa./J. 196/2005, digital registry: 174971 (2005).

reached in a shareholders' meeting. These agreements will remain in effect until the nullity of the meeting is declared.[32]

However, courts have recognized that it is possible to grant injunctions to suspend the effects of an irregular board of directors meeting. In the case reviewed, among other reasons, the court highlighted that: (1) the meeting took place with only two present members when a majority should be present according to its bylaws; and (2) there was no evidence of a prior designation of the person who acted as president in such meeting.[33]

The court determined that such irregularities presume the illegality of the meeting. Therefore, due to the intention to execute the agreements of the meeting promptly, it justifies granting an injunction because the damage in the delay would constitute irreparable damages.[34]

Moreover, the court considered that the circumstances justified the suspension of the resolution's effects, as it implied that the board of directors meeting was illegal due to its violation of the bylaws and applicable legislation. Therefore, it is debatable whether this precedent expands the possibility of using injunctions to suspend acts related to shareholder's meetings, including cases where nullity claims are pursued.

Shareholders may also bring claims based on an alleged violation of their contractual rights as contained in the bylaws of the company or the shareholders' agreement. The type of claim will depend on the nature of the breached obligation, the party against whom the claim is being made (i.e., another shareholder, the company, or the board of directors) and the remedy sought. Examples of such claims include violations of the right to first refusal, drag- or tag-along clauses, and the lack of approval for selling shares.

Recently, a dispute emerged when a legal entity purchased shares of a publicly traded company beyond the maximum limit established in its bylaws to gain control of such company. This led to a commercial trial challenging the validity of these transactions, with a focus on Article 48 of the Stock Markets Law, the statutory limits that prevented the acquisition of shares that give control of the company to third parties or to stockholders themselves.[35]

Article 48 of the Stock Markets Law regulates the power of corporations to include provisions in its bylaws aimed at safeguarding against the risks associated with the loss of corporate control in stock market operations. This Article grants corporations the power to design protective measures through their highest governing body.[36]

32. *Ibid.*
33. Tesis aislada I.15o.C.77 C (10a.), digital registry: 2024265 (2022).
34. *Ibid.*
35. Tesis aislada 1a. VIII/2022 (10a.), digital registry: 2024256 (2022).
36. *Ibid.*

The First Chamber of the Supreme Court of Justice of the Nation determined that Article 48 of the Stock Markets Law is constitutional as it upholds the economic freedoms enshrined in Article 5 of the Mexican Federal Constitution. The Chamber ruled that this provision enables companies to protect themselves against hostile takeovers while also establishing procedural and substantive requirements to safeguard minority rights, prevent shareholder discrimination, and prohibit absolute impediments to take control.[37]

In an M&A transaction context, shareholder disputes can arise for various reasons. For instance, shareholders may seek to prevent the completion of the transaction or to compel the sale of the company. These disputes can also occur after the transaction has taken place, typically concerning issues related to the management and operation of the company.[38]

For example, a dispute emerged between Company A and Company B due to a shareholder's agreement. In 2020, Company B acquired a 50% stake in X, a broadcaster operating seventeen radio stations in Mexico. Company A, the other major shareholder of X, accused Company B of unilaterally appointing new board members and unauthorized usage of company systems and bank accounts. Company B then argued that the shareholder agreement entered into with Company A back in 2020 was invalid.[39]

Company A invoked a multi-tiered resolution clause that provided a fifteen-day conciliation process, followed by ICC arbitration. Anne Mürle acted as the emergency arbitrator and granted Company A's request to compel Company B to adhere to the shareholder's agreement. However, Mürle denied Company A's request to withhold Company B from using X's signatures and bank accounts.[40]

During the conciliation proceedings, Company A appointed Ricardo Alarcón Gaviria, a Colombian Lawyer, while Company B appointed José Ramón Cossío Díaz, a former Justice of the Mexican Supreme Court. The conciliation proceeding was unsuccessful. Through ICC Arbitration, Company A sought confirmation of its position as a shareholder of X and damages. At the same time, Company A filed proceedings in Mexican Courts to safeguard the broadcaster's operations and obtained a favorable judgment that declared that Company B's shareholder resolution, which appointed new members, was null and void.[41]

Ultimately, Company A and Company B settled the dispute and agreed to coexist and grow the business. This case serves as an illustrative example of the

37. *Ibid.*
38. *See supra* n. 9, 379.
39. Jack Ballantyne, *Dispute over Mexican Broadcaster Settles at ICC*, Global Arbitration Review (April 2022) https://globalarbitrationreview.com/article/dispute-over-mexican-broadcaster-settles-icc.
40. *Ibid.*
41. *Ibid.*

types of disputes that may occur between shareholders in the context of an M&A transaction, as well as the use of multi-tiered clauses[42] in such agreements.

[D] RELEVANT CONSIDERATIONS AS TO MEANS OF DISPUTE RESOLUTION

This section examines two key aspects related to M&A transactions and shareholder disputes: (1) the preference for arbitration in M&A transactions; and (2) the arbitrability of shareholder's disputes.

[1] Arbitration of M&A Transactions

Although various types of disputes can arise in M&A transactions, arbitration is often the preferred method for resolving them.[43] Practice shows that "parties almost inevitably agree on arbitration for the resolution of their disputes arising out of M&A."[44] Arbitration seems to be the prevalent choice as a dispute resolution in M&A transactions in Latin America.[45]

Scholars and experts have highlighted the advantages of arbitration in the context of M&A transactions. Parties have the flexibility to choose a neutral venue for arbitration proceedings, which is particularly advantageous given the complex, cross-border, and specialized nature of these transactions.[46] Below, this chapter will further examine additional factors within Mexico's legal system that may favor arbitration in M&A transactions.

Unlike Delaware's Courts, recognized as a leading business jurisdiction with significant experience in resolving corporate and business controversies, Mexico has no special court for these specialized transactions. Therefore, local, or federal civil courts solve all commercial disputes.

As mentioned previously in this chapter, Mexican Legislation does not comprehensively regulate M&A transactions. Many aspects of these agreements are terms of art not provided for in the law. Therefore, explaining and proving industry practices before Mexican courts can turn the procedure burdensome. In contrast, parties can choose arbitrators who have experience drafting these transactions, which inevitably aids in the resolution of the dispute.

Moreover, most transactions, agreements and related documentation are drafted in English, so costly translations that might otherwise be needed for state court

42. Multi-tier clauses are clauses that comprise different steps, each incorporating a form of ADR, and leading to arbitration as the last method of dispute resolution. *See* Craig Tevendale et al., *Multi-tier Dispute Resolution Clauses and Arbitration*: *The Turkish Commercial Law Review*, Vol. 1 No. 1, 31 (2015).
43. *See supra* n. 12.
44. *Ibid.*
45. *See supra* n. 2, 180.
46. *Ibid.*

proceedings are not necessary for arbitration.[47] The Mexican Commercial Code requires that the corresponding Spanish translation must accompany any document drafted in a foreign language.[48]

Arbitration rules provide that all notifications shall be made to the last address of the party or its representative for whom the same are intended, as notified either by the party in question or by any other party. Such communications may be made by delivery against receipt, email, registered post, courier, etc.[49]

In contrast, the requirements under Mexican law for rendering notice to a defendant are highly formalistic. For example, all notifications must be personal. In most cases, the court clerk must ensure that the person/entity to be notified resides there or is the place of business of the defendant.[50] Moreover, considering the international context of M&A transactions, rendering notice to an entity outside of Mexican jurisdiction through a letter rogatory can take months, making the procedure inefficient.

Moreover, one of the biggest takeaways of COVID-19 was a decrease in in-person closings, as it has become accustomed to closing transactions electronically.[51] In addition to speeding up the closing, electronic signing of transactions will continue to favor arbitration as the preferred forum for these types of deals.

Arbitration has always been more flexible than litigation regarding formal document requirements. The Commerce Code provides that parties may use electronic, optical, or any other technology in the formation of acts of commerce.[52] However, courts have not yet directly interpreted the validity of electronic signatures through programs such as DocuSign or AdobeSign, nor the burden of proof that must be met so a court can deem such transactions valid.

Furthermore, it is advisable to include an arbitration clause when anticipating a difficult evidentiary situation in a dispute, especially when important evidence is in the possession of the opposing party.[53] Unlike arbitration, where parties can agree on a document production phase to exchange relevant evidence, Mexican legislation does not offer extensive opportunities for the use of evidence that is not within the control of the parties involved.

For instance, if a party is unable to present a document to support its claim, it must make a sworn statement explaining why it cannot produce the document. If the court deems it appropriate, it may order the person or entity in possession of the document to present it before the court. If the person or entity refuses to comply, the court may impose various measures of constraint, such as fines, a maximum thirty-six-hour arrest, or the use of public force.[54] However, it is uncommon for a court to

47. *See supra* n. 12.
48. Article 1055 of the Commerce Code.
49. Article 3 of the ICC Arbitration Rules. *See also* Art. 3 of the CAM Arbitration Rules.
50. Article 311 of the Federal Procedure Code.
51. Chambers and Partners, *M&A Market in Mexico After the COVID Era*, https://chambers.com/content/item/4731.
52. Article 89 of the Commerce Code.
53. *See supra* n. 9, 11.
54. Articles 73, 95, and 295 of the Civil Procedure Code for Mexico City.

draw legal consequences from the failure to produce a document in the possession of the opposing party, unlike in arbitration where adverse inferences can be used.

Another factor to consider is that M&A transactions often involve multiple contracts and multiple parties. This may be due to the composition of the purchaser, seller, or target company, which may be comprised of multiple entities. Moreover, a transaction may involve various agreements, such as a share purchase agreement, a shareholder agreement, an escrow agreement, or a guarantee, among others.[55]

Most arbitration rules provide for the requirements and procedures for consolidating arbitrations and allowing the joinder of third parties. Consolidation is typically allowed in the following situations: (1) when the parties agree to it; (2) when all claims are made under the same arbitration agreement; (3) when multiple agreements are involved, but the arbitrations involve the same parties, the dispute arises in connection with the same legal relationship and the arbitration agreements are compatible.[56]

If a party wishes to join an additional party to the arbitration, it must submit its request for arbitration against the additional party. The arbitral tribunal will consider various factors in deciding whether to grant the request for a joinder, including the tribunal's prima facie jurisdiction over the additional party, the timing of the request, potential conflicts of interest, and the impact of the joinder on the arbitration procedure.[57]

A claimant will typically prefer to resolve the dispute through a single arbitration proceeding to avoid conflicting decisions from parallel proceedings. Therefore, when drafting transaction agreements, it is important to include compatible arbitration clauses. Arbitration agreements are considered compatible if they specify the same arbitration rules, seat, language, method for the constitution of the tribunal, and number of arbitrators. This ensures consistency and facilitates the consolidation of multiple disputes into a single arbitration, promoting efficiency and coherence in the resolution process.[58]

While these requirements may seem burdensome, it is important to consider that the standards for consolidation or joinder in Mexican courts are generally higher than those set forth by arbitration institutions. Under Mexican legislation, consolidation requires that the decision in one case directly affects the establishment, constitution, or modification of something related to the same facts in another case. Consolidation must be requested before any hearing takes place in either case.[59]

Joinder works similarly to arbitration under Mexican procedural rules as they provide that when a third party has a dispute with a party of the trial, and the judgment is to influence such dispute, the parties may join the third party before the final hearing takes place.[60]

Therefore, in addition to the preference for arbitration in M&A transactions, given the international context of these transactions or the specialization of the arbitrators,

55. *See supra* n. 9, 183-184.
56. Article 10 of the ICC Arbitration Rules.
57. Article 7 of the ICC Arbitration Rules.
58. *See supra* n. 9, 183-184.
59. Article 72 of the Federal Procedural Code.
60. Article 78 of the Federal Procedural Code.

the previously analyzed elements may favor arbitration clauses for transactions related to Mexico.

[2] Arbitrability of Shareholder's Disputes

There are lengthy discussions worldwide as to whether shareholders can agree on an arbitration clause in their bylaws. The main concern is whether some issues of a shareholder's agreement are non-arbitrable and therefore barred from resolution through arbitration.

Authors have pointed out that this is not necessarily an issue given that in Mexico, most of the non-arbitrable matters belong to public law. Some, such as family matters, are expressly prohibited by law from arbitration. Other non-arbitrable matters are criminal law, tax law, and administrative law.[61]

However, some questioned the inefficacy of agreeing to arbitration in shareholder's agreements because they considered that, given the importance of the opposition action and the time it would take to constitute an arbitral tribunal to combat the disputed shareholder decision. However, this discussion was overcome by the development of interim measures in Mexican laws in aid of arbitration and express provisions in arbitration rules for emergency arbitrators.[62]

Therefore, in theory, the same aspects analyzed in the previous chapter as to M&A transaction disputes should apply to shareholders' agreements. However, this discussion is not unfinished, especially considering the public-private nature of some entities. For example, inquiries have arisen in the United States as to whether arbitration provisions set forth in the bylaws of a public corporation can be unenforceable against shareholders, who may want to seek a class action before a court instead of going to arbitration.[63]

[E] CONCLUSIONS

M&A disputes will inevitably arise due to the increasing number of transactions. As new legislation developments emerge in shareholder legislation, it will be intriguing to observe the new precedents set by Mexican Courts on these matters. While arbitration appears to offer advantages for resolving both M&A and shareholder disputes, it is important to note that it is not a one-size-fits-all solution.

---

61. Gonzalo Uribarri Carpintero, *La Relación Entre El Arbitraje y Otras Formas de Justicia Pública y Privada. Una Referencia al Arbitraje Mexicano* (2005) https://archivos.juridicas.unam.mx/www/bjv/libros/4/1653/13.pdf.
62. Francisco González de Cossío, *Arbitrabilidad de Controversias en Materia de Sociedades Mercantiles*, http://www.gdca.com.mx/PDF/arbitraje/ARBITRABILIDAD%20CONTROVERSIAS.pdf. *See also*, Art. 29 of the ICC Arbitration Rules.
63. Mohsen Manesh & Hoseph Grundfest, *The Corporate Contract and Shareholder Arbitration*, Harvard Law School Forum on Corporate Governance (2022), https://corpgov.law.harvard.edu/2022/11/10/the-corporate-contract-and-shareholder-arbitration/.

CHAPTER 19

Technology and International Arbitration in Mexico*

Luis Omar Guerrero Rodríguez, Eduardo Lobatón Guzmán, Andrés Peña Loyo & Fernanda Serrano Cortez

> Any sufficiently advanced technology is indistinguishable from magic.
>
> –Arthur C. Clarke.

[A] INTRODUCTION: TECH OR NOT TECH? IS THERE EVEN A QUESTION?[1]

Tech or not tech? After the last few years of staggering technological advancements, this should not even be a question. Technology has advanced at unprecedented rates during the last few years. Wholesale shifts to economies are easy to recognize when looking in the rear-view mirror. The beginning of one is not so easy to spot while it is in progress.[2] It is clear, however, that we are witnessing a technological revolution that will allow us to see unrivalled economic, social, and cultural changes.[3]

Technology has deeply reached the legal profession and, in particular, it has reached arbitration. It has already started to revolutionize the way we see, present,

* The views and opinions expressed in this article are those of the authors and do not necessarily reflect the position of Hogan Lovells or its clients.

1. Small adaptation of the title released by the IBA Arbitration Conference that will take place in Colombia in March 2023.
2. Joe Hipsky, *Recognizing the Technological Revolution and Preparing for the 'Next Economy'*, Forbes (14 Oct. 2020) available at https://www.forbes.com/sites/forbesbusinessdevelopmentcouncil/2020/10/14/recognizing-the-technological-revolution-and-preparing-for-the-next-economy/?sh=358846563965.
3. Klaus Schwab, *The Fourth Industrial Revolution* 28 (Currency 2017).

advocate, and think about arbitration proceedings, and it seems that technology will revolutionize arbitration even more fundamentally shortly.

This article addresses the impact of technology on the practice of arbitration in Mexico. The following sections delve into the what, how, and why of different pieces of technology and how they have been and will be used in each state of arbitration. Arbitrators, institutions, and counsel already incorporate 'common' technologies such as file hosting systems (e.g., *Dropbox* or *Google Drive*) instead of physical binders, and virtual hearings instead of or complementing in-person hearings. More advanced artificial intelligence (AI) tools are already present in our daily lives and lawyers have seen a substantial change in the practice of law due to its increasing use.[4] Some examples of its use include contract analysis, legal research, and e-discovery, among others.

However, this article also explores the use of other far-reaching technologies that may well change the rules of the game, such as predictive coding, systems for the appointment of arbitrators, case management, cost estimations, systems that can recreate certain events, objects, or places subject to arbitration and, most controversially, AI decision-making or predictive justice. As artificial intelligence makes its way into the legal profession, we will probably see an increased use in arbitration proceedings in Mexico.[5]

To explain the use of these technologies in arbitrations in Mexico, the authors begin by describing how arbitral tribunals have adapted during the past few years to the current realities of technology (section [B]). Then, this article takes us step-by-step through the arbitration and explains what technologies are currently used and what technologies might appear in the future in every step of the proceeding, from preparing for and starting the arbitration (section [C]), to conducting the arbitration proceeding (section [D]) to reaching a final decision and dealing with the post-award remedies (section [E]). Finally, the authors conclude (section [F]).

We certainly do not own a crystal ball to predict what the future of arbitration will look like, but the current trends allow us to imagine what we might see. For now, we can assure you that with the increased use of technological tools, there will be a need for attorneys who are experts in the development of algorithms, machine training, and data interpretation, among others.

[B] THE ADAPTABILITY ARBITRATION

New technological tools have greatly influenced arbitration proceedings worldwide and Mexico in particular. The implementation and use of technology in arbitration proceedings have posed a challenge to the arbitration world. Arbitrators and party

4. 'Theory and development of computer systems able to perform tasks normally requiring human intelligence, such as visual perception, speech recognition, decision-making, and translation between languages.' (*See* John McCarthy quoted in Maxi Scherer (ed.), *Artificial Intelligence and Legal Decision-Making: The Wide Open?*, 36(5) Journal of International Arbitration 542 (2019) https://doi.org/10.54648/joia2019028).
5. Hogan Lovells' Senior Associate Orlando Cabrera also wrote a great article on the subject: *The Future of International Arbitration in the Age of Artificial Intelligence*, 40(5) Journal of International Arbitration 301-342 (2023) https://doi.org/10.54648/joia2023014.

representatives around the globe were – until recently – not truly tech-savvy. Reluctance to use technology, unavailability, lack of expertise, high cost involved and arguments related to the imbalance of arms, and due-process paranoia were some of the problems that arose. In addition, the entire arbitration community had to adapt, up-skill, or re-skill in the use of new technologies to manage the new arbitration trends.

Arbitration laws[6] and arbitral institutions had to quickly adapt their rules and ways of working[7] in the face of a new challenge and the prohibition of holding in-person hearings due to the COVID-19 lockdowns. Arbitral practitioners created protocols aimed at providing certainty to parties implementing technological tools in order to commence or continue with proceedings. The end result was that thanks to the technology available and the flexibility inherent to arbitration, arbitration proceedings never stopped, while the majority of court proceedings in Mexico did.

Mexico has followed these technological adaptation trends but at a slower pace. Unlike other countries' laws, Mexico's Arbitration Law[8] has not been reformed to include any technological solutions during the arbitration proceedings and the rules of the main arbitration institutions in Mexico reacted less speedy to amend their rules. For instance, just very recently (December 2022), the Mexican Arbitration Centre (CAM) amended its institutional rules to adapt to the technological wave.[9]

Technology has been a part of arbitration proceedings for several years. A substantial part of the proceedings is usually online (e.g., filing of pleadings and evidence, communications with the Tribunal, among others), but the use of technology has lately intensified. Pending and new cases were the beneficiaries of the use of videoconferencing through different platforms. Protocols, guidelines, and other useful information to facilitate the remote conduct of hearings became the new tasks for arbitration institutions worldwide,[10] and new techniques to be effective at presentations of cases and cross-examinations of witnesses and experts became the latest toolkit for arbitration practitioners.[11]

The Mexican judiciary has not yet decided on any arbitration-related cases dealing with these new technological trends. Mexico is lagging. By way of example, the

6. *See, e.g.*, Art. 1072b(4), Dutch Code of Civil Procedure.
7. For example, ICSID made electronic filling the new default procedure (*ICSID Makes Electronic Filing its Default Procedure* (13 Mar. 2020) available at https://icsid.worldbank.org/news-and-events/news-releases/icsid-makes-electronic-filing-its-default-procedure); the 2022 ICSID Rule 4 provides that the request for arbitration shall be filed electronically; the LCIA new arbitration rules require the request for arbitration to be submitted electronically; the updated AAA Arbitration Rules set forth the possibility of arbitrators ordering the use of technology in any stage of the proceeding.
8. Mexico adopted the 1985 UNCITRAL Model Law on International Commercial Arbitration in 1993, by incorporation into the Commerce Code. In 2011, Mexican Congress amended the Commerce Code to adopt some of the 2006 amendments to the UNCITRAL Model Law.
9. For example, Art. 20(1) of the CAM Rules now provides the possibility of holding hearings remotely.
10. For instance, members of different firms drafted the Seoul Protocol on Video Conferencing in International Arbitration. The CIARB published the Guidance Note on Remote Dispute Resolution Proceedings, and several law firms, such as Hogan Lovells, also drafted protocols for the use of technology in virtual international arbitration hearings.
11. Omar Guerrero Rodríguez and Eduardo Lobatón Guzmán, *Arbitration: A Good Alternative During the COVID-19 Pandemic*, Mexico Business News (2020).

Mexican judiciary has recently issued binding precedents in matters relating to the use of e-signatures[12] but just a few months ago was still debating what an '*authenticated*' award is[13] and some courts were adopting very old-fashioned and formalistic interpretations[14] that do not align with current tech trends. Just recently, the First Chamber of the Supreme Court of Justice rendered a couple of important decisions supporting arbitration although not technology-related (concerning the meaning of the right to fully present your case and the fact that there is no violation of the Mexican constitution for not having a right to appeal on the merits of an arbitration award).[15]

Since arbitration has been adopting and implementing technological solutions, in the following sections the authors explore the impact of technology in the practice of arbitration in Mexico.

[C] PREPARING FOR AND STARTING THE ARBITRATION

Technology is present before the arbitration even begins. From the selection of the arbitrator to the method of filing the request for arbitration, technology has started to change the practice of arbitration in Mexico. In this section, the authors explore the technological advances in the preparation and commencement of arbitration, as well as the advances we might see soon.

[1] The Steps We Have Taken: Where Are We?

Technological developments have created at least two main transformations in the way attorneys prepare for an arbitration: the selection of the arbitrator and e-filing. In addition, we are seeing an increase in technology disputes.

[a] Arbitrator Selection and Conflict Checks

One of the main advantages of arbitration (over court litigation) is that parties are entitled to appoint an arbitrator who is an expert in the subject matter of the dispute.[16] An expert arbitrator will have a faster and better understanding of the dispute and, ideally, reach a better final decision. Thus, the arbitrator's selection becomes a fundamental task in the preparation of the case.

Law firms and arbitral institutions spend several hours determining who is the best candidate for the case (considering expertise, nationality, language capabilities,

12. The Mexican Judiciary recently determined that a lawsuit filed using an e-signature is valid. *See* Digital Record: 2016520, Thesis: 2a./J. 19/2018 (10a.). '*FIRMA ELECTRÓNICA. ES VÁLIDA LA DEMANDA DE AMPARO DIRECTO QUE LA CONTIENE, PRESENTADA MEDIANTE EL EMPLEO DE LAS TECNOLOGÍAS DE LA INFORMACIÓN, AUN CUANDO NO EXISTA CONVENIO DE COORDINACIÓN CON EL PODER JUDICIAL DE LA FEDERACIÓN.*'
13. *See infra* section [V][A].
14. *See infra* section [V][A].
15. Amparo Directo en Revisión 7790/2019. First Chamber of the Supreme Court of Justice. December 2022.
16. Margaret Moses, *The Principles and Practice of International Commercial Arbitration* 4 (2017).

absence of conflicts, among others) and researching potential conflicts of interest. Now, technology has been able to drastically reduce the amount of time and energy devoted to this task and several organizations/companies can aid attorneys with this key decision.

Kluwer Arbitration developed a tool that links arbitrators, experts, and counsels' profiles with related publications and awards.[17] In addition, platforms like Kluwer Arbitration and Jus Mundi, developed a conflict checker, which identifies relationships between individuals, firms, or states in minutes, revealing potential conflicts of interest, and saving time and costs.[18] There are also other platforms that provide information about arbitrators, including arbitrators' responses regarding their procedural preferences and practices, as well as the names of lawyers who have represented parties in cases before them and other members of the arbitration panel.[19]

Arbitrator Intelligence is another company that collects feedback from arbitration users and lawyers on key elements of an arbitrator's decision, including the duration, case management, procedural orders, document production, jurisdictional awards, injunctive relief, damages analysis, and legal methodology. Then, data analysis provides parties with critical knowledge about the arbitrator's track record.[20] By using this tool, choosing the right or adequate arbitrator for a case becomes a simpler task.

With these tools, in a matter of seconds, arbitration online platforms present to the attorney potential conflicts of interest by showing direct and indirect relationships between the arbitrator and the counsel, detailing the cases in which the arbitrator and counsel have been together. Further, all the research to find 'expert' arbitrators with good case management – which would take a lawyer several hours – can also be done in a matter of minutes by *Arbitrator Intelligence*. The time and cost implications of this are conspicuous. Shortly, we may even see machines making the entire selection of arbitrators for us.

[b] Starting the Arbitration: E-Filing

Arbitration practice in Mexico has also moved from the physical filing of the request for arbitration to electronic filing. E-filing is one of the topics that the main arbitration institutions in Mexico barely regulate. This provides the parties with a wide range of options to file, whether it is physically or electronically. Below we will comment about the rules of the two main Mexican arbitration institutions.

Article 3 of CANACO's Arbitration Rules sets forth that the party recurring to arbitration must file the *written* request for arbitration.[21] Article 2.3 of said Rules

17. Wolters Kluwer Launches Data-Driven Enhancements to Arbitrator Tool within Kluwer Arbitration Practice Plus, *Kluwer Arbitration Blog* (19 Nov. 2021), available at https://arbitrationblog.kluwerarbitration.com/2021/11/19/wolters-kluwer-launches-data-driven-enhancements-to-arbitrator-tool-within-kluwer-arbitration-practice-plus/.
18. Kluwer Arbitration, available at https://www.wolterskluwer.com/en/solutions/kluwerarbitration and Jus Mundi, available at https://jusmundi.com/en/about.
19. GAR's ART goes live! *Global Arbitration Review* (30 Mar. 2017).
20. Arbitrator Intelligence, available at https://arbitratorintelligence.com/about-1.
21. Article 3, CANACO Rules.

defines 'written' as any interchange of telex, telegrams, telefax, e-mail, or any other means of communication that leaves proof of the information contained in such.[22] In this sense, e-filing is available under these rules.

By contrast, the CAM Arbitration Rules provide that the party initiating the arbitration must *submit* its request for arbitration before the Secretary-General.[23] Unlike CANACO's Arbitration Rules, the CAM Rules do not provide a specific definition of 'submit'. However, similar to CANACO's Arbitration Rules, Article 3.1 of the CAM Arbitration Rules provides the possibility to submit any of the filings through e-mail, certified mail, postal service, or fax.[24]

In practice, due to arbitration's inherent flexibility, arbitration institutions have been open to receiving and processing requests for arbitration filed electronically. Arbitration in Mexico has been quick to adapt and the prevalent practice of filing the initial request in physical format became outdated and the main arbitration institutions receive and process electronic requests.

[c] Increasing Disputes about Technology

There has been an increase in disputes *about* technology or involving tech companies. Unlike energy companies, tech companies have not traditionally relied on investment treaties to protect their investments. This is now changing as tech companies are becoming more aware of investment treaty protections.[25]

For example, in 2020, Uber threatened to bring an investment claim against Colombia due to a nationwide ban on Uber's app.[26] Another example is *ES Holdings v. Mexico*,[27] where Canadian and US investors filed a NAFTA claim after Mexico City cancelled a concession to incorporate digital taximeters and develop a ride-hailing app. This is interesting because, while this article discusses the influence of technology on arbitration, it seems like arbitration is also influencing the decisions of tech companies.

[2] The Next Frontier: Where Are We Going?

While the above refinements and improvements are significant in terms of time and cost, we might soon witness additional technologies incorporated into the preparation

22. Article 2.3, CANACO Rules.
23. Article 6, CAM Rules.
24. Article 3.1 of the CAM Arbitration Rules is similar to Art. 3(2) of the ICC Rules (effective January 2021). Art. 4.3 of the LCIA Rules (2020) also provides the possibility of exchange communications trough electronics means. Rule R-44 of the AAA Rules (2022) provides that the service methods set forth in Rule R-4(b)(iii), including electronic service/email, may also be used for any communication.
25. Luis Paradell and Santiago Gatica, ISDS Landscape in Latin America for 2022, *Kluwer Arbitration Blog* (19 Apr. 2022), available at http://arbitrationblog.kluwerarbitration.com/2022/04/19/isds-landscape-in-latin-america-for-2022/.
26. Nelson Bocanegra, Uber quiere regresar a Colombia, considera arbitraje internacional, *Reuters* (3 Feb. 2020), available at https://www.reuters.com/article/colombia-uber-idLTAKBN1ZX2DH.
27. *Espiritu Santo Holdings, LP (ES Holdings) v. Mexico*, ICSID Case No. ARB/20/13.

of a case, which may bring even more savings, as well as legal implications. These are the complete automatization of document review and the use of sophisticated AI predictive tools.

[a] Completely Automated Document Review: Predictive Coding

Specialized software for document review already exists and is commonly used in the legal profession in the fields of investigations, M&A transactions, and discovery in the United States. The new challenge is to apply these programs to arbitration proceedings.

'Predictive coding is a form of supervised machine learning AI by which relevant documents or documents responsive to a document request or a tribunal order are identified by an algorithm.'[28] It is also known as computer-assisted or technology-assisted review.

In arbitrations where attorneys need to review large numbers of documents and other information in preparation for their case, technology-assisted review (such as *Brainspace*, *Relativity*, *Everlaw*, *Logikcull*, *CS Disco*, *Evisort*, and *Kira Systems*) can outperform associates in terms of accuracy, speed and memory.[29] Technology-assisted review works with artificial intelligence by using algorithms to 'learn' what documents are relevant based on a set of documents that are manually reviewed and labelled by a human reviewer. The platform is fed with a data set, and lawyers prepare a protocol with search terms (e.g., words, names, dates) and then select documents to create a sample, which serves as the basis for the machine to predict which documents are useful for the case. The lawyer then reviews the documents to determine whether they are relevant and confirms or corrects the predictions made by the algorithm. The algorithm uses this information to classify the remaining documents as relevant or non-relevant. The process can be repeated as many times as needed, with the algorithm refining its categorization.[30]

Another tool is *Ross*, an IBM product that tries to emulate the legal research of a lawyer. *Ross* uses AI to understand questions, analyse unstructured information, and provide analytical answers to specific cases from case law. *Ross* reads hundreds of databases, processes the information, evaluates the relevant data, and delivers an answer.[31]

Even some law firms are developing similar technological tools. For instance, Hogan Lovells recently launched *ELTEMATE*, a technology product portfolio that includes several AI-based solutions, tools for eDiscovery, reporting, risk assessment,

---

28. ICC Commission Report, *Leveraging Technology for Fair, Effective and Efficient International Arbitration Proceedings*, International Chamber of Commerce (2021), 29.
29. Orlando F. Cabrera C., 'El Futuro del Arbitraje Internacional en la Era de la Inteligencia Artificial' in *Ensayos Sobre Arbitraje Comercial y de Inversión*, 22-23 (2022).
30. Claire Morel de Westgaver, *Artificial Intelligence: A Driver for Efficiency in International Arbitration – How Predictive Coding Can Change Document Production*, Kluwer Arbitration Blog (23 Feb. 2020), available at http://arbitrationblog.kluwerarbitration.com/2020/02/23/artificial-intelligence-a-driver-for-efficiency-in-international-arbitration-how-predictive-coding-can-change-document-production/.
31. Cabrera, *supra* n. 29, at 25.

project management, information analysis, regulatory updates, and mass litigation.[32] In December 2023, *ELTEMATE* launched a legal chatbot called *CRAIG*, which can be used to draft legal documents, summarize facts, extract and structure information into legal documents, and much more.[33]

Currently, most document reviews are made by attorneys individually reviewing each document. With the above tools, arbitration practitioners will likely have to transform this practice and let the specialized software do most of the review, while the attorneys do less. Automated review has evident benefits in terms of speed, accuracy and costs, but there might also be legal implications.

The use of these platforms *may* compromise the outcome of the case and potentially create professional liability for the attorneys. These software programs are increasingly accurate, but by delegating the review task, attorneys may risk that a potential *'smoking gun'* goes unnoticed. The future will oblige attorneys to carefully balance the efficiency and savings of costs and time against the risk of missing a key piece of evidence or incurring some sort of 'unauthorised practice of law' that although unknown in Mexico is regulated in other jurisdictions.

[b] Predictive Tools

Artificial intelligence can also be used as a risk-assessment tool. Parties could use predictive analytics to identify patterns in past disputes that could help predict the likelihood of future disputes in a particular industry or between certain parties. This information could be used to proactively address potential disputes through preventative measures, such as mediation or other ADR techniques. Predictive tools might also begin making their way into arbitration by analysing past decisions and identifying key factors that may have influenced such outcomes. This information could help develop predictive models to anticipate the likelihood of a successful outcome for a given dispute and to identify potential risk factors.

For example, LexisNexis' *Lex Machina* does litigation data mining of court dockets to reveal knowledge about judges and opposing parties. *Lex Machina* can show how likely a judge is to grant or deny a motion for summary judgment[34] and might even suggest the most persuasive language to be successful. This program is already in use for litigation in the US.

Another useful program is Dispute Resolution Data (DRD)[35] which has a database of 3,500 arbitration cases.[36] According to DRD, 52% of these cases ended with a settlement. With DRD, arbitration can be used as an effective tool to settle the dispute.

32. ELTEMATE, available at: https://eltemate.com/.
33. CRAIG, available at: https://craig.eltemate.com/login.
34. Lex Machina, available at https://lexmachina.com/what-we-do/.
35. DRD, available at https://www.disputeresolutiondata.com/about_drd.
36. Brian Canada, *A Data-Driven Exploration of Arbitration as a Settlement Tool: Does Reality Match Perception?* 11 NY Dispute Resolution Lawyer, 46-48 (2018).

A party with a strong position could try to predict, depending on the particulars of the case, when it should settle.[37]

We might see risk assessment tools shortly that could analyse data on the parties to the dispute, such as their financial resources, negotiating history, and track record in arbitration proceedings. This information could be used to identify potential risk factors and to develop strategies for addressing those risks in arbitration.

Overall, the use of AI for risk assessment in international arbitration could help parties anticipate and mitigate risk, and could ultimately lead to more efficient and effective resolution of disputes.

[D] CONDUCTING THE ARBITRATION

Now we turn to the conduct of the arbitration proceedings. In this section, we explore the technological advances in conducting arbitration proceedings and present further innovations we envision soon. We anticipate most of the innovations occurring in this stage. These changes bring with them several logistical and legal issues.

[1] The Steps We Have Taken: Technology Made Us Adapt

Arbitration rules and laws worldwide have been reformed to expressly regulate the use of technology during arbitration proceedings.[38] Mexico has not been the exception. The main technological advances Mexico has seen in the last couple of years are remote hearings and the use of electronic evidence (stored on or transmitted by an electronic device).

[a] Videoconferencing and Remote Hearings

As of 2020, there has been a dramatic change in the use of videoconferencing services, even though these services have been available for many years for the use of remote hearings.

Under Mexican Arbitration Law, the arbitral tribunal has broad powers to conduct the arbitration in such a manner as it considers appropriate.[39] This allows the arbitral tribunal to determine whether to hold remote hearings through videoconferencing. The new CAM Arbitration Rules, for example, now expressly regulate the possibility that prior consultation with the parties, and when there is no express agreement to the contrary, the arbitral tribunal may hold physical, remote or hybrid meetings and hearings, with the use of information and communications technology.[40]

---

37. Cabrera, *supra* n. 29, at 24.
38. For example, Arts 24(4) and 26(1) of the ICC Rules, R-11 of the AAA Commercial Arbitration Rules, and 14. 3 19.2 of the LCIA Rules, allow the use of videoconferencing.
39. Article 1435, Mexican Commerce Code.
40. Article 20.2, 2022 CAM Arbitration Rules.

The use of video conferencing services is not truly a technology innovation in arbitration. The revolution came with the response of States and arbitral institutions to adapt to the use of remote hearings and to protect the awards issued in arbitration proceedings. Parties and arbitrators have been able to quickly adapt to the circumstances and swiftly incorporated the use of videoconferencing throughout the entire proceedings.

The increase in video conferencing services did not come without new challenges. First, maintaining the privacy and security of proceedings, including the need to include cybersecurity protocols. The creation of recordings of the hearings through video conferencing services may compromise the confidentiality of the proceedings.[41] In that sense, some institutions like the Hong Kong International Arbitration Centre emphasize the importance of making virtual break-out rooms password-protected, with separate participant lists provided to the hearing manager in advance.[42]

Second, virtual hearings provoked arbitration awards to face challenges in its recognition and enforcement stage, under arguments of violation of the parties' right to be heard and treated equally.[43] Arbitral Tribunals must be vigilant to each party's particular situation when deciding to hold virtual hearings, ensuring that each party has the ability and technological possibility to fully present its case.[44]

It seems like such obstacles have started to dissipate, as to the authors' knowledge, there has not been any decision to set aside any award on the grounds of using videoconferencing services. On the contrary, many arbitral awards have been enforced, despite one of the parties arguing that virtual hearings violated their rights.[45] However, Mexican courts have yet to deal with this issue. Certainly, remote hearings assist importantly and it could be a great tool but not necessarily a perfect substitution[46] for in-presence hearing.

Videoconferencing has also brought instant advantages. Videoconferencing provides cost-efficient solutions to previous problems. For instance, in regards to transcripts, real-time stenographer providers are expensive. A tape recording of hearings with videoconferencing services may also be used as tapes may be transcribed later at cheaper costs.[47]

41. Nika Madyoon, Virtual Hearings in International Arbitration: Challenges, Solution, and Threats to Enforcement, *Arbitration: The International Journal of Arbitration, Mediation and Dispute Management* 603 (2021).
42. *HKIAC Guidelines for Virtual Hearings*. Hong Kong International Arbitration Centre (2020).
43. Maxi Scherer, *Remote Hearings in International Arbitration: An Analytical Framework*, 37(4) Journal of International Arbitration 438-439 (2020) https://doi.org/10.54648/joia2020020.
44. Madyoon, *supra* n. 41, at 604-605.
45. *See Sino Dragon Trading v. Noble Resources International* [2016] FCA 1131 (Federal Court of Australia); *Hanaro Shipping v. Cofftea Trading* [2015] EWHC 4293 (Comm) (English High Court); *China National Building Material Investment v. BNK International (W.D. Tex. 2009)*; *Teploenergetika v. Ep International*, 182 F.Supp.3d 556 (E.D. Va. 2016).
46. Borrowing the legal jargon of competition law as to perfect substitution when defining relevant markets.
47. ICC Commission Report. *Information Technology in International Arbitration*. International Chamber of Commerce (2017), available at https://iccwbo.org/wp-content/uploads/sites/3/2017/03/icc-information-technology-in-international-arbitration-icc-arbitration-adr-commission.pdf.

Virtual and remote hearings appear to be here to stay. Remote hearings are, in general, cost-efficient and a better alternative for short or simple hearings. Still, they bring several challenges that arbitration practitioners are still unsure how to overcome. For now, a hybrid model, with some virtual hearings and some in-person hearings, seems to be a good time and cost-saving solution.

[b] E-Evidence

The second big change was the increase in the use of electronic evidence. Mexican courts are extremely formalistic in procedural aspects related to the taking of evidence. In commercial proceedings, the parties need to file all documentary evidence, in its original format, in the initial claim, or the answer to the claim.[48]

This particular situation has been an important obstacle for parties in commercial proceedings. Preparing electronic documents to be filed before a court that complies with the requirements outlined in the Mexican Commercial Code has become a tedious and expensive process. Further, state courts have been unclear about the criteria that have to be met by e-evidence to be considered 'original' documents.

An additional obstacle has been the use of technology in evidence hearings, to present witness or expert testimonies. Under the current legislation, parties, witnesses, and experts, in principle, need to be physically present at hearings.[49] The use of communications technology is regulated by administrative rules issued by the Mexican Federal Judiciary Council and the local judiciary councils of each state.[50] This provides little legal certainty to the parties in the conduction of remote hearings. Additionally, courts have been reluctant to allow virtual hearings; their use increased significantly only after the COVID-19 pandemic. A recent study published by the think tank *México Evalúa* reveals that before the pandemic, only seven states had specific regulations and the necessary infrastructure to conduct virtual hearings.[51]

In this sense, arbitration proceedings have always been a safe haven for the taking of evidence. In general, due to arbitration's flexibility, arbitrators are more willing to accept the taking of evidence through electronic means. The increased use of e-evidence, however, did not come without additional hurdles.

Information stored in an electronic format is different from physical information contained in documents. Even considering the flexibility of arbitration, it is important that arbitral tribunals have clear guidelines to interpret the information. Electronically stored information has been identified to have some characteristics (e.g., greater volume and duplicability, metadata, changeable content, difficulty to delete, among

48. *See* Arts 1062, 1378 and 1390 bis 11, Mexican Commerce Code.
49. *See* Arts 1253, 1262, 1390 bis 42 and 1390 bis 47, Mexican Commerce Code.
50. *See, e.g.*, Mexican Judiciary Council, *ACUERDO GENERAL 12/2020, DEL PLENO DEL CONSEJO DE LA JUDICATURA FEDERAL.*
51. México Evalúa, *Las audiencias judiciales virtuales en México después de la pandemia*. (2024), available at https://www.mexicoevalua.org/wp-content/uploads/2024/03/audiencias-virtuales.pdf.

others) that differentiate it from physical documents and that is important to consider.[52] It is thus relevant that arbitration institutions and arbitration laws adapt and provide parties and arbitrators with clearer guidelines for taking e-evidence.

Some further hiccups arise in hearings using e-evidence, including the remote examination of witnesses, the loss of in-person observation, the possibility of witness coaching, handling of exhibits and ensuring reliable access to technology.[53]

There is still room for improvement and the possibility to create and further regulate the taking of e-evidence to create a predictable and reliable environment for the parties. Institutions and law firms worldwide have issued several protocols to address these issues; however, this seems to be missing in most arbitration laws. For Mexico, this is not the exception.

In sum, the way arbitration proceedings are conducted has changed, and possibly for good. Virtual and remote hearings, as well as e-evidence, will continue to be used in most arbitration proceedings to reduce costs and time, and parties will have to continue to improve their abilities to convey their arguments remotely.

[2] The Next Frontier: Technology Will Make Us Better

Despite the steps we have taken to incorporate technology into the arbitration proceedings, there are additional tools that could transform the way we present cases before the arbitral tribunal. We explore these changes in the following sections.

[a] Live Notes: Transcripts, Translation and Interpretation

Stenography is the act of recording spoken words through shorthand using a stenotype machine.[54] Stenography is frequently used in litigation in other jurisdictions like the US and is also used in arbitration proceedings. Currently, stenography remains the most widely used form, both in and out of the courtroom. A very important branch of AI is speech-to-text. Because of the developments in this branch, traditional stenography may soon cease to be used in arbitration.

Software developers have already created speech-to-text technology that listens to the speaker and transcribes the speech in real time and with outstanding precision. There are free apps like Google's *Live Transcribe* that use automatic speech recognition to transcribe speech in the real world to on-screen text.[55]

52. Carole Malinvaud, Will Electronic Evidence and E-Discovery Change the Face of Arbitration?, in Teresa Giovannini and Alexis Mourre (eds), *Written Evidence and Discovery in International Arbitration: New Issues and Tendencies*, 376-377 (2009).
53. Queen Mary University, 2021 International Arbitration Survey (2021), available at https://arbitration.qmul.ac.uk/media/arbitration/docs/LON0320037-QMUL-International-Arbitration-Survey-2021_19_WEB.pdf; Scherer, *supra* n. 43, at 427, 429.
54. Harvinder Singh, *A Book of Stenography*, Introduction (2006).
55. Vignesh Giridharan, *Here's How Google Is Putting AI to Work in Healthcare, Environmental Conservation, Agriculture and More*, Digit (15 Jul. 2019), available at https://www.digit.in/features/software/heres-how-google-is-putting-ai-to-work-in-healthcare-environmental-conservation-agriculture-and-more-49182.html.

There are also speech-to-tech developments specifically for law. For example, *Dragon* is built with a specialized legal vocabulary to deliver optimal recognition accuracy when the user dictates legal terms.[56] While *Dragon* is not designed specifically for arbitration hearings, the fact that it is specifically tailored for the legal profession is big progress.

There is also current technology that provides real-time transcripts of witnesses' testimony in depositions. For example, *LiveNote Stream*[57] is deposition software that lets users broadcast the audio, video, and text of a deposition securely and in real time to all members of a litigation team anywhere in the world.[58]

The innovations may not only occur in creating hearing transcripts but also in translations and interpretations. Automated translation and interpretation tools could be used to facilitate communication in cases where the parties, witnesses, or attorneys in an arbitration proceeding do not speak the same language. Currently, human translators and interpreters are typically used to facilitate communication in these cases.

Machine learning AI is also being used more often to provide automatically generated translations of documents in other languages,[59] and it is also possible that automated translation provides real-time translation of spoken language.

As happens with any machine learning tool, these work with data provided by humans, and such data may not be enough to accurately translate or interpret words, phrases, or idioms that they have not encountered before. Therefore, these tools might not yet be able to fully replicate the capabilities of human translators and interpreters, such as the ability to adjust their interpretation based on the context and needs of the situation. Yet, it might be a matter of time until automated translation and interpretation tools are the new normal in hearing rooms.

The implications for arbitrations in Mexico would be enormous. In Mexico, most arbitration proceedings do not even have live stenography services. Transcribers typically record the hearing and transcribe afterwards. It may soon be time to skip the live stenography step and jump directly into the era of speech-to-text technology. This would of course save costs. The above software programs are relatively cheap when compared to stenography services or court reporters' hourly rates.

[b] A New Way to Create Submissions: Live Memorandums and Audiobooks

One of the main objectives of arbitration attorneys is to grasp and maintain the arbitrators' attention while they review a written submission. To that end, attorneys

56. Nuance – Dragon Legal, available at https://www.nuance.com/dragon/business-solutions/dragon-legal-individual.html.
57. Thomson Reuters, *Live Note Stream*, available at https://legal.thomsonreuters.com/en/products/livenote-stream#features.
58. *Ibid.*
59. ICC Commission Report, *supra* n. 47, at 30.

spend considerable time choosing the right words and carefully persuasively drafting arguments. Despite that effort, the traditional manner in which attorneys present their written submissions may be endangered. Attorneys may soon use additional elements of persuasion: live memos and audiobooks.

First, attorneys may start creating memorandums with rich media. Attorneys will likely leave behind memorandums that contain nothing but words and start to create interactive documents that are more powerful and engaging, creating 'live memos' that incorporate all kinds of rich media content: links, audio and video files, images, GIFs, clickable buttons, and fillable forms. These live memos already exist and are easy to create.[60]

An even more revolutionary and persuasive tool might be to transform memorandums and other submissions into audiobooks. Attorneys could file the written memorandum together with the audiobook of said memorandum. We invite the reader to think about how powerful this delivery method could become. Arbitrators could listen to the presentation of the case in addition to reading the pleadings, providing a faster and better alternative to grasp the parties' arguments.[61]

There are already tools that transform any Word or PDF document into an audio recording. For example, Apple has a tool to convert any book in its store into an audiobook.[62] *Narakeet* can convert any Word document, EPUB or PDF text into an audio recording instantly with life-like text-to-speech voice generators. These tools work with AI that recognizes the text and provides audio with real and natural voices that can be adjusted according to the user's preferences. Some software programs even allow the users to modify the tone of voice, and inflexions, among others.

The above is a new and revolutionary persuasion weapon for the arsenal of any arbitration attorney who wishes to use technology to increase his/her chances of convincing arbitral tribunals.

[c] Innovation in Evidence Presentation

Technology is already being used to optimize evidence presentation in arbitration proceedings. For example, documents can now be displayed on individual screens during hearings so when a document is referred to, everyone in the hearing may look at the same document, without having to individually look for it in their copies, saving time and avoiding mistakes such as looking at a wrong document.

However, technology may be used for more than optimizing old ways of presenting evidence (such as displaying documents on screens). The technology could be used to present evidence more interactively and engagingly, potentially making it

60. For a quick guide on how to create live memos *see*: *5 Interactive PDF Ideas You Can Use Right Now* (13 Oct. 2021, last updated 23 Dec. 22), available at https://flippingbook.com/blog/marketing-tips/interactive-pdf-ideas.
61. We thank Christian F. Zinser for his contribution to this section.
62. *Every book deserves to be heard*, Apple, available at https://authors.apple.com/support/4519-digital-narration-audiobooks.

easier for arbitrators to understand and consider the relevant information presented before them, such as the use of video, virtual reality, or other multimedia tools.

Technology could help recreate or reconstruct events or objects subject to dispute, through the help of forensic animation that 'uses computer technology to recreate accidents or other incidents'.[63] Forensic animation refers to a branch of forensic science in which audio-visual reconstructions of incidents or accidents are created to aid investigators.[64] Therefore, forensic animation can aid attorneys and arbitrators in recreating certain events where the evidence is hard to obtain but can be reconstructed using data and environments from the real world.

Its use in international arbitration may go from helping illustrate technical or scientific concepts to providing a visual representation of them, making it easier for the arbitrators to understand; to show how a product or system operates, allowing the arbitrators to better understand it; or even recreate events leading up to an accident or incident that is subject to arbitration.

The above could not only make the presentation of evidence more engaging but most importantly, it will also help the arbitrators see the facts as they happened, which could put them in a position to better decide the case.

Another technological tool that is used but could be further used in the near future is drones for inspections without the need for arbitrators to make an in-presence inspection. Other technological tools to be used in the future in arbitration proceedings are lie detector or polygraph glasses to help arbitrators determine the credibility of witnesses during cross-examination.[65] These glasses are said to analyse physiological signals that are believed to be associated with lying, which may include changes in pupil size, eye movement, and skin conductivity.[66]

There is still controversy surrounding the use of these glasses since it has not been accepted that they can accurately detect if someone is lying. Thus, their use in international arbitration or any other legal context is highly controversial and not widely accepted as reliable. Still, such perceptions may soon change. For example, currently, a machine can tell if a person is lying in court with 90% accuracy, while humans can tell with 54% accuracy.[67]

In short, the way attorneys present their cases and evidence in hearing rooms[68] may soon change with forensic animation or by attempting to reduce the ability of a potential witness to lie.

63. *Forensic Animation for Legal Cases*, Courtroom Animation, available at https://courtroom animation.com/forensic-animation-legal-cases-guide/.
64. *Ibid.*
65. Robert H. Smit, The Future of Science and Technology in International Arbitration: The Next Thirty Years, in Stavros Brekoulakis, Julian D.M. Lew and Loukas Mistelis (eds), *The Evolution and Future of International Arbitration* 365-375 (2016).
66. For example, EyeDetect is said to be a next-generation lie detector that measures change in eye behaviour to detect lies. *The Best Lie Detector Test is Fast and Accurate*, Converous, available at https://converus.com/eyedetect/.
67. Cabrera, *supra* n. 29, at 20.
68. Telepresence will be one of the future ways to hold a remote hearing closer to what an in-presence hearing will look like. Smit, *supra* n. 65, at 367-370.

[d] *Full-Blown Automated Research and Writing*

Shortly, attorneys may be able to automate completely the research and even the writing of their submissions. Technology aimed at this goal is already being developed.

In November 2022, OpenAI[69] announced the launch of *ChatGPT*, a large language model (LLM) trained to interact with people conversationally. OpenAI reports that *ChatGPT* was trained using reinforcement learning from human feedback. *ChatGPT* is loaded with a large database, and it is trained to learn patterns in language so that when given a specific question or phrase, it can answer or complement it by predicting the subsequent text, basing its prediction on the database provided by OpenAI.[70] In March 2023, OpenAI launched ChatGPT-4, an updated version of the LLM, which is trained with online data to generate more accurate and human-kind responses to user's prompts.

ChatGPT-4 itself explains it better.

Figure 19.1 ChatGPT-4 Explains Itself

You
Write a description of ChatGPT

ChatGPT
ChatGPT is an advanced language model developed by OpenAI, based on the Generative Pre-trained Transformer (GPT) architecture. It's designed to understand and generate human-like text based on the input it receives. ChatGPT can perform a wide range of text-based tasks, including answering questions, composing essays, creating stories, generating code, and more. Its capabilities stem from being trained on a diverse dataset of text from the internet, enabling it to grasp a vast array of topics, languages, and styles.

ChatGPT's design allows it to understand context and engage in conversational interactions, making it feel like talking to a human. It can remember the context of the conversation within the current session, which helps it provide coherent and contextually relevant responses. However, it does not retain personal data after the session ends, prioritizing user privacy.

The model's flexibility and adaptability make it useful for various applications, from educational tools and customer service bots to creative writing aids and technical problem-solving. Despite its impressive capabilities, ChatGPT has limitations, such as generating inaccurate information or biased content, reflecting the biases present in the data it was trained on. OpenAI continues to update and refine the model to address these issues and enhance its performance and reliability.

69. OpenAI, available at https://openai.com/about/.
70. Jonathan Vanian, *Why Tech Insiders Are So Excited about ChatGPT, A Chatbot That Answers Questions and Writes Essays*, CNBC (13 Dec. 2022) available at https://www.cnbc.com/2022/12/13/chatgpt-is-a-new-ai-chatbot-that-can-answer-questions-and-write-essays.html.

OpenAI also developed Harvey, an artificial intelligence software developed for the legal field.[71] Google has also released *Bard*[72] and Microsoft has released *Bing*[73] and Copilot, a chatbot powered by generative AI, created to replace the now-discontinued Cortana.[74] Other companies including Amazon and even Stanford University are also developing AI language generators,[75] and more are already being released.

In the international arbitration context, attorneys could begin using *ChatGPT* and similar language generators to do research. When attorneys ask a question to *ChatGPT* (called a prompt), it will answer. But attorneys could be more ambitious. *ChatGPT* is already trained to create poems, provide itineraries for vacations, and explain a wide range of concepts. Attorneys could ask the system to draft an entire section of a written submission. Arbitrators could ask the system to draft entire procedural orders or sections of the award.

Currently, these systems do not seem to be ready to write entire complex arbitration memorandums. *ChatGPT* has limited knowledge of the world after 2021 and it can generate incorrect information, get answers wrong or misunderstand the prompt. However, it seems to be a matter of time before these language generators can draft coherent briefs.

Using these 'chatbots' to create and draft briefs has interesting legal and ethical implications. Is it desirable that software makes the research and writing for the attorney? The use of these platforms *may* once again have professional liability implications since attorneys are delegating work that, in principle, should be done by the attorney. Regarding this issue, on August 31, 2023, the Silicon Valley Arbitration and Mediation Center published a draft of the Guidelines on the use of AI in arbitration (SVAMC Guidelines), which aim to regulate the applications o of AI in arbitration proceedings. The SVAMC Guidelines are split into three chapters of guidelines: (i) the applicable to all participants in arbitration; (ii) for parties and their representatives; and (ii) for arbitrators.

Leaving the ethics discussions aside, it is uncontested that the use of AI programs will change legal departments. Large companies like JP Morgan are already using software to review documents, saving 360,000 hours of work each year by lawyers and loan officers.[76]

71. Harvey, available at https://www.harvey.ai/.
72. Google, available at https://bard.google.com/?hl = en.
73. Microsoft, available at: https://www.bing.com/search?q = Bing + AI&showconv = 1&FORM = hpcodx.
74. Copilot, available at: https://copilot.microsoft.com/
75. Alex Hughes, *ChatGPT: Everything You Need to Know about OpenAI's GPT-3 Tool*, Science Focus (16 Jan. 2023), available at https://www.sciencefocus.com/future-technology/gpt-3/; Jasper, available at https://www.jasper.ai/; Fireflies, available at https://fireflies.ai/?gr_pk = ZqLO&gr_uid = 5xqA; Notion, available at https://www.notion.so/product/ai.
76. Debra Casssens Weiss, *JPMorgan Chase Uses Tech to Save 360,000 Hours of Annual Work by Lawyers and Loan Officers*, Aba Journal (2 Mar. 2017), available at https://www.abajournal.com/news/article/jpmorgan_chase_uses_tech_to_save_360000_hours_of_annual_work_by_lawyers_and.

[e] Full-Blown Advocacy

The next step that arbitration users could take is to fully automate the advocacy. There are already some creations of software programs that are designed to argue and advocate in court.

In early January 2023, it was reported that the 'world's first robot lawyer' was planning to take two speeding ticket cases in court. This would be possible through *DoNotPay*'s artificial intelligence, telling the defendants how to conduct themselves before their assigned judges.[77]

DoNotPay is a start-up advertised as the world's first robot lawyer.[78] Its goal is to 'level the playing field and make legal help accessible to the most vulnerable in society'.[79] The use of a robot lawyer again has professional responsibility implications. This robot lawyer is not a licensed attorney in the US. There is a discussion on the legality of this robot under the rules of professional responsibility.

In early January 2023, the founder of *DoNotPay* offered USD 1 million to any lawyer or person who would wear AirPods at the Supreme Court and let the robot lawyer argue the case for them. However, after receiving warnings from the State Bar and threats of legal consequences, *DoNotPay* withdrew its offer. In mid-November 2023, a federal judge dismissed a lawsuit filed against *DoNotPay* for allegedly engaging in unauthorized practice of law, considering that the case 'pits real lawyers against a robot lawyer',[80] and that the plaintiffs did not show how they were harmed by *DoNotPay*.

Because of the legal and professional implications, *DoNotPay* may not be ready to take on arbitration yet. Although *DoNotPay* is advertised as a 'robot lawyer,' it is clearly stated in its Terms of Use that the information provided by the website or app related to legal matters, does not constitute legal advice. If any legal advice is needed, the interested person should consult a licensed attorney. It will be interesting to follow up on the outcome of the cases taken by *DoNotPay* before the court.

[f] A New Way to Do Arbitration: Blockchain and the Metaverse

Finally, there are some early ideas and developments that aim to sway and reconfigure arbitration as a whole: arbitration using blockchain technology and metaverse disputes.

---

77. Bailey Schulz, *DoNotPay's 'First Robot Lawyer' to Take on Speeding Tickets in Court Via AI: How It Works*, US Today (9 Jan. 2023), available at https://www.usatoday.com/story/tech/2023/01/09/first-ai-robot-lawyer-donotpay/11018060002/.
78. *The World's First Robot Lawyer*, DoNotPay, available at https://donotpay.com/.
79. *Terms of Service and Privacy Policy* (6 Jul. 2021), DoNotPay, available at https://donotpay.com/learn/terms-of-service-and-privacy-policy/.
80. *MillerKing LLC v. DoNotPay Inc*, U.S. District Court for the Southern District of Illinois, No. 3:23-CV-00863.

[i] Blockchain ADR

Blockchain is a delocalized, shared, immutable and permanent ledger that facilitates the process of recording transactions and tracking assets in a business network. Blockchain is different from other recording systems for the unique manner in which these records are created, preserved and shared in a linear and sequential environment.[81]

Blockchain technology is already in use in the legal profession. For example, blockchain technology is used to create 'smart contracts,' which are essentially computer codes that automatically execute or enforce all or parts of an agreement.[82] Blockchain technology now is also used in arbitration proceedings.

Kleros is a decentralized arbitration service for the disputes of the new economy.[83] It works with blockchain and combines several applications of this technology, in particular, smart contracts and cryptocurrencies. On the surface, *Kleros* functions very similarly to a traditional arbitration: the parties agree to settle their dispute through *Kleros* arbitration; when a dispute arises, one party presents their case and the other party responds; and finally, a group of decision-makers (called jury) decide the dispute.[84] Yet, when we look past the surface, *Kleros* aims at revolutionising the institution of arbitration as it is understood today[85] in a few fundamental ways.

First, *Kleros* challenges the concept of the 'seat' of arbitration. The seat is the internet. *Kleros* is fully online and decentralized. The users of *Kleros* are in hundreds of different locations, but all the action occurs online. In an environment where the parties, the contract, the enforcement, the system, and the award are all online, submitting a *Kleros* arbitration to a physical location seems almost impossible.[86]

Second, *Kleros* has an entirely different system for the appointment of arbitrators. In a dispute, there may be hundreds of arbitrators, who are anonymous, and who *pay* to be elected as arbitrators for a case. If the arbitrator votes with the majority, they receive compensation from the money paid by the minority. If the arbitrator votes with the minority, they lose their fee.[87] This system fully transforms the current system of appointment. The selection of the arbitrator is currently a fundamental task for law firms and arbitral institutions. In *Kleros*, that decision becomes irrelevant. Arbitrators are anonymous and their qualifications are unknown to the parties.

Finally, a *Kleros* award is made without reason, is subject to infinite appeals and is self-enforcing. Today, as a general rule in Mexico, awards are reasoned,[88] not subject to appeal, and subject to recognition and enforcement or annulment. *Kleros* changes

81. Erick Clavel, *Reescribiendo el Arbitraje* in Francisco González de Cossío (ed.), *Todo Arbitraje y MASC* 68 (2022).
82. Dirk Wiegandt, *Blockchain, Smart Contracts and the Role of Arbitration*, 39(5) Journal of International Arbitration 676-677 (2022) https://doi.org/10.54648/joia2022029.
83. Kleros, available at https://kleros.io/.
84. Clavel, *supra* n. 81, at 75.
85. The many legal implications of *Kleros* deserve an article of their own. Here, we only highlight some of the innovations.
86. Clavel, *supra* n. 81, at 76.
87. *Ibid.*, at 79.
88. Article 1448, Mexican Commerce Code.

that. In *Kleros*, parties only receive a notification that informs which party prevailed with a maximum of a couple of lines justifying the decision. Parties can then appeal that decision infinite times. The number of arbitrators on appeal will be duplicated and, therefore, the quota for the appeal also doubles. Finally, since *Kleros* is based on blockchain technology and smart contracts, the award will self-execute as soon as it is rendered.

All of the above is a complete revolution of the system and may well change the future of arbitration, at least for *some* disputes. Currently, *Kleros* only works for very simple disputes where the result is binary: one party wins all and one party loses all.[89] However, it may be the case that, as more users turn to *Kleros*, the technology will adapt to the different types of disputes.

[ii] Metaverse

The other big revolution to the very foundations of arbitration may be found in the metaverse. The metaverse is an alternative virtual universe,[90] where users create an avatar (a digital representation of a person) to interact with other avatars, objects, assets, and places.[91] The metaverse combines virtual and augmented reality to allow people to have real-time interactions and experiences across distance and has gained attention due to the ability to fully own (in this virtual space), objects, experiences, or even land.[92]

Each day, more companies and people engage and become part of the metaverse, and the acquisition of virtual assets and currency has increased significantly. Therefore, the possibility of disputes arising in the Metaverse increases as well. There, arbitration could take on a relevant role. Although at present, the physical format offers many advantages, it is conceivable that in the not-so-distant future, we may be able to conduct arbitration proceedings within the metaverse.

To give an example, in March 2022, the University of Ottawa held a moot court competition in the metaverse. Students, attendees, and the judges interacted and carried out the competition in this virtual space.[93] Another example is that, in January 2022, the first-ever international arbitration gathering took place in virtual reality.[94]

89. Clavel, *supra* n. 81, at 75.
90. Matthew Ball, *The Metaverse: An How It Will Revolutionize Everything* 30 (2022).
91. Sneha Vijayan, *Autonomous Arbitration in the Era of the Metaverse*, Kluwer Arbitration Blog (11 Mar. 2022), available at http://arbitrationblog.kluwerarbitration.com/2022/03/11/autonomous-arbitration-in-the-era-of-the-metaverse/.
92. Deborah Lovich, *What Is the Metaverse and Why Should You Care?* (11 May. 2022), available at https://www.forbes.com/sites/deborahlovich/2022/05/11/what-is-the-metaverse-and-why-should-you-care/?sh = 5440d07d2704.
93. Paul Logothetis, *uOttawa's Faculty of Law Takes Moot Trials to the Metaverse*, UOttawa (March 2022), available at https://www.uottawa.ca/about-us/media/newsroom/uottawas-faculty-law-takes-moot-trials-metaverse.
94. Elizabeth Chan and Graham Rhodes, *Arbitration Tech Toolbox: Lessons from the First Ever International Arbitration Gathering in Virtual Reality*, Kluwer Arbitration Blog (February 2022), available at http://arbitrationblog.kluwerarbitration.com/2022/02/06/arbitration-tech-toolbox-lessons-from-the-first-ever-international-arbitration-gathering-in-virtual-reality/.

Something similar could happen with arbitration institutions: in a not-so-distant future virtual spaces may be created in the metaverse to hold hearings where the parties, arbitrators and witnesses would have the possibility to create their own avatar and interact with each other in a virtual hearing room.

However, issues may arise from the resolution of real-world disputes in the Metaverse, or even those disputes arising in the Metaverse. For instance, in the absence of the parties' choice of law, which law applies when the place of arbitration is the metaverse? or how would an award rendered in the metaverse be enforced? We do not have the answer to these questions, and we might have to find out in the future. Similar to *Kleros*, this could completely revolutionize concepts that are key to current arbitration such as the seat.[95]

Arbitration proceedings could also arise due to disputes that originate in the metaverse. Most of the metaverse platforms include arbitration agreements in their term of service.[96] In that way, arbitration is already relevant for disputes arising out of the Metaverse, at least regarding user-platform disputes. Arbitration could also take place, however, for disputes that arise between users of these platforms derived from their interaction in the metaverse.

Generally, users' transactions in the metaverse are completed through smart contracts. As explained, smart contracts are self-executing, and there are already smart contracts that provide for *Kleros* arbitration.[97] This again brings all the consequences of a delocalized blockchain arbitration, such as the absence of seats, lack of reasoned awards, and lack of necessity of enforcement proceedings, among others.[98]

All this new technology aims to create big changes in arbitration proceedings. From tasks as 'simple' as creating automated transcriptions and translations, to fully revolutionising and changing the way we understand arbitration, technology is making its way into the conduction of arbitration proceedings.

[E] AFTER THE ARBITRATION: THE AWARD AND ITS ENFORCEMENT[99]

The use of technology in arbitration is not restrained to the arbitration proceeding itself, but parties, arbitrators, arbitral institutions and even courts have had to adapt from the traditional recognition and enforcement proceedings to harmonize them with the use of technology. In this section, we explore the technological advances in the drafting of the decisions and the enforcement proceedings and present further innovations we envision in the near future, with their potential logistical and legal issues.

95. *Supra*, section [D][2][f][i].
96. For example, Decentraland, Axie Infinity, Roblox, Star Atlas and Upland.
97. *Supra*, section [D][2][f][i].
98. *Supra*, section [D][2][f][i].
99. For a summary of the state of affairs in Mexico *see*: Omar Guerrero, Fernanda Serrano et al., Nulidad, reconocimiento y ejecución de laudos arbitrales de naturaleza privada en México bajo el prisma de tres sentencias de la Suprema Corte de Justicia de la Nación in Francisco González de Cossío (ed.), *Todo Arbitraje y MASC* 187-221 (2022).

[1] The Steps We Have Taken: Mexico Was Obliged to Modernize its Enforcement Proceedings

The main challenge in Mexico was to modernize some of its concepts to allow enforcement of awards rendered with technology. The main focus has been the use of e-signatures. Recently in Mexico, there has been an important development in the regulation of e-signatures that has had an impact on the way arbitral tribunals can issue awards.

In Mexico, there are several platforms that provide e-signature services that can comply with the legal requirements for simple e-signatures[100] and advanced e-signatures.[101] Therefore, such tools are available for arbitrators when rendering their awards. The problem arises in the recognition and enforcement stage, as local courts have been reluctant to admit e-signed awards for recognition and enforcement.

For instance, Article 1461 of the Mexican Commercial Code provides that the party that intends to initiate a recognition and enforcement proceeding must file the original award 'duly authenticated'.[102] For electronically-signed awards, courts have had a hard time determining what must be understood as 'original'. Further, the authentication requirement was understood by some courts as a formality that the parties must prove, before a notary public or similar, the origin of the signature of the award.[103]

Luckily, Mexican jurisprudence has advanced on this front. Recently, the Mexican Supreme Court ruled that the authentication requirement is unconstitutional, and parties must only comply with the requirement of presenting the original award for its recognition and enforcement.[104]

In this sense, it is clear that post-arbitration proceedings are adapting to the changing environment brought by technology for arbitration. However, there are still steps that courts must take to catch up with arbitration technological improvements. The real question relies on whether the Mexican Judiciary will be able to catch up with the rapid technological advancement in arbitration and will be able to comprehend the complexities that the use of technology in arbitration may bring.

[2] The Next Frontier: Predictive Justice and Robo-Arbitrators

In the future, we may see increased use of predictive machines and 'robo-lawyers' that help reduce the work of arbitrators to reach a decision. If it is possible to have fully

100. Article 89, Commerce Code.
101. Article 97, Commerce Code.
102. Article 1461, Commerce Code.
103. *See*: Digital Record: 2017915, Thesis: I.14o.C.26 C (10a.). '*LAUDO ARBITRAL. AUTENTICACIÓN A QUE SE REFIERE EL ARTÍCULO 1461 DEL CÓDIGO DE COMERCIO PARA SU EJECUCIÓN.*'
104. *See* Digital Record: 2025614, Thesis: 1a. XXV/2022 (10a.). '*RECONOCIMIENTO Y EJECUCIÓN DE LAUDO ARBITRAL. EL ARTÍCULO 1461, PÁRRAFO SEGUNDO, DEL CÓDIGO DE COMERCIO, AL PREVER COMO REQUISITO PRESENTAR EL ORIGINAL DEL LAUDO "DEBIDAMENTE AUTENTICADO" O COPIA CERTIFICADA DEL MISMO, VULNERA EL DERECHO DE ACCESO A LA JUSTICIA TUTELADO POR EL ARTÍCULO 17 CONSTITUCIONAL.*'

automated advocacy, it should also be possible to have fully automated decision-making.

As explored throughout this chapter, artificial intelligence will become an important tool for arbitrators when analysing cases. The amount of time spent reviewing documents and other evidence, and searching applicable case law, among other tasks, would be significantly reduced by using artificial intelligence tools. However, artificial intelligence could go much further with predictive justice.

Programs are being developed and are already in use worldwide to aid judges in reducing the time spent on each case and to standardize the criteria of cases with similar facts and circumstances. For example, predictive machines can predict how judges will vote. One program outperformed humans in predicting how US Supreme Court justices would vote. The program was correct 75% of the time, while eminent lawyers and professors could only achieve 59.1%.[105] Another recent model achieved 79% accuracy in predicting all cases of the European Court of Human Rights.[106] The Argentinean justice system developed *PROMETEA*, an artificial intelligence tool created to optimize the justice service which can predict the solution to a Court case in less than twenty seconds, with an astounding 96% success rate.[107]

Some programs go beyond prediction. An example that is currently used is *iFlyTech* in Shanghai, a software that assists judges with evidence and sentencing criminal cases.[108] The system uses language recognition and natural speech processing to compare all the evidence filed in a proceeding to look for conflicting fact patterns. The machine alerts the judge about inconsistencies, allowing the judge to investigate further. Once sentencing is about to take place, the judge can use another AI tool where the machine starts with a fact pattern (the criminal record, age of defendant, damages, etc.) and then, the algorithm scans millions of court records. With this data, the machine recommends to the judge the years of imprisonment or fine to be paid.[109]

A software like *iFlyTech* could be transplanted into arbitration to assist arbitrators in detecting inconsistencies in evidence, reviewing past decisions, and suggesting a decision.

These predictive machines are very valuable and we can understand why they are being used, since they can produce predictions faster, better, and cheaper than humans and their prediction is key in making decisions under uncertainty.[110] Until now, the conclusions that these artificial intelligence tools generate are generally

105. Theodore W. Ruger et al., *The Supreme Court Forecasting Project: Legal and Political Sciences Approaches to Predicting Supreme Court Decisionmaking*, 104 Colum. L. Rev. 1150-1152 (2004) https://doi.org/10.2307/4099370.
106. Nikolaos Aletras et al., *Predicting Judicial Decision of the European Court of Human Rights: A Natural Language Processing Perspective*, 2:e93 PeerJ Computer Science 10 (2016) https://doi.org/10.7717/peerj-cs.93.
107. Juan Gustavo Corvalán, *PROMETEA: Artificial Intelligence to Transform Justice and Public Organizations*, 6 International Journal of Digital and Data Law 93 (2020).
108. Kai Fu Lee, *AI Super-Powers: China, Silicon Valley, and the New World Order* 115 (Houghton Mifflin Harcourt 2018); George G. Zheng, *China's Grand Design of People's Smart Courts*, 7 Asian Journal of Law and Society, 561, 574-575 (2020)
109. *Ibid.*
110. Ajay Agrawal et al., *Prediction Machines: The Simple Economics of Artificial Intelligence*, 81 (2018).

reviewed by a human, so the artificial intelligence analysis is only used as a guide. Humans keep making final decisions.[111]

However, predictive machines and robo-arbitrators do not yet operate because they currently encounter several problems of both technological and legal nature. We now analyse these complications.

On the technological front, machines have at least three shortcomings, at least when compared to humans. The first is a lack of sufficient information. For a successful AI tool, the existence of abundant data is indispensable. The larger the data sample, the more accurate the predictive value of the model.[112] In arbitration, this becomes a problem. Commercial arbitral awards are generally not public. Confidentiality of arbitral awards inherently limits the availability of data.[113] In investment cases, some arbitration awards and other documents are public,[114] but certainly not all of them. As long as parties continue to keep their awards confidential, machines will have insufficient data to predict many types of conduct in arbitration.[115]

Still, this unavailability of data might be changing. Some arbitral institutions have amended their rules to allow for more publications of awards. The ICC, ICDR, SIAC and SCC publish versions of selected awards with permission of the parties excluding certain data.[116] Further, some organizations have endeavoured to compile information about arbitration.[117] As more information becomes public, the AI model will become more precise.

The second problem is the lack of predictability in arbitration. Currently, particularly in investment arbitration, there is a serious debate about the lack of consistency and predictability of decisions.[118] As arbitration encounters more dissimilar, unique, and non-repetitive cases, AI will encounter greater hurdles in its development.[119]

Part of the reason is that international arbitration lacks a system of *binding* precedent. Almost all legal scholars agree that 'persuasive precedent' rather than binding precedent, is a principle that can be applied in arbitration.[120] Introducing a system of *binding* precedent in the arbitration system seems a difficult task. There is no

111. *Ibid.*, at 69
112. Cabrera, *supra* n. 29, at 6.
113. *Ibid.*
114. Frequently, ICSID, PCA and other arbitral institutions publish awards.
115. Cabrera, *supra* n. 29, at 21.
116. Kathleen Paisley and Edna Sussman, *Artificial Intelligence Challenges and Opportunities for international Arbitration* 37 (2018).
117. Jus Mundi, for example, claims to have the most comprehensive international arbitration database.
118. *See* U.N. *Report of Working Group III on the work of its thirty-sixth session*. Commission on International Trade Law (UNITRAL), U.N. Doc A/CN.9/W.G.III/WP.150, 3,4,11 (2018).
119. Scherer, *supra* n. 4, at 556.
120. Alexis Moure. *Arbitral Jurisprudence in International Commercial Arbitration: The Case for a Systematic Publication of Arbitral Awards in 10 Questions*. Kluwer Arbitration Blog (28 May 2009), available at https://arbitrationblog.kluwerarbitration.com/2009/05/28/arbitral-jurisprudence-in-international-commercial-arbitration-the-case-for-a-systematic-publication-of-arbitral-awards-in-10-questions/.

hierarchy of arbitration tribunals, and there is no compelling reason to simply allow the next to resolve an issue to lay the legal foundation for all subsequent tribunals.[121]

Consistency is also hard to achieve in arbitration. All cases are not only under a different set of facts but also under different individual agreements (commercial) or treaties (investment), different languages, different applicable laws, and different seats, among others.

With more inconsistent decisions, it will be harder for AI to have good predictive models. One could even question the decisions made by AI on these matters, which would be based on existing data, since there is no actual justification to follow previous arbitral decisions, simply because they were decided first. In this sense, human arbitrators still have a big advantage over machines. Humans know things that machines do not know yet and are better at deciding what to do when there is not much data to rely on.[122] Humans have intuition.

The final technological problem is that arbitration decisions are biased by human interference,[123] and AI could perpetuate these biases.[124] Even though artificial intelligence tools might help to be more time-efficient, their use comes with risks. There are already reports that machines could have biases. That is the case of the risk assessment tool named Correctional Offender Management Profiling for Alternative Sanctions (COMPAS) used in the United States to assess recidivism risk.[125] The COMPAS algorithm was reported to be biased against African Americans, as it tends to falsely flag these defendants as future criminals at almost twice the rate of white defendants.[126] Notwithstanding, some cases have started being decided with the important use of AI.[127]

The same kind of biases could be seen in international arbitration. For example, in investment arbitration matters, an algorithm could be biased if programmed with a lot of cases involving a certain country. The result could be that the machine is biased against the country labelled as problematic.

On the legal front, the authors also envision three potential issues. First, predictive machines still maintain a major problem today: they cannot reason. Instead, they simply analyse probabilities. Reasoning of the award is important. Regardless of

121. *SGS Société Générale de Surveillance S.A. v. Republic of the Philippines*. ICSIC Case No. ARB/02/6. Decision on Objections to Jurisdiction, ¶97.
122. Agrawal et al., *supra* n. 110, at 98.
123. A great book that would merit another article is *'Noise', A Flaw in Human Judgment* by Daniel Kahneman et al. (2021). The key theme of the book (as explained by the authors) is: '*wherever there is judgment, there is noise -and more of it than you think*', 12.
124. Richard Susskind, *Online Courts and the Future of Justice* 171, 288 (2019)
125. Julia Angwin et al., *Machine Bias: There's Software Used Across the Country to Predict Future Criminals – And It's Biased Against Blacks*, ProPublica (23 May 2016), available at www.propublica.org/article/machine-bias-risk-assessments-in-criminal-sentencing.
126. *Ibid.*
127. For example, there is a recent news article (2 Feb. 2023) that reads: '*Resuelven en Colombia el primer caso Jurídico con la ayuda de robot ChatGPT,*' which reported that a Judge in Colombia issued a ruling with the help of ChatGPT. Available at https://www.dw.com/es/resuelven-en-colombia-el-primer-caso-jur%C3%ADdico-con-la-ayuda-de-robot-chatgpt/a-64597510#:~:text=Un%20juez%20de%20Colombia%20resolvi%C3%B3,inteligencia%20artificial%20en%20el%20pa%C3%ADs.

the nature of the dispute, parties and attorneys are interested in knowing what they did right, what they did wrong, and even whether the arbitrators adequately heard their case. Only good reasoning will provide these answers and will allow the parties and the arbitration as an institution to improve.[128]

In Mexico, '[t]he award shall state the *reasons* upon which it is based, unless the parties have agreed that no reasons are to be given ....'[129] Likewise, in investment arbitration, the reasoning of the award is indispensable. The ICSID Convention allows a party to seek the annulment of an award based on the grounds 'that the award has failed to state the reasons on which it is based'.[130] However, AI has difficulty generating reasoned decisions since it simply follows the instructions coded in a system of rules or uses probabilities to solve problems in machine learning models.

There is, however, a limited opportunity for Mexico to make AI decisions because parties can agree to have the award without reason. Some attorneys posit that clients do not care about reasons, they care about whether they are going to win or lose and they want to know the answer as soon as possible.[131] Companies and businesspeople may not have in their minds the objectives of reasons: legitimacy, consistency, moral concerns, or the development of law. It is possible that in the future, companies will be willing to sacrifice legal reasoning and submit their disputes to machines.

Legal services platforms today already offer to resolve disputes without humans or with limited human assistance. For example, *Mondria.com* uses algorithms to analyse case information and issues a decision on eBay transactions. If the consumer is dissatisfied with the decision, he can file an appeal that works without humans. *Mondria.com* has already resolved 400 million disputes between consumers and sellers. Already, three times more legal disputes are resolved with virtual platforms on eBay than all the lawsuits heard in US courts.[132]

The second legal issue is that today, arbitration laws may impede robots from making decisions. For example, the French arbitration law expressly requires the arbitrator to be a natural person.[133] Similarly, the English Arbitration Act sets forth that '[t]he authority of an arbitrator is personal and ceases on his death'.[134] While Mexico does not have a similar rule, it does refer to *human* arbitrators. Article 1428 of the Commerce Code provides that 'the *person* who is approached in connection with his possible appointment as an arbitrator ....'[135] Arbitration was designed for an era where technology had a role much more limited than its capacity today. In order to have robo-arbitrators, arbitration laws may have to be amended.

The final legal issue is that an AI-created decision might face serious enforcement issues. Parties may well argue that an AI award must be annulled since the case was not

128. Clavel, *supra* n. 81, at 82-83.
129. Article 1448, Commerce Code; *see also*, Art. 31(2), UNCITRAL Model Law.
130. Article 52.1, ICSID Convention.
131. Maxi Scherer, *The Future of International Arbitration: Virtual Hearings and AI-Arbitrators?*, (2020), quoted by Cabrera, *supra* n. 29, at 30.
132. Cabrera, *supra* n. 29, at 36.
133. Article 1454, Code de Procédure Civile.
134. Article 26, English Arbitration Act.
135. Article 1428, Commerce Code.

decided by the arbitrators but by a machine. To avoid this issue, there will have to exist a clear criterion that a decision dictated by a machine will not be a ground for annulment unless biased algorithms are demonstrated. To detect bias in algorithms, the lawyer will have to understand the algorithm and how it was developed, to identify whether errors are attributable to the programmer or to the data itself.

In conclusion, Mexican courts have started to change their interpretation of some key concepts to modernize and allow the enforcement of arbitration awards even with some technological features. But the challenge of predictive justice and robo-lawyers may require not only the courts but also all users of arbitration to modernize quickly.

[F] CONCLUSION: TECH OR NOT TECH? THAT IS NOT EVEN THE QUESTION

The use of technology in international arbitration in Mexico has come a long way in recent years, and it will continue to play an increasingly important role in the field. The current use of tools such as videoconferencing, e-discovery, and online document management systems has greatly improved the efficiency and cost-effectiveness of arbitration proceedings. These tools have enabled parties and arbitrators to conduct proceedings remotely, saving time and money, and have also made it easier to access and manage large amounts of data.

However, there is still potential for further technological advancements to be implemented shortly. These advancements could include the use of virtual and augmented reality, which could enhance the ability of parties and arbitrators to visualize evidence, blockchain, which could provide a secure and efficient way to manage and track data, and machine learning, which could assist arbitrators in decision-making by analysing large amounts of data.

As technology continues to evolve, arbitrators, practitioners, and parties need to stay informed and adapt to these changes to ensure that international arbitration in Mexico remains a fair, efficient, and cost-effective method of dispute resolution. However, it is important to keep in mind that the use of technology in arbitration proceedings might also have legal and ethical implications for attorneys. Attorneys should be aware of the legal and ethical rules that apply to the use of technology in arbitration proceedings, especially in terms of data protection, confidentiality, and e-discovery.

The use of technology should be embraced by all stakeholders, as it has the potential to greatly improve the arbitration process and make it more accessible to a wider range of parties. The future of international arbitration in Mexico looks bright, with technology playing an ever-increasing role in making the process more efficient and effective for all parties involved.

The ideas put forth in this chapter might seem futuristic and far away from the present, but the reality is that most of the technology already exists or is being developed. For example, the reader might be surprised to learn that the entirety of the conclusion to this piece – except for this paragraph – was written by *ChatGPT*.

Technology revolutionizes everything within its grasp, and technology now has its hands on arbitration. We started this article by asking tech or not tech? Is there even a question? Now we conclude: Tech or not tech? That is not even the question.

CHAPTER 20

Mediation and Negotiation in Mexico: The Three-Cushion Carom

Fernando Navarro Sánchez

One of my dearest childhood memories traces back to the times my family and I visited the city of *Ixtlahuaca*, in the State of Mexico, my maternal grandfather's hometown. He and my grandmother had a house there where they would escape from the tension and buzz of Mexico City on weekends and holidays throughout the decades. As happens with such spaces, they see generations appear and grow. My grandfather had a billiard table, but not the commonly known pool billiard where the goal is to get numbered and colored balls into the holes, but the *carom* billiard, known in Spanish as *carambola*. The *carom* rules are simple: (1) there are three balls and no holes in the table; and (2) each player must hit one ball with the cue, and with that one ball hit the other two in a single shot to score one *carom*. Contrary to the simplicity of the rules, finding the right technique to accumulate *caroms* or *carambolas*, requires high skills and practice. But the greatest challenge comes to every ten caroms, to keep advancing in the game, one must hit a three-cushion carom which means that before hitting the two other balls with yours, your ball must bounce against three of the table cushions. Quite a crafty trick in which my grandfather was a specialist.

When thinking about *mediation and negotiation* in Mexico, the main challenge is to find a frame that embodies a comprehensive approach of Alternative Dispute Resolution (ADR) methods which also considers the views of the arbitration community. This is itself a three-cushion *carom*, where the cushions are: negotiation, mediation, and litigation-arbitration.[1]

1. The procedural and practical differences between court litigation and arbitration will be disregarded for purposes of this chapter. The statements and ideas proposed hereby are assumed equally valid for both processes alike.

[A] INTRODUCTION: HITTING THE BALL

After decades of efforts in the academic space, through legislation, and in legal practice, mediation has slowly become a familiar topic to people in the practice of business and law in Mexico.

In the civil and commercial legal landscape,[2] Mexico has regulated the practice of mediation differently in every state. The first mediation law was enacted in 1997 in the state of Quintana Roo. Ever since, most states have enacted mediation laws dealing with details like defining the process of mediation, who can mediate, and the effects of the mediation agreement. This last piece, the mediation agreement's effects, has had the biggest impact. In Mexico City, public or private certified mediators have the authority to grant the mediation agreement res judicata status. Hence, the enforcement of a mediation agreement is more agile than the enforcement of a regular contract. Industries like banking and mortgage have embraced this mechanism. Some other state jurisdictions allow for a similar mechanism, but the specific requirements for the mediation agreement, and mediators vary in every state. In 2018, the Federal Congress mandated the creation of a General ADR law that would aim at providing a homogeneous standard of practice for the thirty-two state laws. Several initiatives for the *General ADR Law*[3] have been discussed ever since, and at the time of this article, Congress has yet to enact the law.

The COVID-19 pandemic appeared to give the development of mediation a twist and a boost. In every city in the country, tribunals closed their doors temporarily from March 2020 and remained closed for several months to prevent the virus from spreading.[4] The backlog created by such a phenomenon made mediation an accessible alternative. But the development got a twist, because the world and mediation alike, turned to electronic communication, remote mediation and electronic signatures became the norm, at least for the months following the closure. And mediation was boosted since the process became an answer to many of the otherwise stuck processes. It is, thus, a good moment in history to take a snapshot of mediation and its identity as a conflict resolution method in twenty-first-century Mexico.

Having spent the last decade discussing mediation, its merits, opportunities, and challenges, it has become clear that the Mexican legal forum is increasingly familiar with the mediation field. In 2021, according to the National Institute of Statistics and Geography,[5] there were 1,470 public mediators and 182,927 open files for alternative justice processes in a wide range of subject matters, 40% of which were family cases,

2. Criminal and labor ADR processes are regulated at a federal level.
3. In February 2017, Congress reformed the Constitution to include a mandate to enact the *Ley General de Mecanismos Alternativos de Solución de Controversias* in subjects different than criminal law.
4. As an example, federal courts implemented safety measures in different stages. From March 18 to May 5, 2020, only *urgent cases* were listed.
   Fundación para la Justicia y el Estado Democrático de Derecho et al., *El Acceso a la Justicia en México durante la Pandemia de Covid-19* 18 (July 2021), https://imumi.org/wp-content/uploads/2021/08/el-acceso-a-la-justicia-en-mexico-durante-la-pandemia-de-covid-19.pdf.
5. INEGI, *Censo Nacional de Impartición de Justicia Estatal* (Dec. 1, 2022), https://www.inegi.org.mx/programas/cnije/2022/.

30% civil cases, and 10% commercial cases. In comparison, the number of total court cases opened in the same period was 2,130,586 in all subject matters.

The number of mediations is considerable, although it is still low in comparison. Even lower, if we consider that the number of non-adjudicative or consensual alternative dispute resolution processes opened yearly are mere formalities. Indeed, since mediated agreements allow for res judicata as indicated above in many states and cases, it is increasingly customary practice in Mexico for attorneys to formalize a regular or negotiated settlement as mediation for ease of enforcement in case of breach.[6]

When it comes to commercial disputes, despite efforts from various stakeholders and incentives arising from the COVID-19 pandemic and the judicial backlog it caused, authentic mediation processes where parties negotiate with the help of a mediator, remain exceptional.

Commercial parties in Mexico, tend to favor common ground and understanding,[7] and attorneys pride themselves on preferring a *bad agreement over a good fight*.[8] This inevitably raises the question as to why stakeholders of the system do not use mediation more commonly as a catalyst or an extension of the efforts to reach settlements, to build more and better settlements. The answer might have different dimensions, but one theory could be that mediation, either as one single process or *tiered* with other forms of dispute resolution could be more prevalent if we revise how and where mediation is placed in the dispute resolution continuum.

To contextualize the role mediation and negotiation have in the overall spectrum of dispute resolution, and the interaction between both processes as dispute resolution tools, it might be useful to picture two buckets for conflict resolution. The consensual conflict resolution bucket on the one hand, including negotiation and its different versions through the assistance of a third-party neutral, like mediation, and the adversarial dispute resolution bucket on the other hand, including litigation and arbitration.

The scarce usage of mediation may be the result of traditionally using a different way to categorize the dispute resolution methods in the spectrum: direct negotiations on one bucket, and any other formal or structured dispute resolution method in the other bucket. Under this mindset, negotiation, a common commercial practice, when it fails, is followed by more structured and regulated mechanisms, be it mediation, litigation, or arbitration. This means in turn that mediation is often perceived as a choice from a menu of options including adversarial choices. And when mediation is perceived as a choice vis-à-vis litigation or arbitration assuming that the consensual

6. For the purposes of this chapter, we will not consider the use of mediated agreements to formalize settlements as mediations.
7. Eighty percent of Mexican people would tend to foster win-win situations. Habib Chamoun Nicolás, *La Cultura de Negociación en México* (Mar. 1, 2023), https://www.gestiopolis.com/cultura-negociacion-mexico/.
8. Popular say: *Más vale un mal arreglo que un buen pleito*. More than 40% of the population in Mexico would prefer a "bad agreement" over a "good fight," and only around 19% would prefer the latter. Héctor Felipe Fix-Fierro *et al*, *Entre un buen arreglo y un mal pleito* (Jan. 10, 2023), http://www.librosoa.unam.mx/bitstream/handle/123456789/313/Coleccion_Mexicanos_justicia.pdf?sequence=3&isAllowed=y.

options have been exhausted, mediation fades as a less appealing option. On the contrary, if mediation is perceived to be part of the consensual conflict resolution options, along with negotiation, then the disputing parties and counsel may consider mediation as part of such continuum of consensual procedures, as an extended platform and a tool of the familiar broad negotiation phase. And there are compelling reasons that show the ways mediation increases the potential for agreement in negotiations.

[B] THE NEGOTIATION CUSHION

Negotiation is hardly a novel concept. On the contrary, it is one of the oldest types of human interaction. What is more difficult is to find its place in the dispute resolution spectrum. Or affirm if it even is a dispute resolution method in the first place. Some may argue that negotiation is not always included as one of the dispute resolution methods since it assumes that by parties being negotiating, the dispute has not yet arisen.

There are multiple definitions of negotiation and ways to approach it. The iconic Program on Negotiation at Harvard Law School defines negotiation as a "back and forth communication designed to reach an agreement when you and the other side have some interests that are shared and others that are opposed."[9] Nowhere in the concept does the word conflict or dispute appear. Naturally so since negotiation for conflict resolution is only one expression of the process. So, is negotiation a dispute resolution process, or a dispute prevention process? A tough question that explains the difficulties in finding a place for negotiation in the dispute resolution spectrum.

Furthermore, when we find the literature and laws on alternative justice or alternative dispute resolution, there are scarce references to negotiation as a process. The Mexico City Alternative Justice Law, for instance, refers to alternative justice as "procedures different to jurisdictional ones, for the resolution of disputes between private citizens."[10] However, this Law refers to mediation almost exclusively and only mentions negotiation when detailing the mediator's role as a facilitator of the negotiation process. A similar concept for alternative dispute mechanisms is contained in the law for the State of Nuevo Leon.[11] In the State of Jalisco, local law does define negotiation, nevertheless, it fails to refer to negotiation in any further provision.[12] The

9. Katie Shonk, *What Is Negotiation? Program on Negotiation Daily* Blog (Mar. 31, 2023), https://www.pon.harvard.edu/daily/negotiation-skills-daily/what-is-negotiation/.
10. *Ley de Justicia Alternativa del Tribunal Superior de Justicia para el Distrito Federal* Art. 2. (Jan. 8, 2008), http://cgservicios.df.gob.mx/prontuario/vigente/r171503.htm.
11. *Ley de Métodos Alternos para la Resolución de Conflictos del Estado de Nuevo León* Art. 2 (Jan. 14, 2005), chrome-extension://efaidnbmnnnibpcajpcglclefindmkaj/http://www.tcanl.gob.mx/docs/ley_de_metodos_alternos_para_la_solucion_de_conflictos_del_estado_de_nuevo_leon.pdf.
12. *Ley de Justicia Alternativa del Estado de Jalisco* Art. 3 (Jan. 30, 2007), chrome-extension://efaidnbmnnnibpcajpcglclefindmkaj/https://transparencia.info.jalisco.gob.mx/sites/default/files/u37/Ley%20de%20Justicia%20Alternativa%20del%20Estado%20de%20Jalisco_0.pdf.

Mexican Constitution refers to alternative mechanisms more broadly.[13] In all cases, including the Constitution and the domestic laws, negotiation could fit into the definition of alternative justice or mechanisms but is not more exhaustively defined or regulated in the law itself.

Before the ADR legal developments that started in the 1990s, right after the first state mediation law,[14] many civil and commercial local laws referred to the *settlement agreement*, but the regulation dealt with the result (the agreement and its effects) and not with the process itself.[15]

In contrast, legal practice indicates that commercial cases in Mexico are regularly negotiated directly by attorneys and commercial parties themselves. In fact, one of the obstacles to mediation in Mexico may be that cases are often negotiated by the parties and their counsels directly as part of the regular practice of seeking a *bad agreement* over a *good fight* as part of a commercial one-tier effort. If we go back to the analogy of the dispute resolution buckets, direct negotiation being alone on the informal settlement effort bucket, then parties tend to assume that once that bucket has been visited, all that is left is going to the formal bucket. If mediation is in the formal bucket, parties will then have to choose between mediation, and litigation/arbitration. And since they serve so different purposes, parties tend to think that mediation is not worth the try anymore having exhausted the informal/consensual efforts through negotiation. While little empirical research has been done around the practice of negotiation for commercial disputes in Mexico, examples of these tendencies are consistent with the international commercial practice where companies tend to prefer to exhaust all means of possible negotiation prior to trying another mechanism or during the exhaustion of formal procedures.[16]

Moreover, the pursuit of settlements may be well aligned with the Mexican culture. Research made by the renowned Hofstede Institute explains country cultures through six different dimensions.[17] Looking at two of these dimensions may explain this tendency that favors settling conflicts. Mexico scores high in collectivism.[18] A collectivist society has an emotional preference to protect relationships; loyalty and long-term commitments are highly valued. The second dimension where Mexico scores high is "uncertainty avoidance."[19] This means in essence that change (be it in relationships, partnerships, or jobs) creates anxiety and there is a strong preference for stability and long-term commitment. The quest for settlement as opposed to breaking

13. *Constitución Política de los Estados Unidos Mexicanos* Art. 17 (Feb. 5, 1917 last reformed May 28. 2021), https://www.gob.mx/indesol/documentos/constitucion-politica-de-los-estados-unidos-mexicanos-97187.
14. Nuria González Martín, *El ABC de la Mediación en México*, in: Juan VEGA (ed.), *Libro homenaje a Sonia Rodríguez Jiménez* 7 (2014).
15. *Código Civil Federal Arts 2944-2963* (Aug. 31, 1928 last reformed Jan. 11, 2021), https://www.gob.mx/indesol/documentos/codigo-civil-federal-marco-normativo.
16. Anna Howard, *EU Cross-Border Commercial Mediation, Listening to Disputants, Changing the Frame; Framing the Changes* 120 (2021).
17. Geert Hofstede, *Dimensionalizing Cultures: The Hofstede Model in Context—Online Readings in Psychology and Culture 2011* (May 31, 2023), https://doi.org/10.9707/2307-0919.1014.
18. Hofstede Institute, *Hofstede Insights—Country Comparison Tool* (May 31, 2023), https://www.hofstede-insights.com/country-comparison-tool?countries = mexico.
19. *Ibid.*

relationships and moving on to a new stage, is well within the general emotional preferences of the Mexican people.

But all those efforts to reach a settlement are still viewed as part of the commercial efforts. As part of what businesswomen and men are expected to do. Only after exhausting such efforts is that they move on to a new stage. To a formal dispute stage.

This may explain why negotiation is often seen as part of one tiered process pocket (the pre-dispute, commercial stage) and the rest of the conflict resolution methods, starting from mediation in the commonly known ADR spectrum or continuum, as a multi-tiered process. And in turn, this may explain the underuse of mediation.

[C] THE MEDIATION CUSHION

Mediation is, in a literal sense, a space between immediacy. In a more doctrinal view, it is a pause that interrupts the otherwise natural flow of a process. In dispute resolution terms, mediation is a pause in direct negotiation between the parties, and there might be several reasons why the pause may be welcome.

For example:

> The Claimant was an international corporation doing business in Mexico, which had hired the services of a particular mountain resort for the annual retreat of senior managers. The resort, Respondent, had announced a series of renovations to the resort that made it appealing for the retreat. The parties had agreed on a date for the retreat which was shortly after the reopening of the resort with the renovations. The person in charge of the engagement spent a weekend there, one month before the retreat and while several issues were identified, the resort committed to having the place ready for the company's event. The event finally happened. There were numerous issues with uncompleted, unavailable, or misrepresented services, some of which were acknowledged by the resort itself, to the extent that the retreat had to be terminated earlier than scheduled. A discount on the price was offered as compensation. The dispute arose when the corporation sought to claim not only the reimbursement of such a discount but also the indemnity for having caused additional expenses and damages for various grounds.
>
> The parties tried to resolve this via direct negotiations through their in-house commercial and legal departments. One of the parties hired counsel right after and then, another iteration of negotiations took place. However, negotiations did not progress to the point of success. The perspectives of each other on the merits of their case differed while the person in charge of negotiations on behalf of the resort had a strong reputational agenda at stake, and the emotional investment of having been embarrassed in front of senior managers was concerning to the commercial representative of the Claimant. The external counsel thought that the case merited negotiation by another means: mediation. And so, they did. Mediation allowed for the negotiation to find a safe harbor and resolve the matter. The parties were the same and the negotiation was the same. It was the process that changed.

There are three natural reasons for an *impasse* in negotiations (1) structural, (2) interpersonal, and (3) intrapersonal.[20] The dynamics in a negotiation are so varied depending on alternatives, perceptions, agents, timing, and other factors, that even the best negotiators can face roadblocks. Often, experienced negotiators can identify and overcome the negotiation *impasse* and resolve it as a result, or they push hard enough to break it. But when that is not possible, mediation can help. *Impasse* and negotiation failures do not mean that a negotiated solution is not available. Yet, when we frame mediation as a different, formal process that distinguishes from negotiation, instead of a part of the negotiation spectrum, it prevents people from accessing the mediation process. Mediation could help disentangle the roadblock and enable negotiation. No agreement because of negotiation does not mean that no agreement is possible, it just means that it may need a different process.

However, mediation is rarely looked at as an extended negotiation in Mexico, or as a useful tool to negotiate when the latter cannot reach a successful settlement. Literature and legislation in Mexico, tend to describe mediation as a peaceful, amicable path to resolving disputes, in clear contrast to litigation. Examples of language used in the different mediation laws of the Mexican states include: "non-adversarial alternative dispute resolution method,"[21] "culture of peace,"[22] and "peaceful resolution."[23] In academic literature, we find multiple references to the "culture of peace" where mediation is regarded as a public policy tool to transform social conflict to change the tendency away from the culture of litigation.[24] The frame is clearly one where mediation is presented as an alternative to litigation or adversarial dispute resolution mechanisms.

Further, mediation has been traditionally promoted as a process that promises to offer a better path in the context of a perceived justice crisis due to courts' backlog, lack of professionalism, and corruption.[25] It is presented in the different legislative bodies and the preparatory works as an alternative, more accessible path to justice.

Both the quest for peacebuilding and the path to justice through more accessible ways, are undeniably true, righteous, and worthy goals to pursue. By themselves, those goals can make the case for mediation before public opinion. Nonetheless, it may

---

20. Martin Schweinsberg et al., *Negotiation Impasses: Types, Causes, and Resolutions*. Journal of Management *48(1)* 49-76 (Nov 31, 2022), https://doi.org/10.1177/01492063211021657.
21. *Ley de Justicia Alternativa del Estado de Jalisco* (Jan. 30, 2007), chrome-extension://efaidnbmnnnibpcajpcglclefindmkaj/https://transparencia.info.jalisco.gob.mx/sites/default/files/u37/Ley%20de%20Justicia%20Alternativa%20del%20Estado%20de%20Jalisco_0.pdf.
22. *Ley de Métodos Alternos para la Resolución de Conflictos del Estado de Nuevo León* (Jan. 14, 2005), chrome-extension://efaidnbmnnnibpcajpcglclefindmkaj/http://www.tcanl.gob.mx/docs/ley_de_metodos_alternos_para_la_solucion_de_conflictos_del_estado_de_nuevo_leon.pdf.
23. *Ley de Justicia Alternativa del Tribunal Superior de Justicia para el Distrito Federal* (Jan. 8, 2008), http://cgservicios.df.gob.mx/prontuario/vigente/r171503.htm.
24. Paris Alejandro Cabello Tijerina, *La Mediación como una Estrategia de la Cultura de la Paz* in Arellano Hernández, Francisca Patricia and Cabello Tijerina, Paris Alejandro, *Retos y Perspectivas de los MASC en México* (Tirant Lo Blanch 2015).
25. Luis Figueroa Díaz and Margarita Magaña Hernández, *El conflicto y la negociación: elementos para su reflexión normativa en el marco de la justicia alternativa en México*, in *Series Alegatos no. 88* (September-December 2014).

be that those goals are not appealing to the stakeholders who use the legal system. Peace and more accessible justice are not clear incentives for a person seeking to recover an investment or a company claiming the protection of certain intellectual property rights.

In an in-depth empirical study, Howard addresses the hypothesis that the traditional ways used to promote mediation may be misaligned with the incentives of the potential users of the commercial justice systems.[26] Her approach was to focus on the European Union's strategy to boost the practice of cross-border commercial mediation in the region. Howard proposes that framing mediation as an alternative to litigation or highlighting the ability to enforce a mediated agreement are not frames that appeal to the actual users of the commercial dispute resolution ecosystem, i.e., corporate counsel. Howard's work was based on multiple interviews with corporate counsel practicing in the European region.

She introduces the idea that counsels are expected to be good negotiators. Therefore, the use of mediation could be perceived as having failed in their jobs, which consequently prompts such stakeholders to avoid mediation.[27] Consistent with this finding, earlier examples in the negotiation section of this essay show that attorneys in Mexico are confronted with negotiations on a regular basis, and the concept of needing help to land those negotiations successfully is not well perceived. Howard finds that there is a lack of understanding of what mediation can bring to the table.[28] If practitioners and businesspeople do not perceive a benefit from mediation when compared to negotiation, then another layer of obstacles is added to the mix, and fewer are the incentives to go to mediation.

So, peacebuilding and economizing, the goals that are traditionally embodied in the promotion of mediation, surely are good reasons to mediate, but promoting mediation in the law, in academia, and in legal forums by highlighting the benefits that mediation brings to the negotiation table may be a better strategy. Those benefits trace back to the obstacles to negotiation as presented above. Mediation offers unique opportunities to overcome natural obstacles to negotiation and that concrete concept should be the clearest incentive for commercial parties to incorporate mediation in their negotiation efforts.

In the case offered as an example, the negotiation was not successful for a myriad of reasons. Had parties decided that the negotiation stage was exhausted through the direct offer and counteroffer, the Claimant would have had to file for arbitration or litigation, and perhaps then—based on what is seen in practice, in Mexico—incur another round of negotiations and those could fail for similar reasons as in the first time. Instead, negotiation continued to another stage, that of mediation, where parties were able to identify the obstacles (interpersonal and intrapersonal barriers), share information about what mattered to each one the most, adjust the list of participants to

26. Howard, *supra* n. 16.
27. *Ibid.*, 157.
28. *Ibid.*, 165. Howard specifically refers to how the European Union highlights the benefits of mediation "in terms of economizing time and money" and then those incentives alone are not enough to appeal to legal practitioners. They know resolving the matter is less expensive, but they have already tried to resolve it via negotiation.

people that were less conflicted by their commercial objectives and emotions, as well as the balance of power. Ultimately, the negotiation efforts were successful. There is abundant literature on the stages and spaces that mediation creates to allow for such knots to be untied.

Once the platform is set and organizations and attorneys become comfortable with the idea of incorporating mediation into their normal negotiation efforts, mediation happens regularly and without fear of perceptions, even from the offset of the negotiation, as has been demonstrated internationally.[29]

Mediation is not always successful, although numbers show that a big majority of the cases that are mediated worldwide do result in a settlement agreement with numbers in the range of 80% to 90%,[30] and similar numbers have been reported in Mexico.[31]

[D] THE ARBITRATION: LITIGATION CUSHION

Consensual dispute resolution processes like negotiation and mediation satisfy certain needs and can offer a resolution to a wide array of disputes between individuals and organizations. But there is a reason why formal processes to resolve disputes exist and need to be strengthened. Litigation is in its own essence a path to justice, and hence, a path to peace. The legal procedure is, when no prevention or early correction is available, the cure to the battle of the conflict.[32] Litigation is indeed a path to justice. Ideally, a path that is only worth transiting when other less burdensome paths are not available, but it is not better or worse than mediation or negotiation; it is simply a different path to the goal of justice and peace. A good example of spaces where litigation must not only be an option but also a desired path to pursue, is the increasing platform of *strategic litigation* for cases of human rights, gender parity, or environmental causes.

Businesspeople and attorneys under this traditional way to understand mediation as it has been promoted (i.e., an alternative to litigation or arbitration), find a narrow or non-existent mediation door. That slim door is one that lies between the direct negotiation efforts and the well-explored territory of the litigation procedure. Mediation is then seen as something that would only happen if the cost of litigation is not worth incurring or if the litigation is so uncertain or adverse that mediation might be the last resort. The latter is a scenario where it is likely only one of the parties would be interested in trying mediation and not both. Mediation becomes then a rare exception.

29. One interviewee of Howard reflects so by saying that "in one third or 50% of negotiations we would immediately start with mediation rather than beginning with a negotiation ...." *Ibid.*, 172.
30. The Center for Effective Dispute Resolution CEDR, *The Ninth Mediation Unit—2021* (Jan. 31, 2023), https://www.cedr.com/wp-content/uploads/2021/05/CEDR_Audit-2021-lr.pdf.
31. Laura Lucía Romero Mireles, *La Justicia en México, congestionada por litigios entre personas cercanas* (Jan. 31, 2023), https://www.gaceta.unam.mx/la-justicia-en-mexico-congestionada-por-litigios-entre-personas-cercanas/.
32. Sergio García Ramírez (Jan. 15, 2023), https://www.scielo.org.mx/scielo.php?script=sci_arttext&pid=S0041-86332004000100008.

When mediation is framed as a "better" "cheaper" or "quicker" method than litigation, it openly or subconsciously puts both processes in competition, where one excludes the possibility of the other. And then mediation seems to fade as a weaker option because the moment when parties are presented with such a choice, they are ready and well-armed to arbitrate or litigate, on the one hand, and they feel their negotiation efforts have been exhausted on the other.

[E] THE CAROM: THE CALL FOR EVOLUTION

Currently, in Mexico, the moment in history is ready for an evolution of the understanding of each of those processes, as the legal framework for consensual conflict resolution processes and the position of Mexico in the global economy keep evolving. In such a context, below are the proposed conclusions:

(1) Negotiation in Mexico is more mainstream than legal research tends to give it credit. More empirical research around the practice of negotiation as a pre-litigation or pre-arbitration stage would be beneficial to further develop this concept.

(2) Being negotiation a common cultural approach to conflict and legal practice, mediation would come naturally as an extension of such efforts. To do so, mediation needs to be re-assessed and promoted differently in the Mexican legal and commercial mindset. Not as a "better" "quicker" "more efficient" process than litigation or arbitration, but as a "better" "quicker" "more efficient" process than direct negotiation. Stakeholders interested in the improvement of the justice system through the embracement of more mediation should be interested in addressing the advantages and benefits brought by mediation to the negotiation efforts. Failing to rethink mediation and its role in the dispute resolution spectrum in Mexico, may risk marginalizing mediation to a formality that helps strengthen settlement agreements. A formality, by the way, that will depend entirely on the legislative and technological trends.

(3) There is an obstacle to this approach, and that is that offering mediation and merely discussing it can be perceived as a sign of weakness or failure. This could be addressed by rethinking and reframing mediation as part of the same "pocket" as negotiation. As negotiation by different means and with different tools. Going to mediation is not conceding to the idea that negotiations failed, but rather a continuation of the negotiation efforts.

(4) One catalyst of such rethinking is framing the different dispute resolution methods as a menu of paths toward resolution and justice. A menu that includes consensual options and adversarial options and has been referred to

> as Appropriate Dispute Resolution,[33] it may be time to move on from the twentieth-century *Alternative Dispute Resolution* pockets.

A lot may change in Mexico if mediation and negotiation are regarded as part of the same category, of the same stage in the dispute resolution continuum, and as different options—not alternative options—to litigation and arbitration.

33. Francisco Gonzalez de Cossio, *Analisis Económico de los Mecanismos Alternativos (Rectius: Apropiados) de Solución de Controversias* (Jan. 31, 2023), http://gdca.com.mx/PDF/arbitraje/DE%20LOS%20MECANISMOS.pdf.

PART VI Conclusion

CHAPTER 21

Concluding Thoughts on Arbitration in Mexico

Celia Cañete & Gloria M. Alvarez

[A] INTRODUCTION

As of today, Mexico is widely recognised as one of the world's arbitration hubs in Latin America. This is mainly explained by the fact that Mexico is the second-largest economy in Latin America, and among the fourteen largest economies in the world.[1] Its position as global exporter spans across all key industries and is a game-changer in facilitating global manufacturing to achieve today's energy transition. This includes mining, vehicles, computers, oils and petroleum, connecting it with the main economies across the globe.[2]

Mexico has been recognised by the ICC as the most represented nationality in commercial arbitration in Latin America, and the second most represented nationality in commercial arbitration worldwide.[3] Mexico also registered the largest number of ICSID cases in 2023.[4] While the foundations of its arbitration system are well-rooted in

1. The Observatory of Economic Complexity, *Mexico* (2022) https://oec.world/en/profile/country/mex. *See also* Ministerio de Economía, Comercio y Empresa del Gobierno de España, *Informe Mensual de Comercio Exterior* (April 2024) https://comercio.gob.es/ImportacionExportacion/Informes_Estadisticas/Documents/informe-mensual/Informe-Mensual-de-Comercio-Exterior-ultimo-periodo.pdf.
2. The World Bank, *Mexico Overview* (4 April 2023), https://www.worldbank.org/en/country/mexico/overview#: ~ :text = Its%20economic%20growth%20averaged%20just,to%20the%20COVID%2D19%20pandemic.
3. International Chamber of Commerce (ICC), *ICC Dispute Resolution 2023 Statistics* 5, 21 (24 June 2024) https://iccwbo.org/wp-content/uploads/sites/3/2024/06/2023-Statistics_ICC_Dispute-Resolution_991.pdf.
4. International Centre for Settlement of Investment Disputes (ICSID), *The ICSID Caseload – Statistics*, Issue 2024-1, 9 (1 February 2024) https://icsid.worldbank.org/sites/default/files/publications/ENG_The_ICSID_Caseload_Statistics_Issue%202024.pdf.

civil practice and its approaches to dispute resolution and the UNCITRAL Model Law, Mexican arbitration law has evolved due to the subscription of multiple international treaties and conventions over the years.

In Mexico, the constitutional right to submit disputes to arbitration is expressly recognised in Article 17 of the Mexican Constitution, when indicating that '[t]he laws shall provide alternative mechanisms to resolve controversies'.[5] This, together with the decisions rendered by Mexican courts in relation to the use of arbitration, have consolidated Mexico as an arbitration-friendly jurisdiction worth being studied in the international arbitration arena.

This book aims to cover the main issues and singularities of the region, by providing first an introductory overview of the Mexican regulatory, economic and political framework in its Part I (section [B]), followed by an in-depth analysis of the main issues faced in commercial and investment arbitration, as well as the judicial intervention of domestic courts in support of international arbitration, addressed in Part II (section [C]), Part III (section [D]) and Part IV (section [E]) of the book. In order to give a detailed approach to the particularities of the region, Part V (section [F]) elaborates on the specific topics and players of the Mexican arbitration arena. As a means to provide a conclusion that covers the main features of the topics set forth throughout the chapters, we provide a brief review of each Part's content as presented in the book and wrap up with some concluding thoughts on Arbitration in Mexico (section [G]).

[B] PART I: INTRODUCTION AND REGULATORY FRAMEWORK

'Arbitration in Mexico' commences with an introductory overview of the regulatory framework in Mexico. In its first chapter, Bernardo Sepúlveda, Luis Jardón and Camilo Soto's 'Arbitration in Mexico: An Overview' set out the main historical milestones accomplished by Mexico to embrace commercial and investment arbitration. The authors address the main negotiations and treaties signed by Mexico, as well as its most relevant legislative reforms. In addition, they anticipate the changes and challenges that arbitration will have to face in the upcoming years.

In 'Regulatory Framework in Mexico: The National and International Dimensions', Ana Sofía Sapiña Errecart and Cecilia Azar Manzur emphasise that Mexico is a pro-arbitration jurisdiction. From there, the authors outline Mexico's relevant legal framework and explain the key trends that contribute to the increment of dispute resolution. To conclude, the chapter refers to some imminent challenges affecting commercial and investment arbitration in the near future.

[C] PART II: COMMERCIAL ARBITRATION

Following the introduction contained in Part I of the book, Part II focuses its study on commercial arbitration. Elsa Ortega López lays the foundation of the study by

5. Free Translation of Art. 17 of the Mexican Constitution: 'Las leyes preverán mecanismos alternativos de solución de controversias'.

analysing 'The Arbitration Agreement under Mexican Law' through the lenses of both the Mexican Commerce Code and the Federal Civil Code. The author highlights the importance of the legal principle of party autonomy, as well as the essential elements required for the arbitration agreement's validity under Mexican law.

In 'The Separability of the Arbitral Clause and the Competence of the Arbitral Tribunal in Mexico', Salvador Fonseca González further elaborates on matters related to the arbitration agreement. The chapter explains that the doctrine of separability in Mexico is understood within the framework and influence of the adoption of the UNCITRAL Model Law. It also elucidates on the well-established criteria that an arbitration tribunal is empowered to rule on objections to the existence or validity of the arbitration agreement, particularly in light of the reforms made to the Articles 1464 and 1424 of the Federal Code of Commerce, as well as the 2014 Supreme Court judgment in favour of arbitration.

Francisco González de Cossío transfers the study to the two ex officio grounds for setting aside arbitral awards or refusing their enforcement: 'Public Policy and Arbitrability in Mexico'. The author examines the precedents in relation to these two issues under Mexican law and contrasts them with internationally accepted arbitration law concepts; arriving at the conclusion that, in general, the aggregate outcome has proved that Mexico is an arbitration-friendly jurisdiction.

Subsequently, Eduardo Siqueiros T.'s chapter on 'Arbitrators and Arbitral Tribunals'. The author reviews the role of arbitrators in the resolution of disputes in Mexico, as well as the principles governing their appointment, duties and rights according to the domestic reality and the functioning of the Mexican judiciary.

Carlos Manuel Loperena Ruiz and Alejandro Flores Patiño tackle the issue of documentary evidence in arbitration under Mexican law in their chapter 'Document Production'. The authors develop the notion of *document* and the arbitral tribunal's power on the production of documents both under Mexican legislation and the institutional local rules of arbitration, including the provisions related to judicial assistance for the production of documents.

In 'The Measure of Damages in Mexico and their Quantification', Herfried Wöss and Adriana San Román Rivera outline the change in the treatment of damages under Mexican law, acknowledging that Mexican damages law initially resulted in under-compensation but then shifted to the obligation of total reparation. The authors present such a change of direction in relation to the changes in the Mexican Federal Constitution in 2011 and the incorporation of the Factory at Chorzów *dictum* into Mexican civil law.

[D] PART III: JUDICIAL INTERVENTION IN SUPPORT OF INTERNATIONAL ARBITRATION

Part III addresses the role of judicial intervention of domestic courts in support of international arbitration in México. First, in 'Judicial Aid to International Arbitration in Mexico', Carlos Alvarado studies the relationship between State courts and arbitration tribunals in Mexico, providing a balanced view regarding judicial intervention and the autonomy vested in arbitration tribunals. To do so, the chapter reviews the principle of judicial non-interference from the lenses of whether judicial aid is either available or required, including challenge of arbitrators, jurisdictional issues, interim measures, recognition, and enforcement; as well as national courts acting as appointing authority, support to the tribunal in taking evidence and consultation of the tribunal's fees. The author offers a comprehensive explanation of the Mexican judiciary structure as well as their competences and draws examples of the French influence on Mexican arbitration proceedings, including the 'remission to arbitration' as the negative effect of *kompetenz-kompetenz*.

In their chapter 'Interim Measures in the Mexican *Lex Arbitri*', Victor M. Ruiz and Andrea Orta reviewed interim measures when Mexico is the seat of arbitration proceedings. The authors underscore Mexico's adoption of the UNCITRAL Model Law via its amendments to the Code of Commerce and draw attention to Mexico's departure from UNCITRAL regarding certain provisions related to the power of the arbitration tribunal, security for costs and type of interim measures. The authors explore the scope of their application, including court intervention in cases subject to arbitration agreements, interim measures, and recognition and enforcement of awards. The authors give a clear analysis of the substantive requirements for the adoption of interim measures in light of the international arbitration practice (i.e., urgency, balance of interests, no pre-judgment of the merits and a *prima facie* on the merits). The chapter also reviews anti-arbitration measures and their impact in the Mexican context.

Montserrat Manzano and Adrián Magallanes look into the issues derived from the 'Recognition and Enforcement of Arbitration Awards in Mexico,' showing that the region's legal system and case law are up to date with the highest international standards in this regard. The authors analyse the legal applicable framework and case law, concluding that Mexico has positioned itself as a trustworthy country and a solid choice for carrying out arbitration proceedings.

To finish Part III of the book, Vicente Bañuelos Rizo explains the 'Setting Aside Arbitration Awards in Mexico' in Mexico, based on the study of the applicable domestic regulation and case law, as well as the international treaties for recognition and enforcement signed by Mexico. The author displays the different steps and elements to set aside arbitral awards in Mexico, with a particular emphasis on the causes to set aside awards under Mexican law.

[E] PART IV: INVESTMENT ARBITRATION

Part IV of the book shifts the study to the particularities of investment arbitration in Mexico. To do so, Alan Bonfiglio Ríos and Jorge Escalona Gálvez showcase the main international investment agreements entered into by Mexico, in their chapter 'Mexico's International Investment Law Framework: Bilateral and Multilateral Investment Treaties'. The chapter navigates through Mexico's creation and evolution of international investment law and ISDS mechanisms over the decades, resulting in the current Mexican investment protection regime resorting to investment arbitration options.

Then, in 'Mexico's Legacy in the Investment Treaty Practice', Orlando Federico Cabrera Colorado explores Mexico's vast past and current accomplishments in managing foreign investment disputes, and its contributions to international investment law practice. In particular, the author highlights Mexico's influence on foundations such as the Calvo clause, the Hull Formula, the minimum standard of treatment, and the notion of legitimate expectations.

[F] PART V: PARTICULAR ISSUES AND PLAYERS IN MEXICAN ARBITRATION

The book dedicates its final section, Part V, to the particularities of the issues and players that perform in the Mexican arbitration arena. To start off, Marco Tulio Venegas and Michelle Carrillo give an overview of Mexico's relationship between 'Commercial Arbitration and State Entities' in the last thirty years. The authors observe the several factors that lead to unfavourable results in relation to disputes against public entities in Mexico and highlight some pending matters that are still a work in progress but could help improve the situation in the region.

In 'Arbitration in the Mexican Power Sector', René Irra de la Cruz and Elisa Legorreta Pastor provide an in-depth narrative on Mexico's electricity and power sector. which has been crucial to the Mexican arbitration community in developing sophisticated procedural and substantive expertise on the matter. In doing so, the chapter provides for a detailed explanation of the different relevant laws that have constructed the domestic electricity market, as well as the set of common contractual sources between the public and private participants. In addition, the authors discuss some of the recurrent procedural issues arising from these disputes, such as multi-tier arbitration clauses, non-signatories, legal standing to claim, and incompatibility of multiple arbitration clauses.

In 'The Rise in Mexico's Energy Disputes: A Focus in Oil and Gas Cases', Diana María Pineda Esteban and Julia Gonzalez Romero bring the boom of energy-related arbitration cases into focus. The authors review the relevant Mexican regulations affecting energy disputes and address some of the most relevant Mexican oil and gas arbitration cases of the last few years. Moreover, they address the challenges related to the enforcement of international arbitration awards by national courts, as well as the latter's role in the recognition and setting aside of arbitral awards in Mexico.

In 'Shareholders and M&A Disputes', Rodrigo Zamora Etcharren and Ana María Castro Dosal share the rise of corporate disputes in the Mexican landscape, including the relevant legislation and a breakout of the most common types of disputes, usually categorised as pre-and post-transaction, and the type of challenges arising from them. Furthermore, the authors analyse the arbitrability of shareholder disputes when an arbitration agreement is included in the bylaws, as well as the efficacy of said arbitration agreements.

Luis Omar Guerrero Rodríguez, Eduardo Lobatón Guzmán, Andrés Peña Loyo and Fernanda Serrano Cortez shift the study of the book to the impact of technology in the practice of arbitration in Mexico. In their chapter 'Technology and International

Arbitration in Mexico', the authors delve into the use of technology in every step of the arbitration in the past and current years, anticipating those that will likely appear in the near future.

To conclude Part V of the book, Fernando Navarro Sánchez offers the metaphor of a *carom* or *carambola* to analyse the position of Mexico in the triple-edged dispute resolution options available: negotiation, mediation and litigation-arbitration. The author addresses, in 'Mediation and Negotiation in Mexico: The Three-Cushion Carom' the fact that while negotiation is a common practice in Mexico, mediation is often regarded as part of the latter and is yet to acquire the perception of being a different option to which parties can resort.

[G] FINAL THOUGHTS ON 'ARBITRATION IN MEXICO'

In short, 'Arbitration in Mexico' is a book that offers a comprehensive exploration of the landscape of arbitration in the region. Through its insightful chapters, the readers can gain a nuanced understanding of Mexico's evolution, challenges and potential avenues for growth in the arbitration practice.

As set out in the multiple perspectives presented within these pages, it becomes evident that Mexico counts with a robust pro-arbitration framework. Yet, there is still room for improvement and innovation in the Mexican arbitration practice. We encourage the readers to keep an eye out as the region can chart a course toward a future where Mexican arbitration further elevates its position in the global arbitration arena.

www.ingramcontent.com/pod-product-compliance
Lightning Source LLC
LaVergne TN
LVHW020645300926
849161LV00004B/820
* 9 7 8 9 4 0 3 5 2 5 2 7 3 *